MW01180569

ROAD TO DESTINY: TWW

To ANDREW:

I hope you Enjoy The Book.
I want To Thank you For Supporting
me and my Red Devil Teams.

I'll Never Forget the many Times
Donna and I went at your house when
you were growing up. We had many good
Times with your Parents.

I want To wish you and yours the
Best of health. May you have many years
of happiness. Best wishes

"Together we win"
Coach Dave Donnell

Road to Destiny: TWW

By

Coach Dave Darnall

"Together We Win"
TWW

NORTH STAR PRESS OF ST. CLOUD, INC.

Copyright © 2004 David Darnall

ISBN: 0-87839-203-3

First edition, March 2004

All rights reserved.

For comments or further information,
contact the author at
<tww@artelco.com> or <tww@mtco.com>

Printed in the United States of America
by Versa Press, Inc., East Peoria, Illinois.

Published by
North Star Press of St. Cloud, Inc.
P.O. Box 451
St. Cloud, Minnesota 55320
nspress@cloudnet.com

ROAD TO DESTINY: TWW

Written by: Coach Dave Darnall

1994 NAIA II National Champion — 1994 NAIA II National Coach of the Year
Former 20 Year Head Basketball Coach – Eureka College

Road to Destiny: TWW is an autobiography of Coach Dave Darnall, written in a historical flavor of Eureka College basketball during his tenure as Head Basketball Coach. Not only does it include games won and lost, but is peppered with human-interest stories and humor from scouting, recruiting, basketball camps, and Dave's college tenure. The Foreword was written by Dave Corzine, 7-foot center for the Chicago Bulls.

"This is the collegiate version of Hoosiers that places the smallest college in the nation at the heart of basketball's best. Follow the Red Devils in the incredible journey from local to national headlines. Get inside the plaid jacket of Head Coach Dave Darnall who was affectionately known for his tireless recruiting and infectious style. Come back to the Mayberry-like town of Eureka and read for yourself how it all happened.," reviews Dr. Nancy LaCursia, New Trier High School and former Women's Head Basketball Coach, Eureka College

To order your copy of Road to Destiny: TWW or "Together We Win" TWW sport wear, complete this form.

NAME: _____

ADDRESS: _____

CITY: _____ STATE _____ ZIP _____

Road to Destiny: TWW	Quantity _____ at $19.95 each plus $3.00 shipping and handling.

"Together We Win" TWW Sportswear

Item	Size (circle)	Cost	Quantity	Total
Baseball Caps	One Size fits All	$10		
T-shirts	S – M – L – XL – XXL	8		
Cap/T-shirt Combo	S – M – L – XL – XXL	15		
Polo Shirt	M – L – XL – XXL	20		
Sweatshirt	S – M – L – XL – XXL	15		
		$ 3 shipping & handling		

Make check payable to "Together We Win" and mail to Dave Darnall, P.O. Box 13, Eureka, IL 61530
Email: IL, tww@mtco.com or AR, tww@artelco.com   Web: www.coachdavedarnall or www.coachdavedarnall

"I have always known Dave as an intriguing personality. His book is intriguing as well. His is a story of a young man's desire to become a successful basketball coach and his unwavering determination on the path to win a collegiate national championship."

> Ron Felling
> Coach, Lawrenceville High School; Indiana University - Retired

"This is the collegiate version of Hoosiers that places the smallest college in the nation at the heart of basketball's best. Follow the Red Devils in their incredible journey from local to national headlines. And most of all, enjoy the ride through the eyes of those who were there. Get inside the plaid jacket of the Head Coach, Dave Darnall, who was affectionately known for his tireless recruiting and infectious style. Come back to the Mayberry-like town of Eureka and read for yourself how it all happened."

> Dr. Nancy LaCursia
> New Trier High School
> Former Head Basketball Coach, Eureka College

"Coach Darnall's tremendous knowledge and understanding of the game of basketball, combined with his ability to communicate with coaches and players, was the backbone of his great career. I was honored to be associated with him and his camps."

> Jim Les
> Head Basketball Coach, Bradley University
> Former NBA Player

"Take away the million-dollar endorsements, the television contracts, the $2,000.00 suits, the 20,000-seat arenas, and everything else that separates big-time college basketball from the rest of the field, and you are left with the true ambassadors of the game. Coaches that coach for the love of the game and the love of their players. That's where you will find places like Eureka College and Coach Dave Darnall.

> Roger Phegley
> Former NBA and European Player

"Through the years of participating in his summer basketball camps at Eureka College, I am most impressed with the single, most powerful observation I have of Dave Darnall: his sincerity. Regardless of whether he is interacting with the college president, his staff, or the young campers, Dave treats everyone with genuine respect and concern. Perhaps for this precious quality above all others, Dave is extremely successful in basketball and, even more importantly, in his life."

C. J. Kupec
Johns Hopkins University
Former NBA & European Player

"Dave Darnall put tiny Eureka on the basketball map with his winning the National Championship NAIA II and his relentless recruiting. This is a book you've been waiting for—a thinking man's guide to basketball, also a fascinating insight into the author himself. A marvelous, evocative portrait of his profession. Certainly one of the best and incisive sport books in recent years. This volume applies to both heart and mind."

John Schneiter
Coach, Stephen Decatur & New Trier - Retired

"Coach Darnall, an inspiration and a true believer. I was honored to speak at Coach Darnall's camps because he was one of a few coaches that really respected and saw a future in women's basketball. To see his enthusiasm and the way he worked with his staff and participants was a thrill. I hope to get into coaching soon, and if I can do as much coaching as Coach Darnall has and keep the young women as eager and enthusiastic as he has, I will know that he truly knew what he was talking about all those years."

Charlotte Lewis
Olympian

"It's my pleasure to tell the world, 'I'm proud to have Dave Darnall as a friend, both professionally and personally.'"

Duffy Bass
Baseball Coach, Illinois State University - Retired

"Dave was a tireless worker at the collegiate level. He turned the Eureka College basketball program from night to day with his knowledge of the game and his relentless work ethic. This book demonstrates his intensity and desire to succeed.

Chuck Rolinski
Coach Toluca High School - Retired
IBCA Executive Director - Treasurer

"It is an honor for the McKendree College basketball program to be included in the chronology of NAIA basketball and the life work of Coach David Darnall. We enjoyed the competitive challenge of college basketball. Coach Darnall did a magnificent job of building the Eureka College basketball program culminating in a National Championship—a feat that is the pinnacle of coaching."

Harry Statham

Head Basketball Coach, McKendree College

"For all you camp coaches and campers who ever attended a 'Dave Darnall's Eureka College Basketball Camp,' this is a must read. We all had a great time, and this book just reinforces those memories."

Coach Roger "Smitty" Smith

"Dave Darnall was the most passionate coach I have ever seen. He demanded and commanded respect from teammates, coaches, peers, faculty, parents, and community supporters. He did not make the game complex; he stayed with the fundamentals, and his teams did them well. His players believed in him and his philosophy, and won a National Championship as a result. I'm proud to have had the opportunity to coach at the same college as Dave Darnall."

Sandy Schuster

Women's Basketball Coach, Eureka College

"Dave's final team had a starting line-up of five seniors who had played together for four years. They knew each other. They knew each other's moves, each other's strengths and weaknesses, and perhaps even more importantly, were best of friends off the court. This philosophy of building team chemistry is to me the foundation of Coach Darnall's approach to success in basketball. Often criticized for playing only five or sometimes six or seven players in a game, Dave believed and proved that the connection each player had to each other [team member] on and off the floor was paramount. The ability to stay with this philosophy that he had build upon since his early days of coaching proved to be the major reason that Eureka won the National Championship."

Coach Dave Gilliland

"When I think of Dave Darnall, I think of a hard-nose competitor, intense, focused, and riveted to the task before him. My relationship was unlike many coaching relationships in that we not only competed tough, but we would challenge one another on other issues of life."

Jack D. Trager

Basketball Coach, Athletic Director

Greenville College, Emeriti

"I met Coach Darnall my senior year at Eureka College in 1974-1975 when he became Head Basketball Coach and I was lucky enough to be a student helper. Ten years later I would come back to work with him as an assistant coach for nine years of great success on the court and a lot of fun off the court, culminating in a National Championship in the 1993-1994 season."

Coach Dennis Dighton

Former Head Coach Eureka College

"When I was thirteen years old, I thought Dave Darnall was out of his mind. When I was sixty years old, I knew Dave Darnall was out of his mind."

Don Raycraft

"I feel very lucky to have been at Eureka College from the beginning of Coach's tenure to the end. My goal as a child was to play college basketball, coach, and teach. Coach Darnall helped make both of those dreams come true."

Tim McGuire

Coach, Prairie Central High School

Table of Contents

About the Cover

THE COVER OF THIS BOOK WAS DESIGNED to depict Dave Darnall's journey to the ultimate in college coaching—A National Championship. The "Road to Destiny" started for Darnall when he spent all but five years of his young life in the Bloomington-Normal area where the dream of coaching was instilled. The young Coach Darnall in the upper left corner is a picture of dejection after losing his very first game as a coach.

Dave developed the slogan "Together We Win"—TWW early in his coaching career as a means of creating a camaraderie and unity for his basketball programs. It permeated the journey to the 1994 NAIA II National Championship pictured at the bottom of the front cover.

As Darnall traveled the road from the top picture to the bottom, his journey was as eventful as the two opposing emotional pictures demonstrate. He had some bumps, ruts, and some great rides along the way, including meeting Ronald Reagan on several occasions, acquiring many autographed pictures from the governor and president, and receiving several telegrams and letters as the excerpt illustrates on the back cover.

President Ronald Reagan graduated from Eureka College in 1932 while his brother followed in 1933. The Fieldhouse that Dave Darnall coached in at Eureka College for twenty years was named Reagan Physical Education Center in honor of the Reagan brothers.

Numerous friendships of coaches and basketball fans made the trip most enjoyable. It was during this time that the friendship developed between Darnall and professional basketball player, Dave Corzine, leading to Corzine's gracious consent to write the foreword to this book.

The NAIA ring is a credit to Darnall's ultimate success in his coaching career—A National Championship!

About the Author

On a May afternoon thirty-seven years ago, a young Stanford, IL High School coach and ISU alum attended the Eureka graduation of his brother. He later remembered the moment this way:

> I was standing in the Rinker open air Theatre and thought, "This is for me. It has the look; it has the feel. Eureka College is where I want to be."

Almost to the day, eight years later in 1974, he wrote to Professor Owen West, Chair of the Division of Education and Psychology, about having spoken with Dean Clarence Noe of the vacant Men's Head Basketball Coaching job. Within a month, he had been offered and signed a faculty and staff contract, beginning twenty-nine years of distinguished service to the College we've gathered today to celebrate, that of our newest retiree, Professor Emeritus Dave Darnall.

Detailing his career is to encounter the stuff of which legends are made. Over a twenty-eight year tenure as a varsity Head Coach at both the high school and college levels, his teams won over 500 games. In his final, twentieth season as Eureka's Head Coach, he directed his team to a 27-4 record en route to winning the NAIA Division II National Championship and being named NAIA Division II Coach of the Year.

Professor Darnall holds the longest tenure and is the winningest coach in the College's history, compiling a Eureka career record of 383-151 for a startling winning percentage of .717. Along the way, his teams won five Prairie College Conference Championships and three NAIA District 20 title honors, spanning the years he was three times named District 20 Coach of the Year, four time Prairie Conference Coach of the Year. From 1991-94 he was named Illinois Basketball Coaches Association Coach of the Year; in 1994 *College Sports Magazine* named him NAIA Men's Coach of the Year.

He has been elected to no fewer than five Halls of Fame: the Illinois State University Athletic Hall of Fame, the Illinois Basketball Coaches Hall of Fame, the Greater Peoria Sports Hall of Fame, the Bloomington-Normal Officials Association Hall of Fame, and on October 29, 1999, received the highest honor offered a Eureka coach or athlete by being named to the Eureka College Athletic Hall of Fame.

By his inspired teaching and achievement, he has enriched this learning community. How fortunate we are to have been here with him. We will not soon see his like again.

Presented by Dean Allen Schwab, April 25, 2003

THE MOMENT OF DISCOVERY

EUREKA
COLLEGE

300 East College Avenue   Eureka, Illinois 61530-1500

Acknowledgements

Acknowledgements to:

My wife, Bonnie, who went through twenty intense seasons as a college coach's wife. She sacrificed many family events that did not occur due to my absence because of my recruiting, scouting, and coaching of games. Bonnie spent many days and nights alone and represented both of us at our children's school events and many other activities they participated in while I was away fulfilling necessary responsibilities in order to make Eureka College Basketball Program a success.

My children, Tiera and Derek, for understanding my absences at their activities, while I attended the activities of other parents' children. I also thank them and my son-in-law, Brett Charlton, for supporting my teams throughout the years.

My grandchildren, Brett, Carraghan, and Alexis, for entertaining me late at night while I tried to stay awake writing this book.

My mother, Ola; sisters, Judy and Lucia; brother, Bruce; my late father, Delmar; and Grandpa Kerr for their support in their particular ways.

To all my high school and college players who made my "road to destiny" possible.

Coach Dighton who drove many miles on recruiting trips and served faithfully as my assistant for nine years.

Chuck Wertz, who served as my chief scout, spent many hours on the road with me driving while I completed paperwork.

Dan Harrod who supported and accompanied me numerous times.

Many other assistant coaches and student administrative assistants for their hard work and dedication in their given tasks.

Becky Duffield, Pat Prosser, Jane Groeper, and Anthony Glass for supplying information helpful to the writing of this book.

Lynn Beer and Shellie Schwanke from the Eureka College Office of College Relations for all the coverage and news releases on my teams, camps, and me.

Don and Carol Raycraft for their advice and guidance.

The Alumni Office for supplying addresses and phone numbers of participants in the Eureka College Basketball Program during my tenure.

The Admission Directors and their staffs over my twenty-eight years for their help in the admitting procedures of student/basketball recruits.

All of those who took time to contribute their personal recollections.

President George Hearne who has dedicated over forty-three years of service to Eureka College. A very special thank you for supporting me during my tenure.

My friend, Dave Corzine, successful former starting center for the NBA Chicago Bulls. Thank you for taking time in your busy schedule to write the Foreword for this book.

My wife, Bonnie, for her time and expertise in the typing and editing of the manuscript.

My good friends, Jim " Sonny" and Doris Hillhouse, for their special support.

Jerry and Barb Short for their computer expertise.

Dave Kagel for his assistance in the publishing of this book.

Corinne and Seal Dwyer and North Star Press for their publishing expertise.

All the parents and basketball fans that attended our games and joined us at our home for post-game gatherings.

To the over 20,000 campers and abundant camp coaches who made my camps so successful providing for an interesting chapter in this book.

College of the Ozarks and Athletic Director Al Waller, for honoring the 1994 NAIA II National Champions at the 2004 NAIA II National Tournament in Point Lookout, Missouri.

I sincerely thank all of those who contributed to this endeavor. Your input, time, and comments used in writing this book are most appreciated.

A special thank you goes to: Bloomington, *The Pantagraph*, Peoria, *Journal Star, Woodford County Journal, Momence Progress Reporter, Mackinaw Valley News, Roseville Independent,* Kankakee *The Daily Journal,* Galesburg *The Register-Mail*, Monmouth *Daily Review Atlas*, Decatur *Herald & Review, Wheaton Leader*, Dixon *Telegraph, Bellville Journal, U.S.A. Today, Idaho Press-Tribune, Idaho Statesman*, and their respective sportswriters and photographers for providing me information and pictures that made this project possible.

Independent photographers Ray Driskell and Rich Beer.

Eureka College, Northwest Nazarene College, and the NAIA National Office for all of their assistance.

Foreword
by
Dave Corzine

ENTHUSIASM, WHEN I THINK of Coach Dave Darnall that is the first word that comes to mind. Not only does he have an enthusiasm for basketball but also an enthusiasm for life. Dave brings enthusiasm and energy to everything he does, and it becomes infectious. He is the type of person you enjoy being with, a person who is experiencing and enjoying life, both the good and the bad.

Dave is real and he cares. I think that has been the key to the success Dave has had in his life. One saying goes, "People don't care how much you know, until they know how much you care," and it is easy to see how much Dave cares. He cares about his family, friends, team members, and everyone else associated with him and Eureka College. Whether on or off the court, Dave treats his players, coaching staff and friends as family. Myself, along with countless others, have spent many a late night at Dave's house having a great time and feeling like we were home. Dave, along with his wife, Bonnie, and their son and daughter, Derek and Tiera, would always make us feel welcome, I'm sure many times well past the point when we actually were. Many of his past players still have a close relationship with Coach Darnall, long after they have graduated from school. They know they can always come to him for help or advice. His successful coaching and recruiting is a direct result of his caring about his team and his players, along with a lot of hard work of course.

Coach Darnall is the type of person who never puts himself first. Dave did not coach the "Red Devils" with the intent of moving up the coaching ladder, or signing a huge contract, or making a lot of money on a shoe endorsement deal. Dave coached at Eureka College because he loved basketball, the school, and his players. So much attention is devoted nowadays to the contracts and money involved in sports that we forget why we play them, and what they are supposed to be about. Coach Darnall reminds us of that. Although Coach Darnall has had tremendous success throughout his career, and has received many honors, along with a National Championship, you'd never find that out by talking or spending time with him. He doesn't spend much time talking about his basketball successes, although he has much to be proud of in that arena. Dave prefers to talk about what he and his wife, Bonnie, are doing, or his kids and grandkids, or what is going on in your life. Even though basketball so permeates his life, Dave is one of those rare people that can keep it all in perspective and balanced. He has too much energy and excitement for what is happening now, or what he is looking forward to in the future, to dwell on past successes for long.

Coach Darnall's motto is "Together We Win"—TWW—and when Dave says "together" he means it. He includes everyone both on and off the court. Together We Win means that all must contribute and do their part and then the team can be successful. But every team must have a leader, and for Eureka men's college basketball team that leader was Dave Darnall.

It's true that you get out of life what you put into it, and when you look at Dave's life, a very successful coaching career, many good friends, and a wonderful wife and family, you can see that his zest for living has paid off.

When you come away from being with Dave Darnall, you feel better for the experience, and that's how you'll feel after reading this book. I hope you enjoy it as much as I did, and as much as I enjoy my friendship with Coach Darnall.

Introduction
by
Dave Darnall

E VERY BASKETBALL FAN HAS HEARD of Johnny Wooden, Bob Knight/Mike Davis, Adolph Rupp/Tubby Smith, Dean Smith, Mike Krzyzewski, Lute Olson, and Rick Pitino. We are all familiar with UCLA, Indiana, Kentucky, North Carolina, Duke, Arizona, and Louisville but who has heard of Dave Darnall? How about Eureka College? Now, you history buffs should have heard of Eureka College. You see, Eureka College produced the fortieth President of the United States, Ronald Reagan.

Reagan is the only person who ever graduated from an institution of higher learning in Illinois to be elected president of the United States. With all the numerous outstanding graduates over the years from Illinois colleges and universities, isn't it remarkable that only Reagan became president?

Oh, by the way, Eureka College is only the second Illinois institution of higher learning to win a NAIA National Championship in it sixty-six years of existence. In 1946, Southern Illinois defeated Indiana State, 49 to 40, to claim the championship.

Up until the early 1960s, many of the state institutions of higher learning in Illinois were members of the National Association of Intercollegiate Athletics. In fact, in 1961, my freshman year at Illinois State University, the "Redbirds" lost to Lewis College, 74 to 69, in the first round of the NAIA District twenty playoffs.

How about Kareem Abdul-Jabbar, Magic Johnson, Dave Corzine, Shaquille O'Neal, Michael Jordan, Allen Iverson, Scottie Pippen, and Tim

Duncan—have you heard of them? Sure! Anyone reading this book or has any interest in basketball has.

How about Chris Peterson, Chris Eaton, Troy Tyler? You have heard of them too, right? Some of you may have, but most have not. This is what this book is all about. You see, Dave Darnall was named National Association of Intercollegiate Athletics Division II Coach of the Year. In fact, he was also named NAIA Coach of the Year by *College Sports Magazine*. In being selected 1994 NAIA II Coach of the Year, he became the second coach from Illinois to receive a NAIA Coach of the Year honor. In 1955, Leroy Morley, Head Coach at Western Illinois, was named NAIA Coach of the Year. His team finished third in the nation. A third coach, Harry Statham of McKendree College, was named NAIA I Coach of the Year in 2002. His team finished in the top sixteen.

There are five recognized national championships in college basketball. These are: NCAA Division I, NAIA Division I, NCAA Division II, NAIA Division II, and NCAA Division III.

Eureka College, then with an enrollment of approximately 450 students, no athletic scholarships, approximately 5,500 alumni, 139 years old, the first college in Illinois to admit men and women on an equal basis, located in a small community of 4,300 population, became a national basketball champion.

By the way, Chris Peterson was named the Most Valuable Player at the 1994 NAIA II National Tournament. Chris Eaton was selected NAIA II First Team All-American and named the 1994 NAIA II National Player of the Year. Troy Tyler was selected NAIA II Second Team All-American both his junior and senior years. He was also named NAIA Academic All-American the same years.

Oh, yes, it should be mentioned that Darnall had several players who did play professional basketball in Europe. This group included Jerome Westbrooks, who Dave calls "The Michael Jordan of Ireland"; Mark Scherer, currently Head Basketball Coach at Elmhurst College; Paul Missavage, presently coaching in Europe; Chris Peterson; and, Hughley Blanton.

This book is dedicated to all players, coaches, administrators, parents, and fans that enjoy the game of basketball for the real purpose of college athletics. That is to have the opportunity to experience playing college basketball for fun as well as winning while acquiring an education to become a productive member of society. Some feel the goal of "big time" athletics is money and winning.

You small college coaches, I commend you because most of you could draw a larger salary at the secondary level. Your dedication is what this book is about.

You small college athletes who put in a lot of hard work and sweat into your sport as well as having to pay for your education, I salute you for your efforts. You work extremely hard competing with little chance of any professional playing opportunity. Many of you also have to work while attending college in order to fulfill your dream of playing college ball and face years of paying back student loans for your education.

You small college, high school, and junior high school coaches who haven't or won't have the opportunity, or know the right people, to became a "Big-time Coach" if that it your desire, I honor you for your personal dedication and sacrifice for our great game of basketball.

For you college administrators who understand the real purpose of athletics and realize the need for a good relationship between yourselves and the coaching staff, I congratulate you.

Finally, to the fans and parents of small college basketball players, I appreciate the time and financial sacrifices you make to support the athletes and teams. Without you, small college athletics would not exist. Every interested athlete should have the possibility to participate in college sports. It is your support that helps to make this possible.

This book is an autobiography written with a historical flavor of Eureka College basketball during my tenure as Head Basketball Coach. It was written with a genuine attempt to recall the events as they actually occurred. The book was written in third person because I felt that would make the book read more smoothly and be more affective in its message.

I feel this book, *Road to Destiny: TWW*, is a small-college version of *Hoosiers*. "Together We Win!" "Together We Win!"

Team picture with fingers raised in #1. (Photo by Dick Selby, Idaho Press Tribune)

Chapter 1

We Are the Champions

WE'RE NUMBER ONE! We're Number One!" With index fingers pointing to the roof, the 1994 Eureka College basketball team members celebrated their first NAIA II National Basketball Championship.

Tuesday, March 15, 1994, was the day Eureka College made history. After two years of near misses and player illnesses, this team put the college on the national athletic map.

While standing in front of the final night's standing-room-only crowd, holding the National Championship banner, smiling from ear to ear, Coach Darnall realized he had reached the ultimate in his profession—to coach a team to a national title. Later would come the real symbol of success—the championship ring. This championship was the final leg of the road to destiny. It would all begin with childhood dreams.

The *Idaho Press Tribune*, the host city's newspaper, headline read, "Eureka! Devils Win NAIA Title in OT." The *Idaho Statesman* newspaper printed, "Eureka, an NAIA Champion." One of the team's hometown newspapers, *The Pantagraph* of Bloomington-Normal, Illinois, front page sports section headline stated, "Eureka College wins crown—Darnall goes out as national champion." What a coincidence that this was the same newspaper that Dave Darnall thumbed through as a youngster while growing up in Normal, Illinois.

It took luck, perseverance, and numerous breaks to achieve what the Red Devil hoopsmen accomplished on that March night. In reality, team camaraderie and hard work played a greater part to achieve the ultimate.

Just moments before the team took the floor for the last time in Coach Darnall's basketball coaching career, he asked for his traditional ten seconds of silence that was taken before each game. "Let's take our ten seconds. Each one is an individual. Think what you want to think or you don't need to think at all as long as we are quiet, and we do it together." For twenty years, 534 games, the coach recited those few words before he dismissed his team to battle.

Eureka College, a small liberal arts institution of higher education with an enrollment of approximately 450 students, was competing in its third consecutive NAIA—Division II National Basketball Tournament. The National Association of Intercollegiate Athletics—Division II sponsored tournament was in its third year of existence. For the second straight year, the tournament was held in Nampa, Idaho. Eureka was only one of four colleges that had competed in all three tournaments.

Eureka College, with the third smallest enrollment of the 1994 twenty-four team field, and the only team that did not offer some type of athletic aid, was seeded sixth. The Midwestern team had an extremely difficult route to take in order to claim the national crown. There would be the possibility that the Red Devils would meet the 1993 National Champions, Willamette University; the 1993 runner-up, Northern State University; and the host school, Northwest Nazarene College.

This task was not new for the Red Devils. Eureka College, affiliated with the Disciple of Christ Christian Church, does not offer athletic scholarships. This was quite different from the other competing institutions in the National Tournament. Eureka was a member of both the NAIA and NCAA national associations. This meant that the college's athletic programs must abide by the most stringent rules of each association.

One of the smallest four-year colleges in Illinois, Eureka had to play a large portion of its schedules against institutions with much larger enrollments throughout Darnall's career.

Several comparable institutions within a natural proximity refused to schedule Eureka College. Even though no college actually expressed why this competition did not occur, Dave felt their fear of losing to a small, non-conference school would hurt their image in recruiting. Not only was it very difficult to schedule colleges equal in size, but finding opponents willing to travel to the heart of Illinois was probably even more difficult because of the number of colleges in the Chicago and St. Louis areas.

In this season of glory, Eureka College only played twelve home games, two of which were the result of the team's ability to achieve the highest national Dunkel rating of their conference schools. The teams with the highest Dunkel points at the end of the season had the honor of hosting conference tournament games. Eureka finished their season schedule with a rating of 43.6. The next best rating was that of Indiana Institute of Technology, a team with a potent offense averaging 107 points a game. This ranked IIT number one in scoring nationally among NAIA Division II institutions. Tech's Dunkel was 38.5. The Conference tournament champion automatically qualified for the National Tournament.

In 1987, Eureka College won its first NAIA District 20 State of Illinois championship. This qualified the team to participate in the thirty-two team NAIA National Championship Tournament in Kansas City. There was only one NAIA National Tournament at that time. Eureka was one of the smallest colleges in the tournament field and the only institution that did not offer some type of athletic aid. Eureka had only nine regular season home games. The first twelve were played on the road, resulting in a fantastic 11 to 1 record.

As Coach Darnall stated, "All college coaches know it is harder than hell to win on the road." How did Eureka College basketball teams overcome this obstacle? Dave said, "The slogan I had developed while coaching high school and carried over to the college level helped. This slogan was 'Together We Win': TWW."

What did that mean? Darnall explained, "I don't care if you are black or white, rich or poor, protestant or catholic, six-foot-six or five-foot-six, handsome or average looking, an A student or C student—nothing below a C, you have to care about each other both on and off the floor. We have to care about each other's concerns. This doesn't mean you have to run around with each other all the time, but you do have to care about each other."

Dave said the players he wanted on his teams must be "coachable, work hard, be good kids, tenacious, and accept challenges." The TWW philosophy Darnall developed, plus these player qualities, were what he felt made his teams successful over the years. Darnall also wanted his players to come to Eureka College for the purpose of getting their education first and to play basketball second. "They can never take your education away from you, but you might get hurt and never play another ounce of basketball,"

Darnall emphasized. Needless to say, this was also the college's concept. To the best of Dave's knowledge, only three players who attended Eureka College for four years during his tenure did not graduate. Of those, two are only a few hours short. Wonder how this percentage would compare to the graduation rate of major universities who give full-ride scholarships?

The journey to the National Championship seemed long and strenuous for Coach Darnall. In twenty years, there were many obstacles to overcome, such as long hours, disappointing losses both in games and recruits, college conflicts, sleepless nights, long trips, lonely hours, family disenchantment, and even close calls on the road. However, the trip to Nampa, Idaho, on Tuesday, March 8, 1994, made it all worthwhile.

Dennis Dighton, Dave's assistant for nine years, a graduate from Eureka College, and Coach's first administrative assistant in 1974-1975, met the Darnall family at Reagan Fieldhouse around 10:30 on the morning of departure. While he was overseeing the loading of game equipment onto the Peoria Charter bus that was to take the Eureka College party to Chicago O'Hare Airport, Coach Darnall was visiting with a group of well-wishers who had assembled for a small send-off. Most of those in attendance were college personnel and parents because the general student body was off-campus on term break. All of the college's administrative offices were represented. Pat and Lynn from the Business Office distributed a small symbolic memorabilia gift to each member of the traveling team. They were artificial Idaho potatoes made of stuffed pantyhose. Three individuals who had worked closely with Dave in preparing for the long trip, Lynn and Shellie from the Collage Relations Office, and Becky, the Athletic Department secretary, were among those lending their support.

President George Hearne and his wife, Jean, mingled among the enthusiastic crowd wishing the team and coaching staff a safe trip and good luck in the tournament. Dave had high regards for President Hearne who had been a factor in his hiring twenty years prior while serving in the capacity of Director of Admissions. It was Hearne who came to Darnall's assistance on several conflicting occasions with other administrators in his somewhat bumpy road to success.

There was a lot of local media interest in the Red Devils' third consecutive trip to an NAIA II National Tournament. Sportswriters from Bloomington's *The Pantagraph*, Peoria's *Journal Star*, and the *Woodford County Journal* were on-hand to interview members of the team and coaching staff. The local radio's sports announcer was taping interviews with coaches and players. Area fans would be able to hear all of the tournament games that Eureka College played on WIVR. The *Journal Star* sent sportswriter Scott Heiberger to cover the Red Devils' entire participation in the tournament. Several of his articles will be reviewed in later chapters.

Finishing the informal "send-off," faithful Red Devil fans who were accompanying the team and the players headed for the charter for the two-hour ride to Chicago's O'Hare Airport. As bus driver, Phil Foster, patiently waited, the team paused in front of the bus for last minute pictures. Finishing the photo session, the players boarded the charter for the first leg to Idaho.

The bus trip to Chicago was subdued. Passengers were visiting, looking at the passing scenery or taking a nap. The real excitement started as O'Hare became visible from the windows of the big red-and-white bus traveling on Tri-State 294. It soon would be "Big Time." Only once before had a Eureka College athletic team traveled by plane, that being the year before. For some, this was the first time in a plane. For others, it was a repeat of the previous year. Last year's team lost to host school, Northwest Nazarene College, in the quarterfinals to make claim of being in the "Elite Eight."

Upon arrival at O'Hare, the entourage moved quickly to the terminal that would lead to their flight to San Francisco International Airport. Due to the remodeling of Denver International, the flight was detoured to San Francisco. The players, dressed in their traveling suits sporting a Eureka College basketball logo on the multi-colored jacket, looked impressive. The motto, "Together We Win," was definitely evident with coaches and players dressed identically on their flight to destiny.

Approximately forty-five minutes later, the team boarded the California bound American Airline for the second phase of the trip. Dave compared himself to John Madden. He hated to fly. With two faithful companions close by, his wife, Bonnie, sitting next to him, and Dan Harrod, a retired Air National Guard pilot and friend nearby, the flight went fairly smoothly. This was the second consecutive year that he had his moral supporters accompany him to Nampa. Dave kept his mind off the flying by preparing his up-coming practices and reviewing scouting reports. Needless to say, Bonnie was the one sitting by the window gazing at the scenery. A couple of cold beers during the flight helped to settle the coach's nerves. The players, listening to music through their earphones, were busy reading, napping, checking the view, or quietly talking to their seatmate. The most popular time of the flight was when dinner was served. Everyone knows growing boys never get full.

Amy and Dan Harrod seated behind Bonnie and Coach with "Super Scout" Wertz in the aisle.

Upon arrival in San Francisco, panic set in. It was learned that the continuing flight to Boise had been overbooked by some ten passengers. At first there was dismay.

Then it was learned that the airline was enticing passengers with free overnight accommodations in a classy downtown hotel, complimentary dinner, and a free ticket to use at a later date. Several of the twenty-five accompanying Red Devil fans decided that would be a "good deal" since the opening ceremony was still a couple of days away.

Some rushed to the ticket counter volunteering to forfeit their ticket. One was Dave's son, Derek. Being in his early twenties, he thought staying in San Francisco for the night would be a great adventure. There was much disappointment when approximately a minute before take-off those electing to stay back were informed that there were ten "no-shows" and all passengers should board.

The last leg of the flight seemed to pass quickly. The team was anxiously awaiting their arrival in Boise. After last year's experience, Coach

6

Darnall knew that one of the most difficult times in the entire trip was about to occur. That would be getting everyone unloaded, finding their luggage, locating the equipment trunks, and waiting for the fans to get their rental vehicles. For the tournament's participating teams, the NAIA tournament committee did an outstanding job in providing each team with two vans for transportation throughout their stay.

As customary, each team had a sponsor. For the second consecutive year, Eureka was fortunate to have Albertson's as their sponsor. Albertson's is a grocery chain with the majority of stores located in western and southern states. The home office is located in Boise. Duplicating the previous year representing Albertson's, Frank Mattern who was manager of third-party pharmacy, and John Danielson, assistant treasurer, met the team at the airport.

"Hello, Frank, John," Dave said. "Great to see you. Boy, are we happy you guys are our sponsors again this year."

Frank acknowledged the kind words as the hosts directed the Eureka entourage to the inner walkway leading to the escalator for a quick trip to the bottom floor where the team vans were waiting. After gathering luggage and a few fans obtained keys for rental vehicles, the entire group left the building for the final twenty minutes of the journey. With Coach Dighton driving one van and Coach Begole the other, the team left for their hotel in Nampa.

Coach Darnall hopped into the back seat of Danielson's Ford Explorer while Mattern slipped into the passenger seat. John also headed for the team's hotel. Along the way, the three renewed their acquaintance, asking each other about the past year's happenings.

Dave inquired how they became Eureka's sponsors again. This had shocked him since the year before the teams' names had been draw from a "hat." The fellows informed him that a few sponsors, including themselves, requested to have whoever represented the same district or conference as the previous year. The tournament committee decided to grant their wish. It was Eureka College's blessing.

John and Frank, hearing about the Red Devil's thrilling victory over Indiana Tech in the conference championship game that qualified Eureka for the return trip, wanted to know about the quality of the Indiana team.

Darnall replied, "I feel the game against Tech was actually the first round of the National Tournament. We felt the winner would possibly get a bye in the first round. I think Indiana Tech could play with any team out here."

After about ten miles, John pulled into a McDonald's adjacent to the highway and let his passengers out. Frank took Dave in his car the remaining distance to the hotel while John proceeded home.

Upon Darnall's arrival at the Shilo Inn, named Nampa Suites Hotel, the players and coaches had already checked-in and were heading to their rooms. Dave had faxed a room list before leaving Eureka. The players had only to locate their assigned rooms.

The Red Devils' supporters were staying at the Super 8 located at the next exit two miles away. The team and their fans would not see each other until the following evening at the NAIA Tournament Tip-off Banquet held at the Civic Center in downtown Nampa.

After letting Coach Darnall out, Frank drove off while Dave entered the hotel lobby. The night clerk informed Dave he had a fax when he approached the front desk. What a fax it was! Guess who it was from? You lose! It was from former President Ronald Reagan. The hotel personnel were very anxious and excited about giving President Reagan's letter to the Eureka College coach. Who was this guy receiving a letter from a former president?

Even though Coach Darnall had on several occasions received letters and autographed pictures from President Reagan, getting this letter was special. The former president, who is a 1932 graduate of the college, had a deep commitment and genuine interest in his alma mater. The fieldhouse in which the Red Devils play was named after Reagan and his brother, Neil, better known as "Moon." Neil graduated from Eureka in 1933.

Dave knew that the reading of this letter at the following day's practice would motivate his players to play hard throughout the tournament. His players played for their fans as much as for themselves. During the tournament, the team or individual players received over seventy-five faxes and telegrams from their fans back home. Coach would read these messages to his team the afternoon of the games during their "skull session." This seemed to have a great impact upon the players.

By the time Darnall got the letter, checked-in, and got to his room, it was close to 8:00 P.M. As usual, the players were hungry. Dave telephoned his assistant coaches to instruct Coach Dighton to have Coach Begole go to McDonald's and get the players their usual post-game meal—two cheeseburgers, large fry, and a large Coke.

"I don't think the players need anything," Dighton replied. "All they did today since leaving Eureka has been eat." Coach Dighton always felt the players were hungrier to play when they weren't so "fat and full." Besides,

Coach Dighton enjoyed keeping the players "on their toes." Even though Dave felt Dighton's philosophy was probably right, he thought the players should have a little something before they went to bed. It would still be a couple of days before the team would actually play.

It took an hour before Begole would return with the food. Most of the players were in their rooms visiting, watching TV or playing euchre waiting for the food to arrive.

Coach Darnall, wanting the players to settle down after their long day, proclaimed an 11:00 P.M. curfew, meaning lights out. This would give his team over an hour of free time. He wanted his players to start thinking about their mission of the next few days. Several of the six seniors went to the pool area after finishing their meal. Most used the whirlpool. While sitting in the swirling, warm water, they met and chatted with a couple of the officials who had been assigned to the tournament. The game officials were staying at the same hotel. The players and officials visited and exchanged general information regarding background on the team and where the officials were from.

At 11:00 P.M., Coaches Dighton and Begole made bed check finding the fellows were pretty much settled in. The rule was that as long as the players were in bed with lights off, they could leave on the TV Coach Darnall knew the next few days would be hectic and demanding. Practices, "skull sessions," games, and tournament events such as banquets and scouting future opponents would keep the players "hopping." They would need their rest.

With the players in bed, the three coaches went next door to O'Callahan's Restaurant/Lounge for a coaches' meeting and relaxation. Trainer Brown remained in the hotel for supervision. The coaching staff prepared a plan for the up-coming day's happenings as well as drew up the practice schedule.

Even though Bonnie was in Nampa, she stayed at the Super 8 with the players' parents and other Eureka College fans. Other members of Dave's family—Derek, daughter Tiera, son-in-law Brett, who would fly in later, and Dave's nephew Travis, who rode the fan bus—would also stay at the Super 8.

Darnall wanted his players, assistant coaches, as well as himself, to remain focused upon their objective—to win the National Championship. With his family staying with the other Red Devil fans, he would be able to apply his full attention to the job to be done. Besides, this arrangement would demonstrate to his players his commitment to stay focused.

The coach always had a sleeping disorder during the season. This included itching, upset stomach, diarrhea, and sleeplessness. These symptoms occurred both the night before a game as well as the night of a game. Therefore, having a room to himself meant he would not disturb anyone else. The planning for the next few days was extremely important. Darnall felt the main responsibilities of the coaching staff were to see that the players received the proper amount of rest, ate properly and at appropriate times, and be prepared to play. Proper meal scheduling was important so that the players would be able to practice or play games effectively.

The following morning, the players had a wake-up call at 10:00 A.M. Many liked to sleep-in because they had a difficult time falling asleep during such an emotional time. The team would meet in the hotel's lobby at 10:50 A.M. to walk together the few feet to O'Callahan's for breakfast. The Nampa Suite Hotel's lobby would serve as the team's meeting point throughout the tournament.

Upon completion of breakfast, the players again gathered in the hotel's lobby to get instructions for the remainder of the day. Wednesday, March 9th, would be very busy with the Tip-off Banquet climaxing the day's events.

Following the short meeting, the guys returned to their rooms for approximately an hour before they had to reconvene in the lobby at 12:30 P.M. dressed in their practice gear. With Coach Dighton driving one van containing Darnall and the underclassmen, Coach Begole chauffeured the other van with the upper classmen. The team left the hotel for the fifteen-minute drive to Nampa High School. The 1:00 P.M. practice was held at the local high school even though school was in session. However, the physical education classes had been cancelled.

With the physical education students sitting in the bleachers, the team started their warm-up at 1:00 P.M. Following the warm-up, Coach Darnall gathered the team together for his usual pre-practice talk. Darnall explained the possibility of up-coming opponents. He discussed what offenses, defenses, and strategies they would possibly employ in the first tournament game. Not knowing whom the first opponent would be, the coach discussed the personnel of both possible opponents.

Finishing the team meeting, Coach Darnall reached into his folder containing the practice schedule and scouting reports and retrieved the letter he had received the night before from President Reagan. He read it to his players.

RONALD REAGAN

March 8, 1994

Dear Coach Darnall,

I was thrilled to hear that the Red Devils have once again qualified for National Competition! Sounds like you and the boys have done it again!! I don't suppose you are in need of a healthy, feisty, and very "mature" Right Guard!? I'd be willing to help you out just this once for such a big game!

Seriously, I am so proud of you and your impressive team -- not only for your outstanding record and talented athletes, but also for your teamwork, your determination throughout the season, and your fine sportsmanship. I know you will give the championship your best effort and -- win or lose -- you will have worked to the best of your ability and made Eureka proud.

You have every right to be satisfied with your season -- pleased with your great victories and triumphs. I wish you all the best as you face the tough competition in the coming days. You have what it takes to be victorious; so I ask you, please go out there and win one for the Gipper!

Sincerely,

Ronald Reagan

Coach Dave Darnall
Eureka College
300 East College Avenue
Eureka, Illinois 61530

After reading the letter, Coach Darnall instructed his players to warm-up by taking several laps with their arms up. Dave believed in short practices at this stage of the season, meaning approximately an hour. The practice included the execution of offenses and defenses that the team would employ against their opponent.

The first opponent was unknown. Eureka College was seeded sixth in the twenty-four-team tournament; thus drawing a first-round bye. The Red Devils would play the winner of the Westbrook, Maine, and Ohio Dominican game. This contest would be played at noon, Thursday, March 10, the first day of the tournament.

With practice over, the team returned to the Shilo Inn. The players would have some free time. Several of the players went to the pool while others watched TV or took a nap.

Since the Tip-off Banquet was still three hours away, Coach Darnall felt the players should have some sort of snack. He asked Coach Begole to go to the nearby Albertson's, the team's sponsor store, to pick up some fruit and juices. Dave felt this would hold them over until the 7:00 P.M. banquet.

Coach Darnall and Coach Dighton had to leave the hotel to attend the coaches' meeting for all 24 participating institutions' head coaches. The 4:00 P.M. meeting was held at Montgomery Physical Education Building on the campus of host school, Northwest Nazarene College.

Upon Begole's return from Albertson's, he delivered the snacks to the players' rooms and informed them that they should be dressed for the banquet and meet in the lobby at 6:30 P.M. They were told to "look good" meaning slacks, shirt and tie, sweater, or sportcoat.

It was time to leave for the banquet. The team went to their vans for the short trip to downtown Nampa. Their supporters who had accompanied them to Idaho greeted the Red Devil team at the Civic Center. This was the first time the players saw their fans since their arrival at the Boise airport. After exchanging hellos and chit-chatting several minutes, the Eureka College entourage headed toward the Center's main door.

All twenty-four teams, their sponsors, players' parents, their fans and friends of basketball would celebrate the opening of the third NAIA Division II National Tournament. With the ceremony open to the public, an expected crowd of over 1000 people was in attendance. Once inside, the team went to their assigned seating, and the Red Devil fans sat as a group in another designated area. By fate, the Eureka College basketball team and their sponsors were seated directly in front of the head table and speaker's

12

podium. There were approximately fourteen dignitaries sitting at the head table, including NAIA II directors and mayors of local cities. Sitting at their assigned location meant the Red Devil team was at the center of attention. Maybe this was a good sign of things to come. The team enjoyed a great meal, listened to the speakers, and visited with their sponsors, John and Frank. The sponsors knew all of the upperclassmen as well as many of the team's fans because of their sponsorship of the team the previous year.

The tournament banquet concluded around 9:30 P.M. The Eureka College supporters escorted their favorite sons to the parking lot where a few words were exchanged before Coaches Dighton and Begole drove the players back to the Shilo Inn.

As customary, team curfew was 11:00 P.M. Coach Darnall went with John and Frank. John drove the trio to a nearby lounge where they met most of the male Red Devil fans. The women returned to the motel where they got together.

At the lounge, the sponsors, coaches, fathers, and other supporters reminisced about last year's tournament, talked about the past season, and speculated about the up-coming tournament. A cold beer tasted great after the excellent meal at the Center. The assistant coaches were able to rejoin the group after dropping the players off at the hotel. Trainer Brown again supervised the players. The players were given strict instructions! They could go to the whirlpool, stay in their room, watch TV, play cards, or just visit with teammates until lights out at 11:00 P.M. Darnall did not worry about his players' behavior at the hotel. He knew this year's team was on a mission. Being one of only four teams to compete in all three Division II tournaments plus making the "Elite 8" the previous year, the players wanted the championship trophy and rings.

It was an enjoyable evening. The coaches returned to the hotel and proceeded to Darnall's room for a short meeting. The next day's agenda was discussed. Finishing, the assistants returned to their rooms while Darnall turned on the TV, took a sleeping pill and went to bed. He knew the next night before the game would be sleepless. Anxious about winning or losing and worrying about the up-coming opponent would keep him up. Thank God, after several minutes the pill took affect and coach fell asleep.

On Thursday morning, the players were awakened at 9:30 A.M. They again met in the lobby and proceeded to walk next door to O'Callahan's. Following breakfast, the players returned to their rooms to prepare for their departure to the arena, Orrin E. Hills Center Court.

13

The tournament's afternoon session began at noon. Eureka College's first opponent would be the winner of this game between Westbrook and Ohio Dominican. Coach Darnall wanted his players to see their future opponent before a scheduled 2:00 P.M. practice to prepare for the winner.

The Red Devils entered the pass gate located at the rear of Montgomery fieldhouse. Their fans were already seated, also anxious to see who the first opponent would be. The players and their supporters sat together watching the all-important game.

Chuck Wertz, the volunteer chief scout, watched one team while Coach Dighton scouted the other. Coach Darnall, surrounded by the starters, observed both teams while discussing potential match-ups, strengths, and weaknesses of players from both teams.

The team returned to the hotel around 1:15 P.M. to prepare for practice. Arriving at the Shilo Inn, Dave had received several faxes from the fans back home wishing the team luck in their up-coming game. Routinely, Darnall read them to his players during the day's "skull session."

The practice was spent entirely preparing for Dominican. Actually, EC had seen their first opponent play earlier in the season at the Wabash (Indiana) Invitational Tournament.

Returning to the Nampa Suite Hotel, the team quickly prepared to go to the Albertson's corporate headquarters for an early dinner. Sponsors John and Frank had invited the players, coaches, and Bonnie. Equaling the previous year, the meal was outstanding. The sit-down affair allowed the team to enjoy the hospitality of their sponsors. Frank and John gave their guests a tour of their office complex following the meal. It was a magnificent operation with modern high-tech equipment. The visit was an outstanding educational opportunity for the Eureka student-athletes.

The team returned to the hotel to dress into their game warm-ups before proceeding to Orrin E. Hills Center Court for the opening night ceremony. The opening night ceremony included a "Parade of Champions." All twenty-four participating teams marched out onto the game floor to form a giant "NAIA" as their respective school's name was announced.

The "Parade of Champions" was a very special event. However, by the time the presentation took place, six teams had already been eliminated. All teams were required to participate in the opening night ceremony regardless of the day's outcomes. With the teams standing in formation on the floor, the National Anthem was played. The players were then asked to sit facing the south end of the facility to watch a video presentation projected on the gym wall. The tape was a compilation of highlights of all twenty-four competing teams' season games. Each team was featured in approximately a minute segment of their season's highlights. The video was a salute to the champions. At the completion of the video presentation, the teams left the floor in an unspecified manner.

The 8:00 P.M. game put the host school, Northwest Nazarene, against Husson, Maine. Coach Darnall knew the winner of that game could be a future opponent. Knowing this, he wanted his players to see some of the game. At half time the team returned to the hotel in preparation for bed since tomorrow's 12:00 P.M. game would soon be there. Dave took a sleeping pill and went to bed even thought he knew it would prove futile. Pre-game syndrome had already taken hold. Finally in the wee hours of the morning, he drifted off. A good night's sleep it was not!

Eureka College's first game of the tournament on Friday, March 11, was the opening contest of the afternoon session. This meant the players would have wake-up at 8:00 A.M. The pre-game breakfast was served at O'Callahan's at 8:45 A.M. following a short team meeting in the lobby. The players returned to their rooms after breakfast to prepare to go to the fieldhouse. Because of only a ten-minute warm-up period between games, the next game's teams were allowed to take the floor for individual shooting at half time of the preceding game. Since that game started at 10:45 A.M., Coach Darnall wanted his team to be at their assigned locker room, dressed in their game warm-ups, and ready to shoot by 11:15 A.M.

The team boarded their waiting vans in front of the Nampa Suite Hotel at 10:30 A.M. for the ten-minute drive to the tournament site. Would this be their last trip or just another ride on a route to destiny?

Chapter 2

Childhood Dreams

T WEET, TWEET; BOBWHITE, BOBWHITE," were the chirping sounds the Darnalls heard from the pear trees located in their long, narrow backyard. They were gazing through their screened dining room window, watching their sons David and Bruce playing ball on the bright early fall Saturday morning.

"Those kids are going to be ball players some day," Ola told her husband as they shared morning coffee at their dining room table.

"I think so; that's all they like to do," Delmar replied. "Whatever sport season it is, they are doing it."

"I just hope they don't get hurt," said the boys' mother.

"They'll be all right. Just let them play," the boys' father reassured.

The remarkable journey began for David Darnall on March 18, 1942, when he was born the second child to Ola and Delmar Darnall. The family lived in an older two-story yellow house owned by David's grandparents, the John Kerrs. Noted for its "Darnall's Kennel Cocker Spaniels" sign planted in the front yard, the house was located on Main Street, or U.S. 51 and Route 66, which ran directly through Bloomington-Normal, Illinois. The Darnall home was located three blocks from where Dave's name would eventually be permanently enshrined with the highest honor a sport enthusiast could achieve at his/her alma mater—a hall of fame selection.

The unexpected occurred on September 21, 1991, when Coach Dave Darnall was inducted into the Illinois State University Athletic Hall of Fame.

This achievement holds great prestige because David never participated in any of the college's sports' programs.

This honor, bestowed upon him for future accomplishments, all began with his early childhood environment and those people with whom he surrounded himself. While ISU (then called Illinois State Normal University —ISNU) never benefited from David's limited athletic ability, it did provide a source for his tremendous love of athletics.

David had an older sister, Judy, and a younger sister, Lucia. However, it was his younger brother by two years, Bruce, that provided Dave his athletic companion. The elder Darnall worked the night shift at Caterpillar Tractor Company in Peoria, approximately fifty miles away. Most of the day hours were spent by Mr. Darnall either sleeping or caring for some thirty Cocker Spaniels in his kennel. As a youngster, Dave was a very active child playing baseball, basketball, and football with neighborhood friends, John Hendricks, Jerry Whittet, Ronnie Wall, Dick Steljes, and Rod Brent. Besides spending time with Grandma and Grandpa Kerr, the Darnall boys enjoyed playing ball with their neighborhood buddies the most.

At the ages of seven and five respectively, David and Bruce received their first basketball uniforms. These were from Santa Claus. Dave's was red and Bruce's was blue. How fitting since red was Dave's favorite color, and ISNU's colors were red and white. Guess Santa knew! The color red was significant to Dave. He grew up a St. Louis Cardinal (Redbird) fan in baseball, a Chicago Cardinal fan in football, and, of course, an ISNU Redbird fan in college sports. Needless to say, in all neighborhood games, his team had to be the Cardinals or Redbirds.

The phone rang. David and Bruce's mother answered the phone.

"Do you know," the neighbor woman asked, "that your boys are outside in the snow with no clothes on playing basketball?"

"Oh," Ola said, "I guess they couldn't wait until the snow melts."

After a delicious late-afternoon Christmas meal, the boys returned to the outdoor court wearing their favorite Christmas gifts, their basketball uniforms. Before night fell, another neighbor shared her concern to the boys' mother. "No wonder those boys will be sick, out there playing in the cold and snow," the neighbor warned.

The boys' first baseball uniforms were somewhat homemade. Mrs. Darnall cut off the lower legs of some white pajamas and sewed in elastic. This would hold up the boys' purchased red and white socks. They had their first set of baseball pants. With red T-shirts and plain red caps, the uniforms sym-

bolized the St. Louis Cardinals and ISNU Redbirds to the youngsters. The boys were a picture to be seen. A year later they received their first bought baseball uniforms. With stripes on the pants and fancy caps, the boys felt they were in the "big leagues."

The Darnall brothers played each sport as it was in season; football in the fall, basketball in the winter, and baseball in the spring and summer. The only organized sports program for youngsters was American Legion Baseball. It was during this time that Dave met two gentlemen who would have an impact upon his life—Duffy Bass and Guy Ricci. Bass was a young coach employed by University High School, the laboratory school associated with the famous teachers' college, ISNU. Ricci was the Head Basketball and Baseball Coach at Normal Community High School. It was this school with its noted orange and black colors that most students from Normal attended.

Kids had sports heroes during this time. Dave was no exception. In baseball, his pro heroes were Red Schoendienst, Stan Musial, and Enos Slaughter. In football, they were Ollie Matson and Charlie Trippie. In college, they were ISNU's Buck Weaver, Fred Mulberry, and Bob Riggenbach. At the high school level, they were neighbor, Jim Maxey, and Marlow Zehr who both attended Normal Community High School.

Many youngsters, including the Darnall brothers, dreamed of becoming a professional football, basketball, or baseball player. The boys spent hours talking about this desire. However, the high school they eventually attended did not have football, and they never had the chance to formally play the game.

Playing "ball" was the thing to do. In the neighborhood where the Darnalls lived, most parents did not have to worry about their children getting into trouble. Youngsters were playing ball games either in their yards, at the schoolyards, at ISNU practice fields, or at Victory Hall. Victory Hall was located on the street directly behind the Darnall house. The Hall provided many playmates for Dave and Bruce as this was the home for boys from broken homes, those with family problems, or orphans. Superintendent Stark's oldest two sons, Charles and Billy, were classmates and good friends of the Darnall boys.

The brothers and Hendricks spent many hours at Victory Hall, especially during the winter. Its facility was the only location, other than the schools or ISNU, which had a gymnasium. It was not what one would call a regulation gym, but it did provided a place where the trio could play basketball.

"David enjoyed playing basketball in the Victory Hall gym," Bruce said. "He could beat the older guys in 'HORSE.' He always did have a good shot."

The boys missed numerous meals due to coming home late from the Hall. On several occasions their mother went to Victory Hall to snatch them. It was not a pleasant sight for Bruce and Dave to see her come in. That meant that she was upset. Missing their supper, the boys usually were sent to the room they shared on the second floor. There they listened to professional baseball games in the summer and area basketball games during the winter on local radio station WJBC.

Even though the brothers loved sports, they had several other childhood interests. One was their detective agency. Getting FBI Wanted posters from the local corner gas station and looking at crime headlines in the newspaper, the boys searched the area for the "bad guys." With their cap guns in their shoulder holsters and play handcuffs on their belts, the detectives felt secure.

A second interest was the printing of a small two-page, four-by-four-inch paper. The hand-printed paper was a weekly endeavor. The boys would copy headlines from the local *The Pantagraph* newspaper. Selling their paper to the neighbors for five cents an issue, the fellows thought they were rich. The paper went out of business after a full year of existence.

A neighborhood boy, Judd McElvane, who lived a block north of the Darnall home, was very inventive at a young age. He set up a newscast studio in his basement. The Darnalls were members of the late afternoon newscast team. Judd was the newsman, Bruce handled the weather, and Dave was the sports commentator. This adventure lasted over a year until Judd moved to Missouri. Unfortunately, there was never a live-cast.

Ola and Delmar had several close friends with children. The families included the Woods, Fentons, McGaths, and Harrisons. The group got together during weekends and played canasta or pinochle. The Woods had two boys, Larry and Gary. Fentons had three children. Harrisons had one son, Gary, and a daughter. The McGaths had a daughter, Sally.

While the parents played cards, most of the boys and Sally played cowboys. David usually portrayed "Wild Bill" Hickock, wearing his two gun holster belt backwards with a cap gun in each. Wearing a white hat, Dave was the good guy. Bruce, on the other hand, had a black cowboy hat and only carried one gun.

Dave, the oldest of the kids, took Sally and Gary Woods, the youngest of the boys, and who eventually became Athletic Director at Normal Community High School, as his good-guy partners. Every cowboy hero had to have his "Dale Evans." Dave was no different. Gary Woods was too young to be a threat to "Wild Bill" Hickock. Bruce, Larry, and Gary Harrison were designated as the bay guys. The other kids were either not interested or too young to play.

Bruce described another activity. "As our parents played pinochle with their friends, the kids would either play cowboys or 'kick the can.' We'd all go hide, but Sally and David would go off and hide together. They would never come in. A little romancing. We'd all get mad, but David would talk his way out of it," Bruce continued. "He always had a good reason for where they were hiding. This happened time after time."

At this point in time, most kids had household chores to do. The brothers were no exception. The neighborhood games played in the Darnall's backyard had to be played around pear trees and dog pens. The backyard seemed as though it was always full of fallen pears. It was the boys' job to keep them picked up.

Many times balls flew into the dog pens. Dave's father raised pedigree Cocker Spaniels. Sometimes as many as thirty dogs lived in the eight-by-twenty-foot doghouse. It was the brothers' job to feed and water the dogs daily.

Bruce recalled the daily duty because it was a nuisance to the neighborhood ball games. "I can remember David and I having to carry five-gallon pails of water and mix them in with dog food and take them down to the doghouse. We fed them all. Then we would have to clean up the dog poop in all those pens, put it in a garbage bucket, and put lime on it. So we grew up having to care for dogs, learning some responsibilities," Bruce concluded.

It was through the dogs that Dave experienced his second type of competition. Even though Gypsy Joe was the first Cocker Spaniel the Darnalls owned, it was Snappsy that won the awards at the kennel club shows. David and his sister, Judy, showed the blonde pedigree at several kennel shows. This included shows held at Bloomington Miller Park, ISNU farm, and Kankakee, Illinois.

It was at the Kankakee Kennel Club dog show that David received his first major award, an eighteen-inch trophy. He won a couple of small first-place gold cups at the locally sponsored shows, but it was at Kankakee that he established himself as a young showman.

In dog show competition, both dog and handler were judged. Different contestants could show the same dog in various classes. A major aspect of the competition was the way the handler showed the dog. This included how still the dog stood, how the handler held the dog's tail and head, and how the contestant maneuvered as the judge circled the dog. On this particular fall afternoon in 1952, the ten-year old and his dog, Snappsy, were at their best. Dave was awarded the KKC Best Junior Showman Trophy.

The trophy offered by the *Kankakee Journal* was the beginning of many trophies and plaques that would eventually grace David's family room for a variety of other activities.

Dave and his best friend, Hendricks, spent numerous hours together including spending the night at each other's house. The successful Wisconsin lawyer remembered many special occasions. "I recall staying over at your place. I am sure it was one of the first times I had stayed away from home.

We laughed and you taught me how to make 'fart noises.' I recall your dad working nights at Caterpillar in Peoria and not seeing him too much."

John continued, "You guys had the Cocker Spaniel kennel, and we raised chickens. You guys were the ones with the Hudson, the car that was way ahead of its time. You were also the ones with the TV. You had a monster antenna on the roof. I think you had several different types, but they were way the hell up there. It was a little black and white set in a little room off the main floor. You kept it very dark because it was so hard to see. There was so much snow. I think you tried to get Chicago as that was the closest station at that time. I can recall coming over to see the thing, but it was hard to make anything out because of the snow," John concluded.

John and David attended a small school with grades kindergarten through third on the west edge of Normal, named Smith School. Dave remembered how small the building was and his favorite teacher. "My favorite teacher at Smith School was Miss Nafzinger, my second grade teacher," Dave said. "During recess, she would umpire our softball games."

The three-room school building had only a basement for indoor activities. There was one basket hanging at the south end of the room, but the ceiling was so low not much basketball was played.

John's parents, the Howard Hendricks, were also friends of Dave's parents. Both couples were very active in the Smith School's PTA as well as other school functions. They worked hard to promote the tiny school and the school district. The Darnalls and Hendricks were among several sets of parents who campaigned hard to get better facilities for their children. Eventually, a new kindergarten through sixth grade school was built where Bruce would attend.

Sometime during John and Dave's second-grade year, they got into trouble that neither will ever forget. A set of twins reported that the boys had "looked up their dresses." This caused quite a stir. The Darnalls and Hendricks were furious! There were no after-school activities, no Victory Hall, just straight home for the youngsters. To this day, both guys insist that the allegations were false.

Hendricks enjoyed the good "ole" days when he and David had gone to the tiny school. "As I recall, we played a lot of ball—first out in the playground, then in the small basement of the school building. The ceiling was too low, so not too much basketball was played there," John said.

"As I remember, the playground had lots of holes, and we called them fox holes. Some said the playground was an old junkyard. It was out on the playground where we allegedly looked up the sisters' dresses. They were twins and pains in the butt," Hendricks added. "One of the girls called our folks. We could not come to school early and play on the playground, at least for a while," lamented John.

As the buddies grew older, the neighborhood football and baseball games were played at Hendrick's house. With a huge backyard, the playing fields became much larger. John remembered the highly contested games. "What I really recall the most was our regular 1:30 P.M. games, usually at our house. I recall your brother, Bruce, coming to play, but for reasons that escape me now, he would end up crying."

Dave defended his younger brother's behavior, "Bruce was very competitive. He was not afraid to get in there and get hit. Remember, he was a couple of years younger than most of the boys we played with." Dave continued, "He was always getting his butt kicked. Usually he ended up with a bloody nose. Mom always worried until he got home, but he just wanted to play with the older boys. He broke his nose three times by the time he entered high school."

Bruce verified the story like this, "David and I would always play together. He had friends, John Hendricks and few other guys, that we would play football, basketball, and baseball with. I would get a nosebleed, and Dave would be there to help me through it. I would get right back into the ball game again."

It was the Cardinals against the Bears. The big football game took place in the Darnall's backyard. Each team consisted of three boys. The game had been going on for a couple of hours. Bruce, the youngest, had to go "number 2"—poop. He asked his older brother if he could go to the house.

Dave answered, "Bruce, what do you think the pro players do when they have to go to the bathroom? You know they can't leave the field."

Bruce asked, "What should I do?"

"Go in your pants," Dave replied.

Bruce's version of the unforgettable incident was, "My brother was always a 'talker.' That's how he got to be a good recruiter. We had received new leather football helmets and uniforms for Christmas. We were playing snow football with a few neighborhood boys, and I had to go to the bathroom —'number 2,' if you know what I mean. Dave talked me into staying and playing and just going in my pants. He convinced me that was what the pros did when they played a long game. He got into real trouble with Mom and Dad when we went in. I was a mess! After a while, David just laughed," Bruce concluded.

The boys were warned that if a similar incident happened again, the football suits would go. They kept their uniforms—it didn't happen again!

Even though the Darnall children always had a nice Christmas, the family could have been classified as low-middle class economically. "I guess because of my background that is why I became so conservative," Dave said. "I would get one or two pairs of street shoes a year, wore the same couple pairs of pant, which were always kept clean, and got one 'Sunday School' suit each Easter. Maybe that is how I also became so superstitious. I was always wearing the same things when good things happened to me."

Darnall ended his coaching career wearing the same gray pants, white shirt, white sweater, gray plaid sportcoat, and cordovan shoes at each college contest. That apparel was only worn for games.

Ola Darnall was a religious lady. She taught Sunday School at the University Christian Church in Normal. This background provided the family with religious convictions. Bruce attended Sunday School for sixteen years without missing a Sunday. Dave went fourteen years with only missing two.

"As I got older, I hated to go to Sunday School," Dave confessed. It had nothing to do with religion. It was due to my reading skill. We were asked to read aloud from either the Bible or lesson book. With my reading ability, I felt extremely nervous and embarrassed," Dave admitted. "I just couldn't enjoy the class. I was always worried about when I would be asked to read. I would ask the person next to me how to pronounce anticipated words."

Bruce was the opposite. He was a good reader and student. He was usually cast as the lead character in the annual church Christmas and Easter plays.

"Bruce was a chip off the 'old block.' Today, I feel my father would have been an English teacher," David said. "Even though my dad worked in a plant, he was an articulate and intelligent man. Back then, it was very difficult to go to college. Money, the war, and family responsibilities kept him from a college education"

Delmar was not an athlete at Normal Community High School but did receive a varsity letter. He was a top debater on the school's successful debate team. This ability sometimes caused difficulties for Dave.

Since Dave's father spent limited time with his children, he believed in having a one-week family vacation. With two weeks of vacation allotted him each summer from his work, the elder Darnall took his family north to either Wisconsin or Minnesota fishing for one of the weeks. He worked the second week to support their trip. On one of those trips a major incident occurred that would affect the entire family.

A yearly trip to a professional baseball game was also taken. Although a Cubs fan, Mr. Darnall took the family either to St. Louis or to Chicago's Comisky Park. The boys liked the Cardinals and White Sox, so he attempted to please them. Besides, the Cardinals and White Sox were winning more than the Cubs. Bruce and Dave wanted to see their teams win.

The Darnall boys enjoyed spending time with their grandparents during the summer. This was both when the Kerrs lived on Market Street in Bloomington and when they lived on a farm near Carlock. The brothers played cowboys and Indians in the country hillsides and creeks.

BeBe, as the kids called their grandma, was a housewife. She was small and somewhat frail. Grandpa Kerr was a railroad man, an interior passenger car wood finisher. He was an excellent carpenter. One summer he built each boy a soapbox car for the annual "Soapbox Derby" that was held during the Normal Tomato Festival.

"Of all the cars in the race, mine was the best looking," Dave said. "It even had a small wooden grill. No one else actually had a grill." Needless to say, Dave's soapbox car was red!

The Darnall kids loved BeBe. She was gentle, nice, and an excellent cook. On some occasions when their parents were gone, she would "babysit." Bruce remembered one tragic happening. "BeBe was baby-sitting Judy, David, and me. David and I got into it. He knew he could get me angry pretty easily. This time he got me angry, and I chased after him. BeBe came chasing after both of us. As she went into the house, she collapsed and had a heart attack. We had to run to a neighbor's for help. They came over and called the ambulance, which took her to the hospital. She survived the heart attack, but it really upset both of us that we were part of the cause."

Even though the boys do not talk much about it today, they both feel very guilty for their behavior.

Summer was a fun time. The kids from one part of Normal-Bloomington could compete against kids from other parts of the towns in baseball. The community had an outstanding American Legion youth baseball program. Good coaching, good equipment, and good playing areas provided young players with good-quality playing.

One sponsoring business attracted the players' attention. Hubbard's Cupboard gave its team members free sodas after each game. Everyone wanted to be on that team. Only once did either of the Darnall boys play for the Cupboard.

Bruce and David, being different ages, participated in separate leagues. Dave and John signed up together in order to play on the same team. The playing areas were scattered throughout the entire twin cities. The players had to find their own transportation to the fields. The Darnall boys usually rode their bikes. Some trips took them nearly an hour. Even though Bruce, John, and Dave liked to ride their bikes to Bloomington High School, O'Neal Park, or State Farm Park, they loved playing at the "Cabbage Patch." The "patch" was only a fifteen-minute ride from most homes in Normal. Bruce and Dave's favorite coach was stationed there.

Duffy Bass, who eventually became the legendary Head Baseball Coach at Illinois State University, was their idol. A knowledgeable, patient, young coach, Bass won the hearts of the youngsters. The relationship between Coach Bass and Coach Darnall has continued to the present.

Living only a couple blocks from ISNU and about six blocks from Normal Community High School, the brothers spent numerous hours at those locations. During the spring, the boys were Normal Community's batboys. Guy Ricci, Head Baseball and Basketball Coach, took a liking to the Darnall brothers. Coach Ricci took Dave with him on Saturday morning baseball trips to neighboring towns. There, Dave took care of the team's bats. One athletic item Bruce and Dave had plenty of was bats. Oh yes, they were spliced with several nails and wrapped up with plenty of tape, but they worked.

Not only did Ricci coach at the local high school, but he also managed a team in the summer municipal league. The teams were composed of college age guys and older. The games were played at McCormick Field, the home diamond of the ISNU Redbirds. Games would start in the early evening and last until 10:00 P.M. or later. Mrs. Darnall never unduly worried about her boys, knowing they were just a few blocks from home, and were serving as batboys for either Ricci's or Bass's team. The boys inherited more broken bats.

Dave stated, "The association with Coach Bass and Coach Ricci made me think at an early age of becoming a coach." Those experiences helped Dave, as a youngster, to understand the games of baseball and basketball.

In 1954, the twelve-year old was devastated when Coach Ricci left Normal Community High School to become Head Baseball and Assistant Basketball Coach at Western Illinois University. Dave just could not understand why the coach would want to leave Normal. Years later, Dave crossed paths with Ricci on several occasions.

Not only did the brothers serve as batboys at muny-league games, they also chased foul balls on the nights their teams were not playing. Following those games, Warren Crews, who was in charge of the facilities, gave the boys a couple used baseballs. The neighborhood baseball games always had a good supply of bats and balls.

The young Darnall brothers admired their older cousin, Norris. He was the son of their father's sister. Norris was six feet, six inches tall. He played basketball at Normal Community High School and went on to play a year at Illinois State Normal University. Leaving ISNU, Norris played AAU basketball. Dave recalled when his cousin took him on a road trip. "I remembered going to Peoria to watch him play. He was so huge. Back then six-six was tall; almost a giant."

Occasionally, Norris and the boys' father took them to Peoria to watch the Caterpillar Cats play. "That was like watching professional basketball," said Dave.

"When the Cats played Phillips 66, it was the greatest thing I had ever seen. The crowd was large and loud. I wanted to be a Caterpillar Cat. Some of the greatest players in the country, including future professionals, were in that league."

Completing third grade at Smith School, the students had three choices of where to attend fourth grade. Most went to Normal Central. Others chose to go to Metcalf, ISNU's laboratory school, or Holy Trinity. Normal Central was the natural feeder to Normal Community High School.

Central was located approximately ten blocks from the Darnall house. However, if one cut across ISNU's campus, it was only seven blocks. That was the way John, Dave, and the rest of the kids on the southwest side of Normal took.

Being somewhat cocky, the Smith School boys sometimes had run-ins with the college students. Those episodes were usually started by the youngsters. "Recalling our going to and from Normal Central brings to mind that we walked through the campus during the winter," Hendricks said. "We would have some snowball fights with university students. We would throw snowballs and run. Sometimes the students would chase us."

While attending fourth grade at Normal Central, Dave met several new friends. One was Billy Draper. Draper lived on Main Street approximately ten blocks north of the Darnall home. It was while hanging out at

Billy's house that Dave found his first girl friend, a nearby neighbor named Diane. With this new personal interest, plus the addition of several other new friends on the north end of Normal, many of the football games were switched to a vacant lot next door to the Draper's. Across the street, where University High School is currently located, was an ISNU agriculture field. A large "sugar creek" ran through it. A huge concrete sewer tunnel provided a good place for the kids to "get away."

"This may be where I got my first kiss," Dave said. "It was a place we went where no one could find us." It was there that Draper would entertain his young friends.

"Bill was a pretty good singer," Dave said. "Every time we went there he would always sing one song. I think it was called 'Chattanooga Choo Choo.' I guess that was his favorite song."

When Dave and his buddies got older, they started attending the Normal Community football and basketball games. In the fall, the boys wore the distinctive orange and black stocking caps when attending the Friday night football games. The fellows watched their favorite players while still finding time to run around in the bleachers. It was a place where the boys could be with their buddies or with the girls.

A second popular gathering place for the youngsters was the "show." The business district of Normal was quite small. Still there was one intriguing spot, the Normal Theater. Kids from all over the city met every Saturday afternoon. The theater, which has since been renovated, provided the first place shy kids could hold hands.

"This was probably the first place other than the ball fields, I really looked forward to going," Dave said. Of course, the westerns and cartoons were kids' favorite shows—Roy Rodgers, John Wayne, and Bugs Bunny. However, the black-and-white newsreels at times intrigued the inattentive youngsters.

During fourth and fifth grades, most of the athletic competition was during recess, physical education class, or in the neighborhood yards. It was not until the sixth grade, that boys had the opportunity to play organized competitive sports. The school offered baseball in the fall, basketball in the winter, and track in the spring. Ray Temple was the only coach for all of these sports. Most boys could not wait until the sixth grade, including the Darnalls.

Chapter 3

School Days

I BELIEVE I WAS IN THE FIFTH GRADE when I played on our church team," Darnall said. "That was the first organized basketball team I played on. It was the UCC team, standing for the University Christian Church that competed in the church youth league. We were so proud wearing those green jerseys with white UCC letters across the chest."

The team played their league games at the YMCA. Practice was held in the basement of the church, known as the eating area. The ceiling was so low that no baskets were available. However, individual skills in the fundamentals of dribbling, passing, and learning an offense were taught by Coach Ray Blunk.

"I can remember playing some practice games at the Normal Methodist Church," Dave said. "We loved this." The Methodist church was located only one block north of the Christian Church making the practice game site quite convenient for the UCC youngsters.

The first basketball team Dave was associated with won a championship. So did his last! "We won the church league," Darnall said. "Not bad for only eight players."

Bruce Scott, the tallest player; Gordon Graves, the strongest and biggest player; Dave Blunk, coaches' son, and Darnall, the quickest players, were four of the starters.

The UCC youth team repeated as league champions the following year. There were several departures and additions to the team. Among the new players were Brother Bruce, Bill Draper, and Rod Brent.

The sixth grade boys were anxious for the start of school. They could finally try out for a school athletic team. Making a squad in any sport for a sixth grader was extremely difficult. They had to compete against both seventh and eighth graders. Dave wanted his chance.

Baseball practice started. Dave worked hard to make the team. His favorite position was second base. Even though he was a decent baseball player, it was difficult to compete against the bigger, stronger upper classmen. Dave was cut. He had to wait until the following year for another chance.

Basketball was different. Teams were designated as lightweight and heavyweight, not by grade level. A sixth grader could possibly make the lightweight team. Dave made the team as a substitute. In the spring, Dave also participated on the lightweight track team. He experienced success in the broad jump (now the long jump), hop-skip-jump (now the triple jump), and the fifty-yard dash. Most of the members of the track squad also participated in the Junior Olympics. This gave the intercity kids the opportunity to participate against each other during the summer.

Dave continued playing junior legion baseball during the summer. In the evening, Bruce and he served as batboys and ball chasers at the muny league games. During the day, the neighborhood boys played baseball or football at either Draper's or Hendricks'.

The brothers began to spend more time at their grandparents' farm near Carlock, a village approximately fifteen miles northwest of Normal. The boys helped their grandpa with his everyday chores. Normally, a couple other buddies went with them to help out and then play in the countryside. Dave recalled a happening that took place at the farm. It had not rained for weeks. The fields were drying up and no grass was growing. The cattle were getting sick with a couple dying. There was no water left in the field creek. It was a tremendous drought. Grandpa carried water across the road to a cattle trough, but there just wasn't enough water to give the cattle. The well was going dry. Dave's Grandpa told BeBe that if they did not get water within the next day or two, they would lose all of their animals. They went to bed. BeBe, a true believer, said her nightly prayer asking for rain before she fell asleep. Grandpa woke up early the next morning; still no rain. He carried a bucket across the street for the cattle. As he approached the water trough, he saw no cattle. Where did they go to die? He started walking the field. Passing over a ridge headed toward a ravine, he noticed the cattle way down by the timber. The creek ran through this area. He walked down to the creek. The cattle were there drinking water from the rushing stream. Where did the water come from? It had not rained. Grandpa Kerr rushed back to the house to tell Grandma. BeBe gave thanks. Was it a miracle or meant to be?

Entering seventh grade, Dave liked his chances of making the school's baseball team. Even though he had played very little, he made it. He was thrilled! Perhaps the following year he would be the starting second baseman.

Basketball began, and Dave made the starting five as one of the guards on the lightweight team. He finally reached a personal goal—to be a starter on a school's team. In fact, he was a key player.

An average student, Dave was more interested in sports and his friends than his studies. Bruce was the opposite. While in the seventh grade, David heard for the first time his father's famous words. "Sports aren't going to get you anywhere. If you don't start studying, you're going to end up digging ditches." Not that digging ditches was bad, but Dave's dad felt a college education was important. He wanted his children to have easier, less physical jobs than his.

"Being an excellent debater and having good communication skills, Dad would have been a very successful student," Dave said. "I feel he wanted things better for us later in life than what he had," Dave admitted. "That's why he was always on me. Playing ball games were not going to provide me with a living."

It was at this time Mr. Darnall insisted that his older three children go to their rooms each weekday evening to spend time studying. The boys, sharing the same second floor bedroom, spent more time conversing about the day's events and friends than studying.

With summer arriving and numerous friends from the northeast end of Normal gathering, including new friends Don Emmert and Don Raycraft, a larger field in that part of town was needed for the neighborhood ball games. Raycraft lived on a farm on the north edge of Normal. He had moved earlier from Bloomington. The house had a large yard on its east side that provided an excellent football, baseball, or wiffle ball field. Mr. Raycraft raised horses. There was a huge barn located behind the house, and it contained a large hayloft to store the winter feed. After some strong persuasion from his son, Mr. Raycraft agreed to leave the middle of the loft open for a "full-court basketball facility." The boys spent hours in their new "gymnasium." The barn eventually became Don's home. The baskets still hang from the rafters hidden by the upstairs ceiling. Dr. Raycraft, later in Dave's life, would have a significant impact upon his college career.

31

Sometime during the summer, the Darnall boys did a "NO, NO." Bruce explained the incident. "We sat on top of the large doghouse and had a cigarette. I guess we felt no one could see us up there. We got tobacco from our dad's Kool cigarette butts and put it in Mom's empty tampon dispensers. Maybe that's why neither of us smoke now," Bruce emphasized.

Dave was excited for his eighth-grade year to begin. He should finally become the starting second baseman on a good baseball team. After the previous year's lightweight success, making the top five on the heavyweight basketball team was a real possibility. Another successful track season should be repeated. Some of this never happened.

With school resuming, baseball practice started. Several eighth graders had been waiting their turn to be in the starting line-up, Dave being one. In the season opener, he found himself at second base. His good friends, Hendricks, Draper, and Raycraft joined him as starters. Behind the great pitching of right-hander Gary Willis, Normal Central completed an outstanding regular season. In post-season play, the team went on to win the Regional and Sectional Tournaments, advancing to the State Tournament. The "State" was held in Towanda, a small town just a few miles north of Normal. This was Dave's biggest athletic event to date—the first time to compete for a State Championship.

Subsequent State Champion LaSalle-Peru beat Central by the score of 18 to 3 in the semi-finals. However, Central bounced back to claim third place by defeating Virginia. Everything was going well for David; starting second baseman on the State's third place team, and his favorite sport, basketball, had begun. Then a traumatic event took place.

One evening in early October, sitting around the dinner table, Delmar announced to his family, "I have been transferred to Decatur. We will be moving in a few days." Dave was stunned and saddened. He begged his father to stay at the Peoria plant so he could finish playing his eighth-grade year with his friends and continue on to Normal Community High School. David had been looking forward to attending Normal High since he was very young. Knowing some of the high school players and coaches, he could hardly wait to attend. Now it would not happen.

After much pleading and threatening not to go, reality set in. Dave was leaving his friends and his hopes to be a Normal Community athlete behind. The family moved to Argenta, some ten miles east of Decatur, which was the location of the new Caterpillar Tractor plant. The year was 1955.

The family relocated sometime during the end of October. There were only a couple of days before the opening game for the Argenta Bomber's Junior High team's basketball season. The Darnalls had asked Coach Temple to write a letter of recommendation for their son in his attempt to join the Argenta team. Unusual at this late date, Dave was admitted to the heavyweight team. Normally, eighth graders play on the heavyweight team and seventh graders on the lightweight team. In reality, height and weight were the determining factors for which team a boy qualified.

Argenta had a reputation of having an excellent junior high basketball program. The coach was a young, enthusiastic guy named Art Goreham. After a couple weeks of practice, Dave became the team's sixth man. That was his role for the remainder of the season.

The season was both rewarding and disappointing for the new boy on the team. The heavyweight team completed their season undefeated, including winning the County Tournament Championship. They were 15 to 0.

The lightweight team also had a good regular season. The highlight of the season for Dave was the Lightweight County Tournament held the second week of January. Three members of the heavyweight team qualified to participate in this tournament, and Dave was one of those three. The tournament gave him his first opportunity to be a starter at Argenta. In order to qualify as a lightweight, he had to go on a two-week diet before weigh-in. Being approximately five-foot-nine, he had to lose several pounds to stay under the thirty-point maximum qualifying limit. The weight loss was done by limiting the amount of food intake, doing a lot of running, and taking exlax the night before weigh-in. The eighth grader made it by receiving the thirty-point maximum allowed. Dave ended up sick and extremely hungry, but he felt it was worth the agony. The team won the tournament championship. Dave was the leading scorer and rebounder in the tournament.

His performance in the tournament led to more playing time on the heavyweight team. Both teams had great seasons. However, the players were extremely disappointed when the school board decided not to allow the teams to participate in the State Play-off. With the possibility of another five or six games before the conclusion of the State Tournament, the school board felt it was too mentally and physically demanding of youngsters of that age. There was an outcry in the community. The ultimate agony came when Latham won the State Heavyweight Tournament. Argenta's heavyweight team had beaten Latham once during the regular season by twenty points and again by four in the conference tournament. This disappointment left Dave and his teammates with a feeling of emptiness. There could have been a State Championship for them.

In January, the Darnall children got a great jolt. BeBe passed away. The grandkids had all loved her. She was the image of a "grandma."

Adjusting to a new school was to some degree difficult for the "new kid in town." Trying to make new friends, being an outsider on the basketball team, and attempting to adjust to new academic courses provided some obstacles. In small towns, most kids grow up knowing each other. A new student entering a school already in session could find making friends very difficult especially if the new student was somewhat shy.

Argenta with a population of 850 furnished approximately half of the students to the junior-senior high school. Two surrounding towns, Oreana and Greenswitch, provided the other half. Dave met five friends from the town of Argenta. One became his best high school buddy. He was Gene Phillips. Phillips lived about ten blocks from the Darnall home, but later, his family moved to the country south of town. Three neighborhood boys, Woody White, Leroy Moyer, and Mike Stoddard were among the five. Leroy, who was in Bruce's class, was actually a closer friend to Bruce than Dave. Max Justice was the fifth friend from Argenta. He and Dave were the same age, whereas Gene and Mike were a year older and Woody was a year younger. Max was a big kid for his age. He was pretty much "the man" in the eighth grade.

Max was the starting center on the heavyweight team. The forwards were Dave Fombelle, a seventh grader, and Bill Agee, an eighth grader. Guy "Babe" Allen, a seventh grader, and Dick McCammack, and eighth grader, were the guards. McCammack and Darnall eventually became good friends and college roommates. Woody White and Leon Bryant, who also became a good friend and college roommate, were the key players on the lightweight team. During the lightweight tournament, Darnall, Babe, and Dick joined Woody and Leon to compose the starting five.

The junior high and high school were located in the same building. Therefore, junior high kids and high school students ran around together. This was especially true with the freshmen and eighth graders. Once in high school, Dave spent a lot of time with kids in classes behind him.

Argenta was a farming community. During the summer, many boys baled hay and walked beans. The going rate was fifty cents an hour. When not working, the guys enjoyed playing ball. A couple times a week, the Darnall boys hosted neighborhood football, baseball, and wiffle ball games.

Lucia, David's younger sister, enjoyed playing ball with the older boys. During a highly competitive game, she slid into second base and broke her leg. She returned to action after several months of being idle.

In the evening, Dave participated on the newly formed Pony League baseball team, which traveled to nearby communities for competition. Roy Adams coached the Argenta team. Adams, the local postmaster, had no sons but two daughters, Judy and Nancy. Judy was one year younger than Dave and Nancy two years younger. Dave's parents followed his Pony League games during the summer. They became friends with Coach Adams and his wife, Marge. They played cards at each other's homes. Even though Roy had no formal coaching training, the players like him and respected his coaching ability. Mr. Adams made it fun for the boys while producing one of the best teams in the area.

Max was a big, strong, right-hand pitcher that made the Argenta team hard to beat. A majority of the opponents were afraid of his fast ball. He could really "hum" it. Gene was his catcher.

Dave entered high school realizing that he would not be a starter on the basketball "B" team. He was just hoping to see a lot of action. At Argenta there was the varsity or "A" team and the "B" team. The "B" team consisted mostly of freshmen and sophomores. However, a junior could participate on the team. Dale Huff was the Head Basketball Coach, Track Coach, and physical education teacher all of Dave's four years of high school.

With Judy and Dave both in high school, their home became a place where many teenagers gathered. The Darnalls welcomed their kids' friends to their home. Students from all classes stopped by. Some of Judy's friends, including neighbors Judy Stiles and Judy Conner, socialized with Dave's older buddies.

Dave found a couple classes somewhat difficult even though they were not classified as college-prep courses. Against his father's wishes, he enrolled in Industrial Arts I, English I, General Math I, and General Science. Freshmen college-prep courses were English I, Algebra I, and Biology. All students participated in Physical Education. This was David's favorite course in high school inspite of never receiving a grade higher than a B plus.

The lack of interest, personality conflicts, defeatist attitude, the lack of studying, and a couple poor teachers seemed to haunt Dave throughout his high school years.

Summer arrived. Dave again played on Coach Adam's Pony League baseball team. On occasion, Bruce joined his older brother on the team. The brothers liked this. It was the first time they played on the same team since church basketball. Even though Bruce played on a Little League team, his ability allowed him to play at the higher level. Due to age limit rules, this was Dave's last year of Pony League play.

It was during summer baseball that Dave first really noticed Nancy. However, she already had a boyfriend, Babe. The friendliness of Roy and Marge meant that many town kids spent a lot of time at their house. It was a place where everyone was welcome and felt at home. It seemed as though once a week during the summer, Mrs. Adams hauled a carload of kids in their blue Studebaker to a swimming pool. The trips were normally to the Lake of the Woods in Mahomet or the Danville city pool. Both were a good distance away.

Besides playing Pony League baseball, going swimming, and playing neighborhood ball games at the Darnalls, the brothers baled hay and walked beans. They wanted to earn enough money to buy an old car the following year when Dave turned sixteen.

A true learning experience occurred for Dave just before the start of his sophomore year. Playing pool at the local pool hall attracted many of the town's male youths. One late summer night an incident occurred that would always be implanted in Dave's mind. As his dad's curfew approached, Dave told his buddies he needed to head home. None of the guys had a driver's license so he had to walk. Opening the door, he noticed it was misting outside. He began his seven-block walk home. After taking a few steps, he heard a voice. A fellow, who had been playing all evening on the table next to where Dave and his buddies were playing, asked if he wanted a ride home. With it beginning to rain, the naïve young teenager accepted.

The stranger, in his late twenties, asked Dave if he knew how to drive. "Yes, but I am too young to have a driver's license." Dave replied.

"Do you want to drive?" the man exhorted.

Always anxious to drive, the teenager took advantage of the offer. They entered the car. Basic chitchat followed. Approaching the Darnall house, the man asked the young driver if he wanted to drive a little longer. Enjoying driving the big, fancy automobile, David accepted. He still had a few minutes before his dad's curfew. Passing the Darnall home, they headed north of town. After to few minutes, the guy began asking Dave some peculiar questions.

"Bet you're good with the girls. Been lucky lately? How long are you?"

The man scooted toward the center of the seat still asking such questions. Dave now realized this "deal" was not right. The man started for Dave's pants. David knew he was in trouble. This sort of thing was not heard of then. However, his mind was working.

Again the man asked, "How long are you?" as he reached for Dave's crotch.

"This is serious," Dave thought.

Trying to keep his cool and not panic and wreck the car, Dave replied, "Here let me show you," as he took his foot off the accelerator and applied the brakes. Unknown to the aggressor, the teenager grabbed the door handle with his left hand as his right hand approached the zipper of his pants. Abruptly, he leaped out, falling in the ditch. Dave sprung up and started to sprint. Slamming into a barbed wire fence in the pitch dark, the frightened youth scrambled to his feet with bloody hands. With torn jeans, Dave dashed a quarter of a mile up a lane to a farmhouse. Reaching the porch exhausted, he lunged for the front door. At the point when Dave bailed out of the car, the man had leaped out, yelling for the teenager to return. With no luck, he jumped back into the car and sped off.

After what seemed like minutes to the terrified youngster, an old gentleman in his pajamas turned on the porch light and opened the front door. Dave asked if he could call his parents. The homeowner, seeing the young stranger trembling and bleeding, asked, "What in the hell happened?"

David explained briefly as the old man's wife joined them. After seeing the stressed lad, she told her husband to get dressed and take the teenager home.

Reaching home, Dave raced upstairs to the bathroom, removed his soiled clothes, and jumped into the bathtub. There was no bathroom shower. Finishing, he headed to bed.

His dad yelled, "You're late—we'll talk about it tomorrow."

Dave lay down next to Bruce, who shared the bed.

Approximately twenty minutes later, the phone rang. It was now close to midnight. Mr. Darnall answered the phone. A few minutes later he switched on the light and entered the boys' room. "They called me. Are you all right?" Dave's dad asked.

The frightened youth explained the horrible episode.

Mr. Darnall notified the Decatur Police the next morning. Not knowing a name, he gave a description of the car. Investigators arrived in Argenta later in the day to talk to people who had been at the pool hall the previous night. A few days later, the Darnalls were notified that a suspect had been arrested. They were asked if they would press charges. Mr. Darnall said, "Yes!"

The suspect was found guilty and sentenced. A lesson was learned by many of the youth in the community. Do not get into a car with a stranger!

With his sophomore year under way, David enrolled in American Problems, Industrial Arts II, Algebra I, English II, Physical Education, and General Science. Yes, after flunking General Science the previous year, he had to repeat the course. This did not make his father happy.

After a couple weeks of fall baseball practice, Dave found himself a part-time starter at second base. He enjoyed playing the infield. As with many second basemen, he was a pretty good fielder and an average batter who could handle the bat.

During his first two years in high school, David did not have a steady girlfriend. As his senior class prophecy would eventually state, "The girls are clamoring for an autograph from Dave Darnall, Walt Disney's newest star. He is featured in a new T.V. series, *The Many Loves of Dave Darnall*." In reality, Dave did very little dating. He did ask Sally McGath, whose family had moved to Decatur, to accompany him to a couple school-sponsored hayrack rides. He was actually just one of the boys riding around town with his friends. Usually, this was with Richard Wallace in his turquoise and ivory 1956 Chevy or with Phillips or Bill Agee.

"Most of the time we drove around town or sat in their cars, uptown, near the pool hall. Sometimes we cruised 'the gag'—Steak & Shake—in Decatur or went to a stock car race at one of the two tracks located in the area," Dave said. Dave could hardly wait until he turned sixteen and could provide his own "ride."

As basketball season approached, David had to make a big decision, to cut his hair or not. He had a pretty good "duck tail," a typical hairstyle of many "uptown boys." A lot of athletes had the other popular type, the "flat-top." Coach Huff established a haircut rule. His players had to have either a flattop or short cut. After some persuasion, Huff allowed the players to comb their sides back as long as the ears were completely showing. The top had to remain short. Darnall decided he could handle this style.

David's sophomore year was somewhat profitable. He finally made the starting five as a forward on the "B" basketball team. However, he failed to make the varsity squad. This was disappointing as a couple freshmen were selected.

There was a former Argenta player that David really admired. When he "got down," he tried to think of him. Even though the player had a handicap, he was one of the hardest workers and best shooters the youngster had ever seen. His name was Ed Wallace. He was Richard's brother. Ed had lost all the fingers on his left hand in a farm accident. When not playing basketball, he wore a hook.

"Ed was one of the greatest shooter I had even seen," Dave said. "He held the ball with his left thumb and stub and shot with his right hand. He had a faultless shot. His left hand never got in the way as it does with a lot of shooters. It just held the ball steady," Dave explained.

"I described his form in all of my physical education classes and to all of my basketball teams throughout my career," said Darnall. "I would demonstrate how the shot should be executed."

Darnall felt he had a good season, averaging approximately ten points and five rebounds a game. He hoped his play impressed his coach enough to see a lot a playing time on the "A" team the following year. At times, he questioned if he would ever become an important player because some freshmen had already made the "A" team.

"If I could only shoot the jump shot like Ed, I would definitely play on the varsity," said the young teenage player.

As kids, the Darnall boys wanted to be professional ball players. Now beginning to realize this dream would not happen, Dave began to think about following the footsteps of his childhood idols, coaches Bass and Ricci. They had done a lot for him. Perhaps he could do the same for other kids.

His positive attitude sometimes wandered. Dave began running around more with the "boys" and concentrating less on athletics and his studies during the second half of the school year and summer. It was then that the disenchanted teenager started smoking Red Dot cigars while cruising with the fellas. Mr. Darnall tried to remind his son that sports were not going to get him anywhere, but his books would. He wanted his son to put athletics in perspective. Receiving a college education was what was important.

With basketball concluded and track now in full swing, Dave again found some success in the jumping events, while enjoying a new event he had experimented with the previous year, the hurdles. Gene Phillips was a good hurdler. He spent time helping his buddy with his form. Dave was approximately six feet tall, lean, and had decent speed. These qualities made for a good hurdler. Long legs helped make the traditional three steps between the high hurdles somewhat easier. The question was: did Dave want to spend the time and effort it took to be a good athlete and student?

Immediately after turning sixteen, David obtained his driver's license. As with most parents, Ola and Delmar lay awake at night until the kids returned home. The sound of the car pulling into the driveway was "sweet music." That was especially true since their son's unforgettable episode the previous summer.

During the spring, Dave found a part-time job. He became a gardener for two elderly sisters who lived in the country some eight miles east of town. A huge vegetable garden and numerous flower gardens surrounded their farmhouse. To earn more money, he also baled hay and walked beans for local farmers during the summer. With all this work, the Darnalls agreed there was a need for their son to have a car to drive to the various jobs. They were on a limited budget with four children and only one income. As the boys worked on the farms, Judy babysat to earn her spending money. Dave's parents could not afford to help him buy a car. David convinced Bruce that he should help buy the car since he also needed a ride to work. With the money they earned, they purchased a 1950 black two-door Ford coupe, then eight years old. With white fuzzy dice hanging from the inside rearview mirror and a red dome light, the boys were set.

On Saturday nights during the summer, the city of Argenta held a free outdoor movie. It was sort of a makeshift drive-in theater. That is where Dave first showed off his new purchase. No longer did he have to rely on Wallace, Phillips or Agee for transportation. Now he could provide the rides for the younger kids, especially those in Bruce's class. The class was loaded with a lot of cute girls.

Phillips had started dating Adam's older daughter, Judy, during the school year. Now that Dave had his driver's license, he and Gene provided much of the transportation for the younger kids. The trips were normally to Decatur for pizza, roller skating, or to the drive-in theater. Dave hung out mostly with the new in-coming freshmen, Gene, and Eddie Allen. Allen was in Darnall's class and was seeing Gene's sister, Donna. She was considered one of the sharp, in-coming freshmen.

Dave started to pal with Bobby Beadleston, also a freshman. He was considered the best athlete in his class. He and Bruce hung around a lot with the upper classmen.

Nancy and Babe had broken up. David, who had had a crush on her for some time, attempted to entice her to ride in his car whenever the gang went somewhere. The Argenta kids had lost a good friend and transportation when Marge Adams had gotten suddenly ill and past away earlier in the year.

David did not look forward to the start of his junior year—more advanced courses, taking science for the third time, probably little playing time in basketball, and obeying a weekday curfew. Part of his concern was realized when he enrolled in Industrial Arts III, American History, English III, Algebra II, and General Science for the third consecutive year. Driver Education and Physical Education rounded out his curriculum.

Mr. Darnall had always been interested in the education system. He had previously decided to run for the local school board. Since transferring to the Decatur Caterpillar Plant, he worked the day shift. That allowed him to attend evening school functions. Dave's dad had some concerns and a genuine interest in the school system. He felt being a school board member was the best way to address those issues. He had been elected. That became very fortunate for David.

Obviously, others besides David had had trouble with the general science course. The school board decided that any student taking General Science for the third time would be given the option to take a comprehensive test. If the test was passed, the student was exempt from repeating the class and credit was given. Several students elected to take the test. Dave passed the test!

"I'm finally out of the damn freshman class. There isn't going to be anymore science courses of any kind for me," expounded Dave.

Baseball had started with Huff also coaching baseball this year. David found himself the starting second baseman. That pleased him, especially feeling that basketball would be quite different. Bruce joined his older brother on the baseball team. A good all-around player, Bruce also liked second base as well as catching. Midway through the season, he took over at second base with Dave moving to shortstop. The boys were thrilled to be playing together in the same infield. However, once in a while, David did play in the outfield.

"I moved him out because I ended up being a better fielder, but David was a good hitter and could switch hit, so he went to both shortstop and right field," Bruce said.

That was the first time the Darnall brothers played together on a varsity team. Bruce recalls a special moment. "I can always remember my dad walking across the parking lot, through the outfield, and sitting on the bleachers on the first-base side. David was playing right field that game, and

41

I was playing second base. There we were all close together," Bruce concluded.

With basketball season approaching, Dave began to ponder what he really wanted to do with his time. He considered giving up basketball. Instead, he could drive around town after school or go to Manning's. That was the local café where many kids frequented to listen to the jukebox. There also was always the pool hall.

If it weren't for his interest in becoming a coach, he might have just ended up hanging out up-town. Still contemplating the coaching profession, David felt he could at least gain much knowledge by staying close to the game regardless of playing time. There were times that the junior forward thought his coach looked upon him as somewhat of a renegade with his hairstyle, liking the girls, and running around "up-town" with the boys.

Often athletes feel their coaches play favorites. Dave was no different. That was something he swore not to be guilty of if he ever became a coach. Time would tell! Coach Darnall did not escape the accusations. As he found out later, varsity coaches usually played who they thought were the best players and who were going to help win the game—right or wrong.

With basketball season underway, Dave's foresight came true. He was not a factor on the varsity team. He wished he were back in Normal playing with his former buddies. He felt he might have "fit in" better there. Besides, playing for Normal Community High School had been a childhood dream.

Darnall sat and watched his teammates play. He was getting some playing time but not nearly what he had hoped for. He did not realize it at the time, but by observing the games and his coach's technique and strategies, he was actually learning how to coach: learning offenses, defenses, and how to or not to handle players.

The small amount of playing time contributed to Dave's lack of enthusiasm for the game. He felt he was getting nowhere. Ken Wolf, Dave's favorite teacher and his Industrial Arts instructor was serving as an assistant basketball coach. He was a positive influence upon Dave and tried his best to encourage the junior forward. However, with his attitude, Darnall began spending more time hanging around up-town. Dave began to smoke cigarettes, knowing that if he got caught he would have to pay the consequences. However, at that time, he was willing to take the chance.

Sometime during the middle of the season, one of Dave's wishes came true. He had his first date with freshman baton twirler, Nancy Adams.

With Gene, a varsity starter dating her sister, the four began to double date. Dave's attention reversed back to the team and his teammates and less to running around up-town. The change of emphasis was also helped by the fact that Nancy's best friend, Dinah, and Bobby Beadleston, also a basketball player, were dating. With the three of them being freshmen, Dave did the driving.

By the time the season came to a conclusion in early March, Dave and Nancy were going steady. The biggest event of Dave's young life would soon occur. The date was Friday, March 13, 1959. With very little to do in Argenta, most of the teens traveled ten miles to Decatur for entertainment. Judy, Gene, Nancy, and Dave wanted pizza. The place to go was Romano's. Before leaving, the four watched their favorite TV show, *77 Sunset Strip*. That night Dave drove his father's 1955 two-door, Chevy hardtop. Normally when driving to Decatur, Dave took the family car since his old '50 Ford was not too reliable. Besides, the '55 Chevy was considered a "cool teenage car."

They prepared to leave the Adam's house for the short trip to Decatur. Nancy was sitting in the center of the front seat, Judy was sitting in the middle of the back seat, and Gene was directly behind the front passenger's seat. The teenagers enjoyed listening to the radio while cruising. Johnny Rabbitt, a disk jockey on KXOX-St. Louis, and Dick Biondi of WLS-Chicago, were favorites of the day. As with most teens, Darnall had his favorite groups and songs. The Platters with its great hits, "My Prayer" and "The Great Pretender" was among his favorites. Later, it would include the Righteous Brothers' "Unchanged Melody." The radio was tuned into KXOX.

Leaving the sisters' house, Dave drove the four blocks to Route 48, which connected Argenta to Decatur. Turning right on the highway, he accelerated to approximately fifty-five miles per hour in the first half mile. He entered a big curve. A few seconds later "BANG!" An approaching car traveling at a high rate of speed, estimated at seventy miles per hour, crossed over the center line and slammed into the '55 Chevy. The kids found out later that the intoxicated driver, stunned but basically uninjured, left his badly damaged vehicle and ran into an old bean field.

Losing its headlights in the accident, the drunk driver's car caused another collision. A vehicle following Darnall's Chevy, but far enough back around the curve so the driver could not see the original impact, crashed head-on into the unoccupied, darkened, wrecked car. Two people were traveling in that car. The passenger suffered a severe injury, leaving her paralyzed from a broken back and damaged spinal cord.

The entire left side of the '55 Chevy was, in essence, gone. Unknown to Dave, he had swerved a little to the right just before impact. That prevented a "straight head-on" accident. The front end, hood, motor, and left side were smashed. The windshield was half-gone and the left side driver's window was missing. The car was a "total!" A large section of the driver's side front window was lying on the back window ledge. It was a miracle that the jagged glass missed the driver's head as it flew to the back. It was speculated that if Judy or Gene had been sitting directly behind the driver's seat, the jagged glass could have severed the upper body. The left side, outside chrome strip, shaped like a spear was located on the back floor. It was a wonder that the pointed exterior piece did not penetrate the back seat passengers.

Nancy was thrown out of the car through the windshield and landed in a nearby field. Her untied white tennis shoes, remaining on the floorboard, indicated to the by-passers that someone else had been in the front seat. After some time, she appeared, wobbling, in front of the destroyed car. She had received cuts in the head and face area and had bruises all over her body. Judy also received cuts and bruises. Both sisters were in a state of shock and extremely sore.

Gene was the only one who could remember the actual impact, but it was somewhat foggy. He was thrown against the back of the front seat, pushing it forward, and was found lying in the front. The '55 Chevy had no seat belts! Even though Gene was dazed, a by-passer transported him back to the Adams' house in Argenta to retrieve his truck. He then drove to the hospital to be examined and be with his friends.

Miraculously, no one was killed. Dave was critically injured; the worst of the teenagers. He was found slouched over the steering wheel bleeding from his nose, mouth, and ears. The steering wheel had a horn ring with a center emblem that protruded outward. Having an extremely large steering wheel possibly prevented Dave's head from hitting the windshield. However, the protruding emblem caused significant chest injuries.

Dave remained in the car until an ambulance arrived at the accident scene. During that time several travelers stopped to help the injured teens. They were afraid to remove the driver from the smashed Chevy. It would take trained personnel.

The ambulances finally arrived; one coming from Decatur, the other from Argenta. Emergency personnel immediately began to transfer the driver from the badly wrecked car to the ambulance. Dave was gently placed on the gurney and rolled to the back door of the waiting emergency vehicle. He was cautiously placed inside. There were internal injuries, and he was in a state of shock. An attendant climbed in tending to Dave's life-threatening injuries. The Adams girls were placed in the front seat of the ambulance. The two occupants of the third car involved in the horrible accident were transported to the hospital in the second ambulance.

Other than turning onto Route 48 and seeing swirling, bright circles, Dave remembered only two incidents. The first was on the way to the hospital. Dave begged to live. In a prayer, he made a promise to God, "God, please save me. If you do, I will dedicate my life to serve kids."

Dave was rushed to the Emergency Room upon arriving at Decatur Memorial. The staff frantically began to work on the critically injured patient. Afraid to move the teenager, they removed only what clothing was necessary. There was a fear that any movement of the upper body could result in further injury and possibly death. Dave's injuries were diagnosed as internal bleeding, punctured lung, compressed heart, and virtually all of his left side ribs were broken.

The Darnalls and Roy Adams rushed to the hospital upon notification of the terrible accident. They arrived shortly after the ambulance. The sisters were examined and admitted to the hospital. Within forty-eight hours, they were released to recover completely at home. Gene was examined and released in the mid-hours of the night. Dave remained in the Emergency Room throughout most of the night before being transferred to the Special Care Unit early the next morning. His parents stayed by his side for several days.

The first twenty-four hours were the most critical period of the horrible ordeal. In mid-morning, David had surgery to drain the punctured lung and stabilize his internal injuries. He had lost blood and needed a transfusion.

The second recollection Dave had was that of the doctor inserting an instrument into the left side of his chest. The physician accidentally punctured the compressed heart. Dave thought he heard the doctor say, "Oh, damn!" At that point, his entire body emitted fluids, moistening the operating table sheets. Dave went into "the tunnel of death" as he called it. "I was walking in the tunnel," he described later. "The tunnel was a large cylinder, deep and cold. It was hollow. I saw myself walking toward the end," Dave concluded.

The doctors worked furiously to revive him. He was informed later that, in fact, his heart had stopped beating, and he had expired for a short period of time.

Others having near-death experiences have also reported "walking in the tunnel." "It is a memory that will never leave," Dave said. "It often haunts me."

Bruce, who was minister before leaving the profession to become a junior high guidance counselor, reflected on the ordeal. "I can remember when David had his accident. Sometime after the wreck when he was better, he told me, 'Brother, you'll never believe this. I was laying in the hospital bed after Friday the 13th when something happened. I felt like my body was suspended above the bed, and the people worked on me. They were pumping my heart to get me breathing again. I felt like I was going through a tunnel, and at the end I met Jesus. He asked me if I wanted another chance, and I said, "Yes."' Well, I just thought my brother was hallucinating and imagining something like that had happened. As I got older and into counseling, I did a little research on death and dying for a class that I have taught to seventh graders for the past eighteen years. There is a book by Raymond Moody, entitled *Life after Life*, about people, who had been pronounced dead and then revived, that had gone through similar experiences. Some were Christians and some weren't, but I really believe that David had a life-after-life experience."

For the first forty-eight hours, Dave's condition was extremely critical and guarded. After approximately five days, he began to recuperate quickly. The body seems to heal quite rapidly when young and in good condition. Even though the broken ribs caused much pain, the punctured lung, internal bleeding, and compressed heart were responding to treatment with great success. The state of shock had diminished. Spending nine days in the hospital, Dave was released for home recuperation. He was very lucky, or was "it just meant to be."

The accident was a wake-up call for him. "Teenagers feel immortal. Nothing will happen to me; only them—not me," Dave recited later.

Movie legend James Dean was Dave's idol. He often duplicated Dean's dress from the film, *Rebel without a Cause.* The night of the accident he wore a white T-shirt, jeans, white socks, black pointed-toe shoes, and of course, the legendary red nylon jacket.

Dave recalled the frightening evening, "The last thing I remembered was the two swirling circles. As a matter of fact, I saw the same circles illustrated on the back of a James Dean memorabilia magazine, supposedly that was the last thing he saw."

The swirling circles were the headlights of the on-coming car. James Dean was killed in a night head-on collision just at his prime of life and stardom.

"I do not remember the impact or whether I did anything to prevent the accident," David said. "Just those swirling circles and the promise I made to God if he would spare my life. Believe me, you know when your time is up. That prayer was the turning point of my life."

Dave knew he was getting behind in his classes. He needed to get back to school. After two weeks at home, including a week due to Easter Vacation, he returned to school. At first, it was half-days. He was able to attend school full time approximately a month after the accident. Dave's teachers liked him and were willing to assist him with his missed school-work. He was only an average student academically, but he was always friendly, did his homework, attended classes, and was no discipline problem. The loss of class time and the memory of the accident made it difficult to improve much upon his grades. He felt his senior year would be different. He now had a purpose. Dave was determined to fulfill his promise to God. However, he was anxious for the completion of the current school year.

Through insurance, Mr. Darnall purchased a duplicate of his wrecked car. A small out-of-court settlement made it possible for the injured teenager to trade-in his old Ford for a 1955 two-door, Delray. The Gypsy Red and Ivory Chevy became a favorite.

With school out, summer was in full swing. Dave had quit smoking due to the lung problems caused by the accident. Besides, his "promise" prompted him to do it anyway. He was still able to work at the ladies' place

Dave's 1955 Gypsy Red and Ivory Deray Chevy.

in the country. Bruce was now helping his older brother fulltime in the gardens. There was no baling hay or walking beans for Dave. In the evenings, the brothers went roller-skating, to drive-in movies, or just cruised with buddies, Gene, Bobby, Eddie, Woody, Leon, and their girlfriends. Very little time was spent with the "up-town boys."

Dave had just completely recovered when another tragedy struck the Darnall family. While vacationing in Wisconsin, the elder Darnall suffered a severe heart attack. It was shocking because he was only forty-eight. Ultimately, Delmar missed six months of work, including being hospitalized for two months in Wisconsin.

The first week of July, Dave's parents, Bruce, and Lucia traveled to Bolton Lake near Woodruff, Wisconsin, for a two-week vacation of fishing. Judy, already married to Chuck Runyen from nearby Maroa, and Dave, who stayed home to work, planned to join the rest of the family for the final week of the vacation. David liked the idea of staying home the first week since he had the house to himself. He was hosting a teenage party for many of the Argenta area kids when his older sister phoned him. Judy had received a phone call from their mother informing her what had taken place. The four were fishing on the lake when their dad felt ill. With no motors allowed on the lake, he had been rowing the boat. Feeling sick, Delmar went to shore to go to the bathroom. He returned to the boat and immediately keeled over into his wife's lap. Bruce frantically rowed the boat across the lake to the lodge. The lodge had no phone. The owner and Bruce sped off to the nearest bait shop to call for assistance. It took some time for the ambulance to arrive. Meanwhile, Mrs. Darnall remained in the boat holding her husband. Many minutes later, Mr. Darnall was transferred to the Woodruff Memorial Hospital.

Receiving the terrifying phone call from his sister, Dave, Gene, and others attending the party quickly started to clean up their mess. They needed to get the house presentable before Judy and Chuck arrived. The party was over!

The trio left immediately for the eight-hour trip to Wisconsin. Arriving in Woodruff, they went directly to the hospital. Their father was still unconscious.

A couple years prior to this horrible event, the Darnall family had stayed at the same resort. They had attended a fundraising event to build a hospital. Thank God it had gotten built.

Mr. Darnall remained in the hospital until Labor Day. For two months, Dave's mother rented a one-room apartment in Woodruff to remain close to her husband. Chuck brought the Darnall children back to Argenta after a week at their dad's bedside. The kids were scattered among three families during their parents' absence. Dave spent several days with his folks' friends, the George Humphries, before returning home. Bruce stayed at his friend Leroy's house. Lucia moved in with the McGaths in Decatur.

School started with the Darnall brothers participating in baseball. It was a season of changes. First, Dean Strobel became the team's new coach. He was Dave's third Varsity Baseball Coach in the same number of years. Next, Bruce started at second base, and Dave was switched to third. The senior infielder actually enjoyed playing "hot corner" more than second base. The boys had always hoped to play in the same infield—a dream come true.

After a successful baseball season, basketball started. Dave was hoping to be on the starting five. He knew his younger brother would start on the "B" team. There were four seniors on the "A" team competing for a starting berth.

Dave gave it his best effort and was enjoying himself. Things were good for him. His grades were the best since he had started junior high, he had finished a good baseball season, his social life was good, and he had a chance to become a basketball starter.

The goal of all high school basketball players is to have their names announced in the starting line-up. It is a thrill to trot to the center of the court under the spotlight to the applause of the crowd. Dave's wish came true. On opening night, in front of the hometown crowd, Dave was announced as a starting forward for the first time in his varsity basketball career. He had won the battle for the fifth starting position over his friend Leon Bryant. As Dave jogged to the center court when his name was announced, he turned to look for his dad in the stands. Through all the adversity they had endured during the past eight months, tonight was a blessing and an evening to be shared.

For three years, Dave had been mediocre at best in his studies. His father had disciplined him on several occasions for his grades. However, since making his "promise" to dedicate his life to youth, he knew he had to improve his grades in order to be accepted to college. He was now positive he wanted to be a physical education teacher and coach. Besides, he had decided it would be a good way to make a living.

Prior to the game, Dave had butterflies. Coach gave his six-foot senior forward two butterfly tablets. He had become a nervous, anxious person following his car accident. This trait followed him throughout his coaching career. Argenta opened the season with a victory over Deland-Weldon. Dave felt he had held his own in his first ever varsity start. He had a couple rebounds and two points. Seven "Bombers" played. They were the starters, Justice, McCammick, Fombelle, Allen, and Darnall. Bryant and Beadleston came off the bench to see action.

Dave did not start the second game. He was the team's sixth man. Junior Leon Bryant started in his place. A senior and thinking he was as talented as his good friend was, Dave felt he should have been a starter. However, he accepted Coach Huff's decision and played his role.

Mid-way through the season, the Bombers played at Cerro Gordo; a town located approximately fifteen miles southeast of Argenta. As usual, the "B" team game was a preliminary to the varsity contest. Coach Huff sat the bench with the "B" team and its coach. The varsity players were sitting together in the bleachers. The varsity team normally reported to the locker room to dress at the beginning of the preliminary game's fourth quarter. Students wanting to attend "road" games could pay a small fee and join the cheerleaders in riding a spectator bus to the game site. This was the case that evening.

The gymnasium was small with seating only on one side. All spectators faced a stage with both teams' benches placed on the floor in front of it. Argenta varsity players were sitting in the bleachers spread out over two rows. The fan bus arrived during the second quarter of the preliminary game. The Bomber supporters entered and sat around the players. Darnall and several other players were sitting in the first of the two rows. Nancy sat in front of Dave while other girls also sat in front of their boyfriends.

The varsity team consisted of nine players. At times, the Argenta coach dressed some members of the starting five from the "B" team for the main event. That night all would dress. The varsity players left the spectator section and headed toward their locker room at the usual time. As Dave started to enter the dressing room located at the end of the Argenta bench, he was startled by his coach's touch on his shoulder. Huff announced, "You're off the team!"

Dave, totally shocked and stunned, replied, "What?"

Coach said, "I saw you sitting up there with your girlfriend."

Dave responded, "I wasn't sitting with my girlfriend. The fans just came in and sat down among us."

Coach answered back, "You know the rule. No one sits with his girlfriend before the game."

David wasn't done. "There were other girls who sat in front of their boyfriends."

As the two were speaking loudly, the remaining players filed by shocked by what was occurring. The "B" game was still in progress. Dave pleaded not to be dismissed from the team and be allowed to dress for the game. After a short period of time of conversation, Coach Huff finally instructed him to go ahead and get dressed.

As the varsity game starting line-up was introduced, Dave was on the bench. The game was not close. Cerro Gordo was not a very good team. The Bombers rambled to a quick lead and by halftime, most varsity players had played. Dave had not.

The original starters started the second half. With the Bombers leading by a good margin, the Argenta coach had substituted freely all of the varsity players except Darnall. Mid-way through the fourth quarter, the varsity players were pulled, and the five "B" team players inserted. Dave still sat on the end of the bench. Now all players had seen some action except the senior forward. With a big lead and approximately fifteen seconds left in the game, his coach summoned Dave from the end of the bench. Totally embarrassed and humiliated, Dave reported to the score table. The senior took the floor with ten seconds left to play. The game was immediately over. Argenta won by eighteen points. Dave walked briskly to the locker room totally dejected and got dressed. Some of his teammates approached him asking, "What the hell happened?"

Dave, not wanting to discuss the issue, replied, "I don't know."

Mr. Darnall, who had attended the game, was waiting for his son when he got home. David tried to explain the situation—that the fans came in, sat down, and some of the girls sat in and around the players. The elder Darnall did not have much sympathy for his son at that point, thinking that Dave had broken the coach's rule. What David could not understand was why he was singled out. At least two other players who were sitting next to him also had their girlfriends in front of them.

Dave thought he had been made an example. By not being a starter and a senior, coach had used him to make a point to the other players. Once his father found out where several of the other players' girlfriends had been sitting, he too became disturbed over what had taken place.

David never started another game and played sparingly until the last home game of the season. Determined he was not going to quit even though he wanted to, Dave stuck the season out. That incident, more than ever, made him positive he wanted to become a coach. He wanted to prove to everyone that he could make it.

Unbelievably, Dave did not let the basketball situation interfere with his attempt to do better in the classroom. There were no relapses. He finally had decided he wanted to go to college, but was it too late?

There were three games remaining on the regular season schedule—one at home and two away. Then came the Regional Tournament in Bloomington-Normal, his old hometown.

Coach Huff had a tradition of starting all seniors the last home game. Since there was only four seniors on the team, Darnall got to start. Thus, he started the first and last home games of his final year of high school basketball.

The game was against Farmer City. During the contest, Dave played like a man on a mission. He was playing so well that Coach Huff did not take him out even though the Bombers had a big lead. At the conclusion, Argenta won 101 to 52. David was the leading scorer of the game and had double figures in rebounds. He also had the honor of scoring the 100th point. Scoring 100 points in 1960 was a novelty since there was no three-point shot.

Bruce states, "I will always remember David's last three regular season basketball games he got to play his senior year. Coach Huff had a tradition of playing seniors and since there were only four, he got a chance to start. In the last home game, David got thirty-one points. He played the baseline, and he would shoot the baseline shot. Then the next time he would fake and drive the baseline and do a reverse lay-up. He would do some fade-aways. Dave had such a nice shot. He was also able to do reverse lay-ups and do that little fade-away with a kick. He really played a good ball game."

Following the game, Coach congratulated Dave on his game. Dave acknowledged his coach's words but did not want to talk. He felt he could have had a great season if he had not been singled out to make an example for discipline. Besides, he wanted to get home to hear his name on TV. It was the first time it was going to be aired.

The next two season regular games were played on the road. They were against nearby rivals, Warrensburg and Maroa. Dave's performance in the Farmer City game warranted him a starting position against Warrensburg. A repeat performance in the Warrensburg game, merited another starting performance against Maroa in the regular season final. Argenta won both games with identical scores of 63 to 59. In both games, David scored in the twenties; scoring in the mid-twenties against Warrensburg and netting twenty-three against Maroa.

Completing the season, the team traveled to Bloomington-Normal some fifty miles away for the Regional Tournament. Dave was going home. Argenta opened the tournament against Bloomington Trinity Catholic. As a seventh grade lightweight, Dave had played against their lightweights. David had finally become a permanent member of the starting five. The senior forward led his team to a 61 to 54 victory over the highly respected Bloomington team. Dave, the leading scorer, had twenty points on eight baskets and four free throws. It was a great homecoming for Darnall. Several of his childhood friends, including Raycraft, Hendricks, Emmert, and Draper, plus many of his parents' pinochle friends were in the stands to witness his game. That was the first time his old buddies had the opportunity to see him play high school ball. David did not let them down.

A sentence from an article that appeared in the next day's *The Pantagraph* read, "Dave Darnall headed the Argenta attack with 20 points." A picture of him accompanied the article. The caption stated, "Dave Darnall of Argenta appears to be a little ahead of the basketball, but actually he had just attempted to save a wild pass from going out of bounds during regional game with Trinity. Referee is Bob Brodbeck."

The Pantagraph photo file.

Both the statements of Dave's prowess and his picture in the newspaper that he had looked at as a youngster, meant a great deal to the former resident. Publicity was not unusual for several of his teammates, but for Dave, it took until the end of his career to get some recognition.

The Regional semi-final game was a rematch with final regular season foe, Maroa. Maroa had advanced by claiming a very impressive 53 to 47 win over the much larger host, Bloomington High School. David played a significant role in Argenta's 59 to 56 victory over its neighboring rival school. It wasn't as much the eleven points he scored against Maroa as being able to withstand the pressure at the end of the game.

A paragraph from an article in the following day's *The Pantagraph* read, "Maroa controlled the ball until twenty seconds remained and then Jim Thiele missed a twenty footer. Argenta rebounded, and the Bomber's Dave Darnall was fouled seven seconds later. Darnall made both throws of a one-and-one situation to put the game on ice."

Again, a picture of David in action appeared in the same newspaper. For four years, no pictures and now twice in back-to-back issues. The caption under the picture read, "Argenta's David Darnall powers his way around Jim Etnier of Maroa in route to basket in first half."

In the same paper another headline read, "Southern Wins NAIA District Title, Wallops North Central." At that particular time, Darnall had no idea of what that meant. In fact, he did not remember reading it. If Dave did, it only meant Southern Illinois won. Who would ever guess that someday the NAIA District title would mean a great deal to the future coach.

Since Darnall had been inserted into the starting line-up, Argenta had won five consecutive games. They were next going to play the state-ranked Clinton Maroons for the Regional Championship. The Bombers' starters were Justice and Darnall at forwards, Allen and McCammack at guards, and Fombelle at center.

The first half was a seesaw affair. However, Clinton took a substantial lead early in the second half, but the Bombers were not done yet. They started to climb back toward the end of the third period.

The Pantagraph photo file.

54

Then there was the fourth quarter. A paragraph in the next day's *The Pantagraph* described the final period. "The fireworks were reserved for the fourth period. Dick McCammack and Dave Darnall, both, got in some telling licks, and the score knotted at 29 all." The remainder of the quarter was a back and forth affair before Argenta suffered a heartbreak 57 to 55 defeat.

The tournament's leading scorer, Darnall contributed fifteen points in the losing cause. However, he was devastated. After a couple of years of frustration, he finally got his chance to prove what he could do. Then the season was over. He wished it were only beginning. What kind of season could he have had?

The team ended its season with an 18 to 5 record and a legitimate chance to go to State. After the game, the locker room was solemn. The players were in tears. Their heads between their hands bowed in disbelief. "How did we let this one get away?" one asked.

After approximately fifteen minutes, a gentleman walked into the dressing room and headed in Darnall's direction. Still sitting on the bench with his head down, Dave looked up as the gentleman spoke.

"Dave, I am Coach Collie from Illinois State Normal University. I'm interested in having you come to ISNU and play for me," the coach said.

A stunned Darnall responded, "Coach, you don't want me. I only started six games."

That caught the college coach off-guard. After a few seconds, Coach Collie replied, "You had a great tournament. I feel you could play college ball."

The ISNU head mentor went on to tell Dave that he would be contacting him in a few days. Several days later Dave received a letter from Illinois State Normal University's Athletic Department.

Dave gathered his composure and left the locker room to visit with some of his hometown buddies. His parents were talking to their old friends as well. Before leaving the building to board the yellow school bus for the long, lonely ride home, Dave mentioned to his parents what the locker room visitor had said. He then told his dad, "Hell, I couldn't even play high school ball, let alone be good enough to play college ball." They smiled.

That was the first time David gave thought to playing college basketball. With a high school career like his, who would?

What a coincidence this was. David wanted to go back to Normal for college anyway. ISNU was an excellent teachers' college. The thought of rekindling his friendship with his old friends back in Normal thrilled him.

David never had really prepared himself for college. He did not take all of the college preparatory courses he should have. The ones he did, he received only average grades. It wasn't until his senior year that his grades resembled that of a college-caliber student.

Approximately three weeks after the conclusion of the season, the basketball team had an award banquet at the community building in Argenta. The guest speaker was none other than ISNU's Head Basketball Coach Jim Collie. Collie again talked to Dave and teammate Dick McCammack about attending Illinois State Normal University.

Track season started. After missing the previous year due to the car accident, David participated again. It was during track season that he made application to attend ISNU. That was the only college David applied to. He already knew several of the coaches at ISNU: Jim Collie's assistant basketball coach, Warren Crews; Ed Struck, the football coach; Harold Frye, the baseball coach; and Duffy Bass who was coaching baseball at University High School.

In early June, Dave received an acceptance letter from ISNU. However, there was one stipulation. He had to enroll in a non-credit English course during a three-week summer session. Teammate McCammack also decided to attend ISNU and play basketball. He, too, had to enroll in the English class.

Chapter 4

College Years

THE SUMMER PASSED QUICKLY. Dave was preparing to attend the three-week English course at ISNU, fulfilling the requirement necessary for fall enrollment. Throughout the summer, Dave and Nancy were still going together. However, as he was leaving for the special session, he began to see a strain in their relationship.

In 1954, Dave's grandparents sold their farm in Carlock and purchased another one about a mile west of Bloomington. His grandfather now lived there alone. The Darnall family struggled financially since Delmar's heart attack. Mrs. Darnall had started working at a department store in Decatur in December to help with family expenses. Dave and his parents decided it would be better for everyone for him to live with his grandfather rather than on campus.

Mr. Kerr lived in a big two-story farmhouse. There was one bedroom, his, downstairs and three upstairs. Dave's high school buddy, McCammack, also attending ISNU, decided to live at the farm too. He would provide company both for Grandpa and David. The boys shared the largest upstairs bedroom. Since both had cars, the ten-minute drive to campus did not present a problem.

Dave left Argenta for ISNU the last day of July. What a surprise he had when attending the first day of the required English class. Sitting in the back of the room was his old friend, Don Raycraft. About two chairs away from David was a guy from Antioch named Jim Barone. Barone and Darnall would eventually become life-long friends.

Raycraft, Barone, McCammack, and Darnall went to lunch every day at the Sinorak. The Sinorak was a smorgasbord located at the drive-in theatre on the south side of Bloomington. There, the boys ate all they wanted for ninety-nine cents. That was their one big meal of the day.

The class met for two and one-half hours in the morning and a couple hours in the afternoon. Class time and studying left little time for recreational activities. When time did allow, the fellows went to Raycraft's for a wiffle ball game or basketball in the barn.

Dave returned home after the first week of summer school. It was troublesome. He could tell there was a serious problem with his and Nancy's relationship. This agitated him. He had a hard time concentrating. Dave received a "D" in the summer course, passing the class but entering college with an academic warning. That meant that he had to achieve a satisfactory grade-point average at the conclusion of the first semester or be dismissed.

With a week between summer school and the start of the regular school year, Darnall and McCammack returned home to Argenta. Nancy and Dave broke up. She indicated they could remain friends but would no longer be "going together." That ended his "high school years."

It was time to return to ISNU. Dave packed up and headed back. He was disturbed. It didn't take long for him to revert back to his "ole self." He began smoking again, drank frequently, and was struggling in a couple of his classes. The legal drinking age for girls was eighteen and twenty-one for boys. Often the guys asked the girls to purchase beer for them. Dave did. Sometimes it was as a favor, other times for a couple bucks.

Dave and Dick had to have jobs in order to remain in college. David's parents had an old friend named Stan Sleever. He was the director of the food service for the new "tall halls" on campus. The official names for the tall halls were Hamilton-Whitten Halls. They housed approximately 800 female students. David was employed as a "salad boy" working in the kitchen adjacent to the dining area. Dick was a student supervisor for the dishwashing crew located in the basement of the kitchen area. The fellows worked approximately two and a half hours a day receiving their noon meal and minimum wage.

The most difficult class for Dave was English 101, especially after he had received a "D" in the non-credit English 100 summer course. His English teacher was Ms. Lucile Hyneman. She was a middle-aged lady who had spent time in England and was a very friendly, compassionate, intellectual person. Of the numerous English teachers at ISNU, she was the "one" everyone hoped to get. Dave felt lucky, but there was one problem. The class met at four o'clock daily. That was during basketball practice. What should he do now?

After talking to other ISNU students, Dave felt it was best for him to stay in his assigned class. That meant giving up basketball, the one thing he really wanted to do.

Dick, on the other hand, had a ten o'clock class allowing him to practice with the team. However, because of his demanding work schedule both on campus and some weekends back in Decatur, he also chose not to participate.

David, still having the urge to play basketball, decided to form his own intramural basketball team. That was the first time he was in charge of an athletic team. He started his team by recruiting his friends McCammack and Barone. Jack Ary, a cross-country runner, and his former high school classmate, Dale Gerrietts, also joined the newly formed team. The team needed one more player, a center. Darnall was able to recruit a six-foot-three freshman named Bill Zimmerman to play the position. David's friend, Raycraft, would have joined the team, but he had transferred to Illinois Wesleyan at the beginning of the regular school year. There were several different basketball leagues in the college's intramural basketball program. The newly formed Indies won their league.

Even though Dave attended classes regularly, a couple classes were difficult for him. He knew he could not afford to miss any professors' lectures and still pass his tests. His English course was still very difficult for him in spite of having the "best" English teacher. He started talking to a "smart" girl who sat in front of him regarding the English assignments. She lived in the same dorm where Dave worked as a salad boy. On several occasions, he asked if she would proof read his homework assignments after work. She agreed. They met in the dorm's lounge to review assignments before class met later in the day. One day Ms. Hyneman assigned a long written paper as a major assignment.

Having difficulty in writing papers, Dave asked his friend for help. Again, she agreed. For several evenings, they worked in the dorm's lounge on the dreadful paper. They started to date. Dave received an all-important "C" out of the class. With only one "D" and no "As," he made it through his first year of college.

During the summer, David found employment at Revere Copper and Brass Company in Clinton. The drive from Argenta took approximately twenty minutes. David spent most of his time with the fellas. Working eight hours a day, driving home, and then heading out to be with the boys became the daily routine. Cruising "the gag" in Decatur, attending stock car races, hanging out at the Argenta pool hall, or just sitting up-town in cars with the "good ole boys" was the thing to do.

Drinking also entered frequently into his leisure time. The one vise David never became involved with was recreational drugs.

Bruce was no company. The brothers spent very little time together even though they still shared the same bedroom. Bruce was a dedicated athlete and had a steady girlfriend. He was planning to attend Eureka College to prepare for the ministry. The college was affiliated with the Disciples of Christ Church. It was located approximately twenty-five miles west of Bloomington-Normal.

It was time for college to resume. The last thing on Dave's mind was returning to ISNU. Also, his family's economical situation was still a problem. Struggling with his parents, who were extremely upset and disappointed with their eldest son, it was decided that college should be put on hold until, maybe, second semester. Dave remained living at home and working in Clinton until January.

The period between August and January saw no change in Dave's behavior. He was still running hard. Two of his friends and former teammates were attending ISNU. Justice was a sophomore and Bryant, a freshman. They told Darnall he should return to college and live with them in a house located on Mason Street a block away from campus. Phillips was now in barber college and McCammack had transferred to a college in Kansas. Their prodding sounded like a good idea.

Dave returned to school in January. His personal habits had not improved. An extremely nervous person, Dave wondered if he could adjust to college life again. Oh, no, not the social life but to the demands of studying. This would be his last real chance to make something of himself. Was the promise he made while riding in the ambulance on the way to the hospital following the accident just a passing thing or a real commitment to God?

Dave planned to move into an upstairs room on Mason Street with Max and Leon. There also would be a fourth roommate. Across the street from the guys' house was an off-campus rooming house for girls. Thirteen coeds lived in the house.

Dave arrived in Normal on an early Sunday evening. He drove up and parked his car in front of his new home. He had been drinking. He exited his '55 Chevy wearing his new Jimmy Dean red nylon jacket. He had turned his radio to a blaring volume and began dancing to it in the street. His parents were hoping his return to college would help him become a responsible, goal-oriented person. This was not the picture his parents would have wanted to see.

The Cold War with Russia, the problems with Cuba, and the Vietnam Conflict made the draft an issue young men followed closely. Some teenagers feared being drafted for ground fighting forces so they enlisted in a branch of service of their choice. Their enlistment meant two extra years of serving their country, but at least it was in a branch of their choosing.

David didn't believe in guns, including for hunting. Thus, he was not anxious to be in the infantry. He was classified as 2S. That meant he had been given a student deferment. He felt fortunate that his Selective Service classification had not switched back to 1A, meaning "available for process," while sitting out the first semester.

Classes started the following morning. Dave worried about his ability to study after being away from the academic scene for nine months. Lack of concentration and an overall negative attitude, in general, were obstacles he had to overcome to be a successful student.

The first morning, classes were troublesome. Trying to take notes with a hangover was not an easy task. The professors were talking too fast to take notes. David finally just gave up and listened. After attending both of his morning classes, David reported to work. Mr. Sleever had hired him back. He returned to the kitchen as a salad boy—back to cutting the lettuce and making individual salad dishes. The kitchen staff's reaction to his return made his day.

The only girls Dave really talked to since arriving back on campus were those who lived across the street. The boys in his house talked frequently with them. They often crossed paths going to and from classes, stopping to visit. It was at this time that Dave asked a girl named Bonnie to fix him up with one of her roommates. A few of the girls already had boyfriends, but a couple were available. Bonnie fixed David up with a housemate. They attended a movie at the downtown Normal theatre within walking distance of their houses. Yes, it was the same "show" (theatre) that Dave went to on Saturday afternoon as a kid.

Several weeks went by. David was attending classes regularly. He believed students should attend their classes just like athletes should go to practices. Academically, Dave was able to keep "his head above water." Though it had been a shaky freshman year, Dave received only one "D"—in psychology—an area of study in which he became quite proficient later in life. He wanted, at least, to duplicate the previous year's grades.

Since David was a physical education major, he found himself in several classes with numerous athletes. Although he was not an athlete, he did socialize with many of them. Ed Thomas, who lived a few houses away, and Larry Gassen, who worked with him in the girls' dorm food service, were two football players with whom he became friends. Other than room-mates Leon and Max, Dave continued to run around with Barone, Ary, and Gerrietts. He continued to party even though it was against university rules for students to drink alcoholic beverages. Actually, the City of Normal was dry; Bloomington was not.

During the spring, some of the fellas from Dave's house and the girls across the street played touch football in a vacant field adjacent to the ladies' house. It was there that Dave really noticed Bonnie, the girl who fixed him up with her housemate. Following the games, Dave and "Tooles" would talk. After a game in early April, Dave asked her if she wanted to get something to eat. She accepted. They left in his '55 Chevy for the Steak n Shake. David sometimes called Bonnie "Tooles" because her last name was Toole. That nickname stayed with Bonnie for years. In fact to this day, Barone still calls her "Tooles."

The couple started to date. Their dates usually consisted of getting something to eat, walking to the theatre, going to the drive-in in Bloom-ington, or driving to Lake Bloomington some fifteen miles away. There Dave drank a few beers while listening to music. Almost every other weekend a party took place at Lake Bloomington. The "kids" parked their vehicles along the side of an old gravel road, climbed a fence, and hiked up a large hill to a secluded farmer's field. Being on top of the hill, the partiers could see if anyone (the authorities) was coming. After building a fire, the kids sat around drinking beer, telling stories, singing, and snuggling. David and Bonnie joined the other college students at these outdoor parties.

A rumor got out that "drinking" parties were taking place at Lake Bloomington. The Dean of Men's Office notified Dave that hearsay had it he had attended some parties off-campus. Therefore, he was given a warning regarding the university's drinking policy.

A couple weeks after receiving the warning, David attended a party at the RoJo in Kappa. Kappa was a small village of several houses and three bars located approximately ten miles north of Normal. There were approximately thirty college fellas at one of the bars. Many attendees were athletes. However, Dave and Barone were not. It was a boys' night out; a great time drinking, telling stories, and just reminiscing.

A few days later, the Dean of Men's Office again contacted David. He was to report to the office. Someone at the party had gotten caught and squealed on the others. Most of the guys attending the party were also required to report to the Dean's Office. Since David had already been warned, he was in serious trouble. Knowing that he was in deep "shit," he called his dad. What Mr. Darnall was going to learn was something he had not wanted to hear but had worried about.

Mr. Darnall had attended Normal Community High School with Harold Sylvester, Chief of Police of the ISNU Security Department. Once he had given his son "hell" and told him that the incident should wake him up and he would have to pay the consequences, Dave's father called Sylvester. They met. Dave's dream was about to come to an end. Growing up in Normal, being a bat and ball boy at ISNU, idolizing ISNU players and local coaches, wanting to be a coach himself, now he was about to be dismissed from school in disgrace. He had messed up his last chance.

After talking to an assistant dean, Dave was informed he had one final chance. Mr. Sylvester must have come to David's aid. The administration allowed him one final opportunity to reach his questionable goal, obtaining a college degree. Darnall was placed on social probation. That meant any other incident involving school policy would result in his dismissal. David called his father to thank him for meeting with Mr. Sylvester on his behalf.

Bonnie and Dave saw each quite frequently the last several weeks of the school year. He now spent most weekday evenings in the library studying. Bonnie, an excellent student, helped him with his required papers. On weekends the couple frequented the same places as before except for the parties.

With school ending, Bonnie returned home to Secor, a village approximately twenty-five miles north of Normal. She found summer employment at State Farm in Bloomington. David went home for a few days before returning to Bloomington to live with his grandfather. Grandpa owned three rental houses that needed painting. His grandson spent the summer helping him. Dave also enrolled in a couple summer courses at ISNU. That helped to make up a few semester hours of credit that were missed by not attending the first semester.

David was only thirty minutes away from Bonnie but still missed seeing her. He stayed in Bloomington during the week, working and studying. He then went to Secor on weekends.

Darnall was pleased after receiving his second semester grades. Absent from school for a semester, running around partying, being on probation, and with his lackadaisical attitude, Dave felt fortunate to receive all "Cs."

It was on Friday, July 6, 1962, Dave and Bonnie made a memorable trip. The previous night, Dave suggested that they should run off and get married. Bonnie agreed. The couple left Secor in Dave's '55 Chevy. They headed south on US 51 to get married. It was reported that the easiest states in which to elope were Tennessee or Mississippi. Those states, supposedly, did not have as rigorous marriage laws as most states.

In Illinois, the legal age to get married without parental consent was eighteen for females and twenty-one for males. Bonnie was already eighteen, but Dave was only twenty. The couple had decided to secretly get married, not tell their parents, and still live in their respective homes. Basically, they would see each other on weekends until school would resume in September. There was to be no plans for children until both finished school.

The young lovers drove throughout the night reaching Memphis in the wee hours of the morning. All of a sudden, David noticed a flashing red light approaching from the rear. With the sound of the siren and the flashing light, he pulled over to the side of the road.

"Who would know what we are doing?" Dave asked.

Bonnie replied, "The only one we told was Judy."

"I don't think she would have told anyone," Dave responded, "but someone found out."

The Tennessee State policeman approached the kids' car. Dave, trembling, rolled the window down. "What's wrong?" he asked the officer.

The policeman answered, "Sir, where are you going?"

Dave replied, "I don't really know."

The officer looked puzzled and asked to see Dave's driver's license. He then instructed the couple to remain in their vehicle as he returned to his squad car. Glaring at each other, the frightened kids wondered who would have reported them.

The officer returned to the '55 Chevy. "Do you know why I stopped you?" the patrolman asked.

David replied, "No."

"Didn't you see that big stop sign back there?" he inquired.

Again, the driver said, "No."

"What are you doing down here in Tennessee?" asked the officer.

Dave thinking that someone had notified the police that they were missing replied, "We are down here to get married. We were told that Tennessee and Mississippi were the easiest places to get married."

The patrolman said, "Both Tennessee and Mississippi have residency and age requirements. You are not old enough."

The officer explained that a county in Southern Illinois was the easiest place to elope. He told the young couple that he would not give them a ticket for running the stop sign if they would promise to turn around and head back home. Relieved, scared and disappointed, they agreed.

Dave turned his Chevy around and headed back north. They could not believe the size of the stop sign when they saw it. It was a large ground billboard type sign.

"How could we have missed that?" Dave asked. It was a long trip back to Central Illinois.

On the way home, the couple decided they still wanted to get married. What should they do now? After some discussion, it was decided to go back to Argenta and tell Dave's parents their plan. They would marry in a small family ceremony the following Sunday. Reverend O'Brien, Dave's minister as a youngster at the Normal University Christian Church, would be asked to perform the ceremony. The wedding would take place in the chapel of the Normal Methodist Church. Bonnie was a Methodist. David would ask Bruce to stand up with him. Joni, Bonnie's roommate from the Mason Street house, would be her maid of honor. Hopefully, Bonnie's parents, Roy and Dolly, would hold a small reception at their home in Secor following the wedding. They would live with her parents until they could find an affordable apartment in Normal.

Looking back after forty-plus years of marriage, Bonnie comments about their "plan," "What a ridiculous plan! But, we were in love. I would have 'killed' my daughter if she had done that."

The two drove the remainder of the night arriving in Argenta close to noon.

Both were afraid of what Dave's parents would say about their wedding plans. The Darnalls were surprised to see the kids at that time of day, especially looking so tired and grubby. Mr. Darnall asked where they had been. David told his parents of the near twenty-hour ordeal. Finishing his story, he informed his parents of their wish for the following weekend. Caught off-guard, the Darnalls seemed stunned by the kids' desire. Catching their breaths, they agreed to the request. Even though they thought it was best to wait a while, they said they would sign for their son.

Bonnie and Dave rested a few hours and then drove to Secor to tell Bonnie's parents of their hastened decision to get married. She informed her parents that they had already expressed their desire to the Darnalls. Bonnie, being eighteen, did not need her parents' signatures, but she did want their approval. Dolly and Roy were also a little taken back, but after some conversation also agreed to support the marriage.

The wedding took place as planned in Normal on July 15, 1962, at the Methodist Church. Attending the wedding were mostly family members and a few family friends. A wedding reception was held at the Toole home. The newlyweds spent their first night together at the Holiday Inn in

Bloomington. Both had places to be at 8:00 A.M. the following morning— Bonnie, to work at State Farm, and Dave, to classes at ISNU.

Dave fulfilled his commitment to attend his classes. In five years and four summers of his college career, Dave missed only one class. Throughout his years of teaching he also stressed the importance of attendance to his physical education students and players. Dave believed that if a student missed a class of physical education, by the nature of the course, it could never be made up. That also held true in athletics. A missed practice was totally lost.

The newly weds spent their first two weeks at Bonnie's parents home. Early August they moved into a basement apartment approximately six blocks from ISNU campus. It consisted of a tiny kitchen, bedroom, and living area. It was quite small, but the price was right—only $12.00 a week.

This apartment was the new Darnall home for a couple months. Dave's grandpa had told them that if an opening came available at his Locust Street house in Bloomington, they could rent it. The new couple moved into an upstairs apartment during the winter. Mr. Kerr was very generous with this arrangement.

Darnall had a busy first summer of his marriage. Besides being a husband, he helped his grandfather on his farm, attended classes at ISNU, and worked for a spice company—Frank's Spice & Tea Company. His main responsibility was to order and keep the spice rack filled at the new K-Mart grocery store in Bloomington. However, he did solicit other grocery stores in the Bloomington-Normal area to stock Frank's famous Red Hot Sauce.

Bonnie kept busy at State Farm as well as performing household chores. The only real getaway the couple had came during the early part of the summer when they took Barone's girlfriend, Sherri, and traveled to his home on a lake in Antioch, Illinois. The couples enjoyed a few days of boating and swimming.

With the summer ending, Dave started the 1962-1963 college year. This would be his third year in school. He resumed his job as the salad boy at the same dorm cafeteria as well as continuing his duties with Frank's.

Not only was Bonnie working full-time and doing household chores, she also was enrolled in night classes at ISNU. The strategy was for her to work full-time until Dave graduated. He would then obtain a teaching position close to Normal so that Bonnie would be able to complete her degree in Special Education. No time for children. With their extremely busy schedules, the young couple only socialized on weekends.

Sometime during this school year, the Darnalls traded in Dave's '55 Chevy for a two-door yellow 1960 Chevy. That was a move they often regretted.

Somehow Darnall found time to reassemble his intramural basketball team. The squad members were mostly the same guys who had played on his previous team, minus McCammack, who had transferred, and Barone, who had joined the Air Force.

Bruce had enrolled at Eureka College. The institution was a small church-related college with an enrollment of approximately 500 students. He was majoring in English with a minor in Religion. He wanted to become a minister.

Bruce participated in the Eureka College basketball program. As a freshman, he was a member of the Junior Varsity team. Needing games, Bruce told his college coaches, Leo Traister and Loren Logsdon, of his brother's good ISNU basketball team called the Indees. Coach Traister called Dave to schedule a junior varsity game in Pritchard Gymnasium on the Eureka College campus. The gym was quite small with a balcony surrounding the playing floor. Darnall and his team were just happy to have an opponent and a place to play. That was the first time Dave was on the Eureka College campus. Even though it was the first time Dave saw a Red Devil basketball team, it surely would not be the last. By the way, the Indees won. As printed in the Bloomington *The Pantagraph*, a sentence stated, "In Junior Varsity action, Eureka edged by an Illinois State University Normal freshman squad, 64 - 61." It was the one and only "college basketball game" Darnall ever played in.

During the school year, the Darnalls' social life consisted mostly of hosting parties in their Bloomington apartment. It was a convenient place for college friends to gather.

As the 1962-1963 school year came to an end, Dave's grades had improved drastically. They were, by far, the best since he had entered college. He was, however, disappointed that he had received only a "C" in "Theory of Basketball Coaching." A majority of the students were either basketball players or ISNU athletes. Darnall felt a little out of place by not being an athlete but did think he had done as well as some others in the class.

David's study habits began to pay off. Quite often he went to their bedroom after dinner, shut the door, and studied until after midnight. That put a strain on the marriage but was the only way he could academically stay in school. Courses like anatomy/physiology and kinesiology were extremely difficult for him. It should be remembered that he flunked General Science twice in high school and had never taken a biology course. Not only did David have to learn the course content, but also the pronunciation and spelling of the words. That was an added burden.

David contributes some of his academic success to Bonnie. "I didn't run around drinking and partying all week. Instead, I stayed home studying. Bonnie is a very intellectual person and helped me a great deal with my papers," Dave explained.

"My good friend, Gene Phillips, and several other buddies often told me that my degree should have had both of our names on it. I do have to admit that if it wasn't for her, I might not be where I am today," Dave continued. "A good man needs a good woman beside him!"

It was during the summer of 1963 that David started his recreation softball career. Along with his childhood friends, Don Raycraft, Bill Draper, Don Emmert, and Jim Bennett, he was a member of the Eureka Williams' Goodfellows twelve-inch fast-pitch softball team. Eureka Williams was a vacuum sweeper company in Bloomington. The manager of the team was Merlin Kennedy. He worked for the company and was very active in the NAACP. Kennedy called Darnall, "Darrel." That became the name Raycraft and Barone called him from then on.

The Darnalls were good friends of both the Drapers and Emmerts, who also had gotten married at young ages. Both Bill and Don have continued to remain life-long friends. In fact, it was Don and wife, Doris, who took the Darnalls to Talledaga for the races. Bonnie is a die-hard NASCAR fan.

Other than playing softball, David's time was spent attending school for the second consecutive summer. He continued working part time for Frank's Spice & Tea Company. Bonnie remained working at State Farm and also took a class at ISNU.

Darnall enrolled in three courses during the summer. He received one "A"—the only "A" in his undergraduate course work. That class was "Introduction to Art Workshop." Dave enjoyed art. Bonnie and he both have produced art pieces that are currently displayed in their home.

The summer came to an end. David started his fourth year in college. The couple continued to live in David's grandfather's apartment in Bloomington. Gene Phillip's sister, Donna, and her husband, Larry, also a college student, moved into a vacant apartment below the Darnalls. David liked this because he was now able to see Gene and his wife, Jeannie, more often.

The 1963-1964 school year went quickly. However, it did have its tragedies. David was sitting in his anatomy class on the historic Friday, November 22, 1963; the day President Kennedy was shot. Not necessarily a Kennedy fan, Dave was still disturbed by the event. "How could anyone shoot the president?" Dave thought.

His grandmother, Laura Darnall, also died during that winter. She was ninety-four years old and had lived by herself since Dave could remember. His grandfather Darnall had passed away before he was born.

Dave, again, had a good year academically. He received four "Bs" and three "Cs." One of the classes was "Theory of Baseball Coaching." His professor was none other than Duffy Bass, the new Head Baseball Coach at

ISU. That's right—the same Duffy Bass whom Dave idolized as a youngster. His youth's American Legion baseball coach at the "Cabbage Patch." By the way, Illinois State Normal University officially changed its name to Illinois State University in January of 1964.

During the summer of 1964, David again enrolled in summer school courses. This was his third summer of classes. Hopefully, his last! He again played on the Eureka Williams' softball team while working for Frank's. Bonnie was still working to support the family while taking classes at ISU. The plan was still intact.

At least one weekend during the summer, the Darnalls and their friends made a trip to St. Louis to watch professional baseball. Among the gang taking the short vacations were Drapers, Phillips, Emmerts, Paynes, Thomases, and the Jerry Yoders. The couples were young and financially strapped. They did what had to be done in order to make the trip. That meant often piling into a couple motel rooms. Two or three members of the group checked into the motel before going to the ballpark. Upon returning, the rest of the group joined them in the limited number of rooms. The occupants ended up sleeping wherever they could—on beds, chairs, or the floor. By the time most fellows were ready to go to sleep, it was nearly time for breakfast. At this age, the guys could go without much sleep.

Phillips recalled a prank during one of those trips. "I remember going to St. Louis with a bunch of young couples to watch a St. Louis Cardinal game and party. After the game, we went back to the motel and par-tied all night. While some went swimming in the pool, others continued to party in the rooms until the wee hours of the morning. Dave, Bonnie, Jeannie, and I shared the same room. Sooner or later, David was partied-out and needed to go to bed even though the adjacent room's door was wide open and the rest of the gang continued on," Gene said.

70

"I came up with the idea of wouldn't it be nice to show his younger 'reverend brother' that he still needed to work on David's moral life. So we laid an empty booze bottle by his head and placed a Gideon Bible near him. Then a picture was taken. The purpose was to show Brother Bruce he still needed to help his older brother," Phillips continued. "However, the real reason was we would be able to 'pimp' Dave in the future."

The young couple went to Grandpa Kerr's farm several times a month. Occasionally, the trio went to Sinorak for Sunday dinner. Grandpa was good to them. He allowed the kids to stay at their apartment for very little rent. He knew Dave and Bonnie were trying to get their education. That made him proud.

The Vietnam Conflict was drawing national attention, and there was unrest in the country. Some college-age male students were leaving the country for Canada to escape the draft. President Kennedy's policy exempted married college students from the draft. However, this did change unless a dependent was involved.

The use of social drugs became prominent. David was against any type of recreational drugs. To his knowledge he never attended any party where drugs were being used. Plenty of beer, but no social drugs! Being married to Bonnie perhaps prevented him from experimenting with drugs. Over his twenty-eight-year coaching career, Darnall had only one hard, fast training rule—no use of drugs. His policy regarding drinking, smoking, and curfew changed according to the times and level of competition.

David could not wait to finish his final year in college. The struggle would finally conclude in August 1965. He fulfilled his student teaching requirement at Ottawa High School during the first semester. Ottawa is located sixty miles north of Normal. The worst aspect of the assignment was being away from Bonnie for several weeks. He left their apartment on Sunday evening and returned on Friday afternoon unless the basketball team had a game. David received his first professional coaching experience by assisting Coach Harris with the Freshmen-Sophomore team.

David split his student teaching assignment between physical education and driver education. His student teaching experience proved to be somewhat difficult for him. He had attended a very small high school but had to student teach at a large school. That was a big adjustment. Ottawa had ROTC. His physical education supervisor was the director of the program. This program was completely foreign to him. He had a difficult time understanding the program. The large class confusion and having some ROTC responsibilities doomed him. Dave received a "B" in the physical education phase of his student teaching.

David enjoyed his coaching experience. It was everything he thought coaching would be. His coach was pleased with his work with the Freshmen-Sophomore Team. However, the volunteer assignment received no grade.

He had a difficult time teaching the classroom phase of driver education. David's on-site supervisor and he seemed to have a personality conflict. That resulted in a student teaching grade of "C" in driver education. That was not good! If it had not been for the Vietnam War taking many potentially good teaching candidates, Dave would have had a very difficult time obtaining a teaching position.

Tragedy again struck the family in the spring of 1965. Dave's grandfather died of a heart attack. Dave and Bonnie had driven to the farm to see Grandpa Kerr. He was not at home, but Dave knew where the house key was hidden. They decided to go in and wait for his return. Thirty minutes or so passed when they saw headlights coming up the driveway. The driver of the truck let Mr. Kerr off and drove away. Grandpa went directly to the barn to feed his livestock. After a few minutes he came into the house holding and rubbing his left arm. He also complained of chest pain. The kids helped him to the couch. Bonnie immediately ran to the phone to call for an ambulance. Living in the country, it was difficult to explain the location of the house. Bonnie returned to the couch and began to give the elderly gentleman chest compressions. David sprinted down the lane leading to the highway that ran in front of the house where he waited for the ambulance. It had begun to rain. It seemed like hours. Meanwhile, Bonnie was still with Grandpa Kerr. He was intermittently crying, praying, and begging her not to stop the rhythmic chest compressions. She was crying and praying he would not go unconscious on her.

After a second phone call, the ambulance finally arrived. The attendants rushed Mr. Kerr to the hospital. David called his parents in Argenta. They immediately left home and arrived in Bloomington in a little over an hour. They joined Bonnie and Dave at Grandpa's bedside. After some time, he communicated briefly with those around him.

A doctor told them Mr. Kerr was responding to treatment and that the exhausted young couple should go get some rest. Dave's parents stayed by his side.

A short time after arriving back at their apartment, Bonnie received a call from Dave's mother. Her father had taken a turn for the worse. By the time the kids got back to the hospital, Mr. Kerr had passed away. His death affected the young couple greatly.

Dave's spring semester courses were almost unbearable. He was enrolled in "Modern World Civilization," the second course of anatomy/physiology, physical geology, and hygiene. Hygiene was very tough because of Dave's lack of a background in science. Dave had saved these difficult classes until the end so that if his grade point average dropped, it would be too late to cause him to be ineligible for student teaching.

David was not a good test-taker. He had struggled taking tests ever since high school, getting extremely nervous before exams. The time factor disturbed him the most. Dave never understood why college professors discussed certain material in class but then would test on other content.

"I do not believe in 'head' games—students trying to guess what will be on the test," Darnall said. "As a professor, I told my students that I would not play 'head' games with them. I'd let them know what information they would need to know for the test," Dave explained, "but it was their responsibility to study if they wanted to receive a good grade." The tests were demanding, but at least the students knew what to expect. Time was allowed to complete the exams.

David was happy to receive four "Cs." He still needed two more courses before he could graduate. That meant he had to attend summer school for the fourth consecutive year.

The summer was quite busy. Besides attending summer school, playing twelve-inch softball for Eureka Williams for the third and last summer, working part time for Frank's Spice & Tea Company, David wanted to somehow get more coaching experience. He applied to serve as a Youth American Legion Baseball coach, wanting to follow the footsteps of Coach Bass. He wanted to do the same for youngsters as Bass had done for him—teach the proper fundamentals of sports. Whereas Bass ended up as the head baseball coach at a large university, Darnall's ambition was to become a head basketball coach at a small college.

Dave was accepted and assigned as the Legion's adult baseball coach at Oakland Elementary School in Bloomington. He was given a student assistant coach by the name of Cal Hubbard. Hubbard became a very successful high school coach at several high schools including University High School in Normal.

It was during this summer that the Darnalls started a family. No, not a child—a puppy. One morning, Bonnie went to the garage for the car to go to work. She heard some noises. Looking toward the back of the garage, she saw three puppies. Since pets were not allowed in the apartment, she did not know what to do. This presented a problem as they did not want to call the dog pound and have the puppies possibly euthanized.

Over the weekend, they were successful in finding homes for two of the puppies. Bonnie and Dave decided to keep the runt—a tan male. Since Dave enjoyed partying, Bonnie named the dog Boozer. Boozer stayed with the family for sixteen years. He grew old and developed cataracts on his eyes. It was while living in Eureka that he wandered off in an especially heavy snowstorm. It was one that had closed schools for several days. He never returned. The family searched frantically for him for many days. Boozer was not found. His end still remains a mystery.

Darnall and Raycraft were intrigued with a new softball game, six-teen-inch slow pitch. They formed a team to compete in the newly devised sixteen-inch softball league sponsored by the Normal Parks and Recreation Department. The organizer was Dave Anderson, the new City of Normal Recreation Director. Later, Dave worked two summers for Anderson as a playground director.

For the next several years, Raycraft and Darnall's Normal Indees found much success in sixteen-inch softball. Their teams were mostly com-posed of some of the areas best known former athletes and coaches. Among them were Bobby Spahn, Stan Petty, Bill Stark, Bill Jones, Ed Thomas, Dave Blunk, Gary Dahlquist, Brad Miller, Bernie Lewis, Dave Preston, Del Swearingen, Jack Marcoline, Rod Brent, and Mike Payne. Brother Bruce and Jim Barone usually rounded out the team. The Normal Indees' best season came in 1968.

Not caring if he ever returned to college, Dave was anxious to grad-uate. He successfully completed the two summer courses. He was relieved! Dave was ready to start teaching and coaching. He had respected his college teachers, attended classes, and often visited with his college professors regarding his weaknesses in their classes. Some may call this "brown nos-ing." Cited in the *Pilot*, Dave's high school yearbook, he was listed in the Senior Poll as the class' biggest male "apple polisher." Guess it means the same. Yet, having the ability to communicate with his teachers was a big asset. Together with Bonnie's assistance and his willingness to attend class-es, Dave finally made it. It took five years and four summers. He was through. That made his father proud!

Chapter 5

Early Career

WITHIN TWO WEEKS OF GRADUATION, David finally reached one of his childhood dreams—to be a high school coach. As with most youngsters not having the ability to become professional players, he had to settle for his second choice, but, even at that, many graduates, in actuality, never fulfill their career choices. He did. The Vietnam Conflict provided this opportunity. There was a teacher shortage in Illinois, especially of males. This "opened the door" for him.

The Darnalls wanted to stay close to Normal so that Bonnie could continue her education as a full-time student while still maintaining a part-time job. David had four interviews. Not bad for a person who received a "C" and "B" in student teaching, besides taking five years to receive his degree. In fact, he was offered four different positions before graduating and becoming certified.

David had conversed with his father about interviewing techniques. He was not sure of what to say, ask, or how to conduct himself in an interview. Mr. Darnall was a very articulate person with high school debating experience and had served on the local school board. His son felt his dad's wisdom and debating experience would be beneficial to him.

However, his father still did not have much confidence in David's communication skills. "Answer the questions, but don't talk too much," Delmar told his son.

How wrong would his father be? Maybe it was a "chip off the old block," but as time would tell, Dave's future success was largely due to his ability to communicate. Recruiting takes a whole lot of communicating skills!

David's first interview was at Lacon High School, located approximately sixty miles northwest of Normal. He was offered the position after a personal interview. However, the Darnalls felt the daily drive to or from Lacon would be too rigorous for either of them. Darnall turned down the offer.

The second interview was at Cullom High School. Cullom was a small town about fifty miles northeast of Normal. The position consisted of teaching physical education and biology, coaching high school basketball, and a possibility of other coaching responsibilities. He almost accepted the position even though he would have had to teach biology. Biology! Yes, biology, a course David never took in high school or college. Remember his high school General Science experience?

The reason Darnall almost accepted the offer from Cullom was that he thought it might be his last chance to obtain a head basketball coaching position even though there was a teacher shortage. He felt his low grades from student teaching might eventually catch up with him. This was especially true since he had already turned down one offer. However, the fear of teaching biology caused him to make the right decision. He turned down the position.

David was contact by Elkhart High School to interview for an opening in their system as a physical education teacher and head basketball coach with other coaching duties. Elkhart was a small town approximately fifty miles south of Normal on Route 66. The Darnalls drove to Elkhart.

Dave took Bonnie with him when interviewing for several reasons. He felt it was important that Bonnie like the town in which he would be coaching. He wanted her to see what type of housing would be available. Darnall also felt that going together to interview showed family support. Bonnie would be an asset to his candidacy.

The teaching and coaching was to Dave's liking. Even though Elkhart was fifty miles away from Normal, the road was a four-lane highway; an hour's drive. Perhaps the Darnalls could live somewhere in between.

Dave was offered the position. He had a few days in which to make a decision. The Darnalls liked what they saw. So far, it was the best situation for them.

A day or so after the interview while Dave was contemplating what to do, he received a phone call from the principal of Stanford High School. Stanford was a small town located approximately ten miles straight west of Bloomington. The location was perfect. He wanted Darnall to interview for a teaching/coaching position.

The Elkhart school system needed an answer from Dave before his interview with Stanford. It was a big decision. Having confidence he would do well in the interview, the Darnalls decided to reject Elkhart's offer. Dave made the call.

Bonnie, as usual, escorted her husband to the interview. Stanford had an enrollment of approximately ninety students located in the rural community of about 500 people. The position consisted of teaching physical education and driver education, as well as serving as head coach in basketball, baseball, and track. The new employee would also be the Athletic Director. With the coaching staff consisting of only himself, the new Athletic Director would be in charge of a one-man staff—himself! By the way, the coach was also the bus driver for away fall and spring sports.

Superintendent Ron Wepprecht and Principal Richard Vincent interviewed Dave and offered him the vacant position. Darnall accepted and signed his first teaching/coaching contract. It was meant to be. He received $5,200.00 compensation for his teaching/coaching duties.

Stanford was the perfect location for the Darnalls. With the couple finding a small, one-story house at the edge of Stanford, the drive to Normal's campus would take only twenty minutes. It was just perfect for the young couple and Boozer. What a coincidence that this was the same village in which Dave's father had been born.

"Boozer"

Darnall's first decision in his new position was to start a cross-country program. He used this as a conditioning program for basketball. All basketball prospects had to participate in cross-country. The basketball program had been in shambles without a winning season in the past ten years. What a challenge for the young, inexperienced coach!

77

Darnall's first coaching responsibility was fall baseball. There was no football. Baseball, along with the newly formed cross-country program, meant a busy fall for the coach before his beloved sport, basketball, would begin.

Dave loved basketball, but he enjoy baseball as well. Baseball had been fun for him during the summers, in junior high school, and in high school. He also had enjoyed being batboy for Normal Community High School and for a couple teams in the summer Muny League at ISNU. Those experiences provided him with some excellent teachers.

The new coach was anxious for October to arrive. He could not wait for his first basketball practice as a coach. However prior to this first official practice, Dave met with his old high school coach. Coach Huff was coaching at a small high school in Northern Illinois. Even though Darnall had had some issues with Huff while in high school, he respected his basketball knowledge and liked him. As a matter of fact, David used portions of his pre-game warm-up routine all twenty-eight years of coaching, including at the National Tournament.

Darnall's longtime dream finally came true as basketball season got underway. The conference consisted of eight schools of which four had new basketball coaches. Stanford opened its basketball season against Mackinaw Valley Conference foe, Minier. The game was at Minier. Coach Darnall started his career on the road in 1965 and finished it on the road in 1994. What a ride!

As stated in a local newspaper, *The News*, Minier was the team to beat. "On paper, at least, it looks like the Minier Wildcats will give *The News* area its strongest representative in the MVC play," the paper read.

Coach Darnall had eleven players on his first varsity basketball squad. They were seniors: Randy Benjamin, David Dawson, and Bill Dickson; juniors: Ray Irwin, Rich Kindred, Bob Risser, and Dave Rutledge; and sophomores: Dick Barclay, Norman Johnson, Andy Reining, and David Semple.

Johnson reminded Darnall of himself. Norm was extremely interested in sports. He would read all the newspapers and know what was going on in the world of sports. He followed Coach Darnall around just like Dave had done with Coaches Bass and Ricci. Norm even volunteered to go with Coach Darnall when he scouted nearby opponents.

Even at this early stage of Darnall's coaching career, he believed in scouting his opponents. That philosophy continued throughout his twenty-eight years of coaching basketball. Minier High School opened its season a couple days prior to their game with Stanford. Coach Darnall, Norm, and several other players scouted Minier on its opening night. The result of the contest did not bring much comfort to the observers. Minier won.

It was Monday, November 22, 1965; the night before Coach Darnall's first game. Dave experienced the agony that also was prevalent his entire coaching career. That included having no appetite, sleepless nights, unsettled stomach, and having to go to the bathroom quite frequently.

Coach Darnall boarded the team bus for the first of numerous road trips in his illustrious coaching career, hoping his team would perform admirably. He heard how difficult it was to win on the road regardless of the team's ability, and his team did perform, but Stanford did not win the game. They lost by only one point to the pre-season favorite in their conference. The picture on the cover of this book tells the story. The newspaper read, "Coach David Darnall of Stanford High School is a picture of dejection moments after his team dropped a one-point decision to the Minier Wildcats." The score was Minier, 60, Stanford, 59.

Stanford went on to lose its first seven games of the season. How frustrating it was for the first year coach. Had he chosen the wrong field? It sure was not what it was made out to be. Where was the glory and happiness? Not sadness, loneliness, and frustration.

The Green Valley game brought Darnall his first coaching victory. The score was 62 to 55. That was the way it was suppose to be.

Dave scouted the next opponent and felt that team had a great deal more talent than his own. Thus, he would have to employ ball control tactics to win.

The first time Coach Darnall used this strategy was against Danvers High School. The score was Stanford, 2, Danvers, 4, at the end of the first quarter. At halftime it was Stanford, 12, Danvers, 13. The final score was Stanford, 38, and Danvers, 47. Dave's team got beat; however, they had given themselves a chance to win.

The second time Coach Darnall used ball control tactics was against conference contender San Jose. San Jose had a "big" team led by six-foot-six freshman sensation, Ron Eeten. Eeten was at least three inches taller than any of Darnall's players. The next day's headline in the Peoria *Journal Star* stated, "San Jose, Down 19 - 11 at half, Solves Stanford Slowdown 33 - 29." *The Pantagraph*'s headline read, "San Jose Withstands Stall, Turns Back Stanford, 33 - 29." Stanford had been in the game with a chance to win. The fans at Stanford, however, were used to the "run and gun" style of play and were not overly impressed with the young coach's tactics.

The Indians finally won two consecutive games. They beat Green Valley for the second time and followed with a nice win over Hopedale. Stanford then played Delavan. The headline in the next morning *Journal Star* stated, "Delavan Has Close Call in 42 - 35 Win." Portions of the article read,

> Delavan maintained their perfect record here Friday as they came off with a close 42 - 35 Mackinaw Valley victory over the Stanford Indians. Stanford controlled the ball throughout the entire first half of play as they led 13 - 9 and 19 - 15 at the end of the first two quarters of play. Delavan won the game in the final quarter as they made seven charity tosses, three of them in the final minute of play.

Again, Darnall's game plan had allowed his team the opportunity to win the contest against a more talented club.

On Saturday, February 12, 1966, Dave got a phone call he had always feared. The Darnalls were at home in Stanford, enjoying a day away from basketball when they received a phone call from Larry McConkey. Larry and Donna lived in the apartment below the one the Darnalls had lived in on Locust Street in Bloomington. Larry informed Dave that his father had died of a heart attack. Mr. Darnall had climbed the steps leading to an upstairs apartment to collect rent. Since Grandpa Kerr's death in the spring of 1965, Dave's dad had overseen the property. He had collapsed and fallen down the stairs. McConkey found him lying on the entryway floor.

Dave and Bonnie jumped into their car and rushed to Bloomington. As they opened the apartment house front door, they saw the senior Darnall lying at the bottom of the steps. The coroner had come and gone. Dave was in great grief. His dad died at the young age of fifty-five, seven years after his first heart attack in Wisconsin.

Mr. Darnall was taken to Argenta for visitation purposes on Monday, and then brought back to Normal for both afternoon and evening visitations on Tuesday. Funeral services were scheduled for Wednesday afternoon. Needless to say, Dave missed school both Monday and Tuesday as well as basketball practice on Monday. However, Stanford had a home game scheduled Tuesday evening with Minier, the team that had beaten Dave's team by one point in his first game of his coaching career.

Dave and Bonnie had stayed with the rest of the family since the death. On Tuesday, the young coach spent the afternoon at the funeral home.

Should he coach that night? Did he feel like it? After much thought and discussion with the family, it was decided that Dave's father would have wanted his son to coach his team at the scheduled game. Who would know that twenty-eight years later Dave would miss only one game as a coach? It was because he was in the hospital for a suspected second heart attack following a first one three years earlier. However, it proved to be negative. Missing only one class as a college student and only one game as a coach, Dave felt someone was watching over him.

Coach Darnall arrived at the gym from the funeral home just minutes before game time. Not talking much to his players, he asked them to do the very best they could—to reach down for a little extra as this game meant a lot to him. The team took its already traditional few seconds of silence before the game.

They were ready! What a performance! The next morning's issue of the Peoria *Journal Star* had a headline stating, "Minier 76 - 56 Stanford Victim." The article read in part,

> The Stanford Indians rolled past Minier in a Mackinaw Valley Conference game, 76 - 56, here Tuesday. The Indians quickly got off to a 5 - 0 lead and steadily increased that margin, at times leading by 25 points. Minier's defense proved inadequate for a great part of the time, as most of Stanford's shots in the first half came from within a ten-foot range of the basket.

The team won one for their coach. Dave won one for his father. How could a team beat another team by twenty points after losing to them earlier in the season? It was meant to be!

Dave finished his first season as Head Basketball Coach with a five to eighteen record, losing to Tremont, 59 to 39, in the first round of the District Tournament. The new coach was disappointed with his first year's record. He felt he and his team should have done better. Who would ever guess that this year, Dave's first, would be the worst season of his coaching career and only the fourth losing season in his twenty-eight-year tenure?

Even though Coach Darnall had an unsatisfying year as a head coach, he did meet some life-long friends. Believe it or not, they were basketball officials. Dave often kidded, "The stress of winning and losing and them damn officials drove me out of the game." In reality, Darnall had a lot of respect for officials. He knew it took special qualities to fulfill the demands of officiating. Several officials who had an impact upon the young coach were Chuck West, Jim Jones, Wayne Meece, Hy Roznowski, George Bailey, Stan Decker, Joe Bratcher, and Jim Schilkoski.

Lucca's Grill was a corner bar and grill in Bloomington with a great tradition. It was the local "Cheers" establishment, a place where professional people and sport enthusiasts frequented. Dave and Bonnie drove to Lucca's Grill after many games to meet with other coaches, officials, and sport fans. Often they visited with the officials mentioned. On some occasions, Principal Richard Vincent accompanied the Darnalls to Lucca's. Owners John and Tot were among the area's greatest sport fans. Lucca's enthusiastic sports tradition has continued under present owner Chuck Williams.

Not only was David disappointed with his first season as a coach, but so were some of the Stanford fans. That was especially true of the young graduates. It was not necessarily because of the team's won and loss record, but because of the style of play. Most of the fans were not used to the slow-down tactics that Darnall sometimes employed. Stanford fans were not used to winning, which included ten losing seasons prior to Darnall's arrival. Some of the fans really didn't care about winning, but they wanted to see the boys run. "We come to see the boys play, not stand around," a distraught fan complained. Dave felt differently. He thought his job was to win varsity games.

"The real enjoyment of varsity sports comes with winning," Darnall said. "The game is for the players, not the fans. The players, after working hard, want to feel they accomplish something." The winning attitude is what Dave wanted to instill in his athletes. Winning is a positive reflection upon the community, but Stanford now had eleven consecutive losing seasons.

With the basketball season over, Coach Darnall turned his attention and energy to track. As a high school athlete, David was probably more successful in track than any other sport in which he participated. Bonnie, whose favorite sport was track, attended her husband's track meets as much as possible. Darnall's track team was successful. That was partially due to his ability to get some "non-athletes" with athletic ability to join the team. He noticed their talents in his physical education classes. Some of the fellas had had not received much attention or recognition. Track provided self-esteem as well as fellowship. Even though the first-year coach's team did not win any major meets, there were some excellent individual efforts. Dave Rutledge's performance in several events led the Stanford team to a successful season.

It was during May of 1966 that Dave really got the feel for Eureka College. His brother, Bruce, graduated from the institution. Darnall recalled sitting in Rinker Outdoor Theater for commencement. It was a beautiful spring day in a peaceful, natural setting when Dave said to his wife, "Bonnie, someday I would like to be Head Basketball Coach here."

She replied, "David, that's a dream, especially after the season you just had."

"I know, but I want to be a small college coach," he responded.

It was definitely a big dream following only his first year of teaching and coaching. The school year ended, leaving Dave with many "first experiences," and he was glad to see summer. After attending college for five years and four summers, he was tired of school. "No school this summer," he said. Needing money to pay off his college loan, he found summer employment with the Normal Recreation Department. He was assigned to Oakdale School as Playground Director.

The summer proved to be a busy but fun time. Dave, Raycraft, and their buddies had another successful season of sixteen-inch softball.

Darnall started his second year as teacher and coach at Stanford. Duplicating the previous year, he started school coaching both baseball and cross-country. Whereas the baseball team had a good season, the cross-country team had an outstanding one. They completed the season undefeated in dual and tri-angular meets and won the first Mackinaw Valley Cross-Country title.

Darnall was troubled throughout the fall athletic season by the uncertainty of his draft status. The Vietnam Conflict was in full swing. The draft board was now drafting everyone, including married students. In fact, David had traveled to St. Louis the middle of September to take his military physical examination. One day during a discussion with a colleague, Dave mentioned his draft status. The English teacher told Dave that her son was a career military person with the National Guard. He could get Dave into the Guard. Darnall, attending a meeting with her son at the Peoria National Guard Headquarters, intended to sign-up. He would have six month's of training and then just weekend and summer duties. Therefore, his military duty would not interfere with his coaching career. He would not be drafted and sent to Vietnam.

Viewing a film of the Green Beret Airborne training and drilling, David decided that was not for him. He did not realize that this would be the unit he would be joining. Darnall was extremely afraid of heights. In fact, he would not even get up on a house roof. No way could he ever jump from a plane. Besides, he felt the Green Beret boys were "nuts." Even though he was afraid of his escort's reaction to his decision not to enlist, Dave felt it would be best for him to take his chances with the Draft. It was a long, quiet ride back to Stanford.

Coach Darnall was anxious for his second basketball season to start. He was optimistic that his team would have a good season; he hoped to reach the .500 point.

Stanford opened its season with a lopsided win over McLean, 63 to 45. That victory was a great win for Darnall and his players, especially since Stanford lost its first seven games the previous year.

Dave and Bonnie began to establish themselves in the community. It was during this season that the Darnalls set a tradition that would continue for his entire coaching career. He wanted to share his team with the community. The Darnalls invited the players' parents, school personnel, and community fans to their house after every home game. The Barclays, Semples, Rissers, and Shafers—parents of players—and school Principal Richard Vincent were among those gathering after the games.

Coach Darnall continued his slow-down or stall tactics against taller or more talented teams. It was against Armington that the young coach again used his "unique tactics." Armington had three guys six-foot five or six-foot-six. The score at the end of the first quarter was 2 to 2; at halftime it was Armington, 8, and Stanford, 6; at the end of the third quarter it was Armington, 14 and Stanford, 8. The game ended with Armington, 26 and Stanford, 20. Again, Dave felt he had given his team an opportunity to win. However, an increasing number of Indian fans disliked this strategy.

Stanford went into the Beason Holiday Tournament with a 5 to 4 record. Darnall was satisfied. His team made it to the championship game. Their opponent was Minier.

Minier had already beaten Stanford the second game of the season by a score of 50 to 43. Coach, again, felt his team should employ slow-down tactics because leading scorer, Rich Kindred, would miss the game due to having mumps. Stanford lost the championship game 25 to 21.

The Indians lost another heartbreaker a few days later. "Would You Really Believe 5 Overtimes," the newspaper headline read. With three seconds left in the fifth overtime, a Mackinaw player stepped up to the charity line and made two free throws, making the score Mackinaw - 34 and Stanford - 32. The box score read: Stanford - 10, 12, 19, 30, 30, 32, 32, 32, 32 and Mackinaw - 8, 18, 26, 30, 30, 32, 32, 32, 34.

It was not long after the memorable five-overtime loss that Coach Darnall found out how rude basketball fans could be. After a close, slow-down home game, several fans reacted in a way Dave never dreamed possible. Throughout the game, a few young Stanford fans were shouting negative remarks toward him regarding his coaching strategy. The game ended, and Darnall walked off the floor with his disappointed team for their traditional locker room post-game talk. Finishing this, Darnall went to his office adjoining the locker room. Just as he was reaching for the phone to call in the game result, three young adult fans burst through the door and began to swing at the bewildered coach. Some of the players saw the happening through the window that led into the locker room and rushed to their coach's aid. The players grabbed the intruders, forcing them out of the locker room area.

That evening, during a small post-game gathering at the Darnall home, Coach received a couple phone calls threatening him, "If you either stall or use slow-down tactics again, you will not walk out of the gym alive."

Over the next couple of days, Coach Darnall received several letters with the same message. The school administration, aware of the threats, notified the McLean County Sheriff's Office of the situation. For the remainder of the season, a deputy escorted Darnall at all games. The officer sat behind the coach at each contest. The young coach could not believe that this was what coaching was all about. He still believed it was his job to give his team the opportunity to stay in the games with the possibility of winning. The game was for the players, not the fans.

Darnall finished his second season as a head coach with an overall 11 to 13 record. That was actually one loss or one win away from the goal of .500. One loss turned into a win would have given his team a 12 to 12 season. Even thought 11 to 13 was the best record Stanford High School had had in thirteen years, or since the 1954-1955 season, there were people within the community that wanted Darnall fired.

Track season brought some respite from the problems of the past basketball season and the lingering draft situation. Coach Darnall felt that year's track team should be quite successful. His team did not disappoint him. They went undefeated in the regular season schedule. They placed second in the "Tiny State Meet," second in the McLean County Track Meet, and won the Mackinaw Conference title. Duplicating the previous year, the team was led by senior Dave Rutledge. Other outstanding performers who contributed to the team's success were Dick Barclay, Ray Irwin, Bob Risser, Jim Mowery, Jim Williamson, John Owen, and Larry Shafer.

At the conclusion of track season, Darnall decided to resign as teacher-coach at Stanford. It was rumored that he would be fired if he did not voluntarily quit. After talking to his friend, Principal Vincent, Dave learned that Vincent could save his job. However, Darnall figured: why would he want to coach there after the way he had been treated?

Before Dave left Stanford, he had another memorable experience, this one very rewarding. Due to the turmoil in Vietnam, Darnall, a senior class advisor, suggested the seniors do something to show their support of the American soldiers in Vietnam. The class agreed. They unselfishly decided to forego the usual senior trip and donate the money to the Marine Civic Action Fund. *The Pantagraph* headline for an article regarding this decision read, "Seniors Vote Class Fund to U.S. Marines in Vietnam."

Dave started looking for another teaching-coaching position in the Bloomington-Normal area. It was important for the Darnalls to stay in the area as Bonnie was still attending ISU. Coach Darnall looked forward to going into a situation where the program was "down." He enjoyed the challenge of building a program to a "winner."

Even though many people did not appreciate the job he did at Stanford and the fact he did not have a .500 season, Coach felt he had built the program to respectability.

Darnall pulled for the underdog. He gained self-satisfaction in attempting to develop a winning tradition from a losing program. He would face another challenge. He accepted a position as teacher-coach at Gridley High School. His coaching responsibilities consisted of Head Basketball, Baseball, and Track. He also was an assistant in the football program. Dave also served as the school's Athletic Director. He felt the move to Gridley was a professional advancement. Stanford's enrollment was approximately ninety students; Gridley boasted approximately one hundred thirty.

Gridley was located approximately twenty-five miles north of Normal, a community of nearly 1,000 people. The basketball team's record the previous year was 2 to 21, with four consecutive losing seasons. This was going to definitely be another challenge. Exactly what Darnall was looking for.

Bonnie and Dave decided to buy their first home, a small ranch-style house in Normal. They planned to remain in the area for some time. Living in Normal would make it easy for Bonnie to attend college and work part-time at the Normal Police Department. David now started to think about working on his Master's Degree at ISU.

It was approximately a thirty-minute drive to Gridley. The Darnalls moved into their new home immediately following the conclusion of the school year.

Soon Coach Darnall was looking forward to a fresh start as a head basketball coach. However, this would have to wait several weeks due to his assignment as the football team's line coach. Dave knew very little about football. In fact, he was not excited about the position. It definitely would be a new endeavor. Darnall would not realize the importance of this coaching experience for several years to come. Eventually, it became a major benefit for future employment. The season ended one of the best the gridiron boys had had in recent years. The team finished in a tie for second place in the Mid-State Conference.

Coach Darnall had started his basketball practice the middle of October for those players who did not participate in football. The whole team reported to practice on Monday, November 5th. That gave him only two weeks to get his team ready for its first game. A lot had to be done for a team that had compiled a 2 to 21 record the previous year.

Before Dave's first game at Gridley could be played, a tragedy took place. The Darnalls lost a close friend. Leon Bryant was killed in Vietnam. Leon gained national recognition when singer/actress Anita Bryant wore his fatigue jacket while being photographed during her annual goodwill trip to Fort Leonard Wood. Leon was to meet Miss Bryant in Vietnam on her overseas Christmas tour in late 1967. The following is a news release to the press by Anita Bryant regarding the jacket:

> For seven years I accompanied Bob Hope on his Holiday Tours more than any female performer ever did, so he rewarded me the title of "Den Mother."
>
> I remember one Thanksgiving prior to leaving on a Bob Hope tour I sang for troops at Foot Leonard Wood, Missouri, America's largest training post. Many of the men in that audience were later shipped off to Vietnam. I had collected dozens of military patches and insignia from the various outfits I'd visited on previous Christmas shows. I asked permission to purchase a fatigue jacket so I could cover it with my patches and insignia to wear to Vietnam. They were happy to *give* me a jacket (the one I am wearing in the photo) after my concert to the service men at Fort Leonard Wood. To my astonishment, it had my name stenciled above the left pocket: BRYANT. Later I learned the real story.
>
> The jacket belonged to a sergeant named Leon Bryant of Decatur, Illinois. Later his hometown newspaper carried the story: How Sergeant

Bryant came in from a three-week field problem, dirty . . . how the post photographer snapped his picture in the jacket before he even had a chance to wash his face . . . how the garment was given to Miss Anita Bryant for her use in Vietnam.

How did I learn all that? Mrs. Yvonne Bryant, the sergeant's wife, mailed me the newspaper story along with a nice letter from Illinois.

"When you get to Vietnam, please look up Leon," she asked.

In the newspaper article Sergeant Bryant, when asked what he'd like me to give him in exchange for his jacket, had said, "a kiss on the cheek." I resolved to look him up and deliver that kiss, but I never got the chance before Yvonne Bryant wrote another letter . . . "If you ever feel like disposing of Leon's jacket, I would be glad to have it," she wrote. He died in Vietnam November 14, 1967, from gunshot wounds received while on combat operations when hit by hostile small arms fire . . . Leon was carrying a machine gun at the time and one of the members of his squad was pinned down by a V.C. . . . Leon moved forth trying to save his buddy [who] was being attacked by Viet Cong, while all the members of his squad safely took cover . . . Leon did save the life of his buddy but the V.C.'s fired upon Leon, killing him instantly . . . I felt sick—utterly stricken. It was like learning of the death of someone I had known intimately. It hurt to learn that Leon Bryant had a newspaper clipping about the jacket and a letter from me in his pocket when he died. As I imagined the young man who once wore that jacket, I almost felt the weight of it, heavy now with insignia, across my shoulders.

What can one say at a time like that? Nothing. Absolutely nothing, yet I felt led to try to reach Yvonne Bryant by telephone—to try in my own halting way to express our sorrow for her sorrow.

On the telephone, she shared that she and her sergeant were newly-weds and had lived together only a few months before he left for Vietnam.

Her voice was clear and steady.

"Leon was a Christian," she told me. "It's all right. He was proud to fight for his country. We had talked about this, about how it might happen, and he told me how he felt. Leon said he didn't mind dying for America. And Anita, Leon died a Christian. I know he is with Our Lord."

I shall never forget Yvonne Bryant's calm young voice. I had called to offer her comfort, but she had consoled me. In a way, this story represents for me so many other—small incidents and big events—each in its own way haunting—that I will always carry in my heart . . .

As I close each show in Branson, Missouri, with that story, prior to singing the "Battle Hymn of the Republic," wearing Leon's jacket . . .

I thank God for all our servicemen and women who down through history have been willing to pay the price for Freedom, which is never free.

Dave's high school teammate and college roommate left college early. Not able to afford his education, Leon went to work in Decatur. He was drafted into the Army January of 1967. It would be less than a year before he was killed in action. Dave's brother, Bruce, who was then a minister, conducted the funeral service.

Darnall was disturbed emotionally over Leon's death, his fourth high school buddy to be killed in five years. The others were killed in car accidents—Bobby Beadleston in 1964 while returning to college at Southern Illinois; Eddie Allen, a classmate, while returning to Decatur from Taylorville in 1965; and Jim Edwards, a classmate of Bruce's who also ran around with Dave, killed in late summer of 1962 in Lincoln, Illinois.

Bobby and Leon's deaths meant that two of the top seven players on Darnall's senior year basketball team were no longer here. How lucky were Dave and his passengers in their accident? There could have been three. (There's that number three) It was meant to be!

Darnall's Gridley team tied the previous year's record in wins in the second game of the season by defeating Tri-Valley, 65 to54. Freshman standout, Rob Tipsword, led the way by pouring in twenty-two points. Other members of the team were: seniors Dale Aupperle, Mark Widmer, Greg Maurer, Dick Gilmore, Paul Morin, and Steve Phillis; juniors Larry Gilmore, Mike Morin, Pat Kinsella, Curt Fleming, and Brent Ehresman; and sophomores Mark Dalton and Clark Stoller rounded out the varsity team. Henry "Hank" Finck was Darnall's faithful student assistant.

The Darnalls met several life-long friends at Gridley. They were Mark's parents, Dick and Phyllis Dalton, Dr. and Mary Rich, Bill and Nancy Froelich, Harold and Lois Burke, and Mariam and Hubert Hutcheson to mention a few. The Riches would eventually have two children and a grandchild attend Eureka College while Doc served on the college's Board of Trustees.

Bonnie and Dave did not live in Gridley, but the post-game social gatherings continued to take place. With the generosity of the Daltons, most of the after-game parties were held at their home. The Riches, Burkes, and Froeliches also hosted some of the after-game parties. Parents, school personnel, coaches, and community fans attended these post-game functions to rehash the evening's game.

Gridley lost its first game of the season to Minonk in a nail-biter, 53 to 51, in the third game of the year. Gridley, who finished in last place in the 1966 Beason Holiday Tournament, was seeded number one this year. For the second consecutive year, a Darnall coached team placed second in the tournament. Gridley lost to the host team, 53 to 48. The previous year it had been Stanford, a victim to Minier.

One of the most disappointing losses in Dave's young career was to his formerly coached team, Stanford, in the opening round of the McLean County Tournament held on the ISU campus. Shooting only twenty-nine percent, Gridley lost 44 to 41 in a hard fought contest.

The Gridley Redskins finished the season with a 13 to 10 record, the

Gridley's Rib Tipsord guarded by Stanford's Dick Barklay as teammate Mark Dalton comes to his aid.

first winning season in six years. It was a great improvement over the previous year's record of 2 to 21. It was Darnall's first winning season as a coach.

Sometime during that year, Coach Darnall began a tension-releasing ritual that would be his trademark for years to come. The habit started by accident. A player on the court had received an injury, and Darnall thought applying tape would help. While the game proceeded, Dave reached into the medicine kit and got a roll of athletic tape. By the time he got to the injured player to apply the tape, the athlete had decided he did not need it. Instead of returning the tape to the kit, Dave hung onto it as he continued to watch the action of the game. Sooner or later, he tore a piece about two inches long. With the tape in his hand, he left his normal "crutch," a small red towel lying on the bench. That towel had been squeezed, rolled, dropped, and thrown numerous times since the beginning of his coaching career. It would now have some peace.

Taking the tape between his forefinger and thumb, he ripped a piece from the roll. Darnall continued tearing this little piece until it became the size of a fingernail. Each piece torn was rolled up and thrown back over his shoulder. The tradition started. There were numerous tiny balls of tape for the custodian to sweep following the game. However, many times the janitor had help because a few young kids would gather the small balls of tape and put them together to form one big ball. It was then used to shoot at the basket while fans vacated the gym.

To this day, many years later, Darnall is often remembered more for his tape tearing than for his coaching. The ritual was a tension-releasing measure for the coach but was a spectacle for the fans. How many rolls of tape did he throw away?

Dave could not wait for the next year. He was ready to start over after this team's success. He felt top returning players Dalton, Tipsword, Kinsella, Gilmore, and sophomore Dean Kirkton would form the nucleus that would make his next year's team a good one.

The summer was eventful for the Darnalls. Their first child, a daughter whom they named Tiera, was born June 10th. She would eventually also become very involved in athletics. Next, Bonnie graduated from Illinois State University majoring in Special Education. She began her teaching career by accepting a position at the Soldiers and Sailor's Children's Home in Normal.

In the meantime, Darnall and Raycraft, again, managed a sixteen-inch softball team. Their team qualified for the 1968 ASA Illinois State sixteen-inch Softball Tournament held at Humko Park in Champaign, Illinois. In the double elimination tournament, the Normal Indees beat the WKID Good Guys in the first round of the two-day affair. The team qualified for the

Normal Indees Sixteen-inch Softball Team.

finals early the second day. They then spent most of the rest of the day in a nearby bowling alley lounge. That was the most convenient place to go since the team had to check out of its motel by noon.

The Good Guys worked their way back through the tournament to the finals. The two teams would play again. If the Indees won, they would go on to the Nationals; if they lost, the two teams would have to play a third game for the title.

Dave Werkman hit a home run in the bottom of the seventh inning with two outs to give WKID Good Guys an 18 to 16 victory. A third game would be necessary.

The Indees were worn out—too much partying and bowling at the alley. The championship game finally was completed in the fog at 2:55 A.M. It was a long hour-trip back to Normal.

That summer Dave received word from Prentice-Hall, Inc., that an article he had written entitled, "Unique Problems of a Rural Track Coach," would appear in the October Issue of *The Coaching Clinic*. That was the first of ten articles he would have published in national coaching magazines.

The 1968-1969 basketball season started with Chenoa and El Paso favored to win the Mid-State Conference basketball race. Gridley jumped off to a quick start by winning five consecutive games under the direction of its second-year coach. Junior Mark Dalton, senior Pat Kinsella, and sophomore Rob Tipsword led the team. The Redskins fell to some hard times, losing the next four games, including two in the Beason Holiday Tournament. After some soul-searching and attitude adjustment, Gridley won the next four games in a row before receiving its sixth loss. Again, the team bounced back and won its next six games. That gave them a compiled record of 15 to 5 with four games remaining in the season. Splitting those, the Redskins finished with a 17 to 7 record. The team had two outstanding accomplishments. Mid-way through the season, the Redskins had set a scoring record in the McLean County Basketball Tournament, scoring ninety-eight points. The second was the sharing of the Mid-State Conference title with Flanagan with a 12 to 2 Conference record. That was the first Conference Championship for Gridley in several years.

Gridley also was able to claim the McLean County traveling trophy from Chenoa with its thrilling 74 to 66 victory. It was the first time in years that Gridley had held this trophy. As thrilling as the victory was, it was not without an unusual and challenging beginning. Gridley started the game with five technicals. That was due to having the wrong player numbers in the score book. A lesson was learned. Darnall began a ritual that would be carried out at the beginning of each game for the remainder of his twenty-eight-year coaching career. He put all names of his players and their numbers in the score book himself. He followed this by reading off each player's name and number in his pre-game talk. Darnall never started a game with a technical again.

Dave's success as a head track coach continued. As stated in *The Pantagraph* newspaper, "Gridley surprised a field of ten and turned in several top efforts to capture the McLean County Track Championship. Gridley, thus, ended LeRoy's three-year reign."

With three starters returning, including top scorers Mark Dalton and Rob Tipsword, Darnall felt his 1969-1970 team would be his best team to-date. However, this did not materialize. Darnall resigned to accept a similar position at Roseville High School. He became Head Basketball and Track Coach at the school located in Western Illinois. Roseville had an enrollment of approximately 200 students—a professional advancement.

That was the first and only time in his early coaching career Dave entered a situation where the team had a winning basketball record. Roseville had a 20 to 5 record the previous year.

During the summer of 1969, Darnall continued working on his Master's Degree. A class assignment in a Philosophy of Education course was to compose a creative writing relating to athletics. Dave's writing, along with Bonnie's help, was entitled, "The Ulcer." Professor Robert Koehler, course instructor, suggested Dave submit his writing for publication in a national coaching magazine. The article appeared in *The Coaching Clinic*. That was his second writing to be published.

The Darnalls relocated to Roseville at the end of the summer. With three top players—center Dan Livermore, and guards, Terry Gibb and Rudy Carlson—returning, Coach Darnall was anxious to begin his first Roseville basketball season. The expectations were high. Junior forward, six-foot-four Dave Cox, and sophomore forward, Dick Grant, rounded out the starting five. Senior Terry Barr was the first Panther off the bench.

Darnall's team won the first game of the season beating Roosevelt Military Academy of Aledo, 78 to 30. However, his team lost two of its next three games. That left his team 2 to 2 after four games, a disappointment to the coach, players, and fans. Dave felt it took those four games for his team to adjust and understand his coaching style and demands.

Roseville reeled off fifteen straight victories, including winning the Roseville Holiday Tourney and the Bi-County Tournament. After a loss on the road to LaHarpe by one point, 53 to 52, the Panthers went on to win the next eight straight games. Even though the team was winning and having a good season, Coach Darnall was nervous and having trouble with his stomach. With a "triple" Type-A personality and the pressures of the games, Dave's health was being affected. The coach's stomach problems had actually begun the previous year at Gridley. He was a true example of his writing, "The Ulcer."

The Darnalls again hosted a post-game gathering after each home game. One couple who attended the parties—the John Brewers—became life-long friends. Because of the success of the team, the post-game parties were usually cheerful and fun.

Roseville ended its season with a 25 to 4 record. Besides the tournament championships previously mentioned, the Panthers claimed the District Tournament with a 51 to 49 thrilling victory over Stronghurst. The Panthers then had a great, 70 to 66, win over the larger school, Monmouth, in the first round of the Regional Tournament held in Galesburg. In the semi-final game, Roseville faced the home team, state-ranked third, Galesburg High School. Playing probably the biggest game of the school's history, Roseville trailed only by six points at halftime. Unfortunately, the game and the season ended with over a twenty-point loss. The Panther's highly successful season had been the best in the school's history.

The game was not without exciting moments. In an article that appeared in the Peoria *Journal Star*

Hugs for Dan Livermore following thrilling victory over Stronghurst. (Photo by Dave Stauth, *The Register-Mail*)

the next morning: "First year Roseville coach, Dave Darnall, aided the Galesburg free throw attack with a pair of technical fouls drawn in rapid succession when he found a charging call by the officials intolerable and had the audacity to walk out onto the court half as far as Thiel had numerous times in the first half."

Galesburg was coached by the highly respected John Thiel, who was later inducted into the Illinois Basketball Coaches' Hall of Fame. Galesburg, a three-year high school, had an enrollment of approximately 1,850 students compared to Roseville's 205.

"I feel we could have possibly won the state tournament if there had been two classes," Darnall told his audience at the annual basketball awards banquet. "Unfortunately, we are one year too early." The following season was the first time there was a two-class system in Illinois. Coach Chuck Rolinski spearheaded the class system. Class A consisted of small high schools and Class AA for larger high schools like Galesburg.

Coach Darnall's track squad was also very successful. The team, undefeated in its regular season dual and tri-angular meets, won the Bi-County Conference meet, and was second in both the Roseville Relays and Avon Relays. Two members of the team qualified for the State Track Meet. The success of Dave's track teams over the past several years would prove to be very beneficial for him professionally.

Darnall, who had developed ulcers over the past two years, decided he needed to separate himself from the game he loved for a while. After completing only one year at Roseville, Dave resigned without having another job. Bonnie, Tiera, and he moved in with Dave's mother who lived in Oreana in early June. From there, Darnall drove the forty miles daily to Normal to attend summer school. He completed his last two classroom courses required for his Master's Degree. Dave had started writing his Master's thesis entitled, "Trends in Administrative Policies of the Mid-State Conference, 1948-1970," during the school year.

Dave began looking for a less stressful teaching and coaching position. It was late summer before he accepted a teaching/coaching position at Wheeling High School. His duties included being head coach in cross-country and track besides teaching physical education.

Wheeling was a school of approximately 2,700 students located in the western suburbs of Chicago. It was an excellent position for someone who had a true interest in coaching cross-country/track. Dave often said, "This would have been a perfect job for my son-in-law, Brett Charlton, who has guided his Eureka High School Cross-County Team to five Class A titles in six years and a second in the sixth." Dave's success as a rural track coach had paid dividends.

It was at Wheeling where Dave wrote his first basketball article for publication. Missing basketball, even though he was involved in in-door track, Dave stayed in touch with the game during the winter by writing about it and watching local high school games. The article entitled, "The One-Two-Two Adjustable Zone," appeared in the December, 1970 issue of *Athletic Journal*. To Darnall's knowledge, that was the first article published about a match-up zone with the big man on top. He also began writing another article that would eventually be published in October of 1971. During this time, Dave finished his thesis and received his Master's Degree in Physical Education.

It was also at one of those high school games that Darnall first saw a future good friend—a tall skinny freshman for Hersey High School, Dave Corzine.

A second child joined the Darnall family while living in Wheeling. Derek Dean Darnall was born April 16, 1972. He shared his middle name with both his father and paternal grandfather. During this time, Bonnie had continued to teach learning disabilities in nearby Mundelien.

Dave missed basketball a great deal. With his ulcer healing, he decided to get back into the "hardwood wars." He began writing letters of inquiry and applied for high school basketball positions during the spring. After interviewing at several schools, he accepted a position at Momence High School. Darnall was hired as Head Basketball and Baseball Coach with the teaching of physical education and driver education. Dave was actually Momence's second choice out of 100-plus applicants. Its first choice decided to accept an offer at a larger school.

Darnall was extremely happy about his new job. He had confidence in his ability to turn the losing program into a winning one. Coaching at a school that only three years prior had a 0 to 22 record would be a challenge. Resigning at Wheeling to go to Momence meant leaving one of the highest paying school districts in Illinois to one of the lowest. However, money was not the issue. The opportunity to coach basketball was. It was a decision he would not regret.

The Darnalls moved to Momence, a town with a population of ap- proximately 3,300 and a school enrollment of around 350, in early June. Their new home was an older two-story house located on the Kankakee River.

The recently hired coach and his wife attended a "meet the new coach" meeting with future prospects in early May. Dave felt it was important that the players got to know Bonnie because of the family atmosphere she helped to create. He wanted to improve upon the Redskins previous year's record of 10 to 15. This was another challenge to build a second "Redskin" winning program.

Darnall had "open gym" during the summer for his future players. Because of the economic situation of many students in the Momence school district, the players could not afford to attend basketball camps. Besides, basketball camps were a relatively new commodity.

By the time school began in August of 1971, Coach Darnall pretty much knew the talent of his new players. Two other communities, Hopkins Park and The Terrace, also provided students for the high school. Both of the communities were predominately African-American. Many of Darnall's players came from those two areas.

This was a time of much racial unrest. Darnall witnessed for the first time a student up-rising where black students came from one end and white students from the other end to clash in the middle of the main corridor of the high school's second floor. In his mind, he wondered if he would be able to bring a team together.

Darnall opened practice the first of October with several returning lettermen. For the first time in his career, he would be coaching black players. Dave felt that Momence had talent, but the players needed to care about each other both on and off the floor to be successful.

It was at that time Coach Darnall developed the slogan that would become his trademark for the remainder of his career. "Together We Win," was initiated. With this philosophy Darnall eventually led his Momence team to its first winning season in five years. As the Kankakee *Daily Journal* stated in its pre-season review of area teams, "Coach Darnall has only three seniors, so he will be working with a lot of youngsters, which looks good for the future."

Following the first game of the season, portions of another article in the same paper read,

> Momence, expected to have one of its best seasons in years, made a dismal debut Tuesday night when the Redskins were clobbered by Crete-Monee, 74 - 52. In so doing, the Redskins made their new coach, Dave Darnall, wonder what he let himself in for.
> But, at least, Darnall has a good excuse for what happened to his club in his inaugural. It is, temporarily at least, without the services of Leon

Ross, the mainstay of the Redskins' five for the past two years. And whether Ross ever plays another high school basketball game won't be learned until Monday night when, according to reports, an expulsion hearing will be conducted by the Momence Board of Education.

Ross is accused of having participated in a recent student uprising, along with two other members of the basketball team since reinstated and drew a suspension.

Darnall was quoted in the article as saying, "Because of the suspension and the Thanksgiving Holidays, during which we weren't allowed to practice, the reinstated players had virtually no practice for ten days. The school problems weren't exactly conducive to team morale either. I was greatly disappointed in our showing against Crete-Monee, but maybe, we can do a lot better this weekend."

After three straight losses, the Redskins finally won its first game under the leadership of its new coach by beating Conference foe Beecher, 64 to 58. That was the first game Coach Darnall had all of his troops. The game starters were Mike Jeffries, Dan Plein, Rick Wehrmann, Sam Jordan, and Don Murray. Two other important squad members were Leon Ross and Darryl Walker.

Winning only two of the first seven games, Momence went on to win ten of the next eleven. During this winning streak, the Redskins set a school scoring record by tallying 101 points against Hanover. The team also won the Manteno Holiday Tournament. As the headline in a local newspaper read, "Momence Redskins Win First Holiday Tournament Cage Title in Ten Years." Momence won the championship tilt from host Manteno, 55 to 48. Senior Leon Ross led his team in scoring in all three tournament games. He scored fifty-seven points in the three games to capture the "Outstanding Player" award of the tournament.

Then, tough times again hit the team. They lost four consecutive games, the first of which was to St. Anne in the championship game of the Kankakee Valley Conference Tournament. An article written by Kankakee *Daily Journal* sportswriter, Dennis Yohnka, entitled, "'Goaltender' Helps Cards Win KVC Tourney Crown," best described the controversial championship game.

Momence basketball coach, Dave Darnall, might still be grumbling about referee Don Clark's controversial goaltending call as St. Anne coach, Al Hubert, hums another verse from "When You're Hot, You're Hot."

In each coach's mind, he is reliving the turning point in the Cardinal's big 65 - 61 victory over Momence. The triumph in the Momence Junior High School gym gave last year's bridesmaid, Cards, the Kankakee Valley Tournament Championship and left the Redskins with a very bitter taste in defeat.

The controversial call came at 3:51 with the score tied 55 - 55. St. Anne's Marvin Whitlock, who was a surprise starter after his fine semifinal game, gunned up a long 25-foot jumper that appeared to be falling well short of the basket. Momence's Leon Ross, who had been blocking shots with his excellent reflexes and tremendous jumping ability all night, leaped for the ball.

He snared the ball and suddenly a whistle was blown, and most fans looked toward the basket, where the action had been rough all night, expecting a pushing foul. To almost everyone's amazement, Ross was called for goaltending, and two points were awarded to Whitlock.

At that point, Darnall resorted to his already established second "game vice." He reached for his side pocket and broke an ammonia capsule under his nose. A clear head was needed.

The article continued:

"You can quote me on this," Darnall said. "That was the worst call I've ever seen in high school basketball. It actually meant four points because it was two they didn't deserve and two we may have been able to score. To me, that was the turning point of the game. I haven't blamed an official for a loss in my seven years of coaching, and I'm not this time. But this is the closest I've ever come to feeling that a referee decided the outcome of a game."

Redemption for the loss came four games later with Momence claiming a great victory over the Kankakee Valley Conference Tournament Champion, St. Anne, by the score of 60 to 59. St. Anne was led by the future NBA Seattle Supersonic star player, Jack Sikma. He pumped in fifteen points in the losing cause while tallying ten points in the Conference Tournament Championship game.

Momence finished its season with a 14 to 12 overall record, the most wins in approximately ten years.

It was at Momence that Tiera began her cheerleading career at the age of three. She became the cheerleaders' mascot and actually participated in a few of the cheers. Nancy Ross, Leon mother, crocheted Tiera's first cheerleading outfit. The red and white sweater matched those of the varsity

Tiera practicing a Redskin cheer.

cheerleaders. The interest and enthusiasm followed Tiera from Momence High School to eventually becoming a varsity men's basketball cheerleader at Illinois State University. Another Momence cheerleader went on to bigger and better things also. Janet Hubert left Momence after graduation in 1974 for New York. She later starred as Vivian Banks, the mother, in *Fresh Prince of Bel-Air*, made numerous other television appearances and is currently seen in television commercials.

With his first Momence season completed, Darnall was looking forward to the 1972-1973 year. A local newspaper article stated, "Coach Darnall feels that he has some potential, but the lack of height and experience will have to be made up by hustle and drive. Coach Darnall believes that there is a lot of talent on the lower levels and should provide a tough team in a couple of years. He feels this year's team may surprise a few people."

There were only four returning lettermen on Dave's second Momence team. However, after five games, the team was off to a surprisingly good start. A portion of a local newspaper article read, "After pre-season predictions that Momence would win only five games, the squad has started with a 4 to 1 record."

The players that made this happen were seniors Sam Jordan, Darryl Walker, Don Murray; junior transfer Ron Kelly; and sophomore Eddie Covington.

Ted Petersen, who was a senior substitute player on the team, eventually became a starting offensive guard on the NFL Pittsburgh Steeler's Super Bowl Championship teams—Super Bowl XIII and Super Bowl XIV. Two Super Bowl rings! Not bad for a fella who started only about half of his high school football games his senior year.

During his tenure at Momence, Coach Darnall again took some of the young players with him when scouting up-coming opponents. Among the young players who usually accompanied the coach on these trips were Fred Ross, Jerome Westbrooks, and Hughley Blanton. These guys would eventually become significant players on Darnall's team.

Due to the environment in which some of his players lived, including the distance from school and difficult economic conditions, the Darnalls had hotdogs, chips, and soda pop available at their home before games. Some of the players were unable to go home between school and games and came to the Darnall home.

As in the past, Coach and Bonnie hosted post-game social gatherings at their home for players' parents and other Redskin fans. It became a "traveling" event with other hosts being the Jack Cherrys, the successful Football Coach and Athletic Director; the Ernie Monks, the school Guidance Counselor; the Ron Clarks, a member of the School Board; the Howard Strassenbergs; the Jim Vickerys; the Frank Simpsons; the Jack Willises; and "Boo" Lambert.

During this time, the Darnalls occasionally used Dave's players, along with the Clark girls, as babysitters. Jerome "Spanky" White was the most frequently used male sitter. "Spanky" was Dave's basketball manager. White eventually followed Darnall to Eureka College where he served as Dave's administrative assistant, as well as participating in football. Once in Eureka, Jerome's "babysitting duties" expanded to the whole Darnall neighborhood. When Jerome was at the Darnalls's, so were all the neighborhood boys. At one point, Derek made the comment to his mother, "I love Jerome more that anybody in the world."

When asked by Bonnie, "Oh, well what about me and your dad?"

Young Derek responded with, "Well, I love you too, but I really love Jerome!" It was years later that Bonnie would still find army men hidden in her household plants from their war games.

The 1972-1973 basketball team had its ups and downs. As with most seasons, there were a few highlights. The Redskins claimed a great victory over the much larger Kankakee Eastridge High School. The headline of an article in the next morning Kankakee *Daily Journal* stated, "Skins' Whispy Walker Walks Over Eastsiders."

Portions of the article read, "Physically, he looks a little like Abdul Kareem Jabbar, junior size. Artistically, he's a dead ringer. So, Darryl Walker, 6 foot-3 inch, who looks as if he should stay indoors on a rainy day, was the main reason Momence's Redskins achieved

Jerome Westbrooks, 21, attempts to block a shot. Teammate Fred Ross, 13, looks on. (Kankakee *The Daily Journal* file photo)

its first victory in history over Kankakee Eastridge, 42 - 37, Friday night on the Abraham Lincoln court." It was an extremely satisfying win.

Top seeded St. Anne Cardinals played Momence in a rematch from the previous year's disputed Conference Championship. The Redskins were out-manned and dropped a 69 to 43 decision to the Cardinals behind the twenty-nine-point scoring output of six-foot-eight Jack Sikma. Darnall, however, felt his young team had accomplished a great deal. Second place was not bad. St. Anne ran its record to 17 to 1.

Following the championship game, Herb Eller, sportswriter with the Kankakee *Daily Journal* asked Dave his thoughts about St. Anne's Sikma's performance. "We wanted to slow them down, but we couldn't after we fell behind so quickly. Sikma was killing us on the boards. He is the best player I have seen this year. He can dominate a game and is definitely All-State material."

Coach Darnall (above) making a point with Ron Kelly, Eddie Covington, and the rest of the Redskins. (Kankakee *The Daily Journal* file photo)

Hughley Blanton, 33 (at right), goes up for a rebound. (Kankakee *The Daily Journal* file photo)

St. Anne went on to place fourth in the Class A State Basketball Tournament.

Throughout the season, Coach Darnall gave a few of his young talented players some quality playing time. They were the future. Junior Fred Ross, sophomores

Jerome Westbrooks and Kim Wells, and freshman Hughley Blanton saw a lot of action.

Even though the season was suppose to be a rebuilding year, the team made great strides, which made their coach very optimistic about having an outstanding 1973-1974 year. Darnall felt his program was in place. His slogan, "Together We Win," had been accepted.

The lowest point of the season for the Redskins came in the Class A Regional Tournament on their own floor. Grant Park upset Momence in a low-scoring affair 35 to 31. Coach Gary Swartz used the same tactics against the more talented Redskins as Darnall had used in his early career at Stanford. A dejected Dave Darnall stated to sportswriter Herb Eller that his team killed itself with its own poor shooting. "That was our poorest shooting of the year (11 for 38, for a .290 average)," Darnall complained, "and we were just about as bad at the free throw line."

"I don't want to take anything away from Grant Park," he added. "They were really scrappy out there, but our kids wanted this one so that we could end up with 15 wins and we just couldn't get the job done." Momence finished its season with a 14 to 11 record.

That particular game was devastating for Coach Darnall. He did not leave his locker room office until almost daybreak. There was no post-game party that night! In fact, once in bed, he remained there for two days!

Darnall was also Head Baseball Coach. He enjoyed the sport since his days at the "Cabbage Patch." Coaches Bass and Ricci had taught him, as a youngster, a great deal about the game. Anyone who knows baseball will say that a team will go as far as its pitching takes them. Dave had two good pitchers in senior Jack Trudeau and junior Ron Kelly. Right-hander Trudeau hurled a no-hitter as Momence gained the first win of the season, 3 to 0, over Grant Park. It was a great win over the school that had just given Darnall so much agony in basketball.

The Darnalls enjoyed Momence. They decided this was the place to raise Tiera and Derek. The children would be able to participate successfully in the school's activities. In addition, Bonnie had resumed teaching, and they had made some very good friends. Thus during the winter, the Darnalls approached their friend "Boo" Lambert, also a contractor, about building a new home. It was decided the project should start early in summer and be completed around Christmas. That would be their first newly built home.

While coaching at Momence, Darnall became involved with the Illinois Basketball Coaches Association. The Association was directed by the legendary Coach Rolinski, the "father" of the two-class basketball system in Illinois. Through his membership in the organization, Dave met several top coaches and became friends with those who later would become guest speakers at his camps and clinics.

Darnall, starting his third year as the Redskin mentor, thought his young team could be a true Conference contender. With only three seniors returning, he felt his best team was still a year away. Dave thought this year's team could possibly win the Regional Tournament and do well in the Sectional. However, he felt the next year's team would be the one to have a chance to participate in the Class A State Tournament held in the Assembly Hall in Champaign.

The Redskin cage season opened at home against Chicago Holy Trinity. Coach Darnall would be seeking his one-hundredth career victory. The opening night's starting line-up consisted of seniors Ron Kelly and Fred Ross, juniors Jerome Westbrooks and Kim Wells, and six-foot-four sophomore Hughley Blanton at center. Eddie Covington was the first player off the bench.

The Redskin coach would have to wait for his one-hundredth win. Momence dropped its opener to the larger school, 66 to 57. In the second game of the season, Momence defeated Manteno to even its record and give its coach his one-hundredth coaching career win.

Going into the KVC Tournament, Darnall's team was 12 to 2. That was the best start Momence had had in years. The team was also tied for the league's lead with preseason favorite St. Anne.

The Redskins, reaching the final game, played host school Kankakee Bishop McNamara for the Conference Tournament Championship. The veteran Irish team was too much for the youthful Momence club, downing the Redskins, 65 to 44, for the title. The loss snapped a nine-game winning streak. It was the third consecutive year Momence finished second in the KVC Tournament.

A week later, the two schools had a rematch. As before, the game was played at McNamara. That was the Redskins' first contest since its defeat in the tournament championship game. The tide would turn. As the *Progress Reporter*, Momence's local newspaper, headline read, "Momence Gains Important Revenge With Conference Victory Over Irish, 56 - 50." It was perhaps the sweetest win for Darnall and his assistant coaches Tim Umphrey and Fred Bell since Dave's arrival at Momence.

Portions of the article went on to say, "After the near miserable showing and being walloped by the Macs in the finals of the KVC Tournament just a week before, the complete turn-around, again on the same foreign boards, established the "Skins" as the team to beat for the title."

Headline of the Kankakee *The Daily Journal* article the next morning read, "Redskins' Win Over Irish 1st Since '67." Portions of the article written by Paul Rix read:

> You'll have to go back a ways to find out when Momence basketball fans might have felt as good as they did Friday night at Bishop-McNamara. It was quite an occasion for them.
> It was also quite a night for Dave Darnall, who freely admits that in nine years of coaching, Friday's victory was his greatest ever.
> It was the first triumph by a Momence basketball team over McNamara since that 83 - 76 contest back on February 17, 1967.
> Darnall was most succinct following the game: "This was my greatest victory. We did everything I said we had to do to beat McNamara. We sharpened up our offense, got lay-ups, set picks, and we played great defense."

The two teams played for the third time four weeks later in the championship game of the Regional Tournament. This time the contest was held at Momence. The Redskins dropped a heartbreaker, a game that haunted Darnall the remainder of his career.

The headline of an article covering the game in the *Progress Reporter* was, "Redskins End Cage Season With Record of 22 Wins, 5 Losses, Losing to Irish." Portions of the article read, "It was a mild night outside for the general public, but a cold one inside for the Momence Redskins in an almost successful effort to win the Class A Regional basketball title before a noisy crowd of some 2,000 fans in the Momence Junior High gym Friday. The final score of 43 - 41 in favor of the Irish left the Skins with a season record of 22 victories against only 5 losses, their best mark in at least recent decades. McNamara enjoyed a .500 shooting average, while Momence suffered from only .340 percent."

The season had come to an end. Redskin fans, however, had a lot to be proud of. Their team finished with a perfect 8 to 0 Conference record for its first Kankakee Valley Conference Championship ever. It was a record-breaking season, the best record of any Momence basketball team in twenty years. It also included being second in the KVC Tournament, and second in the IHSA Regional Tournament.

Coach Darnall and his players would have to wait until the next year to make their trip to the Assemby Hall (State Tournament). This year's team made great strides towards reaching their goal, especially since there were only three seniors.

An extremely gratifying article about the progress of Darnall's program had appeared during the season in the Kankakee *Daily Journal*. It discussed the changes taking place in Momence basketball. The article written by Larry Henry was entitled, "Skins Adopt New Tag—Winners." It read:

Perhaps you recall the popular story, "The Miracle of 34th Street." In case you don't, it's about an old gent who claims he's the real Santa Claus and nobody believes him.

Currently, there's a new miracle in the making, only it's billed, "The Miracle of Highway 1." Here, too, there's a Santa Claus character involved. Nobody believes him, either.

The Highway 1 St. Nick, however, is black-haired, beardless and his joviality during the winter months centers around how often five youngsters in short pants can put a ball through a hoop, not how many good girls and boys he can delight with gifts. He can be a little gruff at times, therefore.

In all likelihood, Dave Darnall probably doesn't quite picture himself as Santa Claus. But if Santa is a miracle-worker, then Dave Darnall is eligible to check out a sleigh and eight tiny reindeer next Dec. 25.

Darnall, you see, coaches basketball at Momence High School. Before the season began, there were people who thought he might be smart to sign up for unemployment compensation under the Santa Claus Act, to hell with the roundball.

The Redskins were not picked to win many games. But this is not unusual. Momence is never favored to win many games. Look back over the record for the last 20 years and you'll understand why.

They were in a rut.

Since 1952, the school has produced 15 non-winning cage teams. Before Darnall unpacked his furniture in the east Kankakee County town in 1971, the best records in 20 years were something like 14 - 11 or 14 - 12, of which there had been three. There were years when the football team won more games, as in 1969, when the cagers were 0 - 22. The gridders did better than that in the Kankakee Valley Conference alone, winning two games.

The year before Darnall came to Momence, the Redskins enjoyed a banner year. They won 10 and lost only 15.

Darnall said he understood what he was stepping into when he accepted the job, for which he was No. 2 in line (No. 1 was John Keller, who had taken Effingham St. Anthony to the state the year before. Keller eventually took the head job at Mount Zion). But he had been out of basketball coaching for a year and was anxious to get back in. "And I like a challenge," he said.

With vocal chords humming that first year ("I was called for four technicals, for which I caught a lot of hell," he said) and psychology "psyching," Darnall got the Redskins up to 14 - 12.

The next year, he did even better. He got only one technical. And though the Redskins didn't win any more games (14), They lost one less.

Which brings us to this year. And "The Miracle of Highway 1."

This was to be the year Darnall would double his pleasure (eight technicals), double his glum (seven victories? Six? Five?).

Everybody's surprised.

The glum has turned to gloom. But not for Darnall. For the opposition. They can't believe the Redskins. Neither can Darnall, if you want to know the truth. Neither can some of the players ("I thought we'd maybe win a half-dozen ball games," said one disbelieving Redskin.) And, apparently, neither can some of the fans. Or, if they do, it's just been too bloomin' cold for them to stick their heads out the door.

"We're lucky to average 500 fans for a home game," sighed Darnall. "When Grant Park played here, they brought more fans than we did."

Seems like it's about time for Momence fans to wake up to the fact that things are happening down there in the gym, then. Like their ball club is flaunting an 8 -2 record and running neck-and-neck (with Bishop McNamara) for the lead in the Kankakee Valley Conference, where they were picked to finish next-to-last.

It's quite an accomplishment, too. When Darnall opened the season, he had three lettermen back, only one of whom, Ron Kelly, was a regular last year. The lettermen were also the extent of his senior players.

Creating something out of nothing is not a new trick for Darnall. He's done it at practically every school he's been to. The year before he went to Stanford, his first coaching job, the school had a 5 - 18 record. Under Darnall, the school was 11 - 13, the best it had compiled in years.

Gridley was 2 - 20 the year before he checked in there. Darnall produced another 13 - 10 record his first campaign there and was 17 - 7 the next year. That was the first time they'd won a conference title in 10 years.

At Roseville, the following year, he was 25 - 4. Then he was at Wheeling the year after, coaching track and cross country and taking a respite from the rigors of basketball.

But one year away from the hardwood was all he could take. Momence basketball fans, wherever they are, should be happy he got restless for the cage wars.

Now Darnall's aim is to put Momence on the basketball map, to bring the cage program up on a par with the Redskin football program, which is one of the best in the area. What a fitting finish that would be to "The Miracle of Highway 1."

Even though the basketball season was over and baseball season was under way, Darnall was still thinking about how much progress his young cage team had made. Knowing his next year's team had a great opportunity to go to the State Tournament, Dave could not wait for the following season to arrive. Then a phone call came, "Hello, Darrel, this is Raycraft!"

Chapter 6

Eureka! We Found It!

THE ALL-IMPORTANT PHONE CALL came in early May. Dave was sitting in the Momence High School teachers' lounge during his prep period, working on his baseball practice plan. A voice over the intercom system announced, "Coach Darnall, phone." Dave placed a cigarette in the ashtray and strolled to the lounge phone. On the other end was his lifelong friend, Professor Don Raycraft.

"Hello, Darrel. How'd you like to be the Head Basketball Coach at Eureka College?"

Darnall was caught off-guard. Thinking it was an impossible dream, he replied, "Is the job open?"

Dr. Raycraft, a teacher in the Eureka College Education Department and a student teacher supervisor, said, "The job is available. Leo Traister, longtime coach at Eureka, has resigned as Head Basketball Coach."

Dave, uncertain about the genuine possibility of having a chance for the position, asked, "Do you really think I have a chance?"

"I'll tell you what to do," Ray replied.

Dave was very content with his current position, especially since his basketball team had just completed the best season in the school's history. Losing only three seniors, the coach felt he had a great chance to go to "State" the following year. The Momence mentor believed his next year's team could match neighboring school St. Anne's, 1972-1973 accomplish-

110

ment when future NBA star, Jack Sigma, led his high school team to a fourth place finish in the Class A State Tournament. It's the dream of all high school coaches to participate in the state tournament. Darnall was no different.

Dave asked his friend for details on the vacancy. He inquired about the application procedure just in case he decided "to go for it." Raycraft emphasized he knew the "inside" to obtaining the position. The professor continued to tell his old buddy what to do.

The conversation was completed. Several teachers, who had overheard portions of it, asked, "What was that all about?"

Dave proceeded to tell his colleagues about the opening at Eureka College.

Eureka College was not new to David. The Darnall family had attended University Christian Church while living in Normal. Both Eureka College and University Christian Church were affiliates of the same denomination—Disciples of Christ. As previously mentioned, Bruce Darnall had graduated from the small liberal arts college. His interest in religion began as a youngster. Bruce was involved in church activities, and David and he attended Sunday school regularly at University Christian.

Leota Cox, the Darnalls' next door neighbor while living in Normal, had indicated to Dave's parents that she would help finance any of their children who chose to attend Eureka College and study religion. Bruce had taken advantage of her generosity.

Fate would step in. Dave recalled that while coaching at Stanford he attended Bruce's graduation from Eureka College and had remarked to Bonnie that he would someday like to coach there. Of course, numerous high school coaches hope one day to become college coaches. Respectively, it is like high school athletes wanting to become college players, and college players wanting to become professionals. Remember childhood dreams?

Dave left the teachers' lounge, walking briskly to his office in the locker room to prepare for his next class. His mind, however, was not on the up-coming class but whether or not to apply for the vacant position at Eureka College. Anxiously waiting for the day to end, Darnall wished he could go home immediately and talk to Bonnie about the opening.

Dave told Bonnie about his conversation with Dr. "Ray" as soon as he arrived home after baseball practice. A few minutes of exchanging words went by when it was decided that it would probably be a fruitless endeavor. However, what did they have to lose to send a letter of inquiry and a resumé? Dave would request that his credentials be sent from Illinois State University.

That evening Darnall sat down and wrote a letter of application and up-dated his resumé. Bonnie, after proofreading both, typed the documents so that they could be mailed the next day. Dave thumbed through his current year's scrapbook looking for articles to include with the letter and resumé that would reveal the great success his basketball team had experienced. The articles would, in addition, indicate any honors either he or his team had achieved. The article "Miracle of Highway 1" was a great asset.

Raycraft informed his old friend that he should send the information to Clarence Noe, Dean of Faculty at Eureka College. The professor instructed Darnall to send carbon copies to Dr. Owen West, Chairman of the Education Department, and Judge Sam Harrod, Chairman of the Board of Trustees. Harrod, who had long-standing family ties to the college, was a staunch sports fan. Dave followed Dr. "Ray's" instructions faithfully. Later he found out, indeed, those were the exact moves needed to obtain the Head Basketball coaching position at the small liberal arts college.

Leo Traister, also a Eureka College alum, once was Head Football, Basketball, and Track Coach—all at the same time. He resigned as Head Basketball Coach to spend more time on his Athletic Director responsibilities. Traister continued to serve as Head Golf and Assistant Football Coach as well as assisting Coach Darnall.

A week following the mailing of his letter, Dave received a phone call from Dr. West requesting he come to the college for an interview. As in the past, Coach wanted Bonnie to accompany him. He thought her presence would be a positive influence on the committee.

Dr. West greeted the Darnalls upon their arrival on the college campus. Dave introduced Bonnie to their host. West proceeded to describe the details of the vacant teaching/coaching position. Several people interviewed Darnall during the visit. One of the first to talk to him was George Hearne, both Director of Admissions and Dean of Students. The coaching position required a great deal of recruiting. Hearne, who had been associated with the college some fifteen years, was extremely interested in the quality of the coach to be chosen and his ability to recruit new students.

Completing his interview with Dean Hearne, Dave next met Clarence Noe, Dean of Faculty. Dean Noe was a very dedicated individual who also had been with the college for numerous years. Darnall felt very comfortable with both and thought the interviews went well.

Dave and Bonnie were escorted to the President's Office to meet Dr. Ira Langston. The interview lasted only minutes. Dave was very impressed with the president. He felt, if chosen, he could definitely work with this man.

A couple questions kept coming up during the interview process. "What would you do to turn the basketball program around?" "Do you feel you can recruit students to come to Eureka College?"

Darnall had often thought about what he would do if he ever had the chance to become a college basketball coach. First, he would conduct a basketball camp. Second, he would hold a coaches' clinic at the college. Those events would expose coaches to the campus; thus, making them aware of the college's program. Both camps and clinics would assist in recruiting.

"The number one asset in recruiting is knowing the high school coach. It is usually through him that college coaches become familiar with prospective players," Darnall said.

Dave felt he would enjoy recruiting since he believed in his system, enjoyed visiting with coaches, and felt at ease talking to players. "If a coach cannot sell his program or institution, then he will not last long as a college coach," Dave stated.

Later, President George Hearne commented on his interview with Dave:

> When Eureka College opened its search for a men's Basketball coach to begin his duties in 1974, I was then Dean of Students and Director of Admissions. As Director of Admissions, I was very interested in the search because I was acutely aware of the important role that intercollegiate athletics can play in new student recruitment. A successful athletic program is, in itself, a positive support for recruitment of athletes and non-athletes alike. If the head coach is an aggressive recruiter for his team, that adds immeasurably to the potential success of enrolling additional new students.
>
> I recall a mixture of impressions from my interview session with Dave Darnall. He was obviously intent and aggressive, anxious to move into college coaching, and well prepared for the interview. It would be hard, after talking to him, to consider any other candidate. He made a strong case in support of his past achievements and his goals for success at Eureka College. There was no question of his commitment to recruit actively, and there was clear evidence of his many contacts which would help in that process.
>
> I was also impressed with his past experience, coaching students from a variety of economic and ethnic backgrounds. This was not true for most of the other candidates being considered, and made him a stand out in our evaluations.

I, frankly, did not expect him to stay at Eureka College for a long time. He had not had long tenures at any high school. I perceived him to be an able and aggressive young man who would want to make a mark as a head coach in a small college, and move on from there to larger programs. That was my only observation that proved to be inaccurate. I did not perceive, at that time, the dedication that he would have to a long career of service to Eureka College.

The Darnalls had the opportunity to visit briefly with their friend, Dr. "Ray," in the late afternoon. The evening was spent with Judge Sam Harrod and his wife, Nancy. They escorted the candidate to dinner at the Chanticleer. It was a well-known lounge-restaurant located at the north end of Eureka. The establishment would become quite familiar to the Darnalls over Dave's tenure at the college.

Dave and Bonnie enjoyed the evening of conversation with the Harrods. Later, it was discovered that this gathering was very influential in his hiring. The Darnalls and Harrods eventually became friends.

A full day of interviewing concluded, the Darnalls returned home to Momence. Unaware of the number of candidates considered, Dave felt his chance of being hired was pretty slim even though he felt comfortable with his interviews. He was just a Class A high school basketball coach with eight year's experience.

A couple days passed before Dave called Raycraft to see if any rumors had leaked regarding other candidates. "Ray" informed his pal there was at least one other interviewee. He was Wally Keller, Head Basketball Coach at Kewanee-Weathersfield High School. Dave and Wally had crossed paths before. Darnall was Head Coach at Stanford and Keller had been the main man at Deer Creek-Mackinaw. Both schools, belonging to the same conference, meant that the two coaches had coached against each other on several occasions, specifically the five-overtime loss Dave experienced at Stanford.

It was approximately a week after his visit to the college that Dave received a phone call from Dr. West offering him the position of Head Basketball Coach, Assistant Football Coach, Intramural Director, and Assistant Professor of Physical Education. Darnall was caught off-guard and requested a twenty-four-hour delay in his decision. Hanging up the phone, Bonnie and he discussed the pros and cons of leaving the high school scene for the college ranks. The first consideration discussed was the next year's Momence basketball team that had a great opportunity to participate in the state tournament. Three years of working hard to build the basketball program to one of the top small high school programs in the state, did Dave want to let it go? He was hesitant to leave these good players. The Darnalls felt that maybe it would be best to leave the decision to his players.

There were other issues to be considered also. Dave would take a pay cut leaving the state school system for the private institution of higher learning. Bonnie, currently teaching special education at the elementary level, would have to find a new teaching position in the Eureka area. Having two small children meant some family adjustments including daytime babysitting. Then there was leaving their first newly built home, a house they designed and dearly loved.

It was a sleepless night for both of them. Throughout the night, Dave pondered the positives and negatives of leaving Momence for the college level. Leaving their lovely home, taking the pay cut, Bonnie needing to find a new job, and mostly leaving his players made for a difficult decision. It must be remembered that the college level is what many coaches strive for.

Sometime during the night, Dave decided he should share his dilemma with his returning upperclassmen players. It would be, "Fellas, I could coach you one more year here at Momence, or I could leave you for a year or two to go to Eureka College where we could rejoin for four more years." This might make his decision a little easier.

Dave believed that the possible continued relationship with some upperclassmen players for four more years was better than for just one or two. He knew leaving a top-notch team after all his work to another coach would be difficult.

The next morning, Coach Darnall had a team meeting with his players. He informed them of his opportunity to become a college coach. Dave explained the concept he had thought about the night before. Most of the upperclassmen, still hating to see him leave, realized they could join him at Eureka College if they chose after a year or two. That would give them four more years with their coach. However, it was difficult for some returning players to understand the possible move. Darnall reflected that he had had the same feeling when Coach Ricci left Normal Community High School for Western Illinois University.

The decision had been made. Dave was going to leave Momence High School to become Head Basketball Coach at Eureka College. He was going to give up security of tenure for a one-year contract and a decrease in salary. However, he would fulfill a dream he had had some eight years prior while attending his brother's graduation. Professionally, he knew it was a step up. Financially, it was a step down. That was somewhat difficult for many people to understand. How could a college coach be paid less than what a high school coach received?

Later that day, Dave phoned Dr. West to inform the Department Chairman that he would accept the contract and return to campus for the signing. It was a very difficult decision to make; however, the Darnalls agreed that professionally it was a "move up the ladder" and something David just could not turn down. Darnall signed his first college contract around the beginning of June 1974.

Don Raycraft expressed his amazement at Darnall's selection as Head Basketball Coach at Eureka College, "I called him on the telephone at Momence High School to tell him about the basketball opening at Eureka College. I told him what to do; step by step. When Darnall got the college basketball job, many considered it the greatest upset in collegiate basketball history."

While driving to Eureka to sign the contract, the Darnalls wondered what it was that convinced the search committee to select Dave as the new coach. Not having a winning season in eight years nor participating in any playoffs for numerous years, perhaps there was a feeling among the college Community that a young, enthusiastic coach would be best at the helm.

Judge Harrod shared his recollection of why Darnall was selected as the new Eureka coach:

> I was a member of the search committee and Chairman of the Board of Trustees. We received more than 75 applications from all over the United States, including a PHD with a 75% winning record.
>
> The sheer force of Dave's tremendous dedication to excellence and his determination to lead his players to excellence, both on the floor and in the classroom, were most impressive.
>
> For the final round of selection, our committee met late into a mid-week evening. At 9:45 we agreed unanimously on Dave as the most out-standing in the highly qualified field of professional coaches and educators.
>
> Dave Darnall was affectionately respected as "The Miracle of Highway l" at Momence High School in Illinois, when he was chosen to become the Head Coach of the Men's Basketball Team and a member of the faculty at Eureka College, in the spring of 1974.

It was learned later that Darnall's answer to the question, "What would you do to turn the Eureka College basketball program around?" seemed to be what led to his appointment. Not only was initiating a basketball camp and coaches clinic impressive ideas, but his plan to make the team not only his team, but also the community's team, was impressive to several.

The Darnalls planned to have an "open house" at their home after every home basketball game for parents, faculty, staff, administrators, season ticket holders, friends, and members of the community. Dave wanted the team not only to be his team, but also the fans' team.

The Darnalls did this at Momence and felt that having people over after games helped turn around an disinterested and racially biased community into a community and student body that supported their basketball team totally together. It was with this thought that David developed his motto, "Together We Win." Could this be achieved at the college level?

Darnall's thought regarding establishing a basketball camp at Eureka College actually came from his being hired as a future camp coach at ISU, his alma mater, for the up-coming summer, not knowing at that particular time that he was about to become a college coach. Dave felt working at a camp provided the experience needed to direct one if he ever became a college coach. Who would guess the opportunity would come so quickly?

As a member of the Will Robinson's Illinois State University Basketball Camp staff, Dave had the opportunity to meet several potential guest speakers for his future camps and clinics. Among those basketball celebrities were Gene Smithson, Assistant Coach at ISU; Dwayne "Moose" Roe, former Assistant at Oral Roberts University; Ernie Kivisto, Head Coach at Aurora East High School; NBA Chicago Bulls forward and Aurora College super star, Mickey Johnson; and former Harlem Globe Trotter, Leon Hillard.

Coach Darnall, not having played college basketball, enjoyed going back to his alma mater to coach youngsters on the floor he never played on.

The idea of hosting a basketball clinic actually came from his attendance at two clinics the previous year. The well-known Chuck Rolinski's Clinic was a one-day clinic featuring several of the state's top coaches. The young coach had also attended Pat Riley's Eureka High School Clinic. Darnall felt that if he ever had the opportunity to be a college coach, he too would hold a basketball clinic. He thought that possibly the springtime would be a better time to hold a clinic than in the fall. Maybe more coaches would be free to attend. Besides, there were already several basketball clinics in the state held in the fall.

Those three ideas—the camps, clinics, and an open house after games—along with his enthusiasm and his potential to become a good recruiter were why Dave was selected Head Basketball Coach at Eureka College.

Recruiting is a very important factor of being a successful college coach. As a later chapter will reveal, Coach Darnall eventually became one of the most effective small college recruiters in the Midwest. It was this recruiting talent that led him to the ultimate goal of college coaches—a National Championship!

Chapter 7

Dave Darnall's Eureka College Basketball Camps

DARNALL DID START A BASKETBALL CLINIC and camp as he promised in his interview for the Eureka College Head Basketball coaching position. With Rolinski's clinic held in near-by Toluca in the fall, Dave scheduled his clinic in the spring as planned. The inaugural clinic occurred at the conclusion of his first campaign as a Red Devil coach.

In the early seventies, there were very few basketball camps in Illinois. Those camps were conducted mostly at large universities as Illinois State University, Bradley, and the University of Illinois. Very few small college basketball camps existed. It also was against the IHSA rules for high schools to sponsor basketball camps.

Eureka College is located approximately twenty miles from both Illinois State and Bradley. Darnall, however, had enough confidence in his ability to establish and direct a successful basketball camp that neighboring competition did not concern him. He had a year to plan and organize the first camp.

Imagine the sound of 300 basketballs being dribbled across campus by kids dressed in gold mesh jerseys ablaze with "Dave Darnall's Eureka College Basketball Camp." Their destination being Dickinson Commons for lunch. That was the scene that eventually appeared several weeks each summer. The campus came alive with aspiring young basketball players, male and female, fifth through eleventh grades, over 300 campers per week for

NBA player Jack Sikma with a young Tiera and Derek.

three weeks, dashing between the gym, dorms, and mess hall. Each was eager to learn "pointers" from NBA professional players Darnall had arranged as featured guest speakers—such as Dave Corzine, Mickey Johnson, Roger Phegley, C.J. Kupec, Jim Les, and Jack Sikma. Words of wisdom from an excellent coaching staff, guest high school coaches, and professional women players Charlotte Lewis, Cathy Boswell, and Pat McKinzie were also heard.

Campers from all over the state, plus a few outside of Illinois, were given a basketball, a mesh shirt, and assigned a dormitory room upon arrival. The next six days were filled with lectures, fundamentals, drills, and scrimmage games con-ducted by a coaching staff of over thirty professional coaches representing all sections of the state. Lots of physical activity, fun, new friendships, and a scattering of homesickness were the ingredients of a summer camp. All camp coaches had two things in common—they enjoyed basketball, and they enjoyed the youngsters.

Successful Dave Darnall's Eureka College Basketball Camps did not just happen. Years before, Darnall had thought colleges would be ideal places to host camps. He felt basketball camps would be an excellent recruiting tool as well as helping youngsters improve their basic basketball skills.

His first scheduled boys' camp was held the summer of 1975. Fifty-five campers attended. Over the years, the program grew to include three camps, two for boys and one for girls. Then came a fourth basketball camp—a twelve-team boys' junior high camp. Each camp was consistently filled to capacity.

A clinic was held prior to the first camp. The first annual Eureka College Basketball Coaches' Clinic took place the first Saturday in May, 1975. It was held at Reagan Center on the college's campus. Dave turned to the coaching friends he had met through the IBCA for his clinic's speakers. It was a top flight, all star cast featuring Gene Smithson, Assistant Coach at Illinois State University; Ron Ferguson, Head Coach Class AA State Champions Thornridge High School; Ron Felling, Head Coach Class A Lawrenceville High School; Chuck Rolinski, Head Coach Toluca High School; and Dwayne "Moose" Roe, Head Coach Olympia High School and former Assistant Coach at Oral Roberts University. Approximately 100 basketball coaches from throughout the state attended the one-day clinic.

The first basketball camp held at Eureka College was during the week of June 15 to 21. The actual name of this camp was Eureka Junior Pro Basketball Camp. Dave's friend, Ron Felling, was affiliated with the Junior Pro Basketball Camp Association. Junior Pro furnished basketballs, camp

First clinic speakers: Chuck Rolinski, Gene Smithson, and Ron Felling with Director Dave Darnall.

First Basketball Camp—1975.

nylon mesh jerseys, official Junior Pro jacket patches, and official Junior Pro certificates of completion, membership cards, jump ropes, and newsletters.

Felling went on to accumulate four Class A State Basketball Championships, including back-to-back titles, while at Lawrenceville. He later became a long-time assistant coach at the University of Indiana.

There were eight coaches, including Darnall, on the first Eureka College camp staff. Other members of the official staff were Allen Pickering, Head Coach Lincoln Junior College; Craig Gerdes, Head Coach Eureka Middle School; Ken Miller, Head Coach Coal City High School; Larry Rosenthal, Head Coach Palestine High School; Bill Harrison, Head Coach Gilman High School; and Eureka College players Tim McGuire and Doug Brown.

Darnall turned to recent acquaintances for his first guest speakers, two of whom he met at the Illinois State University camp the previous summer. They were Leon Hillard, Harlem Globe Trotter and one of the premiere ball handlers in the country, and Ernie Kivisto, Head Coach East Aurora High School and member of the Illinois Basketball Hall of Fame. Successful area high school coaches Dave had met during the basketball season, Wayne Hammerton, Head Coach Peoria Richwoods. Chuck Westendorf, Head Coach Washington High School, also spoke.

The second annual Eureka College Basketball Clinic was held in May of 1976. Dave again gathered an all-state cast, mostly from coaches he had met through the IBCA. They were Tony Yates, Assistant Coach University of Illinois; Wes Mason, Head Coach Bloom Township High School; Bill Gleason, Head Coach Loyola Academy; Ken Trickey, former Head Coach Oral Roberts University and Iowa State University; Jeff Carling, Head Coach Centralia High School; and Ernie Kivisto.

Duplicating the prior year, the clinic attracted approximately 100 coaches. Many young coaches were busy coaching spring sports—baseball, track, or golf, conflicting their ability to attend the one-day event. Darnall felt the two clinics had served their purpose of meeting and getting acquainted with area high school coaches for recruiting purposes. He decided that this year's clinic would be his last. Dave had been disappointed with attendance having such an outstanding clinic card.

The second yearly basketball camp was held in June of 1976. The camp staff grew from eight to seventeen. The number of campers increased from fifty-five to 150. With the encouragement and insistence of camp coaches Al Pickering, Ken Miller, and Roger Smith, Darnall decided to deviate from the Junior Pro Program and rename the camp Dave Darnall's Eureka College Basketball Camp.

A significant addition to this year's staff was Smith, Head Coach at Flanagan High School. There were several outstanding coaches joining the staff, but "Smitty" eventually worked every basketball camp until the sessions dropped to only the Junior High Team Camp in 2000. Sixty-eight camps; seventeen months; one year and sixteen weeks!

The 1977 basketball camp was attended by 250 boys. In three years, it gained 200 campers. The camp was reaching its maximum with the available facilities. The additional 100 campers forced the staff to be increased to over twenty professional coaches.

An additional twelve student coaches were needed to complete the camp staff. The student coaches were mostly basketball players. They served as dorm counselors as well as assisting the professional coaches on the floor. The great demand to attend Darnall's basketball camp compelled him to increase the camp to two sessions of one week each. Turning away over 100 prospective campers gave him the impetus to do this.

Starting in the summer of 1978, Dave directed two sessions of boys' camps. Thirty professional coaches were employed to coach the 500 campers. Approximately fifteen student coaches were needed to assist the professionals.

It continued to be a very busy summer. The Darnall children were active in gymnastics and attended the Gym Corner in Eureka directed by Kim Smith. This interest led Dave to establish the Eureka College All-American Gymnastic Camp with Miss Smith. He served as Director of this camp for several years. Then on top of the second session of boy's basketball camp and the gymnastic camp, he added a third sport camp.

There was a growing interest in girls' basketball, so Dave decided to establish a basketball camp for girls. The camp provided a good opportunity for those girls who wanted to improve their basketball skills. It also served as an excellent recruiting tool for the college, in particular, the women's basketball program. A good experience at camp made for potential students to the college. That is what Director of Admissions Hearne liked.

Coach Darnall scheduled two excellent guest speakers. Charlotte Lewis, a member of the USA Silver Medal Olympic Team, an All-American at Illinois State University, and a resident of near-by Peoria, was a model of inspiration and incentive for the young girl cagers. Roger Phegley, first-

NBA player Roger Phegley speaking at boys' camp with Coach Darnall at his side.

round draft choice of the NBA Washington Bullets, a college All-American from Bradley University, and a native of East Peoria was also an excellent messenger for the girl campers. Phegley, thus, spoke at the girls' and both boys' camps.

Darnall assembled an excellent coaching staff for his first girls' camp. Some members of the staff were Roger Smith; Maury Hough, Oblong High School; Bonnie Yocum, Tremont High School; Gregg Johnson, Eureka High School; Cathy Camargo, Peoria Bergan High School; Bruce Darnall, Lake Mills, Wisconsin, High School; Britta Johnson, Lake Mills High School; Betty Gardner, Saybrook High School; and Bonita Howard, Eureka College Ladies' Basketball Coach. Also on the staff was Dave's former high school teammate and college roommate, Dick McCammack, O'Fallon High School.

During the first years of the girls' camp for security reasons as well as Dave's belief that the girls needed to be entertained in the evening, all basketball games were concluded by 8:00 P.M. A social activity followed. All campers and camp staff were required to attend. An entertainment film was shown on Sunday night. Monday evening consisted of a "Watermelon Feast" —all the watermelon the girls could eat. Tuesday night was set aside for a

camp "Pool Party." The girls enjoyed this since it provided an opportunity for them to dunk their favorite coach. A snack of potato chips and lemonaide was served poolside. Wednesday evening was the girls' favorite. That was the night of the camp "Gong Show." Each dorm floor was responsible to perform an act. That meant approximately twelve performances. Student coach "T" Moore, in his white brim and sunglasses, was Master of Ceremony, Chuck. Student trainer Henry Hunsinger was "Gene, Gene the Dancing Machine." A panel of four judged each act. The popular panel members were student coach Jane Brooks, Miss America in her bathing suit; Roger Phegley, Mr. NBA Basketball; the Man-with-the Tan, Eureka Middle School Coach Craig Gerdes; and Mr. Hollywood, the charming student coach Doug Brown. Scott Runyen, Dave's nephew and

Master of Ceremony "T" Moore.

125

assistant student director served as a substitute on the panel. Thursday evening, the last night, was set aside for the camp "Pizza Party." Music and dancing followed the pizza party in Harrod Lounge.

Dave started his fourth sport camp in the summer of 1979. This time it was a girls' volleyball camp. With the success of the other camps, besides the need to recruit more females to the college, the addition of a volleyball camp made sense. Darnall was always thinking about recruiting students to help increase the school's enrollment. This was something the administration liked.

Darnall knew very little about the actual teaching of volleyball fundamentals. He did, however, possess the knowledge and knack to organize and direct new camps. He had to rely upon a qualified camp staff to teach the fundamentals and game strategy. One such person was Nancy LaCursia. She would eventually become a vital member of the college's faculty. LaCursia was Head Coach of Volleyball, Basketball, and a physical education teacher at near-by LeRoy High School. A few years later, she fulfilled the same responsibilities at Eureka College.

Dave felt the need to have noted guest speakers. Young people are often fascinated by their appearances. It was very difficult at first to find well-known female basketball or volleyball players due to the lack of professional status at that time. However, through Nancy's affiliation with Illinois State University, Darnall was able to obtain some excellent female collegiate and European basketball players. One was Pat McKinzie, granddaughter of legendary Eureka College Coach Ralph McKinzie.

Dave was more fortunate in acquiring noted male speakers. It was somewhat unusual to be able to obtain professional players as guest speakers when neither the college nor camp had any real ties to the NBA. Darnall had the good fortune to develop the right connections to fulfill this important aspect needed for a successful camp.

Mickey Johnson, six-foot-seven Chicago Bull forward, was the first NBA player to speak at Darnall's camp. Later, NBA players Roger Phegley, Washington Bullets; Dave Corzine, Washington Bullets; C.J. Kupec, Los Angeles Lakers; Jack Sikma, Seattle Supersonics; and Jim Les, Utah Jazz, became camp guest speakers. Johnson, Corzine, Phegley, and Les later played for other NBA organizations. All players, except Sikma, became annual speakers until their retirement from the game.

One reason why Dave believed his camps were so successful was the dedication and loyalty of the camp coaches.

"The coaches worked the camps because of the love of the game and the enjoyment of working with youngsters, not because of the money. A coach's base salary for the first seven years of existence was a mere sixty-dollars a week. The coaches received a five-dollar increase for each camp they worked thereafter. The supervisor of each division received a ten-dollar bonus," Darnall said.

An important factor for some coaches was the generous allotment for their entertainment and refreshment. Professional coaches assembled each evening somewhere off-campus after the campers had "lights-out." This was a "coaches' meeting." Student coaches and student dorm supervisors remained on campus at all times overseeing the dorms. Coach Darnall was always nearby. He left Eureka only twice in the longevity of the camps— once to attend a Miss Woodford County Pageant in a nearby community in which Tiera was participating and the other in 1990 when he had a heart attack. Most of the professional coaches lived in the dorms for the week.

A typical camp day resembled the following schedule:

7:30 - 8:30 A.M.	Breakfast
8:30 - 8:50 A.M.	Coaches' Meeting
8:50 - 9:00 A.M.	Camp Attendance and Announcements
9:00 - 11:30 A.M.	Morning Session
11:30 - 12:45 P.M.	Lunch
12:55 - 1:00 P.M.	Camp Attendance and Announcements
1:00 - 3:45 P.M.	Afternoon Session
4:00 - 10:00 P.M.	Scrimmage Games
10:30 P.M.	Dorm Lights Out

The morning and afternoon sessions always began with "TWW" (Darnall's trademark) drills. These consisted of group reaction drills, slide drills, ups and downs, and forward-backward sprinting. It was a way all campers, regardless of their assigned divisions, did something together. Basketball fundamentals were then taught with individual and team drills following.

With the new interest in team camps, Darnall initiated both a Varsity and Freshmen-Sophomore Team Camp. These coincided with the individual camps. This extended the camp enrollment to 330 campers per week. The individual camp scrimmages were played first in the evening. These games were divided into three divisions—CBA, ABA, and NBA—according to age. CBAers were the youngest with the NBA consisting of the high school age campers. The ABA was for junior highers. Team camp games concluded the evening.

The professional coaches remained on campus until at least 11:00 P.M. They were responsible to help the floor supervisors bed down the campers. The coaches then gathered in the main campus lounge or "quad" area before leaving campus for their "meeting." The first night was to the Darnall home. Bonnie served the customary ham salad sandwiches. That was the night the returning camp coaches became reacquainted and the new coaches and with the veteran staff members. The evening was spent talking about the week's up-coming agenda, discussing the past year's basketball seasons, telling stories, playing "ship-captain-crew," playing carding, and watching TV while eating and drinking a few "cold ones." The second night was set aside for the traditional initiation pizza party for first-time coaches. It was held at The Outpost on the south side of Eureka. At twelve o'clock midnight all new coaches lined up for the legendary initiation drink, called a "Prairie Fire." It was administered by Smitty and The Outpost owner, Mike Schrementi. Given the support of a drum roll by the veteran camp staff, the rookies downed their surprise. With hot lips and burning mouths, the bewildered coaches were congratulated by their comrades. Following the initiation ceremony, the coaches then went to the Darnalls' for their nightly camp "meeting."

The third and fourth nights usually had the coaches returning to the Darnalls' a little earlier. The usual activities were again pursued. However, some of the coaches ventured on to Peoria to find their own entertainment.

All coaches remained on campus the last night of camp. A coaches' meeting was held in the campus lounge to select the All-star Team players in their respective leagues for the next morning's All-star games. The Team Camp coaches elected schools to receive special camp trophies in six categories. They were Most Improved, Best Defensive, Best Offensive, Best Sportsmanship, Best Rebounding, and Best Passing. These trophies were presented to the respective team winners at the Team Camp closing ceremony. A special award was bestowed to one member of each team who was designated the team's Most Productive Camper. Special T-shirts were given to the winner of the Team Camp "Shoot-out" and "Free Throw" contests.

The coaches, spending a week together working with the campers and socializing with each other in the evenings, developed a bond that some say resembled a "fraternity." Some professional coaches, as well as student coaches, gathered at the end of each camp at The Outpost to "officially close" the camp. Since the student coaches were required to stay on campus all week, they had little time to socialize with the professional coaches. This gathering gave them that opportunity. Smitty traditionally closed camp by blowing his whistle and announcing, "Camp is officially closed," as those surrounding him made a toast with a cold glass of Bud Light.

One of the most tedious times at camp was the Monday morning picture session. It was not easy to organize over 300 campers for a camp photograph. This was especially true when it was vital to have the tallest campers standing at the back of the group. Getting the campers to stand still was another unbelievable task. It took a minimum of fifteen minutes to get the job completed.

Check-in was another tense occurrence at camp. To register 300 campers, pass out properly fitted camp jerseys with their names marked on them, give each a basketball with his/her name on it, and then move them into dorm rooms took a lot of organization, patience, and time. Registration time allotted was three hours. It took Bonnie's expertise with the assistance of a couple helpers and the coaches to make it all happen. This was not counting the hours it took beforehand to insure that the campers were placed in rooms with requested roommates, beside others from their hometowns, or beside other friends. Getting the correct jersey size was also a major accomplishment, especially to some mothers.

It was through Roger Phegley that teammate seven-foot Dave Corzine became a fixture at Darnall's camps. Corzine, as did Phegley, spoke at both the boys' and girls' camps from 1982 until their retirement. That is how the two Daves became friends. Corzine was a member of the Chicago Bulls during the 1982-1983 NBA season. He lived in the City of Chicago. Eureka was only a two-hour trip for the Bulls' center. That made it possible for him to become a regular at camp. Corzine normally spent the night at the Darnall home on the day he spoke. The camp coaches enjoyed this immensely. Between Phegley and Corzine, they were able to get a feel for the life of a NBA player. The camp staff spent hours listening to professional basketball stories by the two pros. Corzine developed a friendship with Smitty. Smitty was an avid card player; so was Corzine. Many camp coaches enjoyed playing cards at the Darnalls' during their nightly camp "meetings." Smitty and Corzine usually organized the highly contested games. All the camp coaches wanted to get a little of Corzine's NBA money. The Chicago Bull usually walked into Darnall's house with a huge white tube sock full of

NBA seven-foot center Dave Corzine with campers.

change. The camp coaches got "fired-up" when they saw that. What high stakes! Smitty would then announce, "Let the game begin!" The card sessions would last for several hours.

Talking about the relationship between Smitty and Corzine, honorary camp coach Sam Harrod witnessed a sight he and all the other attending camp coaches will never forget. He related it this way:

> The first time I met Dave Darnall, one of his first goals was to start a series of summer camps on the Eureka College campus for boys and girls, beginning with basketball and later expanding to other sports. He had several objectives in mind. First, he wanted to bring in young athletes so that they would become familiar with Eureka and later consider enrolling as students and players. He also wanted to make effective use of the campus during the summer months. And, he wanted to offer summer jobs to coaches who would also develop a positive attitude for Eureka.
>
> One summer night, after a long day at one of Dave's camps for youngsters, Corzine and Phegley were out with a bunch of us relaxing

130

with a cold beer at The Outpost. One of the regular camp coaches, Smitty, looked at Corzine and asked, "Dave, when you're in the lane and Kareem tries to come across on you, what do you do?"

Corzine at 7-0 and about 280 pounds raised up to his full height and replied, "Smitty, pretend I am in the lane and you are Kareem. Come across on me." A big man, himself well over 6-2 and 225 pounds, Smitty took a half-step forward when Corzine hit him it the mid-section with a tremendous forearm shiver. Smitty was propelled clear off his feet, went three feet in the air, and crashed to the floor on his back, stunned.

Corzine smiled down at him and explained patiently, "Smitty, that's what I do when Kareem tries to come across the lane on me!"

For the 1982 girls' camp, Darnall was able to obtain two outstanding guest speakers. The two returned yearly for several summers. One was Pat McKinzie. McKinzie's grandfather was a former star athlete and icon coach, including President Reagan's football coach at Eureka College. McKinzie was a college All-American at Illinois State University and a European professional player. The second excellent lecturer was Coach John Schneiter. The dynamic speaker was the girls' head coach at the prestigious New Trier High School. As a teenager, Dave had admired Coach Schneiter because he guided his boys' Running Reds Stephen Decatur High School team to a State Championship. The youngest coach in Illinois to accomplish that feat, Schneiter coached the Decatur school located only a few miles from Darnall's hometown of Argenta.

Dave withdrew from the directorship of the gymnastic camp after a couple years. The strenuous basketball seasons, year-round recruiting, directing the boys' and girls' basketball camps and the volleyball camp became too much. Darnall, soon after, turned over the directorship of the volleyball camp to the new ladies' volleyball and basketball coach at Eureka College, Nancy LaCursia.

It was for the 1982 camp that Dave hired a future prominent camp coach, Dave Gilliland. Gilliland eventually became Assistant Director of the Team Camps as well as a personal friend. He told the story of how he became a Dave Darnall's Eureka College Basketball Camp coach:

> I remember that in 1979 I happened to be at The Outpost tavern in Eureka and met Dave Darnall for the first time. As usual, on that particular evening he had a large group of fans and friends around him. I have often described this group, of which I am now a close member, as his entourage. I was, as a twenty-one-year old still in college, fascinated by the amount of fun, closeness, and comradeship displayed by the mem-

bers of this group that evening. I told Dave that first evening that I wanted to be a coach at the camp. I had no idea what was to lie ahead in either my coaching career or in my association with Coach Dave Darnall and Eureka College. Little did I know what a large part of my life and career both Dave and the camp would end up playing.

However, Dave's tenure as a camp coach became very tenuous after his very first camp. Coach Darnall's son, Derek, age nine, was moved up to the middle-age group boys where he fell into Gilliland's group of twelve- to four-teen-year olds. Of course, Coach Gilliland required as much of this group as the older boys and was a stickler for detail in drills and hustle. Derek proved to be a little too slow in one of the drills. Coach Gilliland instructed him to run five laps around the gym with his arms up. Poor guy had no idea it was Coach Darnall's son. But guess who discovered the "punishment" in progress and came tattling—Tiera! The young teenager was outraged and was hell-bent to save her brother. It took quite a while for her to like Coach Gilliland after that. The three have had many laughs over the years about the incident.

"Dave Gilliland played an important role in the EC basketball program," Darnall said. "Not only has he been a camp coach and an official, but he has been a supporter of the program. Dave has sent several of his high school players on to me. He also got to know my college players personally and became a good friend to many."

There were many additional outstanding coaches who joined the camp staff over the year to share their wisdom and expertise with both the girl and boy campers, including Dave's future assistants Rodney Todd and Dennis Dighton.

Numerous dedicated coaches spent weeks at Darnall's camps teaching fundamentals of basketball to eager learners. All professional coaches who worked a basketball camp are listed in Appendix F.

Four of the seven original camp coaches from 1975 were still staff members on Darnall's last individual camp in 1999. They were Allen Pickering, currently vice president of Lincoln College; Ken Miller; Tim McGuire; and Craig Gerdes. Pickering and Miller worked at least one week of camp each summer for the entire twenty years.

"Over the years, there have been many coaches who have been responsible for sending their players to my camps," Darnall said, "but Gilliland, McGuire, Tim Meiss, Harry Kuntz, Bill Mulvaney, Roger Wiseman, Mike Allen, Mark Berry, and more recently Chris Carter must be

NBA sharpshooting guard Jim Les.

commended for bringing the most. Each has had over twenty-five here during one summer of camps many times."

Darnall was able to obtain Bradley University's All-American guard and NBA player Jim Les as a guest speaker. This was achieved through camp coach Larry Denzel, a Eureka College alum and Les' uncle. The spunky guard dazzled the young campers with his ball handling drills while he stressed there was still a place in the game for small players. Jim spoke at both Darnall boys' and girls' camps for several years. The charismatic Les is currently the successful Head Basketball Coach at his alma mater.

During the middle and late eighties Darnall introduced "team" camps to his already existing individual camps. The concept was that the high school coach would accompany his/her entire high school team to the camp. The first Varsity Team Camp started in 1985 with twelve Class A teams. Rich Vana, then Head Coach at Manito-Foreman High School (now Midwest Central), served as Dave's first Team Camp supervisor. Three years later, Darnall organized and directed the first Girls' Basketball Team Camp. It, too, consisted of twelve Class A teams under the leadership of Eureka College Basketball Coach Nancy LaCursia. The following year, 1989, brought about Darnall's first Freshman-Sophomore Team Camp. Duplicating the other team camps, this camp also consisted of twelve Class A teams. Ken Miller became the Fr-So Team Camp supervisor and later replaced Vana as the Varsity Camp supervisor. Dave Gilliland, Head Basketball Coach at Burlington Central by that time, served as assistant Team Camp supervisor in both of the boys' Team Camps.

During the Girls' Camp orientation in 1990, Darnall suffered a heart attack. He spent a week in the cardiac unit of St. Francis Hospital in Peoria. It was determined that the attack was stress related, but, fortunately, no damage had been done. He felt blessed that Dr. Craig Kurtz had been available when he arrived at St. Francis.

"Not only is he a great doctor, but he equals that as a person. It takes someone special to have to deal with me," Darnall said. "After attending to me for a week, I made him an 'honorary camp coach' without having to have a 'prairie fire.' I gave him a Dave Darnall's Eureka College Basketball Camp coach's shirt. Learning a little about my camps while I was in the hospital, Dr. Kurtz later sent his children to my camp. We have crossed paths several times outside his office."

The camp ran quite smoothly with Bonnie, Dighton, LaCursia, Smitty, and the remainder of the staff responding to the situation.

The 1993 girls' camp was his last girls' camp. Darnall, feeling the strain of all his college responsibilities, decided to turn the leadership over to the capable hands of Lady Red Devil Head Basketball Coach Sandy Schuster. Schuster and her Assistant Coach Karen Sweitzer had been extremely vital to the Girls' Basketball Camp in Darnall's latter years as Director. Dave felt confident in Schuster's ability to maintain the girls' camp as one of the best in the State. He also felt the switch might help the two lady coaches in their recruiting efforts.

Among the first in the State to have a Team Camp, Darnall expanded his endeavor by organizing and directing a Junior High Basketball Team Camp. It also consisted of twelve teams that followed the same format and daily schedule as the other Team Camps. This camp, however, was conducted over only four days and not in conjunction with an individual camp. The Junior High Camp still exists at the writing of this book.

During the 1986 camp, the coaches invented a new sport—"Human Bowl." A coach working the second session of the boys' camp noticed that the local bowling alley was closed. He thought, for staff morale, Darnall should rent the bowling alley to hold a "Human Bowl." What is "Human Bowl?"

First of all, no bowling balls are needed. The coaches are the bowling "balls." The one major piece of equipment needed is a head protector. A couple of the coaches had played football at Eureka High School and knew one of its football coaches. Obtaining six football helmets was not a problem. Coach Darnall had contacted the owner of the alley to see if he could rent the facility for a nominal fee, especially since it would be used only for a few hours at night after the campers were in bed.

Twenty-four professional coaches participated in the first "Human Bowl." They attempted to get guest speaker Dave Corzine to take part in the new event. Using good judgement and not wanting to risk injury, Corzine politely declined and just watched instead.

The bowling alley had six lanes. Four coaches comprised a team. Removing their shoes, the first member of each team stepped up on the alley and placed a football helmet on his head. It was time to go. The coaches ran down the alleys with their arms at their sides and dove head down into the pins. The number of pins that fell was counted. Ten frames were played.

The most difficult part for the coaches of the entire adventure was to remember to keep their heads down so as not to hit the top ledge of the pin housing. The only casualty of the evening was when a six-foot-seven coach failed to get his head down early enough to prevent hitting the ledge. Two non-participating coaches served as the "first aid squad" and hauled the injured bowler from the pit. The result was a cut to the bridge of his nose from the helmet and required a trip to the hospital emergency room for stitches around 1:00 A.M.

"Strike!"

To close the bowling session, the coaches voted for the "Best Performers." Needless to say, the injured bowler was disqualified, and the awards went to a young coach who performed a "flying leap and dive" into the pins and a veteran coach, both scoring a perfect ten.

The following week was the girls' camp. The camp coaches had heard of the previous week's activity and wanted to duplicate it. Again, the alley and helmets were procured. This would become the second "Human Bowl" and last! Never again! It was a "twice" in a lifetime event. The coaches actively tried to out-do other bowlers for some outlandish performances. Fortunately, this evening ended with no casualties, unlike the week before.

A couple years later *America's Funniest Home Videos* was soliciting tapes. Bonnie sent in a segment of the video she had taken of the unique event. For several weeks, the program used a brief portion of the video for their nationwide advertisement. Corzine had even viewed the advertisement while in Florida and called the Darnalls.

Even though the segment was televised on the show, it did not win. The coaches, to this day, do not understand why the program used a portion for advertisement purposes but deemed it not good enough to be selected as the funniest video of the telecast.

Some of the coaches felt a few of the show's episodes appeared to be staged. "Human Bowl" definitely was not! In actuality, it took place several years before the program was aired.

The camp coaches were as cohesive as any fraternity. As ten years of camps approached, they were anxious to plan a ten-year reunion. This was held the summer of 1984 at the Eureka American Legion Hall with seventy-five camp coaches attending along with still-active NBA players Dave Corzine and Roger Phegley. The Legion hosts, also Red Devil fans, were Mel Tedford, Bob Duncan, Cy Cawley, Jeep Zimmerman, and Jim Maloney. The highlight of the evening was a "professional belly-dancer." What a disaster! Or maybe, as Bonnie observed, lucky. She was quite a large lady with a lot to be desired in her dancing skills. It became a comedy act, and the coaches actually thought Dave had hired that particular dancer on purpose. It resulted in a lot of laughs and the coaches keeping "in-line."

Camp Coach Dan Veach served as Master of Ceremony. He wrote a very fitting poem honoring the camp. It signified the closeness of the camp staff.

DARNALL'S CAMP (THE PLACE TO BE)
By Dan Veach
June 15, 1984

It's lonely and tranquil after a week of basketball as you see;
David Darnall's Camp, the place all American youth should be.
Eyes crimson and swollen, bodies badly abused as the week unfolds;
But alas it's ten-year reunion time and everything goes.

If attention coaches you are giving me not; in time I'm certain you will.
I shouldn't talk about this but it seems I can't be still.
You see, once each year we meet at a camp; its founder a man Darnall.
And laying aside all innuendoes, after one week, it's a living hell.

Conservative coaches we are but also broad-minded and cool;
Hey guys, anyone for a midnight swim? Who's that in the pool?
Fighting a hang-over until noon from last night's beer;
Then it's chow at Reagan—which place tonight—Outpost or Chanticleer?

And, oh the next morning! Something mortal eyes shouldn't see;
It's one of our coaches blowing chow in front of Eureka Rotary.
It was horrendous enough what the Rotary eyes shockingly saw;
But how could he do it right in front of his father-in-law.

Am I getting your attention coaches? I've so much more to say;
And because of my benevolence I'll go on without delay.
It's 8:30 coaches meeting time, and half again are late;
Darnall nervously itching and becoming increasingly more irate.

As he scowls and leans upon his podium then just profoundly stares
And at once breaking the serene silence while scratching his head declares
"Who drove over the bridge, through the flowers, and left cans of beer?
Come on coaches, use your heads—President Reagan once lived here."

Somehow we all get it together and innocently smile;
Those damn student coaches, you can't trust them even for a while.
That makes everyone feel better and things are again sparkling and clear
Nothing else will go wrong until 2:00—Oh, crap, the guest speaker's not here.

Miraculously and even prodigiously we fight on through the week;
Drinking, coaching, trading stories, doing all with almost no sleep.
Walking zombies, we motivate, teach and coach for all to see;
The way most of us feel, is Darnall's Camp really the place to be?

On the serious note though, the camp experience none of us would ever trade
Because of our love for the sport and lifetime friends we've made,
As the week is passed on I've survived and sip one final beer;
Smile, sit back, relax and say, "It's been great—See you 'dunkers' next year!"

Over those first ten years, many special occasions, happenings, and events took place. The stories were often written down and kept for a "Camp Trivia" test given to the coaches attending the reunion dinner.

The camp coaches gave Dave a refrigerator painted maroon and gold, the college's colors. Of course, it was not just an ordinary refrigerator. Marv Holmes, the Director of Maintenance and an honorary camp coach, had refitted the old refrigerator with a tapper. It was placed in the Darnalls' laundry room where it was easily accessible to the coaches for a cold beer. The prized possession is still in use today.

The second Dave Darnall's Eureka College Basketball Camp Reunion was held during the summer of 1994. The twentieth anniversary dinner was held in Toluca, a small town thirty miles north of Eureka. Toluca is known for its two famous Italian restaurants, Mona's and Capponi's. The banquet was held at the St. Anne Hall with Mona's catering the dinner. The meal, alone, was worth the trip to Toluca.

Dan Harrod, Darnall's friend and honorary camp coach, served a Master of Ceremony. A twenty-year camp trivia test, administered by coaches Ken Miller and Mike Pryor, was given to the 100-plus coaches and former NBA players, Dave Corzine and C.J. Kupec. Examples of the trivia questions are as follows:

Who is the camp "prairie fire" champion and how many did he drink?
Who went swimming in the City of Washington Square's fountain?
Who made the slam dunk in Derek's basketball hoop with a boulder?
Which speaker was shot to death in a domestic quarrel?
Who was the coach who over three days never changed clothes, shaved, or called a foul?
What camper mooned Coach Darnall?
What team had a "swimming pool" on their dorm floor?
What camper's mother caught camp coaches coming in at 5:45 A.M.? She was picking up her son for an early morning Driver Education session.
What coach has a close relationship with Molly Putts?
Who invented the "power nap" and "power nap plus booster"?
Who drove a motorcycle through Gunzenhauser Hall?
Who won the aqua-suck contest?

Who were the three student coaches who drove the school bus to Darnall's house in the middle of the night?

Who received $100 from Corzine and Phegley for drinking a pitcher of beer through a straw in three minutes?

What coach had to receive a pint of blood upon returning home from a week of camp?

Who pulled Bonnie's shirt off at The Outpost with Smitty coming to the rescue?

Who stole Darnall's car and parked it in a dealer's parking lot?

Who was the coach that up-chucked in front of his father-in-law while he was attending a Rotary Club luncheon at the Commons Food Center?

Who was the coach that required stitches to his nose after being injured at "Human Bowl?"

Who was the coach that stole his car back from a locked parking lot after being towed away and then had to pay a larger fine?

Who was the coach who broke Bonnie's glass-top kitchen table by slamming a stainless steel bowl on it?

Where is the whistle with the hash browns in it hidden in the Reagan Classroom?

Who were the two coaches "on a mission" from one end of Peoria to the other?

Chuck Wertz, who served as the director of the morning camp coaches' golf scramble, presented the golf awards to the winning participants following the test. Coach Darnall then handed out some of his own special awards to Roger Smith for working the most camps, and Ken Miller and Al Pickering for working at least one camp each year for all twenty years. Gilliland concluded the camp reunion by presenting a very special gift to Coach Darnall. Gilliland blindfolded the camp originator and led him to the Hall's parking lot. There the camp coaches presented Dave and Bonnie with a new shiny red golf cart. Dave was shocked! Gilliland had spearheaded the project with help from his assistant coach and golf pro Randy Schairer. Under Gilliland's leadership, past years' camp coaches made donations for the purchase of the cart. Bonnie was aware of the camp coaches' generous gift, but Dave was totally surprised. The Club Car had the emblem of the college's Red Devil on the front with "Coach Dave Darnall" and "Eureka College" in gold lettering on the sides. Darnall had often talked about buying a golf cart for Bonnie and him to use in Fairfield Bay, Arkansas. The still shining cart is housed in the garage of their new home at the "Bay."

With the presentation completed, Coach Smitty announced, "Let the games begin!" The rest of the evening was spent playing cards, ship-captain-crew, toasting drinks, and telling stories.

Darnall's basketball camps have truly been family affairs over the years. Not only has Bonnie served as Assistant Director and Camp Secretary, but she has also been in charge of camp registration and, most importantly, been surrogate mother. Tiera has helped with registration and assisted her mom with the late-night snacks. Derek's duties were varied. His favorite (ha!) was inflating some 900-plus basketballs yearly for numerous years. He also served as the camp's night supervisor for many sessions. Needless to say, he had attended the camps as a camper for more years than he was eligible. Sister Judy's sons, Scott, Tony, Rodd, and Todd, had all worked numerous camps. Scott was Dave's first administrative assistant and head dorm supervisor, maintaining that position for years. Sister Lucia's sons, Travis and Lance, were student dorm supervisors and at times helped their cousin Derek blow up balls. Her daughter Tiffany was often an assistant to Bonnie. Bruce was a camp coach for several years while his daughter, Laura, served as a girls' camp coach and student dorm supervisor. His wife, Gloria, had been a dorm supervisor. Sons, John and Mark, and daughter, Sarah, were too young to be members of the camp staff but were campers for numerous years. Bonnie's niece, Lisa, a college alum, was on the Girls' Camp coaching staff several times. The most recent additions have been son-in-law Brett Charlton who has served both as a trainer and a gym supervisor at the high school. Grandson "Little" Brett, six, became an honorary member of Brandon Fenton's Pontiac Junior High School Team at the 2003 Junior High Team Camp.

Mounting pressures to admit additional campers to each of the three camp sessions resulted in the decision to drop having guest speakers in 1992. That provided the necessary time to have scrimmage games for the increased number of campers.

Throughout the years of camps, many incidents have occurred from which stories could be told. One keeps coming back to Dave. It happened during the first session of the 1994 camp. Due to the renovation of a dorm normally used located close to the Fieldhouse, another dorm located further away had to be utilized. The substitute dorm was named Gunzenhauser. "Gunz" housed upperclassmen during the school year. In the latter part of October, its basement served as the community's "haunted house." Graffiti appeared all over its basement walls. A painting of a clown was among the drawings.

Carraghan and Brett ready for Grandpa's Camp.

Darnall had made the basement off-limits to all campers during the three weeks of camps. However, kids will be kids. If there is a place they are not suppose to be, they'll go there. These young campers were no different. They had to explore.

Several weeks prior to the camp, there had been incidents in nearby Peoria involving a person dressed as a clown attempting to pick-up young boys. This had been highly publicized in all local media.

Each evening Coach Darnall made his security rounds between the dorms, student union, outside courts, and the Fieldhouse while scrimmage games were being played inside. Camp coach personnel were coaching games, officiating, supervising dorms, or just enjoying watching the campers play. That particular evening, while on his "beat," Dave stood in front of the Fieldhouse surrounded by numerous young campers when a female security guard came running up to him shouting, "The clown has been spotted in Eureka!" The frantic guard went on to say, "He's driving a four-by four. The police are looking for him. Watch your kids!"

All of sudden, between ten to fifteen campers went scattering. Dave, showing no real emotion, told the guard, "Keep quiet! Don't say anything around the campers; they'll get all shook up. I'll take care of it."

Darnall calmly proceeded into the gym, quietly telling camp coaches about a clown that was suppose to be in town. Still remaining cool, since he was skeptical of a predator clown in Eureka, he asked for the coaches' cooperation. He instructed them that, if they saw any person dressed as a clown and driving a "pick-up," they should immediately contact him.

Within minutes of Dave's notification of the clown sighting in Eureka, he was receiving phone calls from parents. One asked, "What in the hell is going on over there?" Their sons had called home telling them, "A clown is on campus trying to pick us up." They also reported that he had been in the basement of their dorm writing on the walls.

Darnall was told some parents were on their way to Eureka. Following several calls, Dave went to Gunzenhauser to try to assure the campers living there that everything was all right. However, by then, the word had spread throughout the camp to be on the lookout for the clown. He surely would be coming to the campus. Darnall learned that not only had some campers seen the basement walls of "Gunz," but that prior to coming to camp some had seen a couple of movies featuring men dressed as clowns kidnapping or killing young boys. *The John Gacey* (mass murderer in Rockford area) *Story* was one. The residents also talked about the clown being spotted in the Peoria area as reported by the news media. The rumors and hysteria continued.

Dave left Gunzenhauser to return to the Fieldhouse area where Dean of Student Development Dale Martin was waiting to inform him of the clown sighting in town. Darnall replied that he already knew of the situation and told the dean to have the security people keep quiet around the campers. He did not want to stir the campers up any more than they already were.

By this time, several parents had arrived on campus. They were noticeably upset with the Camp Director. Dave told the irrational parents that there was no clown on the campus and that the camp area was closely supervised by some fifty professional and student coaches.

Shortly before "lights out," Bonnie made her nightly visit to the campus. Dave informed his wife of what had been taking place. Bonnie started to laugh.

"What the hell are you laughing at?" Dave asked, more than a little irritated.

"David, I saw Harlan leave earlier this evening in his clown suit," Bonnie replied.

"What was he driving?" Dave questioned.

"His pickup," Bonnie answered.

Harlan, also known as "Rollo the Clown," was a neighbor of the Darnalls. He actually lived directly across the street from them. "Rollo" went to children's birthday parties and to homes of children who were ill to promote cheer and laughter. In fact, he had been hired by the college to entertain the children of the faculty and staff at the college's annual beginning of school dinner. However, as this was still early in Harlan's clown career, "Rollo" was not well known in the community.

"Go call Harlan and tell him to call the police as they are looking for him," Dave instructed Bonnie. "I'll go back to Gunzenhauser and talk to the kids and the parents. When you get done talking to Harlan, start telling the coaches to notify the campers on their dorm floors who the clown is."

"Rollo" had attended a youngster's birthday party and was driving by the local trailer court, located a block from campus, when someone spotted him. By the time it was "lights out," all the campers had been informed of the clown's identity and that they were safe and sound. Even with this guarantee, a couple campers' fathers spent the night in Gunzenhauser.

As though Darnall did not have enough to worry about at camp time regarding the campers, he also had his "big kids," the coaches, to worry

"Rollo the Clown" Harlan Pierson.

143

about. There were always prankster coaches who forced Dave to be on his toes. Several stories can be told here while others are better left "unwritten."

It was in the wee hours of the night when Bonnie and Dave heard something in their kitchen. Dave quietly got out of bed and cautiously crept down the hallway to the kitchen entryway. There he spotted two student coaches approaching the refrigerator.

"What the hell are you guys doing?" Dave shouted to the intruders.

"Oh, coach, we just came to get something to eat," one replied.

"How did you guys get here?" Dave asked.

"We walked," said one of the students.

"Okay, get some ham salad and chips and get back to campus," Dave instructed.

After a short time, the student coaches, with sandwiches in hand, left by the front door to head back to the dorms.

"I really don't know if they came here for food or beer," Dave told Bonnie as he slipped back to bed.

A few minutes later, the Darnalls heard a motor running. Again, Dave left bed, this time running! He ran to the back door. To his astonishment there sat a big yellow school bus. In briefs only, Darnall sprinted to the running bus.

"Open that door! What the hell are you doing?" he shouted to the occupants.

There were the two house intruders—one behind the wheel, the other in the front seat. Dave entered the bus. Hiding behind the front seat was a third student coach.

"Your asses are in deep s-h-i-t!" Darnall told the stunned trio. "I'll talk to you tomorrow. Get your asses back to campus now."

Back in the late seventies and early eighties, adult coaches who maintained the proper license drove the school buses that were used to transport campers to the other three gymnasiums in town. Two buses were parked in front of the Fieldhouse for early use in the mornings. Somehow the young coaches had acquired a set of keys for their short journey to the Darnall home. Did they really think Darnall would not spot the big yellow bus in his driveway? Sure!

One night during the week, some adult coaches traveled to nearby Peoria for a couple hours of their own entertainment. However, all professional coaches were required to stay on campus until 11:00 P.M. to assist in bedding down the campers. On that particular night, several coaches visited

144

an establishment in Peoria that remained open until 3:00 A.M. Upon leaving the lounge, a young coach noticed that his car was missing.

A stolen car? That is what the coaches thought, but after some conversation with the Peoria authorities, it was learned that the car had been towed away because it had been parked in a NO PARKING area. The police informed the owner that the car could be picked up at a specific location in the morning for a monetary fee.

The coaches, thinking the fee was unreasonable, decided they should go get the car immediately. It was located in a fenced, offbeat parking lot. The car owner proceeded to climb the locked fence to reach his car. One problem remained. How was the car going to escape the chained gate? After much thought, a tool was used to snap the chain. With the gate door now open, the proud coaches drove the car away from its prison.

The college had visitors early the next morning—law enforcement officers. By checking the license plates and making a couple calls, the police traced the car to the campus. To make a long story short, the owner was able to keep the car, but there was an additional fee. In other words, it was a pretty expensive night!

How about another car story that caused Dave a severe headache? With "lights out" and campers nestled in bed, the professional camp coaches went to the Darnalls' for food and drink. They discussed the day's happenings, played cards, ship-captain-crew and sat around visiting. Coach was always the last one to arrive at his house as he walked around the campus for about an hour after "lights out" to make sure that everything was quiet. By the time he arrived home, parking spots in his doublewide driveway, as well as all parking areas in front, back, and to the side of the corner-lot house, were usually taken. He'd park anyplace he could squeeze into. However, the car had to be accessible just in case there was an emergency and he had to make a "mad dash" to campus.

Dave arrived home around 11:45 P.M. on that particular night. His house was already full of coaches. Darnall parked his car at the end of the driveway. Normally, he put the car in the garage before going to bed. That was usually after most of the coaches left to return to campus. However, a few stayed until the wee hours of the night. Dave was extremely tired this night and went to bed without putting the car away.

He woke for another exciting day of camp after just a few hours of sleep. Darnall walked out the back door to head for the coaches' breakfast meeting at the college's Commons. He was startled by the absence of his car.

"Where is the car?" he shouted to Bonnie as she stood in the doorway.

The stunned coach headed for the garage hoping that someone had put his car away for him. The car was not there! Had someone come by, noticed the keys in the ignition, and drove off? Did a coach drive it back to campus?

Dave then had to drive their old van to the campus. No one said a word at breakfast about the missing car. Darnall questioned the coaches at the staff meeting to no avail. The morning session ran smoothly, but the missing car did not show up.

Now thinking this was not a coaches' prank, Dave notified the local police of the missing car. Again at lunchtime, no one said anything about the stolen vehicle. A short time after speaking to the campers to start the afternoon session, Darnall received a phone call in his office.

"Hello, Dave, this is Tim Leman. Are you missing your car?"

"Hell, yes," Dave replied.

"It is out here in our lot," Tim said.

"I'll be right out," said Dave.

Darnall's car was spotted in the lot of local car dealership by one of its employees. It was sitting in the Used Car section among numerous other vehicles for sale. To this day, Dave is not sure who was responsible for the act. No one has come forward, but Darnall feels he might have an idea of who the culprit was. "I think a professional coach was the instigator," Dave commented, "but I think probably a student coach actually drove my car to the lot and was returned to campus by the 'planner.'"

Another incident that caused some embarrassment for the Camp Director occurred when one of his camp coaches got sick at lunch. As mentioned, some coaches would stay up quite late at the Darnall house after the campers went to bed. A few would party pretty hard after the initiation party at The Outpost.

When the coaches ate their meals at the Commons, they usually sat together taking up five to six tables. At lunch the day following the initiation party, a coach from Kentucky suddenly jumped up from his table and ran out the main door. He sprinted around the corner of the main building, leaned over and "barfed." Straightening up, the now relieved coach looked toward the building only to see many shocked eyes looking out at him. He was standing directly in front of the windows that looked out from the Rotary Club's private dining room. What was even worse was that the first person he saw was his father-in-law. The coach, totally embarrassed, decided not to return to the dining hall but headed directly back to his dorm room. When asked about the incident, Coach Darnall's comment was, "I don't know if he was really sick or if it was the 'prairie fire' and too much partying the night before. Regardless, it had to be a shock to have your father-in-law see you puke."

In the earlier days of the camps, Coach Darnall established a five-member All-Camp Derelict Coaches' Team. The team consisted of professional coaches who at some time, while being a member of the coaching staff, did something outlandish. For an example, one member of the team was a young coach, who after a couple years of coaching and teaching, decided he would rather serve his country than teach. He enlisted in the Marines. The coach was to report to boot camp just a few weeks after the conclusion of camp.

Preparing for his soon-to-be new profession, he got a burr haircut prior to working camp. One late night while at coach's house, the new military recruit decided he wanted to get a head start on his training. Dressed in a white T-shirt, a pair of camouflage pants he had bought at an Army Surplus, and some black boots, the eager enlistee started his conditioning program in Darnall's family room. He completed 100 push-ups, at least the same amount of sit-ups, and numerous jumping jacks and then was ready for shooting practice. Grabbing a play rifle of young Derek's, the new Marine ran out the backdoor to board a parked jeep. Another young camp coach owned the open-air vehicle. With the owner behind the wheel, the anxious soldier jumped behind the backseat and imitated a gunman shooting out of a military jeep with an attached machine gun. The dual drove off, traveling in Eureka for about fifteen minutes shooting all imaginary enemies they could spot. Obviously, this was another day and time than today. An episode such as this would not be considered today even by an impulsive, young camp coach.

By the way, this fellow is the same coach who owns the camps' "prairie fire" record of five consecutive drinks within seconds. Now, one can see why this guy was a member of Darnall's All-Camp Derelict Coaches' Team.

Hearing about Dave's special team, a young rookie coach strove to become a member of this unique group. Asking what it would take, a veteran instigator coach suggested that the anxious rookie should catch a live duck at Lake Eureka and put it into the classroom desk drawer where Darnall held his early morning staff meetings. Every morning around 8:15 A.M.,

Dave held a coaches' meeting in Reagan Fieldhouse covering the day's schedule. The veteran coaches thought this would be a good way to say "Good Morning" to Darnall.

One late night several coaches went to the lake located on the outskirts of Eureka to witness the rookie coach's catch of a duck. Professionally, the fella was both a football and basketball coach. Not very nimble at six-foot-three, 250 pounds, the aspiring rookie gave his best effort to catch a prize duck. Following an hour of falling on his face while chasing resting ducks and a couple unintentional trips into the water in front of his hysterical observers, the exhausted hunter decided to give up his quest to become a member of Darnall's distinguished team.

Bonnie's favorite camp story came from a "game" (or maybe she should say "games") invented by the men and women coaches at a girls' camp. Needless to say, Smitty, Corzine, and Dan Williams were instigators. The air of competition did not end on the gym floor. It was decided that the Darnalls' glass-top kitchen table would be a perfect place off of which to try to suck a silver dollar. The women coaches quickly developed a technique with their lips to pop the silver dollar up and off the table. It became quite a game with the male coaches betting on which woman coach could "suck" the dollar up the quickest.

"I could never get the hang of how they could do it no matter how hard I tried," Bonnie commented.

Well, the game didn't end there. Once the ladies were doing it easily, it was decided to blindfold them and have their male counterpart direct them from under the glass table to the silver dollar. Shouts of, "Left, Right, Up-Up, Down-Down, Go for it, Now," could be heard all over the Darnall house. But did it stop with the blindfold? No!

"What are all those wet towels doing on the washer?" Bonnie asked Dave the next morning. Dave had no idea either. It seemed that both Bonnie and Dave, who would often just go to bed when tired, had missed the next adaptation to later be named "Aqua Suck." When the blindfolded version had become too easy, the coaches took one of Bonnie's large stainless steel bowls, filled it half full of water, and placed the silver dollar in the bottom; thus, "aqua suck" and a lot of wet towels!

It wasn't until later the next day that one of the lady coaches confessed what had transpired, but the true confession did not spill forth. It wasn't until possibly a year later that Bonnie and Dave learned the final version. Bonnie had thought it funny that she swept up uncooked oatmeal from around her stove when she hadn't cooked any for a long time, but the thought passed quickly with all that was going on. Can you guess where it came from? You got it! When the "aqua suck" was not a challenge anymore, they cooked oatmeal and put it in the bowl with the dollar in the bottom. Bonnie's final lament was, "I can't believe we didn't hear them and missed all of that! They even cleaned up their mess."

"T" Moore tells a camp story about himself and two NBA guest speakers. "One late afternoon around dinner time, some of the professional coaches escorted the day's speaker, San Antonio Spur Dave Corzine, and Roger Phegley, who had come to hear his teammate speak, to the Chanticleer. Even though I was only a student coach, Dave allowed me to go with the NBA players and camp coaches. After several pitchers of beer and a lot of "bull," a coach told me I couldn't drink a pitcher of beer through a straw in three minutes. Corzine and Phegley thought that was a hell of a challenge. They liked the idea so much that they told me if I did it, they would give me a hundred bucks. Hell, they forgot I was a black college kid from south Chicago. A hundred dollars to them was like a million to me. I accepted. Guess what? I stumbled out of the place a hundred bucks richer."

Of course, the camp coaches love to tell stories about Coach Darnall. One that has been passed along for many years is that of NOSNOW's basketball. At the opening of each session, each camper is given a basketball and shirt with his/her name written on it with permanent marker. Keeping track of his/her basketball is the camper's responsibility but not always an easy task with 300-plus balls bouncing around or stashed in a corner. When a camper lost a ball and it was turned in, Coach Darnall would call out the camper's name and have him/her reclaim it during announcements at the beginning of the morning or afternoon session. As it was related by the coaches, Coach Darnall stood in front of the afternoon session shouting, "NOSNOW, NOSNOW." No one stepped forward. Again, Coach Darnall repeated, "NOSNOW, NOSNOW, come get your ball." Getting a little irritated but thinking the camper was too embarrassed to come up, Coach Darnall tried one more time, "NOSNOW!"

That time a young man finally came to the front and said to Coach Darnall, "Coach, I didn't know it was me. You kept calling NOSNOW. My name is MONSON. You are looking at my name up-side-down."

Sure enough, when Coach turned the ball around to face him, it plainly read MONSON. Campers and coaches, alike, had a good laugh on Coach Darnall that afternoon. Would you believe Coach still has the ball?

"NOSNOW" left it in the gym when he left camp, and again, it has never been reclaimed.

Coach Darnall's All-Camp Derelict Team is a thing of the past. In the last few years of the camp, there was no longer a team. Many of the camp coaches returned each year; thus, age became a factor. The camps' "good old boys and girls" were each year becoming older and more subdued.

"It's not like it used to be," Darnall said, "but that is probably good. Age and maturity has taken its toll. Now, all we do is sit around and tell stories of the more exciting past. Besides, some members of the college community may not see the humor in some of the events."

The 2004 Camp will be Darnall's thirtieth year as Director of a camp. When asked if there would be a thirtieth Reunion Party, Dave just shrugged his shoulders and said, "I guess we will just have to wait and see."

Chapter 8

Recruiting: The Backbone of Success

Y OU ARE ONLY AS GOOD AS YOUR TALENT." That's a philosophy accepted by most coaches. High school coaches, however, have to rely on whoever goes out for the team in their particular school. This puts them at a disadvantage. Parochial schools have a small advantage in that they are able to recruit any student in their particular town or area. However, most students who attend a parochial school are of the school's particular religious belief. Then, the biggest recruiting task for public school coaches is to persuade all students in their school with athletic ability in that particular sport to try out for the team. This isn't easy. Students having cars, they work, or they do not want to make the commitment it takes to be an athlete; this makes the task difficult for some coaches.

College coaches, on the other hand, have an advantage. If they are willing to work long hours, believe in their institution, be organized, and have the support of family and administration, they can recruit good athletes to their programs.

There are some college coaches who enjoy the coaching of basketball on the floor but detest the wars of recruiting. That was not the case with Dave Darnall. He enjoyed talking to high school and junior college coaches and their players. He also liked visiting with the prospective student-athletes and their parents in their homes.

Darnall's passion for recruiting paid high dividends. In January of 1994, President Hearne established a new position for the soon-to-be-retired

151

coach. Dave, with the approval of the Dean of Admissions, became an Athletic Counselor. This new responsibility, his teaching of physical education classes, and the directorship of his basketball camps kept him busy until his total retirement on January 15, 2003. The new recruiting responsibility consisted of the recruitment of women volleyball, basketball, and softball student-athletes. Plus, he assisted in recruiting for the men's basketball program.

Coach Darnall, unknowingly, started his recruitment of Eureka College basketball players while serving as Head Basketball Coach at Momence High School. Dave was attending the Chatsworth Holiday Basketball Tournament to scout a future opponent, St. Anne High School. A six-foot senior guard from Forrest High School caught his eye. Tim McGuire, a sharp-shooting guard, was the best pure shooter Dave saw all year.

"Three Generations," Tim McGuire, Dale Huff, and Dave Darnall.

At that time, no one would have believed McGuire would soon become Darnall's first recruit for Eureka College, a place neither had considered. What's even more ironic was that years later, two of Tim's sons would follow him to his alma mater. And, quite unexpectedly, it just so happened that McGuire's high school coach was none other than Dale Huff, Darnall's own former coach at Argenta High School. Dave called Coach Huff for assistance in arranging a home visit with the McGuires once he officially become head coach at Eureka College.

Darnall phoned McGuire shortly after. He used the same "pitch-line" with Tim that he continued to use for the next twenty years. In fact, in June of 1992, Darnall released a document on the technique of recruiting. The manual was entitled *Eureka College Student Recruiting Techniques Manual*. He listed the following key points for fellow recruiters:

Recruiters must be positive, enthusiastic, excitable, courteous, neat, and a team player.

Recruiters must be knowledgeable about their college in general, and their field in particular.

Recruiters must take pride in their program. They must feel their program is as good as any other institution's, if for no other reason than their own teaching or coaching abilities.

Recruiters must not degrade other schools or their programs, should explain why they think their program is better.

Recruiters should not say another college or particular program is better than theirs.

The phone rang and Mrs. McGuire said, "Hello, McGuire's"

The new coach replied, "Hello, this is Dave Darnall, Head Basketball Coach at Eureka College. Is Tim home?"

"Tim . . . phone . . . a college coach," she shouted.

"Hello," answered Tim.

"Hello, Tim, this is Dave Darnall, Head Basketball Coach at Eureka College." Dave then proceeded with what would become his "patented" recruiting speech. "Tim, I want you to come to Eureka College to get your college education and play basketball for me. Eureka College is a small four-year liberal arts college located in Central Illinois. It's located between Bloomington and Peoria. It is about fifteen miles from Bradley University and about twenty miles from Illinois State University. We have an enrollment of approximately 500 students."

Darnall knew all high school basketball players had heard of Illinois State University and Bradley.

"Eureka is a member of the NAIA (later it became dual members of NAIA and NCAA). We have a very unique calendar. It's called the Intensive Study Program. If you went to Illinois or Illinois State, you would take five or six courses for sixteen weeks," Dave explained without hardly pausing to take a breath, "but at Eureka College you'll take only two or three courses for seven or eight weeks. That means you have only three books to read, three finals to take, and three term papers to write at one time. You see, we have taken the traditional semester and broken it into half. Therefore, we are on four eight-week terms."

Without letting Tim say a word, Dave continued trying to sell Eureka College. "Under our system, the teachers have twice as much time to work with you individually because they are teaching half as many students as they would on a semester system."

"Our basketball program will be one of the top small college programs in the state if we get players like you. We will get some good players," Dave persuaded.

Still not letting McGuire talk, the enthusiastic Eureka College coach continued, "We'll treat you just like you're playing major college basketball. When we go on the road, the only responsibility you'll have is to be on the bus on time and play the game."

The basketball team, at that point, traveled exclusively by Peoria Charter bus. Darnall severely missed that the latter part of his career.

"We'll carry everything for you," Dave continued. "When you walk into the locker room, there will be your shoes, socks, jock, towel, pants, jersey, and warm-up. When the game is over, all you have to do is drop your clothes, shower, and go to the bus. You don't even have to carry a duffel with you."

It was Coach's plan to pack all game equipment in army surplus trunks. The administrative assistants and freshmen players would carry the trunks. Needless to say, Dave did not mention that to his first recruit.

Tim was still held speechless, as the new coach was not done yet. "We'll have a steak dinner before the game." However, Darnall did not mention that it would be at a Ponderosa or Bonanza and probably chopped steak.

Darnall became known as a "real dealer" by having the ability to make good deals at the restaurants and motels on their trips. He usually was able to obtain a couple free meals for the coaches or free drinks for the team. Any deal was welcome. The small college was on a limited budget.

Coach Darnall then informed Tim that the team would be staying in the best motels, Holiday Inns and Marriotts. He finished his first recruiting speech by talking about the Reagan brothers.

"As you probably know, Ronald Reagan is a graduate from Eureka College. The fieldhouse we play in was named after him and his brother, Neil, who is also a Eureka grad," said Darnall.

"I would like to come to your house and visit with you and your parents about Eureka College," concluded the coach.

After several minutes of listening to Coach Darnall and not saying anything, Tim replied, "Okay."

It was what Dave was hoping for. He replied, "How about . . . ?"

Dave developed several home visit techniques with recruits and their parents that he faithfully followed. He prepared well, made a point to be on time and look neat, was friendly, confident and positive, and never felt he was wasting his time or theirs. Dave also liked for Bonnie to accompany him on his home visits when possible. He felt she was an asset. This, of course, was a throwback to when he took her with him on job interviews. Bonnie was a very valuable part of Dave's career and helped to create the family atmosphere. She was like the mother away from home. Recruits' mothers liked that feeling. Dave was lucky. Some coaches' wives would not want to make the trips or be willing to fill that role.

Over the years, Dave had other people accompany him on home visits. They were admission counselors, assistant coaches, or sometimes a faculty member. On this, his first college recruiting trip in early July to the McGuire's, he took Bonnie.

The second technique Dave felt was important was his approach. He developed several guidelines. They were:

> Introduce yourself and anyone accompanying you.
> If they don't offer you a seat, sit in the closest place.
> Start off with general chitchat, but not for over ten minutes.
> Start talking about Eureka College by mentioning it is a small Liberal arts college in Eureka, Illinois.
> Explain the connections to the college—not just as a recruiter or coach, but as it being a part of his family. Brother Bruce graduated from EC, and Dave was later able to say that four nephews and a niece had attended as well.
> Explain what makes Eureka College unique, including the Intensive Study Program.

The third major point explained at all home visits was why people went to college. The reasons were discussed in priority order according to Darnall. There were:

> To get an education—at Eureka College the student could get a quality education with a personal touch—not be just a "number."
> To be active—a person had a better chance to be active in a small school—less competition numbers wise.
> At Eureka College the students had their own social life, but they also had two major universities on each side. The students went to these, and their students came to Eureka.

After Darnall concluded his original opening pitch and what made Eureka College unique, he turned his efforts to what the student might want to major in. He then discussed that particular field and its opportunities.

Coach explained the "open house" that Bonnie and he hosted after every home game. Parents got the opportunity to be part of the basketball program. They were able to meet other parents, college professors, season ticket holders, community people, and college administrators.

Darnall continued to tell the McGuires that they might say, "We have followed Tim for all these years. Now we are no longer part of his athletics." He then countered, "But here at Eureka, you are still part of the program." It was coach's last selling point.

Mr. McGuire replied, "Coach, we have already talked about that. After all these years of following Tim, we didn't know what we would do. This sounds good."

Dave gave his farewell and left feeling good about his first of countless home visits. Tim visited the college's campus a few days later. McGuire became Darnall's first recruit.

Eureka College did not have an official NAIA "Letter of Intent." Darnall felt it was important for the athlete to sign something, however. Athletes wanted to sign a "Letter of Intent." It was what the "big boys" did. Darnall composed one. Needless to say, Dave's "Letter of Intent" was not binding, but it looked official. The players who signed the letter didn't care. They got to sign a "Letter of Intent."

Oh, by the way, there was an admission deposit. Coach Darnall had to ask for a $100 check. Did scholarship players have to do that?

Dave always wanted to make it a special occasion when he signed an athlete. Selecting an institution of higher learning was one of the most important decisions a young adult had to make. Darnall felt the decision should be a memorable one for the recruit. He normally went to the student-athlete's home for the signing of the "Letter of Intent." However, on some occasions, the "signing" took place at the Admissions Office on campus.

Parents often wanted to have a picture of their son's signing the "Letter of Intent." When the "signing" took place at the Admissions Office, someone from the college Relations Office was there to take a picture.

A few years later, the college Admissions Office devised their own "Letter of Intent" to enroll at Eureka College for all incoming students. Coach changed to the universal letter when signing his recruits.

Coach Traister and the Admissions Office were already recruiting Doug Brown, a six-foot-four forward from Mazon High School, when Darnall was hired. It was up to Dave to sell his program to Brown. He signed and deposited; thus, becoming the new coach's second incoming freshman basketball recruit.

Coach Darnall ended up signing seven freshmen and four transfers for his 1974-1975 varsity team. Not bad for his first year of recruiting, especially since he had gotten such a late start.

Darnall felt if he had had a whole season to recruit, he could have had a "banner year" in his first full year of recruiting. He knew the success of any of his teams would reflect the success of his recruiting efforts. Dave's recruiting efforts paid dividends over years for continually being on the road. His 1975-1976 basketball team finished the season with a 19 to 6 record. Quite a turnaround over his first year's record in the college ranks of 9 to 16.

Darnall had also brought with him from Momence his high school student administrative assistant—student manager, Jerome White. Jerome was an excellent recruit for both Darnall and the college in general. "Spanky" became Dave's basketball administrative assistant as well as played football. He also was Bonnie's chief "sitter." Derek and all the neighborhood boys looked forward to Jerome spending time with them.

During that first summer, the Darnalls were invited to the Sam Harrods' home on several occasions. One such visit took place immediately after Dave's hiring. Sam remembered the time vividly, "Soon after coming to our home, Dave asked to borrow our phone. Naturally, I consented, thinking that he probably wanted to call his family. Much to my amazed surprise —but also satisfaction, Dave was on our phone for more than an hour, making one long-distance call after another, recruiting new basketball players. Ever since, Dave has been the most determined recruiter I've ever heard of. He often conducted practice, then drove clear up to Northern Illinois or Wisconsin, or clear down to Southern Illinois or St. Louis, to watch a player in a high school game and stayed late into the night recruiting the player and his parents. Then, Dave still had a long, lonely, tiring drive home, only to get up early the next morning to teach his full schedule of regular classes."

What was supposed to be an evening of socializing ended up as a night of making calls to student-athletes. Darnall made calls from a list he had made, one from the Admissions Office, and one Harrod had prepared. The judge had sent numerous letters and newspaper clippings to the area's outstanding athletes.

One phone call the new coach made at Harrod's was to senior captain Kip Blakesley asking the six-foot-two guard's help with prospective players when they visited campus. Darnall wanted Blakesley to speak to the visiting recruits. This call was his first contact with Blakesley as the new coach had not yet met the returning captain.

Dave first talked about his planned basketball program at Eureka College. He informed the East Peoria native that his goal was to win the conference and qualify for the NAIA District 20 post-season playoff tournament. Blakesley thought the new coach was "nuts" especially after seven consecutive losing seasons. However, as time would tell, only two points separated this goal from reality.

Darnall spent his entire first summer recruiting players. Gregg Johnson became Darnall's first transfer. Johnson, who transferred from Illinois Wesleyan, and his father visited with Darnall shortly after he was named the new mentor at the college. Gregg was no stranger to the new coach. Gregg's high school team, Abingdon, played twice against Darnall's Roseville team. One of the occasions was the championship game of the Roseville Holiday Tournament which the host school won. However, Johnson had made an impression on Darnall. Dave remembered speaking to Gregg after the game.

"You played a great game," Dave said. "I wish you played for me." Who would ever have guessed that five years later that wish would come true?

Darnall's first full recruiting year provided a record number of incoming players. Coach felt if he had numbers, he would find enough talent to put a respectable team on the floor. That proved to be true. The 1975-1976 basketball campaign brought about the first winning season in eight years.

Forty-eight new players greeted the second year coach on opening day of practice. Seven returning players, plus the forty-eight, gave him a total of fifty-five players to choose from in order to turn the Eureka College basketball program around. In fact, Darnall had to establish a third team in order to attempt to satisfy as many players as he could. He had a Varsity Team, Junior Varsity Team, and a Freshmen Team.

"This may have been the only four-year institution in America with three teams," Darnall said. "Needless to say, not all fifty-five players were happy."

Jim Barnhart, sports editor of the Bloomington *The Pantagraph*, wrote an article entitled "Name any town—Darnall has been there." It described Dave's amazing recruitment feat of forty-eight new student-athletes to Eureka College. Portions read:

If Eureka College basketball coach Dave Darnall hasn't made it to your hometown, just relax. He'll be along any day.

The Marco Polo of Illinois college basketball, Darnall has worn out six lifetime pens signing basketball recruits.

Darnall has brushed more highway dirt out of his clothes than you've driven on.

The human road atlas has put 15,000 miles on his car this past school year just contacting high school basketball players.

Forty-eight of those players have said they'll be at Eureka College when school starts later this summer. All but five are from Illinois.

Even more amazing is that Eureka College has 160 incoming freshmen this year and 110 of them are football or basketball players. There'll also be 25 transfer students. Darnall and football coach Tom Hosier have done their homework . . .

Don't get the idea the Woodford County school is going to be an athletic factory. Less than 24 percent of those athletes will be majoring in physical education.

The best things in life may be free but not at Eureka College.

There is no free board and room; not even free tuition.

"We don't have any scholarships at all," said Darnall.

"Some are paying their own way; some are on Illinois state scholarships; some are on opportunity grants; and some will work their way through . . ."

Darnall promises nothing but an opportunity to play.

"Academically, we're very strong," said Dave. "If we have some who see they don't have the ability to play, we hope they'll stay in school and get their education . . ."

The 33-year-old Darnall, who was born and reared in Normal and who lived there all his youth except for four years he spent at Argenta High School, doesn't back off from contacting any athlete.

"I realize there's a certain type of player I can't get," said Darnall. "Players like Chris Schroeder of Roxana and Brad Droy of Triad, but I still contact these kids because some year I might get lucky and get one . . ."

According to Darnall, Eureka College is not going to run before it can walk. "We have to build a winning tradition before we worry about a tough schedule," said Darnall.

Nor does Darnall see a continual mushrooming in the school's enrollment figures. "The philosophy is that the college doesn't want to get too big," said Dave. "We like to have small classes and a personal relationship with the students," said Dave. "You get too large and you lose that. We're not out for just numbers; we'll stay at a certain level . . ."

I can recall Darnall taking his first coaching job at Stanford.

This department knew he was a winner when he stopped in at *The Pantagraph* and asked what we wanted from him in the way of news. He wanted to know when he could call and what he could call about. That is the first and only time any college graduate has done that. At that age, he knew public relations is about 50 percent of coaching.

Dave Darnall has never had a bad press and Eureka College is reaping the benefits.

A full-page picture of the fifty-five players that reported to Darnall's first official practice appeared in the school's newspaper. An article accompanying the picture was entitled "Eureka! A Bumper Crop."

"That it was," Darnall said. "Just what we needed to turn the program around and get the first winning season in eight years."

Darnall's recruiting efforts were not overlooked by college President Ira Langston. The president sent a letter to his coach complimenting him on his recruiting feats. The letter read:

"Eureka! A Bumper Crop"

Dear Mr. Darnall:

Today I expect to get the official report on opening fall admissions at Eureka College. We already know that it will be a good report and it will be so to a great extent because of the tremendous energy, intelligence and effort which you invested in the process. Your work has been of a kind and at a level to be recognized and rewarded by a bonus. Unfortunately for us all, we have no funds for investment, worthy though it would be and so well deserving as you are. Even so, I wanted to take this method to assure you and your colleagues who worked in admissions of my very substantial appreciation for the outstanding job, which you have done.

I know admissions efforts were only a means to a larger goal for you and that is as it should be. Be assured now of my best wishes for a great season of basketball for you and the team.

Sincerely,
Ira W. Langston
President

Darnall stressed when he interviewed for the position of coach that he would establish a hospitality room at the State Basketball Tournament. That recruiting tool proved very beneficial for Darnall and Eureka College.

Darnall reserved a suite at the Howard Johnson Motor Lodge in Urbana where the Illinois State Basketball Tournament was held at the U of I Assembly Hall. The Eureka College's hospitality room was located down the hall from the Illinois Basketball Coaches Association's hospitality room. Dave got to meet numerous coaches while serving them snacks and cold drinks. Darnall felt he could "kill two birds with one stone." His room's placement meant that most coaches walked by Eureka College's room on their way to the IBCA's. Darnall sent an "acquaintance" letter to every high school coach in the state inviting them to the Eureka's hospitality room. Dave also invited any of their senior student-athletes to attend a hospitality time for them in the mornings prior to the start of the afternoon sessions. He sent personal letters to any player from whom he had received a basketball questionnaire. The number was over a hundred.

"One of the first players to take advantage of this invitation was future Hall of Fame member and former assistant Eureka College coach, Stan Prosser," said Dave. "I still remember the skinny, long-legged kid walking through the door. His height really impressed me. There was not much room between his head and the top of the door frame."

Coach Darnall attributes the hospitality rooms as a major factor influencing the number of student-athletes who enrolled at Eureka to play basketball over his first several years of coaching. "With the help of Hearne, Traister, Assistant Coach Paul Brown, and player representative Gregg Johnson, we were pretty thorough and had the right combination to be successful," Darnall said. Needless to say, the nights at the tournament were very short for the Eureka College recruiters.

161

Eureka College was a member of the National Association of Intercollegiate Athletics. The NCAA prohibited some of this type of off-campus recruiting. The coaches' hospitality room was an annual event until Eureka College also joined the NCAA in 1978. Eureka then became dual members of both national associations and had to follow the strictest rules of both organizations. The "open-hour reception" for prospective student-athletes followed the guidelines and continued for numerous years.

The early coaches' receptions provided Darnall the opportunity to meet some future longtime coaching friends and camp coaches. A few of them were Allen Pickering, Roger Smith, Maury Hough, Tom Cirks, Larry Rosenthal, and Gary Carlton.

Included in the large 1975-1976 recruiting class were two former Momence players, Jerome Westbrooks and Darryl Walker. Westbrooks, who was a junior when Darnall left Momence, became a professional basketball player and teacher in Ireland. He has since joined teammate, Stan Prosser, in the Eureka College Athletic Hall of Fame.

Walker played two years for Dave at Momence before furthering his education at Illinois State University. He transferred to Eureka after a year at ISU. The summer prior to his enrollment, Walker got himself into serious trouble. That was uncharacteristic of Darryl. His family turned to the Darnalls for help. Darryl's father had been ill for quite some time, and his mother was confused as to what to do. She called Dave and Bonnie for assistance. Darryl revealed his astonishing story told here to emphasize the togetherness and caring the Darnalls had fostered.

After my first year at ISU, I returned home and began to look for a summer job. After a few days of job hunting, I received a phone call from my old high school coach asking me to transfer to Eureka College and play basketball. I told him that I really liked ISU but would think about it. The thought of playing for a small college didn't sit well with me, but it would give me a chance to get back on the hardwood. I had the entire summer to think it over so I put it aside and continued to look for a job.

The year was 1974 and a new steel fabrication company had opened its doors and was hiring in large numbers. I filled out an application and was called for a physical examination. After the exam, the physician sat across from me, shook his head and said, "Son, you have to stop burning the candle at both ends." He told me my heart rate and blood pressure were too high. He and I both knew that my exam told a very clear story of the lifestyle I was living. My year at ISU had been divided into studying hard and living in the fast lane with an equal amount of tenacity. Rather than face the facts, I became angry at the doctor and blamed him for my not being hired.

Little did I know but all the pieces were in place for the biggest fall of my life. I left the doctor's office and got into my car, destination unknown. As I rode around, I saw a kid who had transferred to Momence two years before I graduated. We spent the next few days together and decided to drive from Illinois to California and back. We had no money between us and had no intentions of doing anything legal to cover the expenses. Approximately two weeks after we decided to go on this wild and reckless escapade, we found ourselves in a Wisconsin jail.

I was eighteen years old and was facing several years in a state prison. Four weeks prior to this time, I had just completed my first year of college with a grade point average that ranked me in the top half of my class. I had never seen the inside of a jail cell and never imagined that I would. Within an hour after being arrested, my partner in crime and I were separated. Eventually, I was allowed to make a phone call. I phoned my mother and told her the news. This hurt her deeply. Once my mother calmed down somewhat, I instructed her to contact Coach Darnall. It was obvious to me that I was in a jam that was too tight for me to get out of alone. I needed someone with a mature, level head that would stick by me. Coach Darnall turned out to be much more than a basketball coach. He and Bonnie became a comfort to my mother and also stood by her.

As the weeks went by with my eyes never seeing the sun rise or set, I was able to get a message to my partner. The message was to meet me at church service on Sunday. When Sunday came around, he was there, and we got a chance to talk. As soon as I saw him, I knew he had changed or perhaps I was seeing a part of him that I had never noticed before. To my amazement, my old high school friend had become comfortable in the environment we found ourselves in. My life was at a crossroad and I, like my friend, had to decide what direction it would head in. Our meeting at church was the last time I saw him.

The days passed at a snail's pace, and the court appearances dragged on. Finally, it was time for my last court appearance. I entered the court room and was directed to my seat. As I approached my seat I raised my head just long enough to acknowledge my mother, two of my sisters, the girl who would one day become my wife, and Coach Darnall and Bonnie. My father was not there. He had suffered several strokes and a battery of heart attacks; as a result my dad was confined to a wheelchair and his mental state had deteriorated to an extent that rendered him to be only a shell of his former self. Coach Darnall had provided my lawyer with a copy of my transcripts, and a personal letter from a prominent judge who was very influential in Central Illinois at the time. The judge ordered me to stand and face the bench as I was sentenced. My full attention was on this man who sat before me in his black judicial robe. He reviewed a stack of papers in front of him. His head slowly raised and our eyes met. He began to speak.

163

"I have had many men standing before me charged with the crime you have committed," he said as we continued to stare into each other's eyes. "All the other men who I have seen who have done what you have had criminal records that covered several pages. You, on the other hand, had no record at all before now. You went straight to the top and committed a crime that everyone graduates to after a life of crime."

The judge broke the stare and dipped his head as he shook it from side to side. When his head returned to its original position, his scornful eyes showed contempt and condemnation of my actions. He began to speak, "Your grades at this point are better than mine were . . . I sentence you to seven years!"

The words he spoke seemed to snatch life from my body. The courtroom went black, and my legs could no longer hold the weight of my body. As I started to sink, I grabbed the table in front of me to keep from falling. My head was spinning like a top as I heard the judge say, "Stayed sentence, five years probation."

My attorney gripped my arm and began pulling me back to an erect position. The light in the courtroom once again began to register and objects in the room came back into view. My legs remembered what they were designed to do, and they began to counteract the force of gravity. I am not sure whether the judge waited for me to gain my composure or if my fainting spell took place between the natural pause of his speech. Nevertheless, he began to talk again.

"I am not giving you probation because I think you deserve it. I am doing it because of those people back there." The judge motioned toward Coach Darnall and my mother. I didn't turn to look because I knew my mother was going through pure hell, and I did not want to see it. The judge's attention turned from Coach and my mother back to me as he said, "I am releasing you to these people. I have a letter in front of me from a judge who is willing to take personal responsibility for you. You will return to Illinois and report to the local probation department."

In closing, the judge said, "Darryl, rarely does someone come before me with people who care about him the way these people care about you. You are fortunate to have such people in your life. I hope you realize what you have and conduct yourself accordingly. Court dismissed!"

Once I returned to Illinois, I went home to see my father. Because of his poor health, we were worried that if we told him of my experience, the shock might cause him to take a turn for the worse. He was never told. After a short visit with my father, I headed off for Eureka.

I did transfer to Eureka College and, yes, became a part of the basketball program. It wasn't until later that I came to realize that none of what Coach Darnall had done was really about basketball. It was about a wonderful man helping a kid whom needed his help. I can never repay him for what he did. What I can do is to continue to help others in the same spirit that I was once helped.

With the cooperation of Admission Director George Hearne and then presiding Woodford County Judge Sam Harrod, Darryl was given an unbelievable second chance. He is now a Eureka College alum and has gone on to prove his worth. He has spent many years in the social work field dedicating himself to helping others in need. The other fellow involved was sentenced to quite a few years in prison.

A future outstanding player among Darnall's fifty-five new basketball candidates was Reggie Holmes. The coach did not talk to Holmes before his visit to the college. Darnall said, "Reggie is by far the most outstanding 'walk-on' I have ever had. He went on to be a NAIA All-District player and a member of the college's Athletic Hall of Fame."

Holmes' high school teammate, Tony "T" Moore, joined him a year later. Moore, in his own right, had an excellent college basketball career and served on Darnall's camp staff for years. "In all my years of coaching, 'T' and 'Little Butch' Cassidy have stayed in touch more than any other of my former players. In fact, Bonnie would always say when the phone rang after midnight, it was probably 'T.' "

Darnall's recruiting efforts were not overlooked by the future president of the United States. Mr. Reagan sent Dave a letter October 1, 1975, complementing him on his recruiting feats. This was the first of several correspondences Darnall was fortunate to receive throughout his career from the president.

Dave's second full year of recruiting provided twenty new student-athletes for the college. He knew some would decide that playing college ball was too demanding and time consuming, and therefore, would exit the program. For others, the experience of being part of the team was rewarding enough to "stick it out." Those who were patient and willing to work usually benefited. Coach Darnall told all recruits, "Each player has an equal opportunity to make the team. There is no one getting money to play ball. Nobody has an athletic scholarship. Sure, the upperclassmen have more experience, but if a freshman is better, he'll play. I owe nothing to anyone. Everybody is equal."

Dave's philosophy was to play the best players regardless of their year in school. "At the college level, the name of the game is to win," Darnall said. "I demand discipline, hard work, and teamwork. Because of my conservative background and wanting to control everything, I know everyone couldn't play for me. Players must have good attitudes," Coach concluded.

RONALD REAGAN

SUITE 812
10960 WILSHIRE BOULEVARD
LOS ANGELES, CALIFORNIA 90024

October 1, 1975

Coach Dave Darnall
Eureka College
Eureka, Illinois

Dear Dave:

Already the Red Devils are facing another season of basketball. I hear you have a good group of returning lettermen as well as some added height on the team this year. Sounds good!

Just wanted to wish you luck on your upcoming schedule and tell you to keep up that team spirit. I must say, with 53 out for basketball this year, you've apparently generated a lot of it already. Keep up the good work and 'all my best wishes for the year ahead.

Sincerely,

RONALD REAGAN

The Nike Coaching Clinic held in St. Louis was one of the largest in the Midwest. The 1976 season now completed, Dave attended it. The attendance fee for the two-day affair was $25.00. Darnall knew Eureka College had a limited recruiting budget, so he decided to bypass the actual speaking sessions. Instead, he mixed with the coaches at the "smokers." Dave spent

Friday night and most of Saturday talking to high school coaches. Public relations was the name of the game. The Clinic provided a source where he was able to obtain names of players to contact later. With Bobby Knight of Indiana and Johnny Orr of Michigan as keynote speakers, the Clinic was highly attended. Four hundred is probably a modest guess.

Knight was the first speaker on Friday night. He started around 7:00 P.M. and was to go until approximately 8:00 P.M. Orr was to follow Knight. The oral presentations were given in a large banquet room with several doors leading into it. Most coaches were seated, while Dave stood in one of the doorways. The doorman left the door open to the hallway after Dave explained that his college was small and on a limited budget. He could not afford the fee with all the other expenses such as the motel room, transportation, and food. The doorman was sympathetic and allowed him to stand in the entrance with it being the only door left open. Darnall had just used his talent to recruit.

An hour passed when the Clinic Director interrupted the fiery coach, informing him that it was time for the next speaker. Ten more minutes passed before he again was reminded of the time schedule. Knight, noticeably upset, announced that if anyone wanted to hear more from him, he would continue in a smaller room down the hall. At least half of the audience followed the Indiana coach to the other room. Coach Orr was introduced to the remaining coaches in the half-empty room. The young college coach, in amazement, had learned that Bobby Knight had "balls." "How could you do that to a fellow conference coach?" Darnall said to himself as he followed the parade of coaches to the smaller room. He again stood in the open doorway. The gathering became a question-and-answer session. Coaches were allowed to ask basic questions, most of which the answers were already known. After about fifteen minutes of the boring questions, Darnall raised his hand from the back of the room. "Coach Knight, you mentioned that your kids don't smoke or drink. What would happen if you had an older player who was married and he had wine with his wife at Christmas?" There was no answer. The question was passed over. "Next," said the assistant helping to pick questions from the group.

The session continued with Knight in a comfortable position leaning back with his legs stretched out, feet crossed on a small table in front of him. After twenty minutes or so, Darnall again raised his hand. The assistant pointed to the standing coach in the doorway. "Coach, I'm from the Bloomington-Normal area and knew Bob Bender and his dad pretty well," Darnall said. "Why is he leaving Indiana?"

Oops! Extremely upset over the asked question, Knight shoved his chair back and jumped to his feet. "Who are you?" Knight shouted. "Some damn reporter?"

Darnall replied, "No, just a small college coach trying to be like you." A couple of questions later, the session ended.

Coach Darnall would definitely never be invited to be one of Coach Knight's assistants, but he did make a hit with several coaches attending the session. "Pretty good question," one coach said.

"Yeah," Darnall replied, "but I don't think he was wanting those kind of questions."

Dave spent the rest of the evening with the other coaches relaxing. There was very little sleep for the young, eager Eureka coach. Some names of players Darnall was able to obtain that night ended up being Red Devil players. The trip was well worth it.

President Langston was extremely happy with the way the basketball program was heading and the number of new students it was providing the college following the two outstanding recruiting years. The president expressed his satisfaction with Coach Darnall in a memo to the second year coach. Portions of the memo read, "We are much pleased with the progress which is being made in your department under your energetic and resource-ful leadership. Be assured of our best wishes."

At the time of the memo, Dave did not realize the up-coming school year, 1976-1977, was going to be Ira Langston's last year as president. Serving twenty-three years as the college's president, Langston retired. It was truly a well-deserved rest, but selfishly disheartening for Darnall. The first three years of Darnall's employment at the college were quite enjoyable, very little stress. That would not be the case over the next several years.

Darnall knew recruiting was the "lifeline" to success. He used every "tool" he could—holding coaches' clinics, directing camps, hosting post-game parties, organizing hospitality rooms at the State Basketball Tournament, and attend-ing coaching clinics were just a few. The high school coach was the key to suc-cessful recruiting. Dave wanted to "rub elbows" with as many as possible.

One of Coach Darnall's twenty new recruits for his 1976-1977 team was a six-foot-two guard from Mendota High School named Tom Cassidy. Cassidy was the fourth youngest of a family of fourteen children. A good Catholic family with all the values every family would like to possess. The Darnall family became good friends with the Cassidys. Darnall immediately gave Tom the nickname "Butch." He could not believe Tom had not acquired the name before. The nickname stayed with him. However, after his younger brother also came to Eureka, Tom became known as "Big Butch."

Dave remembered sitting in the big old two-story brick house visiting with Mr. Cassidy and Tom. In the background, listening to every word, was the youngest Cassidy offspring, Jeff. Having a cold beer with the senior Cassidy, Darnall went through his patent home-visit speech. Darnall ended his talk with the last statement he always told the prospective student-athlete.

"Tom," said Dave, "I want you to come to Eureka College to get your education. Something might happen where you might never play an once of basketball, but no one can take your education away from you."

An hour and a half later, Tom agreed to visit the college. A date was set when he and his father could make the hour and a half trip to Eureka.

One statement Coach Darnall will always remember Mr. Cassidy making to his son, "I don't care what college you choose, but whichever one you pick that is where you are going to stay."

Dave felt that showed a lot of class. Mr. Cassidy explained, "Too many parents just let their kids do what they want to do. If they don't like something, they just leave. That's not the real world."

Darnall's top recruit that year was one of his former Momence High School players, Hughley Blanton. Blanton was the sophomore sensation on Dave's excellent last high school team. The Darnalls felt Hughley was "like one of ours." They had developed a close relationship with "Spanky," Westbrooks, and Blanton. Hughley, actually, had first seen Eureka College when he helped move his former coach into his new home in Eureka. He stayed a couple days with the Darnalls and had a chance to meet Red Devil Captain Kip Blakesley.

"Instead of just saying 'yes' and coming to Eureka College, Hughley made recruiting him difficult," Dave said. "He made me work awfully hard. Several trips back to Momence and numerous phone calls."

Blanton had many college offers since he was selected a Class A All-State player. His decision got down to NCAA Morehead State or follow his high school coach to Eureka College. "We finally won," said Darnall. "It was a relief. The recruiting effort was worth it, not only because he was a great Eureka College player and a NAIA All-District player, but because Bonnie and I had the chance to spend four more years with him."

It was also during this year that Dave made one of the most unusual recruiting trips of his twenty-year tenure as a college basketball coach. That, however, ended up not being for a player, but for a student administrative assistant. Coach Darnall was recruiting a player from Notre Dame High School in Quincy. George Hearne informed Dave of another student from the same school that had shown interest in Eureka College. Hearne wanted Darnall to speak to Bruce Bangert while visiting Notre Dame. Bruce was interested in majoring in communications in college.

Just minutes before Darnall was to leave for the three-hour trip on an old two-lane road, he was informed that the basketball player was no longer interested in Eureka College. Hearne still wanted Dave to speak to Bangert, but Dave wanted to spend his time on basketball players. Unenthusiastically, Darnall made the grueling trip to Quincy. He was originally scheduled to return to Eureka that evening. That didn't happen! Several hours and about six beers later, the Eureka coach decided he'd better find a motel in Quincy and return the next day.

Bruce recalled Dave's recruiting trip this way.

> Meeting Dave was, at best, a coincidence. Dave was recruiting a friend of mine in high school. When my friend decided to go to Kansas, Dave had to drive three hours to talk to a kid who wouldn't play ball. He planned on talking to my family and myself for 15 minutes. Dave can't talk for just 15 minutes. My dad offered him a beer. Three hours later, my dad decides this would be a good place for us to visit. One week later, I'm going to Eureka. Dave's only non-player recruit—by mistake!

To this day, the Bangerts and Darnalls are good friends. For years after Bruce graduated in 1981, the Bangerts returned to Eureka yearly for at least one of Dave's basketball games and post-game parties. Bruce described those trips.

> Trips to Eureka for my dad and myself were on the same level as Christmas—you look forward to it every year with great anticipation. Every year since I graduated, except one when Dad broke his hip, it was time to go back to where it all began. A trip to the game and a trip to Bonnie and Dave's house. Every time we went to Eureka, we were around friends. Friends that we would have for life. It's funny, when Dave announced that he was retiring, my dad wondered, "What are we going to do after a game now?" The home on Pearson Street is home to thousands of people. It's the reason Dad and I have been going back for all these years. It's kind of funny. An unscheduled trip by Dave in 1977 to my house has kept my dad and I making scheduled trips to his house, year after year.

Bruce gained the nickname "Preacher" because he volunteered to give the pre-meal prayer at the new student orientation picnic. The nickname has stayed with him over the years. As a matter of fact, many of his fellow students didn't know his real first name. Oh, yes, Bruce also became a valuable member of the basketball program as an administrative assistant. Dave's trip was not in vain.

Over the years, some student-athletes were recruited to play basketball, but after a year or two on the team, decided for various reasons to give up playing to become part of Darnall's administrative staff. That provided great experience for those wanting to become coaches. Several students have even come to Eureka College planning on helping in the basketball program. "Spanky," "Preacher," Kirk Doehring, Scott Raycraft, and Dave's first administrative assistant-student manager, Dennis Dighton were a few. Dighton was a senior when Darnall arrived on campus. Yes, he is the same Dennis Dighton that served as Darnall's assistant coach for the last nine years of his tenure. Dighton then succeeded Darnall as the head mentor upon Dave's retirement from the game.

The 1978-1979 recruiting year brought about one of the most publicized players in the area to enroll at Eureka College. Mike Sain was a five-foot-ten, 135-pound point-guard from Decatur Eisenhower High School. Sain concluded his high school career by being named Second Team All-State behind Isaiah Thomas. Mike also came from a very athletic family. His father had been an outstanding baseball player in his time. His cousin, Bill Madlock, who was raised as a sibling by Mike's parents, was a three-time major league batting champion and an All-Star Game MVP. Two of Mike's older sisters are married to former star athletes from Decatur and another sister married Jimmy Parker, brother of former Pittsburgh Pirate star Dave Parker. Mike just continued the "pattern."

Mike had been recruited by some eighty universities and colleges throughout the country. Coach Darnall spotted Sain while he was playing in the Christmas Holiday Tournament in Normal. This was the same tournament where Darnall had spotted Tom Cassidy the year before. Coach Darnall had a chance to meet and speak briefly with Mike after the game.

Dave's assistant, Kip Blakesley, was with him at the time. Kip's first reaction was, "He looks awfully small. I don't think he can make it."

Dave replied, "Yeah, but he can shoot the rock and is really quick."

Blakesley, himself, had been a six-foot-two point guard for Darnall and could shoot and pass, but quick he was not. Mike proved Kip wrong.

"Maybe that's why Blakesley is out of coaching and in business," said Darnall. "Just kidding!"

Dave spent the remainder of the season attending Sain's games when his own team was not playing. Blakesley attended the games of the other student-athletes they were trying to recruit. Coach Darnall would approach Sain after the other college coaches finished talking to him. There were always three or four coaches in line to speak to the All-Stater. Dave "batted clean-up," and they would normally proceed to the Sain's home after the game. There, Dave could also visit with Sain's parents. Mr. Sain and Coach usually enjoyed a few cold beers as they conversed either about Mike's future or just had general chitchat. It was during those visits that Dave and the Sains developed a genuine friendship. The late Wardie Sain was a very wise gentleman and insisted that Mike consider all factors about the college he would choose, not just the basketball program. It was said that Mike was told to "go where you are going to be happy, not where you are going to be used."

Mike, who went on to be inducted into Eureka College's Athletic Hall of Fame, explained why he chose to play for Coach Darnall and attend Eureka College. "Coach Darnall was the only coach I truly trusted. My trust grew the first night he visited my home, and my dad offered him a Stag beer, and he sat there and drank it! Any man that could drink a Stag beer—you have to taste it—and keep a straight face had to be okay. My dad agreed. Coach didn't lie and say I'd start now. I respected him when he said, 'If you earn it, you'll play.' That was all I needed to hear."

Darnall recalled a side-story to Sain's recruiting. On one trip to Decatur, Dave took two of his former Momence players who were currently on his Eureka College team with him. Jerome Westbrooks and Hughley Blanton were watching not only the action on the floor, but also had spotted two nice-looking girls across the gym. When the game ended, Darnall's boys wanted to speak to the girls they had been watching. The college players started to walk toward where their coach and Mike were talking. To their surprise, the two cute girls were also heading to the same destination. Sain continued the story, "Hell, Jerome and Hughley didn't care if I could play or not. They had spotted two 'chicks' they wanted to 'hit on.' They were my forty-year-old married sisters. Those guys didn't even know my number until half-time."

After meeting Jerome and Hughley, Mike introduced his married sisters, Juanita and Paulette, to Coach Darnall. To the dismay and shock of Jerome and Hughley, the good-looking gals they had been staring at all evening were married with children. Sain, Westbrooks, and Blanton became good friends at Eureka College.

The 1981-1982 recruiting year produced the first brother act for Darnall. Jeff Cassidy, Tom's little brother and the youngest of the Cassidy clan, followed in his older brother's footsteps. Unfortunately, Tom did not get to play on the same team as "Little Butch" as he graduated in 1980.

Jeff gave his memories of being recruited by Darnall:

> Since my brother had played for Coach Darnall before me, my family and I were already a part of the "Eureka Family" when I was recruited to play for Eureka College. Coach had already sold himself and the program to my father and since I was not "highly recruited" by many schools with the caliber of the program at Eureka I was more than eager to sign on.
>
> My father made it clear that once I was in place at EC there would be no "jumping ship" and my entire career would take place at EC. To this day I'm not sure whether he respected coach that much or he knew how many credits and dollars could be lost during a transfer. Seriously, once I committed to Eureka my father basically said, "Mr. Darnull (he's terrible with names) will be in charge of you for the next four years and he will let me know if he has any problems with you. Got it?" I got it!

My father is old school, and he was very impressed with Coach Darnall from the start. Dave visited our family several times during the recruiting of my brother Tom and each time his relationship grew stronger with my father and mother. I'll always remember how impressed my father was of Coach Darnall's office upon his first visit to Reagan Center. Coach had newspaper clippings all over the walls of his office, and I mean taped all over the place. The articles were about previous big games; the signing of some all-state player to EC; the signing of some no name kid from some no name town to EC; and a whole potpourri of other amusing articles. To many it would have given the appearance of a man who did not know how to decorate. My father, however, knew right away that this was not a pretentious man, but a man who took great pride in all of his players and their accomplishments no matter if he was an all-stater highly recruited by big schools, an inner city player out of Chicago, or a hick from down state.

Dave, accompanied by Bonnie or an assistant coach, attended for years the Chicago Athletes for Better Education scrimmages held on a Saturday at Loyola University. The scrimmage games started around 8:00 A.M. and ran continuously on an hourly basis until mid-afternoon. There were at least three games being played simultaneously. Dave described the chaos, "The players wore paper numbers. Following their games, many took them off. With so many college coaches and players roaming around, a lot of confusion took place. I found it extremely difficult to locate, wait my turn, and then finally talk to any prospect. There may have been three or four players I wanted to talk to running all over the place and talking to other coaches. By the time I left the place after being there all day, I had a major headache. It was like a big "meat market."

Bonnie or whoever went with Coach watched the on-going scrimmage, spotting players for Dave while he tried to talk with players from a previous game. Even though it was a very stressful day for everyone, it did pay dividends. Darnall was able to recruit several good student-athletes from the events.

"Little Butch" Cassidy remembered an especially good story from a junior college "audition" day. That trip was to a series of junior college scrimmages at Eastern Illinois University in Charleston. Following one of the games, Coach and Jeff dashed to a large locker room where several of the players were dressing. Coach spotted a six-foot-three, strongly built athlete he wanted to talk to.

He began, "Hi, I'm Dave Darnall, Head Basketball Coach at Eureka College. I am interested in having you come to Eureka and play for me. We are losing several kids and need some big kids like you to help us. We are one of the top small college programs in the state and plan to remain so. Eureka College has a very unique calendar called the 'Intensive Study Program,'" Darnall ran off quickly. "What do you want to major in?"

"Coach," the young man said, "I'd really like to play for you, but I am an Eastern Illinois wrestler."

Coach was speechless and took a few seconds to compose his thoughts. "Oh, I am sorry." He then tried to escape the locker room without the other occupants seeing him. Dave quickly slid out the nearest exit. Cassidy had beaten Darnall to the corridor. Reaching the hallway himself, Dave saw "Little Butch" laughing his ass off.

"Don't say a thing," Darnall instructed. "I just screwed up."

By the time the duo returned to the gym floor, they both were laughing profusely. It became a story they have retold many times.

"Little Butch" often said that some of the best times of his college career were spent on the road with Coach Darnall. "He would have me drive so that he could get more time in on those damn note cards he always carried. Once we were close to our final destination, he would begin to 'brainstorm' the recruiting session. Who else would be recruiting the kid? Was there any connection between the recruit and EC already? Was it going to be more important to sell the player or the parent? And countless other things that Coach would come up with. No angle was overlooked on getting the inside track with a recruit. Finally before we would actually go to the visit, he would have me pull-off at a gas station or café in town to check himself out. Was his hair okay? No dandruff on the coat? Was I presentable?"

The 1982-1983 recruiting campaign brought about several outstanding players. Not only did Darnall have success at the Chicago scrimmage, but he also spotted a Chicago area player while attending the prestigious Pekin Christmas Holiday Tournament. It was Greg Nunn, currently a successful State Farm agent in Seattle and seen on national television in an advertisement for his company. He was equally successful on the basketball court. Known on campus as "Sugar," Nunn became a two-time NAIA All-District 20 player and a member of the college's Athletic Hall of Fame.

Rick Taylor teamed with Nunn to perhaps become the best backcourt duo in the college's history. The six-foot-two guard's recruiting story is one Dave often talks about. "It all started over Thanksgiving Vacation. I went to Edwardsville, a three-hour drive, to watch a skinny kid from Alton play. The weather was terrible. Following the game, I went into Alton's dressing room to talk to Rick Taylor. He had returned a basketball questionnaire that I had sent him earlier. Therefore, I felt he might be interested in our program. I approached Coach McAfoos and introduced myself. I asked if I could say hello to Taylor. Coach McAfoos replied, 'Rick is a major college player. You'll be wasting your time.' So I went out to my car and drove all the way home. What a wasted eight hours I thought."

It was the beginning of April when Dave got a phone call. "Hello," Coach Darnall said.

"Hello, this is Rick Taylor," the person on the other end replied.

"Rick, how you doing?" Coach Darnall said. "Wait a minute; I need to go to the other phone." Dave, forgetting who Rick Taylor was, started looking through his basketball questionnaires to find "Taylor." Upon finding his questionnaire, Coach Darnall picked up the phone to continue the conversation. "Rick, what's happening?" Darnall said excitedly, "It's good to hear from you. I have been wondering what you were going to do next year."

"That's why I called you," Rick replied. "I have three full-ride scholarships at large schools, but I think I want to go to a small college and play right away. Would you still be interested in me?"

Darnall nearly fell out of bed. That's where he made most of his recruiting calls. He said, "I think you can help our team next year. I would like to come down and visit with you and your family."

"That would be okay," Taylor replied. Darnall then got directions to Rick's home and set up the home visit for two days later.

Coach Darnall, accompanied by his assistant Rod Todd, enthusiastically made the three-hour trip to Alton, located across the river from St. Louis. Dave knew if he did a good job recruiting he could possibly get an "impact" player. Taylor had the talent needed for a team's appearance in the National Tournament.

Darnall introduced himself and Coach Todd to the family upon their arrival at the apartment where Rick, his mother, and a sister lived. The coach, mastering his recruiting speech, spent nearly two hours informing the Taylors about Eureka College and his basketball program. Dave convinced Rick to fill out an application form before he left. This was needed before he could be admitted or considered for financial aid. Darnall returned to campus feeling confident with the job they had done and thought he had a chance of getting him.

A few days later, Taylor was admitted to Eureka College. Dave returned to Alton, this time taking Rick his admittance letter. Now it was up to Taylor. Darnall convinced Rick and his mother that Eureka College was the best place for him to further his education and play basketball. Rick signed the admissions "Letter of Intent" to enroll in the college and gave his new coach a partial payment on the required deposit. That was the first time Darnall received a deposit from a recruit without the student-athlete visiting the campus. Rick planned to make his first visit to Eureka College during Coach Darnall's basketball camp in early June. The delighted coach made several phone calls back to the local media announcing Rick's signing with Eureka College. That announcement gave the institution some good press. It was a huge feather for Darnall's program.

Then two weeks came and went and no Rick Taylor. Coach Darnall called Rick's home continuously, but there was no answer. Some three months later, still no contact with Rick Taylor. Dave finally decided Taylor was not going to attend Eureka College after all.

Four days prior to the start of the school year, Darnall decided to make one more attempt to reach Taylor. The skeptical coach made the phone call on a Thursday. "Hello," Coach Darnall said. "Rick, is this you? Where have you been?"

"Coach," Rick responded, "you'll never believe what has happened to us."

Rick went on to explain that a few weeks after he had signed to enroll at Eureka, his mother, sister, and he visited some relatives in Ohio. They took a bus. There was a tragic wreck. The bus caught fire and burned. His sister was killed, his mother was severely injured, and he received several cuts.

Darnall felt terrible for Rick, but asked if he was still planning to come to Eureka. Taylor said that he was. He got on a train Saturday morning to make his first trip to Eureka and the campus. Rick went on to become a tremendous asset to Darnall's program and earned NAIA All-District 20 player honor his senior year. He became "Ice" for his resemblance to NBA superstar George Gervin. Thus, "Sugar and Ice"—Greg Nunn and Rick Taylor.

There was one recruiting trip to Chicago that Coach Darnall was not anxious to make. He had scheduled a home visit at Cabrini Green. The recruit was concerned with Darnall's welfare and told the coach he would meet him at a particular corner about two blocks away at 6:00 P.M. Arriving a little early, Dave noticed a parking space on the opposite side of the street near the designated corner. Driving on, looking for a place to turn around, he came to an alley. Pulling over to the side of the street, he notice two women approaching the car. One displayed a bare breast. Dave was shocked! He turned into the alleyway to turn around. One of the women began to open the door. Darnall waved her off as he began to back up into the street and head in the direction he had just come. Yelling vulgar words, the "lady of the street" flipped the startled driver "the bird." Upon returning to the designated spot, Darnall picked up the young man. The recruit directed him to the housing showing him where to park his car. The location was an area where very few white people lived.

Since it was early summer, Darnall passed by many residents sitting along the apartments' concrete outdoor walkway as they made their way to the student-athlete's apartment. He was very uncomfortable in the unknown surrounding. "Hello. Hi. How are you?" Coach said as he passed the many sitting residents. There were very few vocal responses but several nods.

Darnall finished his visit with the prospect and his family. He then headed back to his car with the escort of the recruit for security. On the way back, they noticed several police cars. Dave felt very uneasy. This was a long way from Eureka in many ways!

Coach had scheduled another home visit approximately fifteen miles away. Upon reaching the second recruit's home, Dave was informed by the mother that Bonnie had called and wanted him to return the call. Darnall normally left his wife with a schedule of his home visits, including the name of the recruit, the address, and phone number. This was done in case of an emergency at home.

He called Bonnie collect. She wanted to know if he was all right. Dave replied, "Why?"

Bonnie said, "There was a news report on TV that two people were killed at Cabrini Green around 6:30 P.M. I just wanted to make sure you were okay."

"I did feel uncomfortable," Dave confessed. "I noticed several police cars with flashing lights when I was leaving. It will be nice to get the hell out of here and back to Eureka."

Both prospects attended Eureka College. The second recruit graduated and is a very successful businessman in the Chicago area. The first lasted only a few weeks. Dave's visit to Cabrini Green was both his first and last trip to the controversial housing project.

A recruiting trip that keeps coming to Darnall's mind involves his good friend Dave Gilliland when he was coaching at Brussels, Illinois.

Brussels is located in the southwestern corner of Illinois, near where the Illinois and Mississippi rivers join at Alton. The high school had an enrollment of approximately seventy students. The team was led by senior center Dave Tepen. Darnall thought Tepen would be an excellent recruit for Eureka College. He scheduled a home visit to meet the Tepens. The only problem was that there was no easy way to reach their home. The Tepens lived out "in the hills."

"Most of the students lived outside of the town," Darnall said. "There really wasn't much of a town, just a school building, Catholic Church, a distinguished old hotel-restaurant, a couple of bars, and a post office. They were all located along the one and only road that ran through the village. There was also an old, frequently visited bar located out in the county called the "Meppen Tap." That is where Darnall, Mr. Tepen, Dave Tepen, Coach Gilliland, and Dennis Dighton ended up spending most of the night after leaving the Tepen home. Dighton at that time was an assistant coach to Coach Gilliland.

Coach Gilliland loves to tell the story of the recruitment of Dave Tepen.

The only way in and out of Brussels is by ferryboat or a bridge at the northern part of the county. Not many coaches get here. We had several tremendous players on a squad that went all the way to the Sweet Sixteen. Our center on that team was a young man named David Tepen. He was six-foot-six, dominated the boards, and most of all, was a super person with a heart of gold. Needless to say, Dave Darnall wanted "Tep" as a Eureka Red Devil.

Now, there aren't too many places that Dave Darnall hasn't been in this state, but Brussels in Calhoun County was one of them. Dave made a preliminary trip to see this place others and I call "the Kingdom," and he immediately made a connection to its people. One of the first places that I took Dave in the county was the Barefoot Bar and Restaurant in Hardin, right on the banks of the Illinois River. The Barefoot is known for its delectable catfish dinners and its cold Busch and Budweiser bottles of beer. In fact, a large percentage of Calhounians enjoy their beer. At this first encounter with the county for Darnall, we talked about the recruiting of Tepen, and ironically, the name of a person from Dave's past, Dennis Dighton, then a coach for us at Brussels, was mentioned. A few years later, Dennis became a major part of the Red Devil program as Dave's assistant.

Tepen and his family lived in a settlement a few miles outside of Brussels called Meppen. To get to the Tepen farm, one must travel a one-lane dirt/gravel road up into the hills and valleys. Darnall who had been to all parts of the state hung onto the dashboard as we wove and rolled up to the Tepen farm. The Tepens were and are a great family and wonderful people. Coach Darnall got his first taste of one of Meppen's favorite beers that evening, Stag. As I've seen so many times, in five minutes Darnall was like one of the Tepen family. He could recruit from the inner city of Chicago, and he could recruit in the remoteness of Calhoun County. There was instantly a good feeling between the Tepens and Coach.

Not long after Dave's initial visit to Brussels, he returned to sign Tepen to a "letter of intent" to go to Eureka College. Darnall always had a knack for making Eureka College seem like Indiana University. When he left your living room after signing one of these papers that actually had no binding power at all, you thought you were attending the greatest college in the world to play basketball.

On the night Tep signed, the news had already spread all over the county, and everyone knew that a real college coach would actually be spending the night in "the Kingdom." And for sure, everyone in Meppen and Brussels knew it. After the signing and a few Stag beers at Art Tepen's house, we proceeded to go to the Meppen Tavern, an old country bar nestled along the Calhoun cliffs. All around, folks knew that Art, Coach, and I would be there. The tiny tavern was packed, and to say the least, the beer flowed freely. Coach, at once, was a celebrity. A true college coach was in our midst. Needless to say, it was late in the evening when the whole gang left Meppen. Years later, old guys who still hang out at Meppen, talk about that night and the fun we had.

There is a sad epilogue to the Dave Tepen story. Dave did attend Eureka College and played on the basketball team for three years before transferring to Eastern Illinois University at the beginning of his senior year. Tragically, he was killed by a freak fire accident at a service station in Charleston in early November, 1986.

All of us who knew Tep, including Coach Darnall, lost a little of ourselves after that.

Darnall was able to "lay low" for a year. He felt the addition of more players for the 1984-1985 basketball season might result in morale problems on the team.

He began recruiting again in full force during the 1984-1985 school year. Heading the new crop of players was Tom Dooley, an All-State Class A player from Vandalia. Darnall spent nearly as much time recruiting Tom as he had Sain. He made numerous trips to both Dooley's basketball and baseball games. Mr. Dooley and Coach Darnall shared many beers over the years. Tom had an outstanding career at Eureka College in spite of two major injuries. He is a member of the Hall of Fame and currently a successful businessman in the Decatur area.

Darnall spent a lot of time in the Decatur area that year. Besides Dooley, he was also recruiting Jeff Wooters of Shelbyville and Mike Coffman of Niantic. When Darnall made a home visit to the Coffman's, Mike's older sister Jackie also sat in on the presentation with the rest of the family. She had been out of school for a year. After listening to what Dave had to say about Eureka College, Jackie decided she wanted to visit the campus with Mike. That turned out to be a very worthwhile recruiting trip. Mike became a fraternity brother of Tom Dooley. Both Mike and Jackie graduated from Eureka. Mike is currently a CPA in the Decatur area, and Jackie, who married Dooley in September of 1994, is an elementary teacher. "Sounds like 'all in the family,'" Darnall said.

In April of the same year, Coach attended another "meat market." Only this time it was a Junior College scrimmage. A large number of JC players were trying to find places to finish their college career. Approximately a hundred players from throughout the state participated in the all-day event held at Kankakee Junior College.

Dave was, basically, looking for one type of player. He needed a power forward who could rebound, execute the offense, and play defense against opponent's muscle men and not worry about scoring. Darnall felt he needed this player to fill the missing piece in the puzzle. An experienced power forward is what was needed to be a NAIA District 20 contender.

Following one of the scrimmage games, Dave tracked down a six-foot-six, well-built forward from DuPage Junior College named Rob Kroehnke. Darnall was able to talk "Kronk" into visiting Eureka College. Rob visited campus and liked what he saw. A couple of weeks later he "signed" to attend Eureka. Rob ended up being just what the "doctor ordered."

Dave came across a familiar name while watching the scrimmage games—Buerkett. Several years prior, he made a home visit to the Buerkett home in Hillsboro. He was recruiting Dyke who eventually attended St. Francis College in Joliet. However, younger brother Eric was also known to Darnall. He remembered him both as a young kid while talking to his older brother and as a college player for Greenville College. As a freshman, Eric had started for Conference foe Greenville. Buerkett transferred to Lincoln Land Community College after one year at the four-year institution. Darnall had been impressed with Eric's "coolness" and leadership ability while playing at Greenville. Eric decided to finish his college career at Eureka.

Darnall followed up with another excellent recruiting class for the 1986-1987 basketball season. Heading the list were All-State Class A players Brad Bickett of Ohio, Illinois, and Kevin Root of Hoopeston. Both players led their respective high school teams to the final four of the Illinois Class A State Championship. Brad and Kevin were selected on the State Class A Tournament Team. Darnall spent numerous hours recruiting the two quality players including several home visits.

Bickett, a two-time NAIA District 20 player and member of Eureka's Athletic Hall of Fame, is now a successful high school coach. He remembered Darnall's visit to his home.

> Dave, I guess, made his first visit to my family farm in Ohio in April, and it was his recruiting spiel, his talk, that really sold me on Eureka College. The things that he had to say about the College and about the Eureka College basketball family really told me that this may be the place I wanted to go. It was a small college, and I didn't know if I could be successful in a big college atmosphere. I thought that a small four-year school would be beneficial to me. My parents really pressed that they thought Dave Darnall was a good guy, and Eureka College may be the place for me. So, I chose Eureka College in the latter part of April, and I think it was a great choice for me.
>
> I look back and see how Dave got my family involved in his deals and other things he would do after the games at his house and realize how much my parents were involved. The family atmosphere of Eureka College, and the small school excitement of the basketball program that he ran was really enjoyable for me and for my family. That's what is exciting. He didn't just get me involved. He got my folks, my brother, my sister, and my nieces and nephews. Everyone just loved Eureka College basketball and that's the thing that sold his program. He worked hard at it, and that's what made Dave successful. He got players that probably no other small school could get because of his tough recruiting work. He sold Eureka College. He would talk about the steak dinners and the baked potatoes and charter buses and all the stuff Dave would sell to you. And the big arena you would get to play in and all that. He was a talker. He could sell Eureka College. He sold it to some kids that probably could've went other places.

Root is both Eureka College's single-season assist leader and career assist leader with 579. He returned to Hoopeston to become Athletic Director and Head Basketball Coach for the Cornjerkers. The successful coach should someday be inducted into the Eureka College Athletic Hall of Fame. "He was the greatest passer I saw at that time," Darnall said. "Just ask our big men. He made some of them look awfully good." He deserves a membership in the Hall.

Overnight, Eureka College basketball became known throughout Illinois and the Midwest. A NAIA National Tournament appearance provided that. Most good high school players wanted to be associated with a college program that received national attention. The 1986-1987 championship season fueled Darnall's recruiting "fire power."

Darnall said, "First Team NAIA All-American Scottie Pippen's Central Arkansas team failed to reach the 1987 NAIA National Tournament, but little Eureka College did." He used this new recruiting line the remainder of his career when talking to prospects.

The coaching staff was able to make some Christmas break recruiting trips during the 1986-1987 campaign. Once the playing season resumed, their attention returned to their current team and scouting future opponents. Recruiting efforts would be through phone calls and letter writing.

Darnall attended the Breese Mater Dei Holiday Tournament. He spotted a six-foot-seven center from Mascoutah High School named Mark Blunt. He was unable to speak to the senior but did send a letter and basketball questionnaire. Originally, Blunt had decided he was not interested in Eureka, but through Coach's persistence, Mark ended up coming to Eureka. He had an excellent career as a Red Devil player. He also served a year as a student coach.

DeLeon Lavender of Alton was a top recruit for Darnall that year. Lavender attended a Eureka College practice at Dave's invitation when Alton native Rick Taylor arranged for Eureka to practice in the Alton High School gym while the Red Devils were on a four-day, two-game trip to the St. Louis area. Both Coach McAfoos and Taylor talked to "D" about the Eureka College basketball program. Darnall had a good visit with the six-foot-four talented center. He made several home visits meeting the Lavender family before "D" finally decided to further his education and play basketball at Eureka College. It was a good decision for the well-liked Alton kid. The Eureka alum is a successful businessman with State Farm Insurance Company and a member of the Hall of Fame.

Coach Darnall finished his 1986-1987 recruiting year with several more new players. As time would tell, it was a good thing he had a good recruiting class.

The 1988-1989 recruiting season also brought about numerous trips for Darnall. One was quite unusual for him. Darnall traveled two and a half hours to Oakland, Illinois, for a home visit with a six-foot-two guard named Lance Craft. Craft was considered one of the top small college prospects in Eastern Illinois. He had previously visited the college. Darnall had hoped to sign the sharp shooter during this visit. However, he left without doing so. But wait, let's have the story retold by Craft himself.

Well, there we sat—Mom, Dad, two sisters, and my high school girl-friend—in the log cabin home I grew up in. I had just come home from a regional track meet. I had talked to Coach about three times on the phone. Man, this guy was good. He was a true salesman, and he had me on cloud nine, thinking about playing big time basketball for Eureka College, clothes all laid out for every game, new shoes paid for by the basketball program, NAIA sitting right between NCAA Division I and NCAA Division II, and no other school was really interested or pursued me like Coach Darnall. I wanted to go where I could play right away. Coach convinced me the opportunity to prove myself was there and with hard work and dedication by my sophomore or junior year, I would see playing time but no guarantees of course.

As we sat there, I kept thinking if I really wanted to go two hours away from home to play basketball. My dad and Coach continued to discuss the opportunities over several beers. I could tell he and Coach would get along. Finally, Coach asked if I was prepared to sign a "Letter of Intent." I was still hesitant. My dad kept asking if I was sure I didn't want to sign, and my mom was saying we'll talk about it and see what happens.

As my father and I walked Coach to his car, we thanked him for coming all the way to talk to us. Something made me want to say I would sign and get it over with and if it didn't work out, I could always come back, but I didn't say anything. As we waved goodbye, my father said, "You sure you don't want to sign tonight since he's here?" and I said nervously, "You know, I like what he said. I kind of want to go to Eureka but I don't know. I don't know what to do."

With a little encouragement from my father, there we were jumping in Dad's run-down Ford pickup truck chasing Coach Darnall down in his new Red Ford Mustang, flyin' down the country roads flashing our lights trying to get Coach to pull over. After several miles and flashing our lights, we finally got Coach's attention enough that he pulled over. When we approached the car, he had his driver's license out thinking we were the police and he had been pulled over for speeding, only to realize it was my dad and I, and we had chased him down to sign the letter before he got too far out of town. So coach got the letter out, along the side of the road, and, on the hood of Dad's pickup truck, I signed the "Letter of Intent" to play basketball for the Eureka Red Devils that evening.

The next three recruiting years provided Coach Darnall with some excellent talent to conclude his college coaching career. The rigorous pace of coaching, recruiting, scouting, teaching classes, working as Intramural Director, and directing one the largest and most successful basketball camps in the state were beginning to take its toll.

It was for the 1989-1990 season that Coach Darnall signed one of the purest shooters ever to play for Eureka College. That was Jon Guderjan. Not only was Jon an excellent player, but he also had a super personality to go with his talent. The First Team Class A All-Stater was also an outstanding student; therefore, in great demand. Jon required much recruiting time because of those qualities.

Not only did Dave spend many evenings watching Jon play basketball, but he also spent several cold, windy afternoons watching him play baseball. On one occasion, Darnall's point guard Kevin Root asked to accompany his coach to watch Guderjan play a baseball game. The two players had "hit it off." Jon had told Coach Darnall that Root was his idol ever since he had seen him play at the State Tournament three years prior.

Dave recalled the first home visit to the Guderjan's. Jon lived about thirty miles north of Eureka in the country. The trip took Coach approximately thirty minutes. Mrs. Guderjan greeted Darnall at the back door. She led coach to the family room where he shook hands with Jon and Mr. Guderjan. Jon introduced Coach to his high school girlfriend. Larry offered Coach a beer. Dave asked if he was going to have one. Larry replied, "Yes." Coach said he would join him. Who would guess this would be only the first of many the two would share during Jon's recruitment and over the many years to come? Sipping a beer, Darnall started his standard recruiting presentation. After an hour of serious dialogue, Coach and the Guderjans began general talk.

That was not the first time Coach Darnall had experienced a high school girlfriend being involved in the recruiting process. He made a point of telling the new recruits not to let anyone keep them from going to the college of their choice, especially a girlfriend. He remembered telling Jon about all the nice looking girls on campus. Jon's response was, "I'm not interested. I have a girlfriend."

"That could very well change when you get to college," Coach replied.

"Not me," Jon shot back.

Well, by the time basketball season started, Jon was dating a college coed. "What's that—about two months?" Darnall asked, smiling.

Darnall made five more home visits before Jon finally decided to attend Eureka. Jim Mattson, WHOI Peoria television sports director, was on hand to witness Jon's signing with Eureka College. That was a first for Coach Darnall. The Guderjans and Darnalls became good friends and still meet for dinner whenever possible. Jon became one of the all-time career leading scorers on his way to becoming a NAIA All-District player. The Hall of Fame member is currently a successful businessman with State Farm.

Perhaps the most talented accumulation of players ever gathered in one year for Eureka College was the 1990-1991 crop. Those freshmen formed the foundation for the team that became the most successful team in the history of Eureka College. Even though only five members of the incoming players remained on the team for all four years, they set a precedent for all remaining recruiting classes.

Darnall concentrated his recruiting efforts on five players—Chris Eaton, Dennis Huttenlocher, Chris Peterson, Duane Schmedeke, and Troy Tyler. Three of these had attended his basketball camps—Tyler, Peterson, and Schmedeke. Of course, Dave made numerous home visits for these five recruits.

Chris Peterson was from Brimfield, a small town approximately thirty miles from Eureka. The sharp-shooting guard was recruited by numerous small colleges. He ended his high school career as a Class A All-State player and participated in the Illinois Basketball Coaches All-Star Game. Not only did Darnall like Chris's basketball ability, but he was also impressed with the point guard's leadership qualities.

Chris had still not decided to go to Eureka College when Dave asked him to talk to a player from the nearby community of Wyoming, Chris Eaton. Dave knew if he got the six-foot-seven center along with Peterson, he would have a great one-two punch. Coach made several visits to the Eaton's home. On a couple of occasions, Bonnie accompanied her husband. Mrs. Eaton was a single parent, and Dave thought Bonnie would be a reassuring factor in discussing Chris's future at Eureka College. Chris's grandparents also lived with them, and he had an older brother in the service.

Darnall was pretty persistent in the recruitment of Eaton. With several other area colleges wanting the six-foot-seven center, Dave knew he better stay in constant contact with Chris. One college coach in particular had made some derogatory comments about Eureka College. Several recruits had mentioned this to Darnall. However, the negative approach to recruiting did not seem to diminish the success of his recruiting. Most athletes were able to put it aside. After several weeks of continuous contact and persistence, Eaton finally decided to sign the "Letter of Intent" to attend Eureka College. What a relief for Darnall!

The Class A All-State player did not disappoint his college coach. The Eureka College Hall of Fame member received the highest honor a college player could receive when he was selected the NAIA II National Player of the Year. Eaton was also named a NAIA II All-American.

Peterson also earned National honors when he was named the 1994 NAIA II National Tournament's Most Valuable Player. The Eureka College Hall of Fame member played professional basketball in Ireland for a couple years and is still playing on a traveling USA professional team.

Troy Tyler, the only Class AA player of the five, was from nearby Washington. The six-foot-four forward was a high school All-Stater and participated in the IBCA All-Star Game. Troy was not only an excellent basketball player, but he was also an outstanding student receiving an academic scholarship to attend Eureka College.

Coach had known Troy for several years. As a kid, Troy had attended his basketball camps. Darnall's recruitment of Troy was an on-going process taking place over several years. Recruiting actually began at camp when all the camp coaches could see that the youngster had a lot of talent and someday would become an excellent player. Troy remembered his recruitment to Eureka College.

> Initially, I blew off Coach Darnall and Eureka College, for my dream was to play big-time college basketball. After one game my senior year, Coach Darnall walked into the locker room congratulating me as I stood there in a towel. The next thing I knew, Coach Darnall had me scheduled to visit Eureka College.
> My father accompanied me on my first college visit. It was a success and stimulated more interest. A few weeks later, Coach visited our house. My dad asked him if he would like something to drink—milk, orange juice, soda, tea, or water? Coach Darnall replied, "Do you have a beer?" I can remember thinking to myself that he and my dad will get along just fine. Interestingly enough, Coach and my dad became good friends.

Darnall was thrilled when Troy finally decided to further his education and play basketball at Eureka College. Tyler had an outstanding career both athletically and academically at Eureka. The pre-med major had the distinct honor of receiving the National Frank Hesselroth Leadership Award given to the top NAIA scholar-athlete in the entire United States. Troy was also named NAIA II Second Team All-American both his junior and senior years as well as being selected a NAIA II Academic All-American both years. He is the all-time leading scorer at Eureka College and member of the school's Athletic Hall of Fame. Troy's younger brother, Jeff, also followed in his footsteps and became an important member of the Red Devil basketball team.

Darnall also made several trips to the homes of the other two members of the "fabulous five," Dennis Huttenlocher and Duane Schmedeke. He was extremely pleased when both decided to come to Eureka College. He then felt he had the nucleus of an outstanding ball club.

With the outstanding recruiting class of the previous year, Darnall had the opportunity to ease up on his recruiting activities during the 1990-1991 season. Dave actually recruited only one player persistently who ended up being a four-year letterman and a factor on the championship team.

Dave Gilliland, then Head Basketball Coach at Burlington High School, recommended a point guard from Shabbona High School by the name of Chris Hopwood. Dave attended an area All-Star game where he was impressed with Hopwood's play. Coach made several home visits before Chris decided to join the program at Eureka College. As with many of Dave's players' parents, the Darnalls and Hopwoods became good friends and have remained so over the years since.

Then during the 1991-1992 recruiting year, Coach Darnall returned to his old recruiting form. He signed six good freshmen players plus two transfers. Dave, for the third time in his tenure, recruited an administrative assistant. This time it was the son of Dr. Raycraft, the person responsible for his hiring at Eureka College. Scott was an avid basketball fan and fit right into the program.

One of the new recruits was a player for Dave Gilliland from Burlington named Adam Ferguson. The six-foot-three "jumping jack" was a Class A All-State player and also participated in the IBCA All-Star Game.

Darnall accused Gilliland as being a "mother hen" for the numerous hours he spent helping his players find a suitable college including taking Ferguson to ten different schools. "His players don't know how lucky they are to have him as a coach," Darnall said. "Some high school coaches don't bother trying to find places for their kids."

Darnall signed Ferguson at the player's home with Gilliland and two newspaper writers witnessing the signing. The four went out for dinner and a couple beers following the penning.

"What a relief!" Darnall told Gilliland. "Thanks for all your help, but sometimes you can be a pain in the ass."

Gilliland just shook his head before a large gulp of cold beer and replied, "I know."

Two other top recruits that year were Greg Crider, a six-foot-one guard from Dunlap and Peter Vaughn, a six-foot-six forward from Normal U-High. Both players went on to have outstanding careers on the hardwood and became successful professional people. Crider is the enthusiastic Head Basketball Coach at Tremont High School, and Pete is a businessman in Connecticut.

The 1992-1993 recruiting year was Darnall's last as the Head Coach at Eureka College. Seven new players entered the program. Even though none made a major contribution as freshmen, several became stars as their careers progressed.

Stote Reeder headed the new group of Red Devils. The six-foot-one sharp-shooting guard from Sullivan was also a Class A All-State player and participated in the IBCA All-Star Game. Reeder was recruited by several colleges, forcing Darnall to spend a great deal of time in the Reeder home. His recruitment extended over a five-month period. That provided Darnall with many opportunities to visit with his parents. The Reeders became regulars in Eureka. Not only did they come to all of Stote's games over his four-year career, attended post-games parties at the Darnalls' home, but they also followed younger son Chet's career as a Red Devil.

Stote is currently Athletic Director and successful coach at nearby Flanagan High School. The Reeder family has now become Falcons fans also.

Two other newcomers that went on to play four years of varsity basketball were six-foot-five Chris Carter of Bloomington and Doug Hattermann, a six-foot-six forward from Bartonville Limestone.

The 1993-1994 school year was the last for Darnall as Head Basketball Coach at Eureka College. He started the recruiting year "hot and heavy." However, by the middle of December, he was feeling the stress of winning and losing along with some health problems. Dave decided he could not maintain the pace he had been going at over the past twenty years to build and keep the basketball program as one of the top small college programs in the country. In a family discussion, Dave decided to retire at the conclusion of the current season.

Prior to the Christmas break, Coach Darnall informed President Hearne of his intention to retire. A long discussion took place. President

Hearne suggested a news conference to be held on Monday, January 31, at Melick Library to announce Coach Darnall's retirement from the game he loved. Hearne wanted to introduce the twenty-year veteran to the press corp. Dave had high regards for President Hearne, both as president of the college and as a personal friend. He was delighted to have him involved in his retirement announcement.

It was at the meeting with Hearne that President Hearne suggested that Dave consider becoming an "athletic counselor" along with his teaching responsibilities. His recruiting responsibilities would be the recruitment of women's volleyball, basketball, and softball players as well as men's basketball players. He told Dave he wanted to share his idea for the new position in Admissions with the dean of the college and the dean of Admissions.

Coach Darnall had a good working relationship with Women's Basketball Coach Sandy Schuster and Softball Coach Karen Sweitzer. Due to their coaching duties, which included assisting each other, recruiting time was very difficult for them to find. They were very supportive of the new position for Dave.

Coach Darnall had recommended Coach Dighton as his successor in the meeting with Hearne. He also publicly recommended Dighton as the new Head Basketball Coach at his news conference. He knew recruiting basketball players for his loyal nine-year assistant would not be a difficult task. Since Dave enjoyed recruiting student-athletes, he felt it actually would be fun.

Traveling the recruiting roads for twenty years was both lonely and dangerous. Basketball being played in the winter meant long trips in a diversity of weather conditions. Snow, ice, rain, wind, and fog were adversities that college coaches had to conquer in order to win the recruiting wars. Darnall was lucky. In addition to his assistant coaches, he had several other individuals who volunteered to join him on the long tedious trips. First, it was Bonnie. Even though she taught school, kept house, and did most of the raising of their two children, she squeezed in time to go on the road with Dave. She was usually "bribed" with dinner out.

Ron Eeten, teacher-coach at Eureka High School, was the second volunteer to find time to travel with Darnall. Eeten, who played against Darnall's Stanford High School team as a student at San Jose High School, had been a member of the Illinois State University basketball team when in college. He saw limited playing time and at times had wished he had gone to a smaller school. A teammate of his was Doug Collins. Ron described his experience of helping Dave recruit for Eureka College.

Dave was such a good recruiter that he was able to convince great players to pass up scholarships to attend Eureka College. In every one of these situations, the young man would have an outstanding career at Eureka and memories that would last a lifetime. I often wished that someone like Dave had been around when I was making my college choice. I, like so many other small school players, picked too big of a school to attend and enjoyed very little success. It has amazed me for several years that some of the larger schools, like Illinois, Bradley, and ISU, weren't trying to lure Dave into their programs. They had a gold mine in their own backyard and didn't realize it.

One recruiting story that has stayed with me over the years is when he asked me to speak to a promising sophomore while he spoke to his senior teammate. I agreed that this young man showed lots of potential, and I did my best to leave a bright picture of Eureka College. Two years later, I found out that this young man, Russell Cross, was rated as the number one player in the nation and had signed a scholarship to Purdue University. I reminded Dave that even though I felt I was a good recruiter, maybe in the future he could assign me players a little closer to our level.

The late seventies and early eighties brought several other volunteers —Les Bauman, a local farmer; Mel Tedford, an employee of Caterpillar; and Dave Knopp, a professor in the college's Business Department.

Tedford enjoyed accompanying Darnall to high school games in the Chicago area. He was fascinated by the talent level of the inner city teams. He told about a trip the two made to Chicago.

We went to Percy L. Julian High School to see them play. We were recruiting the third and fourth best players on the squad while NCAA Division I coaches were sitting only a few feet away watching the top players. We were sitting among several large university coaches watching Julian's Robert Haile play. Sitting next to Darnall was Tony Yates, Assistant Coach at the University of Illinois. Dave knew Tony. The two conversed freely throughout the game. This surprised me. I felt like I was in the "big-time." By the way, Haile did come to Eureka College.

"Haile played three years of varsity basketball," commented Darnall. "He is a Eureka College alum and currently a Chicago police officer.

In the last several years of Darnall's tenure, family friend Bill Eaton journeyed with Dave on several trips. He enjoyed going to post-season high school All-Star games where he helped Darnall identify potential players. Also, two of Dave's players' fathers traveled with him on occasion. Larry

Guderjan and the late John Tyler. Both lived close to Eureka and accompanied their sons' coach to area high school games.

Chuck Wertz, who really enjoyed scouting more than recruiting, joined Darnall on the road more than any other volunteer. Wertz spent nearly eight years scouting and recruiting with Darnall. Their friend Dean Nohl went with the two on some scouting trips when both teams needed to be watched.

Throughout the countless recruiting and scouting trips, many stories could be told. Dave's chief scout, Chuck Wertz, was involved in quite a few of them. "He was so valuable to the success of our teams," said Darnall. "He took vacation days from work for scouting and recruiting purposes."

On one such trip, Dave was to pick Chuck up from his job at Diamond Star Motors to scout Harris-Stowe in St. Louis. In the meantime, a snowstorm had begun, and Chuck was hesitant to head out in the storm and get stuck somewhere.

"I really don't want to go in this storm. Besides I doubt they will be any real competition for you," protested Chuck.

Darnall's reply was, "Well, it's up to you, but I'm going whether you do or not."

Chuck was sure that Dave would get stuck, alone, somewhere, so he agreed to go along. The trip down was as bad as Chuck had imagined, but they did arrive safely. Their first stop in St. Louis was a Jack-in-the-Box for something to eat. While sitting at their table, they were approached by a suspicious character who muttered something unintelligible to them.

"I kept my nose in a newspaper and tried to ignore him," said Wertz, " but Coach, of course, says, 'What? I didn't hear you.' The guy mutters a little more clearly, 'Want to buy a watch?' Coach looks at me and then tells the guy, 'Uh, no thanks. I've got a good watch.' He muttered at us some more and then, thankfully, walked away. I told Coach, 'Let's get out of here!' We took off to resume Coach's mission—once he starts, you can't change his course."

The game only reinforced Chuck's initial reaction that the two didn't really need to scout Harris-Stowe, especially in that kind of weather. They would not be a real challenge for the Red Devils. With the game over, the two exited the gym to entirely different weather conditions. It had completely cleared. Wertz reported that Coach made fun of him all the way home for not wanting to go in the first place.

One recruiting-scouting trip illustrates the frantic pace Dave set during the season in order to win games. Bonnie accompanied him on this particular three-day, three-state, hundreds of miles journey on the third weekend of November 1991.

Coach had scheduled a game with St. Norbert College of Green Bay, Wisconsin. Of course, he had to scout the opponent! But first he had to conduct practice and then make a stop at a Thanksgiving Tip-Off Tourney on the way north. Dave left practice in the capable hands of his assistant Dennis Dighton as Bonnie and he left Eureka around 5:00 P.M. The first stop was the high school Tip-Off Tourney at Princeville, Illinois, some fifty miles northwest of Eureka. They were there for two games. Dave talked to one of the recruits following the first game while Bonnie continued to "scout" the second recruit playing in the second game. When the final game ended, Dave dashed to the locker room to again talk to a prospective EC player. The couple left the gym around 10:00 P.M. and headed for Rockford located close to the Illinois-Wisconsin border. It was their destination for the night. They checked into a motel close to midnight and then proceeded across the street to an all night restaurant for dinner. By the time they hit the bed, it was 1:30 A.M.

They rose early, ate breakfast, and left for the next 180 miles north to Green Bay to see St. Norbert play an afternoon game. Dave scouted St. Norbert while Bonnie studied in the stands for her comprehensive Master exam.

The next leg of the three-day trip was to turn around and beeline for St. Louis, approximately 470 miles south. Coach needed to be at Maryville College by noon on Sunday. The St. Louis school was hosting a "Tip-Off" Tourney in which a future EC opponent, Westminster College, was participating. The Darnalls left Green Bay about 4:00 P.M. and arrived in St. Louis around midnight.

They were able to sleep in the next morning before heading to Maryville for the 1:00 P.M. game. Two hours of basketball, and the Darnalls finally headed back to Eureka, another 160 miles, arriving home around 7:00 P.M. They had finished the four-game, three-day, three-state, fifty-hour trip.

Another marathon trip involved both Chuck and Jane Wertz and Bonnie. During the 1992-1993 season, Eureka was scheduled to play in the Franklin (Indiana) Tournament. Eureka was to play DeFiance as their first game of the tourney. Darnall *had* to scout the opponent. He found DeFiance was going to open its season with a Friday, 6:30 P.M. game at Mt. Vernon Nazarene College in Ohio. The trip to Ohio would be over 425 miles one-way. The plan was for Chuck and Dave to drive eight hours to the game, watch the two-hour game, and then drive the eight hours back. It was another mission for Darnall. The two returned to Eureka by 4:00 A.M.

However, the journey was not over. Four hours later the men were to be on the road again—this time to the Judson Tip-Off Tournament in Elgin, Illinois. The four-team tourney involved all teams that Eureka was scheduled to play later in the season. The extremely tired fellows were unable to drive. So they enlisted Jane and Bonnie to chauffeur. Bonnie became the first designated driver. They reached the Judson site and scouted the teams until the conclusion of the final game at 4:30 P.M. Then it was Jane's turn to drive the next two hours to West Central Illinois for a 6:00 P.M. first game of the Princeton Tip-Off Tourney. Now it was recruiting time, not scouting. Dave talked to one player following the first game and two after the second game.

Hungry and tired, the couples checked in to an economical motel around 10:30 P.M. Dinner came at a twenty-four-hour restaurant across the street. That was usually the "wonderful meals" Bonnie was bribed with! The quartet finished the late dinner and immediately headed for the motel.

The next stop was at Monmouth College. It was only an hour and a half away. Lindenwood College of St. Louis was playing Monmouth at 2:00 P.M. Lindenwood was a future opponent of the Red Devils. The "scouts" were, however, getting closer to home.

Two hours after the game, they dropped the Wertzes off at their home, and Dave headed for practice being only a few minutes late. Coach Dighton had everything under control, working the team on the motion offense.

Dave arrived home around 9:00 P.M. He had finished the whirlwind weekend. He had scouted six teams, recruited at two high school games, conducted a two and a half-hour practice, and traveled approximately 1,200 miles. "I'll do anything that is not legally or morally wrong to win a game," said Coach Darnall. Oh, by the way, Darnall had a class to teach the following morning.

Chuck also tells a story that again demonstrated just how determined Darnall could be when he sets his mind.

This is about a trip we made to Goshen, Indiana. Goshen was to scrimmage their alumni on a Saturday afternoon. Since this would be the only chance to see them, Coach and I left early Saturday, planning to view the scrimmage and then return to Eureka late the same night. We arrived in Goshen and located the gym with some time to spare. We rested outside for a while, but then became suspicious as Coach said, "You know, there aren't many people around." He went in to see what was going on. When he returned he said there was no scrimmage. It had been postponed until the next day. I thought we should return home and scout them another time, but there was no way. Darnall said, "If we leave without seeing Goshen play, the College will be upset. We've just got to see them tomorrow."

Astonishingly, we decided to stay. However, we made this decision before realizing we weren't really prepared to stay. We had to plan our strategy. The next thing we knew we were in a Dollar General pooling our money to buy the cheapest things we could to make our stay "comfortable." We decided on a small tube of toothpaste, a package of two toothbrushes, a can of spray deodorant, and a small bottle of after-shave. On the way to the checkout, Coach remarks, "We forgot the most important thing. I can't wear the same underwear for two days in a row." So we found a three-pack of underwear to share. Finally, we were set to spend the night in Goshen for a total of $8.85. Boy, can we be fugal!

We then found the least expensive motel, a Best Western. So, here we were two guys in a strange town, no real change of clothes, and not a lot of cash. In order to preserve our clothes, we stripped down to our underwear and hung our clothes up neatly. There we were watching TV in our BVDs.

Around dinnertime, we again began pooling our money. Rather than dress and further wrinkle our clothes, we decided to order pizza, but decided we needed some beer to go with it. I reluctantly dressed and found a package liquor store to buy a twelve-pack of beer. Our money was pretty much depleted. The pizza had arrived by the time I got back. Boy, talk about class! Two grown men in underwear, eating pizza, and drinking beer while watching TV. What more could you want?

Later, Eureka lost to Goshen, but it wasn't because Coach and I hadn't done our part.

One of Dave's first recruiting trips in his new position as Athletic Counselor was back to his old high school to watch a girls' volleyball game. First of all, he knew little about volleyball at that point, but it was going to be good to be going "back home." He was anxious to see, hopefully, some of the hometown folks. His first stop in Argenta was at the Kenny Boyds' for a short visit before going on to the high school. As he walked into the foyer, he noticed and had a short visit with someone he knew. It was Marty Stiles, Judy Boyd's sister who worked at the high school. He was sure he would see more. As he proceeded on, he gazed at the many trophies and senior class pictures. There he was, in the Class of 1960. He picked up a program and proceeded to make his "grand entrance" into the gym he had seen little playing time in. But this time, he had a Championship ring on his finger! Dave waited through the first game but saw no one he knew; and then the second game in which Argenta played. Still no one! What a disappointment for the native! But wait, the night and his ego were saved; a group of fellows from near-by Maroa had come to support their volleyball team. They approached the bewildered recruiter who was sitting high in the bleachers by himself, "Coach, I know you don't know us, but we attended your basketball camps for a couple years. It was great!" Coach perked up and visited a while with the group. He finally had to excuse himself because the game was over and he had to go to work.

Basketball started a month later. Darnall was off to Peotone High School to see a girls' basketball game. He did not mind the two-hour trip. In fact, he was looking forward to it. The Momence High School girls' team was going to provide the competition. However, this time he left "the ring" at home.

Looking around the half-empty gym, again there were no familiar faces; there were no known names in the program. But it had only been twenty years! Was it a duplication of the Argenta trip? No one knew the "Coach." What happened to the "Miracle of Highway 1?" Hold it! Why was he sent there in the first place? Wasn't it to recruit a Peotone basketball player? Back to reality for Darnall!

Wendy Schmaedeke decided to attend Eureka College following two campus visits. She was a 1999 graduate. Isn't that what it was all about anyway?

Coach Darnall summarized his thoughts on recruiting after twenty-eight-plus years of "pounding the road." "If one believes in his/her institution and the program they are trying to sell, recruiting can be fun, worthwhile, and satisfying. If one has the support of the administration and his/her family, the job can be done without much stress. If not, it will be a calamity. I only wish some of my colleagues understood this," Dave concluded.

President Hearne summarized Dave Darnall's prowess as an athletic recruiter. He expressed his thoughts on Darnall's efforts and contributions in recruiting student-athletes to Eureka College.

> I worked directly, or in a supervisory capacity, with the Admissions area for most of my career here, prior to becoming president in 1985. I have remained intensely interested in the Admissions program since then. There has been no athletic coach at Eureka during that time who ever worked as tirelessly, traveled as extensively, made as many phone calls and home visits as Dave Darnall. At the expense of his personal health and family, he was determined to build a program that would be able to challenge for championships year after year. Eureka College does not provide athletic scholarships. Dave did not allow the fact that a prospect had been offered an athletic scholarship elsewhere deter him from trying to persuade the student of the advantages of coming to

Eureka College. Throughout his career, there have been many who have chosen to turn down athletic scholarships because they wanted to be here under Coach Darnall.

A first impression of Coach Darnall, because he is so intense and tries to cover a wide variety of things in a short time, could lead one to think he was not highly organized. Nothing could be further from the truth. I credit a great deal of his success—in coaching, recruiting and public relations—to his organizational skills. He anticipates and plans for every detail that might be important in winning a game or recruiting a prospect.

We used to have some serious conversations about his recruiting travel and telephone call expenses. Since those were being met out of a limited Admissions Office budget, I had a major concern. At times I would note that he would travel to Southern Illinois to see a prospect, and call other prospects in the Chicago area, while in the south. I also noted that he would travel from that Southern Illinois town up to Northern Illinois and then back to the south. I thought he could cover things much more efficiently while in a particular area. He would then explain to me why each of these was done in the order it was, a part of a careful plan to make each contact when it needed to be made. His explanations were usually convincing.

What happened within a very short period of time was amazing. his recruiting success led first to a full junior varsity program, and then we had to establish a freshman team program as well. In later years, we moved away from the freshman program in order to provide resources to support a growing women's athletic program, but the foundation for success had been established.

Dave was a gifted, dedicated recruiter. His recruitment of each individual was like an extensive game plan. He knew the College and what was attractive to students in general. He also knew the things that might be particularly attractive to each individual. He made connections between the prospect and faculty in the area of interest. He made a point to know the family very well, often visiting several times in their home, as well as visiting with them on the phone, at games, and on the campus. He knew that success depended on his being there early in the recruitment process, and then staying regularly in touch with those he wanted to have at Eureka. He knew the importance to a prospect, as the walked around campus, of stopping to introduce him to faculty and staff, and especially to the president.

In the spring of 1992, we asked Coach Darnall to put in writing a recruiting manual making available to others some of the secrets of his success. It was an extensive and detailed document that can provide enormous assistance to anyone involved in the recruitment of students.

Chapter 9

The Building of a Respectable Program

THE ROAD FROM MOMENCE TO EUREKA was somewhat straight and smooth, while at other times it was hilly and curvy, similar to that of Darnall's tenure at Eureka College. The two towns were a hundred miles apart and took two hours to drive. Darnall's career as a coach lasted twenty years and required thousands of miles on the road. Who would have guessed a trip in a U-haul would lead to Dave's final trip to destiny two decades later?

The Darnalls moved into their home in Eureka in early July with the help of several of Dave's Momence players. Four-eleven Pearson soon became the social center of the coach's new town. The tradition established several years prior of a post-game party following every home game would continue. Just different people in a different town. The unfamiliar neighbors would soon provide new friends and fun for the Darnall children. Just as the after-game gatherings at the house would create new friendships.

Darnall spent most of the summer preparing for his fall classes and recruiting. The recruiting wars over the years sometimes were vicious. In order to obtain the Head Basketball Coaching position, Dave had to also serve as an assistant football coach. He did not mind becoming the Intra-mural Director, but coaching football was not to his liking. He felt fortunate when new football coach Tom Hosier assigned him to work with defensive coordinator Jack Marcoline. Darnall knew Marcoline from playing sixteen-inch softball together.

"If it hadn't been for Jack, I don't think I could have survived the year," Dave said. "He really helped me not to get overly stressed since I knew very little about the game. He was very lenient with me, especially on those damn Sunday afternoon film sessions. I didn't even do that in basketball, let alone in football."

It was during football season that Darnall met two gentlemen for whom he had a great deal of respect. They were the legendary Coach Ralph McKinzie and Steve Thomson. Both were Eureka College alumni. McKinzie has been President Ronald Reagan's football coach at Eureka. He was still serving as an assistant coach and trainer for the football program. Thomson was a successful businessman in the Bloomington-Normal area and was a member of the college's Board of Trustees. It was though his help that the football press box was built.

Coach Darnall was known as a disciplinarian. That included long, hard practices with the players giving 100 percent. At his first practice, Darnall told his players, "When I am on the floor, I am the man. When I am off the floor, I am no better than anyone else. When I tell you to do something, you do it. I don't have time to argue with you. After practice, if you want to come to my office and talk to me about something, you're welcome. I have an open door policy. If I made a mistake, I'll correct myself in front of the team at the next practice."

Some may say that's "old fashioned," but Darnall followed that policy throughout his twenty-year tenure at Eureka College. As time went by, players became more independent, making this philosophy harder to maintain. In order to adhere to Darnall's slogan "Together We Win," the players sometimes had to give up their individuality for togetherness. To this day, Coach still feels that philosophy established his first year at Eureka resulted in a National Championship.

Darnall believed that in order to have a good season, a team must play defense. His high school teams played solid defense by employing the 1-2-2 adjustable zone defense. "It will work at this level too," Dave said. "However, it might be a little harder to sell at the college level. Everyone plays man-to-man."

Eureka College was no different. It had, basically, played man-to-man in the past. That would change during Darnall's first year. The Red Devil players would have to adjust. Another change took place. This one was on offense. Most college teams liked to get the ball and go—fast break! Coach was more deliberate. He wanted his team to run a "controlled fast

199

break." If they had it, take it. However, if they did not have the lay-up, he wanted them to pull it out and set up the offense. Darnall told his players, "I want good percentage shots only."

If his team did get a fast break, Darnall believed that the ball should be taken down the side, not the middle. Nearly all coaches thought the fast break with the ball being in the middle was the way to go. Darnall was definitely in the minority. He thought by taking the ball down the side, five players could fill six lanes. That was because one player fills two spots. That player is the first of three when the ball is taken down the side, as well as serving as the first person when the ball is taken down the middle. In other words, there are six lanes filled by five players. Three down the side and three across the middle of the floor. The change was made.

The players also had to learn a new man-to-man offense. It was the "Power I" offense. It was the offense that Dave had developed and wrote an article on while teaching at Wheeling High School. It had been published in *Scholastic Coach*.

There were numerous great games and many memorable occasions that took place in Coach Darnall's first six years at Eureka College. All cannot be covered or discussed in this book. Therefore, a summary of some of the contests will be delivered while others may not.

1974-1975 Season

THERE WERE TWENTY-FIVE GAMES on Darnall's first college schedule. That included a three-game trip to Kentucky. Eureka was a member of the Prairie College Conference consisting of Blackburn, Eureka, Greenville, Illinois College, and MacMurray. The Conference winner received an automatic bid for the NAIA District 20 (State) Playoffs. Eight teams participated in the tournament with the winner advancing to the NAIA National Championship Tournament in Kansas City.

Eight returning players greeted the first year coach as official practice got underway. They were joined by twenty new faces. Three returning starters formed the nucleus of Darnall's first team. They were seniors Kip Blakesley, Dan Nafziger, and Elton Bryson. Sophomore six-foot-six Jeff Smith was a part-time starter. Darnall was assisted by Athletic Director Leo Traister and student assistants Paul Brown and Dennis Dighton.

Reagan Fieldhouse.

The Red Devils would open their season in Reagan Fieldhouse, named after alumni Ronald and Neil Reagan, against Aurora College. Prior to Darnalls arrival at Eureka, Aurora had been led by Chicago Bull Mickey Johnson.

The night before the game was a sleepless night for the new college coach. Lying awake with an upset stomach, worrying about winning and losing, became standard for the rookie mentor.

Dave's first coaching apparel was the fashionable polyester leisure suit with a large open collar. A superstitious person, it remained his game attire until Bonnie forced him to up-date his coaching outfit several years later.

Darnall experienced pre-game anxiety opening night. That meant several trips to the bathroom. The chain-smoking coach passed out Vitamin C tablets to his players and gave his first pre-game talk in the Reagan Fieldhouse classroom. He followed that by announcing the starters. They were seniors Blakesley, Nafziger, Bryson, sophomore Smith, and freshman six-foot-three Brian Wright. Thirteen players dressed for EC's home opener.

The number 13 again surfaced. He finished his first pre-game speech with what would become his famous motivating last words. Taking the cigarette from his mouth, placing it in the small ashtry on the desk in front of him, Darnall said, "Let's take our ten seconds. Each one is an individual. Think what you want to think or you don't need to think at all, as long as we are quiet and we do it together."

Snuffing out the cigarette, Coach departed the classroom and made his first of what would become numerous walks down the back stairs to the sparse crowd awaiting his team. He wondered if he had made the right decision leaving Momence as he gazed at the empty gym. Perhaps there were a hundred fans in the bleachers. A far cry from what he had experienced the year before. The situation was something Darnall planned to change.

Dave started his high school career at Stanford with a 60 to 59 loss. He did not want a repeat in his first college game. Employing the 1-2-2 adjustable zone defense and the Power I offense, the Red Devils won their first game under the direction of their new mentor. The Red Devils were led in scoring by seniors Elton Bryson, fourteen points, and Dan Nafziger, thirteen. The victory was the first of what would be 383 wins under the reins of Darnall. Who would guess that after twenty years of directing the Eureka College basketball program, Dave would become one of just a few coaches that started with a win and finished their college coaching career with a national tournament victory? A feat seldom accomplished.

Dave mingled among his players in the locker room following the game praising them on their accomplishment. He hoped the feeling he was experiencing would be a frequent one.

The first post-game celebration at the Darnall home was about to take place. Dave notified the local press of the game results and hurried home for a cold beer. The tradition at Eureka had begun. Everyone, including parents of players, faculty, staff, season ticket holders, and local fans were invited. Approximately fifteen people attended the first post-game party. That number would drastically change during Darnall's twenty-year tenure eventually attracting up to a hundred people. What an understanding wife!

The Red Devils lost the following two games before bouncing back with a 79 to 71 victory over pre-season favorite Illinois College. Nafziger led the way with twenty-one points, mostly coming from great passes from senior point guard Kip Blakesley. Sophomore Jeff Smith led the team in rebounds.

It took only two home games before it became evident to the local fans that the "new man" had two unusual traits—tearing tape and rolling it into tiny balls and popping ammonia capsules when he got excited. The spectators' only question was when would it happen.

Darnall realized quite quickly how difficult it was to win on the road. That became evident during the first multi-game road trip. The team traveled to Kentucky by charter bus for a three-game series. They lost all three. That was not the way to start off the second half of the season.

They had not won any of the games, but they did stay in nice motels with indoor pools as the coach had promised in the recruiting spiel. Sounds like the Holiday Inn commercial, huh?

Coach Brown and Darnall shared one room while their wives stayed in another. Administrative assistants Dennis Dighton and Jerome "Spanky" White roomed together. Four players were assigned to a room. Dave managed to get one complimentary room. He became pretty efficient in the negotiating process as the years past.

For many of the players, that was the first time they had been in Kentucky. In fact, several had never been out of Illinois. The trip, at least, served as an "educational" experience.

It was after the first game of the trip that the traditional post-game meal of two cheeseburgers, a large fry, and large Coke was really established. Another important procedure was also changed following that game. While the players sat in their rooms eating, the coaches and administrative assistants removed the soiled and wet socks, jocks, and towels from the traveling trunks and scattered them throughout their rooms to dry. The following morning, the administrative assistants folded the now dry accessories and placed them back into the trunk for the next game. Once the team arrived at the game site, the gear was randomly distributed. That was mind boggling to Bonnie. She was astounded that the guys would wear somebody else's dirty socks and jocks, let alone the towels. "Sounds like a mother wouldn't you say," Dave commented. "Thanks to her continuous harping, the procedure was changed. The player's initials were placed on their items with black permanent marker and were, along with the towels, washed after each game.

The Red Devils finally got their third win of the season. It was against the talented McKendree Bearcats. The hugely successful program under the leadership of Coach Harry Statham was known throughout the country. Even though McKendree had never made a trip to the NAIA National Tournament in Kansas City until 1988, they always qualified for

NAIA District 20 (State) Playoffs. The rivalry of McKendree and Eureka continued throughout the years.

Gregg Johnson led the home team in their victory over the Bearcats by pumping in thirty points. The six-foot-two junior guard transfer from Illinois Wesleyan was rapidly becoming the scoring leader of the team. One of the game officials was Ed Mittage of Chicago. He went on to referee thirty-four games at Eureka College over a seventeen-year span. Dave and he eventually became good friends.

The Red Devils' first road victory under the new coach came at Greenville College. The overtime win was the second of four in a row. The other two Eureka College victims were Blackburn College and Culver-Stockton.

The Conference title came down to a road game at Illinois College. The winner automatically qualified for the NAIA District 20 Playoffs. Not ever participating in a playoff, Eureka was about to play one of its biggest games in its history. Coach Darnall had gotten his team within one game of what he had told senior captain Kip Blakesley was his goal that summer. Remember Blakesley's response when he heard Dave say that? "I don't think you know about our team," Kip had said. He thought Darnall was crazy.

The Conference championship game turned out to be what a championship should be all about. The Red Devil coach was jumping up and down throughout the whole game. Several times Darnall had to pop his ammonia capsules. The emotional and vocal coach tried to keep both his players and officials in the game.

Eureka College lost the title game and the automatic playoff bid to the Blue Boys by the score of 72 to 70 in overtime. The score was tied 62 to 62 at the end of regulation time. With two seconds left in the extra period, Dave Hobson threw back a long rebound shot for the winning basket. Darnall's heart sank. So close to Eureka College basketball history. The charter bus ride home was very long and silent. It was a sleepless night for the coach. Who would guess that twenty years later another championship game would be decided in overtime? However, that time the " EC good guys" won the game that had a much higher reward. The Red Devils finished the current season under the leadership of the rookie coach with a 9 to 16 record.

Throughout the season, not many of the freshmen saw much action. One that did was Darnall's first recruit, Tim McGuire. Tim shared a story of one of his frustrated rookie classmates.

"My roommate, Steve Gorman, didn't get to play much," said McGuire. "He got so upset after one of our away games when the administrative assistants passed out our McDonald's hamburgers and his had a bun, pickles, ketchup, mustard, but no meat. He said that he could stand not playing, but now *no food!*"

1975-1976 Season

COACH DARNALL'S SECOND EUREKA COLLEGE basketball squad became the first winning team in nine years. Its 19 to 6 record produced the most wins in the school's history. The team was led by returning lettermen Gregg Johnson, Jeff Smith, and Tim McGuire. Combined with an outstanding recruiting class of forty-six new prospects, the three players helped turn the Red Devil basketball program from a loser to a winner—the beginning of NAIA national recognition for Eureka College basketball.

Darnall added a freshman team to his program. Now there were three EC teams with separate schedules. That was done in order to keep the some fifty-plus players that were out for basketball content. It was in reference to this recruiting class that *The Pantagraph*'s Jim Barnhart wrote "Name Any Town—Darnall has been there." He called Dave Darnall "The Marco Polo of Illinois college basketball."

The question was often asked, "Why should an athlete spend more to go to a small private school like Eureka College instead of a larger state institution?" The answer most often given was "because they get a chance to participate."

"A lot of kids will get a chance to play here that would not have a prayer in a large school. That is exactly why I added another schedule. Now we have three teams in our program," Darnall said.

Most of the players in this "bumper crop" were also good students. Dave was asked about the year's recruiting class by the local press. "We did not just get jocks. The kids we got were all top-notch kids. Many of the players are high academically and came here on academic scholarship," Dave replied. "We have four players on the team who are in pre-med and four Presidential Scholars out of the ten Presidential Scholars in the whole school."

The team opened its season with an impressive 73 to 70 victory over Illinois Institute of Technology in the McKendree Tournament. Darnall's

Momence High School player, Jerome Westbrooks, came off the bench to score seventeen points to lead his team to the sweeping win.

The chain-smoking, delighted coach talked to the press following the emotional win. The next morning's *The Pantagraph* reported, "The Red Devils overcame a 62 - 50 Illinois Tech lead with less than nine minutes to play in the game. Eureka Coach Dave Darnall went to his bench at that time and inserted an entire freshmen line-up to key the comeback. Mark Fernandez hit a seven-foot jump shot to give Eureka a 72 - 70 lead with a minute to play, and Tim Peters added an insuring free throw moments later."

The Red Devils lost the championship game to the high scoring McKendree Bearcats, 107 to 89. Darnall had considered employing his slow-down tactics, especially since they were on the road. However, he decided to go ahead and let his "boys" run. He would put the idea on the "back burner."

Eureka bounced back with a nice victory at Aurora College to start an eight-game winning streak. Among the eight consecutive wins were impressive home victories over Knox College and a rematch game with McKendree College.

The post-game party at the Darnall home following the Knox game was well attended. By now the mere number of fifteen who attended the coach's first gathering had tripled. Players' parents, the Fernandezes, McGuires, Prossers, Johnsons, and Smiths were among the partygoers. The Hearnes, Traisters, Marcolines, Hosiers, Browns, Sam Harrods, Dobbersteins, Beers and Brunkharts, all members of the college community, joined in. There was even a larger, more jubilant group following the great McKendree victory.

Included in the eight-game winning streak were three games played in the St. Louis area during the first part of January. The team was staying at the Airport Marriott. As Coach Darnall had promised, it was one of the best motels in the St. Louis area.

With the first contest scheduled for 7:30 P.M. on New Year's Day, Darnall knew his players would sleep in on game day. Therefore, he had reserved a private room for a New Years Eve party for the entire Eureka entourage of players, parents and fans. The motel had an indoor-outdoor swimming pool. That was the first time most of the players saw such a facility. Some of the players, showing how brave they were on the bitter cold day, swam under a wall to the outdoor pool filled with plastic balls. The purpose of the balls was to keep the outdoor pool warm.

Following their dinner in the motel's restaurant, the team attended the New Year's Eve party that had been underway since 8:00 P.M. Darnall had the motel cater some hors d'oeuvres for the private party. The parents and other fans also supplied food and snacks. Liquid refreshments were available. Most of the Eureka group strolled around visiting and wishing each other a "Happy New Year."

Coach Darnall announced a team curfew of 1:00 P.M. With numerous parties taking place in the motel, he felt it was best to set a time limit for "cruising." One intriguing party took place in the Ballroom. It was a $100-a-person affair. This was "The New Year's Eve Party" of St. Louis. With a well-known orchestra and complete television coverage, it was the place to be.

The Darnalls and Browns were extremely curious and wanted to sneak away from the Eureka College gathering for a few minutes to go down stairs and observe the "party of parties." Throughout the entire evening, people were roaming everywhere, so the two couples thought that possibly after midnight no charge would be taken at the extravaganza. They were right. At 12:00 A.M. the doors opened. As the coaches and their wives entered the ballroom, to their surprise they saw three to four players dancing with well-dressed middle-aged ladies. Soon the players noticed their coaches. Bonnie and Suzie were surprised, but not Dave and Paul. They knew the boys too well.

The players strolled over to the coaches with the ladies not too far behind. Coach Darnall asked them if they were having a good time. The players answered, "Great!"

Dave informed the lads that Paul and he were going to have one dance with their wives and then return to the Eureka party upstairs and that they also had one dance left. The Darnalls and Browns admitted that the whole scene was pretty impressive.

As the players, coaches, and their wives walked to the elevator for the ride upstairs, Coach Darnall asked, "Okay, fellas, how did this all come about?"

Looking at each other to see who was going to speak, one player finally spoke up. "To tell the truth Coach, we were riding the elevator down to the lobby when these four ladies invited us to the ballroom celebration. We just couldn't pass it up."

Darnall replied, "We'll talk about this after our party. When did you go down?"

Looking around, one player finally responded, "Around eleven o'clock."

At 1:00 A.M., Coach sent his players to their own rooms with lights out at 1:30. The fans stayed in the assigned party room until approximately that time also. With the team and supporters returning to their rooms, the coaches and their wives went to Dave's from for a final drink. Thirty minutes passed before Bonnie and Suzie went on to their room around the corner of the hall. Two more hours passed when the coaches heard glass breaking in the hall. After a few seconds, Dave raced to his door to see what was happening. He saw glass on the hallway floor but no one in sight. As he rounded the hallway corner, he saw Bonnie down the hall standing in front of one of the boys' room.

Dave thought, "Oh, no," and rushed down to ask Bonnie what was going on.

She said that she had heard something too and had walked down in front of the guys' rooms just to "listen." While standing there a man came running down the hall, going from side to side, and knocking the decorative lights from the walls. When he reached her, she backed up against the wall. He paused long enough to say to her, "Just don't mind lady; just don't mind." He then proceeded on with his destruction.

Bonnie walked down to the front desk to report the incident while Dave checked the players' rooms. All were quiet. They were thankful Bonnie was not hurt, but also relieved that they could testify that the boys had no part in the episode. They later were informed that the vandal was a recently fired employee of the motel.

Several years later, McGuire told his coach of another happening of that night. Guess he didn't want to get any of his teammates in trouble, "Together We Win." However, Darnall questioned how he had any blame! McGuire related the story. "I don't remember if it was 'Bean' (Jeff Smith), Reggie, or Terry Teegarden, our student trainer, but someone picked up a girl at the St. Louis Airport Marriott during the New Year's Eve festivities. He thought she was a nice girl until in the motel room a gun fell out of her purse. Another nice deal Coach got us into, we thought. Where was Coach? Probably working on perfecting the Power I."

With the ninth win of the first ten games, the Red Devils matched all of their wins of the previous year. The Eureka College basketball program had taken the turn that the young coach wanted. Coach Darnall was quoted in *The Pantagraph*, "I think we have to be respected now a lot more than we were at the beginning of the season. One of the reasons for our success is we don't have one or two real good players we depend on. We have eight or nine who all have been having very good games. That makes all our recruiting efforts seem worthwhile at this point."

Nine of Eureka's fifteen varsity players were freshmen recruits.

On the road again. The Red Devils traveled to Rockford College following the St. Louis trip for the eleventh game of the season. Unfortunately, the result was not to their liking. They lost, 85 to 63. Perhaps the loss was a wake-up call for the team. The Red Devils won their next five consecutive games, giving them an unbelievable 13 to 2 record.

The next loss came at the hands of the pesky Illinois College Blue Boys. An article in *The Pantagraph* summarized the battle.

> The loss was the first in Conference play for the Red Devils in four outings, while Illinois College is unbeaten in two games. Eureka College is 14 - 3 for the season. Both teams hit 26 field goals, but the difference came at the foul line, where Illinois College hit 16 of 25, the Red Devils managed 13 of 19.

Will this scenario be heard again?

Eureka College bounced back with four consecutive wins. Then there were losses again to Illinois College, McKendree, and MacMurray before ending the season with a thrilling home victory against Monmouth College, 75 to 73, and a 19 to 6 record. Gregg Johnson led the way with twenty-three points. Jeff Smith chipped in with fifteen.

The home loss to Illinois College that eliminated his team from any Conference Championship for the second straight year was especially hard on the coach. Whereas post-game parties after victories were always fun and rewarding, those after losses were usually down beat with Darnall attempting to explain why his team lost. He enjoyed having people over to his home after games because it was his belief that his team was the community's also. Darnall also felt the need to be surrounded by people both in the celebration of a victory or the "agony of defeat." However, losing the Conference title the first two years of his college coaching to Illinois College had taken a toll on the coach. Darnall took every loss personally. He felt he must have done something wrong.

Dave reflected back to a creative writing piece he had penned while attending graduate school entitled "The Ulcer." Perhaps it summarized his feelings at this time.

The Ulcer

Although many of my friends complain of their mistreatments, none are quite so abused as I. You see, I am the ulcer of a coach.

For days before a game, I am tormented by worry—will the plans of strategy be effective, will the boys carry them off, what if an injury occurs, will John be eligible, and many others not yet thought of. Sometimes I wish my coach would just stop thinking, maybe even sleep a little.

I am also dragged along on a cold, bitter night to watch a game I could care less about. When the team is poor, I feel a little better and know my next few days will be more relaxed, but if the team is good, I just shudder and wish we had never come. My coach then feels all his worries are justified and adds to those he has already conjured up. Others don't help by telling how big a game is coming up—we know— they all are.

Finally, the day of the game comes and I wonder if I'll survive. I am starved all day except for an occasional butterfly pill, which is suppose to make me feel better. The game brings no relief. It's up and down and up and down, and when I almost feel it's no use, I'm given a big whiff of ammonia. After all this, I just hope and pray for the game to end.

Yet, even this does not end my misery. Winning just prolongs the agony. I'm jumped about, flipped, and flopped. Not only is my tormentor even more excited, but others are pounding him on the back, shaking his hand, and sometimes even hoisting us high in the air. Following this I'm dragged off to some celebration party where my nagging appetite is "nourished" with—ugh—pizza and beer. It would almost make me wish the game had been lost. But that is no more pleasant for he then droops his shoulders and stoops a bit which makes tight quarters for me. Even though he takes me straight home to bed, there is no rest. The game is played over and over again wondering how it could have been won and why it was lost. When sleep comes at long last, I think to myself, "I wish he would learn that it is not so important who wins or loses, but how you play the game."

1976-1977 Season

COACH DARNALL ENTERED HIS THIRD YEAR of college coaching with twenty new faces greeting him. He was, at least, winning the recruiting war. Not only was Dave able to get quantity, he was also obtaining quality. Gregg Johnson stayed around to assist his former coach. With the addition of Johnson and former player Doug Brown, Darnall felt he had the necessary components to bridge the gap between himself and his young players.

Communication and respect between the coaching staff and players are vital aspects of a winning program.

Four of the new recruits remained active all four years and contributed quickly to the success of the team over that period. They were Hughley Blanton, who had played for Darnall at Momence; Tom "Butch" Cassidy of Mendota; Tony "T" Moore of Chicago; and Chuck Topp of Rockford.

The annual maroon and gold scrimmage was held before the actual first regular season game. Two area icon sport figures served as honorary coaches. One was Ralph McKinzie. The other was Fred Young. Mr. Young was a well-known Bloomington-Normal area former athlete, official, and Sports Director of *The Pantagraph*. It was an honor to have both gentlemen in the gym.

The team opened this season against Indiana Institute of Technology in the Oakland City Tournament. It was the first time Darnall had heard of IIT, but it surely would not be the last!

Would Darnall's third year as Head Coach at EC be lucky for him? Remember, his favorite numbers were three and thirteen. His players rewarded their coach with an outstanding game winning, 102 to 80. Sophomores Reggie Holmes and Jerome Westbrooks led the scoring parade with twenty-two and twenty-one points respectively. Senior center Jeff Smith chipped in sixteen.

The next night wasn't so lucky for the Red Devil coach and his team. He lost the championship to the host school by the score of 79 to 72. Freshman Hughley Blanton, making his first start of his college career, contributed to the winning cause with seven points.

A late change in the Red Devil schedule had them traveling to Bolivar, Missouri, as a Homecoming foe for Southwest Baptist. A team had backed out of a contract leaving the NAIA District 16 champion and National Tournament participant in Kansas City the previous year without an opponent for its big weekend festivities.

Coach Darnall was contacted about the void in Baptist's schedule. As history will prove, Dave was not one to refuse to play anyone who would play home and home or give a guarantee. Darnall knew he was getting his team into deep shit. However, Southwest Baptist guaranteed their guests six motel rooms for the night before the game, four meals for the entire twenty-one traveling party, a two-hour practice session on the game floor, and nine hundred dollars—enough to charter a bus for the team with a little left over. That was too good of a deal to pass up. Besides, many players hadn't been to Missouri just like some had never been to Kentucky. The bottom line for Darnall, however, was he could use the trip as a recruiting tool—the opponent, the way the team would travel, and where they would stay. How many teams got paid to play a NAIA National Tournament participant—a top team in the country?

The Red Devils arrived in Bolivar around 4:00 P.M. after a six-hour trip. The dorms, fraternity houses, sorority houses, and other college buildings were all covered with Homecoming decorations.

"What the hell did Darnall get us into?" Westbrooks asked his good buddy McGuire after seeing all the unusual scenery. Sayings like "Bury the Red Devils," "Stomp the Red Devils," and "Dunk the Red Devils" were just a few of the messages the team saw throughout the campus.

"Damn, I don't know, but it doesn't look too good for us," McGuire replied.

The team had an early dinner at the college's dining hall before arriving at the fieldhouse at 7:30 P.M. for a short practice. When playing against "big competitors," Darnall liked his players to get familiar with the game floor. He maintained that philosophy throughout his college career.

Darnall had his players work a lot on the 1-2-2 adjustable zone defense in that practice. He had several drills where the players had to move with their arms extended full length above their heads. His players were trained to play a long time with their arms up. That was vital in the success of a zone defense.

Coach Darnall was uncharacteristically relaxed for a night before a game. The coaches had held a short coaches' meeting in the motel lounge before turning in for the night. Dave explained to his staff that they had nothing to lose and everything to gain. They had to give the NAIA Playoff team a good game. They had to take the crowd out of the game and not be embarrassing— no "blow out." That would hurt their new reputation as a respectable basketball program on the more upward.

The Red Devils arrived at the fieldhouse close to 6:00 P.M. Darnall liked to be at the game site an hour and a half before tip-off. He began his pre-game talk about fifty minutes before game time. His pre-game ritual normally took twenty minutes. That gave the players twenty minutes of warm-up with still ten left for final details. That procedure remained constant all of Darnall's twenty years of college coaching.

Coach announced the starters for probably the "biggest game" in his three years at the Eureka helm. They were Smith, Holmes, Westbrooks, McGuire, and Blanton. The ten seconds of silence was taken.

Darnall gave his last words to his bewildered players before they took the floor in front of a sell-out Homecoming crowd of over 3,500. It was by far the largest number of fans that a Eureka College team had played in front of. "Don't embarrass yourself, the team, or the college," Darnall instructed his players.

The game was on. Southwest jumped off to an early lead and held a 32 to 27 lead at the intermission. The Red Devils were holding their own. They were embarrassing no one. The normally fiery coach was pretty calm. He mostly gave praises to his players and reminded them to stay with the game plan. Darnall ended his half-time talk by saying, "Fellows, you have the opportunity to put Eureka College on the basketball map. This is by far the biggest game in the school's history. Can you imagine beating the NAIA State of Missouri champs? What a great trip home it would be."

Dave Darnall must have said the magic words. His Red Devils immediately jumped on the Bearcats, scoring the first ten points of the second half. They went on to hang on for an astonishing 69 to 64 victory. The on-floor celebration before the shocked Homecoming crowd was fairly short. The locker room jollification, however, lasted for at least a half-hour.

"I can remember the atmosphere in the locker room after the game just like it was yesterday," Dave said some twenty years later. "Who could ever forget seeing Tim McGuire pounding his head on his locker yelling, 'This has got to be a dream, this has got to be a dream' as the players were yelling, slapping hands, and hugging each other."

The Eureka College basketball program made history. It truly turned the corner for the program. The recognition Darnall wanted for his basketball program suddenly happened.

Dave finally had to get his players "back to earth." They still had a six-hour ride home during which no one would sleep. There was constant noise as a few tried to play euchre. Darnall by-passed the traditional McDonald's post-game meal and treated them with two Big Macs, large fries, and two large Cokes. That treat was financed by the $900 check Darnall grabbed as he left the visitors' locker room. The night surely wasn't what the Athletic Director expected when contacting the Eureka coach for the important Homecoming game.

By the way, freshman sensation Hughley Blanton, in only his second start of his career, led the Red Devils in double figures. He pumped in sixteen while teammates Smith and Westbrooks chipped in with fifteen apiece. Stan Prosser, Darnall's John Havlicek, contributed to the winning cause with eleven.

Two games later, the Red Devils again faced an institution with a considerably higher enrollment. That time it was the University of Illinois—

Chicago Circle. They had thousands more students than the tiny four-year liberal arts college located in the cornfields of Central Illinois.

However, before that game, Eureka played its home opener in front of a good enthusiastic crowd. The fans wanted to see the team that just put Eureka College on the basketball map. They were not disappointed! The Red Devils squeaked out a 61 to 60 victory over Aurora College on Tim McGuire's two free throws with twelve seconds remaining to play.

Portions of an article by Dave Wieczorek, sportswriter for *The Pantagraph*, best described Darnall's feeling following the game. "Sometimes a team can play its best game and still lose. Sometimes a team can play its worst game and still come out smelling like a rose. . . . . The Eureka College Red Devils did the latter in a non-conference game with the Aurora College Spartans."

It was during that frustrating game that two new behavior traits developed that remained with Darnall until his retirement. The first was the "right foot stomp." Feeling helpless, Dave responded to the unsatisfactory play of his players by stomping his right foot to the floor in front of his bench chair. The second occurred by accident. With his team playing extremely lackadaisically, Darnall had to waste a timeout to get his players' attention. He was beyond "pissed-off" at the five players who were playing. Darnall had the five form a circle around him halfway out to center court. The remaining members of the team surrounded them. There he could give his players a piece of his mind without the fans completely hearing what was being said.

Not only was the coach upset with the play he was witnessing, but also he was really peeved that he had to waste a timeout. Darnall wanted to keep those until the end of the game. If the players were playing well, regardless of the score, he rewarded them by allowing them to sit on the bench during timeouts. The players did not want to gather-up during timeout on the court.

The Pantagraph's Dave Wieczorek wrote a feature article following the Aurora game entitled "Tape shredder Darnall a Eureka College winner." Portion of it read,

Many coaches have been described as married to their jobs because of the amount of time they spend on it. Eureka College basketball coach Dave Darnall may be one of those coaches, but more likely he is stuck to his job—literally.

Darnall is in a sticky situation every game his team plays, whether the Red Devils are losing by a point with 10 seconds to go, or ahead by 10 points with a second to go.

Darnall, you see, is a tape shredder. At the start of a game Darnall begins ripping off strips of athletic tape from a fresh roll and rolls it into little balls. By the final buzzer, he's usually down to the end of the roll.

"I'm a nervous type of person and ripping up the tape relieves the tension," said Darnall in his Reagan Center office. The office walls are decorated with newspaper clippings about Eureka College players.

Darnall probably has a unique habit, but he has also been innovative in other ways, which have led the Red Devils to a 3 - 1 record this season. He has molded a fine defense.

Eureka College is coming off its best season in 30 years. Darnall has brought a winning program to Eureka College just like he did at Gridley, Roseville, and Momence High Schools.

Now to the game between the NCAA Division II institution of 20,000 students and the NAIA non-scholarship school of 450. University of Illinois-Chicago Circle is currently a NCAA Division I participant.

Coach Darnall told his players in his pre-game speech that they had the opportunity to make a name for themselves by beating the likes of schools as Illinois-Circle, that basketball people would take notice. McGuire commented on Darnall's pre-game talks, "Coach was always pumping us up before a game. Telling us how great our opponent was even though we had played them two weeks earlier and beat them by 30! Did we have stupid written on our foreheads!" Darnall never took anything for granted, and surely didn't want his player to do so.

Perhaps playing their best game of the season and with the support of their noisy home crowd, the Red Devils raced to a 40 to 25 half-time lead. EC was never seriously threatened the remainder of the game as they claimed a 71 to 57 victory over the much larger scholarship school. The post-game party at the Darnalls' was crowded. The Red Devil enthusiasts wanted to talk about the team's two great wins, Southwest Baptist and University of Illinois-Chicago Circle.

With another win under their belt, the Red Devils' next game was against their menace, the McKendree Bearcats. Just hours before the game, Coach Darnall received a handwritten note from a new coaching friend. The well-known Duncan Reid, now at the University of Kansas, took time to write the young coach.

Dave,
What are you trying to do, start a dynasty? You'll have too much pressure on you if you go 27 - 1. Stay around 15 - 10 and enjoy - enjoy.
Duncan
We're 5 -1 and pressure is on.

Who would guess that this would eventually happen? Not Darnall.

The bubble was about to burst. The Red Devils were spanked at home by the mighty Bearcats, 99 to 72. One very unusual aspect of the game was the visitors shot twenty-five free throws, making twenty-three, while the home team made six of seven. The post-game party was nothing like the one following the Chicago-Circle game. Could the humiliating loss become a wake-up call for perhaps an overconfident Red Devil team?

The players had three weeks for final exams and Christmas break before resuming their schedule with a game against Maryville College of St. Louis. The game was played at Illinois State University's Horton Fieldhouse as a preliminary game to the ISU-Bradley game. Whereas Dave Darnall never played college ball at Illinois State, he did at least get to coach a college game on the Redbird floor.

Darnall felt the long lay-off hurt his team but was happy to gain a 73 to 58 victory over Maryville. The Red Devils, actually, trailed at halftime by one, 24 to 25. Dave felt one of his "great" half-time lectures might have woke up his "sleeping" team. EC reeled off eleven consecutive wins, including the Maryville triumph. Perhaps the Red Devil players didn't want to hear anymore of Darnall's half-time lectures.

Four of the victories in the string of eleven were against the other Conference schools. That gave EC a 4 to 0 record in league play after the first round. One of the victories came on the road against the reigning Conference Champion, Illinois College. Stan Prosser pumped in twenty points to lead his team to the 62 to 57 victory. The Blue Boys were the pre-season Conference favorites to repeat.

Then it was time to have a Conference rematch with Greenville College on their floor. Darnall had great respect for Panther coach Jack Trager. "Regardless the talent we had, Coach Trager's teams were always ready to play us," said Darnall.

That proved true as the Greenville coach used one of Darnall's tactics against the highly talented team—ball control. The score at intermission was Eureka, 12, Greenville, 10. Trager had his ball club in the game.

Greenville got an early second-half lead forcing the Red Devils out of their well known 1-2-2 adjustable zone. The Panther's game plan was to shoot nothing but lay-ups. The strategy worked! Greenville gave EC its first Conference loss of the season.

The Red Devils lost back-to-back road games after that. The second loss came at the hands of Knox College. Eureka bounced back with a short three-game winning streak, including wins over Conference foes Blackburn and Illinois College. Beating Illinois College was especially gratifying for the Red Devil coach since the Blue Boys had beaten his team the two previous years for the Conference title.

The Red Devils lost two out of their last three regular season games. The one win was a "biggie." Eureka College beat MacMurray, claiming the Conference Championship and qualifying for the NAIA District 20 Playoffs. That was the first post-season play for the Red Devils since 1950.

The losses came in low scoring affairs against McKendree, 32 to 21, and a hard-fought, heartbreaking, one-point loss at Monmouth. The game was the last time the two institutions would play during Darnall's tenure. It was Monmouth's turn to play at Eureka the following year, but that never materialized.

The Red Devils finished regular play with a 20 to 6 record. That was the most wins in the college's history and Darnall's first twenty-game winning season. The Conference Champions led the NAIA District 20 in defense, ranking them fourth in the Nation. National recognition was now established on the Eureka College Basketball program.

Participating in the NAIA District 20 Playoffs was what Dave and his players had striven for. Their hard work had finally paid off. A couple sentences in an article entitled "Playoffs—Eureka in NAIA field with 57 - 53 victory" by Phil Theobald, sportswriter for the Peoria *Journal Star* best signified the coach's satisfaction of the Red Devils' season.

> Three years ago Dave Darnall took over as Head Basketball Coach at Eureka College and announced his intention to make the Red Devils into a NAIA basketball force to be considered.
>
> Three years later, Darnall has 'em in the District 20 Playoffs thanks to Tuesday's 57 - 53 victory over Illinois College at Reagan Center for at least a share of the Prairie College Conference Title.
>
> But what now? Can Eureka honestly hope to do much business against the likes of Illinois Wesleyan or Quincy? "Maybe not this year," said Darnall, "but we're right on the timetable I had for us when I came here . . ."

What a coincidence, or "was it meant to be" that Darnall would win his first Conference Championship and make his first trip to NAIA Playoffs in his third year at the helm? Oh, those numbers 3 and 13!

Six teams participated in the NAIA Playoffs with the winner having the honor of playing in the elite NAIA National Tournament in Kansas City. The Red Devils left the day before the game so as to practice on the game floor that evening. It was something Darnall wanted to do before playing a "big game." The practice, however, was to no avail. The talented Quincy College Hawks rolled over the undermanned, inexperienced Red Devils, 82 to 52. Quincy's legendary coach, Sherril Hanks had guided his third-seeded Hawks to a great win over Tulsa in regular season play. The tournament loss for Eureka, however, was just the beginning of many NAIA Playoff appearances and ultimately a National Championship.

Illinois Wesleyan was seeded number one with the support of the six-foot-ten NAIA All-American Jack Sikma. The St. Anne product had grown a couple inches since he played against Darnall's Momence teams.

Jeff Smith was selected on the ten-man NAIA All-District Team. He was the first Darnall-coached player to achieve that honor. However, he surely would not be the last. Coach Darnall received his first Prairie Conference Coach of the Year award. The team also had their annual sports banquet at the college's Commons. Following the banquet, players, parents, and fans gathered back at the Darnall home. This event became a Eureka College basketball tradition.

A very special occurrence took place on the Eureka College campus during that school year. Coach Darnall had his first opportunity to meet former California

Coach Darnall, Ronald Reagan, and Nancy Reagan.

218

Governor Ronald Reagan, Nancy Reagan, and brother Neil Reagan. The Reagan brothers are Eureka College alumni and had returned to campus to kick-off the college's "Million Dollar Campaign." Dave had no idea that he had just talked to the future president of the United States.

A major change was announced that year also. Eureka College President Dr. Ira Langston was going to retire. Dave hated to hear this. He had great respect for Langston and hated to see him leave the college Presidency. Dr. Dan Gilbert became the new president.

1977-1978 Season

GREAT EXPECTATIONS WERE MADE for the 1977-1978 basketball team. Ten returning lettermen and another good recruiting class reinforced that thought. Only NAIA All-District player Jeff Smith had departed. Six-foot-eight freshman center Ed Brady and sharp shooting Junior College transfer Joel Micetich were among the good recruits.

Darnall added a couple new faces to his staff—Kip Blakesley returned to be his former coach's number one assistant and Bruce "Preacher" Bangert became an administrative assistant working in several areas of the program.

A pre-season article appeared in *The Pantagraph* informing the Red Devil fans what they should expect to see during the year. First of all, they were suppose to see their favorite team only once before January 11, and that being against the tough CCIW school, Millikin University. Portions of the article entitle "Eureka College cagers face tougher schedule" read in part:

> "We have the most talent here that we've had in four years," said Darnall, "but we might not have as good a record because we've upgraded the schedule immensely."
> Eight of the first nine Eureka Games will be on the road, with only tough Millikin visiting the Red Devils in between.
> "Those first nine will tell a lot," said Darnall, an Illinois State University graduate. "If we're 6 - 3 we'll probably do pretty good the rest of the season. If not, then the schedule will prove what I've been saying."

Coach Darnall often wondered if the Eureka College administrators that had kept questioning his basketball schedules ever read the area newspapers. It seemed most reporters and Red Devil fans understood the difficulties of scheduling and felt most of the schools on the schedule were quality institutions with good basketball programs.

The team opened the season at the Central Methodist Classic in Fayette, Missouri. Behind the twenty-three-point performance of Stan Prosser and the additional twenty points of Reggie Holmes, the Red Devils gained a 72 to 60 victory over Columbia College. Holmes, Prosser, Westbrooks, McGuire, and Cassidy were the opening game starters. Blanton was the first player off the bench. The Red Devils played the host school for the tournament championship. It was not meant to be. Eureka lost their first game of the season, 106 to 100, in double overtime. That was a heartbreaking loss for Darnall and his troops.

Paced by Tom Cassidy's twelve second-half points, the Red Devils bounced back to beat a good Aurora College team, 92 to 68, in the third game of the season. That win was followed by an outstanding, 66 to 53, win over an always tough Marycrest College team.

It was then time to take on the much larger University of Illinois-Chicago Circle in the "Windy City." Dave knew that game would be a real challenge for his team since they wouldn't have their vocal fans supporting them.

The team and cheerleaders boarded a Peoria Charter bus on a cold and snowy Thursday in December. The normal three-and-a-half-hour trip, including stopping for a pre-game meal, took twice as long. The weather conditions forced the game to be delayed by thirty minutes. The Red Devil players were physically cold and played that way. They got behind early in the game and could never fight their way back. EC lost, 81 to 69. The scholarship school got its revenge.

The journey home proved to be even longer than the trip to Chicago. How about some thirty hours longer? Yes, it took a day and a half to reach Eureka's campus. Twenty-one team members and six cheerleaders left the "Windy (Snowy) City" at 10:30 P.M. and arrived at Dwight around 3:30 A.M. Interstate 55 (old Route 66) was down to one-lane with numerous vehicles in ditches. The five-hour trip to Dwight normally took about one hour. There, the Illinois State Police blocked the interstate. Nothing was going either way.

The Eureka entourage spent over two hours in either the bus or a near-by restaurant before being relocated to a local church basement. A "Sunday School" room became their new home. Each person was given a blanket. Most of the group had not yet slept and were anxious to get a little "shut-eye." Darnall desperately wanted to take a shower. He could hardly wait until the local general store opened and he could walk downtown to get some new BVDs for himself and toothbrushes for everyone.

Coach Darnall notified his Athletic Director of what was taking place and asked him to call the Dwight bank to arrange for a small loan for their expenses the next couple of days. The people of Dwight were extremely gracious. They cooked and brought food for all the stranded travelers. Food was available at all times. The students spent their first day napping, talking, playing cards, or backgammon. Around 5:00 P.M. on Friday, Dave was notified that the roads would remain closed until at least the following day. Eureka's home opener on Saturday against Millikin would have to be postponed until later in the season. Maybe it was meant to be. The phone call to the Decatur school was made.

It was then Friday night. The traditional night college students "let their hair down." Darnall's young athletes were getting restless. The Eureka College students wanted some action. Coach announced he was going to take his group to a local bowling alley on the bus and any other stranded travelers would be welcome to join them. Around 7:30 P.M., a bus full of people started its five-minute trip to the alley. Upon arriving, Dave noticed the parking lot was empty. The bowling alley was closed; he had failed to check before hand—a detail Darnall seldom missed.

"Now what do we do?" Darnall asked Assistant Coach Kip Blakesley.

"I don't know," Kip replied.

Someone in the back of the bus mentioned that a lounge was open downtown. That remark brought about a loud applause from the bus's occupants. So Dave agreed to go. The lounge was a neat, clean establishment with both food and game tables available. Since the drinking age for beer and wine was nineteen in Illinois and Eureka College at the time had an "open door" alcohol policy regarding those items on campus, Darnall felt he was in compliance with school regulations. Besides, many colleges allowed beer and wine on their campuses at that time.

Coach Darnall had only a few training rules. They were: "Don't do anything that is going to embarrass the team, the college, or yourself; be in your room on a given time before big games; no smoking in public; and absolutely no use of recreational drugs."

Drinking wine and beer was not against his policy.

Pitchers of beer were $3.00. Since he was very conscious about money, Dave felt pitchers of beer were a better deal than individual bottles.

221

The local lounge was doing an excellent business before the busload of fifty people arrived. Now, they were having a fantastic night. Business was so good the owner gave one free pitcher for every three bought. Everyone in the establishment was mixing with each other. Laughter could be heard everywhere. The loss was forgotten by all except the coach.

The busload returned to the church after a couple hours of fun. Food was available for anyone that was hungry. Around 1:00 A.M., Coach Darnall informed the players and cheerleaders that they should go to the team's assigned area and try to get some sleep. Some members of the group were already attempting to sleep. The room was extremely crowded with everyone lying on the floor. Darnall lay awake throughout the night. Even though he was extremely tired, Dave felt he should remain awake to "monitor" the mixed group. He could hear whispers of people talking and shuffling movement throughout the night. He could hardly wait until daybreak. Coach was ready to be home. Oh, how good a shower would feel! Finally, morning came, and the sun gave rise to the first clear day in three. It was still extremely cold, but the sun brought hope that the bus would be able to leave soon.

It was shortly after lunch on Saturday that the team boarded the charter bus for the slow trip home. Some snow along the roadside was as high as the bus. The normal hour-trip turned into three. The Red Devils finally arrived home.

Four weeks would pass before the next game. Eureka went into Christmas break with a disappointing 3 to 2 record. Still no home game. The Red Devils returned to action by claiming three victories in a five-day trip to the St. Louis area. That meant eight consecutive road games before the home folks would see the team compete.

North Central from the prestigious CCIW conference provided the competition for the January 11th home opener. The Red Devils did not disappoint their fans. They jumped out to a 46 to 29 half-time lead behind the fourteen-point performance of Hughley Blanton. Blanton went on to score a game high twenty-four points to propel his team to a "big win" over North Central, 84 to 62.

Eureka College split the next four Conference games. Darnall was very disappointed with the results of these games. He felt his team should have been at least 3 to 1. The team was now playing in spurts. Three good games; then three not so good. A good, 83 to 63, victory over Blackburn behind the twenty-three-point scoring output of Hughley Blanton and twenty-one points of Reggie Holmes was sandwiched between the second spurt—three more losses before finishing the season with two wins.

One of the last two victories was the make-up game against Millikin University that had been postponed due to the snowstorm. Darnall commented on the win. "They were ready to play the 'Big Blue.' We didn't have the type of season we wanted. I guess by beating Millikin, the players figured we did better than our record indicated. We played two CCIW schools and beat both," said Darnall.

Eureka College claimed the impressive 76 to 71, five-point victory behind the scoring power of Stan Prosser and Tim McGuire, twenty-three and twenty points respectively. Leading 73 to 71, the Red Devils put the game out of reach with two free throws by "T" Moore and one by Joel Micetich.

EC lost six out of the last nine games, including three Conference games. They finished with a dismal Conference record of 3 to 5 and a very disappointing 15 to 10 overall record. It was a long off-season for the coach.

The 1977-1978 campaign was the last year for the Prairie College Conference. There were several rumors as to why it disbanded. One was Illinois College's refusal to play Eureka College, supposedly over an incident during the football season. Some indicated that Eureka's basketball program was becoming too competitive. In any case, Blackburn also dropped Eureka from its basketball schedule. MacMurray and Greenville both continued to schedule Eureka until some years later.

1978-1979 Season

A CHANGE TOOK PLACE DURING THE SUMMER that would affect all Eureka College athletic programs. The college applied for and was admitted into the NCAA Division III. A major reason given for this decision was to move the athletic program to a more "prestigious academic level." A few members of the administration felt this was needed for various reasons.

The move meant that both NCAA III and NAIA II rules and regulations would govern the basketball program. It did not necessarily mean the EC basketball program would make dramatic changes. The college, however, would have to declare its intention of what post-season tournament it would participate in if qualifying. Since Darnall felt the NAIA National Championship was the second most prestigious basketball championship in the United States, he chose the NAIA. Hopefully, no one would override him. Dave was a NAIA "man."

It was unusual for an institution to be a member of both national associations. It meant the college had to follow the strictest rules of each. The new restrictions by the NCAA Division III gave the head coach more headaches. The one new rule that did not matter was the prohibiting of any type of athletic aid to the student-athlete. Eureka College did not permit athletic scholarships anyway. The Red Devils definitely had a disadvantage in competing with most other NAIA colleges and universities. Very few people were aware of the rigorous regulations Eureka College had to follow.

The annual Maroon and Gold scrimmage game gave the Red Devil fans their first opportunity to view their favorite team. McKinzie and Young were joined by former Illinois State University coach Don Karnes as an honorary coach. Darnall observed the game from the bleachers, hoping to select the starters that would turn around the disappointing previous season. Besides some very good returning lettermen, Dave added several freshmen who could contribute immediately in his pursuit to return to the NAIA Playoff. Larry Thomason of Bartonville Limestone and two of Wes Mason's Chicago Heights Bloom players, Sam Reed and Monte Bell, were among the good recruiting class. Darnall did not want the "cupboard to run dry."

An article written by Phil Theobald entitled "Darnall Plans to 'Feast' on Red Devil Victories" appeared in the Peoria *Journal Star*. It best described the team's outlook for the 1978-1979 season as well as summing up Dave's recruiting efforts. Portions read:

Dave Darnall's desk was his dinner table Thursday. On the menu was a cold ham sandwich, Coke in a paper cup and a cigarette for desert.

"I don't have time to go out and eat," said Darnall, head basketball coach at what he believes is the smallest (enrollment 425) four-year college in Illinois.

"We had a 15 - 10 record last year and that was a disappointment," said Darnall. "We'll be better . . . more inside scoring and quicker, so if they slow it down to bring us out of the zone, it won't be a disaster."

Darnall's teams have averaged 18 victories over the past three seasons. No longer do most Mid-State 10 Conference coaches, when approached at recruiting time, tell him to go fish.

"We really hafta beat the bushes for players," said Darnall, indicating he often sends out for two cold ham sandwiches because neither does Assistant Kip Blakesley have time to go out and eat.

"Our problem is we've got to talk to so darned many players to get a few," added Darnall, who unlike some others in his position is realistic enough to forget at the start about hustling potential NCAA Division I players.

"Last year we talked to, oh, 100 players," said Darnall. "We got 17. A lot of the ones we wanted got away . . . and we know the players we're interested in usually wait for a better offer. That's why some kids don't sign with us until July."

Darnall took another bite of the cold ham sandwich, "We had 400 kids at our summer basketball camp," he said. "It all helps. We're making progress."

He wrapped up the remains of the cold ham sandwich and looked at the Red Devil's schedule, perhaps thinking in terms of filet mignon.

The Red Devils opened their campaign by participating in two early season invitational tip-off tournaments. The first one was the Judson Turkey Classic. Their first opponent was Grand Rapids Baptist. Darnall, in his traditional pre-game talk, challenged his players to play hard and execute their offenses and defenses. No words were held back. The chain-smoking coach told it like it was or like it would be if they did not play well. Winning is the "name of the game" at this level.

The pre-game lecture worked. The Red Devils scored ninety-eight points and won by a thirty-five-point margin. The championship game was to be against the talented Judson Eagles. Holding a slim one-point lead at the intermission, Eureka College went on to claim the title by defeating the host, 72 to 68. Sam Reed led a balanced Red Devil scoring attack with a fifteen-point performance. Senior Reggie Holmes was named the tournament's Most Valuable Player while Hughley Blanton and Joel Micetich were selected to the All-tournament Team.

In the first round of the William Penn Tip-off Tournament held at Oskaloosa, Iowa, Eureka College was paired with Grinnell College. Behind the eleven-point first-half performance of Hughley Blanton and additional ten points from Micetich, the Red Devils jumped out to a 33 to 24 half-time lead and held on for an eighteen-point victory.

The championship game was a showdown between EC and the host school. Portions of a newspaper article that appeared in the following morning's *The Pantagraph* best described what took place the previous night.

Eureka College, sparked by five reserves, came back from an early 19 - 3 deficit to edge William Penn, 46 - 43, in Saturday's Championship game of the William Penn Tip-off Basketball Tournament. The Red Devil's Tony Moore, 6-foot junior guard, came off the bench to become the game's only double-figure scorer with 10 points. Moore and Eureka College starter Hughley Blanton were named to the All-tournament Team.

Down 19 - 3 with 12 minutes left in the first half, Red Devil coach Dave Darnall sent five reserves—Moore, Dave Chandler, Ed Brady, Stan Prosser, and Mark Anderson—into the game. The five non-starters outscored William Penn 20 - 8 the rest of the half to cut the host's lead to four points.

Darnall, still disgusted with his starters and happy with the way their replacements had performed, stayed with the five that brought his team back in the second half. He did, however, substitute during the final twenty minutes. With five seconds left on the clock, Chandler made the first end of a bonus situation to seal the Red Devil victory, 46 to 43, and claim their second tournament championship within the first week of play.

The Red Devils returned home to play two games in front of their hometown fans. They won both. The first post-game party at Darnalls' was heartily attended. Not only were the fans celebrating the 95 to 70 victory over Aurora College, but many people unable to attend the tournament games were anxious to know the details of those two tournaments.

A newspaper article by Bryan Bloodworth, sportswriter for the Bloomington *The Pantagraph* entitled "Attitude Spurs Red Devils to 6 - 0 Start on Season" signified the great start Eureka College experienced. It read in part:

> Eureka College basketball coach Dave Darnall doesn't have the answers to all the questions, but he can sure tell you why his Red Devils are off to a 6 - 0 start.
>
> "It's our attitude," he said matter-of-factly between bites of a hamburger before running his team through practice Tuesday at Reagan Center.
>
> "This team has a much better attitude than last year's. Last year everyone was a little more worried about themselves than the team. This year they're concerned about the team first.
>
> "This is the best start I've ever had personally as coach and I'm sure it's one of the best Eureka College has had in a long time," said Darnall, who is in his fifth season at the helm. "I don't know if the school has ever won two tournaments in the same season, but I never have as a coach."
>
> While most coaches complain about the lack of depth, Darnall just sits back and smiles.
>
> Two examples indicate just how much depth Eureka College has. Stan Prosser, a 6-foot-6-inch forward, is a three-year all-conference performer, but this season he's not starting.
>
> "He could be a starter," Darnall says, "but we have been using him off the bench to give us the extra boost we need. Sam Reed (a freshman

from Chicago Heights Bloom) has been starting and we use Stan as a safety valve. We don't lose anything with either one in there."

Prosser, one of three seniors on the squad, has accepted the assignment without any gripes.

"At first I was a little upset and couldn't figure it out, but as long as I get in the game, I don't mind," he said. "There aren't any hard feelings when one guy goes in for another. It's easier to accept when you know you have someone just as good sitting on the bench that can do the job."

Another article that appeared in the Peoria *Journal Star* written by Phil Theobald reinforced Prosser's extreme value to the team.

Last season, a few of those who didn't start for Eureka burned off their extra energy by griping a lot. Stan Prosser did start—as he had the previous two seasons, each of them ending in all Prairie College Conference honors for the 6-6 forward from Villa Grove High School.

Prosser hasn't started this season. "He's been sort of a John Havlicek player for us," said Darnall. "Stan has actually had more playing time off the bench than some starters . . . and he's been giving us a lift."

The Red Devils went on to win four in a row before suffering their first defeat of the season at the hands of Concordia-Milwaukee on the road. One of the wins was against the highly respected McKendree Bearcats. Year after year, Coach Harry Statham has his quality teams ready to play Eureka College. The game was played in front of a near-capacity house. The two potential NAIA Playoff teams provided an exciting evening of basketball. The Red Devils gained a little revenge after suffering two defeats to the Bearcats the previous year. Coach Darnall had given one of his most rigorous pre-game talks of the season. He reminded his players of the two losses and how important the game would be in determining the playoff field.

Dave was very nervous before the game. With the players heading to the back stairway of the building, the coach visited the bathroom for the final time. He then trailed his team to the gym entrance. Stomping out his last cigarette, he entered his work area. There was a championship atmosphere. His team was ready. An 81 to 68 victory over a class program was waiting. What a post-game party at the Darnalls' followed!

A three-week lay-off preceded the team's two-game trip after Christmas break to the St. Louis area. Several fans accompanied the team. They all stayed at the Collinsville Holiday Inn that featured an indoor pool. That arrangement was exactly what Darnall promised in his recruiting talks. The fans provided food for all.

Eureka College gained two wins on the trip and went on to claim five consecutive victories before losing in a heartbreaking two-point triple-overtime to Iowa Wesleyan.

One of the five wins was against Marycrest College. Eureka played an inspired game and went on to win, 79 to 58. Following the contest, Darnall was asked by *Journal Star* sportswriter Phil Theobald his thoughts about the game.

"Overall, I was impressed with the way we played. We got that nice lead, and we ran with 'em when we had to," Darnall said.

Coach was also quoted on his 1-2-2 adjustable defense. "Our philosophy," said Darnall, whose team leads NAIA District 20 in defense, "is that if we are going to get beat, we'll get beat by the twenty-foot shot. We don't want to give anybody anything inside."

Theobald also asked Marycrest's Coach Ned Era to reflect on the game. Coach Era favorably compared Eureka, shooting sixty-two percent from the field, to once-beaten Briar Cliff, ranked No. 5 nationally among NAIA schools. "They beat us by twenty last week," said Era. "Briar Cliff could play Eureka, and it would be a good matchup." He did, however, indicate that the Red Devils were less physical underneath.

The triple overtime loss to Iowa Wesleyan was devastating to Darnall. It left him both physically and mentally drained. The coach said, "That was one of the longest trips home after a game in my entire career. Not only because of the strain of the game but also because of the hazardous winter road conditions."

The team began to travel on some road trips by vans. The reason was Title IX. Eureka College couldn't afford to send both their men's and women's teams on the road in charter buses. However, when both teams played the same opponent on the same night, they traveled by charter together. The night of the Iowa Wesleyan game was, unfortunately, not the case. Coach Darnall did not like to drive the school's vans, so he bought one himself to drive on road trips. His assistant coach drove the college's van.

The team finally arrived home to Eureka around 2:30 A.M. There had to be at least ten inches of snow on the ground. The wind was blowing, and it was a very cold Saturday night. The players exited the vans and headed for their dorms. Coach Blakesley and several players lived in the TKE house located directly across the parking lot from Reagan Center. As Coach Darnall stepped from the van into the snow, two gunshots rang out from the backside of the TKE house. Dave, tired and stressed, and knowing a couple of players were upset both with the loss and their playing time, dove head first into the snow bank.

Darnall shouted to his assistant, "Kip, get the hell over there and find out who in the hell is shooting at me!"

Blakesley took off running. Darnall jumped up and quickly brushed the snow from his maroon leisure suit. Kip, by then, had reached the TKE house and headed back to the head coach. He was laughing his ass off.

"What the hell are you laughing at?" Darnall shouted.

Blakesley replied, "Coach, someone was shooting at a thrown volleyball."

"What?" Dave asked.

Kip went on to explain that one of the TKEs, probably after a few beers, was shooting out his window at a volleyball tossed in the air by a fraternity brother in the snow-covered backyard.

"Who in the hell would be shooting a gun at this time of the night?" Darnall questioned, not amused by the whole ordeal. "I thought guns were prohibited on campus." He then turned and headed to the gym to help unload the game equipment and clean up.

The Red Devils won the next four games before losing to Millikin in a road game. They ended their regular season schedule by squeaking out a one-point win at Concordia-River Forest.

One of the victories had been over prestigious Grace College. The Indiana school was considered one of the top small college basketball programs in the country. In fact, several years later, Grace would win the inaugural NAIA Division II National Championship.

Reggie Holmes led the way with fourteen points, helping the Red Devils conquer a 60 to 54 overtime victory over the visitors. Teammate "Butch" Cassidy contributed to the scoring attack with eleven points. It was a fun party at the Darnalls' after the game. It was time to celebrate a 17 to 2 record overall and 7 to 0 at home.

A second great win during that stretch was a 68 to 54 rematch victory over Iowa Wesleyan. The triple overtime loss still haunted Darnall as his team took the floor. So did the dive in the snow. The revenge win gave the coach a little comfort.

It was about that time that an article by Tim Yonke appeared in the Kankakee *Daily Journal*, discussing Momence's connection to the successful Eureka College basketball program. The article entitled "Cage fever runs rampant at Eureka" surrounded the Red Devil's new star Hughley Blanton. Portions read:

Basketball fever is reaching epidemic proportions at little Eureka College with the help of the "Momence Connection."

The Red Devils are currently the No. 1 team in NAIA District 20 with a record of 17 - 2. While the school has an enrollment of just 400, home games draw more than 1,000 fans to Reagan Center gym.

Two of the reasons why Eureka a playing with the best small colleges in the state are its coach and his star player—former Momence Coach Dave Darnall and ex-Redskin standout Hughley Blanton.

"Hughley is having a good year for us. On most teams he'd be a superstar but he plays within the team concept here," Darnall said.

Averaging 12 points and nine rebounds, Blanton has used his 6-6 frame in a less than showboat fashion.

"He's improved over the last couple of years but I don't think he's reached his maximum. He doesn't play with a whole lot of emotion, and at times, he's not aggressive. We're hoping next year he'll break out," said Darnall.

Darnall is already thinking of next year and drooling. That's when another member of the Momence Connection—6-4 Jerome Westbrooks—returns to the Red Devil lineup for his senior year. Darnall redshirted Westbrooks this year since Jerome was changing majors and would have to go another year to complete his degree anyway. As a junior last year, Westbrooks averaged 12 points a game as a forward opposite Blanton.

"I don't have to tell you that we're really looking forward to them playing together again next year," Darnall said.

So are about 1,000 loyal Eureka fans.

The team finished its regular season play with a 20 to 3 record, which included all eight home game victories. Two home games had been cancelled due to bad weather conditions. Coach Darnall felt those could have resulted in wins for the Red Devils especially with the great fan support that was prevalent in the other home victories. The opponents, supposedly, were unable to fit the make-up games into their schedules.

Would there be post-season play for the Red Devils? Since Eureka College was no longer affiliated with a conference, they had to depend on being selected by the District Playoff Committee. Darnall felt his team proved its worth but knew being from a small rural community with no major newspapers or radio covering them exclusively, it would be an uphill battle. Eureka did not have much clout even though it had the best won- and-lost record in the district and was among the leaders in several statistical categories, including leading in defense.

It was a tense twenty-four hours for Coach Darnall and his Red Devils between their one-point win over Concordia and the hearing of their playoff fate. An article entitled "Eureka College District 20 Pick" that appeared in *The Pantagraph* best described why Darnall was worrying. Portions read:

> Eureka College was chosen to participate in the National Assn. of Intercollegiate Athletics District 20 (Illinois) basketball playoffs for the second time in three years Sunday, but the suspense didn't end early for Red Devil Coach Dave Darnall.
>
> Eureka, which sports a 20 - 3 record, was the last team picked for the six-team field and will play third-seeded St. Xavier of Chicago at 7:30 P.M. Saturday in the Chicago State University gymnasium.

Darnall had been the first to petition the committee on behalf of his team for one of the at-large berths. When Quincy, St. Xavier, and McKendree were picked, Darnall admitted he was concerned and worried they would not make the field. Needless to say, Coach Darnall was thrilled and relieved when his team was selected as the final playoff team. He knew the game with St. Xavier would be difficult, but after last season's absence from the tournament field, he was just happy to be playing one more game.

A charter busload of team members and fans left early afternoon for the three-and-a-half-hour trip, including stopping for a pre-game meal, to Chicago State's fieldhouse. The game was being played there because St. Xavier's gym did not meet NAIA regulations.

The first half was thrilling. Paced by the twelve-point scoring attack of Hughley Blanton, the Red Devils trailed the third-seeded Xavier by only four points, 49 to 45. Coach was pleased with the play of his players. However, he was upset with the officiating. Reggie Holmes picked up three quick fouls in the game, two of which were very questionable in Darnall's mind. The NAIA All-District player saw limited action. Joel Micetich also got into early foul trouble. The Eureka College fans were also frustrated with the Chicago area officials.

The Red Devils proved they belonged in the playoff field even though they lost, 79 to 76. The game was close throughout, but without the services of starters Holmes and Micetich, both had fouled out, Eureka could not overcome the "home court advantage." St. Xavier played the entire game with their top seven players—no one fouled out. Both teams scored thirty-three baskets with the home team winning at the free throw line. Blanton led the Red Devils in scoring with eighteen points. Stan Prosser chipped in fifteen. Prosser and Holmes each hauled down nine rebounds as Eureka dominated the boards, 41 to 28.

The long, but gratifying season was over. The many hours spent recruiting and the demanding season wore out the Red Devil coach. Bonnie and Dave needed a vacation. They had never really taken a vacation other than the Biloxi trips with the Dick Daltons of Gridley. This summer was going to be different. The week following the completion of Dave's summer camps, the Darnalls and Gregg Johnsons spent a week at Table Rock Lake, Kimberling City, Missouri.

The well-known Branson area would, twenty-seven years later, host many Red Devil players and fans. The 1994 NAIA II National Champions would celebrate the tenth anniversary of their great accomplishment at the 2004 National Tournament held on the campus of the College of the Ozarks.

1979-1980 Season

COACH DARNALL HAD RECRUITED SEVERAL excellent high school players, but it was Decatur Eisenhower High School's standout playmaker who had earned "City Player of the Year" honors that stole the show. The five-foot-ten sharp-shooting guard would eventually end his college career as EC's all-time scoring leader.

Mike Sain was recruited by numerous colleges throughout the country, but it was Dave Darnall who "captured his attention." That was to the complete dismay of his hometown college, Millikin University. A portion of an article that appeared in the Decatur *Herald & Review* written by Forrest R. Kyle described the bewildered Millikin coach's thoughts.

> "We've lost several players whom I think had a genuine interest in Millikin but ended up getting full-ride athletic scholarships," Ramsey said. "The biggest disappointment, however, was losing Mike Sain."
> Sain, Eisenhower High's sharp-shooting guard, was wooed by several schools—some which offer a full-ride athletic scholarship —but ended up announcing he would attend Eureka College.
> "We wanted him in the worst way," said Ramsey.

Darnall commented on his signing of Sain. "He was sought by many colleges, including a number of Division I schools such as Eastern Illinois and Western Michigan. We felt very fortunate that Mike chose to play ball with us."

Sain, in turn, commented on why he decided on Eureka College to further his education and play ball. "I just felt I had the best opportunity at Eureka, and everything was more agreeable to me there. I had met the players and got to know them pretty well and really liked them."

Two other top recruits added to Eureka College's basketball roster were First Team Class A All-state forward Tracey Trimpe of Havana High School and Bob Barnett of Oregon High School. Barnett was named to the Chicago *Sun Times*' All-state First Team and the Tribune's Second Team. He had signed a baseball contract with the Philadelphia Phillies and was a promising young right-hand pitcher for a couple years before hurting his arm, cutting his career short. One reason the super athlete chose Eureka College was the college's unique school calendar called the Intensive Study Program. It allowed Barnett to attend three-fourths of the school year and pitch professionally the other quarter and summer.

Coach Darnall was disappointed when the faculty voted to change the system to a semester schedule years later. It has been a great incentive when recruiting. However, since he was out of coaching, the former head coach remained silent during the debate for change.

The 1979-1980 season was very rewarding but also disappointing for the Red Devil team. An article by Phil Theobald of the Peoria *Journal Star*, "Opponent, Red Devils Hope to Have Your Number (20)" related Darnall's hopes and concerns for his shortest team in several years.

At Eureka College, basketball coach Dave Darnall has his players repeating, "If we're gonna get beat, get beat by 20." Sounds almost as if close doesn't count.

But for the Red Devils it does. "By 20, we don't mean points,'" said Darnall. "We mean if they're going to beat us, they'll have to beat us by shooting from 20 feet.

"We like to call the lane 'No Man's Land,'" added Darnall, whose team won 20 games last year for a NAIA District 20 Playoff assignment.

Problem is, the lane may not be exactly a friendly place for the Red Devils to spend much time in this season. "It's the smallest team I've had in my six years here," said Darnall.

"The lack of height scares me," he added, "especially against some of the stronger teams we play. We've got to have some players come through for us."

"My main concern is what happens close to the basket," said Darnall. "We need scoring punch in there and we need rebounding."

The Red Devils opened their season with a novelty of a two-game home "stand." After claiming a twelve-point decision over Greenville, the Red Devils turned their attention to the tough CCIW foe Millikin University. Eureka wanted a little revenge after the previous year's beating in Decatur by the Big Blue. Coach Darnall wanted to prove to Mike Sain that he made the right choice in choosing Eureka over his hometown college. His team corroborated Sain's decision.

It is difficult to do justice to the magnitude of the game between the two colleges located only fifty miles apart. Bill Flick, *The Pantagraph* sportswriter witnessed the highly contested game. Portions of his article "Eureka College shocks Millikin" follow.

It wasn't a showdown between the state's two best basketball teams. It wasn't a long-awaited battle for a conference championship. It wasn't even a conference game.

But you never would have guessed it after Eureka College scored an impressive 63 - 45 victory over Millikin University Tuesday night.

At first glance to a latecomer, it must have appeared the Red Devils had upset the nation's top team or, better yet, won the national championship.

They didn't, but what the Red Devils did accomplish meant nearly as much. "I'd have to say this was probably the biggest win Eureka College has ever had," said Darnall, coach of a school which has long suffered from an identity crisis.

"Millikin is from one of the best conferences in Illinois (the College Conference of Illinois and Wisconsin) and we beat them. Convincingly. Eureka College. Little Eureka College."

A team traditionally known for excellent outside shooters, Millikin was bottled by a defense which never quit.

Eureka College controlled the tempo of the game throughout. The teams were tied . . . six times in the first half and settled for a 23 - 23 knot.

Early in the second half, the Red Devils' zone prevailed. The Big Blue never seriously threatened again.

Six-foot-six senior Hughley Blanton led Eureka College offensively with 19 points on seven-of-11 shooting from the field. But 6-4 sophomore guard Sam Reed played a major role, scoring 18 points with all but two coming in the second half.

"Tonight we had two 'big-time' papers here, a television station and the game was carried on radio. I don't ever remember all that in one game."

The second post-game party at the Darnalls' was a blast. The champagne was flowing, while the question "How far can this team go?" was constantly asked. It was a great social gathering but left the coach with a huge headache.

The first of three consecutive road games was underway. New Assistant Coach Reggie Holmes drove one van carrying the upperclassmen and "Preacher" Bangert, while second-year student coach Pat Hayes drove for Darnall, the underclassmen, and trainer Henry Hunsinger. Dave continuously talked to Hayes about his concern of his team "coming back to earth" after the "big" Millikin win.

The basketball program was on a limited budget that year. Instead of stopping and eating a pre-game meal, it was decided to buy a meal following the game. The team would take snack lunches prepared by the college's cafeteria staff for its pre-game meal. The journey to Grace College in Indiana led the EC party through Darnall, Blanton, and Westbrooks' old hometown of Momence. A few miles further came the Indiana border and its "Naked City." The world famous nudist colony was located approximately twenty-five miles straight east of Momence. The colony was well known throughout the Momence-Kankakee area.

By then, the players were getting hungry. It was time for their pre-game snack-meal. But where could the two vans pull over so the occupants could eat? Guess what!

Someone, unnamed here, suggested the parking lot of "Naked City." A roar could be heard all the way back to the Christian college campus. The main man, not wanting to upset his players before the night's battle and as a little reward for their last great win, agreed. The vans pulled into the establishment's parking lot. The players, wanting to stretch their legs, immediately jumped out. Twenty healthy lads started to roam. The coaches also leaped from the vans, not to stretch their legs but to gather the wandering boys.

"Everyone over here," Darnall shouted. "We stopped to eat. That's all."

By that time, several of the guys were approaching the locked entrance gate. Hearing their coach's words, all team members returned to their vans to do what they had stopped for—eat!

It is not really known if the trip was too long, the change of the pre-game meal, an over-confident team, or the good play of the host school, but Grace College hammered the weary Red Devils, 91 to 70.

Following the game, Darnall asked his assistants Holmes and Hayes, "What the hell happened out there tonight? Do you think the fellows had their minds on something other than the game?"

There was no answer. To this day, Darnall still wonders what happened—what went wrong.

The other two road games resulted in a couple of wins. The Red Devils bounced back from their dismal performance to beat a good Marion College of Indiana, 73 to 68. The other victory came at the expense of Trinity Christian.

The Red Devils next competed in two invitational tournaments. The first was at Eureka College and the other at the University of Chicago.

In the only invitational tournament held at Eureka College during his tenure, Darnall's team raced by St. Louis Christian to set up the title match against Judson College. The Eagles qualified for the final game by beating Edgewood College, Wisconsin, 89 to 55. In a hard fought contest, the Red Devils downed their opponent, 81 to 68, for the tournament championship. Eureka College had a balanced scoring attack with four players scoring in double figures. Joel Micetich led his team with twenty points while Blanton chipped in with nineteen.

It was time to go to the "Windy City." Eureka was going to play in its first and last University of Chicago Holiday Tournament during Darnall's tenure. It was a tournament of academic prestigious colleges—just what Eureka College's new president wanted.

Grinnell College, Iowa, was EC's first opponent. Blanton, Westbrooks, and Sam Reed scored twenty, eighteen, and sixteen points respectively to lead their team to an 85 to 47 victory. Coach Darnall was really proud of his "Momence Connection." The fellows' success at Eureka was the dream Darnall had shared with his Momence players when he was trying to decide whether to stay there or accept the Eureka College offer.

The Red Devils played the host school in the championship game. With the president of Eureka College in the stands, EC played a flawless game to claim the championship. Eureka hit all but three of its first twenty-three shots from the field for a twenty-two-point lead at intermission and romped to a 91 to 69 win over the University of Chicago. Leading the parade of twelve, Red Devil scorers were Sam Reed and Hughley Blanton who netted twenty-two and twenty-one points respectively.

In a post-game press conference, Coach Darnall was asked by Mike Conklin for an unspecified Chicago newspaper his thoughts about the game.

"We've got the quickness and depth to play up-beat this year," said Darnall. "We've also got five seniors who've been with me all four years, and that develops a lot of understanding on the floor, which really helps on defense. Our problem has come in the tournaments at the end of the year," continued Darnall, whose teams have qualified for two of the last three NAIA District 20 Playoffs. "We always seem to get a tough seed and play the strongest teams right off the bat."

Dave had planned to return the following year to defend the title. It wasn't to be. Eureka College was not invited back. Darnall thought that was somewhat unusual. It was a perfect example of the dilemma he faced when trying to fill the Red Devil basketball schedule. Darnall had no idea why his team wasn't invited back or, in fact, why any other schools like Eureka wouldn't play them. Could it be they were just getting too competitive?

"I guess you'll have to ask the University of Chicago why we weren't invited back just like the other Central Illinois schools that refused to play us while I was coaching," Darnall said.

The Red Devils had three weeks for Christmas break before returning for two road games. One was close to Chicago and the other south of St. Louis. Eureka won a two-point squeaker against Aurora College before breezing by Harris-Stowe, 81 to 60. "T" Moore scored twenty points, including four free throws in the last twenty-eight seconds of overtime to lead the Red Devils to the 71 to 69 victory over Aurora College. Blanton put nineteen points in the scoring column.

The Red Devils next recorded two lopsided home victories before traveling to Sheboygan, Wisconsin, to participate in the Lakeland Tournament. The first game was against NFL former quarterback Dave Krieg's alma mater, Milton College. Behind the twenty-three-point performance of Sam Reed, Eureka nosed out an excellent Milton team, 64 to 62. The Red Devil victory resulted in a match-up with the host school for the championship. That game was one Darnall will always remember.

Dave witnessed one of the poorest officiated games since he started his college-coaching career. Eureka led at halftime by eight, 38 to 30. The second half play began to get ugly. The teams got away from the ordinary "playing hard." Shoving and pushing began to take place. It was rougher than a football game. As the score became closer in the latter stages of the game, a closely guarded Lakeland player, moving beneath his basket, got frustrated with the pressure Cassidy was applying. He hauled off and socked him in the face. Cassidy was knocked out. "Butch" dropped like he was shot, unconscious and bleeding. The Eureka bench emptied followed by Lakeland's. A total rumble broke out. The attacker ducked under the basket. Several Red Devils followed. Blanton reached him first. After several swings had been made, Darnall was able to restrain his angry player. Players from both teams were scattered all over the floor. Cassidy's sister, Patty, sprinted from the bleachers to the side of her severely injured younger brother as she was yelling obscenities at the officials. Darnall ran to his laid-out player after setting Blanton down. "T" Moore, Eureka's black point guard and a close friend of "Butch" went berserk, screaming and shouting at Lakeland's black player who had decked his white buddy. Cassidy was the most likeable player on the team. Definitely the wrong man to hit. An ambulance was summoned to transport the stunned Cassidy to a hospital. Patty accompanied her brother to the emergency room. The assistant coaches from both teams finally restored order.

The game resumed with only a short time left to play. Eureka College was assessed two technical fouls: one for the bench going on the floor and the second for Tom's sister running onto the floor to aid her brother. Dave was angry.

"How come the player that hit 'Butch' and started everything wasn't given a technical and thrown out of the game?" Darnall shouted. "Why didn't Lakeland's bench get a technical when they went on the floor?" There were no answers.

Lakeland got the win by a score of 80 to 70. Hughley Blanton and "Butch" Cassidy were selected on the All-tournament Team. When Tom's name was called, the Eureka players told his nephew, six-year-old Todd, to go to the center of the court to receive his uncle's plaque.

As the players were heading to the locker rooms in the same downstairs area, words were exchanged and shoving resumed. Lakeland started to run to their locker room. Eureka still extremely upset over the cheap shot injuring "Butch" and the poor officiating, took off in pursuit of the Lakeland players. Darnall, Holmes, and Hayes chased after their players. Finally, Darnall persuaded the team to get back into their locker room. Coach Holmes and Coach Hayes escorted the team into the dressing room. Darnall's black players, Blanton, Westbrooks, and Moore, were extremely upset over the whole ordeal.

Darnall contacted the hospital to inquire on the status of his player. He was informed that Tom suffered a broken jaw and a slight concussion. His face was severely swollen. Coach was told Tom would have to remain in the hospital for a few hours.

To illustrate Coach Darnall's feeling about the rough play and the officiating, especially during the second half, forty-six free throws were shot by both teams combined. Lakeland shot twenty-seven and Eureka nineteen. Blanton, who plays center, shot twelve in the second period. Perhaps getting "pounded" in the second half, added fuel to why he was so upset. Blanton had five field goals the first half with no free throws; he had only one basket in the second half.

The team went to a fast-food restaurant for their traditional two cheeseburgers, fries, and large Coke post-game meal. Then it was a trip to the hospital to retrieve Tom for the long journey home. The Red Devils arrived home both physically and mentally drained. They had just lost their second game of the season after eleven consecutive wins.

Eureka College returned home to play a good Iowa Wesleyan team before hitting the road with games against Greenville College and the always tough McKendree Bearcats. The Red Devils were ready to play in front of the hometown fans. With five players scoring in double figures, led by Blanton's twenty, EC trounced the Tigers from Iowa, 94 to 71. "T" Moore, starting in place of his injured "brother," contributed to the winning cause by pumping in eighteen points from nine field goals.

Eureka traveled to Greenville and lost a heartbreaker to the Panthers, 76 to 74. Dave knew Greenville was going to give his team a good battle but had hoped to escape with a victory. He stated after the game, "Jack is an excellent coach and always has his teams ready to play us. I respect his program a lot."

It was then time to take on Coach Statham's powerful Bearcats at McKendree. The headline and portions of an article in the next morning's Peoria *Journal Star* best described what took place. "Eureka Slowdown Fails. Eureka College went to a slow-down game Tuesday night at Lebanon in an effort to offset a McKendree front line averaging 6-8½-inch height, but the strategy backfired as the Red Devils dropped a 32 - 25 decision."

In Darnall's mind, it was not a matter of bad strategy. Instead, it was a way to give his team a chance to win against a well-coached rated team on the road. Eureka College had not beaten in years the always-talented Bearcats that usually played run and gun on their tiny floor in front of a near capacity crowd, so why not try to slow down the "well-oiled train." Perhaps McKendree's "fast running train" would "jump the track." It would be a later date when another Red Devil team would try to "put the brakes on" again.

Eureka College bounced back after the double defeats by winning seven out of the last eight remaining games on its schedule. The first two came at the Principia Tournament. The Red Devils beat Greenville in a rematch by the score of 78 to 63. That win came only six days after their two-point loss at Greenville. Hughley Blanton poured in thirty-two points as the leading scorer of the game.

Blanton came back the following night to net twenty-six points on the way to an 80 to 77 victory over the host school to claim the Principia Tournament championship. That was the third invitational tournament championship for the Red Devils that year. Hughley Blanton's twenty-nine-point average for the two-games earned him the honor of Most Valuable Player of the tournament. Sam Reed joined his teammate on the All-tourney Team.

A home win over St. Ambrose preceded another heartbreaking two-point loss to Iowa Wesleyan. Bill Maas hit a twelve-footer at the buzzer to lift the home team to a 61 to 59 win over EC. The Red Devils recovered to win the last four games of the season. They included a great home win over CCIW foe North Central and a sweet two-point victory over St. Ambrose on the road to conclude regular season play. Then 21 to 5, one of the best records in the District 20 or state, the Red Devils were waiting for a NAIA Playoff bid. They had to wait 365 days!

Darnall knew politics played a great deal in the selection of the six-team field. The bigger, more prestigious schools had the clout. He was especially envious of Illinois Wesleyan. Darnall felt their representatives pulled a lot of weight in the decision making. Darnall also felt there was something wrong with a coach having to stand in front of a committee and plead his team's position. That was particularly true when a coach could "cut down" another college's program or schedule.

The headline of an article that appeared in *The Pantagraph* stated, "Eureka College fails to receive playoff bid." The article relayed some of Darnall's frustration. It read in part,

> If nothing else, Eureka College basketball coach Dave Darnall has learned one thing about the selection for teams to participate in the NAIA District 20 Playoffs—expect the unexpected.
> After compiling a 20 - 5 record entering Tuesday night's finale at St. Ambrose College, coupled with a 20 - 4 mark and a narrow 79 - 76 loss at St. Xavier in the playoffs a year ago, Darnall and his Red Devils figured they had an excellent chance of returning to the playoffs this year.

But the unexpected happened to Darnall and his squad Sunday when the Red Devils failed to receive one of the six District 20 berths.

"I'm very, very disappointed," Darnall said, "Our team definitely deserves to be in the playoffs.

"I feel especially sorry for our six seniors," Darnall said. "They (the seniors) have won 75 games in the last four years and have had three 20-victory seasons yet they don't get into the playoffs.

"It (the selection process) just doesn't make sense," Darnall said. "We beat Aurora (71 - 69 at Aurora) and Aurora beat Illinois Benedictine twice yet they both get bids ahead of us."

The Red Devils also hold victories over College Conference of Illinois and Wisconsin opponents Millikin (63 - 45) and North Central (77 - 70).

"I really don't understand the whole thing," Darnall said.

Eureka College's unsuccessful, but warranted, bid to the NAIA District 20 Playoffs triggered a reevaluation of the selection process. Two highly respected District 20 coaches also expressed concern for Eureka's oversight and supported the reevaluation. It resulted in an implementation of the Dunkel Rating System the following year. The system was undoubtedly a fairer way of determining the playoff field but brought with it a whole other set of headaches for Coach Darnall.

An end-of-year, all-sports banquet was held honoring all Eureka College sport participants at Dickinson Commons. The guest speaker was Basketball Hall of Fame member and former great player and captain of the Boston Celtics, Bob Cousy. Hughley Blanton was named to the NAIA District 20 (Illinois) All-star Team. The six-foot-six senior center led his team to the best record in the school's history, 21 to 5, and they were unde-feated at home for the second consecutive year. Blanton's accomplishments during his Red Devil career validate his worthiness for induction into the Eureka College Athletic Hall of Fame.

Chapter 10

The Middle Years

C OACH DARNALL PROCLAIMED the years between 1980 and 1986 the "middle years" of his coaching career at Eureka College. They produced some excellent players and good ball clubs that continued to build upon the process Darnall set forth in bringing the program to respectability. He felt the six years were very productive, resulting in a combined record of 106 to 51 and five NAIA District 20 Playoff appearances. They were important years in the overall development of Eureka College's basketball program.

1980–1981

FOR THE FIRST TIME, THE 1980-1981 playoff field would be determined by the Dunkel Rating System. The failure of the selection committee to pick Darnall's good Red Devil team made the disappointed coach determined to learn how "to play" the new system. The Eureka College mentor was not going to "take any chances." The rating system was, basically, based on three factors: 1) who won the game, 2) the point spread, and 3) the strength of the team's schedule. Darnall could never understand why the home court was not a factor.

Regardless of the system's weaknesses, Dave and many other coaches felt the Dunkel was a better method of choosing the playoff field than the old method of a selection committee. Individual biases were eliminated. The Dunkel system, however, proved to cause Darnall many headaches. There was the scheduling problem, the point margin whether winning or losing, and the playing time for the players. The point margin factor often limited substitutions. These haunted the coach the entire time.

"Even though the Dunkel caused me pain, it was still the best method," Darnall said of the selection procedure. "There never would have been a "Kansas City" or a "National Championship" for us without the Dunkel."

Prior to the first season of the "middle years," the Darnall family had the good fortune to attend a special occasion. It was during the summer of 1980, and they were invited to the wedding of Jimmy Parker and Nancy Sain in Pittsburg, Pennsylvania. Jimmy was the younger brother of Pittsburg Pirate star Dave Parker while Nancy was sister to Mike Sain and National League batting champion, Bill Madlock

The Sains and the Darnalls became friends with the recruitment of Mike to Eureka College. Sain and Darnall had a friend-friend relationship as well as a player-coach one. Dave had this type of relationship with many of his former players.

Darnall often said, "On the floor, I'm the "man"; off the floor, I'm no better than anybody else."

There was no question who was in charge on the court. Most of Darnall's players understood this double image. The ones that could not usually did not make it through the program.

Earlier in the summer, Darnall, College Maintenance Director Marv Holmes, "T" Moore, Joel Micetich, Tom Cassidy, Sain and his hometown buddy and Red Devil teammate Greg Hunt took Coach's old brown van for a three-day trip to Pittsburg to see the Pirates play. The trip was memorable for Darnall.

"Even though it has been over two decades, I remember several things about the journey like they happened yesterday," said Darnall. "First of all, I remember sitting directly behind home plate with the players' wives, families, and friends. Needless to say, Bill had gotten the tickets for us. In fact, he came by during batting practice and spoke to us."

"It was a rainy afternoon," Darnall continued, "and the game was delayed. So guess what happened? Mike suggested we go to the locker room. I thought he had to be kidding, but he said to follow him."

The group followed Sain to the locker room entrance where a guard was present. Mike introduced himself as Madlock's brother. The guard left and returned a few minutes later with Madlock. Bill said, "Let them in." Coach felt like a kid. Who would believe he was in the 1979 World Series Champions' locker room? Not him!

Sitting around a table in the middle of the locker room playing cards were Madlock, Dave Parker, Jim Bibby, and another Pirate.

"Who in the hell is that?" Parker asked Madlock. "He looks like Bowa. Get the hell of out here," Parker told Darnall.

"Dave is my brother's basketball coach," Madlock told Parker.

"Hey, okay," Parker replied.

Sain introduced the Eureka gang to several members of the Pirates. They remained in the locker room for about twenty minutes of the hour delay.

"When we left the ballpark, the traffic was unbelievable. Mike said he knew a shortcut," Darnall said. His directions left the group stuck on a railroad track. Darnall had made a sudden turn at Sain's command. Now the wheels were caught between the tracks. Darnall rocked the van back and forth. It would not budge.

"What the hell do we do now?" a nervous Darnall asked. "Who knows when a train will come."

Having a few beers at the ballpark, the boys did not want the police to come to check out the problem. It was finally decided that the passengers would have to lift or shove the van from the rails. Several minutes of groans and shoving passed before the stuck wheels broke loose and the guys were on their way.

The Madlocks served post-game snacks to the Illinois visitors at their beautiful home. The group was awed by Bill's memorabilia. A replica of the World Series trophy, Batting Champion silver bats, and his All-Star Most Valuable trophy were just a few.

The group spent close to an hour at the Madlock home before going to their motel. The next day, they returned to the Madlocks' place. Bill chatted with Mike's friends before departing for the ballpark for an afternoon game. Meanwhile, Mrs. Madlock was outside weeding a large flowerbed adjacent to the back deck. Cassidy, Micetich, and Darnall, wanting to show their gratitude for her hospitality, volunteered to help.

Holmes said, "I do that for a living 365 days a year," and remained in the house with Sain, "T" Moore, and Hunt. Twenty minutes or so of pulling weeds passed when Coach looked over to Butch and Joel and quietly said, "Wouldn't Abraham Lincoln be proud of us now?" Following a few minutes of quiet giggling, the trio returned to rooting up the ugly weeds in the garden.

The Illinois crew, again, sat in the Pirate players' family section. After the game, Mrs. Madlock had prepared a wonderful "spread" back at their home. "It looked like a smorgasbord," Darnall commented. "I'll never forget the way the Madlocks treated us. It was a thrill to have Bill and Dave Parker serve us steaks from the grill, especially after my initial impression on Parker. In fact, he was on my ass all evening about looking like Larry Bowa. It must have been the nose and hair. I don't think Bowa was one of Parker's favorite opponents."

The second trip back to Pittsburg later that summer was for the wedding. The elegant affair was held in the Madlock estate's backyard at 6:30 following a doubleheader with the Chicago Cubs. The guest list was a mixture of baseball greats, hometown friends, and relatives. Darnall said, "We were the only 'common' people there," referring to the distinguished other guests.

"I was awed by being surrounded by professional baseball stars the likes of Madlock, Parker, Willie Stargel, Jim Bibby, Tim Foli, Phil Garner, and John Milner, just to mention a few," said Darnall. Tiera, Derek, and Derek's friend David Matthews along with all the other youngsters at the wedding received a Bill Madlock autographed bat. It hangs in our Arkansas family room even today."

The reception was held at the Ramada Inn. The new couple traveled to the reception in Madlock's restored 1934 Ford. The whole affair was "breathtaking" for Dave. He wanted to take a camera to the reception, but Bonnie refused saying it would be "tacky." As it turned out, the Darnalls were the only guests without one. Only visual memories remain.

Coach Darnall had spent much time attempting to bring several quality student-athletes into his basketball program. However, the 1980 recruited group ended as a weak class. Only one recruit, Greg Bange, played all four years. An article by *The Pantagraph* sportswriter Randy Kindred entitled "Red Devils successful, but recruits stay away" illustrated Darnall's disappointment in his recruiting efforts. Portions of the article read:

> While there may be several factors necessary for building a successful well known basketball program, there is one thing which is absolutely essential.

It doesn't take a John Wooden to figure out that the best way to gain recognition and prestige for a basketball program is to do what Wooden's teams at UCLA did more than most other teams—win.

Well, they've tried it at Eureka College. It hasn't worked. Despite winning 95 games and losing just 32 the past five seasons, Red Devil coach Dave Darnall is still experiencing the same headaches he did 95 victories ago. Especially when it comes to recruiting.

"Probably the main thing that hampers our recruiting is that we can't offer a full athletic scholarship to anyone," said Darnall. "We lose a lot of kids to bigger schools because they can get full rides there and we lose others to junior colleges because it is cheaper."

In spite of all the victories and titles, recruiting has remained an uphill battle at Eureka College, a battle that this year has been tougher than most, according to Darnall . . .

But Darnall does see one glimmer of hope on the horizon for gaining recognition for Eureka College. "Maybe Ronald Reagan (a Eureka College graduate) will be elected president," Darnall joked. "At least then people might know Eureka College exits."

Dave geared up for the upcoming season by speaking at Coach Rolinski's Toluca Basketball Coaches Clinic. Over two hundred eager coaches listened to the outstanding group of coaches that Rolinski had assembled as clinic speakers. It had been at the Toluca clinic that Darnall as a young coach gained much basketball knowledge.

Another article appearing at the beginning of the season was "Eureka College has inexperienced cagers" written by Mark Miller for *The Pantagraph*. It read in part:

"I think inexperience is one thing and our size - we won't be as big as we have been in the past,' said Darnall in his office Tuesday.

"I think it will be difficult for us realistically to have a season like we've had the last two years because of the experience factor, but the kids think they can have that kind of year and I have a lot of confidence in them."

With little experience and shorter players, Darnall has had to make some adjustments. Coming up with the right combination is always the test of a good coach.

"I think we will have to rely on our defense which traditionally we've been pretty good at," he said. "We'll have to rely on getting down the floor before the other team does and we'll have to be careful of turnovers. When we get the ball, we'll have to get a shot.

"I think another key is teamwork. Our slogan here is 'together we win.' It's on our program and I really stress that. I don't think one or two individuals will lead us. It will be a real team effort. A different person could lead us every night."

Sam Reed, a six-foot-four forward, was the only returning full-time player from the previous year.

Coach Darnall and his new assistant coaches, Pat Hayes and Joel Cowan, took their team to Rockford to participate in the a tip-off tournament. The starters against Northeastern Illinois, a Chicago-area institution with an enrollment of approximately 10,000 students, were Mike Sain and Monte Bell at guards, Tom Fisher and Reed at forwards, and Ed Brady at center. Mark Scherer was backup to Brady, and Tracey Trimpe, six-foot-four forward from Havana, was the sixth man. With the fifteen-point performance of Brady and an additional fourteen points apiece by Sain and Reed, the Red Devils jumped out to a 45 to 31 half-time lead. Sain's twenty-six-point barrage led EC to an impressive 92 to 71 victory over the larger scholarship school in the first round of the tournament.

The following evening, Eureka beat Rockford College, 87 to 80, to claim the tournament championship. Sain had pumped in twenty-eight points while being named Most Valuable Player of the two-day event. Brady joined his teammate, Sain, on the All-tourney team.

The 1980-1981 team went on to have an overall 17 to 9 record. Other than the Rockford Tournament championship, the Red Devils picked up third place trophies at both the Judson and Principia Invitational Tournaments. Those were not really what Coach had hoped for.

The one goal that Darnall dearly wanted to achieve was for his team to return to the NAIA District 20 Playoff. Coach stated his feeling about the Red Devils' return to the playoff field.

"I know this year's team is not as good as last years, but I'm thankful we're back in. It was because of the Dunkel Rating System. It's hard to 'play' the Dunkel, but we did. I'll 'play' it the rest of my career. I have to."

Dave, to this day, feels one of the major reasons of the switch in the playoff selection procedure was the failure of his excellent 1979-1980 team to make the field.

One of the Red Devil losses came at the hands of Millikin University. The Big Blue wanted a little revenge from the previous year's 63 to 45 defeat. Besides, they wanted to show "hometown boy," Mike Sain, he should never have left Decatur for Eureka. Millikin gained the 60 to 53 win, but Sain was the game's leading scorer when he tossed in nineteen points for his Red Devil team's losing cause.

Eureka's menace, Jack Trager's Greenville College Panthers had beaten EC three straight times during the season. Two losses came in the first rounds of invitational tournaments. Two of them were also in overtime. Finally, Eureka bested the pesky Panthers on the fourth try, 94 to 84.

"I always fear Greenville," Darnall confessed after one of the losses. "Coach Trager is an excellent coach and gets the most out of his kids. They're always ready to play us. So are their great fans. Do you know what it is like to go into a noisy gym and have a rubber chicken thrown at you?"

Dave went on to explain. "The teams sat on one side of the gym while the spectators sat directly across the floor. During warm-ups, I sat there watching a rubber chicken coming my way. Sometimes it was right at my feet. Some guy in the bleachers had a fishing pole with a rubber chicken attached to the line. The fisherman would wind up and cast the foul toward our bench. The damn chicken looked real. I'd chuckle. The players wanted to step on it as he reeled it across the floor, but they didn't. The fisherman would cast again, and again, and again!"

It was during the 1980-1981 season that the Eureka College fans were first able to hear some of the college games. WRBA, a relatively new Eureka radio station, broadcast half of the Red Devil's scheduled games. The close games, such as those against Greenville College, kept the sport enthusiasts at the "edge of their chairs."

Throughout the season, Darnall spent hours on the road recruiting new prospects and scouting future opponents. Dave felt he needed several more quality players to move to the next level, a national tournament appearance. There was one period of time the coach was out of town for part of the day for twenty-five straight days.

"Thank God for administrative assistants Hayes, Cowan, "Preacher," and Jeff Stephens," said Darnall. "Those guys accompanied me on the trips. Not only did they provide company, but they were also my chauffeurs."

In the middle of the season, the Red Devils lost five consecutive games before putting together a six-game winning streak. EC won the last three games of the season before meeting Quincy College in the first round of the NAIA District 20 Playoff.

Eureka qualified for the playoffs by finishing seventh in the rating points with 31.1. Northeastern Illinois was eighth with 31.0. Fourth tenths of a point separated the last two qualifying teams and two other teams that just missed out by having 30.9 and 30.7 points. It could then be seen why Darnall preached all season, "Every point in a game makes a difference. Winning and winning big is important. If you lose, make it close. Beat those you are supposed to beat. Stay close to the ones you aren't."

The playoff game was a "dream come true" for "Preacher" Bangert. Growing up in Quincy, he and his father watched the Hawks in action regularly.

Just as the Red Devils arrived at the game site after spending the night in Quincy, so did a big red-and-white charter bus. It was loaded with loyal EC fans. Words of encouragement were shouted as the players left their vans to enter the gym's back door.

There was no yelling or screaming by the coach during his pre-game talk. Darnall was just happy to be there. "Remember the game plan," Darnall told his team. "Be patient on offense, take only good shot selection, and pack down the defense inside. Now let's take our ten seconds. Each one is an individual. Think what you want to think or you don't need to think at all as long as we are quiet, and we do it together."

The team left the locker room. Darnall went to the toilet for the final time, then followed the same path his players had taken only minutes earlier. Twenty minutes of action and approximately an hour later, the Red Devils returned to their temporary home trailing the scholarship host school, 37 to 26.

"Stay with the game plan, be patient on offense, take only good shots, move in that damn zone," were phrases the players heard from their encouraging coach. "We're still in the game. Bust your butt. We can do it," could be heard as the players slid out the locker room door.

With Quincy's outside shooting faltering with just three for eighteen, and the Red Devils narrowing the gap to 43 to 38 in the first ten minutes of the second half, Coach Hanks ordered his Hawks to keep the ball outside. He wanted to pull the Red Devils out of their effective 1-2-2 adjustable zone defense. The Quincy coach wanted Darnall to have his players switch to a man-to-man defense. The Red Devils, however, held fast. Coach Darnall instructed his team to stay in their zone. Dave remembered what had happened several years prior when a very good EC team employed a man-to-man defense and got demolished by Quincy, 82 to 52. Unfortunately, there was no shot clock. Darnall felt if his team could stay within five or six points with four minutes left to play, perhaps they could pull-off a close win.

The Hawk fans were booing Darnall for his strategy. They wanted to see their bigger and stronger players take EC players "to the bucket." For example, Quincy's post-guard, six-foot-four Cary Doehring, against EC's five-foot-ten Mike Sain. Actually, it was Quincy that was employing the stalling tactic. Quincy held the ball outside for seven minutes. The court looked like a "chess board"—everyone standing around waiting for the next opponent move. Even some Red Devil fans were getting antsy. Remember those young fans back at Stanford?

Darnall ordered his players to "pick 'em up" with less than four minutes left. Go man-to-man. The Hawks started to play "power" basketball, forcing the smaller opponents to foul. Sam Reed hit a jumper with fifteen seconds remaining in the game. He had pumped in twenty points for EC. Quincy went on to win 46 to 40.

In Darnall's mind, the only way his team could have kept close was to stay with the game plan. To prove his point, the coach stated, "With slow-down tactics, the Hawks took some bad shots anxious to score. They hit a chilling three for twenty-one in the second half. They had a hard time scoring against our zone. The much taller Hawks dominated us on the boards, 33 to 22. We shot zero free throws while they shot ten."

Asked about the officiating after the game, Darnall replied, "In reality, the officials did a pretty good job. I know one of the officials, Bob Brodbeck. He is a good official."

The 1980-1981 season came to an end with a Red Devil basketball team social gathering at the Darnalls'. The players enjoyed "the home cooking." Wardie Sain's barbecue ribs, Jim Bangert's hot sauce mini-wieners, and Coach Darnall's baked beans were several hits.

1981–1982

NINE LETTERMEN GREETED THE EIGHTH-YEAR coach on opening day of practice. Coach Darnall and assistants Hayes and Cowan were hoping for a banner year in their recruiting efforts, but as time would tell, Derrick Martin and Tony Shelly would be the only ones to participate all four years. A third recruit, Scott Burgess, became a student coach after playing for three years. The coaches did receive good news with Bob Barnett's return to action after recovering from an injury and Mark Scherer's complete recuperation following a mysterious illness that had limited his play the previous year.

An article in *The Pantagraph* by sportswriter Randy Kindred entitled "Darnall's Red Devils 'Unique'" presented the season's outlook. Portions read:

Most of Eureka College's successful basketball teams the past seven years under Coach Dave Darnall have been built around the center positions.

With all-state performers like Jeff Smith, Hughley Blanton, and Reggie Holmes occupying the middle at one time or another during Darnall's tenure, the Red Devils have grown accustomed to having their key man at center.

But this season there is no Smith, Blanton, or Holmes returning, a fact which sets this year's squad apart from Darnall's past teams.

"It'll really be a challenge this year," said Darnall . . .

"I never realized how much you miss having a center until this year.

"We've moved Mark Scherer (6-6 junior from Roanoke-Benson High School) to center and he's really more of a forward than a center."

Since the letterman Scherer lacks experience at center, Darnall said veteran players like Mike Sain, Monte Bell, Sam Reed, Tracey Trimpe, and Bob Barnett will have to lead the team while Scherer gains that needed experience.

"I think our biggest strength will be our guards," said Darnall. "Sain (a junior letterman) averaged 20 points a game last year and I think he is a potential all-stater this year.

"Bell (a senior letterman) has started for two years and at 6-3, has good size . . . Trimpe is an excellent shooter and Barnett is real strong and very aggressive . . .

"I think the key to our game this year will be our shooting percentage every night," said Darnall. "As small as we are this year, we'll have to shoot well to win consistently."

Starters Scherer, Barnett, Reed, Bell and Sain led their Red Devil teammates to an impressive 86 to 67 victory over St. Ambrose in the first round of the Rockford Invitational Tournament. However, the following night did not go as well for EC as it dropped the title game to the host school, 90 - 70.

Eureka College split the next two games before claiming the Judson Tournament Championship. The Red Devils opened the tourney by knocking off Mt. Mercy with Sain "tickling the twine" for twenty. They came right back beating the host school for the title. Sain, again, led the Red Devils in scoring with nineteen points, while Reed and Trimpe each canned eighteen.

With a tournament championship under its belt, EC traveled to Aurora to take on the Spartans. The Red Devils dropped an 89 to 81 decision to Aurora. The loss left Eureka with a disappointing 4 to 3 record. It was a long ride home.

The next day, Coach Darnall started practice by holding a team meeting in Reagan Fieldhouse's classroom. That was the same place he held his pre-game talks. Coach wanted an atmosphere where the players were used to his direct talk. In no uncertain words, Darnall let his team know his displeasure with its play. With only one player minus from the previous year's team, the coach expected to be "sitting" better than where they had been the year before. If the Red Devils were going to get back to the play-offs, things were going to have to change—not only the winning effort, but also the point spread. So far, the team was not "playing" the Dunkel very well. In fact, Eureka's rating points were fairly low.

The Red Devil players must have gotten their coach's message. EC won eleven out of the next twelve games, including five consecutive games after Darnall's stern lecture. That was the results the coach was seeking.

It was during the first part of the season that a special fan enjoyed a Red Devil game. Bill Madlock had the pleasure of watching Mike Sain swish the nets for a bunch. The star Pittsburg Pirate third baseman and three-time National League batting champion joined the Sains and the rest of the Red Devil fans at a post-game party at the Darnalls'. The following day, the All-Star Most Valuable Player was the guest speaker at a Eureka American Legion sponsored banquet honoring him for his participation in the state's Legion Baseball Program. Legion baseball coach Cy Cawley presented Madlock with a "plaque of appreciation" for his banquet appearance. Bill generously donated all of the day's proceeds to the Eureka American Legion Baseball Program. He also assumed all of his own expenses.

One of the games in the string was quite unusual. Eureka College traveled to Oak Park for a contest with undermanned Rosary College. It turned out to be a historical, unbelievable night. As an unidentified newspaper stated, "The Red Devils could have gone to sleep Wednesday night against Rosary. And Rosary College apparently did . . . for the first 36 minutes and 17 seconds of the game."

Eureka scored the first basket, and Rosary, who had lost twenty-two straight games, went into a delay. Coach Darnall decided to leave the Red Devils in his well-known 1-2-2 zone defense. His team made six steals, turning five into field goals for a 10 to 0 score at halftime.

The Rebels stayed with the stall in the second half, running the first twelve minutes off the clock without trying a shot. Again, the Eureka coach ordered his team to stay in the zone. With 3:43 remaining in the game, Rosary finally began to run a bona fide offense with Phil Hesslau missing a twelve-footer. Eureka grabbed the rebound and scored instantly. Rosary, then executing their offense, made their first basket of the contest with two minutes to play. The final score was Eureka, 19 and Rosary, 4.

The press asked Dave what he thought about the unusual game. "The crowd hated the stall," Darnall said. "People were booing and really getting nasty. It was even worse in the second half. But I said the heck with it, and we just stayed in the zone. I think they stuck around to see if the game was going to be a shutout. We might have made history. I guess they just felt they couldn't match-up with us and decided to stall."

Around that time, a small announcement appeared in a local newspaper under the heading of "In Passing" regarding Coach Darnall's success at Eureka. It stated, "You hear of winning records, but how about Eureka College Head Basketball Coach Dave Darnall? He's now the 11th winningest coach in the nation (in NCAA Division III) with a 7-year record of 121 - 57."

When asked about the accomplishment, Dave sounded like a coach. "It's a nice honor, but qualifying for the NAIA District tournament is what's on my mind," he replied.

Coach Darnall spent Christmas vacation criss-crossing the state attending as many holiday tournaments as possible. He knew with ten juniors and seniors there was a need for a good recruiting year in order to keep the program on the "upward swing." Some of the tournaments the coach attended were the Pontiac, Pekin, Macomb, Breese Mater Dei, Fairbury, Princeville, and the Bloomington-Normal Classic—now called the State Farm Classic.

Prior to Christmas, Dave attended an excellent small high school tournament hosted by Spring Valley High School. It was at an earlier tournament there that Darnall first met radio station WLPO LaSalle-Peru sports announcer Lanny Slevin. The personable Slevin was influential in the recruitment of Tom Cassidy of Mendota and, eventually, was helpful with Jon Guderjan of Mid-County and Cassidy's younger brother Jeff. He also provided names of several other Eureka College basketball recruits.

Like most small college coaches, Darnall was a "jack of all trades." He coached, scouted, recruited, taught classes, and was Intramural Director, as well as father and husband. It was a busy life. The pressure to win was largely exerted by himself. He loved the winning and experienced the agony of each defeat. He was well aware that the pressure of all college coaches, both small and large, could be alleviated by the recruitment of good players and having supportive financial resources.

It was at that time of the season that an article by Phil Theobald regarding recruiting appeared in the Peoria *Journal Star*. "Wanted: Tall Guys

Who Appreciate Reaganomics" appeared with an accompanying picture of Darnall. The caption said, "We've got 15 varsity players right now and probably six or seven of them attend Eureka on some type of need (grant or loan). I'm not sure how many we'll have next year or the year after that."

The concern came from a federal administrative shift. President Ronald Reagan's push toward a philosophy of private institutions depending upon the private sector for support had put a crimp in Darnall's recruiting pitch.

The article continued to state, "The administration theory is that too many schools have become dependent upon government aid and, as a result, are unable to roll with the punches of tight economic times."

"In the meantime, what does Dave Darnall tell a recruit? What can he tell a recruit?"

Without athletic scholarships to offer, Darnall had been able to, at least, tell recruits of various state and or federal programs. If recruiting had been difficult before, it was then going to become much more difficult.

There were two great home wins in the eleven victories. They came against DePauw and McKendree College. Led by Sain's twenty-three points, Eureka College claimed a "big win" both on and off the floor (in Dunkel points) over DePauw. The Red Devils played a nearly flawless game in securing the 79 to 68 victory.

Five days later, a near capacity home crowd witnessed an exciting game between their beloved Red Devils and the highly respected McKendree Bearcats. In his pre-game talk, Darnall reminded his players that beating a team like McKendree would do wonders for their Dunkel rating. EC played a near perfect game against one of the consistently best small college teams in the country. The Red Devils' offense was at full cylinder as they scored a surprising 106 points. All five starters scored in double figures, led by Sain's thirty-four.

Coach Darnall congratulated his "warriors" on their great win in the locker room following the game. Shaking hands and giving hugs, the jubilant coach shouted, "This is a great win for Eureka College basketball. You took a giant step toward the playoffs. Don't let yourselves down now. We must now finish the season strong."

The post-game celebration at Coach's house was crowded. Bottles of champagne were popped and food was plenty. At 10:15 P.M. most of the guests surrounded the two TV sets to watch the local sports broadcast to get a glimpse of the footage of the all-important game. The party lasted until the wee-hours of the morning.

Next, the Red Devils suffered a road defeat at the hands of St. Ambrose before finishing the season with four consecutive wins—two at home and two on the road. Following the St. Ambrose loss, Darnall did not have an answer. "The loss is as bad as the McKendree win was good," said the coach. "Everything we gained in Dunkel points by beating McKendree, we lost tonight."

Fortunately for the sake of their coach, fans, the college, and themselves, the Red Devils did bounce back from the Ambrose loss to claim the season's four remaining games. One of those wins came against Chicago- based Roosevelt University. All five starters scored in double figures with Mike Sain, again, leading the parade with thirty. Following the game, the Chicago-area officials, Ed Mittage and Ron Steigerwall stopped by the Darnall home before heading north. Mittage and Darnall became friends and eventually vacationed in Arkansas together after Darnall's retirement from the game.

The last game of the year was at Greenville. It was a game that Eureka College was not looking forward to. "It's hell getting down to the last game of the season knowing if you lose, there is no playoff," Darnall said. "It's like a one game season now."

Dave had a lot of respect for Panther coach Jack Trager. "I don't care what talent he had, they always played tough. It's extremely difficult to beat them at home," said Darnall.

The first half was a low-scoring affair with the visitors holding a slight 29 to 33 lead. The Red Devils stretched the lead in the second half and went on to win, 59 to 46. Sain pumped in twenty-five points, but it was the six rebounds by power-forward Bob Barnett in the final minutes that sealed the victory and relieved the worried coach's mind. The win provided for a happy but long ride home.

It was then time to find out the eight team NAIA District 20 Playoff field. Coach Darnall was happy the Dunkel point system was the method of selection. *The Pantagraph* headline read, "IWU, Red Devils in NAIA playoffs." The article from Illinois Wesleyan's sports information office explained the results of the District 20 meeting. Portions read:

> Illinois Wesleyan University was seeded second for the eight-team playoffs of the District 20 (Illinois) of the National Association of Intercollegiate Athletics Sunday . . .
> Eureka College, which jumped from 12th to eighth in the Dunkel ratings to win the eight and last berth in the playoffs, drew top-seeded Quincy for a first round game at 5:30 PM Saturday in Quincy . . .

Eureka College coach Dave Darnall considers his team better than the 1980-81 crew that lost a six-point game at Quincy in the first round of the district playoffs. The Red Devils have won nine of their last 10, including four last week.

"We're getting better team play than last year. We had one or two players doing most of it last year, but we have six contributing about equally this season," Darnall said.

Quincy, however, is considered to be much better than last year since adding former Quincy High School stars Keith Douglas and Mike Rudd in January.

The *Quincy Herald-Whig*'s sportswriter Chuck Brady wrote an article entitled "Hawks wary of possible Eureka slow-down." Portions read:

Not many of this season's Quincy College basketball players were around a year ago when the Hawks encountered Eureka's Red Devils in the first round of the NAIA District Playoffs, but Bill Lillwitz and Brent Clemmons are probably bringing their new teammates up to date.

And if they don't, coach Sherrill Hanks can handle the refresher course in 1981 history . . .

"Quincy completely ignored us last year and was saying who's Eureka, and we gave them a scare," said Darnall this week after the playoff pairings were set.

Hanks isn't real sure Darnall will change his style of play and has spent considerable time this week drilling the Hawks in coping with a slowdown game. Of course, it's much easier to deal with such tactics when you own a comfortable lead.

Eureka has won nine of its last 10 coming down the stretch and defeated all the right teams necessary for climbing from 12th to eight place in the Dunkel ratings.

Big victories were a 19-pointer over McKendree and a 23-pointer over Roosevelt University, which had held the No. 8 spot.

"A loss in any one of those games would have kept us out of the playoffs," admits the Devils' coach.

Those articles proved two things. Darnall had a pretty good understanding of how the Dunkel Rating System worked and what he was preaching to his players the last half of the season wasn't just a "bunch of bull." Dave often upset parents, fans, and even opponent coaches with his game strategy, the lack of substituting players, and the game's final point margin. He, however, defended his stance by saying, "It is my job to try to take my team as far as possible. The Dunkel system has forced me to do what I am doing, and I won't change. As long as the Dunkel determines the teams that participate in the playoffs, I'll 'play' it."

The article had also described the uphill battle the Red Devils would face playing the No. 1 seed team on their floor. Athletes sometimes have an inflated ego. It's hard for them to believe that there is someone better than they are or another team better than theirs. Darnall had several with this attitude on his team. "They just wanted to go to 'full blast.' They had a 'they can't beat us' attitude. Darnall liked their mental toughness, but it did present a problem for him. What should the game plan be?

Coach wrestled with that question. He truly felt a "slow paced" game with his team very patient on offense was the best way to beat the bigger, stronger Quincy team. However, could some of his players execute that style of play? Following much thought, Darnall decided that for the benefit of the team, not necessarily himself, to go ahead and play a "regular game." That would make the fans and most of his players happy.

The Red Devils started the game in their normal zone defense and attempted to have good shot selection. The first half was a spectators' game —a lot of scoring with both teams shooting well. EC stayed close, trailing only by five points, 42 to 37, at the intermission. Eventually, the Hawks' talent and depth took over. Eureka dropped the contest, 85 to 71, and finished the season with a 19 to 6 record.

Most of the Eureka College fans were satisfied with their boys' play. At least, they didn't stand around like the previous year. Darnall was asked to compare the two Quincy games.

"To me it makes no difference. We still got beat. Last year by 6; this year by 14," Darnall said. "In reality, we had a better chance of winning last year. Maybe down the line I'll be able to prove it. I'm sure the fans liked watching the game more this year."

Eureka College coaches were able to convince the administration to do away with the All-sports Honor Ceremony in order to hold individual sport banquets. Coach Darnall invited renowned WMLA Sports Director, Bloomington-Normal, Art Kimball to serve as Master of Ceremony for the men and women's basketball banquet. The teams, families, and fans were invited to the Darnalls' following the affair.

The 1982 Eureka College commencement left a lasting impression on Coach Darnall. President Ronald Reagan, 1939 alumni, was the keynote speaker at the ceremony. The crammed packed fieldhouse was surrounded by law enforcement and secret security personnel when three giant government helicopters landed on the playing fields behind the fieldhouse with the President and Nancy Reagan in one.

The faculty and graduates congregated for the procession at a dorm a short distance from the crowded facility. The parade of dignitaries followed several bag pipers in full dress. The line had to proceed through a metal detector as it filed into the building. As Assistant Professor Darnall went through the security device, a loud sound went off. Within seconds, several security agents carrying weapons grabbed the stunned coach and threw him up against the wall. The surrounding faculty members were awed by the whole ordeal. Darnall tried to identify himself.

"Shut up!" an agent instructed as others began to frisk the shocked coach.

Dave finally said, "I'm the basketball coach here," to deaf ears. The agents found what they were looking for. It was his "pick" that he had inadvertently left in the pocket of his pants under his black ceremonial robe. Yes, it was his hair pick! Ever since coaching at Momence, Darnall had used a metal hair pick to "comb" his hair. The metal pick had triggered the alarm. It could only happen to Coach. Several years later, President Reagan returned to the campus, but that time Darnall left his pick at home.

Darnall had another summer of basketball camps. NBA players Roger Phegley and Mickey Johnson returned as guest speakers. A new NBA player also became a camp speaker. Seven-foot Dave Corzine, center of the San Antonio Spurs, became a dedicated camp speaker at every one of Darnall's basketball camps until his retirement after thirteen years of the NBA wars.

John Schneiter of New Trier High School also became a regular speaker at the girls' camp that year.

"When I was a young coach and coming through the ranks, John was my idol," Dave said. "Not only was he a great floor coach, but he could really motivate his players to play hard and execute his game plan. I loved to hear him talk to his kids along the sidelines. He also had time to talk to us "podunk" small-time coaches."

Dave's children were growing up under the unwatchful eyes of their father because of his total involvement in his quest to put Eureka College on the basketball map. Tiera had graduated from junior high where she participated in volleyball, track, and had been a cheerleader. Her dad was able to watch her some in volleyball games and track but almost none as a cheerleader. Derek had played baseball in the summer little league program for the second year. Dave was able to catch some games. However, because of his summer camps and recruiting home visits, he missed several. In the fall and winter Derek participated in the Biddy Basketball program for the first time. Darnall was only able to watch his son play only occasionally due to the conflicts with college practices and games.

1982–1983

PRIOR TO THE START OF OFFICIAL BASKETBALL practice, the Darnalls had the opportunity to enjoy a life-long dream of Dave's. He was a die-hard Cardinal baseball fan and was able to watch his "Redbirds" play a game in the 1982 World Series. Dick Dalton, a long-time friend from Gridley, had been able to obtain four tickets to the sixth game at Busch Memorial Stadium. The Daltons and Darnalls had a great two-day trip to St. Louis.

Several coaching changes took place at Eureka College that year. Nancy LaCursia was named women's basketball coach. She was no stranger to Darnall since she had worked Dave's basketball camp. In fact, it was he who had recommended her to the administration for the open position. What a good decision the college made!

Coach Darnall also had a couple changes in his staff. A 1978 ISU graduate and coach at Neponset High School, Rodney Todd, was appointed Dave's assistant and women's softball coach. Administrative assistants Jeff Stephens and Dean Vigna became student assistant coaches. All three coaches had served on Darnall's camp staff.

The Eureka College coach had an outstanding recruiting year. For the first and only time, Darnall "signed" a younger brother of a former player. Jeff Cassidy followed the path of his brother Tom. The fourteenth child of the George Cassidy's not only became a player, an assistant coach, but also a life-long friend.

A review of the upcoming season was made by Mark Lanz, sportswriter for the *Woodford County Journal* entitled "Red Devil cage team blends experience, youth." Portions read:

> Eureka College basketball coach Dave Darnall is counting on an experienced core of veterans to bolster his lineup and give an outstanding group of freshmen a chance to get their feet on the ground in the upcoming Red Devil season.

Darnall, who in eight years has compiled a 139 - 64 record (12th best in NCAA Division III over the period), has a tough early-season schedule to look forward to.

"If we can come out of the early part of the season with our heads above water, then in conference play, I think we'll be all right," Darnall said . . .

Leading the returnees from last year's 18 - 7 team . . . is 5 foot-10 inch senior guard Mike Sain. Sain a deadly outside shooter, has led EC in scoring for the past two seasons, last year averaging 19 points a game.

"Mike is a little ahead of his time," said Darnall. "With the three-point play, he would be awesome, but this year we play only one game in which the three-point play will be used."

Also back is starter Mark Scherer of Roanoke, a 6-6 senior, who will be moved from center to forward this year. Scherer led the team with 56 percent shooting and was third in rebounds.

Another returning forward is 6-4 Bob Barnett . . .

Two veteran guards will share time in the backcourt, Greg Bange and Greg Hunt . . .

Starting center at this stage of the season is 6-7 freshman Keith Kovanda from St. Viator High School. . . . Also sure to see plenty of playing time is a 6-6 freshman, Pat Fuchs.

"Last year was one of the best, if not the best, recruiting year we've ever had," Darnall said. "With seven of the top 15 players on the varsity being freshmen, our future looks very bright."

The coach was hoping his team would hit the magic number twenty in victories. He was disappointed that the Red Devils would only claim sixteen but was happy his team qualified for the NAIA District 20 Playoffs for the third consecutive year since the implementation of the Dunkel.

The Red Devils opened the 1982-1983 campaign at the Rockford Invitational Tournament against Hamline, Minnesota. Coach Darnall's opening lineup was the three holdover starters from last year Sain, Scherer, and Barnett. The other two were Greg Bange at guard and Kovanda at center.

Mike Sain continued where he left off from the previous year. Scoring a game-high thirty points, he led Eureka to a 77 to 66 victory over Hamline. Scherer added nineteen points, while freshman reserve Pat Fuchs helped the Red Devils to a 39 to 29 advantage in rebounding by grabbing fourteen. Senior substitute point-guard Greg Hunt dished out ten assists.

For the second straight year, EC scored seventy points but lost the title game to the host school by twenty points. That was only the beginning of the bad news for the Red Devil fans. Their team dropped four of the next five games, giving Eureka a 2 to 5 record after seven games. That included losing two games at the Judson Tournament, placing them last.

The Red Devils finally got on the winning side by claiming two games on a trip to Wisconsin. Those led to five consecutive wins before dropping two more. The hometown fans did not get a chance to see their struggling team until the tenth game of the season on January 13th. It was the first game after Christmas break. The fans were pleased in what they finally witnessed.

Mark Scherer pumped in twenty-one points to lead EC to a sweet, 99 to 67, victory over Cardinal-Stritch. This was especially a good win since the Red Devils had lost two important members of their squad. Barnett reinjured the knee that cut short his promising professional baseball career. His athletic participation was over. Greg Hunt started his student teaching assignment the first part of January interfering with his basketball playing.

It took into two months of the season before the Red Devil fans could discuss the game results and season to-date at the coach's house. That night the mood was happiness since EC had won three straight games.

Over Christmas break the coaching staff was busy on the recruiting trail. However, the Darnalls, the Todds, and the Roger Smiths spent a couple days in Chicago. The first evening, December 30th, was spent at Chicago Stadium watching the Bulls and San Antonio Spurs in action. Two of Darnall's camp guest speakers were playing against each other—ex-teammates and friends Dave Corzine, then with the Bulls, and Roger Phegley with the Spurs. Corzine obtained the game tickets for the Eureka fans. At that time the Bulls' tickets were not as difficult to get. Both players had outstanding first halves. They were the leading scorers for their respective teams. Following the game, Darnall, Todd, and Smitty headed for the Chicago locker room. Coach was in "prime form" convincing the security guards that he was supposed to meet Corzine in the Bulls' dressing room. Actually, the Chicago center had told the guys to come to the locker room after the game.

The trio sliced past the guards at the locker room door, walked by the press, and entered the dressing room. The trespassers filed by several Bulls' players and headed for Corzine. He greeted his fans with an offer of a cold beer from an ice bucket. The intruders delivered their congratulations and engaged in small talk before Corzine told them that he would meet them on the playing floor. The trio then proceeded back to the stadium floor, crossed the court, and headed like "three little kids" for the visitors' locker room.

There they greeted Phegley. The Spur guard also offered the camp coaches a cold beer.

"Boy, it's not like this in our locker room after a game," a kidding Darnall told his pal Smitty. "Maybe I should be a pro coach."

The three "musketeers" spent ten minutes with Phegley and then returned to the playing floor where their wives were waiting.

Coach Todd had felt ill most of the evening and thought he needed to return to the motel located just off Tollway 294. It was a small neighborhood motel with little rooms and very dimly lit. The three wives almost "killed" Darnall when they first opened their separate outside room doors. However for Coach who had spent numerous nights in motels like this one while on the road recruiting and scouting, including that very one, it was just fine. In fact, with as much as he was on the road, this type of motel was about all Darnall's recruiting budget allowed.

Barb Todd described the motel that Darnall reserved for them in their "Big Chicago Weekend." "It was the worst "flee-bag motel I've been in," Mrs. Todd said. "The place had paper thin walls. We were up most of the night hearing noises from next door and had to put a chair under our door knob that wouldn't lock."

Darnall used his persuasive talents to talk his assistant to "gut it out" and join the group, including Corzine and Phegley, at the Ultimate Sports Bar & Grill in downtown Chicago. It was a place Corzine frequented.

"Todd," said Darnall, "this is a once in a life-time deal. When will we ever again get a chance to go out with two NBA players and their wives to have a couple beers?"

The ailing coach agreed.

Corzine was a little poorer because of fines levied on the seven-foot center for a couple technical fouls in the game, but was still a generous host. Following a hearty meal, several cold beers, and listening to some good NBA stories, the three couples headed back to their "luxurious" neighborhood motel on the outskirts of Chicago.

The next day at 5:00 P.M., the Smiths and Darnalls left the motel for a long, long night of fun at Corzine's New Years Eve party. Todd was too sick to make the event; he "got" to stay back at the motel! Coach Nancy LaCursia and her male friend also joined the group at Corzine's. Dave was sure they would be the only "common folk" at the extravaganza.

The two couples and Bulls' trainer Mark Pfeil were the first to arrive around 5:30. It wasn't long before Smitty and Darnall were in heaven. They were surrounded by such NBA players as David Greenwood, Orlando Woolridge, and Mark Olberding. Shortly after, some of Corzine's former teammates and current Spur players arrived. Among them were George "Ice" Gervin, Johnny Moore, Paul Griffin, and the Phegleys. They were most gracious and spent time conversing with the Eureka "boys."

There were plenty of refreshments for everyone. Darnall and Smitty enjoyed the cold bottles of beer while their wives were indulging in "Long Island Ice Tea." It was one of very few times that Bonnie drank enough to have a hangover. Dave switched to it before the evening was over also. Ouch! Smitty, worrying that Corzine would run out of beer, took a case with him and hid it in some bushes outside the back door. The cold weather would keep the brew cold.

At the stroke of midnight, the Corzines passed out bottles of champagne to their guests. It was estimated that seventy-five bottles were handed out. A fireworks display equal to some seen at a small public Fourth of July showing was shot off from the back tennis court.

Following the shower of fireworks, Coach Smith thought he would like to see what a NBA player's limo was like. He took his wife to the "Iceman's" ride. The chauffeur invited the couple into the luxury loaded black vehicle. Smitty just wanted to see how the "big boys" traveled. The three chatted while Smitty enjoyed a little of Gervin's liquid refreshment.

Around 2:00 A.M. the beer supply was running low. Corzine noticed a case was missing. Through a process of elimination, Corzine zeroed in on Smitty as the culprit. The host strongly suggested that his buddy share his stash. Smitty had been generously supplying Darnall, Phegley, and a couple other NBA players from his hidden treasure. Host Corzine got what was left.

The Central Illinois guests were one of the firsts to arrive and one of the lasts to leave. Smitty and Darnall did not want to miss a thing. The couples arrived back at the motel around 5:00 A.M. It was a New Year's Eve to be remembered.

The two losses that the Red Devils had incurred came at the hands of Iowa Wesleyan on the road and Conference foe Blackburn. In a rare home loss, the Blackburn Beavers knocked off the Red Devils to become the Conference favorite. Coach Darnall rallied his troops to claim four straight victories, including Conference wins over MacMurray and Principia. Eureka College had an overall 11 to 7 record with eight games remaining on their regular season. The Red Devils lost three of those with the first coming from DePauw, Indiana.

It was then time for a rematch with Iowa Wesleyan. This time it was in a legitimate gym, meaning Reagan Fieldhouse, not the Tigers' undersized "pit." Darnall felt that place should have been outlawed.

"I think it was the second hardest place to play in or win at other than McKendree," Dave said. "None of my teams had ever won at McKendree, but we were able to sneak out a couple in Iowa. However, the Iowa Wesleyan so-called "gym" was the worst I had played in since being at Eureka."

When the Red Devils played at Iowa Wesleyan earlier in the year, Darnall was so totally dissatisfied with the officiating that he helped the winning cause by getting a technical foul.

"I am damn tired of coming over here and getting screwed," Darnall said after the game between the two schools. "Something has to be done."

The rivals eventually agreed that each school would hire one official to do the games in both Illinois and Iowa. The Illinois official would have to travel to Iowa and Wesleyan's to Illinois.

History was made during that game between the two schools. It was only fitting that Mike Sain made the first three-point field goal in Eureka College's history even if it was in defeat. Iowa Wesleyan used the three-point shot on a trial basis.

"If Sain had played his entire college career with the three-point field goal in effect, his scoring record would have never been broken," Darnall said. "Ninety percent of his shots came from that range."

Coach Darnall gave a stern talk before the second contest with Iowa Wesleyan. He wanted a little revenge. The coach reminded his "warriors" of the "shaft" they had gotten in Iowa. He hadn't needed to—they remembered. The coach also challenged his players as to their desire to make the playoff. Their record was surely no indication of that desire. Darnall knew a few more losses would have killed their Dunkel points.

The Red Devils were ready to play. Darnall's pre-game speech must have motivated the team. It was perhaps the best game they played all year. Scherer and Sain led the way by pouring in thirty-six and twenty-nine points respectively. EC came away with an impressive 102 to 78 win over the Tigers. It might have been the first time all season that the post-game gathering at the Darnalls' seemed like a celebration.

The winning streak stopped at one! It was a game where the Red Devils could have gained important Dunkel points. A win against one of the Districts top teams, McKendree Bearcats, would have jumped EC dramatically in the Dunkel. The two teams played an even first half. That pleased the Eureka mentor as it had been years since a Red Devil team had claimed a victory in the Bearcat Den.

The second half was a seesaw affair. Trailing by nine points late in the game, the Red Devils cut the lead to four with a minute left. Despite the disbelief and disenchantment of a couple of his players, Darnall ordered his men not to foul. His team had to stay close.

"Go after the ball," Darnall shouted, "but don't foul," as the Bearcats went into a delay game. In dismay, the players followed their coach's instructions. Hustling, diving, reaching, the Red Devil players went for the ball, but to no avail. Eureka College lost, 67 to 63, to McKendree. But wait! Did they lose? Darnall said, "Not overall."

The tremendous competitor Scherer damn near went berserk. A couple older players were noticeably upset. They could not understand why their coach would not allow them to foul. Most of the players could not comprehend the Dunkel. They had been taught since youngsters that the name of the game was to win, not stay close.

Darnall knew McKendree was an excellent free-throw shooting team and did not want them to go to the line with the clock stopped. It would just add to their lead and increase the scoring margin.

"Where in the hell is the shot clock when you need it?" Darnall questioned Coach Todd late in the game. That was an issue that many coaches felt would soon be addressed.

Soon after the defeat by McKendree, Sports Editor Jim Barnhart of *The Pantagraph* wrote an article on the Dunkel Rating System and Darnall. It was titled "How close is close?" It came as close as any article to explaining the Dunkel. It read in part:

Close counts in love, horseshoes, and . . . uh, uh, the Dunkel Ratings?

Let's imagine you're a college basketball coach. Your team has trailed by as many as nine points but you cut the opponent's lead to four with about a minute and 15 seconds to play.

The opponent has the ball. So, you apply defensive pressure—right?

Wrong! Not if you're coaching Eureka College and the opposition—in this case, McKendree College—is, in your opinion, a 5-point favorite.

McKendree spreads out its offense but you sit back in a zone. Then, with nine second left, McKendree calls a timeout. After the timeout, you retreat back into your zone. McKendree gets off a shot but it misses and you lose 67 - 63.

Some of your players are admittedly confused. They've been taught that winning is paramount and now they've been held on a leash, unable to harass McKendree into mistakes and a possible victory.

However, if you're Eureka College coach Dave Darnall, you justify your conservative performance by pointing out your team gains 1.5 points in the next Dunkel Ratings. Had you lost by six, you would have dropped, you claim.

The Dunkel Ratings, which originated in 1929, are being used for the third year to determine the representatives for the upcoming NAIA District 20 playoffs.

The ratings, which originate in Florida, do not take road or home games into account when they judge teams. The system, which operates with a formula known only to Dick Dunkel, Jr., judges teams on the strength of their opponents and how well they outscore them.

Darnall believes you can gain points by beating teams up to as many as 30 points. Another District 20 coach told me he believes 23 points is the cutoff.

No coach in District 20—including Darnall—will tell you he understands how the system operates. But Darnall, who admits he faces a hard sell in explaining to his team why it's good to come close and remain in that position, says he has a good idea of what goes on behind the scenes . . .

"McKendree was five points ahead of us in the ratings. So, I figure Dunkel believes they're five points better. I told the kids that if we stayed within four points of them, we'd gain in the rankings. We lost by four and moved up."

Wasn't it possible for his team to erase that four-point deficit and beat McKendree, thereby moving further up the ladder? Darnall insists he couldn't take that chance . . .

"They're a deadly free throw shooting team," said Darnall. "We couldn't foul them and have them build the lead to 10 or 12 points . . . they hadn't missed all night at the free throw line."

"We go into every game to win; I'm one of the worst losers out. You just can't go out and foul if you're not under the point spread . . ."

If you play and beat a team twice, you must have a larger point spread in the second meeting, according to Darnall.

"I've never been through a season when points meant so much. When it depends on how badly you have to beat someone, that isn't good. I don't like to beat someone badly."

Following a home win over Conference foe Principia College, 91 to 55, another article appeared in *The Pantagraph*. The headline stated "Eureka College sixth in rating." Portions read:

Eureka College basketball team made a big move from a tie for ninth to sixth place in the latest Dunkel Rating in District 20 of the National

Association of Intercollegiate Athletics. The Red Devils saw their rating rise from 31.3 to 34.2.

Dave was right. Winning big against some teams and staying close even in defeat to others can raise a team's Dunkel points. McKendree was ranked sixth with 38.4 points.

The Red Devils finished the regular season play by winning three out of the next four games after the Principia victory. Unfortunately, the defeat was to Blackburn College, leaving Eureka to finish second in the Conference race. During the game, Coach felt he had to make a change against the bigger, stronger Beavers. The Conference champions were beating the Red Devils on the boards. The change did not sit well with one particular Red Devil player. Displaying his displeasure and frustration of being substituted, as well as the loss, the disgruntled player yelled profanity concerning Coach Darnall in the direction of both the Eureka and Blackburn fans entangled in the small Eureka section. As the player left the floor he shouted, "Our F_ _ _in' Coach" and demonstrated the same lack of respect. Darnall had already left the floor following the devastating defeat. However, Bonnie heard and saw it all. She was outraged. Ignoring the grip of Tiera sitting with her, Bonnie leaped from her front row seat and pursued the player to the locker room. Bursting through the locker room door and racing down a flight of steps, she charged up to the player and grabbed him by the front of his shirt and shouted, "You bastard!"

The other players, in shock and disbelief, stood stunned observing this unbelievable sight. It was not something they would have ever dreamed Bonnie would do. Darnall, not knowing what was happening, ran over to the commotion. Sain and Scherer followed their coach, informing him of the earlier public display. Coach extremely upset and drained by the loss told Bonnie to leave the locker room and instructed the player to get his ass over to the other side of the room.

"This is an example of why we got beat," Darnall shouted. "Players worrying more about their playing time than whether the team wins or loses. No damn wonder this is a disappointing season."

An angry Darnall instructed, "Get the hell in there and get your showers so we can get our asses home." It was a long ride home.

With some attitude adjustments, the Red Devils bounced back to win the two remaining regular season games.

During the 96 to 74 win over Conference opponent MacMurray College, Mike Sain became Eureka's all-time career leader in points scored.

His 1,106 points surpassed Rick Schwab's (1963 to 1967) 1,605 career points. The game was temporarily halted so that Schwab could present the game ball to Sain.

Eureka College finished the 1982-1983 regular season campaign with a somewhat disappointing 16 to 10 record. Would that be good enough to get into the NAIA District 20 Playoff? Yes! For the third consecutive year, they had made it. Notice that No. 3.

EC was able to hang onto its sixth spot in the Dunkel ranking they had gained the previous week. A game in Bloomington against third-seed Illinois Wesleyan was about to occur.

Red Devil fans had long wanted that match-up. Wesleyan and Eureka, only twenty-five miles apart, had not met since the l942-1943 season, the year Darnall was born. They had split a two-game series. The subsequent disbanding of play between the two institutions was Wesleyan's choice.

"Only their Athletic Department can answer why," Darnall said. "but I believe their feeling was that they had everything to lose and nothing to gain by playing us—just like the old ISNU and Wesleyan match-up."

This year didn't prove Wesleyan's hesitation, but ten years later might have.

The Titans knocked off the Red Devils, 82 to 68. Not only did the season come to an end, but also the career of a great Red Devil player, Mike Sain. The Eureka College Athletic Hall of Famer dazzled a whole lot of people. He concluded his eligibility by being named on the All-District 20 team.

Dave was only able to see his children participate in their activities a few times during the basketball season. Tiera was a Eureka High School JV cheerleader, while Derek played on a fifth-sixth grade traveling basketball team. In the opening game, Eureka defeated Lostant, 55 to 15, with Derek leading the way with sixteen points. The young Darnall and his friends Chad Heffren and Eric Lockart led their team to a successful season. For Darnall it was a pleasure to see his kids participate. His only regret was that he didn't do more of it.

Coach Darnall had a busy spring and summer. He saw Tiera win her first championship in the high hurdle event in the Woodford County track meet. There were the successful camps in June. He also finished up an outstanding recruiting year.

Then came his second trip to Pittsburg to watch the Pirates play. Joining Darnall and Sain on the trip were Mike's buddies Jeff "Little Butch"

Cassidy, Dennis "J.J." Johnson, and "T" Moore. Coach Todd, Terry Dobberstein, and camp coach John Dodd made for a full load in Darnall's old brown van. The trip was a replica of the first with several cold beers, going inside the Pirate locker room, and sitting with the players' families directly behind home plate. The new travelers were treated royally by the Madlocks. Even though the Cassidy brothers were never teammates at Eureka, they both became friends with Mike Sain. Sain played with Tom during his freshman year and with Jeff his senior year. He commented about the brothers, "They're like two peas in a pod. The look alike, they act alike, they talk alike, and they both chew that damn snuff."

Darnall was able to watch his son play baseball on the Eureka Pony League team during that summer. The young shortstop amused his father with his slick fielding and speed on the base paths. "I wish he had played baseball in high school," the elder Darnall said, "but I think it was boring to him—too much standing around. Sports like basketball and football were more competitive and physical. He liked that."

1983–1984

THE FALL SEEMED TO BE BUSIER than ever for Coach Darnall. Dave was able to watch Derek compete in the youngster's first interscholastic athletic program, fall baseball. The star pitcher on the team was Brett Charlton. Does that name sound familiar? It should. Brett would eventually become Darnall's son-in-law.

In a 12 to 4 victory over St. Mary's, the Darnalls witnessed their infielder become the hitting star for the Hornets with three hits. In the last regular season game, Eureka coasted to an 18 to 4 win over Deer Creek behind the hitting of Derek and Brett. They each had two hits. The team finished another successful regular season under the leadership of Coach Craig Gerdes with an 11 to 7 record.

Dave's good friend and an avid Red Devil basketball fan, Ron Eeten, hosted an informal cookout in late September for the team and community supporters at his Eureka home. Darnall had had a banner recruiting year and with so many new faces, Eeten wanted the hometown fans to meet the players. The outing was very successful.

Coach Darnall was optimistic and anxiously awaited the start of his tenth season at the Red Devil helm. Twenty new players, including junior college transfer Tony Tuttle, greeted the coaching staff at the first official practice. Tuttle joined former Lynx teammate Alonzo Echols at Eureka. Echols had transferred to EC the previous year and served on Darnall's administrative staff as he was being "red shirted." Both players had played for Darnall's good friend and camp coach Al Pickering at Lincoln Junior College.

The competition of making the fifteen-man varsity team was fierce. The coaching staff sensed some dissention among the players. Darnall felt he had possibly assembled the most skilled athletes that had ever entered his program. The first couple of weeks of practice proved that point. Dave was worried that a few new players didn't understand his slogan "Together We Win," that the team was more important than the individual.

Several of the hopefuls were extremely upset when their names were omitted from the varsity squad. A couple players immediately quit, while one was dismissed. The coaches had completed a meeting in Darnall's office following the announcement of the 1983-1984 varsity team. They left the office and walked to their parked cars located in the college's parking lot in front of Reagan Fieldhouse.

"Damn, Coach come here," Coach Todd yelled.

Dave, walking toward Todd's parked car asked, "What's up?"

"Look at this," Rod said.

"I wonder who in hell did that," Darnall shouted. "Somebody didn't like our decision."

Coach Todd had found a five-pound weight from the weight room smashed through his car's windshield. As it turned out, it was a disgruntled prospective player who had committed the vandalism. The player was dismissed from the team and soon after withdrew from school.

The 1983-1984 season saw Eureka College join the reorganized Prairie College Conference. The new conference consisted of six schools: Blackburn, Eureka, Greenville, Maryville, MacMurray, and Principia. This conference stayed intact until the 1990-1991 basketball season when Maryville withdrew. Maryville refused to play Eureka College, as Eureka had beaten Maryville consistently over several years and, in some cases, badly due to the use of the Dunkel Rating System. The other five members stayed together for one more year until Principia College also refused to play Eureka. Soon MacMurray joined the other two institutions and decided not to schedule the Red Devils anymore. A couple years later, Blackburn followed the pattern and dropped

Eureka from its schedule. The dropping of those NCAA III schools from the Eureka College schedule bothered Darnall. He felt those institutions were the type of schools Eureka should be playing, not scholarship schools. Perhaps his program had reached a level that they didn't want to deal with. Maybe it was distance. "I don't understand their thinking," Darnall said. "We built our program on hard work and intense recruiting and now those teams won't schedule us. They make all kinds of excuses. What is the real reason?" It all added to Darnall's scheduling nightmare.

The season ended below expectations. The Red Devils did win the Rockford and Judson Invitational tournament championships, but they finished third in Conference play and failed to make the NAIA Playoff field.

Their overall record of 16 to 10 was disappointing to both the coaches and the players. The team started ablaze, claiming five consecutive victories, including the tournament titles. The Red Devils then turned cold as ice, dropping six straight games for a 5 to 6 record.

To illustrate the uncertainty of which player should be leading the way, Darnall uncharacteristically had ten different starters throughout the year. Greg Bange served as Darnall's John Havlicek all season. The starting line-up for Eureka's first game of the season against Cardinal-Stritch was Keith Kovanda at center, Pat Fuchs and Alonzo Echols at forwards, with Tony Tuttle and Tony Shelly at guards.

Peoria *Journal Star* sportswriter Phil Theobald penned an article entitled "Eureka not waiting for future—young Red Devils, Darnall savor surprising tournament title" referred to the season and Rockford Tournament Championship. Portions read:

> "We're looking ahead to the next few years," said Darnall. "I don't like to stick my neck out, but I think if we can stay away from ineligibilities and injuries, we're on our way to becoming state contenders."
>
> Big words, those. Big team, the Devils—with four players close to 6-foot-7, according to Darnall, and reason to suspect this won't be the rebuilding year most expected.
>
> Eureka traveled to Rockford last weekend to open the season in a four-team tourney, and won impressively. "We're still awfully young," said Darnall, "but I think we've got a potentially great group of players."

Eureka College ended the six-game losing streak with an easy home non-conference victory, 104 to 48, over an out-manned Milwaukee School of Engineering. Darnall was asked for his reaction to the game.

"We needed a game like that," said the EC coach. "After losing six games in a row and only playing one home game out of eleven, we needed a lift."

Dave continued, "The first part of our schedule was tough. Those were against some very quality ball clubs and all on the road. We wanted a win going into Conference play."

Asked about starting two freshmen, six-foot-seven Wright and six-foot-four Haile, for the second straight game, Darnall said, "I made the move after the Huntington game. I didn't feel we were getting the effort and team unity that we should have. I think an attitude adjustment is on the way."

The Red Devils won eight of the next nine games, including the MSOE win. Darnall, again, made some line-up changes during that period, including replacing Haile with another freshman, six-foot-four Michael Harris. Late in the season, six-foot-four Jason Gorham replaced Harris. Sophomore point guard, Jeff "Little Butch" Cassidy, got his first start of the year in the Red Devils' last game of the season. EC won the home finale against Greenville, 67 to 44.

The single loss in the nine-game sequence was on the road to Iowa Wesleyan. The Red Devils dropped a heartbreaking one-point decision to the Tigers in the "pit."

"It's easier to lose by ten or more than by one or two," Coach Darnall said. "If you get beat by a larger margin, then you usually know the other team is better, but if you lose by a small number, you start second guessing yourself and use 'if this and if that.'"

During that time Darnall found some time to attend a couple of Derek's seventh-grade basketball games. His son's team started the season with a 6 to 0 record. Derek and Chad Heffren started as guards, Eric Lockart and Ken Terpin were the forwards, with Rick Bauman at center. Jayme Roberts was the first substitute. Derek, Chad, Eric, Rick, and Jayme were all good friends. Their parents were also friends.

In a 44 to 34 win over Deer Creek, Derek led the Hornets in scoring with twenty points. Against Germantown Hills, the young Darnall scored a game-high twenty-two points to lead his team to a 43 to 25 victory. Even though Derek was capable of scoring, his father felt his greatest asset was his ball handling—passing skills and his quickness both on offense and defense.

There was one great win in the Red Devils' "spurt." It was an astonishing 77 to 59 triumph over McKendree College. Alonzo Echols pumped in career high thirty-two points, while teammate Tony Shelly contributed twenty-three. The post-game party at the Darnalls' following the great victory was by far the most highly attended all season. It seemed that the quality of the opposing team brought more spectators to the game and, consequently, more to Coach's home after.

EC split the remaining six games of the season. One of the wins came in a rematch with Iowa Wesleyan. Alonzo Echols led the way with twenty-one points to give Eureka a little revenge, 94 to 84, for its one-point loss earlier in the season at Iowa.

Unfortunately, the three losses came in Conference play—one against Blackburn and two against MacMurray, placing the Red Devils third in the league. The defeats also prohibited EC from making the NAIA Playoff for the first time since the Dunkel took effect.

In Eureka's final game of the season, Greenville's starting point-guard, Eric Buerkett, scored seven points. Darnall had met him as a youngster when he was recruiting Eric's older brother. As time would tell, Eric transferred and became a valuable part of the Red Devil basketball program.

Two special events occurred during the 1983-1984 year. On February 6, 1984, President Ronald Reagan addressed his alma mater in the first of a series of lectures sponsored by *Time* magazine in celebration of its sixtieth anniversary. The Distinguished Speaker Program was intended to bring to campuses throughout the United States a variety of newsmakers who had appeared on the cover of *Time*. This date, February 6, also marked the seventy-third birthday of the president and the 129th of Eureka College.

That time, Darnall was very conscientious and left his hair pick at home. He definitely did not want a repeat of several years before when he set the security alarm off.

The second special occurrence for Darnall was his promotion to Associate Professor of Physical Education by the Faculty Status Committee and approval by the general faculty. He was very gratified by this promotion.

The Darnall family found time during Easter Vacation to travel to Willow Springs, Missouri, to purchase a car. Not just any car, but a 1955 Chevy. It would take years for the Delray to be restored to an exact replica of the gypsy red and ivory Chevy, Dave's first car in high school. Bonnie often said that if their bed collapsed, it would smash thousands of dollars in car parts. The car was finally completely restored in 1993.

Bruce took his brother, Chuck Wertz, and Mike Lockart to the Indianapolis 500 on Memorial Day. The quartet enjoyed two days at the track and can testify that the rumored sights are true. Bruce, a racing enthusiast has attended the world's most famous race for years.

There was no rest for the coach during the summer. Following several weeks of camps, the Darnall family made a trip to Florida to Disney World and Magic Kingdom. On the return, they stopped at Fairfield Glade in Crossland, Tennessee. Dave and Bonnie bought a one-week timeshare with Fairfield Communities. This move eventually led to their new home in Fairfield Bay, Arkansas.

Somehow, Dave also found time to be a guest speaker at Dave Gilliland's Raider Basketball Summer Camp in Bussels, Illinois. Dennis Dighton, Darnall's first administrative assistant during the 1974-1975 season, was the assistant coach at Bussels High School. At the time, Darnall did not realize how fortunate the 150-mile trip would later become to his program.

1984–1985

THE 1984-1985 SEASON BROUGHT ABOUT a rule change that would effect some college basketball games. A forty-five-second clock was used for the first time at the college level. This rule change was to the liking of Darnall.

"This will help our zone defense be more effective," Dave said. "Instead of teams holding the ball or trying to pull us out of our zone, they will have to attempt to attack it."

Remember the playoff game with Quincy?

"I can anticipate an attitude change in our players regarding our zone already," Darnall continued. "They only have to bust their butts for forty-five seconds instead of a couple of minutes like they have been used to. Teams will now have to challenge our zone."

As the season began to get underway, Coach Darnall had a second article published within a year in a national coaching magazine. "Eureka's Fast Break Down the Side" appeared in the October issue of *Scholastic Coach*. The magazine later became the number one coaching magazine in the country.

Dave did not think he needed a big recruiting class since the previous two years provided both quantity and quality. Or did he? Devastation took place. A former EC football player decided to transfer to Southeast Missouri State. Several of his TKE brothers followed him. During Darnall's tenure at Eureka, many basketball players were members of the Tau Kappa Epsilon Fraternity. Five basketball players, including three part-time starters were among the group. One TKE player did stay. "Little Butch" Cassidy showed his loyalty to Darnall and remained at Eureka. Also, remember what his father told him when he was looking for a college? "I don't care where you go, but wherever it is, you are going to stay there the full time," Mr. Cassidy had told his son. Dave thought he was a "wise man." Jeff respected his father's words. "Little Butch," however, was interested in becoming a coach, so he decided to bypass his playing career to become an administrative assistant. He joined student coach Scott Burgess on Darnall's staff. The move by Cassidy proved invaluable to Darnall and solidified a relationship that is strong to this day.

Dave is still not sure why the players left the college and gave up basketball. There were rumors, but none verified.

Two new Red Devil players were transfer students. Lincoln Junior College graduate John Jones joined ex-teammates Echols and Tuttle at Eureka. Al Pickering supplied his friend Darnall another quality kid.

"Every student-athlete that came to our college was top-notch," Darnall said. "The basketball players were also disciplined and understood the game. Al did a great job at Lincoln."

Kirk Doehring, Darnall's administrative assistant, convinced his cousin that he should finish his college education and basketball career at Eureka College. Cary Doehring, remember him? He had a great deal to do with Quincy College's win over Eureka in the 1980-1981 NAIA Playoff game. Doehring left Quincy, played a year of Division I ball, laid out a year, but still had one year of eligibility left. The six-foot-five guard was a great addition to the Eureka program.

The Red Devils played their first seven games of the season on the road. That was not necessarily unusual, but six in three invitational tournaments were. The first game was at the Marian Tournament against the much larger school of University of Wisconsin-Superior. The starters for the game were Jones at center, Harris and Echols at forwards, and Rick Taylor and Cary Doehring at guards. In reality, six-foot-five guard Doehring was the tallest player on the EC starting five. This was also the first college career start for the six-foot-three sophomore Taylor, but it surely would not be his last.

Taylor and Doehring pumped in twenty and sixteen respectively to lead their team to a great win over the tournament favorite state school, 84 to 64. The following day, the Red Devils played another large Wisconsin state school for the championship. That time it was against the University of Wisconsin-Milwaukee. The school, with an enrollment of over 20,000 and currently a member of the NCAA Division I, outlasted the tiny college, 90 to 82, for the title. Cary Doehring was named to the All-tourney team.

Eureka College returned to the Rockford Invitational Tournament to defend its championship. With a win over Hamline University, the Red Devils took on Rockford for the championship. Greg Nunn, making his first college career start contributed thirteen points as EC claimed the tournament championship by outscoring the host by four. Rick Taylor led the team in scoring with seventeen points on the way to become the tournaments MVP. Echols joined his teammate on the All-tournament team.

The Red Devils knocked off Concordia College before competing in their third invitational. Senior forward Derrick Martin made his first start of the year, contributing to the EC scoring attack by pumping in sixteen points in the lopsided, 87 to 60, win.

Darnall's team bested Roosevelt University in a low-scoring affair in the first round of the Judson Tournament. Dave was interviewed by *Woodford County Journal* sportswriter Joe Bates about his team's win.

"Our zone defense was again the key," Darnall said. "John Jones had an exceptional overall game. Roosevelt has a tremendous amount of talent. This was an excellent win for us. It puts us in the position to win our second tournament championship of the year."

The Red Devils did not let their coach down, but they did have him sweating the first half. Holding only a two-point lead at the intermission, Darnall gave an inspirational half-time talk that challenged his players to prove they were a quality team.

"I'm tired of all the bull _ _ _ _ on how good you are," Darnall shouted. "You guys think you're good; prove it!"

After making a few offensive adjustments, the coach instructed his team to "get the hell out there and kick some butt."

Behind the tournament's MVP's game-high twenty-seven points, the Red Devils beat host school Judson for the tournament title. Alonzo Echols, again, made an All-tournament team along with the MVP Cary Doehring.

Eureka went into Christmas break with an 8 to 2 record. After playing eight of the ten games on the opponents' floors, Peoria *Journal Star* sportswriter Dave Reynolds wrote an article entitled "There's no place like the road," about the Red Devils' early season schedule and results. Portions read:

> Most basketball teams subscribe to the phrase, "There's no place like home." After all, isn't a friendly, supportive crowd supposed to be worth 10 points or so?
>
> Not to the Eureka College men's team. The Red Devils began the season with a seven-game road trip and won six of them, including two

tournament championships. Then in their home opener earlier this month against Washington University, they played their worst game of the year, losing 81 - 70.

The Red Devils finally won one for the home folks, 72 - 48 over George Williams, but then took to the road again in a big way, trouncing Maranatha 81 - 67 in their last outing before the Christmas break.

"I'm not sure that we don't play as well, if not better, on the road," said Coach Dave Darnall. "Our kids are kind of unemotional. When they're home, they feel the pressure from that emotional crowd buildup. When they're on the road, they're more relaxed.

"It's very frustrating for me because I'm kind of an emotional guy and I can never see any emotion in them. I'm not sure if they're motivated like they should be."

Darnall should know a thing or two about motivation. His 10-year record at Eureka entering this season was 172 - 83, a winning percentage of.675. That ranks him in a tie for 15th among active Division III coaches . . .

In his last eight years, Darnall has guided five Red Devil teams to the state NAIA playoffs, but he's never had a club in the NAIA national tournament in Kansas City's Kemper Arena, and, despite this season's 8 - 2 start, he's not so sure that this is the year . . .

"As a team, we really haven't taken control yet. We've been winning by just two or three points. And if we're going to be an NAIA contender, we've got to do more than survive."

The rest of the season went in spurts—two or three wins in a row, lose two or three in a row.

EC opened the second half of the season dropping three games in a five-day trip to Indiana. The Red Devils returned home for Harris-Stowe before hitting the road again for two. The home court remedy was just what the "doctor ordered,"—the floor, the fans, and the officials. Sophomore Greg Nunn paved the way with eighteen points as Eureka broke its three game losing streak defeating Harris-Stowe, 88 to 72.

"It's great to win a game," Darnall said following the contest. "Right now even a win over a junior high team would be good. Our team must develop the winning attitude again. We need to win several games in a row to turn this thing around."

That's exactly what Darnall's team did. They won three straight Conference games. Doehring and Taylor had consistently carried the scoring load on their "shoulders." However, they were finally getting some help. In the four consecutive wins, Nunn poured in eighteen, twenty-two, nineteen, and fourteen points.

It was around that time that the two future Red Devil stars started to really be known by their nicknames. The names remained with the two for the rest of their careers and even after college. Sophomore guards Rick "Ice" Taylor and Greg "Sugar" Nunn would become perhaps the best set of guards to ever wear the maroon and gold.

Rick's nickname, "Ice," was the result of his resemblance to NBA superstar George "The Iceman" Gervin. "Sugar" came from Nunn's sweet jump shot. "Sugar" and "Ice" would dazzle the fans for two more years.

The winning streak came to an end at McKendree College. The Bearcats blasted the young Red Devils, 92 to 62. Darnall had started senior Doehring, freshman Matt Krieger, and sophomores Nunn, Taylor, and Wright. The three sophomores and Darnall would not forget the humiliating defeat.

Blackburn College took a big step toward the Conference championship by knocking off the previously undefeated Red Devils at home by the score of 61 to 52.

Eureka bounced back with a smashing 101 to 52 home triumph over Conference foe Principia College. That started a string of four victories, including an impressive 114 to 65 win over Iowa Wesleyan. Playing in front of the home crowd, the Red Devils perhaps played their best game of the season. The point spread definitely helped Eureka's Dunkel rating points. However, it wasn't like Darnall was trying to "run up the score." In a true rarity, the EC coach played all fifteen varsity players and all contributed to the final tally by scoring at least two points or better.

As happy as the fans were at Coach's house after the Iowa Wesleyan game, they were equally depressed after the Blackburn loss. Then the Red Devils lost at MacMurray. The future professional baseball player, Bill Sampen, tossed in twenty-seven points as the Highlanders claimed a 97 to 83 victory. That set up a match-up with Blackburn for the Conference title. The hometown fans showed up in force to witness the all-important game. Despite a game-high twenty-five-point performance by Tony Tuttle, Eureka was not able to overcome the visitors in a double overtime battle. Sophomore Greg Nunn had the opportunity to seal the victory for the Red Devils with two free throws in the closing seconds of regulation play. Unfortunately, Nunn missed the charity tosses, sending the game into overtime. Fortunately, he would have the chance to redeem himself for an even more important championship. The 83 to 81 loss resulted in the Red Devils finishing second in the Conference.

EC closed out its regular season play with a Conference forfeit win. The unusual "win" was the result of a measles epidemic on the Principia campus. The student body had been quarantined for several days. The strongly religious school affiliated with the Christian Scientist church believed in spiritual healing and not with medical doctors. The forfeit gave the Red Devils a 17 to 9 record in regular season play. Would that be good enough to get them back into the playoffs?

To Darnall surprise, his team was seeded sixth in the eight-team NAIA District 20 Playoff field. Eureka College traveled to the Chicago area to take on No. 2 seed St. Xavier. Even though the Red Devils were only four points down at the intermission, they could not overcome the Cougars' twenty-one for thirty-two free throw shooting. EC outscored the home team by one basket from the field, but only shot eleven free throws, connecting on only eight of those. The Red Devils ended losing to the scholarship school, 83 to 72.

Coach was asked to comment on the game by Joe Bates, sportswriter for the *Woodford County Journal*.

"We proved we were worthy of the playoff bid," stated Darnall. "If that was the number two team in the state, we were able to play with them. We held our own pretty well under the circumstances; we had a good show."

Establishing a precedent, the annual end-of-season basketball banquet was held solely at the Darnalls' home. Coach LaCursia's Lady Red Devils joined the men's team for the outdoor potluck and awards presentations. Dave obtained donations from the local IGA, E-Tribe, and the college's food service to help supply additional food and beverage for the gathering. Former players and their parents also joined with the current set of players and parents for the festivities. Needless to say, no one left hungry.

The season was over, and it was time for Darnall and his "boys" to make their annual trip to Chicago to see the Bulls in action. Those making this trip were Coach Smitty, Bob Gold, Chuck Wertz, George VanWinkle, Joel Micetich, and Roger Phegley. Yes, the former NBA Roger Phegley. Phegley had just retired from basketball due to a knee injury after spending a year in Europe. Joining the group at the stadium were Bruce and camp coach Jack Gronholz, both from Wisconsin.

The guys enjoyed a couple cold beers at Darnalls' before leaving for the two-hour trip to Chicago. Stupidly, they also took plenty of cold ones with them to enjoy while playing cards on the way north. The driver was careful not to partake with his passengers. The travelers had finally reached the Eisenhower Expressway around 6:00 P.M., still a half-hour away from the arena, when one of the passengers announced he had to "pee." Unfortunately, there was bumper-to-bumper traffic with vehicles only creeping, and no exits in sight. Darnall tried to get the "man in pain" to just hold it.

"Either you stop on the shoulder, give me an empty bottle, or I'm going in here," the distraught rider demanded. Darnall had no choice. The only option was the "bottle." To illustrate the severity of the situation, it took four bottles. With the full bottles placed in the four cup holders in the card table, Darnall drove carefully to the parking lot adjacent to the stadium. The bottles were the first things to depart the van. Dave, wisely, would not reveal which passenger had to fill the bottles.

Corzine had left the game tickets at the "will call" window for his fans. The "Jordan Phenomenon" had just begun and seats were at a minimum. The Eureka group had no idea where their seats were located. Would you believe it was the very top of the stadium?

"I mean the last row in the whole damn building," commented Darnall. "You know, nose-bleed territory. But that's all right, some didn't even get in. I think Corzine did it on purpose."

The fellows were sitting so high that they wished they had brought binoculars with them. Darnall turned to Phegley and said, "How soon do they forget! Just think, a little over a year ago, you were down there on the floor."

Several spectators sitting close by heard Coach's remarks but could not believe the man sitting next to the speaker was a former NBA player. They could not be convinced.

As soon as the game was over, Darnall, Phegley, Bruce, and Smitty dashed for the game floor and then on to the Bulls' locker room. It was no easy task to get from the roof to the basement of the huge building. Then came the security guard obstacles. They didn't buy who the quartet was or why they should be allowed into the Chicago locker room. Finally, one of the guards consented to get Mark Pfeil, the Bulls' trainer. Mark knew Phegley and had met Darnall and Smitty previously at Corzine's. Pfeil became the "man of the hour." The foursome passed Jordan, who was surrounded by the press but took time to acknowledge Phegley as the four slid by and hurried on to their own hero. Corzine offered the "boys" a cold beer.

"You better after the tickets you got for us," Smitty jokingly threw at Corzine.

Corzine was half dressed by the time the group had entered the locker room. He suggested that they go to Burton's Place, one of his favorites, in downtown Chicago for something to eat and drink.

"Phegley, grab my bag and come with me," Corzine ordered. "The guys can follow us."

They left the locker room and headed toward the ramp leading to the empty playing floor. The others from the Eureka group were waiting patiently. They all proceeded to Darnall's van and left for Burton's. It was, again, an exciting and fun trip for the Eureka guys.

1985–1986

SEVERAL CHANGES TOOK PLACE AT EUREKA COLLEGE prior to the beginning of the 1985-1986 school year. George Hearne, a man dedicated to serving the institution, was named the twenty-fourth president of the college. Darnall was thrilled with the appointment. He felt his working atmosphere would improve and become less stressful. He thought hard work and dedication would be more appreciated.

Coach Darnall had some changes in his coaching staff also. Dennis Dighton returned to his alma mater to become Dave's number one assistant. Coach Todd left the coaching profession to enter the business world. Jeff Cassidy became the head junior varsity coach and student varsity assistant. Darnall and "Little Butch" spent numerous hours together on the road that year recruiting and scouting.

"The boy could talk," Dave said. "I guess that's what you learn to do when you're the baby of fourteen children. Not only could he relate to new recruits, but he also served as a liaison between the coaching staff and players. Being a former player and possessing leadership qualities, he was respected by his peers."

Mark Wilmington joined Kirk Doehring as a basketball administrative assistant. Darnall felt the assistants were the unsung heroes. They never got the credit they deserved for helping to put together a quality program.

Darnall knew he had some excellent small college players returning, but also knew he needed a few good freshmen and a couple of experienced junior college players, particularly a strong power-forward to keep the program moving forward. Coach achieved both of those objectives by recruiting six-foot-six JC transfer Rob Kroehnke and freshmen Tom Dooley, Jeff Wooters, Mike Coffman, and Tim Ricketts.

Dave, again, was able to see his freshman son participate on the fresh-soph football team prior to the official start of basketball season. Football was Derek's favorite sport even though the youth recreation league of Eureka had not initiated a football program at that time, and he had not been able to play organized football before that year. The younger Darnall was a starter on both the offensive and defensive units.

Twenty-two candidates greeted the coaching staff on the first official night of practice. That included nine lettermen. Selecting the fifteen varsity players was an extremely difficult task for the coaching staff.

"In all my years as a college coach, the hardest task I had was to pick my top fifteen," Darnall said. "As I always told each year's squad, the fifteen who dress the first game won't be the same fifteen who will dress the last game." That year was no different.

The Eureka College basketball team that year took a giant step forward in becoming one of the best small college programs in the Midwest. No, that did not mean that the Red Devils won their first ever NAIA Playoff game or even the first game of the season. It meant the team:

1. had the best record and most wins in the school's history—21 - 5;
2. earned a berth in the NAIA Playoff field—selected 5th, the highest for a Eureka team;
3. was Conference champions—10 - 0;
4. was undefeated at home—10 - 0;
5. led the NAIA District 20 in defense;
6. led the NAIA District 20 in offense-defense margin;
7. led the Conference in defense; and,
8. had the longest winning streak in the college's history—16 games.

The Red Devils' opened by traveling to Kirksville, Missouri, for a night game against the much larger institution Northeast Missouri State. It ended up being a nightmare for the small college team.

"I should have known it was going to be a long day after the trouble we had getting there," Darnall said. "Mentally, everyone was pretty much drained by the time the game started."

Dave was referring to the problem the team had getting to Kirksville. Coach Cassidy drove one van carrying the upperclassmen, while Darnall and Dighton escorted the underclassmen. The team had to make an unscheduled stop in Macomb after traveling the two-lane roads for a couple of hours— "Little Butch's van broke down.

"What in the hell do we do now?" Darnall asked Dighton.

By then, the vans were pulled over to the side of the road. They examined the vehicle, but both coaches did not know a damn thing about cars. Some of the players thought they did, but it was soon determined that they needed professional help. A gas station was spotted a couple of blocks away from the stalled van. Dave drove his van to the station for help. A mechanic returned with Coach to take a look at the damage. The evaluation was not good.

"It's going to take time," he said. "You have a major problem."

An impromptu coaches' meeting took place. It was decided that Darnall and Cassidy would take the top eight players plus the game equipment and charge forward. Coaches Dighton, Doehring, and the seven remaining players would stay behind. Darnall's van took off, leaving all their clothes back in the baggage trailer that was attached to the broken vehicle.

The first group of Red Devils checked in to the motel, settled in, and proceeded to the motel's restaurant for the pre-game meal. They finished around 4:30 P.M., returned to their rooms to relax, and then left at 6:00 for the five-minute drive to the opponent's fieldhouse. Still no second van!

The top eight players dressed. Coach Darnall had a short pre-game talk before his "underdogs" took the court for an adjusted warm-up drill.

Then it was 7:20, ten minutes before tip-off, and still no van, including Coach Darnall's game suit. Darnall proceeded to take his half-team back to the locker room for his last minute instructions. Finishing the quick meeting, the players returned to the floor while Darnall headed to the bathroom for the final time. All of a sudden, the seven players and two coaches from the second van burst through the dressing room door. The players started to put on their uniforms.

"Big Daddy," Kirk Doehring's nickname, "go get my suit," the sitting coach instructed. "The rest of you guys get your butts in gear and get out there."

Darnall, who had been dressed in an old sweat suit and basketball shoes, could not wait to get rid of his "grubs." He definitely was not the image of a college basketball coach.

The first game starters of the optimistic season were John Jones at center, Al Wright and Rob Kroehnke at forwards, and "Sugar" Nunn and "Ice" Taylor at guards.

The day's events had taken a toll on the Red Devils. Despite "Sugar's" twenty-five points, the larger scholarship school's basketball team was just too much for the out-matched Red Devils.

"We just didn't play very well," Dave told the press following the game. "Too much confusion both on and off the floor. You're not going to win many games shooting thirty-seven percent from the field and making only thirteen out of twenty-four free throws."

In the locker room, the coach talked to his players. "We've got to forget about tonight," Darnall said. "I guess it was not meant to be. To beat a team like Northeast, we have to have everything going for us. Tonight we didn't."

Dave continued, "We've got to bounce back and beat Iowa Wesleyan tomorrow night. Losing to them will kill us. If we go one and one on this trip, it'll be okay. We need to go back to the motel, get something to eat, and 'hit the hay.'"

EC bounced back the following night to even up its record by knocking off Iowa Wesleyan, 72 to 54. The team went on to win five out of the next seven games. The only problem was that both losses came in the first rounds of invitational tournaments. They lost to Rosary at the Judson Tourney and to Anderson College at Rose-Hulman's. However, the Red Devils did rebound in both tournaments to claim third places. Those were not the places Darnall had wanted. He was disappointed that his team did not play for the championships.

Eureka College's first home game had brought a smashing 85 to 45 victory over Concordia-River Forest. The hometown fans had been anxiously waiting to get a peek at their team. The Red Devils did not disappoint them as the dynamic backcourt duo, "Sugar" and "Ice" pumped in twenty and sixteen points respectively.

The first post-game party at the Darnalls' was well attended. It turned out to be a good celebration of the team's first two victories and reminiscing about the team's ordeal on the Northeast Missouri trip.

The last game before break and for third place at the Rose-Hulman Tournament was against Manchester College. The highly respected NCAA III school put up a good fight, but fell eleven points short. Rick Taylor, perhaps, played the best game of his career to that date. He sank twenty-six points while dishing out six assists in EC's, 79 to 68, win. Freshman forward Tom Dooley, making only his second start of his career, contributed to Eureka's scoring attack by netting eleven points. The Red Devils were left with a 6 to 3 record entering Christmas break.

Dave was ready for the four-week interval before the first game of the second part of the season. There was a stretch of time that Darnall had been away from home for twenty straight evenings.

"Thank God for 'Little Butch' and Chuck Wertz," the coach replied when asked about his horrendous schedule. "Jeff drove while I worked on some of my papers. So did Chuck."

When Darnall had to leave early from practice or miss it altogether, he did not worry what was happening in the gym. He had a lot of respect and confidence in his assistant coach Dennis Dighton.

"I didn't have to worry about how practice was going or whether the kids were learning anything," said Dave. "Dighton has a great basketball mind and is a great 'X' and 'O' man."

Darnall was also able to see his children participate in their school activities during the break. Tiera was then a varsity cheerleader while Derek was the starting point-guard on the fresh-soph team. He could shoot the "rock," but his quickness, passing, ball handling, and defense were his specialties.

"Everyone wants to score," the younger Darnall told his dad. "Someone else has to do the other things that win games. I guess that's me."

Dave felt that Derek had internalized the "Together We Win" attitude. He also saw it shown in a freshman class writing assignment. The students were to write about their saddest and most enjoyable experience. Derek's response meant a lot to his dad. It read:

> My saddest moment was when my grandmother, mom, and I went to the nursing home in El Paso. When we got there, my grandpa had just died. It was hard watching Grandma and the friends he had at the home.
>
> One of my most enjoyable experiences was last Thursday when Eureka played Tremont in a freshman football game. It was great because on the first kick-off, Andy Shields and I were back to catch the ball and run it back. Andy caught the ball and started running to the right out-of-bounds line. I saw three Tremont guys coming from that side running right next to each other after Andy. I dove right at their legs and knocked all three on top of me. He got all the credit, but it was still fun. Actually, the whole game was one of my most fun times.

"Even though I haven't been there all the time, Tiera and Derek both seem to have their priorities right. Bonnie has done a great job of raising our kids in my absence."

The Red Devils started the second half of the season with a two-game, four-day trip to the St. Louis area. Coach LaCursia's Lady Red Devils accompanied the men's team to the Gateway City. The men's coaching staff and Marv Holmes, who had also traveled with the teams, spent the first evening in Darnall's twentieth-floor complimentary rooms. The Cunningham Suite was a luxurious two-room suite with a breathtaking view of downtown St. Louis.

Coach Darnall and his players both had benefited from the long lay-off. The Red Devil team seemed rejuvenated and focused. They reeled off fifteen consecutive victories before losing the final regular season contest on the road to the highly regarded Washington University by five.

EC's trip to St. Louis was successful with convincing wins over Lindenwood College and Webster University by the scores of 96 to 63 and 93 to 78 respectively. Then came a great home revenge victory over Anderson College. Eureka had lost to the Indiana school three consecutive times before the 78 to 69 win. However, the victory did not come easily. Darnall had emphasized the significance of the game in his pre-game talk. It was a super chance to gain valuable Dunkel points. Coach thought he had his "warriors" ready to play. He was wrong! The team came out of the locker room flat and disorganized. Twice Darnall called his patent timeouts on the court. He raised hell with both the team's effort and execution. It made no difference. The Red Devils trailed at intermission, 31 to 24.

Darnall was livid in the locker room. The emotional coach let his players know his dissatisfaction of their first-half performance. Throwing a piece of chalk at the blackboard, the perplexed coach stormed out of the room leaving the players time to talk about their play. It was like day and night when they returned to the floor as the final score indicated. It became a good night for the Dunkel as well as the post-game party at the Darnalls'. The Red Devil fans had waited a couple years for a triumph over Anderson.

Three straight victories followed. The middle win was not only important for the team, but it was equally big for their coach. The Red Devil players handed Darnall his 200th college win. It is a milestone numerous coaches strive for, but only a few achieve. With Nunn, who was named NAIA District 20 Player of the Week, and Taylor pumping in twenty and nineteen respectively, EC breezed by Maryville College, 82 to 47, in St. Louis.

At the next home game against Greenville College, President Hearne honored his coach by presenting Dave with a plaque for his accomplishment of 200 wins. Hearne also handed Darnall a telegram from President Ronald Reagan also congratulating him for the achievement.

An article entitled "Darnall wins 200th game" by Joe Bates appeared in the *Woodford County Journal*. It read in part:

> When the Eureka College basketball team defeated Maryville 82 - 47 on Thursday, Jan 23, head coach Dave Darnall accomplished something many coaches only dream of—winning 200 games at one school.
> And what makes Darnall's accomplishment even more outstanding is the fact he has won 200 games and has yet to lose 100 . . .

Darnall's 12-year record at EC was 201 - 97, a winning percentage of .674 . . .

Darnall was also honored by receiving a telegram from President Ronald Reagan, a former EC graduate. "He gave me some nice remarks and he wished the team well," stated Darnall about what the telegram said. Reagan also hoped EC would be able to qualify for another state playoff berth this season . . .

The citizens of Eureka should also be pleased to hear Darnall plans on finishing his coaching career at EC. "I definitely plan on staying in Eureka," said Darnall. "I'd like to last 20 years as a coach here. It (coaching) is still very demanding; I don't know if I can last eight more years.' Darnall's goal is to reach victory No. 300.

Although he may never be mentioned in the same breath with Bobby Knight of Indiana or Dean Smith of North Carolina, Dave Darnall certainly ranks among the best Division III coaches around.

```
IPM35IL
1-0047961024 01/24/86
ZCZC 199 GOVT DLY WHITE HOUSE DC JAN 24
PMS PEORIA AGENT, WESTERN UNION
FOR DAVE DARNALL, (WILL CALL -HOLD FOR
DLY)
PEORIA, ILLINOIS
BT

DAVE:

CONGRATULATIONS TO YOU AND THE RED
DEVILS ON YOUR 200TH VICTORY. I KNOW I CAN
SPEAK FOR ALL EUREKA ALUMNI IN
EXPRESSING OUR PRIDE IN YOUR
ACHIEVEMENT. THE COLLEGE AND THE TEAM
ARE FORTUNATE TO HAVE SOMEONE WITH YOUR
DETERMINATION AND CAPABILITY AND I KNOW
THAT YOU WILL ONCE AGAIN TAKE THE RED
DEVILS TO THE DISTRICT PLAYOFFS. GOD BLESS
YOU AND I LOOK FORWARD TO MORE GOOD
NEWS FROM YOU AND THE TEAM.

    RONALD REAGAN

NNNN
1058 EST
IPM35IL
```

287

The party after the game celebrated both the Greenville win and Coach's 200th milestone. Dave's friend, Bill Eaton, made a wooden countdown board reading "Darnall's Countdown to 300." The flip chart was placed in the Darnall family room where it became a ritual to flip the numbers after each win on the road to 300.

When asked about possibly reaching his 300th, Darnall replied, "I hope I'm able to endure until I reach my 300th coaching win at Eureka College. Anything after that would be gravy."

With the Greenville win under their "belt," the Red Devils were ready to take on McKendree on Eureka's "turf." A near-capacity crowd witnessed the game that would affect the weekly Dunkel standing. Coach Darnall felt his fellas were ready for the challenge and, consequently, gave a "low-key" pre-game talk.

"You want to prove you're a team to be reckoned with, beat McKendree," Darnall said. "You guys want recognition, a win tonight will give it to you. Go out there and show me what you're made of."

The Red Devils, playing a hellish 1-2-2 adjustable zone, held the Bearcats' potent offense to a mere twenty-three points at the intermission and held an eight-point lead. EC did not disappoint its fans and claimed a narrow five-point victory, 72 to 67. McKendree had been rated fifth in the Dunkel points, while Eureka was sixth.

It was back to Conference play for the EC team. It won seven consecutive league games, finishing Conference play at 10 to 0. The championship had been one of the team's goals. It, however, did not come without a fight. Two close road victories—one against Greenville and the other with Blackburn—sealed the title.

Eureka escaped Greenville with a one-point, 51 to 50, win. Dave was thrilled that his team had won, but on the other hand, they had lost. EC's point spread was not enough to appease the all-important Dunkel system.

In Eureka's first win over Blackburn, the coach credited the crowd for the victory. "It was a tremendous crowd and the TKE Fraternity was unreal. They are like the sixth man. The Eureka High School pep band also really got us fired-up. It was a tremendous atmosphere."

However, that huge support would be lacking on the second outing at Blackburn. They were on their own with their usual traveling fans. The two point, 54 to 52, victory sufficed. It gave the Red Devils the outright Conference Championship.

Prior to the Blackburn game, *The Pantagraph* sportswriter Bryan Bloodworth wrote a great article on two of Eureka's players. Portions of "Sugar, Ice nice for Red Devils" read:

Sugar and Ice. The combination has served as a winning mixture for Eureka College's basketball team.

Sugar is the nickname of 6-foot-2 junior guard Greg Nunn while 6-3 junior guard Rick Taylor carries the Ice tag. Together, Sugar and Ice have made things very nice for the Red Devils.

Eureka College has won 14 straight, the longest winning streak in school history, for a 19 -3 record. The school record for victories in a season is 21 . . .

Sugar, er Nunn, paces the Red Devils with a 21.1 scoring average while shooting 59 percent from the field. He ranks second in the state in scoring among National Association of Intercollegiate Athletic players and fourth in field goal percentage.

Taylor carries a 17.4 scoring average and makes 56 percent of his shots. He also leads the team with 105 assists.

"They're as good a set of guards as I've had here," said coach Dave Darnall. "They both work to the maximum of their abilities and they're both solid students . . ."

The dynamic duo has helped Eureka College to a No. 5 ranking among NAIA District 20 teams. Quincy College leads the rankings.

"That's the highest we've ever been ranked…This could be the most outstanding year in history for a Eureka College basketball team. We have never finished higher than sixth in the state in the rankings . . ."

Darnall admits he didn't harbor such hopes at the beginning of the season.

"I was expecting a good year, but I had no idea we would have this kind of season. I'm still in shock," Darnall continued. "I was worried about our scoring. I knew Nunn would score, but I didn't realize what we would get out of Taylor."

Eureka College's 17-man roster is loaded with 11 juniors, which made many believe the Red Devils were a year away from an excellent season.

"I thought that too," said Darnall. "But we got on a roll, so we stopped thinking about next year and decided to take things while we could."

How far could they go next year? That was yet to be determined.

Eureka College closed out the season by dropping a hard-fought battle against prestigious Washington University in St. Louis by the score of 67 to 62. The team finished its regular season with an outstanding record of 21 to 4. It awaited the NAIA Playoff pairings.

Red Devils' Dynamic Duo, "Sugar" and "Ice." (Photo by Maureen O'Connor of *The Pantagraph*)

Since Illinois Wesleyan's withdrawal from the NAIA, the spring meeting was held on Eureka College's campus. Eureka was centrally located among the District 20 schools.

The Red Devils just missed it. No, not the playoff field, but they were seeded No. 5 and failed to host a first-round game. That was one factor Darnall felt was needed for any real chance to qualify for the National Tournament in Kansas City. A team had to have a couple home games in the playoffs.

Quincy College grabbed the No. 1 seed with Eureka's first opponent Olivet Nazarene coming in fourth. The Dunkel Rating System gave Olivet 38.1 points and Eureka 38.0. One-tenth of a point kept the Red Devils from hosting a first-round game. Rosary was seeded third with 38.9, while McKendree came in sixth at 37.9, followed by St. Xavier with 37.7. The slim separation of total Dunkel points made Darnall stress how important each point of a game was. The close scores in the Greenville and Blackburn games and the loss to Washington had "done them in." That would have to change in the future.

The team left for Kankakee the day before the game so as to practice on the game floor, a tradition Darnall started in the middle 1970s. Several Red Devil fans arrived at the motel about the same time as the team returned from practice. It was nice to have Ernie and Sheila Monk of nearby Momence, long-time Darnall friends, also join the group. During the afternoon, Gail and Bill Eaton, Dan Harrod, and Bonnie had tried to purchase maroon and gold hankies to wave at the game. Eventually, they settled for yellow and white wash clothes and maroon dye from K-Mart. They found a local laundromat and dyed the white clothes maroon. A small stir was caused with the other patrons who were all African-American when Dan explained, "We just came in to 'dye.'" The Eureka fans were always looking for ways to support their team.

The home-court advantage was present throughout the contest. Olivet jumped to an early lead and held on to defeat Eureka, 78 to 70, despite "Sugar" and "Ice" pumping in nineteen each.

The loss brought the successful season to an end and the annual basketball potluck to Darnall's backyard. Coach was both happy and tormented. Next year he would just have to emphasize the Dunkel system to his players more forcefully and "take no prisoners." The Red Devils would have to master the Dunkel Rating System.

Eureka College led District 20 in two categories—Darnall's pride and joy, defense and offense-defense margins. Greg Nunn was selected First Team NAIA All-District as well as being named the Conference's MVP. The second member of the dynamic duo, Rick Taylor, was named NAIA Honorable Mention All-District and First Team All-Conference.

"Those two boys are, perhaps, one of the best set of guards in small college basketball," Coach Darnall commented about his prize players.

A few days after the conclusion of the season, Coach was asked for his thoughts about the past year. "I feel the team took great strides in reaching our ultimate goal, a national tournament appearance," said Darnall. "I have a vision that someday one of my teams will be holding a championship trophy above their heads as the cameras flash. We'll just have to wait and see. Next year is my thirteenth year here. My lucky number—maybe something good will happen."

Many coaches put pressure on themselves because they hate to lose and have high expectations for their teams. That was the hyper Dave Darnall. The burning desire to succeed drove him beyond limits at times, causing some physical problems. A skin rash covering much of his body resulted in much discomfort and agony. Even medication did not help. The only relief came when he was completely away from the coaching/teaching scene. Dave requested a one-week medical leave over Easter Vacation and took his family to Gulf Shores, Alabama. The one-week in the sun away from the rigors did wonders. However, once back in the "fast lane," the disorder reoccurred. It became a motivating factor in the Darnalls' purchasing a condo in Arkansas the following year.

Soon came the annual pilgrimage of Corzine's Eureka fans to a Bulls' game. The group made a quick stop in Coal City on the way north to pick up Micetich and the two Ken Millers. This time Corzine did a magnificent job in obtaining tickets for the group. However, because two additional members joined late, the group had to secure two tickets from scalpers. Some spectators would have "died" for the tickets the travelers had. They were seated right "smack dab" in the middle of the Bulls' families. Chuck Wertz was in heaven. Sitting right next to him was James Jordan, Michael's father. To this day, he still has the hat Mr. Jordan had autographed for him. Coach sat next to Corzine's parents. The trio enjoyed talking about Dave's trips to Darnall's basketball camps.

Following the game, the group made a quick trip downtown Chicago to the Ultimate Sports Bar & Grill before ending at Corzine's three-floor condo on Lakeshore Drive. There were two bedrooms located on separate floors with huge mattresses in each. A third bedroom housed Dave's huge racecar set. That amazed the visitors. The single Corzine also loved to play cards with the camp coaches and knew they enjoyed ganging up on him for some of his NBA "change." As the night's game went on in the host's kitchen, Smitty asked, "Corzine, where's the beer?"

"In the frig," he replied. "Help yourself."

To Smitty's amazement, the only items in the refrigerator were beer, oatmeal cookies, and sour milk. "Eat out a lot, big boy?" he asked.

"Yeah, especially during the season," Corzine answered and a few minutes later proceeded to order several large Domino pizzas for his guests.

It was, again, another memorable trip to Chicago for the Eureka group.

SUMMERS WERE ALWAYS BUSY FOR DARNALL. There were camps and recruiting as usual. That year Tiera participated in her first Miss Woodford County pageant. She didn't win, but did gain valuable experience. There would be another year.

Also, although the Darnalls would not actually arrive at their twenty-fifth wedding anniversary until the next year, they did take a four-day, three-night Caribbean cruise. It was a great get-away for the Darnalls, but Dave hated his first ride in a commercial airplane. He was afraid of heights and was claustrophobic. What a mess! He swore he would never get into a plane again. We'll see.

Chapter 11

District Champions:
The Unforgettable Win

T HE 1986-1987 SEASON was the year Coach Darnall hoped his program would move to the "next level"—a national tournament appearance. He had thirteen returning lettermen, including all five starters and two consecutive NAIA Playoff appearances to support this thought. Dave felt Eureka, at least, might have a chance to host a playoff first-round game for the first time ever. The coach knew, however, this probably wouldn't happen since McKendree, Olivet Nazarene, St. Xavier, and St. Francis also had many returning experienced players, and some of those schools offered athletic aid.

What a coincidence it was that Darnall had thirteen returning lettermen in his thirteenth year as head coach at Eureka. As mentioned, thirteen and three were Dave's favorite numbers. Even though his car accident had happened on a "Friday the 13th," the superstitious Darnall felt he was both lucky and blessed to have survived the wreck.

For years, his given license plate number was DDD 131. He had requested DDD 122 for his zone defense but was issued 131 instead. The significance of the number issued by the State of Illinois would not be known for years. By the way, in Darnall's third year at Eureka he got his first twenty-win season at the college level. Twenty is a magic number among players and coaches.

The current team was actually assembled over the past several years. Would the chemistry be there now? Most of Darnall's past teams had followed the "golden rule"—"Together We Win," but still couldn't get past the

294

first round of the playoffs. The coach continued to believe that was the key ingredient to a District championship and a trip to the Nationals.

Coach Darnall had had a banner year recruiting. The most heralded was Brad Bickett, an All-Stater who helped lead Ohio High School to the State Class A finals in Champaign.

Bickett was quoted in the Dixon *Telegraph*, "I've been very impressed with (Coach) Dave Darnall and his staff there. I just don't want anything too big. I'd rather go to a place where I can get a good education and be a part of a basketball program on the rise. I've gone to the Eureka Basketball Camp for the past couple of years and know it like the back of my hand. They (Eureka) finished 21 - 5 last year and have the type of winning tradition I'm looking for."

Kevin Root was another top player that chose Eureka College. The six-foot-one guard from Hoopeston was selected Special Honorable Mention Class A All-State and First Team Class A All-State Tournament. Root was excited about his decision to sign with Eureka. He was quoted as saying, "It's close to home, and I know people there more than some other colleges."

In preseason newspaper publicity one article was titled, "Eureka Looking to Build on Last Season's Success." That was Darnall's hope.

Another article headlined, "Talented Red Devils adopt 'On the Road Again' theme," by Randy Sharer, sportswriter for *The Pantagraph*, described Eureka's schedule. Portions of the article read:

> The Eureka College basketball team might be better than the Red Devil squad which won a school record 21 of 26 games last year, but the team's record may not be as good because of a schedule with two Division II teams and only nine home games in the season, according to 13th year Coach Dave Darnall.
>
> "Other than our conference, we have a hard time getting people to schedule us," Darnall said. "A lot of schools our size feel they've got nothing to gain and everything to lose by playing us."
>
> Darnall also pointed out that when schools around the Chicago and St. Louis areas need a non-conference game, they'd rather play in their own areas than travel to Eureka.
>
> So with the theme song, "On the Road Again," the Red Devils began their quest for a third straight NAIA State Playoff berth and second straight Prairie College Conference title tonight at Kirksville, Mo., against Division II-foe Northeast Missouri State.
>
> Eureka College's first 12 games will be on the road. It won't Play at the Reagan Center until Washington (Mo.) visits Jan. 20.
>
> Making those road trips less painful will be nine lettermen including NAIA all-star Greg Nunn and honorable mention all-star Rick Taylor, known as "Sugar" and "Ice," respectively.

Official practice started with Darnall thinking he had thirteen returning lettermen. However, this would not hold true. Four senior letter winners, including a couple former starters, decided to pass up their final year. Eric Buerkett, planning to become a coach, decided to replace "Butch" Cassidy in the varsity student coaching position. Several younger lettermen also chose not to participate any longer. However, Mike Kerestes, Chris Cox, and Dave Gibson remained in the program as administrative assistants.

The reduced number of experienced players worried the coaching staff. Were there enough experienced players left to come off the bench to give the team a lift when needed during the regular season? The new crop of recruits would have to be ready sooner than expected.

The team left early Thursday afternoon for Kirksville, Missouri. It was the day before the season opener. Darnall wanted his players to re-acclimate themselves to the gym floor before they had to play Northeast Missouri State. That's what the "big boys" got to do, and this was a "big time" game for the small Eureka College cagers. The coach wanted to prevent stage fright against the NCAA II full-ride scholarship institution. A victory over a university of that size would aid Eureka's Dunkel points. High Dunkel point rating was a vital factor in making the trip to Kansas City. Besides, the coach did not want a repeat of the previous year when half the team was late because of the van breakdown.

Later that evening after player curfew, the coaching staff met in the motel's lounge to review the game plan. They were joined by several fans that had accompanied the team on the two-game trip.

Darnall knew it would be a sleepless night for him as it was before most games. That was especially true knowing the tremendous impact the game result would have on the Dunkel. If they could only squeak out a win!

The players slept in the following morning. Dave had arranged a buffet brunch for 11:00 A.M. and a pre-game meal for 3:00 P.M. at the motel. A normal pre-game meal consisted of meat, baked potato, vegetable, small salad, roll, and tea or soda. Darnall always ate with the team but chose to drink milk because of his stomach.

The team departed the motel at 5:55 P.M. for the five-minute drive to the campus. Coach usually wanted to arrive at the game site an hour and a half before tip-off. That night was no different.

After dressing, the team had its traditional pre-game meeting. Normally, these lasted twenty minutes, starting fifty minutes before game time. Darnall wanted twenty minutes for warm-up. Announcing the starting line-up was the first item on the agenda. All five starters from last year's team returned—Wright, Kroehnke, Nunn, Taylor, and Dooley. However, six-foot-six sophomore forward, Jeff Wooters, would be starting in the place of his fraternity brother, Tom Dooley. The six-foot-three Dooley, a sophomore forward from Vandalia, had been slowed by a back injury. Darnall called Dooley the team's "John Havlicek"—the person who filled the all-important sixth-man role. It was Darnall's belief throughout his coaching career that the team's sixth man was as important as the starting five, if not more so. Players Jerome Westbrooks and Stan Prosser were not only starters, but had gained recognition by being "Havliceks."

Darnall's pre-game talk included the necessity of a win if the team wanted some national recognition. A win would definitely help the Dunkel situation. The coach challenged his team, "You want recognition; you talk about going to the Nationals; you want to play big schools, cut out the damn talking and get the hell out there and do something about it."

After taking their traditional "ten seconds," Darnall instructed his team to "kick some ass." "Kronk" was ready. Leading the "EC chant," the six-foot-six senior led the team out of the locker room. Darnall proceeded to go to the bathroom for about the fifth time in the past forty-five minutes. That was something he said he would not miss when he got out of coaching. In fact, maybe it would be one reason to leave the coaching ranks!

The Red Devils were ready. Eureka College, who held a three-point lead at half time, had a seesaw battle with the hosts for the lead in the second half, falling behind by as many as five points. Trailing by one, "Sugar" Nunn's two free throws with forty-seven seconds remaining gave his team the lead for good as the Red Devils went on to claim a 72 to 69 victory. "Ice" Taylor sealed the win with two more free throws with twelve seconds left for the three-point margin.

The team went berserk. Bench players sprinted to the floor. High fives and backslapping was the scene. Darnall and his assistants were shaking hands and praising the seven players who had played the game. Sophomore Tim Ricketts was the only other player to play in addition to the top six. Nunn led the winners with twenty-five points while Taylor added eighteen points and had seven assists. Rob Kroehnke had a team-high ten rebounds and Alan Wright had grabbed six.

"I told the players after the game that in my thirteen years here at Eureka, this was in my mind probably the biggest win we had achieved," said a jubilant Darnall. "To beat Northeast Missouri State on their court was an awfully big win for us."

The celebration continued into the locker room with players running around chatting with each other. After several minutes, Darnall tried to calm the fellows down, including himself. Finally, quiet came. Coach congratulated his team on its tremendous victory. He told the players that they had made him a believer. They had accepted his challenge with flying colors. He did, however, remind them that the win tonight would mean nothing if they lost the following evening. He had to get them back to reality.

That would be one thing that would finally get to the coach. There was no time to enjoy the accomplishment. He always had to worry about the next game. Only in retirement would memories of games like this be able to be enjoyed.

Coach Darnall rewarded the players by up-grading the normal post-game meat to two "quarter pounders" with cheese, large fries, and a large Coke! Meanwhile, the coaching staff joined the fans that had traveled to Kirksville for a cold beer in the motel's lounge.

However, their night's work was not done. Upon returning to Darnall's room, they had to do the game stats and prepare game plans for the next game—Simpson College of Indianola, Iowa. "No rest for the weary." Darnall spent a sleepless night—unable to sleep because of replaying the night's game plus worrying about the up-coming game against Simpson.

Dave planned a time schedule that allowed just enough time to arrive in Indianola, have a pre-game meal, and reach the Simpson campus an hour and a half before tip-off. Darnall hated to arrive early at the game sites, forcing the players to just sit around. However, he didn't want to be so rushed that he wouldn't be able to go through his normal pre-game routine. Dave was not one to change. In fact, it was said he was very superstitious and "set in his ways."

The team went directly to the gym upon completing their pre-game meal. The traveling trunks were moved to the locker room and the uniforms placed on the benches by the staff. The players only had to grab theirs and put them on. The trunks being empty, Darnall moved them to an area away from the lockers and took a quick nap. This was the same pre-game syndrome he had when at home—being extremely tired just prior to a game. While Coach Darnall was napping, Coach Dighton brought the players into the locker room at 6:30 P.M. to prepare for the pre-game meeting at 6:40.

Coach Darnall announced the starting line-up. It was the same as the night before with Dooley still being the sixth man. Coach reminded his players that the previous night's win didn't mean a damn thing if they lost that night. He asked the team if the Northeast win was a fluke or if it was for real. Tonight's game would tell. Another challenge was made.

The Red Devils were again ready to play. They held a 34 to 25 half-time lead and went on to a three point victory, 74 to 71.

Eureka led throughout the second half, but Simpson pulled to within two points with twenty-one seconds remaining. "Ice" preserved the lead by making three free throws in final seconds of the game. Simpson made a quick basket, stole the ball, and took a desperate three-point shot at the buzzer that went long. Nunn led the Red Devils in scoring with twenty points while Taylor chipped in nineteen. Alan Wright had fourteen points and eight rebounds while teammate Tom Dooley added twelve points and eight rebounds.

The Red Devils returned home that evening making the long van trip back to Eureka in approximately five hours. The journey was a happy one with very few players napping. The team again got the "royal treatment" of two "quarter pounders" with cheese, large fries, and large Coke. Actually, it was two large Cokes!

The players enjoyed Sunday off before a one-day practice preparing for the next foe, Concordia College. Darnall and his scouting buddy Chuck Wertz had an opportunity to scout Concordia in a scrimmage game. Throughout this season, as well as his entire career, Dave scouted nearly every opponent before they played. On several occasions during the season, he turned over practices to Coach Dighton so Wertz and he could leave early to reach a scouting destination. For some reason, Dave thought it was more important for him to personally see the up-coming opponent than to be at practice. He believed strongly in a good game plan and strategy, and the only way that could be done properly was for him to see the opponents. Dave had confidence that his assistant coaches could take charge of practice and fol-low a practice schedule he had prepared earlier.

To this day, Dave has on file the practice schedule of each of his col-lege practices. He took a three-by-five-inch index card, wrote down the time to start and the length of each drill, offense, or defense he wanted to cover in practice.

The trip to Concordia-River Forest was made by charter bus. Darnall liked that. He still got a thrill when "boarding" the bus. That was "big time." Because of a junior varsity contest preceding the varsity game, the two teams were allowed to travel together by bus.

The Red Devils came out sluggish. Even though they held a 29 to 23 half-time lead, the coach wasn't impressed. Taylor led the team to the six-point intermission lead with twelve points. Coach had a serious half-time discussion. No words were held back. The players knew their shit was in trouble. Darnall's neck veins were sticking out.

The Red Devils played with much more intensity the second half. Maybe they were afraid there would be no cheeseburgers, fries, and large Coke after the game! Darnall had been known to go directly home after a road game, skipping the post-game meal if he was extremely upset with the team's performance, saying "Sometimes the only way to get to you guys is through your stomachs." Boys do like to eat! The Red Devils outscored the Cougars 35 to 24 in the second period to gain a seventeen-point victory. "Ice" led the way with twenty points while Dooley chipped in eighteen. Eureka College's "John Havlicek" was back!

Next, Eureka participated in three consecutive invitational tournaments before Christmas break. Coach called the games the "turning point" of the season. "If we can win all three tournaments," Dave said, "we could be looked upon as being for real."

The first was the Judson Tournament. In what surprised Dave, their first opponent was host Judson. It was reported that Greenville had agreed to participate in the tournament only if they didn't have to play Eureka in the first round since they would already play twice during the season in the Conference.

Behind a fifteen-point first-half performance from "Sugar," the Red Devils took a 40 to 24 lead into the locker room at intermission. Eureka went on to win, 70 to 51. With Dooley now completely recovered and starting in the place of Wooters, all five starters from last year were again starting together. The team was back to full strength.

EC won its first tournament of the season with a 61 to 37 triumph over the out-matched Panthers of Greenville. Wright and Nunn paced the Red Devils with eighteen points each. The win gave Eureka a string of five consecutive road victories.

After a week off, "the Eureka good guys" returned to action by participating in the Wheaton Invitational Tournament. Wheaton College is a member of the prestigious CCIW. Darnall was thrilled to participate in the tournament; so was Rob Kroehnke. Rob had gone to high school in Wheaton, and living not far from the campus, it was like "coming home" for him. Today, Rob is a teacher/coach in the Wheaton school system.

"A championship title here would be a wish come true," said "Kronk" prior to the tournament.

The Red Devils moved into the title game of the Wheaton Tournament with a 79 to 60 victory over Grand Rapids Baptist. Senior Greg Nunn led four teammates in double figures with eighteen points. He was followed closely by Taylor with seventeen and Wright with sixteen.

Rob Kroehnke, "the home town boy," added twelve points, thirteen rebounds and six assists for the winners. A good night's work! Dooley had a re-occurrence of his old injury and was not able to start in the championship game. Freshman Todd Ritsema got his first start of his career.

Eureka then met the host school for the title. Wheaton had beaten MacMurray, 91 to 69, to earn the right to play for their tournament championship. Dave knew this was a big game for Eureka College. It could make or break their season. In order to gain Dunkel points, you had to beat good teams regardless of where the game was played. Darnall never understood why Dunkel didn't consider where the game was played, especially since his team always had to play so many road games.

Alan Wright made a three-point play with less than a minute remaining to give Eureka College the lead to stay as the Red Devils defeated the host team, 73 to 70. Wright scored on a slam-dunk, was fouled, and converted the free throw. After a Wheaton basket, Tim Ricketts sank two free throws with no time remaining. The Red Devils were undefeated in seven games.

An article appeared in the *Wheaton Leader* describing Wright's performance throughout the tournament, "Alan Wright led Eureka's Red Devils (an unlikely nickname for where Ronald Reagan went to school) with 26 points and 11 rebounds. Wright's shooting was as accurate as a TOW or Hawk missile on both days, earning him a place on the All-Tournament Team. Eureka teammate Rick Taylor also received All-Tourney recognition."

"Lucky 13–All the way for Darnall," written by Robin Wettstein of the *Woodford County Journal* expounded on Darnall's favorite number, thirteen. Darnall stated, "It was the 13th tournament win in my 13 years as coach."

His other favorite number, three, would later stand for the three invitational tournament championships in that year.

The Red Devil players received a well-deserved six-day lay-off before heading to the next tournament. Unlike the two previous tournament appearances, the team journeyed to the game a day ahead of time. They arrived at Terre Haute, Indiana, after a four-hour trip and in time for an evening practice at Rose-Hulman College.

After checking into Larry Bird's motel and unpacking, the team left for the gym and their hour and a half practice. The evening at the motel was pretty standard for an on-the-road game. Of course, the coaching staff again discussed the game plan and strategy.

It was again another sleepless night for Coach Darnall. As usual, the up-coming game was big. In fact, every game was big since the Dunkel system had been adopted to select the eight teams that would make the NAIA District 20 Playoffs. However, for Darnall this game was even bigger. It was against old conference rival Illinois College.

Illinois College had refused to play his teams since the 1977-1978 season. Who would guess the two highly respected colleges would ever play again? It took an out-of-state tournament for a rematch of the former conference opponents.

Just moments before the game in Darnall's final talk to the players, he mentioned the history of the rivalry. That may be the last time they would have a chance to demonstrate perhaps why Illinois College did not want them on their schedule. Coach was extremely nervous as his team took the floor just prior to tip-off. With his last bathroom stop over, Dave got to the bench just as the starters were being announced. His were the regular five. Dooley was ready to go!

The first half proved to be a reason Darnall had worried. The game was tied 43 to 43 despite a twenty-point performance by "Ice." The injury-free Dooley had contributed eleven points. Darnall again used a very verbal lecture during his half-time speech. He wanted to motivate his team to "step it up a notch." The thought of losing to Illinois College was too much. It is hard for some players and coaches to recover from a tough loss. Players usually can bounce back quicker than most coaches. Darnall always took losses personally. If his team lost any game, he felt they weren't properly prepared. He should have been able to do something to prevent the defeat. If they lost to Illinois College, it would haunt him forever.

The Red Devils answered the call. They came out the second half ready to play. Their intensity increased dramatically, especially defensively, moving quicker in the 1-2-2 adjustable zone and allowing the Blue Boys very few offensive boards. Sophomore Tim Ricketts led the second-half assault with ten points while "Ice" finished with a game high twenty-five. Dooley chipped in seventeen points. The winning margin was nine points, 87 to 78.

The locker room was jubilant. Darnall praised the players on their second-half performance. After a few minutes of celebrating, it was time to get back to reality. The game the next day would be another big one. Darnall again gave the message, "Tonight's win doesn't mean a thing if we get beat tomorrow." The players had heard that before. If only they had a couple days to enjoy the victory and reflect upon the next game. Instead, they headed for the bleachers to scout their opponent for the up-coming all-important game. Darnall was sure it would be Rose-Hulman unless a hell of an upset took place. Hulman's opponent was Maryville College. Dave wanted his starters sitting close by so that Coach Dighton and he could relay messages to each about the player they would be guarding and the offenses to be employed.

Leaving shortly after halftime, the team returned to the motel to await their post-game "meal." Darnall and Dighton did the stats. Parents and fans also returned and gathered in Darnall's room to celebrate. It was at that time the EC supporters decided the team needed new warm-ups. The current suits were approximately six years old and extremely out-dated. Many were too small for their wearers, leaving some players with "high waters." It was Larry Murison, a cheerleader's father, who suggested the need and took it upon himself to see the project was completed. Parents Kroehnkes, Wooters, Dooleys, Roots, Bicketts, and Bayleses quickly agreed. When everyone left, the staff completed the game statistics and prepared a game plan for Rose-Hulman.

The championship game was the last contest before Christmas break. The team would be off for four weeks. After nine consecutive road games, the team needed the break. However, the hometown fans would still be anxiously waiting to watch their undefeated Red Devils.

Again, it was a sleepless night for the coach. Darnall's stomach was so upset the day of the game; he passed up the team's pre-game meal. Instead, he took his pre-game nap. Coach Dighton brought him a vanilla shake. That became the normal routine on almost all over-night trips.

In Coach's pre-game talk, he emphasized the importance of the game. Three tournament championships, undefeated, the Dunkel, the four-week lay-off to think about it, and the long trip back to Eureka especially if they lost. The team responded. The Red Devils held an eight point half-time lead, 38 to 30. Several newspaper headlines described the results: "Eureka College advances record to 9 - 0" in the *Woodford County Journal*; "Eureka College wins Rose-Hulman Tourney" in *The Pantagraph*; and "Unbeaten Eureka men take 3rd title" in the Peoria *Journal Star*.

The *Journal Star*'s article read in part:

> Rose-Hulman Tournament MVP Greg Nunn's 23 points Saturday night led the unbeaten Eureka College men to their third championship of the young season, 76 - 72 over the host school at Terre Haute, Indiana.

"This is the first time maybe in College history that we've been 9 - 0 at the Christmas break," exclaimed jubilant Red Devil Coach Dave Darnall after Rose-Hulman was turned back despite freshman Mike Webster's 38 point performance.

Rose-Hulman's Mike Webster set a NCAA III shooting record connecting on twelve three-point field goals. Most people thought Coach Darnall was probably crazy not to go to a man-to-man defense. Darnall explained his defensive strategy, "I didn't want to get beat at the foul line. We needed our "horses" to win this game. I didn't want any of them fouling out. The 1-2-2 adjustable zone defense got us this far. We were going to live or die with it."

The locker room celebration was extensive; everyone congratulating each other. Darnall praised his team not only for their effort that night but also for the whole first half of the season. The trip home was exciting and fun. The players were finally enjoying their tremendous start of the season.

An article by Jim Barnhart in *The Pantagraph* portrays the image of the 1986-1987 Red Devils. The article entitled, "Eureka College team nomads of basketball," read in part:

Standard equipment for members of Eureka College's undefeated basketball team is a compass, a suitcase, a globe, a State Farm atlas, and a pup tent.

The Red Devils get to go public in Reagan Center about as often as the president with the same name.

Eureka College spends more time on the road than a Greyhound bus. The Red Devils have wrung more water out of their socks than most people have sailed on. They've worn out six lifetime pens filling out travel vouchers.

Eureka College, which has won nine games, doesn't play at home until Jan. 20. Coach Dave Darnall will have to put his team on a bus, drive the players to the city limits, and then return to campus so the Red Devils will remain in their comfort zone.

However, Darnall will tell you this is nothing new—this globe trotting.

"In my 13 years here, I don't think we've have more than 10 home games in a season," said Darnall. "We have a hard time getting home games."

Darnall doesn't believe a heavy road schedule is a detriment early in the season.

"The team isn't tired yet," explained Darnall. "It's not like it would be in February when the season has dragged on a little. The coaches aren't as tired early even though they have to drive vans . . .

"Later in the season, when we go on the road in the conference (Prairie College Conference) we'll charter because we'll have the girls' team with us. The coaches won't be driving vans."

"I've never had a group with such a team concept," said Darnall. "I tried to push them hard early and now I'm letting them catch their breath.'

Eureka College is ranked No. 2 among state NAIA (National Association of Intercollegiate Athletics) schools, according to the Dunkel ratings.

"McKendree is No. 1," said Darnall. "We've never been ranked in the top four before and we hope to stay there. If we can finish in the top four, we can get the home court advantage in at least one game in the District 20 NAIA playoffs. We've never had that before."

Yeah, but wouldn't you play better on the road?

The publicity continued to flow. Another article emphasizing the amazement of nine consecutive road wins was written by Dave Reynolds of the Peoria *Journal Star* on the day the Red Devils returned to action. It was "The road seems like home to Eureka." Portions read:

There's no place like home, right? Well, don't tell the Eureka College basketball team that.

The 9 - 0 Red Devils haven't played in the Reagan Center yet and will play three more games on the road before their home opener Jan. 20 against Washington University.

Indeed, nine of Eureka's final 14 games are at home. But first there are three road games . . . Today's game is the first for the Red Devils since Dec. 13 when they won the Rose-Hulman Tournament at Terre Haute, Ind.

"The layoff scares me," said Darnall. "We were playing pretty good and then we're off for 3½ weeks. It's gonna affect us."

Darnall's hope is that the effect isn't too lasting. Eureka, 21 - 5 last year en route to a Prairie College Conference Championship and an NAIA state tournament berth for the fifth time in six years, has a good shot at its best season ever.

"We've never been to the NAIA national tournament (in Kansas City)," said Darnall. "I'm always very cautious (about predictions), but if we ever had a chance, this might be the year. But we would probably have to beat McKendree on their home court to do it."

Eureka is ranked second in the state to McKendree, which leads the NAIA in scoring with a 107.3 average. The Red Devils, however, are ranked eighth nationally in defense, yielding 61.7 points.

Darnall and Dighton spent Christmas vacation attending the usual high school Christmas tournaments. It was felt that the team needed to add a few quality players next year since there were four seniors on the team. Darnall and his chief scout, Wertz, also spent several nights viewing up-coming opponents.

The players reported back to campus after their three-week lay-off for a week of double practices before taking another road trip; this time to the St. Louis area. Yes, "On the road again!"

The teams again stayed in the Marriott Hotel adjacent to Busch Stadium. This was super "big time" for the men and women players. Darnall also had a "big-time room." It was even more elegant than the Cunningham Room. He was given the best of the best, the Chairman of the Board's suite. The magnificent suite had three rooms that spanned across the end of the top floor of the multi-floored hotel. It contained a kitchen, a large dining room with a long formal dining table connected to a spacious living room, and a luxuriously decorated master bedroom. The bathroom was a "sight to be seen" including a large whirlpool tub.

"It was so nice of the Marriott to give me that as a complementary suite for several days," Darnall remarked. "Needless to say, I hosted the post-game party for the Red Devil fans that made the trip. I'll never be able to afford to stay in a room like that." Seventeen years later, the statement is still true!

Greg Nunn scored twenty-one points in a 70 to 60 victory over Concordia-St. Louis in the first of the two-game trip.

"We've been off for three and a half weeks and we played like it. I'm disappointed in our performance. We didn't play sharp tonight at all," Darnall lamented following the game.

University of Missouri-St. Louis provided the next competition. It was the second NCAA II team the Red Devils played that year. Dave was very nervous about the game. He laid awake most of the night stewing over the importance of the contest. He then slept most of the day, skipping the team's pre-game meal.

Darnall spent most of LaCursia's Lady Red Devil game in the bathroom. Pre-game syndrome had definitely set in.

The Eureka Coach was irritated within the first few minutes of play. His two tallest players, Wright and Kroehnke, were in foul trouble and played sparingly the first half. Darnall felt his players were called for violations that the taller, stronger Rivermen were getting by with. It also became an omen of foul trouble that would haunt the Red Devils in another important game later in the season.

The Red Devils trailed at intermission, 51 to 34. In spite of an outstanding twenty-four-point effort by sophomore Tom Dooley, EC was unable to pull out a victory. Both Kroehnke and Wright went to the bench midway through the second half. With UMSL shooting twenty-six free throws to Eureka's fourteen, the Red Devils lost their first game of the season, 104 to 75.

Coach Darnall was extremely disappointed; not in losing but that his team was unable to play the type of game UMSL was able to get away with. "If it's going to be physical, then allow both teams to play physical, not just the home team," Darnall emphasized. "I don't know if we could have beat UMSL there or not, but I damn well know we couldn't win with our horses on the bench," concluded Darnall.

With one more road game before their home opener, the Red Devils traveled to Blackburn College for their Conference opener. The winning streak had snapped at ten. The business on hand now was the Conference Championship. Blackburn was always a challenge at home, and Dave saw that contest as no different. His team had to play well in order to gain the win.

Leading by the score of 41 to 31 at the break, the Red Devils had to rely on Dooley's three-point field goal with forty seconds remaining in play to escape with a 78 to 74 Prairie College Conference victory. Wright paced EC in scoring with twenty-one points.

The long-awaited event was about to take place. Darnall was finally going to have a home court advantage and a gym full of home fans. After twelve consecutive road games, would the thirteenth (Darnall's favorite number!) be lucky for him and his team? He was sure hoping!

The first opponent was the prestigious Washington University Bears of St. Louis. The school was noted for its academic reputation as well as its athletic prowess. Just a few days earlier, Washington U. had defeated the highly respected Illinois Wesleyan Titans. It would be a real "feather in Eureka's hat" in the eyes of some Bloomington-Normal area fans if the Red Devils could knock-off the St. Louis school that had just beaten Wesleyan.

After nine weeks, Darnall suffered through his pre-game syndrome at home in his own bed. Assistant Coaches Dighton and Buerkett were already at the gym when Bonnie, as usual, drove Dave to the Fieldhouse at 6:00 P.M., an hour and a half before the game. After assisting in handing out the players' equipment, Dave went to his office to stew, making several trips to the bathroom before his 6:40 team meeting. Darnall worried his team might disappoint its fans that had waited so long to see it in action.

Darnall announced his starting line-up. As usual, it was Wright, Kroehnke, Nunn, Taylor, and Dooley—four seniors and a sophomore. He then proceeded to harshly lecture his players about the importance of the game.

"If you want recognition, this is the type of team you have to beat," Dave said. "No bull shitting around. I don't want to have to call time out and meet you on the court," Darnall emphasized.

After taking the traditional ten seconds, Dave shouted to his team, "Go out there and kick some ass."

The game turned out to be exactly what is was billed to be. A barn-burner in front of a capacity crowd. An article in *The Pantagraph*, "Eureka College upsets Washington," best described the game and Coach Darnall's feeling about it. It read in part:

> Eureka College's basketball team opened its home in grand fashion last night at Reagan Center.
>
> The Red Devils, who played their first 12 games of the season on the road, upset Washington University of St. Louis, 68 - 64, in a non-conference game. Washington is rated 16th nationally in this week's NCAA Division III poll.
>
> "I honestly didn't know if we could beat them. I was just hoping the kids wouldn't embarrass themselves," said Eureka College Coach Dave Darnall, whose team belongs to the National Association of Intercollegiate Athletics. "I told the guys before the game we had nothing to lose and everything to gain."
>
> "I told them it was a game we weren't supposed to win and to just go out and do their jobs. I told them we had to play hard and that's exactly what they did. We gained confidence as the game went on, and suddenly we found ourselves in position to win.
>
> "That's probably the first time in my 13 years here that I've played a man defense the entire game,' said Darnall. 'but after watching Washington play at Wesleyan and at Millikin, I knew the only way we could beat them was to play a man-for-man. They have outstanding shooters. Tom Dooley did an outstanding job on Suiter."

The nine-week delay for a post-game celebration at home was well worth the wait. Close to a hundred people were at the Darnalls' home that night. Beer and champagne flowed freely. Toasts were made not only for the night's victory, but also for the eleven victories prior to the home opener.

Darnall sold his program by saying that his team was also the fans' team and encouraged people to become involved with the program including the post-game celebrations. It brought together faculty, staff, parents, relatives, friends, camp coaches, and local fans from the community. Some of the most loyal were: President Hearne, Trustee Steve Thomson, the Wertzes, Eatons, Mormans, Golds, Gareys, Baylesses, Dan Harrods, Jeff Vicek, Barths, Beers, Marches, Eetens, Coach LaCursia, Murisons, VanWinkles, Pat Riley, McCanns, McQuades, Raycrafts, Marv Holmeses, Lockhards, Baumans, Nohls, Garkeys, Sam Harrods, Roger Smiths, Bakers, Yoders, Dave Gilliland, Ken Miller, and Becky Riddel. Of course, the parents were the most supportive. Those who often joined the post-game gathering were the Kroehnkes, Wrights, Roots, Dooleys, Coffmans, Wooters, Bicketts, Buerketts, Ricketts, and Mrs. Ritsema.

It was a testimony to how far the Eureka College basketball program had come in thirteen years. Besides, how many college fans get to go to the coach's house after a game?

Many of the men stood in the laundry room around the old maroon-and-gold keg-holding refrigerator that the camp coaches had given Dave at the Tenth-Year Reunion. The women were busy in the kitchen placing food and snacks on the breakfast bar. Everyone brought something so it was not a "food" burden for Bonnie. However, for many years she had felt she had to have her house "spotless" before the crowd came over, often not getting to the game until midway through the first half. She finally decided that was foolish. With so many people, they didn't notice anyway. In fact as the years went by, Bonnie was often late getting out of the gym. By the time she got home, Tiera had taken over or the guests had made themselves at home and the party was well underway. Needless to say, the bathrooms were always busy. This particular party lasted well into the wee hours of the morning.

The Red Devils had a second game at home before another three consecutive road games. Principia was having a mediocre season. Dave knew his team was capable of winning at home unless they had a big letdown after the tremendous victory over Washington University. The boys were ready to play. Jumping out to a 52 to 33 half-time lead, the Red Devils scored 64 points the second half while holding Principia to 23 points. The 116 to 56 point spread was the largest of the season. Thirteen different players contributed to the scoring attack.

Then it was back "on the road again" to Maryville College for another Conference game. Maryville was having a good season with a 2 to 1

Conference record. It was another important away game for EC. Dave warned his team about a letdown. The contest ended up being much closer than he had wanted. Eureka edged the hosts 63 to 61. It was one of those games that "takes a toll" on a coach. It did on Darnall!

The next scheduled game matched Eureka College against the No. 13 ranked NAIA team in the nation, McKendree College. The Dunkel Rating System rated McKendree No. 1 in the District (State) with Eureka in the top four.

Darnall was deeply concerned how his team could be victorious at McKendree twice in the same year. Eureka had not won a game in the Bearcat Den in the past twenty years. How could his team do it now and possibly again in the playoffs?

A main reason Dave "played" the Dunkel system was to obtain a home-court advantage in post-season play. That upset many coaches of mediocre teams since Darnall's teams had to play for the point spread. With McKendree's high national ranking, Darnall felt that even if his team beat them, they would not overtake the Bearcats in the Dunkel ratings. History had shown on several occasions where Eureka College had beaten an opponent yet failed to be selected over them in a playoff field.

The team left Reagan Fieldhouse around 1:00 P.M. in two college vans for the five-hour trip to Lebanon. The trip was going to take longer due to bad weather, which included several inches of snow already on the ground. Coach Dighton was driving the first van with Darnall riding "shotgun." Coach Buerkett drove the other van. The upperclassmen rode with Buerkett while the underclassmen rode with Dighton and Darnall.

The team arrived at the Springfield Bonanza around 3:30 P.M. for their pre-game meal. It took approximately an hour to eat and be on the road again. Upon returning to Interstate 55, the vans headed south to St. Louis. The team had traveled only several minutes when a near catastrophe happened.

Traveling in the middle lane of the three-lane highway, Dighton's van crossed the bridge of Lake Springfield first. Two semi-trailer trucks traveling in the right lane were passing the vans. Normally, vehicles pass in the left lane. Thank God, not this time!

Yards remaining from the end of the bridge, the first van veered sharply to the left just missing the end of the bridge railing and heading directly toward the median ditch filled with several feet of snow. The van miraculously did not turn over but sped on into the opposite lanes of traffic.

Occurring during rush hour, several on-coming vehicles had to veer sharply to prevent smashing into the out-of-control van. The bruised van ended up backwards.

The incident happened within view of the Springfield State Police Headquarters. An observer in the headquarters saw the accident and quickly dispatched an officer. One of the passing truck drivers stopped immediately to render whatever help he could. Seeing the driver unconscious, he raced back to his truck and radioed for medical assistance.

The players in the second van, led by Kroehnke, dashed to the snow covered vehicle to also assist. Coach Dighton was unconscious, but none of the players were injured. The snow in the median ditch was probably a life-saver. It had slowed the van down and kept it from overturning. In fact, the vehicle was basically undamaged.

An article in a local newspaper entitled "Red Devils uninjured in wreck" described the happening as such:

> Ten members of the Eureka College basketball team and coaching staff escaped injury Tuesday after a coach driving their van lost consciousness, Illinois State police said.
> Assistant Coach Dennis Dighton suffered what Illinois State patrolman Sgt. Gary Locke described as "a possible seizure." The van, traveling at approximately 55 mph on Interstate 55 south of Springfield en route to a game with McKendree College in Lebanon, went out of control and veered across the median into a northbound lane, according to the police report.
> "At the time it happened, I thought he was gone,' said Eureka College head coach Dave Darnall, who was riding in the van's passenger front seat.
> "With one hand I grabbed the wheel, which wasn't easy because he was on it, and with my other hand I pushed on the brake. I think the snow helped to slow us down. We were so lucky because we just missed a bridge."
> The Red Devil's game was postponed and will be rescheduled.

However with the season coming to an end, the contest with McKendree could not be rescheduled. Eureka College would have to travel to Lebanon again next year.

A game between two of the state's best small college teams would not take place, or would it? With no injuries and no real damage to the van, maybe the whole incident was meant to be!

Next on the list for the Red Devils was Conference foe Greenville College, again on the road. However, this time the team traveled by chartered bus. Playing excellent defense and receiving a game-high twenty-two points from "Sugar," EC was able to post a 73 to 47 win.

A home game followed. In spite of an outstanding individual scoring performance by MacMurray's Scott Fearrin who tallied twenty-eight points, Eureka beat the Highlanders, 81 to 72.

MacMurray's defeat was followed with another home victory in a 75 to 61 besting of Iowa Wesleyan. Alan Wright led the Red Devils to the nonconference win with a team-high twenty-five points. The victory moved Eureka's overall record to an impressive 17 to 1.

Playing their third consecutive home game, EC had a rematch with Conference foe Blackburn College. Eureka started the second round of Conference play with a perfect 4 to 0 record and in first place. The Red Devils came out of the gate quickly to claim a victory over the Beavers for the second time in the season, 89 to 59.

Eureka traveled to Principia for its sixth Conference game of the year. Even though they had beaten the Panthers earlier by a lopsided margin, Darnall did not want the players to take anything for granted. Alan Wright responded with a great individual effort to lead his team to a nine-point advantage at half time. Eureka went on to win, 79 to 67.

A home rematch with Maryville College was a battle of the Conference's two top teams. The only Conference loss for Maryville was at the hands of the Red Devils. Maryville wanted a little revenge, but it was not to be. Behind the career high nineteen-point scoring performance of Rob Kroehnke, Eureka gained an 82 to 46 victory over their visitors. The loss eliminated Maryville from the Conference championship. Eureka remained undefeated in league play with two games left.

For the good of his team's standing, Coach Darnall had also been forced to "play the Dunkel game" with Maryville. It meant beating them by a decisive margin. That was necessary because of the close score in their first contest. Darnall played only nine players in the thirty-six-point win. The rationale was extremely difficult for Maryville's head coach to understand. The necessary point to be made was that with only a two-point victory over Maryville earlier and later a thirty-six-point win, the Dunkel would reflect that Eureka College had improved and was playing well toward the conclusion of its season. That was extremely important when deciding who was seeded in what spot in the NAIA Playoffs.

The next game was again against Conference foe Greenville College. Fortunately, this time it was at home. The Red Devils had no trouble winning the game. Paced by Nunn's game-high thirty points, Eureka beat the Panthers, 94 to 61. That kept them undefeated in Conference play with a non-conference contest against Harris-Stowe next.

Duplicating his thirty-point performance against Greenville, "Sugar" again led his team to victory. It was Eureka, 100; Harris-Stowe, 62. That gave the Red Devils a 22 to 1 record, winning twelve consecutive games going into the last scheduled Conference game of the year against MacMurray. The game was played at MacMurray, always a dangerous place to play. Darnall warned his team of the past difficulties of winning at Jacksonville. A win against MacMurray meant an outright Prairie College Conference Championship and an undefeated 10 to 0 Conference record.

It wasn't meant to be. The Highlanders led, by Scott Fearrin's thirty-two points, including seven three-point goals, beat the non-inspired Red Devils, 73 to 64. Darnall was noticeably upset but appeared more subdued following the defeat. He felt the defeat would perhaps bring the team back to reality. He decided the team might be getting a little complacent and "cocky." He hoped this would be a wake-up call if they were to achieve their goal of participating in the NAIA National Tournament in Kansas City.

The team had been rated third in the District prior to the game. Dave knew a loss to MacMurray would really hurt his team's Dunkel rating. He tried to use this as a motivating tool in his pre-game speech but it was to no avail. The guys just didn't respond to the challenge. The loss probably meant a drop to fourth in the District (State) rating. The result would be that Eureka would possibly have to win two playoff games on the road to qualify for the Nationals.

The ride home from Jacksonville was long and solemn. The punishment from Coach Gay and his Highlanders was felt. Even though this bus trip back was actually only two hours for Darnall and his team, it seemed an eternity. Arriving at the college, Coach Dighton first disposed of the game equipment and then took his dejected head coach home. Coach Darnall was deeply depressed and disappointed. Dave entered the house and was greeted at the door by Bonnie. She had attended the game along with parents and other loyal fans and knew the dismal results. She attempted to console her husband, but nothing seemed to help.

Dave had received a NAIA National Press Kit earlier in the day. The packets were sent to the highest rated four teams in the District. The requested information was to be returned to the National office within a week. That would be the day of the second round of playoff competition. This seemed like an omen to Coach Darnall. Not only was he superstitious, but he didn't like to count on anything until it happened. The loss to MacMurray only reinforced his beliefs and resulting behaviors. Thus, he procrastinated in filling out or gathering the documents requested in the packet.

It became another sleepless night for the coach. The negative memories of the game, how this devastating defeat would affect the Dunkel, if his team could bounce back in two days to end the regular season with a victory never left his mind.

The worry was for naught. Playing at home on Senior Night, both the team and fans were ready for the season finale. A standing-room-only crowd had gathered to honor the seniors who could put the college on the basketball map. Seniors Nunn, Taylor, Kroehnke, and Wright knew that this year's team with its current twenty-two victories had won more games than any other team in the history of Eureka College.

In his traditional pre-game talk, Darnall, ranting and raving, reminded his team of the importance of the season finale against Lindenwood. The results of the night's non-conference contest would be huge in the final Dunkel rating for the District 20 team. The announcement of the eight-team playoff field and the seeding of those teams was to be announced at the next day's (Sunday) NAIA District 20 meeting.

After taking the "ten seconds of silence," Darnall again instructed his players to "go out and kick ass." A loud applause was heard as the team ran through the double doorway leading to the gym. A few minutes were taken to honor the seniors, and then came the final tip-off.

Jumping off to a 59 to 33 half-time lead, the Red Devils had come ready to play. At half time, Darnall emphasized, as he had done all year, the Dunkel Rating System. Not only was winning important, but the point spread was also influential. In some situations, a team must beat another by a pre-determined amount of points or lose valuable points in the ratings. Frequently, the seeding of the top two teams are separated by only tenths of a point, as was the case the previous year.

Even though the second half wasn't played as well as the first, Eureka College claimed a 104 to 72 victory.

The overflow crowd at Darnall's home was both congratulatory and excited about the night's win. However, the main topic of discussion was the next day's NAIA District 20 meeting. The long-awaited NAIA meeting was scheduled at the Holiday Inn in Champaign. For the first time ever, Eureka College could be seeded as high as fourth in the District. Throughout the night, Dave made several phone calls to local newspapers to acquire scores from games of other potential playoff teams.

McKendree, rated fourth in the Nation, No. 1 nationally in offense averaging 105 points a game, and on the strength of a 28 to 4 record, was awarded the No. 1 seed in the eight-team tournament. To Darnall's delight, Eureka College was given the No. 2 nod in the National Association of Intercollegiate Athletics District 20 State Playoffs. They would host seventh seeded Roosevelt University of Chicago on Tuesday. It would mark the first time Eureka College ever hosted a NAIA District 20 Tournament event even though they had participated in the playoffs six of the previous seven years.

In a newspaper article interview in Bloomington's *The Pantagraph*, Darnall expressed his feeling about the day's meeting and the much antici-pated up-coming playoff game.

> "Not only are we happy about receiving the highest seed we've ever had, but we're also thrilled to be hosting a first-round game," said Eureka College coach Dave Darnall.
> "That's a big plus for our team, the school, and the community. In the past, we've always had to go on the road to play in the tournament, so we know how hard it is to win on the road.
> "By playing one, and maybe two games at home, we feel we have an excellent chance to reach the championship game."
> The Red Devils have won 19 straight at home. Their last loss at home was in the final home game of the 1984-85 season.
> Eureka College has won nine straight at home this year.

At the same meeting, Eureka's superstar guards Greg "Sugar" Nunn and Rick "Ice" Taylor were named to the District 20 All-District Team. The ten-player team was voted upon by the District 20 coaches.

Dave was anxious to return to Eureka. He knew his players and many loyal fans would be calling about the playoff match-ups. As predicted, the calls had been coming in. Bonnie had already fielded some without being able to give any information. That would be Dave's pleasure!

Sunday was a day off for the players but not for the coaches. After returning from Champaign, they still had to prepare game plans. Monday was a light practice, mainly discussing Roosevelt's personnel, offenses, and defens-es. The team also began to work on their offensive and defensive strategies.

The Eureka coach was unusually nervous the night before the first playoff game. Darnall had been waiting for this for thirteen years. It was not only a sleepless night, but also a pacing one!

315

Dave spent most of the game day in bed. He was extremely tired as the result of lack of sleep the night before and anxiety. At 6:00 P.M., Bonnie drove him to the gym. Darnall's assistants were already there when he arrived. Some of his players, showing signs of nervousness, had also arrived. Coach headed directly to his office with a severe headache. A few minutes later, he headed downstairs to the training room where the players received their uniforms. Darnall spoke briefly to the players as they grabbed their equipment. The next stop was the men's faculty bathroom. At 6:45, Coach met his team in the classroom for his pre-game talk. Dave, as usual, announced the starting five. He reminded the players of how hard they had worked to achieve the seeding and not to waste it. They needed to win two at home and then take their chance on the road for the championship.

A standing-room-only crowd, in spite of it being the beginning of the college's ten-day term break, gave a hearty welcome to its beloved team as it took the floor on that historic evening. Although the Red Devils had been seeded second, many people, including Darnall, felt they were a "long shot," at best, to win the State tournament and go to the Nationals. The reasoning was based upon Eureka being the smallest college in the playoffs and the only institution that did not give some type of athletic aid or scholarships. Most of the players on the other playoff teams received "full rides," including athletic scholarships, state aid, and federal aid. This remained true throughout the rest of Dave's tenure at Eureka College.

The team was ready to play. It was show time! An article written by Joe Bates of the Peoria *Journal Star* best summed up the night's happening. Entitled "Eureka men win first-ever NAIA playoff game," it reported in part:

> In his 13th season as head basketball coach at Eureka College, Dave Darnall has won 234 games.
> And victory No. 234 may be Darnall's biggest as his Red Devils won their first-ever NAIA District 20 State Playoff game Tuesday, 91 - 70, over Roosevelt at Reagan Center.
> The Red Devils have qualified for the playoffs seven of the last nine years and eight times overall. But they entered Tuesday's game with a 0 - 8 post-season record.
> Eureka, seeded second in the eight-team tournament, will take a 24 - 2 record into Saturday's semifinals where the Red Devils host sixth-seeded Illinois Tech (11-19) who edged third-seeded St. Xavier, 72 - 70, Tuesday.
> Eureka scored the first 11 points of the game while holding Roosevelt scoreless for nearly four minutes.

"We played good defense early," Darnall said. "We executed very well. I think we were patient and our shot selection was good."

While Eureka received typical performances from all-state guards Greg Nunn (26 points) and Rick Taylor (23), it was a less-heralded player who helped spark the Red Devils to their 20th straight home win.

Rob Kroehnke, a 6-foot-6 power forward, scored 14 points, grabbed a game-high 15 rebounds, including nine at the offensive end.

"Kroehnke is a blue-collar worker," Darnall said of the senior. "Overall, this has to match his best game of the season. He's a hard worker. His heart's about as big as an NAIA basketball."

The Darnalls' home was crowded after the game. With several days before the next game, Dave and the Red Devil fans could enjoy the historical win. As before, the added discussion asked who would be Eureka's next opponent. With the services of a newspaper sports' department, it was learned Illinois Tech would be next. Dave and "Scout" Wertz had seen both Illinois Tech and St. Xavier. Darnall was hoping to hear of an upset.

An article appeared in *The Pantagraph*, written by Jim Barnhart, the day of the Illinois Tech game. It was the summary of an interview with Coach Al Pickering of Lincoln College regarding the legitimizing of the Red Devil team. The article was entitled "Eureka College good, says Coach Pickering." It read in part:

Lincoln College basketball coach Al Pickering, who moved into the mainstream of academic life when he was recently named school dean and started wearing a tie, gives high marks to Eureka College's excellent team.

Pickering insists Eureka College is for real.

"We scrimmaged them in the pre-season and they were playing well at that time," said Pickering. "It was obvious they had played together for some time and as seniors. When you have seniors who've played together, it shows up early."

Pickering has been equally impressed with Eureka College coach Dave Darnall.

"Dave is one of the hardest working coaches around," said Pickering. "He's on the road constantly and active in his recruiting. You can ask Dave if he's seen a certain 6-7 kid at so-and-so school play and either he's seen him or he's going to see him. He knows where they all are.

"They're just a fun team to watch. One of my kids—John Jones — was there last year and he had high respect for the way the Eureka College kids play. They beat him out of a job when he was a senior and he still respected them."

If Eureka College wins Saturday at Reagan Center and then triumphs next week and advances to the nationals at Kansas City, will Darnall get a long distance phone from you-know-who?

Darnall followed his usual routine prior to the tip-off. One more win and the Red Devils would reach the unbelievable—the title game.

For the second consecutive game, the Red Devils' opponents were comprised of players on athletic scholarships. This however, was nothing new for Eureka College.

Darnall gave an inspirational pre-game talk. He reminded his players that they were playing a full-ride institution, they were playing before a packed house, and most important, they had the opportunity to make the championship game. Behind "Sugar" and "Ice," the Red Devils jumped out to a 43 to 30 half-time lead. It was the two timeouts that Dave called in the first twenty minutes that he credited with making the difference.

"I had to do something to get the kids to play the way they are capable of playing," Darnall said. "So I had to call an early timeout."

Typically, Dave only called timeouts in the first half to raise hell or to change the game plan. This time, as usual, it was to raise hell. Meeting the players at the middle of the court, not limiting his choice of words, Dave let his team know his feelings about their play. The team responded not only once, but twice.

"The little meetings are not something I would want their mothers to hear," the coach said, "but they help to get their heads out of their butts and back into the game."

Darnall's timeouts had been criticized earlier by a former college president. However, the strategy had been used many times by the coach and would be used many more times in his coaching career.

A newspaper article that best described the game's highlights was one by Jim Benson of Bloomington's *The Pantagraph* entitled "Timeouts spur Eureka College." Mr. Benson's article read in part:

They looked the same when they returned to the court White uniforms with "EC" on the shorts. But every time Eureka College basketball coach Dave Darnall called a timeout last night, the Red Devils were a different group than the one that slumped to the bench moments before.

Eureka College picked up the pace after calling three timeouts, and the result was an 80 - 60 victory over Illinois Tech in the semifinals of the National Association of Intercollegiate Athletics District 20 state playoff at the Reagan Center.

"Sometimes we just get caught up in it," said Red Devil guard Greg "Sugar" Nunn. "We have a tendency to try and do it ourselves. After a timeout, we get back to the team concept."

That concept has helped Eureka College, seeded No. 2 in District 20, put together a 25 - 2 record and extend its home-court winning streak to 21 straight.

The Red Devils face top seed McKendree Thursday night at Lebanon for the state crown. The winner advances to the national tournament at Kansas City.

The excitement on the floor and in the locker room following the game was tremendous. With several days until the championship game, the coach allowed his players to enjoy the moment with their fans and each other. In fact, Darnall was more beside himself than the players. Finally after thirteen years (favorite thirteen!), Dave had achieved one of his far-reaching goals—to play for the District Championship. Even though he would have liked to have played the game at home since they were undefeated there and winless on the road in playoff competition, the coach was just thrilled to be playing for the championship. Could a miracle happen?

The post-game party at the Darnalls' was boiling with excitement. Wall-to-wall people greeted the victorious coaches when they arrived. Smiling and raising their arms in a symbolic victory sign, the coaches accepted the cold drinks offered enthusiastically. Within a few seconds, two bottles of champagne, compliments of President Hearne and Bill Eaton, were popped. Toasts were made, and then the bottles were passed. The first swallow was Coach Darnall's with the bottles then proceeding among the revelers. It didn't take long until they were empty and a third, compliments of Dan Harrod, was sent on its way. Not only did the win produce the opportunity for a state championship, but it also resulted in the most wins for a Eureka College basketball team ever.

At 10:15 P.M. the two TV sets in the kitchen and family room were tuned to the local stations. The fans crowded around and were not disappointed in the excellent coverage of the game. Darnall had already called *The Pantagraph* for the McKendree-Olivet-Nazarene result. McKendree, leading the nation in scoring with an average of 105 points a game, beat the highly talented Olivet, 134 to 96. Yes, the Bearcats scored 134 points! That added even more dimension to the speculations of the up-coming game by the fans at the Darnall home. The anticipation was already in full swing.

The team took Sunday off and returned to practice on Monday and Tuesday. Unfortunately, the up-coming week was third-term finals week for the

Eureka student-athletes. The two primary examination days were Thursday, the day of the game, and Friday, the day following. The players were allowed to alter their final exams by taking them before they left for the game. The general student body, however, was denied any alterations to their schedules by the administration. That did not sit well with many of the 450 students as it meant some would not be able to make the trip to McKendree, a three-hour plus drive from Eureka. Several college administrators and a couple Board of Trustee members were able to make the contest. Some faculty members had been able to obtain "proxies" for their exams and also had made the trip.

On Sunday, the players' day off, Darnall and his staff planned their strategy for the McKendree game. Dave had scouted McKendree twice during the season. He was well aware of their personnel as well as their offensive and defensive schemes. The plan finally decided upon was identical to the one Darnall had planned to use in the cancelled January 27th game. All along, Dave had thought it unlikely his team could beat the powerful Bearcats twice on their floor in the same season. He felt the cancellation of the first scheduled meeting was a "blessing in disguise." It was meant to be!

Dave was known as a pessimist. He never counted on anything until it happened. In fact, many people felt he lacked confidence in his team as well as himself. His answer to that was, "I just don't want to get my hopes up high just to be disappointed." That was one reason, and probably the primary one, that Darnall didn't return the information requested by the NAIA National Office.

Over the weekend, Dave had even made plans with his good friend Dan Harrod to leave for Fairfield Bay, Arkansas, the day of or the day after the State championship game. It was an "insulating" back-up plan in case they lost to McKendree. The Darnalls had purchased a time-share unit in the resort-retirement community approximately five hundred miles from Eureka. Would it become his escape?

The players had "returned to earth" by Monday. Darnall believed in having hard practices a couple days prior to a game. The practice on the day before the game was usually light with a game review and shooting. Monday's and Tuesday's practices were, basically, going over McKendree's personnel, offenses, and defenses; and the execution of their own game plan. The game plan was simple. Play their normal 1-2-2 zone defense; pack down inside; make McKendree beat them by shooting outside. McKendree could "out-man" the Red Devils, and Darnall did not want to get beat inside. Even if his team got behind, Coach wanted his players to stay with the game plan.

Offensively, Dave wanted great shot selection. Don't shoot before ten seconds left on the shot clock unless there was an uncontested lay-up. Be very patient—a "flash-back" to his old high school coaching days.

The execution of this strategy took much discipline and practice. Players can't just go out on the floor and say, "Okay, we'll wait until ten seconds are left on the clock before one of us shoots." Darnall wanted McKendree to play defense. A team that averages 105 points a game likes to run and "put the ball up." Coach felt if McKendree had to play a lot of defense, once they got the ball, they would rush their offense resulting in bad shot selections.

Darnall was not an easy coach to play for. He demanded a lot and discipline was just part of his "request." Coach had several players who liked the McKendree style of play—run and shoot, but this was not Darnall's style. He believed in control, discipline, good shot selection, and defense. Dave felt that if his team could hold McKendree to under eighty points, they would have a slight chance to win. It would be a tremendous upset.

In an article by Randy Sharer of *The Pantagraph* entitled "Eureka College seeks state title against high-scoring McKendree," Mr. Sharer interviewed Darnall regarding the highly publicized up-coming game. Portions of the article stated:

> In a season of firsts, Eureka College will seek its first victory at Lebanon in 16 years.
> The Red Devils have never won a District 20 title, but they had never posted a 25 - 2 record either until this season. Likewise, McKendree has never won the District 20, and its 30 - 4 record is Harry Statham's best in 21 years as coach.
> "My feeling is that if we hold them under 80 points, we have a chance," said Darnall, whose team averages 79.2 points and allows 63.9. "If they score over 80, we're in trouble.
> "They put the ball up right away," Darnall said. "They have excellent shooters and three (point) range players. They don't wait to set up an offense."
> McKendree shoots .525 from the field including .541 from three-point land.
> "Our philosophy is we have to be patient and try to make them work on defense, which they don't like to do. We hope to make them impatient on offense and make them put the ball up even quicker than normally."
> The prospect of playing in the soldout 1,000-seat Bearcat Den doesn't thrill Darnall, but his team has played 16 of its 27 games on the road.
> "Maybe that will pay off for us," Darnall said.

The team planned to leave Eureka the day prior to the game. Darnall wanted his team to practice on the game floor before tournament play. He made a point of doing this for most tournaments and when playing larger institutions like Northeast Missouri State, University of Missouri-St. Louis, and Southern Illinois-Edwardsville. Since McKendree's gym was so small, the familiarizing of the floor was really important to Darnall. He wanted his players to realize how difficult it was going to be to execute the game plan. He also wanted his players to get used to the baskets and practice the movement of the zone on this distinct floor.

The team planned to make the three-hour trip to Lebanon in two vans. They were to stay at a Ramada Inn in Fairview Heights approximately ten miles from McKendree College. However, Dave's good friend and Eureka College alum and Trustee, Steve Thomson volunteered to transport the team to the game in his luxurious motor home. The players thought that was "first class."

A college-sponsored send-off for the team was held at noon the day prior to the game. President Hearne gave a short send-off message, and Coach Darnall thanked the approximate 200 fans that had gathered for their support. After a few minutes of picture taking in front of the motor home, the Red Devils boarded for the trip to Lebanon. Darnall rode "shotgun" as the players fanned throughout the motor home.

For the time being, Dave was at ease. Prior to leaving Eureka, he had chatted with Harrod. They made plans to go to Darnall's condo in Fairfield Bay, Arkansas. It was term break at the college, giving Dave a week out of school. A long, hard season was coming to an end and a little golf and boating would be welcomed. The campaign had taken its toll on the coach. Darnall was going to go somewhere—Kansas City or Arkansas!

The trip to Fairview Heights was pleasant. Dave spent most of his time conversing with the driver, Steve Thomson. The anxiety wouldn't hit until evening, and there was a lot to do before bedtime. The team had an hour and a half practice at the game site that evening. It was a routine practice of shooting and working on offenses and defenses to be used the following night. The team returned to the motel with lights out at 12:00 midnight. The coaches, Trainer Mundle, and Thomson slipped down to the lounge for a short time. The topic of conversation was, of course, the next evening's game and the chances Eureka might have to pull-off an upset. Could the Red Devils stick to their plan?

As usual, it was a sleepless night for Darnall. He had said, "If I ever got to the championship game, I wouldn't be nervous; just take my chances."

Who was he kidding? Like all the other games, Dave was obsessed to win. However, playing a team like McKendree on the road or larger NCAA II schools on their regular schedule that they were not expected to beat, seemed to make it a little easier on the coach.

The next morning the players slept in. Checkout of the motel was not until 1:30 P.M. However, Darnall fretted over what to do with the team from 1:30 until the pre-game meal at 4:00 P.M. He considered taking the team to the mall but didn't really want them to be on their feet for a couple hours. The next option was to have the players remain in the motor home. Not bad, but probably too boring. He was afraid that just sitting around could cause the guys to be stagnant and flat. While contemplating what to do, Coach Dighton looked out the motel window and noticed a cinema a couple blocks away. Guess what was playing? *Hoosiers!* After a quick call, it was determined that the next showing would be around 2:00 P.M.

"Perfect!" said Darnall.

The players had heard about the movie but had not seen it. As it turned out, they were essentially the only people in the theater for the 2:00 viewing. It was their "personal movie of inspiration."

Exiting the theater, "Sugar" turned to "Kronk," "Tonight will be our 'Hoosiers.' We are going to do the real thing."

"Kronk" replied, "I hope you're right. I have the same feeling."

Seeing coach, "Kronk" continued to express his new feeling of confidence, "We are not going to _ _ _ _in' lose tonight!"

With the movie over and time more than appropriately filled, the team went for their pre-game meal. They continued to discuss what they had just witnessed. Darnall prayed for a replay!

The Red Devils arrived at the gymnasium around 5:30 P.M. However, Dave kept the team in the motor home until 6:00. Then they filed into the small gym.

Several hundred Bearcat and Red Devil fans were already at the locked door. Unfortunately, most were for McKendree. Eureka was allowed only about a hundred tickets. The game was a sell-out. That left many people who had traveled to the game site hoping for "no show" tickets, to stand outside the gym and just experience the championship atmosphere.

As the Red Devils entered the hallway leading to the tiny gym and the extremely small locker rooms, they noticed numerous posters on the walls. Several indicated and congratulated McKendree's success for the night's game. Premature? A superstitious Darnall sure hoped so.

In fact, Darnall later learned that a group of fans from Eureka had arrived early in Lebanon and had stopped at a local establishment called "Ron's" for something to eat.

Inquiring what was in the backroom, the proprietor showed the visitors. The area had been decorated for the post-game celebration banquet for the District 20 State Champions. Signs reading, "McKendree—District Champions," "Congratulations Champs," "We're No. 1," "Good Luck in Kansas," and "Kansas City, Here We Come" were scattered on the walls of the room.

Darnall would have been very skeptical of this type of pre-planning. He was way too superstitious. In fact, he failed to fill out the NAIA information sheet because he felt the anticipation would jinx his team leading to defeat and a huge letdown.

The players took their duffel bags into the visitors' locker room and then withdrew to a small area outside where they could visit with some of the Eureka supporters. Eureka fans had been assigned a small section in the bleachers adjacent to the visitors' locker room. One fan drew quite a bit of attention. He was Russell Roseman, a seventy-five-year-old gentleman and the team's elder statesman. The coaching staff remained busy inside laying out game uniforms. It wouldn't be long before they would be ready for the team to rejoin them in preparation for the big game.

The tiny dressing room was solemn as Coach began his pre-game talk. Hoping this would not be, but knowing realistically it could be his final pre-game talk of the season, Darnall was pretty low-key. No ranting and raving, no challenging the players to prove who they were. They had already proven that. He just reminded them to stay with the game plan, not to panic whatever situation might develop. He ended by praising his team for what it had already achieved this year. Out of the ordinary, Darnall was acting pretty calm. He even bypassed his usual locker room snooze on the traveling trunks. It left him a little tired, but he just kept reminding himself that in a day or two Harrod and he would be heading to scenic Arkansas. He was afraid to let himself anticipate Kansas City.

Coach repeated the words he had said for over 325 times before at Eureka College, "Let's take our ten seconds. Each one is an individual. Think whatever you want to think, or you don't need to think at all, as long as we are quiet, and we do it together." The team responded with total silence. That game would be the true test of his now well-known motto—"Together We Win"— TWW. The team took the floor to the applause of around 100 Eureka fans in the standing-room-only, sell-out crowd. Dave stayed behind for his last pre-game trip to the bathroom. He also slipped on his well-worn gray plaid sports jacket, one that he had worn to every game for the past several years.

Shortly after the Red Devils had started their warm-up, the Bearcats took the floor to a thunderous ovation from the overwhelming home-court crowd. "I never, in over twenty years of coaching, have seen such an enormous greeting for a team when they took the floor as I did tonight," Darnall said after the game. "It scared the hell out of me. I'm glad my players weren't like me."

The crowd stood most of the game. There wasn't room for another person. The noise level had to reach the team. "It was the loudest game I ever participated in," Dave said following the game. "I couldn't even hear what Coach Dighton was telling me, and he was sitting right next to me," he commented. It was definitely a championship atmosphere.

Eureka fans cheering their Red Devils in the crowded Bearcat Den.

Eureka started the game as planned with the 1-2-2 zone defense and spread offense. They waited until approximately ten seconds was left on the clock before taking a shot. That took a lot of discipline, but the plan was working the first half. The Red Devils held the Bearcats without a basket for the first seven minutes of the game. Who would have believed? Eureka took a narrow 26 to 24 half-time lead to the dismay of the majority of the fans in the packed house. The scene was unbelievably dramatic, but the drama only increased as the second half was played out.

To relate the happenings of that evening, articles written by sports-writers covering the game do best.

Randy Kindred's article "Eureka College stuns McKendree" appeared in *The Pantagraph*. It read:

Greg Nunn had been there before. That's what had him worried.

"It was against Blackburn two years ago," the Eureka College senior guard said. "The exact same situation. I missed two and we wound up losing in double overtime."

That time, a conference title was on the free-throw line with Nunn in the waning seconds. Last night, a state championship hung in the balance when Nunn toed the line at McKendree College's berserk Bearcat Den.

With his team trailing by a point and four seconds remaining, Nunn calmly swished both shots this time to give Eureka College a 63 - 62 victory and the National Association of Intercollegiate Athletics District 20 title.

The win, Eureka College's first at McKendree in 16 years, earned the 26-2 Red Devils a spot in the NAIA National Tournament, which starts Wednesday in Kansas City. Pairings for the 32-team tourney will be released today.

"That (the Blackburn game) was the first thing that popped into my mind when I was fouled," Nunn said. "But then I realized we were only two shots away from Kansas City. I just prayed to the Man upstairs and he came through for me."

That, in turn, allowed Nunn to 'come through' for Coach Dave Darnall, who has spent 13 years at Eureka College trying to get in position for a trip to Kansas City.

When Nunn delivered and then McKendree's final shot bounced off, Darnall had what he called "the biggest moment of my life."

It was so big, he collapsed immediately following the final buzzer.

"I think I was in a state of shock," he said later. "I jumped up real quick and then I got lightheaded. I didn't know where I was for a few minutes, but it's OK now."

Actually, it was more than OK. It was a dream come true, and it was made possible by a perfectly orchestrated and executed game plan.

The Red Devils stuck to it from start to finish and even then, needed Nunn's heroics to knock off the nation's 10th ranked team in its own crackerbox gym.

"Even when we got behind by six (midway through the second half), we never got out of the game plan," Darnall said. "We knew we had to play zone defensively and force them to shoot from the outside. We felt they'd get anxious and take some bad shots, which they did.

"Offensively, we had to be patient and not take a shot until we had run at least 25 seconds off the (shot) clock. When we did that, it made them play defense and they love to play offense."

That they do. The Bearcats entered the game averaging 105.6 points per game, highest in the nation on any level, and shooting .525 from the field.

Last night, McKendree had its lowest point total of the year and shot 38 percent from the floor (22 of 57).

Other articles relating the drama of the night before were "Eureka! Devils to KC" by Joe Bates for the *Journal Star* and "Eureka College wins heart-stopper; lands berth in national tourney" by Robin Wettstein for the *Woodford County Journal.*

A sportswriter from the McKendree area, David Wilhelm of the *Belleville Journal*, wrote in "Bearcats' dream season comes to quick halt:"

The hush that rested on the campus of McKendree College last Thursday was evidence of what had just taken place inside Bearcat Gymnasium.

There were no bands of students parading around proclaiming a Bearcats' victory or chanting "K-C, K-C." Drivers quietly pulled their cars out of a jam-packed lot without tooting horns or waving banners outside the windows.

MEN'S BASKETBALL

Eureka College had just rained on McKendree's parade with a 63-62 victory that ended the Bearcats' dream for a berth in the NAIA National Tournament at Kansas City, MO. Despite all their accomplishments, the Bearcats and their fans were in no mood for a celebration . . .

Like most teams that went up against McKendree at Bearcat Gymnasium, Eureka had to play a nearly flawless game to come out on top.

The last several minutes of the game were hectic. Darnall refused to change his game plan regardless being down by as many as six points. It paid off. McKendree called timeout just prior to Nunn's free throws. They wanted to "ice" the all-district player. In the Eureka huddle, Darnall was talking a mile a minute. "Sugar" attempted to calm his coach by guaranteeing both his free tosses would "tickle the twine."

Nunn reassures Coach Darnall he will make the free throws as "Ice" listens intently.

"Don't worry coach. I'll get these," Nunn reassured. "I've got some making up to do from a couple years ago. This is our Hoosiers."

Darnall couldn't stand to watch. There was still the flashback to Nunn's sophomore year. With his head bowed and face covered with a towel, he responded to the Eureka fans' cheers. Dighton shouted to him that Nunn had made the first shot.

Then again McKendree called timeout, hoping the strategy would work that time.

328

As the six-foot-two guard stepped to the line and gave a confident wink at his cheerleader girlfriend, Darnall again buried his head. Nunn calmly swished the second, and Dighton reported to Darnall, "We're up!"

Dave removed the towel from his eyes in time to see McKendree make the inbound pass to near mid-court. The Bearcats immediately called another timeout to set up the last shot.

Coach tried to calm his excited players. "The game is not over; don't foul. Don't give them an easy shot." Darnall shouted above the roaring of the crowd. The team put their hands together as the main man yelled, "Let's go!" The players returned to the court.

The ball was thrown in to Ted Longust. That was the last Darnall saw for a few seconds. He couldn't watch the twenty-five-footer. The ball never found the hole. It bounced off the rim as the horn sounded. Jumping up quickly, Darnall collapsed to the floor limp. It was too much for the coach. His "lights went out."

After several seconds of not knowing what was going on, Dave recovered to join the ongoing celebration. Eureka College fans had rushed to the floor swarming their heroes. The players were patting each other on the back, shaking hands, and giving hugs.

Coach Darnall (above) assisted by medic after fainting as the last shot of the game was taken.

Bearcat fans were totally stunned. They could only stand or sit and watch the visitors' celebration. They were in a state of shock. How could this happen? This was not supposed to be.

Tears of joy flowed as the District 20 State Championship plaque was presented to Coach Dave Darnall and his team. It took at least fifteen minutes following the game for the trophy presentation, but it would be

Above: Hugs from Bonnie after victory over McKendree.

Below: NAIA District 20 State Champions. (Photo by Ray Driskell)

another thirty minutes before the Red Devils and their loyal fans left the floor. The excitement didn't cease, and the time was being savored. The players hoisted their coach to their shoulders to ceremoniously cut down the net cords. After Darnall's first cut, the players lifted Coach Dighton, and then each other until nets were removed from both ends of the court.

"It took a lot of discipline and execution to be down by one with twenty seconds left and be able to run the clock down to four seconds for the last shot or be fouled without losing the ball when being

Players hoisting Coach Darnall for the net-cutting ritual.

pressed," the beaming Darnall commented to those surrounding him after the game. "We talked about that and worked on the situation, hoping we would be prepared if needed."

A fifty-five minute on-court celebration finally came to an end. The victorious Red Devils headed to the locker room to dress. The dressing room again became a scene of exhilaration. The Eureka College fans had still not left for the three-hour trip home. Instead some had gathered around the motor home and spectator buses organizing a motorcade. Applause broke out as the team left the now conquered tiny gymnasium and headed for the motor home. Not only a super fan, but also a thoughtful one, Thomson had warmed up the vehicle to the delight of the Red Devils.

Robert Kroehnke, Rob's father, drove downtown Lebanon to purchase some champagne for a later celebration. He stopped at Ron's Lounge, the same establishment that the Eureka fans at visited prior to the game. There was no party. The back room was empty. The celebration was taking place on Thomson's motor home and on the fans' buses.

The caravan left McKendree College close to 11:00 P.M. It took a half-hour to reach Interstate 55. The caravan would not arrive on campus until around 2:30 A.M. The motor coach led the caravan closely followed by the huge Peoria Charter fan buses. Then came numerous cars and vans—a scene from *Hoosiers.*

The ride home was an ecstatic one for the players. They replayed the game and praised each other's accomplishments. The sounds of "Lean on Me" by Bill Withers and "Kansas City" by Wilbert Harrison blasted from the motor home's stereo. Throughout the season, the players had adopted "Lean on Me" as their theme song. It coincided with Darnall's philosophy of "Together We Win." The team was close. They depended on each other. They supported each other. They did not care about color, class, religious background, or economic status. They cared about each other on and off the floor. They had the character of real champions.

Before leaving for McKendree and while the team was boarding the motor home in Eureka, Dan Harrod had slipped Dave a tape of "Kansas City." The song was now going to serve as the team's second theme song and would be heard numerous times over the next couple of weeks.

This was a first for Eureka College athletics. No athletic team had even participated in a national tournament. The Red Devils were going to Kansas City. Forget Fairfield Bay for Dave and Dan. However, qualifying for the Nationals now presented a problem for Darnall. The superstitious coach had not responded with information to Kansas City. He had feared it might jinx his team and definitely did not want to experience what McKendree was feeling that night. He realized that he had "homework" to do much later that night.

It was also on the ride home that Darnall realized that he had just witnessed another *Hoosiers* only this time on the small college level. Dave believed that "it was meant to be." The accident earlier in the season with no injuries prompting the cancellation of the first McKendree game and then the viewing of the movie earlier in the day just could not be a coincidence. Darnall did not understand why this had all happened, but it did.

The caravan arrived in Eureka around 2:30 A.M. Horns were honking as it traveled down Reagan Drive to cheers of those both in and out of the vehicles. The first two campus buildings reached by the caravan were the TKE House and Reagan Fieldhouse. Celebrating was seen everywhere as the team's motor coach pulled up. The passengers of the other buses and vehicles quickly exited to join the other fans to cheer the Red Devils. Several hundred people now gathered, cheering as the team stepped from the motor coach. The players hoisted the "prize" in the air to the delight of the fans.

Coach Darnall thanked the crowd for their support and praised his team for its "greatest win ever at Eureka College." It was a victory that would go down in history.

After fifteen minutes of celebrating, the students were ready to move to the TKE House where the partying would continue for most of the night. Finals or no finals, tonight was a night for celebration—not studying.

Darnall's assistants were busy with the game equipment when he went to his office to finally assemble all of the National Tournament forms he had ignored earlier.

Numerous adult fans went on to the Darnall house for their long-awaited celebration party. Even at that hour, they wanted to "relive" the night's happening, toast the champions, and begin planning the unthinkable trip to Kansas City. Yes, that's right! Eureka College was headed to the National Tournament! Who would have believed they would be one of the top thirty-two teams in the country?

Chapter 12

Kansas City—Here We Come!

THE PARTY LASTED ALL NIGHT FOR SOME. Darnall celebrated, but he also began to work on the papers that had been due in the NAIA office several days prior. The hyped-up coach finally went to bed around 11:00 A.M. to catch two hour's sleep before meeting with Athletic Director Warner McCollum. It was a meeting neither had really thought would take place. Now questions needed to be answered and other factors determined. Who would be in the traveling party? When would they depart for Kansas City? Where would they stay? How would they travel? How much would the trip cost the college? These were just a few they began to work on. A meeting with President Hearne, Dean of Faculty Gary Gammon, College Relations Director Lynn Beer, Financial Officer Geneve Sager, McCollum and Darnall was organized for later in the day to finalize all of the arrangements.

The players wanted to fly. Darnall, another "John Madden," didn't. He was afraid and preferred to go by charter bus. In determining the miles from Eureka to Kansas City, it was discovered that the required distance to be reimbursed for flight fell about fifteen miles short. If one traveled the realistic route by interstate, traveling around St. Louis, the mileage qualified for reimbursement. However, the AAA Motor Club charted a more direct route using mostly two-lane roads. Thus, flying was ruled out, which did not disappoint Coach Darnall. Traveling by Peoria Charter would later prove to be the best choice anyway.

The team was assigned the Americana Hotel in downtown Kansas City for their lodging. This was at the expense of the NAIA. Meals were the responsibility of each of the participating schools. It was decided that the twelve players that dressed for the District 20 Playoffs would also represent Eureka College at the Nationals. Darnall had dressed fifteen players during the regular season, but NAIA regulations allowed for only twelve in tournament play. The official party was composed of the twelve players, three coaches, a trainer, scorekeeper, and a student administrative assistant, for a total of eighteen people. Eureka College absorbed the cost for three individuals since the NAIA would only reimburse for fifteen people. Joining the official Eureka College party would be Dick Lien, sportswriter for the Peoria *Journal Star*. Unofficially, Derek and two buddies, Bob Gold and Chad Heffren, ended up accompanying the team. The boys planned to stay with Coach Darnall. The youngsters' parents were responsible for all other expenses.

Eureka College was scheduled to play their first game on the second day of the tournament, Thursday, March 12. That meant that the team would depart Monday morning and arrive in Kansas City early that evening. Darnall had given his players Friday off—no practice. He knew they would be in no shape either physically or mentally to handle a practice. Being up most of the night, along with the mental drain of the whole affair, the fellows needed some rest and time away from the game for a while. They would resume practice on Saturday and Sunday with Monday being a travel day.

Coach Darnall still had a full day even though he had cancelled practice. He went to his office to finish the required NAIA paperwork before "over-nighting" it to the National office. He was grateful for the help of McCollum and Athletic Secretary Kris Wilson.

Darnall was unable to scout their first opponent Auburn-Montgomery as he customarily did. He would have to rely on information he could obtain from previous opponents. It took several phone calls before Dave found a couple of coaches willing to share scouting information.

Auburn-Montgomery, a scholarship school of approximately 4,500 students, was led by six-foot-eight center Orlando Graham. Graham had transferred to Auburn after establishing himself as a top rebounder in the Missouri Valley Conference as a member of the West Texas State team. The Senators were also blessed with having two strong forwards, both over two-hundred pounds who could also leap. Their guards were quick and good shooters. Both were over six foot tall. On the bench, they had three players

335

over six-foot-six. The team overall was quick, strong rebounders, and liked to get up and down the floor. Coach Darnall compared them to McKendree but more "athletic." Would the game plan that was so successful with the Bearcats be used against their next opponent? Would it be effective?

Dave said, "Hell, yes! We can't run up and down the floor with those big boys."

Another question was how was Dave able to assemble a group of guys that just put Eureka College on the basketball map. How did he get the guys he would ask for one more victory? That question was best answered by an article written by Jim Barnhart, Sports Editor of the Bloomington's *The Pantagraph* entitled "Darnall literally drives self for the college." The article read:

> Dave Darnall is literally stoop shouldered from getting in and out of automobiles, and the Eureka College basketball coach's most used line is, "Fill'er Up."
>
> Half the population of Eureka believes Darnall works at a local service station. Continual use of his credit cards have worn out several billfolds.
>
> Darnall could write a book about his exploits while beating the bushes for high school talent and the trips that take him to and from the far reaches of the state.
>
> During the recent holidays, Darnall visited nine high school tournaments and put nearly 1,000 miles on his automobile. The first day of the tourneys, Darnall went to Fairbury, Charleston, and Breese (Mater Dei) in that order. He was on the go so much, he couldn't remember where he had been or where he was going.
>
> But, what he thought was a wasted trip four years ago, turned out to be the cornerstone in his efforts to build Eureka College into the team that won the District 20 NAIA championship at McKendree Thursday night.
>
> Darnall drove 140 miles to Edwardsville that Thanksgiving night four years ago to see Alton and guard Rick (Ice) Taylor open the season.
>
> "When I tried to talk to Rick after the game, the coach told me I was wasting my time because the kid was a Division I player," said Darnall. "So, I just turned around and drove 140 miles home. I never did get to visit with him.
>
> "About the middle of April, I got a phone call from Rick and I didn't remember who he was. I had to look in my files. He told me he had scholarship offers from three schools but he wanted to go to a small school. I drove down there and visited with him.
>
> "A week later, we signed him. He was never on our campus until the day he enrolled."

Less than a month after the ill-fated trip to Alton, Darnall went to the Pekin Holiday Tournament and came away impressed with Greg (Sugar) Nunn, who teams with Taylor at the guards.

"I saw Hillcrest play and I really liked Nunn," said Darnall. "He shot the ball well and had a great attitude. I visited the family several times."

Darnall later went to Belleville West to see a game against East St. Louis, but the youngster he went to see did not impress him as much as a substitute, who played the last three minutes.

The sub was Alan Wright, now the Red Devils' 6-7 center.

"I really liked the way he ran the floor," said Darnall. "I asked Coy (Nunn), his high school coach, how his grades were. He told me the grades were good and to go ahead and talk to him. So, I did and we got him."

Darnall saw 6-6 forward Rob Kroehnke at a junior college all-star game in Kankakee. "I got three kids out of that game," said Darnall. "One is my scorekeeper, one is my student assistant, and one is Kroehnke. I didn't think I had a chance to get Kroehnke. He finally agreed to visit and somehow I talked him into coming."

The fifth starter is Tom Dooley, a 6-3 sophomore forward from Vandalia.

"I had had a couple of players from Vandalia," said Darnall. "Millikin wanted him bad and he told me it was between us and Millikin."

"I saw him play at least 10 times and I visited the house constantly. I also visited a lot of lounges in Vandalia with his father. I got to know the family really well."

Darnall hopes the upcoming trip to the NAIA finals in Kansas City will be the beginning of an excellent basketball tradition at Eureka College.

"I go out and visit a lot of kids," said Darnall. "I run into Millikin all the time. But, I never see Wesleyan. This is because Wesleyan has an excellent tradition and can be very selective. I have to work at it and I gotta be there all the time."

Darnall believes the successful season was preordained.

"We won six games when the other team had the ball with less than 10 seconds to go and could have beaten us," said Darnall.

"Then, we had that accident during the regular season on the way to McKendree and had to cancel the game. Luckily, no one was hurt but it's like we were to play McKendree for the state title. It was almost like someone wanted us to do it."

Darnall calls himself a realistic coach.

"I knew I had a good group of kids," said Darnall. "But our main goal was to win 20 games, get in the playoffs, and maybe host a first-round game. I never thought we would be going to Kansas City."

When Eureka College returned home from McKendree in the wee hours Friday morning, the team and Darnall couldn't sleep.

337

"I didn't make any kind of plans at all in case we won. I didn't want to jinx us. So, I don't know when we go, where we go, and how we go. Guess I'll have to call Wesleyan and see how to do it."

Coach knew that in order to be successful, they would have to prevent Auburn-Montgomery from getting the ball in the "paint." The zone should help achieve this as well as possibly keep Eureka's two big boys, Kroehnke and Wright, out of foul trouble. Both points were crucial for a victory.

The offense would virtually be the same as they employed against McKendree, a spread alignment using what Darnall calls the "Wheel Offense." The motion offense engineered by Coach Dighton would be used as a backup.

There was no official send-off duplicating the departure for McKendree. The college was still on term break. The Red Devils quietly slipped out of Eureka around 8:00 A.M. on Monday morning. The trip lasted approximately eight hours. The team arrived at the Americana Hotel around 4:00 P.M. The players were able to relax for a couple hours before dinner. The team ate dinner in the hotel's dining room. This was big time—both the meal and the facility. Most of the teams staying at the Americana ate there also. The hotel provided "specials" for the tournament teams.

The Red Devils spent the evening in their hotel.

The following morning the team had brunch at 11:00 A.M. Practice was planned for 2:00 P.M. at Rockhurst College located a few miles away. Eureka was one of only a very few of the thirty-two teams that arrived on Monday. The Red Devils were the only team that traveled to Kansas City by charter bus. That proved to be fortunate and very convenient as the teams had to travel to various functions at other locations. Most of the other teams traveled in "old yellow" school buses arranged by the NAIA.

Eureka's first practice in Kansas City lasted an hour and a half. Dick Lien accompanied the team to the practice.

It was time to get ready for the NAIA Tip-off Banquet held in the Celebrity Room at the Gold Buffet. Imagine thirty-one yellow school buses traveling down the road with one red-and-white charter with "Eureka College" on the nameplate? There were many envious players in the other thirty-one. It was at that time that the players were glad they came to Kansas City by bus. They felt special!

The Tip-off Banquet was the true opening of the tournament festivities. All thirty-two teams were honored. The Master of Ceremony was Bill Grigsby, Advertising Coordinator for the NAIA National Championship. Bill

338

Grimes, president of ESPN Sports, Inc. was the featured speaker. ESPN televised the championship game. Over a thousand people attended the "dress-up" affair. The players looked good—suits, sport coats, ties. This was "big time;" a once-in-a-lifetime occasion. The banquet lasted almost three hours.

The teams' sponsors paid for the banquet tickets. Eureka's sponsors were David Block and James Block of Block and Company, Inc. Realtors. They also served as honorary bench coaches.

Eureka College did not play until the second day of the tournament. Therefore, Coach Darnall allowed his players to "hang-out" with each other in the hotel until midnight. The Eureka coaching staff joined other coaches in the Americana Hotel's lounge for a little relaxation and to discuss the upcoming events.

Dick Lien, the *Journal Star*'s traveling sportswriter, summarized the first day in "Red Devils got here playing Darnall's way." It read in part:

In the Rockhurst College gymnasium—except for the pastel walls, this might have been Hickory High School's home in the film "Hoosiers"—Eureka College basketball coach Dave Darnall did his best Gene Hackman imitation.

"Fellas, don't be forcing shots," Darnall said, effectively ending some playground styling in the early moments of practice Tuesday afternoon, "or your butt's gonna be sitting with me."

Eureka, the second smallest of the 32 teams in the National Association of Intercollegiate Athletics basketball finals, got here playing the coach's way—and he is not about to change now.

The odds will be against Darnall's team in its NAIA opener too, when the Red Devils (26-2) play 14th seeded Auburn-Montgomery (23-7). . . . The tournament will be played downtown at 17,000-seat Kemper Arena, where the Big Eight Conference tournament was played last week and the site of the NCAA Final Four in 1988.

"Seventeen thousand. . . . Our guys are not gonna even be able to imagine what playing there is gonna be like," Darnall said.

With a few reminders this was a national tournament.

Darnall's day had begun at 7:00 A.M. when he was awakened by a call from a reporter for *USA TODAY*, wanting to know if President Reagan had called the basketball coach at his alma mater after the Red Devils qualified for the NAIA finals.

"I told him I didn't get a call and I didn't expect one," Darnall said. He smiled. "I made a joke out of it. I said, 'Maybe if we win this tournament. . . .'"

"You're going to get your butts blown out if we don't spread out and make ourselves play bigger than what we are," Darnall told his players during a break in practice. "We're talking about some big boys here."

"They've got a lot of talent," Alan Wright, Eureka's 6-foot-7, 195-pound center, told another visitor, "but we've got a game plan."

Against McKendree in the District 20 championship game, the game plan had been to take 25 seconds off the 45-second clock before shooting—reducing the scoring opportunities for a more talented team.

"People have said we could probably beat McKendree at McKendree only one time out of 10, and that might be right," Darnall said after practice. He leaned forward. "But that one counted."

After practice, the Eureka players dressed to join the other 31 teams for a buffet dinner at a Kansas City restaurant.

"Coats, ties, the whole caboodle," Darnall said, rising from his front seat on the right side of the bus to announce the uniform of the day. "We're going to be looking sharp, boys. This is the banquet."

And this is the NAIA nationals. Right there alongside 33-0 Oklahoma City, the top-seeded team, are the unseeded Red Devils from Woodford County.

Right there with the 9,344 students of Wisconsin-EauClaire and the 7,519 of Minnesota-Duluth are the 460 student of Eureka and 430 of Northwestern College of Orange City, Iowa.

The first-round games started Wednesday morning at Kemper. Since practice wasn't until 2:00 P.M., Dave allowed his players to sleep in until brunch at 11:00. Once practice was over, the team returned to their rooms to prepare for dinner at a nearby pizza place and then on to Kemper. Tonight was going to be another memorable evening for all the tournament teams. It was the evening of "The Parade of Champions." In spite of a few teams already being eliminated, all teams were required to participate in the pageantry.

Many dedicated Eureka College fans had been filtering into Kansas City throughout the day. Bonnie, Tiera, Dave's mother, Ola, and supporters Jan Gold, Annette Morman, and Dan Harrod, who had volunteered to chauffeur the ladies to Kansas City, arrived early. Harrod had put his "lawyer-persuasive tactics" to work. He had contacted John Bearce, a Central Illinois car dealer, and convinced him that "some" local business should provide transportation to the National Tournament for the head coach's family. A member of Eureka College's Board of Trustees, Bearce happily agreed. Professor Kevin McQuade of the theater department and his wife, Linda, arrived midday as well as the school's official photographer, Rich Beer, and Don Pioletti. President Hearne flew in early in the evening. Dave's brother, Bruce, and sister, Judy, and her husband, Chuck, also arrived in time for the evening's honoring of the teams.

The players, cheerleaders, and many of the fans boarded the charter around 6:00 P.M. for the fifteen-minute drive to the arena. Number-one seed Oklahoma City was playing Northwood Institute of Midland, Michigan, in the first game of the evening. Darnall wanted his players to see the 33 to 0 team as well as experience the atmosphere of the National Tournament. That was the first time the players had seen a game in the tournament, which had begun at 9:00 A.M. with Minnesota-Duluth against Georgetown, Kentucky.

The "Parade of Champions" took place immediately following the Oklahoma City-Northwood game. The thirty-two teams, dressed in their warm-up uniforms, marched onto the arena's floor when introduced. Each college's head coach and season record was announced as the team took the floor. The teams were placed on the court to form a huge, floor-size, NAIA. Dave savored the special moment.

NAIA Parade of Champions.

"I just stood there quietly, looking up at the ceiling of the magnificent building, thanking God for answering my dream," Darnall said following the ceremony. "I just wanted to cherish the moment since I'll probably never experience it again."

As the teams left the floor, the lights were shut down and a spectacular Fiftieth Anniversary celebration for the NAIA began. It was climaxed with a huge cake holding fifty foot-long candles rolled to the center of the court. What a great year for Eureka to qualify!

Dave had asked the fans, whom he felt had spent a considerable amount of money as well as taking time from work, to congregate in his room, possibly for the last time. He had something special to share with them. He also planned to use it as a special motivation for his team at his pre-game talk in the morning. It was a Western Union Mailgram out of Bridgeton, Missouri, from the president of the United States, Ronald Reagan, and Eureka's most famous alum.

The Mailgram read:

1-0075871070002 03/11/87
0TWX WHITEHOUSE WSH DLY PD
021 DLY GOVT WHITE HOUSE DC MAR 11
PMS COACH DAVE DARNALL // DLR DON'T DWR//
EUREKA COLLEGE
EUREKA, IL 61530

CONGRATUATIONS TO YOU AND TO THE RED DEVILS ON YOUR VICTORY IN THE NAIA DISTRICT TITLE GAME. I KNOW YOU AND THE TEAM WORKED VERY HAD FOR THIS ACHIEVEMENT AND MY BEST WISHES ARE WITH YOU FOR FUTURE VICTORIES. AGAIN, CONGRATULATIONS, AND BEST WISHES FOR CONTINUED SUCCESS.

RONALD REAGAN

Darnall also had a newspaper article he wanted to share with the fans. Eureka College basketball had finally made it to the "big time." An article written by Roscoe Nance entitled "Eureka finds its chance to win post-season glory" appeared in *USA TODAY*. It read:

President Reagan is the best known alumnus of Eureka College (Ill.). But Eureka won't be trying to win one for the Gipper in the National Association of Intercollegiate Athletics basketball tournament that starts today in Kansas City, Mo.

"Were trying to win one for everybody," said Coach Darnall.

Eureka (26-2) plays Auburn-Montgomery (23-7) Thursday in the opening round. It will be the first NAIA appearance for both schools.

Reagan, a 1932 graduate, played on the school's football and swimming teams. His brother Neal also attended Eureka and is on the board of trustees.

Eureka plays its home games in Reagan Fieldhouse.

Darnall, surprised just to be in the 32-team tournament, doesn't expect a call from the President.

Eureka had played in the district playoffs seven of the last nine years without a victory. No one was more surprised than Darnall when Eureka beat McKendree 63-62 to win a trip to Kansas City.

"I never even looked at the literature I had gotten on the (NAIA) tournament," said Darnall. "I didn't even know when the tournament was. All the other schools made preparations for banquets and room in their trophy case. We did nothing. That way, we have no disappointments."

"If we win one game, we'll pinch ourselves. It would be nice to get in the Final Four. The we might get a call or something."

"I don't know if it has hit us yet," said Darnall. "As we were eating Monday night, a player said to me, 'Coach, we're in Kansas City.'"

After everyone had left, Dave and the younger boys stayed up watching TV into the mid-hours of the night. Dave was reviewing his scouting reports and game plan when Derek related an incident that had taken place earlier in the day. It was one that left the biggest impression on him of the entire trip.

"Dad, you won't believe what happened to Bob, Chad, and me. We went over to that park across from the auditorium where 'Menudo' was in concert tonight. We were watching some of the kids coming to the concert. Some of them were even dropped off in limousines. We weren't really doing anything, just hanging out. Then, we noticed some black guys in the park. There were about eight to ten of them carrying sticks."

At this Dave's interest perked, "How old were they?"

"Probably between thirteen and seventeen," replied Derek. "All we could think of was, 'How are we going to get back to the hotel?' They were between us and the hotel."

"So, what did you do?" asked his dad, realizing his concern was a little after the fact.

"Well, we knew they weren't playing around and were serious when we heard one say, 'Let's get them!' So we took off running. They were chasing us, and we knew it might be ugly if they got to us."

Dave listened intently as the boys continued to relate how they had run through a water fountain and down approximately eight steps of a waterfall before being chased into an elegant lobby of another hotel. Now what, especially since a couple of the boys had followed them into the lobby and were waiting for their next move? "They just stood by the phones and kept watching us," Derek reported.

To their immense relief, the boys chanced to notice five of the Eureka College basketball players (three black and two white) standing outside the hotel at the street corner. "Then we saw our guys and ran to them as fast as we could. We told them what had just happened so they came back to our hotel with us," concluded Derek.

The "escape route" for Derek, Chad, and Bob.

It seemed when seeing the well-built players standing six-foot-two to six-foot-eight, the gang turned and went back into the park area. What an adventure for the boys from rural Illinois!

Darnall wasn't as nervous as usual the night before a game. Perhaps it was because they weren't supposed to be there in the first place. He finally fell asleep around 3:00 A.M. receiving four hours of rest.

The players ate their pre-game breakfast meal at 8:00 A.M. and then prepared to leave for Kemper Arena at 10:00. If they won the game, the team would stay to watch the following contest between Biola, California, and St. Joseph's of Maine. If they lost, the Eureka College entourage would go somewhere for a late lunch and commiserate. Needless to say, everyone was hoping lunch would be delayed to an early dinner.

The players experienced flashbacks to "Hoosiers" as they entered the huge building and walked down the long hallway leading to their locker room. The Red Devils felt the same emotions the Hickory High School players had to have felt when they entered for the state championship. It was an awesome feeling—once in a lifetime.

Once the team reached the locker room, they placed their personal belongings in lockers and proceeded to the floor to wait for some free shooting during half time of the St. Thomas Aquinas, New York, and William Carey, Mississippi, game. Since there were only ten minutes scheduled between games, the up-coming opponents were allowed to shoot at the intermission of the current game.

The team returned to the locker room to possibly hear their coach's last pre-game talk of the year. Hopefully not!

Darnall calmly reminded his players to follow the game plan. "Duplicate the same execution you did against McKendree," Darnall instructed.

The Senators' quickness, strength, height, and talent dictated the only way Eureka could possibly be victorious. Reality must be faced. Darnall had his team take their traditional ten seconds of silence before exiting the locker room. His last words were, "Fellows, don't embarrass yourselves. You're a good team. Go prove it."

The players went through a modified pre-game warm-up. The last drill was a five-man, two-line, three-ball passing drill that Darnall had used for years called "Kansas." What an appropriate drill for the team to end their warm-up! He had named the drill after the Kansas coach he had learned it from who had been a featured speaker at a basketball clinic.

As each member of the starting five was introduced, their fans sitting behind their bench gave their "hero" a standing ovation. There weren't many—approximately 100 Eureka fans total—but they were vocal.

Coach Darnall caught himself gazing around the arena at the crowd and at the huge scoreboard hanging above center court while the players were being introduced. What a spectacular sight! How many coaches strove to reach that moment and failed?

In spite of only about four to five thousand spectators attending the morning's first session, it was the most people before which the Red Devils had ever played. One spectator in the crowd was a special Eureka College supporter. He was Raymond McCallister. The elderly gentleman had driven down from St. Louis to see his alma mater in action. The college's chapel was named after him.

The scoreboard provided an image Darnall remembers even today. There on the four-sided electronic board appeared Eureka as the home team. At the time, it was Darnall's proudest moment as a coach.

Auburn-Montgomery won the tip-off. Eureka fell back into their well-known 1-2-2 adjustable zone. It didn't work! The Senators powered the ball inside to take a quick lead never to be relinquished. Dick Lien gave a firsthand account of the game in his article "Eureka falls 85-54 in NAIA tourney" for the *Journal Star*. It read in part:

> The shot was there 10 second into the first Eureka College possession. Guard Greg Nunn knew he shouldn't have taken it, but he did. And he missed.
>
> So much for the Red Devils' game plan in their first-round game Thursday morning against powerful Auburn-Montgomery in the National Association of Intercollegiate Athletics basketball finals at Kemper Arena.
>
> "The game plan lasted about a minute," Red Devils' Coach Dave Darnall said after the Alabama school posed an 85-54 victory. "But I can't complain . . . a game plan's not worth a darn if your kids can't execute it, and Montgomery wouldn't let us execute it."
>
> Eureka hoped to control the tempo against the bigger, quicker Senators. Only lay-ups during the first 25 seconds of any possession, Darnall had asked.
>
> The plan dissolved altogether 30 seconds after Nunn missed a 10-foot shot in the lane when Eureka guard Rick "Ice" Taylor put up a three-pointer in the right corner. He missed too.
>
> Eureka fell behind 7-0 in the first 2:20, rallied within 13-11 but trailed 33-20 at halftime. The Red Devils were outscored 52-34 in the second half, which was played at sprint pace after Eureka left its 3-2 zone.
>
> "I've played against teams that good before," Taylor said, "but I've never played against teams that are so physical. They kinda let you play down here, and that was to their advantage."
>
> "You know, it just wasn't one or two physical players, it was the whole Montgomery team," Nunn said. "Those guys set picks and it's a head-on collision with no call. I actually thought we needed some football helmets out there."

"There was one time I was on the free throw line and one of their guys was on the baseline and we met about halfway to the basket . . . believe me, there'd have been scrambled eggs if we were carrying grocery sacks."

If the Eureka guards felt knocked around by Montgomery, the other two seniors, Rob Kroehnke (5 points, 4 rebounds) and Alan Wright (2 and 2) did, too. And they were the only players in the game who fouled out.

"I'm disappointed, but I'm not empty at all," Darnall said. "I've fulfilled every realistic goal of my career. If I got out of coaching now, I wouldn't feel cheated at all because I was able to bring a team here."

In the locker room after the game, Coach addressed his dejected players. "Needless to say, I am disappointed in the loss, but I am proud of you for the way you conducted yourselves on the floor under adverse conditions. You had a great season. Nobody can take that away from you. You'll be the first team to ever be inducted into the college's Athletic "Hall of Fame," he continued as several of his players wept quietly. Darnall also had a few tears in his eyes knowing this sensational season had come to a close.

"Let's go back, shower up, and get some pizza," said Darnall.

However, just before the team left the locker room, their sponsor Jim Block said his company and he would like to take the team to dinner at a local bar-grill. The players thought that would be great but wanted the early pizza left in the plans.

The team remained in the arena for approximately an hour after the game. Some talked with newspaper, TV, and radio personnel while others visited with their fans and parents. A few caught a glimpse of the Biola-St. Joseph game that now did not make any difference.

Coach Darnall was interviewed by several newspaper reporters and radio announcers. An unidentified reporter "special to *The Pantagraph*," asked Darnall what his thoughts were at that time. Darnall replied, "We had a great season. We have no regrets and no one can take away all the positive things we've accomplished. We're just a little disappointed we didn't have a better performance here."

When asked about his game plan, he replied, "We went into the game with the same plan we used against McKendree (in the District 20 finals). We wanted to keep the tempo slow and play good zone defense, but we lost our concentration early and weren't patient enough. We took a couple of shots we shouldn't have. They were able to get a couple of fastbreak baskets, and we were never able to get into our game plan."

347

Darnall was also asked if he would do anything different if he had a team qualify for the National Tournament again. He answered, "If we ever come to Kansas City again, I'm bringing football equipment. It was a very physical game—by far the most physical game we've played. I thought we were in the NBA."

The team went back to the hotel and then headed to the pizzeria for a late lunch. The disappointed Red Devils finished eating and returned to say goodbye to those fans who had to return to Eureka for work or family reasons.

Several fans, especially parents, were able to remain in Kansas City with the players. They wanted to celebrate a "season to remember." They joined the team that evening for dinner. Jim Block greeted his guests upon arrival. The first hour was set aside for cocktails, mostly beer. The team then sat down to an outstanding meal furnished by Block. The McKendree game continued to be a topic of conversation.

As the evening progressed, the discussion went from the season's accomplishments to the closeness of the team. The mood became quite sentimental with stories being told on each other and themselves. Tears of sadness and melancholy could be seen. The players comprehended this had been their last game together. For some it had been their last and for others, they would have to wait until next year. But their feeling of "Together We Win" would never end.

The group left the establishment around 11:00 P.M. and returned to the Americana. There the players and fans continued to intermingle, going from room to room. Lights were out at 2:00 A.M.

The Darnall family and team passed the afternoon watching the second round of the National Tournament. No more pressure, no more scouting, no more wondering whom the next opponent would be. The day concluded with a fantastic meal in the Americana's dining room.

Throughout the day, Dick Lien of the *Journal Star* talked to Eureka College players and coaches. An article entitled "Red Devils leave KC with heavenly memory" summarized the historical trip. (A dedicated sportswriter and editor, Mr. Lien passed away in December of 1996 while accompanying the Bradley University team on a road trip.) His article read in part:

> "Somehow it didn't seem sad. I couldn't ask for anything more than this basketball season," Eureka College senior Rob Kroehnke said. "Coming to Kansas City to play was everybody's dream."
> It was a dream that ended abruptly Thursday when the Red Devils lost 85-54 to Auburn-Montgomery in the first round of the National

348

Association of Intercollegiate Athletic finals. "The seniors will have to leave it to the coaches and players who are still here to bring us to the next level—to come here and win one, I guess." Kroehnke said.

Forty-five minutes after the game, Kroehnke and his teammates were still talking to family and friends, in no hurry to leave Kemper Arena and the memories of this tournament.

"For most of these guys," Coach Dave Darnall said, "playing in the nationals is going to be one of the three greatest memories of their life—along with their wedding and the birth of a child."

Kroehnke was one of four seniors playing their final game for Eureka. The others—Greg "Sugar" Nunn, Rick "Ice" Taylor, and Alan Wright—felt the same.

"Anything we would have done here would have been gravy," said Taylor, a guard from Alton. "It was an overall good season. Nobody expected us to be here."

"The best team in Eureka College history," said Nunn, from Markham. "It must be . . . no other team has made it to the Nationals. Getting here was more than I honestly expected."

And Wright, a center from East St. Louis: "I feel glad I went to school here. If I hadn't come here, I wouldn't have made it this far. It's been a very positive experience."

"President Reagan congratulated us for the season and wished us luck," Darnall said.

Darnall said the team will remain in Kansas City today.

"I don't know where we go from here because the seniors were very important to our success—and there's somebody down at the Class A tournament right now watching some player I might like to recruit," Darnall said.

"But right now we just want to think about this season. It's been one all of us will never forget."

Dave knew the secret of the 1986-1987 campaign was largely due to his past recruiting efforts. The length of this season caused Darnall to be greatly behind his competitors. However, his commitment to his team took priority over any recruiting. That prevented him from attending high school games the later part of the season. In hopes of "catching up," he sent three dozen hand-written postcards to his top recruits from Kansas City.

The team started home early Saturday morning. It was a sad moment as the Red Devils boarded the charter for their eight-hour trip to Eureka. They reached their destination around 6:00 P.M. without a greeting party. However, several signs displaying congratulations were spread about town. Weuthrich-Sanken's read "Congratulations to College BB Team State Champs—WOW!" Another said "Great Year E College BB Team, Thanks!"

An official college reception for the honored team was scheduled a few days later when classes had resumed from term break. Students, faculty, staff, administrators, parents, and fans attended the reception. Athletic Director Warner McCollum introduced Coach Darnall. Darnall, sporting a red NAIA baseball cap, introduced the members of his staff and team. Speaking briefly about each, he praised their individual contributions to the team as well as the team's over-all accomplishments. He then presented President Hearne the NAIA District 20 State Championship plaque for display in Reagan Center's Lobby.

In turn, Bonnie was presented with a large bouquet of flowers, and Dave was given a small monetary award to be used for his basketball program from the college Relations Department for the unprecedented nationwide publicity the team had provided.

Coach knew exactly what he would use the money for. He wanted to purchase a new trophy case to permanently house the year's memorabilia, including three invitational tournament trophies, the Conference trophy, the District 20 State Championship plaque, and numerous souvenirs from the National Tournament. However, establishing this exhibition was not an easy task since a couple people in the athletic department were against this type of singling out. Thanks to the Director of College Relations, it was approved as the college's administration saw the benefit of the achievement display.

The post-season honors began to roll in for both Coach Darnall and his team members. Greg "Sugar" Nunn and Rick "Ice" Taylor were selected NAIA First Team All-District 20-State. Nunn, Taylor, and Alan Wright were selected First Team All-Conference. Kroehnke and Dooley were selected Honorable Mention All-Conference. Coach Darnall was named Conference Coach of the Year.

The team ended by leading the NAIA District 20 in defense with 63.7 points a game and finished twelfth in the nation in both Team Defense and Team Scoring Margin—14.92. They had the fewest number of losses of any NAIA school in the state.

The Red Devils' 1986-1987 basketball season had officially closed with an unprecedented 26 to 3 record. However, as time passed, the stories and memories of this unforgettable season were retold and passed on, further laying the foundation for the road to destiny.

Chapter 13

Troublesome Times

T HE UNBELIEVABLE SEASON WAS OVER. It was now time for Dave to enjoy some time with his camp coaches and family before the rigorous pace would start again with a new school year. Dave knew the next season would be a rebuilding year, but he felt the combination of some good, experienced players and a talented recruiting class might surprise a few.

Darnall and other Corzine fans made their annual trip to see the Chicago Bulls. It was the normal gang except this year Dave Gilliland and Mike Pryor met the rest at the stadium.

Darnall had notified Corzine only a couple days prior to the game that the guys were coming up. Coach went to the "will-call" window to pick up the tickets. What tickets? There were none. Whether Corzine had forgotten or whether there were none available, Darnall didn't know. The game was a sell-out. The Jordan phenomenon was in full swing. Dave did not know what to do. Someone suggested that they get a message to Bulls' trainer Mark Pfeil, telling him of their predicament. Pfeil knew Smitty and Darnall and had helped them before at the stadium. Thankfully, Pfeil helped solve the problem. He was able to obtain standing room only tickets. This was fine with the camp coaches. They just wanted to get inside to see their buddy play.

Corzine and his friends headed downtown Chicago to Burton's Place following the game. The group spent a couple hours eating, drinking, and talking before heading home.

Corzine, in return, made his annual trip to Eureka for camp. It was during this camp that Tiera was crowned "Miss Woodford County" in a pageant held in Metamora. As Corzine had known Tiera for several years, he wanted to also watch the competition. The two Daves decided to drive the fifteen miles to the pageant in Darnall's '55 Chevy. Corzine wanted to drive. By the time they reached Metamora's central park, all of the seating had been taken. In fact, many spectators were sitting on blankets on the grass. Darnall joined them, but Corzine spotted a large tractor tire sandbox. The Chicago Bull found his seat. Imagine a seven-footer sitting in a tractor tire. His huge body hung out all over the place—legs and arms dangling.

The new queen was announced. Great job, Tiera! The two Daves went to the stage for the congratulatory hugs and kisses. Bonnie and Grandma Darnall and Brett were already there. To further celebrate, the group made their way across the street to Myers' Homestead for a toast. Owner Frank Myers had been a co-owner of the Chanticleer in Eureka with his brother Bob for years before locating in Metamora. He had been a good friend to Darnall and the camp coaches who frequented the Chanticleer.

Back at camp, everything had run smoothly. This had been only the second time that Dave had been off campus during a basketball camp. He had a great group of guys who could handle the well-oiled routine of camp.

Finally with camps finished, the Darnalls took a well-earned vacation. Dave, Bonnie, Derek, Cousin Travis, Tiera, and her friend Brett Charlton headed south. The destination was Hot Springs, Arkansas. On the way down and back, they made a stop at Fairfield Bay where the Darnalls had a time-share. They loved the mountains, lake and golf courses. Impulsively, Dave purchased a condominium at the "Bay." This was a place Dave felt would satisfy his need to "escape" following the basketball wars. He was all smiles, but not Bonnie. She cried all the way to St. Louis. Would they ever be out of debt? In the long run, it turned out to be a wise decision. Thirteen years later, they sold the condo and built a beautiful home with a "postcard" view. There's that number thirteen again!

The 1988 school year began, and the glory and excitement of the previous year was gone. Troublesome times would begin. Dave's tenure at Eureka College, on the whole, was most pleasant. However, troubling events and situations began to take a toll. Everyone experiences ups and downs in their employment duration. This year Darnall was going to get his share. Some issues just kept resurfacing as they did throughout his tenure, but others were new.

As the old saying goes, "You have to take the bad with the good." Coach Darnall understood this reality. There are two sides to the coin. Along with the great times, the "troublesome times" seemed to creep in. Who lived in a perfect world? Not Darnall. It would be untruthful to say everything was good and went smoothly during his years at Eureka College. Some incidents were directed at and solely affected the Coach, but the calamity that befell the 1988-1989 team affected many. Quoting the title of Bobby Knight's famous book, *Season on the Brink*, could describe the catastrophic season Dave Darnall calls his "disaster season."

Some coaches, going from a number one team in the state to the last, would have looked for "greener pastures" when they could. Darnall, however as he did throughout his entire coaching career, enjoyed the challenge of taking a losing team and moving it to the top—a state title or a national championship.

On several occasions Darnall had stated, "There is no one that has more Eureka College blood running through his veins than I except for George Hearne." Ever since his brother enrolled in Eureka College followed by his nephews, niece, and former Momence players, as well as his own employment, Dave felt a sincere love and devotion to the college. Yet even with the love, dedication, and family ties to Eureka College, there were times he felt betrayed and threatened. He felt, at times, there were a few members of the college community attempting to make his job more difficult or, perhaps, attempting to obliterate his employment.

Darnall realistically knew that most working people felt some frustration in their working surroundings. But for Dave, who was always somewhat paranoid and sensitive, these situations were extremely difficult to handle. A very conscientious person, trying times made an impact on Darnall. Not that he should agree with all decisions that pertained to him, but he did feel honesty, integrity, and fairness should be considered. These were questioned at times. Also, there were times when Coach Darnall felt that an extremely successful basketball program was not to the liking of a few on campus who felt there was an over emphasis on a particular athletic program or head coach rather than the academic world. Darnall responded to this thinking by saying, "I personally feel both are extremely important. Athletic success and a good education should go hand in hand. That is what I have striven for at Eureka College. To my knowledge, there have only been three or four basketball players who were in the program for four years that did not graduate. Those fellows were only a few hours short and found good employments before receiving their degrees.

In addition, alcohol-related events, scheduling of games, class load, scheduling of classes, changes in teaching assignments without consultation, and differences of opinion regarding Darnall's on-court demeanor were constantly surfacing.

Sometime in the late 1970s, a policy was established that alcohol—beer and wine—could be served on campus. This was mainly due to the reduction in the drinking age from twenty-one to nineteen years old by the State of Illinois. Prior to that, alcohol had been prohibited on campus. In fact, the use of alcohol was so frowned upon that Coach Darnall had gotten a memo from President Ira Langston in February 1976, indicating that he had received a rather strong protest regarding an ad for beer appearing in the basketball program. He instructed his coach that "until a decision is made to allow for advertisement of alcohol beverages in the college's publications, please see that no more will be run." Coach Darnall, who had high respect for President Langston, understood the situation. There may be financial contributors to the college that would be hesitant to donate to the Christian school for advertising alcohol.

Then in June of the same year, President Langston rescinded his request and permitted the advertisement. Even though Dave then had permission to go ahead and use the ad, he knew it was best for both the college and President Langston to eventually have it replaced. The ad last appeared in the 1978-1979 Basketball program.

By the action of the Board of Trustees in a meeting held in late September of 1979, the alcohol policy was rescinded to become effective January 1, 1980. This was in response to the state law raising the drinking age back from nineteen back to twenty-one. For several years, there was confusion because of the change in policy and philosophy

Darnall had this to say of Dr. Langston. "What a pleasure it was to work for him. He appreciated my efforts without a hassle. I never felt 'under the gun' or that I always had to defend what I was doing. He understood the purpose of athletics and wasn't afraid to defend its importance. I had no idea how much I would miss his leadership over the next few years." President Langston retired at the conclusion of the 1976-1977 school year. A real loss!

In some small colleges, athletic assistants are either part time or assigned to areas outside of athletics. This was true in basketball as well as football. In 1983, a young man was hired to be an assistant football coach and assigned other responsibilities in the Dean of Student Development Office. From the start, Dave felt the young coach was extremely cocky and did not really understand the concept of Eureka College. He came from out of state and did not have the loyalty to Eureka College that others did. The coaching staff and a few fans usually got together after football games to rehash the day's events. Beverages including beer, wine, and soda, along with hors d'oeuvres, were usually served. This particular post-game party was held at an assistant football coach's house. Darnall, even though no longer coaching football, and the assistant basketball coaches were invited as were the football coaches to Darnall's house after basketball games. The group was in an outdoor surrounding having conversation. The issue of recruiting and the make-up of the college student body were being discussed. The young coach from out of state made the statement, "The only students that go to Eureka College are the ones that can't go anywhere else."

Coach Darnall in defending the college replied, "That's not true. I have a nephew who is a top student in the science area, and he could have gone anywhere he wanted."

Dave had spent many hours selling Eureka College to young people as well as having quite a few members of his own family attend. His understanding and view of the college was quite different from what the staff member/assistant football coach had just indicated. "If you believe in what you are saying, maybe you should find somewhere else to work," Dave defended.

POP! The young man when challenged suddenly reached across a table and struck Darnall in the face. Dave went to his knees. The trainer and the host ran to his side. The bleeding Darnall was stunned. Blood flowed from his nose and a small cut above the eye.

"That's it; the party's over!" the host shouted. "Out of here," he ordered the aggressor. The other guests also obeyed the request of the property owner. Darnall was escorted to the house by the trainer who secured cold, wet towels for his bruised and bloody face. The Darnalls also left for home after the first aid was administered. The sore coach went to bed. Two days later Dave taught his class with sunglasses covering the swollen eye. Embarrassed, he told his students that he had been involved in a little accident.

In a memo to the faculty dated September 19, 1983, the college president addressed the incident to the college community. Parts of the memo read, "Recently there was an extremely unfortunate episode involving two members of the campus community which has received wide-spread attention and discussion among students, faculty, and staff." The memo went on to read, "It is important that all members of the community be concerned over the incident, and that everyone known received our immediate and thorough attention. It is also important that I re-affirm that Eureka College does not condone and will not accept action of physical abuse on the part of any member of the campus community."

Dave had never been in any altercation where someone got hit since his childhood. He had never hit anyone and avoided any situation where that sort of conduct occurred. The blow to his face was a complete surprise as well as being very embarrassing. Darnall never really knew what the end result of the episode was. The young coach remained on the staff but did not return to Eureka College the following year.

A couple weeks later, Dave received a memo from the Student Development Office. This troubled him. Darnall definitely did not want to become involved in anymore controversies following the recent incident. The memo chastised him for not intervening with visiting adult football fans that were evidently conducting a "tailgate" party in a parking lot across from the football field. Darnall responded that he had recently defended the college in one situation and was reluctant to become involved in a public situation. In addition, there were other college personnel also aware of the situation, including the writer of the memo, who did not take the initiative to approach the group. Did they receive a memo also? Why were he and his assistant singled out for no action? There was no further correspondence between the Student Development Office and Coach Darnall. It was presumed that the administration understood Dave's position.

One troublesome issue constantly surfaced throughout Darnall's tenure. That was the scheduling of basketball games. Dave continuously attempted to explain the difficulties; it had been to no avail to some. It was not until his last few years that most administrators finally understood the laborious task of scheduling some schools.

The coaches did their own scheduling of games in each sport. In many colleges, this responsibility lay with the Athletic Director. Over the years, most of Eureka's coaches preferred to take care of scheduling themselves. If the coaches had trouble filling their respective schedules, they would ask for assistance from the Athletic Director.

The first year or two following Darnall's arrival, filling the game schedule was no problem. As a matter of fact, coaches from many institutions were calling him for games. That changed after his second year. Darnall now had to become the initiator. He received very few phone calls requesting a "home and home" series. Dave was continually asked questions about his basketball scheduling by some members of the administration after the 1976-1977 season. The number one question was why he did not schedule certain schools and why he did schedule others. That issue was extremely stressful and frustrating for Darnall. The coaches from neighboring colleges, who refused to schedule Eureka, certainly caused him distress.

One of the first correspondences regarding this issue was sent by the Dean of Student Development. The letter was dated September 14, 1978. It read:

> I have just received our '78-79 basketball schedule. Dave, we need to take a hard look at where we are going with our basketball scheduling philosophy. Basically, I have very little to say in the negative sense about our other sports schedules. However, our basketball schedule is a bit "bush."
>
> We must work to re-establish or establish home and away relationships with Knox, Monmouth, Illinois College, Wesleyan, Blackburn, Culver-Stockton, etc. We are not going to gain anything of value out of relationships with Harris-Stowe, Trinity, MSOE, St. Louis Pharmacy, Missouri Baptist, etc.
>
> I trust you and the Athletic Director could give this top priority as you two get together to develop the '79-80 budget. It's crucial that Eureka align itself athletically with good academic schools. Generally it is safe to say that those schools with good academic programs are going to challenge us athletically as well.

The "academic" issue was quickly noted.

"To my knowledge, I never refused to schedule a game with any school of our stature throughout my tenure," Darnall said. "I don't remember turning down any institution that would play us on a home and home basis. Our schedule was usually dictated by who would play us. Look at the large institutions such as Southern Illinois-Edwardsville, University of Missouri-St. Louis, Northeastern Illinois, Northeast Missouri State, University of Illinois-Chicago, University of Chicago, and the University of Wisconsin-Milwaukee that we did play. Most of these colleges would not play here; just at their places or in a tournament. Yet, we played them because they were excellent schools, and they would play us.

Coach Darnall received a letter from the Dean of Faculty's Office February 25, 1980, concerning the reason why the Red Devils did not make the 1979-1980 State Playoffs in spite of an outstanding 21 to 5 record. The implication of the letter was that it was due to the image of the opponents. That was brought about because of a comment that appeared in a local newspaper made by an Illinois Wesleyan personnel regarding the Red Devil schedule. The memorandum to Darnall was as follows:

> I read with interest your comments as reported in this morning's *Pantagraph*. I know it was disappointing to you not to receive an invitation to the district playoffs, but I don't believe the selection process is as mysterious as you suggested.
>
> I am convinced that our schedule is the basic problem we confront. No matter what our win-loss record is, we will not get into the playoffs with any regularity if we continue to schedule as many low quality teams as we have in the recent past . . .

Darnall responded to the letter from the Dean's Office by sending the dean a couple documents from outside sources in support that Eureka College should have been selected to the tournament field but was omitted because of politics, not having the "clout" that some of the larger colleges had. The first was the following letter from Jack Trager, Head Basketball Coach at Greenville College:

> Dear Dave:
>
> I want to express my concern to you in regard to your 1979-80 basketball team not getting a bid to the District 20 Playoffs. Your schedule was strong enough to warrant a playoff spot. When a team has a 20 - 5 record on any schedule, they should be given more credit and attention than your team was given Sunday.
>
> Past history has shown the present selection system is not good. It is time for a change. I have recommended to Rich Swanson, District Basketball Committee Chairman, that we look seriously at a point formula that several districts have gone to and are happy with.
>
> The present system has built in bias like, conference schools vs. independents, southern schools vs. northern schools, as well as various personality dislikes. This cannot continue to jeopardize the ball players.
>
> I truly am sorry for you and your team. You definitely deserved a spot in this year's playoffs.

The second support came in the form of portions of an article ran by Chuck Brady in the *Quincy Herald-Whig*. The article quoted Sherrill Hanks, Head Basketball Coach of Quincy College. Darnall felt, year in and year out, Hank's program at Quincy was the best NAIA program in the state.

"Four of the five members of the selection committee were from the Chicago area; so you can picture what chance we had," said Hanks of the Hawks' hopes for the top seeding . . .

Hanks thought another slight of a downstate team was the group's failure to select Eureka College as one of the six playoff teams. Eureka has one of the best records in the District, including wins over a number of larger schools.

Illinois Benedictine, which lost twice to Aurora in conference games, edged Eureka when it came down to the final choice.

Coach Darnall had received a letter February 28th from the former Dean of Faculty under the administration that had hired him. It was the contents of this letter that Darnall tried to keep in mind during the time he was constantly badgered about scheduling from the second administration. The personal, handwritten note read:

Dear Dave,

Congratulations to you, your staff and all members of your basketball team for another excellent basketball season. I am aware of your disappointment in not being selected for post-season play. I share this disappointment with you.

Your reaction and comments to the press were most commendable.

Your satisfaction, however, with the effort of the team members and the growth they have shown is, undoubtedly, the most important thing anyway. I'm sure all will have good memories of the season.

I want you to know how much all of us appreciate your hard work and the excellent results you achieve. It should be a great source of satisfaction for you.

Have a good recruiting season now. Thanks for everything you do.

In contrast, on March 12, 1980, Darnall received another letter from the current Dean of Faculty regarding the over-all basketball program. Several issues were covered including assistant coaches, transportation, publicity including radio coverage, recruiting, and scheduling. One paragraph was most disturbing:

I think we need to continue to explore the question of the scheduling. . . . The President and I both feel that it is not so important to consider the type of teams we play, how strong they may be, or how good they may be, as it is to consider the kind of schools we schedule to play. We want to schedule schools that are strong, healthy, and have the kind of reputation that we cherish for ourselves. I think in the long run this will strengthen not only your basketball program but the college as a whole.

"We had just been denied a playoff berth because some felt our schedule was not strong enough, and now we weren't to be concerned about the 'type of teams we played, how strong they may be, or how good they may be;' just 'the kind of school' they were?" questioned Darnall.

Coach Darnall and the athletic director continued to work on "the schedules," and Dave hoped that the scheduling problems would cease. For a few years, this seemed to be the case. Then another memorandum! It popped up just prior to the opening of the best basketball season in the history of the college and its first NAIA National Tournament appearance. Coach Darnall and the new athletic director received a memo in September of 1987 from a new Dean of Faculty regarding why Eureka College did not schedule nearby NCAA III institutions, Monmouth College and Knox College. It was starting over again.

The Eureka College athletic director sent a letter to the athletic directors of both Monmouth and Knox requesting the institutions renew the rivalry the colleges once had. The requests were denied. The dean was informed of the correspondence. For whatever reasons, the coaches at the two colleges just refused to play Eureka at that time in men's basketball. Darnall believed he had not refused to play any opponent regardless of the enrollment of the institution; the level of competition, whether NCAA or NAIA affiliated; whether the school offered full-ride athletic scholarships, partial athletic aid, or no athletic aid; or what the team's previous season record was as long as they would play home and home or offered a guarantee.

Dave had even contacted several NCAA I institutions in the early 1990s to schedule games. Sometimes those institutions would schedule an early season game against opponents that were not a NCAA I school. Dave had conversation with Valparaiso, Indiana State, Southern Illinois, and Western Illinois as well as others for possible contests. Even though at that time those schools did schedule games of that sort, Eureka was unable to obtain one for their schedule.

Darnall's former player, Mark Scherer, had been a grad assistant coach at Western Illinois before moving on to becoming an assistant coach at Valparaiso and is currently Head Basketball Coach at Elmhurst College. He indicated to Darnall that Eureka College would not be a good opponent for a NCAA I institution. Most small schools just play the game, get their guarantee, and go home, but not Darnall. He played to win.

Toward the end of Coach Darnall's tenure, Eureka College made inquiries and even applied to several athletic conferences for admittance.

Those conferences were the CCIW, SLIAC, Mid-West Conference, and the Northern Illinois Intercollegiate Conference. There was no chance for admittance to the CCIW. Both the Mid-West Conference and the SLIAC Conference were not interested in Eureka College's participation.

"Monmouth, Knox, Illinois Wesleyan, Illinois College, Blackburn, Maryville, MacMurray, and Principia, schools belonging to three of those conferences, were not scheduling us before, so why should they want us in their conference?" Darnall asked. "They are institutions we should be playing, both because of the level of competition and their proximity."

If one would look back to the 13 NAIA District (State) appearances and the four National Tournament appearances that Eureka participated in during Darnall's tenure, it would be found that Eureka was almost always the smallest institution in enrollment and normally one of a very few that did not give some type of athletic aid. They were also probably the only institution that was a member of both national affiliations—the NCAA and the NAIA. That meant Eureka College had to follow the strictest rules of each association.

Why wouldn't several of the similar institutions as Eureka College within the radius of 150 miles not schedule Eureka in men's basketball? Dave Darnall attempted to answer this question hundreds of times over his tenure.

"There are several reasons the way I see it," Dave said. "Teams did not want to get beat by a school enrollmentwise smaller than they were; coaches didn't like my competitiveness and demeanor; they didn't like the way I 'played' the Dunkel Rating System; coaches felt Eureka had too much of a home-court advantage with our excellent fan support; some schools thought we gave athletic aid because of the quality of players I was able to recruit year after year; a few colleges felt they had nothing to gain and everything to lose; since a lot of schools recruited the same players I did, they didn't want to play against the players I got and they didn't; some coaches felt they would have a better chance of winning against schools located closer to them; and lastly, some college coaches just didn't like me," Darnall concluded.

"I have attempted to relate this message for years to different members of the administrations I have worked under. However, some just could not understand," Dave said. "I do feel, however, that George Hearne knew the reasons why we had difficulties scheduling with some area institutions."

In 1996, Eureka College gained membership in the revamped Northern Illinois Intercollegiate Conference. With the addition of Clark College of Iowa and Eureka College to charter members Aurora University, Benedictine University, Concordia University, and Rockford College, the conference was renamed the Northern Illinois-Iowa Conference. Dominican University later joined the conference.

"That was a good move on Eureka's part," Darnall said. "The institutions we are now affiliated with are of high academic quality and are very competitive athletically. They have the same philosophy as Eureka College." Knox College and Blackburn were also added to the Eureka College basketball schedule after Darnall's tenure.

Between 1979 and 1985, Coach Darnall received several handwritten notes regarding various topics pertaining to him from the then president of the college. Even though Dave did receive several notes of appreciation and encouragement, others were especially troubling.

One such letter was especially grueling. The note followed a sequence of two games. The first was the Red Devil's home loss to Washington University of St. Louis, which was a big no-no if they were to gain post-season play. They had to win the next game at home. Also, the Dunkel Rating System was in effect, and the point spread was influential. The next opponent was George Williams. It was a must win game!

To understand how the note related to the George Williams game, portions of an article by Randy Kindred of *The Pantagraph* must be reviewed:

> Adrenaline flows one way in Dave Darnall's body—constantly.
>
> And although his Eureka College basketball players may not have realized it, they benefited from Darnall's unlimited energy source here last night in a 72 - 48 nonconference victory over George Williams College.
>
> The Red Devils, a talented but reserved group which possesses the demeanor of Secret Service agents, decided to relax a bit after building a 50 - 23 lead with 13 minutes, 27 seconds to play at Reagan Center.
>
> Just as that happened, George Williams put together its only positive stretch of the night and whittled Eureka College's 27-point lead to 17 (52 - 35) in just less than four minutes.
>
> It was then, with 9:40 remaining, that Darnall called a timeout and delivered a fiery, inspirational message to his squad. The Red Devils responded by scoring nine straight points to break the contest open for good.
>
> "We've got a great group of guys, but they're non-emotional type players." said Darnall . . . "Sometimes they don't get themselves motivated like they should. When the momentum starts changing and they get complacent, the coaching staff has to stir them up a little and that's what I did. It was an excellent timeout for us."

The president obviously disagreed with the way Darnall handled his players. He felt Dave was extremely hard on players, including dishing out verbal abuse. He also did not approve of Darnall's conduct on the floor, which included mannerisms and floor demeanor. He always found ways to let Dave know. Was it a true personality conflict, some kind of power struggle, or was he doing his job? In any case, his hotly penned note read in part:

> Dear Dave,
> After watching your tirade last night at the time out in the second half with our team ahead by 17 points, I decided that just had to share with you privately my personal disgust with that coaching technique. I don't agree with yours and Dick's (a nearby Division I coach) "publicly humiliate them than hug 'em" style of coaching. And I don't agree with *The Pantagraph* reporter's characterization of that being "inspirational" and your calling it a "good time out." Not only did the players you were "chewing out" have their heads down in embarrassment, but a lot of fans felt the same way. Hooray for the nine straight points afterwards. It didn't impress me . . .

The note was received with as much disgust as it had been written. Darnall knew the relationship he had always established with his players transcended the coaching "tirades" as they had been called. He resented the private "tongue lashing" and suspected it may not be the last as he was not one to change, especially in his own domain. He was right.

One especially chastising note came after a newspaper article appeared regarding Eureka College and Ronald Reagan's contributions to the college. The president felt the article had given misinformation, and somehow Dave was responsible. He instructed, "Obviously now, please don't try to correct this with the author, just be sure you know the facts." But several sentences later, he followed with, "I have no intention of 'fussing' at you about this misinformation. I am assuming you didn't tell _____."

Dave may have been overly sensitive, but then what was the real purpose of the note?

Another note came with some words of praise, but the final paragraph let Dave know of the president's continued awareness of his coaching style and manner. It read in part:

> Dear Dave,
> Since I have told you from time to time about my disagreements with your coaching style and other things, I thought I should also tell when I appreciate things you do . . .

I wish I had dealt more directly with you early in these areas I had trouble with, but it seemed to bother you so much.

Darnall disagreed greatly with the president's interpretation of his style, mannerisms, and behavior, especially toward his players. However, he did admit that on occasion he may have "gone overboard" but felt it was needed to change the way things were happening. "Do you think that NCAA I coaches who yell at their players don't care about them? You've got to be kidding. They care a great deal. Just because they expect precise execution and yell at them during games doesn't mean they don't care. They expect perfection. So do I."

"Not everyone could play under me. But if they can stick it out, I'll guarantee you, they'll be a 'winner,'" emphasized Darnall.

"I spend a lot of time with my players both on and off the floor," Dave insisted. "I have an open-door policy at school and at my home. If anyone who questions my relationship with my players would come over after a game or to one of the post-season potlucks, they could see the relationship my family and I have tried to establish with them and their parents."

Troy Tyler commented on these, "One thing special about Eureka College basketball was the social occasions associated with it. Annually, Coach Darnall had his basketball picnic. It was during the spring, and it gave us a time to reflect on the previous year and set goals for the upcoming year. It was also a time of camaraderie and companionship, not to mention some very good food."

Tim McGuire, Darnall's very first recruit, expressed his gratitude, "I think the only person that ever made more meals for us players than Bonnie, were our mothers. How she put up with Coach for all those years is beyond me. It was great having someplace to go that seemed like our own homes. We all are forever indebted for all the hospitality shown to us by both Bonnie and Dave."

Tom Cassidy gave a very personal recollection of how Darnall's caring affected him and his family. He related that he had some great memories of his days as a player at Eureka College and of the teammates he had, but the invitation his parents received to attend the "roast" of Coach Darnall as he was retiring from coaching was especially touching.

"My father was very ill and in the early part of 1994 and was bedridden most of the day. He was weak and did not have much energy to even move around the house. My mother had mentioned to me that they had also received an invitation from Coach Darnall to the roast and that my little brother Jeff, who also graduated from Eureka College, was going to be a speaker at the roast. I asked my mom if she and dad wanted to go, and she replied, 'It would be a lot of fun but I don't think your father is well enough to make the trip but I'll ask him.' My father and Coach Darnall had built a solid and respectful relationship over the years and my father wanted very badly to attend the roast."

He continued, "As I mentioned previously, my father was very ill and extremely weak. His recovery from the day he decided to go to Coach Darnall's roast to the day of the roast was remarkable. My father was able to endure the ride to Eureka, Illinois, and he

Bonnie preparing a snack for Red Devil players after a holiday vacation practice.

was very excited about being present for Coach Darnall's evening. I truly believe that the recovery of my father was due to his wanting to be present at the honoring and recognition of achievements for Coach Darnall and show Coach how much he respected him and appreciated him for helping his two sons during their tenure at Eureka College."

Later, Darnall received a last note from the same president, then an administrator at another institution, regarding the National Championship. "I will have to admit that I was shocked when I received a congratulatory letter for the National Championship. I respect him for acknowledging the accomplishments of the players and coaching staff," Darnall said. "Even though we viewed many things differently, hopefully he saw that my goal was to help Eureka College basketball gain the respect it deserved.

At one time in the early 1980s, Dave did feel it was possibly time for him to move on because of the differences in opinions regarding his coaching philosophy and style. He interviewed for the head coaching position at the University of Illinois-Chicago. Bonnie and he visited the campus but believed Eureka was still the place for them and their family to be. He withdrew from the candidacy.

At the time, he had asked the director of admissions to write a letter of recommendation for him. Dave felt the letter proved that he really cared about Eureka College and the student-athletes he recruited. One paragraph stated, "Dave Darnall has impressed me with his desire to do his very best for Eureka College and its students. I have felt this about Dave since I first met him and I feel even more strongly about it now."

"If I were only looking out for myself, I would have left Eureka College for a more prestigious or higher paying position years ago. I loved Eureka College, and I enjoyed being with the type of guys I recruited, so I stayed," Darnall said.

Brad Bickett later gave support to Dave's commitment to his players with this comment, "I just want to thank Dave for giving me the opportunity to be a successful player and for giving me the opportunity to graduate from Eureka College. He has supported me now that I have gotten out into the coaching and teaching field. My kids still go to basketball camp down at Eureka College. I want my kids to hear Dave Darnall speak. I want them to see the type of basketball program he has run. It was just a great career for me, and I look back, and if I had to do things over again, I wouldn't change anything a bit. I would still want to play for Dave Darnall and remember that Together We Win. Thanks a lot, Dave."

Teaching "load" was a factor that became extremely stressful for Darnall. That particular issue probably disturbed him, personally, more than any other single issue. Besides game scheduling, it seemed to be an issue that was always causing turmoil throughout much of his tenure. For Darnall, who had other duties and responsibilities of coaching and recruiting, the scheduling of classes, class load, and the specific classes to be taught were major problems.

"I'll tell you one thing," said Darnall, "if all I had to do was coach one or two sports and recruit for those sports like a couple of our past football coaches, I might still be coaching today. However, I just wore out. That, along with some small health problems, was my incentive to retire early."

To understand the dilemma Darnall felt with the teaching load issue, it is necessary to explain the teaching credit hour system at Eureka College. A full teaching load was between twenty-four and twenty-six hours per school year. Eureka College was on a four, eight-week-term school year, called the "Intensive Study Program." Darnall loved this system as it allowed his student-athletes to concentrate on only two or three, maybe four, courses per term. Physical education teachers received half-hour credit for each activity course taught. The number assigned to coaches was based upon the length of the season. If the season spanned sixteen weeks as in basketball, the coach was given eight hours of teaching credit. In Darnall's case, this was one-third of his teaching load.

Changes causing a great deal of frustration were either proposed or made to Darnall's teaching responsibilities in 1987, 1990, and 1992. He was not one for change in any venue, but hated it in his teaching area. Dave prepared for his classes thoroughly. He viewed some of the changes as unreasonable and resulted in constant re-preparing for new classes.

The first, in 1987, began with a memo from the Dean of Faculty to the Chairperson of the Athletic Committee regarding the amount of teaching credit for the Director of Intramurals, a position Darnall had held for thirteen years. The Director was given one credit for each of the four terms, equaling four hours for the school year. The students received one-half credit hour per term, equaling two for the school year. In general, the memo suggested that Darnall's credit for directing intramurals be reduced to two hours, the same as the students', and at mid-year no less. Dave protested the proposed change. First, he felt the students should receive four credit hours for the course that spanned the entire year. Second, it would mean he would have to teach an additional class to maintain full-faculty status. Dr. West intervened. The dean agreed tentatively to let the intramural issue remain the same. It was also during this time that the Student Development Office was lobbying to oversee the intramural program. This didn't make sense to Darnall as intramurals were the "middle phase" of the total physical education triangle. First is the physical education classes for everyone; next is the intramural program for those with an extended interest in a particular activity; and finally, interscholastic athletics for the more highly skilled.

This seemed the beginning of others being concerned over Darnall's teaching load. His feeling was that as long as he fulfilled the duties he had been hired to do, it was no one else's concern.

Then in late 1988, the Dean of Faculty requested Dr. West and Coach Darnall explain why two hours of credit was being given to Dave for supervising students enrolled in three two-hour camp classes and for administration of the basketball camps. Again, the man had no real concept of what was involved in these duties. The classes were official college courses, one of which was required for a major in Physical Education—Fitness Leadership. Darnall's explanation was to no avail. He lost his two hours of credit. This opened the door for more teaching responsibilities to be assigned to him.

"That's all I need," Dave said, "as if I don't already have enough to do. Credit or no credit, the camps benefit this college tremendously and take a lot of my time. Even though I am compensated for directing the camps, I am not for the three courses. Other summer course instructors are paid for teaching their classes. I did expected to receive credit hours for the effort instead of pay."

Shortly after, Dave heard an administrative comment had been made that he was not "carrying his load." Darnall was furious! He fired a memo to the dean. Portions read:

> I have never complained before regarding my recruiting hours while working hard and long both on campus and traveling throughout the state for this college. However, the determination of my "work load" has now made me keenly aware of the time spent in this area with no 'credit.' This now is a major concern.
>
> I would like to share with you my Monday of April 25, 1988. From 9:00 - 10:00 AM, I taught a class. From 10:00 - 10:30 A.M., I did a current student's class schedule. I was with a recruit from 10:30 A.M. to approximately 2:00 P.M. From 2:30 - 3:15 P.M., I did another student's schedule. I then dashed home, changed clothes, and left my house by 3:30 P.M. for a recruiting visit. I arrived at the recruit's home at 6:30 P.M. and talked with the recruit and his parents until 9:00 P.M. I left his home at 9:00 P.M. with the recruit still unsigned. I had driven 10 miles when I was chased down by the father and recruit. He signed along the road. I returned to their home to call two newspapers, and again left their home at 10:00 P.M. I drove until 11:45 P.M. and then stopped to eat supper. I arrived home at approximately 1:15 A.M. Do you know what I received as credit hours for the 15+ hours of work for Eureka College? A one-half hour for teaching the activity class at 9:00 A.M.!

The next shock came when Dave looked over the new schedule for the 1988-1989 school year. To his amazement, he noticed that three activity classes had been added to his teaching load for the second semester since the original class schedule had been produced. When he voiced his dismay to another physical education teacher, she explained that she or another faculty member had originally been scheduled to teach the classes but that she had been informed they were given to Dave to meet his "load limit."

These were not only added without Dave's knowledge, but also without the knowledge of the Education Department Chairman. It was a good thing Dave had taken a look at the revised schedule!

In a response from the Dean of Faculty, it was admitted that Dave did have a teaching load of 27.5 credit hours. This was in direct violation of the *Faculty Handbook*, which stated a member should carry between twenty-four and twenty-six hours. This rest of the dean's explanation of the added classes was unsatisfactory to Darnall. In desperation he finally contacted the president. The result was an additional memo from the dean suggesting that the two of them meet after graduation to discuss adjustments to Dave's schedule. It was a welcome suggestion to Darnall, but why did it take the president to intervene to solve the problem?

Classes and schedules remained steady for the next two years, and then another controversy arose. This time regarding the number of days and time of day that a certain class was taught. The "Methods of Teaching Physical Education" had been taught three days a week—for two hours on two days and one hour on the third. It had been that way for years even by the retiring Leo Traister, whom Darnall replaced as teacher.

Prior to the construction of the next year's class schedules, the various department chairs and members of their departments would meet to establish what courses would be taught by whom and make suggestions as to the time and meeting days of the class. This was the procedure Darnall and his department had followed. The three days a week and time remained consistent. It was one that had worked well for both Traister and Darnall in their coaching and recruiting schedules. However, the suggestion was not followed, and the class was changed to five days a week to meet the needs of one transfer student who had a conflict with the previous schedule. The student's advisor within the Physical Education Department had initiated the change. The mastermind of the college's overall class schedules was the Assistant Dean of Records. Darnall felt that the impact or burden on the current teacher and the other students taking the class had not been considered, and this troubled him. Most of the other students' schedules had been planned well in advance; actually since being freshmen, so as to work in all of the required classes. It should be realized that any time a transfer student enters, a scheduling problem can exist.

Finally, a meeting was held with the Assistant Dean of Records, the Chairman of the Education Department, and Professor Darnall. In a memo following that meeting, the Assistant Dean of Records summarized several points from each side. He indicated that he accepted the decision of the Division to confirm the schedule as it was originally presented. He stated that he was not interested in any rationale but only with the decision, as he had no authority to participate in faculty matters. However, he did present his rationale for the proposed change in response to Darnall's rationale of why the class scheduling should not be changed. He then conceded, "In any case, the Division decided to recommend no change in the schedule. The issue is, regardless of what weekly schedule was adopted, there was at least one student who would have had a conflict. At this point, the Division seemed to favor no schedule change because only one student's involved. The decision seems to be more a result of coalition of persons who agree on a wide variety of reasons rather than one which asserts support for the EDU 423 schedule."

The statements were becoming more pointed and personal rather than objective. It was an issue Darnall wanted to see resolved; of course, to his reasoning. His final rationale was that the schedule conflicts had also occurred the previous year and that the schedule was adjusted. He argued that it should not be changed again because it did not allow for continuity and planning to take place.

The meeting concluded with an understanding that the Division had not authorized the Assistant Dean of Records to change the schedule for EDU 423.

Darnall, taking the dean at his word, thought the issue was dead. How wrong he was!

Two weeks before the first basketball camp, Coach was preparing for 900 campers and another ninety coaches on his camp staff. Darnall was shocked when the Education Division Faculty received a memo from the Assistant Dean of Records. In it, the Assistant Dean reversed his decision using the excuse that it was apparent that the Division had not agreed upon an advisory plan scheme for the majors in physical education with teaching certification. He noted that the eight students enrolled in the course had eight different schedules. As long as there was such a diversity of students enrolling in EDU 423, there was going to be a scheduling problem with the course. He concluded that as this had happened for each of the past two years, it would most likely continue to occur until the advisory problem was solved.

That was exactly what Darnall had been professing. "The schedule got changed last year. If it hadn't, there would not have been a conflict this year if proper planning by the student and advisor had been done. Changing again this year will give more conflict. It is not the students who started here as freshmen who are having conflicts. They did plan ahead. It is the one transfer student now that is causing conflicts for the students who have planned."

Dave became more and more agitated. He called Bonnie at her school to vent. "Bonnie, I received a memo saying they are going to change my Methods class. I am really 'pissed-off.' I just don't understand," Dave said. "He (Assistant Dean of Records) said he was not going to make a decision and asked the Department to make the decision. That decision was made with the agreement of the department chairman, PE coordinator, and teacher of the class, and all members but one. So why did he then take it upon himself to reverse the decision?" Dave asked. Dave just couldn't work this through!

"I don't know, but I understand your frustration," Bonnie said, trying to comfort him. "We'll decide what to do when I get home. I don't understand why you always have to go through these things." She was as frustrated and bewildered at times as Dave.

While all this turmoil was going on, Dave was working hard on finalizing his recruiting and preparing for his three basketball camps. He was becoming totally emotionally drained and physically exhausted.

Dave still could not reconcile himself to the Assistant Dean of Records' decision, and it continually troubled him. He finally decided he had to request a meeting with the Dean of Faculty. Not surprising, the meeting left Dave still unsatisfied. He then followed up the meeting with his own memo to the Dean of Faculty and copies to the chairman of the Education Department, the college president, Professor Emeritus Leo Traister, athletic director, and the women's athletic coordinator. The memo expressed his extreme offense to the decision reversal by the Assistant Dean of Records without the Division's approval and consequent knowledge. The problem was becoming "major" in the eyes of the Coach.

Six days later Dave began a long week of his first boys' camp of nearly 300 campers and thirty-five adult coaches. As usual, both the days and nights were long. Sleep was minimal. The two demanding weeks of boys' camps was followed by the one week of girls' camp. It was during the orientation speech on Sunday, June 24, 1991, that Dave felt a sharp pain in his chest and was extremely dizzy. He immediately stepped back from the podium and sat down. Coach Dighton responded quickly to finish the speech. Dave went home to rest, not recognizing the symptoms for what they were. He came back to campus again that evening around 9:00 P.M. to perform his usual nightly duties. Upon returning home about 12:00 A.M., he went directly to bed. He returned to campus the next morning to have it all happen again. How were these symptoms not recognized before? Denial! Not me! Dave was hospitalized in Peoria with a heart attack. He spent a week in the cardiac unit, missing the entire week of girls' camp, only one of two times he was away from campus during camps. The diagnosis was: one and possibly two attacks, but luckily no damage had been done and no blockage was detected. It was strictly stress related. Wonder what stress Darnall had!

It was during his stay in the hospital that Dave began to wonder if it was all worth it. For sixteen years he had dedicated himself to the college and his teams only to feel that his efforts were unappreciated by some in the administrative circle. Could he just be feeling sorry for himself?

It was also during this time, either while Dave was in the hospital or shortly after his release, that a decision was made not to change the original class schedule for the "Methods" class. To appease the conflict of the transfer student, she was allowed to do an independent study. How easily this could have been determined in the first place!

Dave prayed that the teaching load and class scheduling conflicts were behind him once and for all. The "good" lasted another two years before another major conflict erupted. This time Dr. West, Dave's former Department Chair, was not by his side. He had retired. The new Department Chair was one of his colleagues from the Physical Education Department. It seemed every two years a problem arose with his teaching schedule. It was during this most recent controversy that Dave seriously began to consider getting out of coaching. It was getting too difficult to always have to defend his workload. Darnall wanted to avoid another heart attack.

Dave's father had his first heart attack around the same time of year and at the same age as Dave. Cardiologists talk about the heredity factor. The elder Darnall had his second heart attack seven years after the first and passed away. This timing troubled Dave immensely. Would the saying, "Like father, like son," hold true?

Dave's personal conflicts were soon compounded with those of some of his players. Prior to the opening of the 1987-1988 basketball season, a tragic incident took place involving a girl and several guys. This occurred both on and off campus. It had a tremendous impact upon the basketball season. It also caused a great deal of controversy and turmoil on campus.

There were approximately eight male students embroiled in the incident. Several participated in the basketball program. Ramifications of the incident led to a full law-enforcement investigation. The case was taken to a Grand Jury but no charges were forthcoming.

However, the college gave the students involved the option to withdraw or face disciplinary action. Half of the students chose to leave school while the others decided to plead their case before the Disciplinary Board. The Dean of Students and Dean of Faculty presented the college's view. The students were allowed to have a representative from the faculty. Several of the students requested a local lawyer, who was also on faculty teaching a business law course, to be at the hearing with them. Another asked his faculty advisor to accompany him. The students were also allowed to have character witnesses as well as their parents and family present throughout the hearings. The process took several intense days.

The Dean of Students was a young man who had graduated from and had played football at Eureka College. Darnall knew him well. At one point in an informal setting, Dave and the dean had some brief discussion of the unfortunate incident. Each shared some personal opinions about the situation. To Darnall, it was just two colleagues chatting.

However, shortly thereafter, Dave received a memo from the Dean of Faculty chastising him for his opinions of the disciplinary investigation indicating he was using "political pressure or lobbying" and was not in charge of the investigation. His suggestion was for Darnall to "actively educate the habits and character of your students and players."

The memo totally caught Darnall off-guard. He had not thought the informal conversation had been interfering with any procedure or unduly influencing. As far as educating his students and players in matters of morality and character, it was an ongoing process.

"It bothered me to think that the dean would think that I didn't talk to my players about morality and character. In fact, just a couple days prior to the whole incident in a team meeting I discussed behavior along with grades, training rules, and conditioning."

"It is like telling your own children to do something or not to do something, but you can't be with them twenty-four hours a day. You just hope that you have taught them well and they will use wise judgement. But, there is no guarantee. I don't know any parents that can honestly say that their child would or wouldn't do something to their disliking or disappointment. If they can, they must be in a different world than I am," continued Darnall. "These were good kids from good families who made a terrible mistake. I wanted to give support where I could and help to get them back on the right track."

The result of the hearing was that the students would be suspended from school for eight weeks—one term, and then they would be on probation for the remainder of the school year if they chose to remain.

"I think when all was said and done, the college handled the unfortunate situation admirably. I salute the administration for its closure of the incident," Darnall concluded. I also admired the students who chose to stay at Eureka for their intrepidity.

It was then time for basketball to start again. However the 1987-1988 basketball season was going to be a challenge for Coach Darnall. Basketball coaches have a desire, maybe even a need, to control most things surrounding them. Their livelihood depends upon it. Their happiness and professional stability also depend greatly on the performance of five people running around in shorts. Bonnie often said their lives were controlled by an orange bouncing ball. Even family events were planned around it—weddings, births, among others. However, the events at the beginning of that year were totally out of Dave's control and it would become "disaster management."

Dave never really felt any outside pressure to win. His intensity came from within. Coach was driven to win and wanted someday to have Eureka College stand on top of the basketball world as one of the best small college basketball programs in the country. Isn't that what all coaches and alumni want?

"It doesn't matter who wins or loses, it's how you play the game."

"That's malarkey at the college level," said Darnall. "Just ask the coaches who gave it their all but still got fired because they didn't win a certain amount of games or beat a key opponent. Administration and fans want good, positive publicity in the newspapers, on the radio, and television. That's just the way it is."

This year would be a true test!

Coming off the best season in the college's history—the only team to make a national tournament appearance—with several returning quality players, Dave had been optimistic. He had also had an outstanding recruiting year, so there were some good young players waiting in the wings to fill the vacancy created by the graduation of the four outstanding seniors. But due to the unfortunate incident earlier, three returning players and one transfer did not participate this year. To make matters worse, the Red Devils lost their only returning starter, Tom Dooley, in the second game of the season when he broke his hand in a freak accident. It took him out of action for six weeks.

The adversity the team experienced forced Darnall to look at the new class of hopefuls. Six-foot-four DeLeon Lavender and six-foot-six Mark Blunt were the leading candidates.

"DeLeon was a player I had recruited for two years," said Darnall. "He was my No. 1 recruit. We expected him to come in and contribute to the varsity right away."

Regarding Mark, Darnall said, "I knew Mark was going to be able to help the varsity even as a freshman. I am happy that someone of his quality chose Eureka College."

By the way, Mark's sister, Kim, also an excellent athlete joined her twin brother at Eureka in January after transferring from Southern Illinois-Edwardsville. She eventually became Darnall's student secretary.

To help bring stability to the young team, Rob Kroehnke was hired as a student coach replacing the graduated Eric Buerkett. Mike Knoerle also joined the staff as a student administrative assistant. The native Tolucan had gained much basketball savvy while playing under the legendary Central Illinois coach Chuck Rolinski.

Basketball practice opened with only five returning lettermen reporting from the 1987 NAIA District Champions. This included the soon to be injured Tom Dooley.

"What a shock," said Darnall of his depleted team. "I really expected a lot more experience. We will just have to do the best we can with what we have. Some of the new recruits will have to step forward and be ready to go right away."

The 1987-1988 campaign opened with the Red Devils playing at Northeast Missouri State. This was the first game of a two-game trip to Missouri and Iowa. The starters were Todd Ritsema at center, Jeff Wooters and Steve Redman at forwards, and Tom Dooley and Jeff Gray at guards. Despite the scoring efforts of guards Gray and Dooley, who scored eighteen and sixteen respectively, the Red Devils were totally out-classed in the 80 to 65 loss. A little revenge was sweet for the home team.

The following night was another disaster for the inexperienced Red Devils. Team leader Dooley was going up to block a shot when he got entangled somehow with the rim and the net causing a severe break at the base of the middle finger. He did not return to action until after the first of the year. Dooley's injury was bad enough, but EC dropped its second game of the season, 66 to 53, to Graceland College.

The remainder of the first half of the season did not get much better. Darnall was disappointed. He wasn't used to going into Christmas break with a 3 to 6 record. In fact, the team had lost twice a many games already as they had all the previous year. Not only did the losing bother the coach, but he also began to see a few of the players slipping from the team philosophy, "Together We Win." Squabbling was starting to take place between teammates. A couple of players began to worry about playing time rather than winning the ball game.

"Hopefully, the break will give us a chance to rejuvenate our dedication," said Darnall. "We have got to do something to change the season around. It's probably a good thing we're going to have some time off."

Even though Coach Darnall felt it was work watching his own basketball team play at times, he enjoyed watching his son play for the Eureka High School's basketball team whenever he could make a game. The five-foot-nine junior point-guard was the "quarterback" of the team. Not only was he capable of scoring, but it was his floor game that his dad enjoyed watching.

The break also allowed Dave to catch a couple of Tiera's games at Illinois State University. She was in her second year as a cheerleader.

Dave was happy with a couple of his freshmen players, particularly Lavender and Blunt. However, he could see that for the program to reach the level it enjoyed only a year before, he had to have a couple of good recruiting years. This meant Coach Dighton and he had a lot to do over the Christmas break. Between the two of them, they were able to attend some eight high school holiday tournaments. They also were able to catch a couple of regular scheduled high school games during the break.

The team reported back to campus after Christmas for a week of double practices to prepare for a two-game, four-day road trip to the St. Louis area. Coach Darnall was hoping his players were ready to turn the season around. Dave was optimistic about a revival in the team's attitude and performance, especially with the return of Tom Dooley.

The first opponent of the trip was Concordia Seminary of St. Louis. This was a game that should have broken their losing streak. It wasn't meant to be! The Preachers defeated Eureka, 97 to 89. Dooley led the Red Devils in scoring with twenty-eight points in the losing cause.

Darnall was irate after the game. "In all due respect to Concordia, who played an excellent game and worked hard, they should never have beat us. In my fourteen years of coaching at Eureka, this had to be one of the toughest losses for me to swallow. There was absolutely no way we should have lost that game."

"The team's attitude and performance was no better tonight than what it was before vacation," Darnall told the press. "If we don't do something soon, this will be a disastrous season. I'm not even concerned about post-season play. We need to worry about winning a few games."

The Concordia game was supposed to be a much easier game than the Southern Illinois-Edwardsville game coming next. The NCAA II school had an enrollment much larger than Eureka College and gave athletic aid. The EC team had a day off before the Southern game. The coaching staff had planned a practice session at SIU's fieldhouse. They really felt the team needed it now.

Darnall was in a sour mood. He was totally dissatisfied with the way things were headed, and at practice in no uncertain words, he let his players know of his dissatisfaction with their effort.

The game lived up to what Darnall had feared. Eureka College was out-manned as well as out-classed. The Red Devils gave the Cougars a pretty good game before intermission, but the host school's superior talent took over in the second half for a 95 to 62 victory.

Eureka next traveled to Westminster College for a nonconference game. The highly academic institution always produced a quality basketball team. This year was no different. Again, EC played below par and lost a nineteen-point game to the hosts, 78 to 59. The five-hour trip home was pure misery for the coaching staff. The question was how could they stop the five-game losing streak.

"Somehow we have got to get the old fellowship back with our players. They need 'Together We Win,'" Darnall told Coach Dighton. "We've got guys who are too damn worried about how much playing time they are getting instead of winning. That hasn't happened before. We've got to put an end to it."

A couple players had complained about their playing time on several occasions since Christmas break. In fact at the Southern Illinois-Edwardsville game, Coach Darnall and a player had a heated discussion after the game in the locker room. Darnall had always had an "open door policy," meaning a player could come into his office and talk to him and Coach Dighton anytime they wanted. However, there was not to be conversation on either the practice or playing floor between a coach and player regarding any personal or team problem.

Darnall felt it was always best to have his assistant present anytime he and a player were going to discuss a player's concern.

To further illustrate what was taking place, Coach Darnall had received at least two phone calls from parents regarding the playing time of their sons. Can you imagine parents calling a Division I college coach to complain about how much playing time twenty-year old men are getting? In fact, Darnall was being accused of playing only the boys that their parents came to his home after games. Things were beginning to deteriorate fast.

It didn't take a genius to see that the Eureka College program was in turmoil. It was definitely going in the wrong direction. Losing fosters team dissension and negative attitudes. Darnall's patience was "running thin." He was struggling within himself as to what needed to be done to change the direction the team was heading.

At a practice following the Westminster game, the discord on the team finally came to a "head." Coach, was not only upset over the past games' performances of his team and the attitude of a few players, but they were now having a very bad practice. For a team that just lost five consecutive games, Coach expected more. He ordered his team to line-up along the end line for some reaction drills.

Darnall shouted in frustration, "You damn guys just don't have the balls enough to look at yourself in the mirror and say I am not doing the job."

A player yelled back, "You don't either." This was the same player Coach had received some dissatisfaction from over his playing time the previous year and again some this year. He was really the only player on the championship team that Darnall felt didn't buy into the "Together We Win" slogan.

Darnall immediately yelled back, "Get your ass out of here; you're done!" Coach feeling the pressure of the dismal season, had a short fuse. He had just run out of patience.

A few seconds later another player starting speaking on his teammate and fraternity brother's behalf. Darnall also dismissed him from practice. A few words followed. A couple other players stepped in to assist the suspended player from the floor.

He was not a player who had been a troublemaker. To the contrary, he was a dedicated and outstanding player and individual whom later became a member of the Eureka College Athletic Hall of Fame. However, the temperament of the season had been set; it was going to be a long one.

The team returned to practice after a few minutes of a "cooling down" period. The practice ended up productive in spite of its beginning.

All the Red Devils needed now was another road game, but that is what they got. It had been four consecutive away games since the break. MacMurray was the next opponent. The Red Devils seemed to play a little better, but the result was just the same. They were defeated, 74 to 69. Freshman Mark Blunt did his best to reverse the outcome by scoring a team high twenty-two points, but it just wasn't enough.

Eureka College finally had another home game. This was exactly what they did need. It was good to play Blackburn College in front of the hometown fans. Tom Dooley and Jeff Gray scored twenty-three points each to lead the Red Devils to a 79 to 74 victory stopping the six-game losing streak. The win gave Eureka a 1 to 1 conference record.

The post-game gathering at the Darnall's was scarcely attended. This was not a surprise to either Bonnie or Dave. Only the true "die-hard" fans came to be with the dismayed coaching staff.

The winning was short lived. Total disaster struck! The Red Devils lost five consecutive road games. Most were conference games leaving EC with a 1 to 4 conference record. The other losses were to the always tough McKendree Bearcats and the Iowa Wesleyan Tigers.

The discord on the team was still there. Coach Darnall had never had to dismiss a player from his squad. This illustrated the type of student-athlete he recruited and a fact he was proud of. However, he began to consider the possibility.

Eureka College finally returned home after the Iowa Wesleyan loss for a rematch with MacMurray College. Tom Dooley and Mark Blunt pumped in twenty-four and twenty-one points respectively to lead their team to a much needed 77 to 61 victory. It was only the Red Devil's sixth win of the season with five games remaining to play.

It was then back on the road again as Darnall's troops took on conference foe Blackburn College. The result was not to the liking of Coach Darnall. His team dropped a three-point decision to the host school by the score of 80 to 77. The loss left the Red Devils with an overall record of 6 to 16 and just four games remaining. There was absolutely no NAIA post-season play this year. In fact, it became counting the games left.

It was finally at this time Coach Darnall decided to make an unfamiliar move. He was going to suggest the junior player withdraw from the team. It had reached the point where the player could not conform to Darnall's decisions regarding playing time and what was to be done on the floor. It was causing so much discord on the team that something had to be done. Coach called the player, along with Coach Dighton, into his office to discuss his future. Coach told the player he could drop off the team on his own or be dismissed. It was difficult for both of them. However, Coach was confident this was in the best interest of the team.

The Red Devils went on to win all four of the remaining games, giving Eureka College an overall season record of 10 to 16 and 5 to 5 in conference play.

"I should have made that decision earlier," said Dave. He hoped he would never have to make that kind of decision again, but was determined not to let any similar situation linger. "I just didn't have the guts to make the decision. I learned my lesson."

"This was a learning year in lots of ways. Something we won't want to forget. We want to learn from our mistakes and efforts. We'll be back," Coach Darnall promised. "You'll see a different team next year!"

Darnall hoped that the troublesome times were behind him. Nothing could be much worse than the season just closed. The next two years went fairly well. Then the "class scheduling monster" reared its ugly head again in 1992.

Everything had been going too well. He should have anticipated something. When the team returned from the first NAIA II National Tournament held in Stephensville, Texas, Dave learned that several changes had been made in his teaching load for the up-coming year. Darnall was irate. "Who initiated this change?" Dave queried his athletic director.

"I don't know," he replied, "but I'll check with the department chairman."

Dave immediately called the department chair's office to set up an appointment to discuss the issue. He was extremely upset over what he thought was a very sneaky operation. Would he be able to keep his cool in the meeting? He was worried.

The decision to change some of Dave's teaching responsibilities was supposedly determined by several people. Noticeably absent from the decision-makers was Darnall. He was given to understand that he was not consulted or informed of the possible changes before he guided his team to the National Tournament because it might upset him. "Damn right!" said Darnall.

Dave believed the process followed to change his teaching responsibilities had been extremely unethical. He couldn't fathom changing someone's load and responsibilities without consulting him or her. If they had been so concerned that he was going to be upset, why make the change?

Several changes were made. First, he was released from his Intramural Directorship. It was finally going to be under the Student Development Office. This had been proposed several years previous in 1988. This meant Darnall had to add four more hours' credit in order to maintain full faculty status. "After eighteen years as director, wouldn't you think someone would have said something to me before I was stripped of my directorship?" Dave asked.

All physical education majors were required to enroll in the intramural course. The students' major responsibilities were to implement the intramural program. What had been a "practicum" experience was now changed. Darnall was assigned to teach a classroom phase of intramural management. He would receive two hours credit toward his total teaching requirement. This left him two hours short. To make up for the two hours, he was assigned to teach "Organization and Administration of Physical Education." It was a course previously taught by his assistant, Coach Dighton.

"I can't believe they would take the course away from my assistant coach and add it to my load," Darnall said. "This whole thing is a nightmare. This means less hours for Dighton."

In addition, another slight came by taking away his supervising of student teachers for which he received one-hour credit. That was replaced with a three-quarters-hour credit mini-course in track and field. That sequence had previously been taught by the athletic director. All in all, it meant Darnall had three new class preparations. What was really going on? It seemed like déjà vu.

The meeting with the Department Chairman gave no satisfaction. Darnall then proceeded to contact the Dean of Faculty. That meeting produced the same results. They had made the decision without his input or knowledge, but it would stand. That left Dave with no other option. He finally asked to meet with President Hearne. He had a great deal of respect for the president and hoped he would, at least, understand his complete frustration and dismay at the manner in which the changes were made.

President Hearne listened to Dave's concerns. The mutual respect the two had for each other helped to produce an agreeable solution to the controversial changes. Darnall agreed that being relieved of the intramural

381

director duties, in the long run, might result in less stress for him. Preparing and teaching the classroom phase of the intramural program was fine. Having been a former track coach and enjoying the sport, teaching the track and field mini-course was also acceptable. However, the teaching of "Organization and Administration of Physical Education" still greatly disturbed him. It was decided that Dighton would continue to teach the course.

The president was aware of Dave's interest in the recruitment of student-athletes. He knew Dave enjoyed the recruiting process and was very good at it. Recruiting of new students to the college was always a major concern. The success of the Admissions Office was vital to the survival of the small college.

Eureka College had recently hired a couple new coaches. The president suggested Dave receive two hours credit to act as an admission consultant. He would assist the other coaches with the techniques of recruiting. Dave enthusiastically endorsed this suggestion. He also offered to write a recruiting manual regarding recruiting techniques for the college. It was eventually titled "Eureka College Student Recruiting Techniques Manual," totaled sixteen pages, and is on file in the college's Melick Library.

Always the diplomat, President Hearne suggested Dave arrange another meeting with the Dean of Faculty regarding his teaching responsibilities. He wisely followed the president's advice. The meeting took place at an off-campus restaurant over Cokes. Both talked freely with little animosity. Both left with positive feelings. Darnall hoped the issue of his teaching responsibilities was finally put to rest. He did not want to go through this type of agony again before retiring. Three times in six years was enough.

However, one more disappointment was around the corner. The day before the team was to fly to Boise, Idaho, to compete in the NAIA II National Tournament, the Dean of Faculty's Office called Darnall to arrange a meeting between him and the dean. The topic to be discussed was Dave's professional promotion. The meeting took place just before the team's last home practice in March of 1994.

Ten years earlier with the support of then Department Chairman Dr. Owen West, Assistant Professor of Physical Education Dave Darnall was promoted to Associate Professor. Promotions are usually based on several factors: years of service at the institution, the degree held by the candidate, professional publications, professional recognition at local, state, and national levels. Dr. West had initiated the process for Darnall's promotion. The Faculty Status and Development Committee, consisting of five faculty members plus the Dean of

Faculty as an exofficio member, determine all promotions. The committee makes a recommendation to the Dean of Faculty for approval.

After serving the college for ten years as an Assistant Professor, followed by ten more as an Associate Professor, Darnall felt he deserved to be considered for promotion to full professorship. He based this upon several factors:

1. Twenty years of teaching and coaching at the college.
2. Authored ten published articles in national coaching magazines.
3. Inducted into two athletic hall of fame—Illinois State University and Illinois Basketball Coaches' Association.
4. Recruitment of numerous student-athletes for the college
5. Named NAIA II Coach of the Year for the third consecutive year by the Illinois Basketball Coaches' Association.
6. Selected the Annual Tri-County Sports Award Male Coach of the Year given by the Greater Peoria Sports Hall of Fame.
7. The basketball coach with the most wins in the history of the college.
8. Guided three past teams, not counting the current team, to appearances in the NAIA National Tournament.
9. Selected NAIA District 20 Coach of the Year three times.
10. Director of one of the largest and most successful basketball camps in the State.
11. Other coaching awards including conference coach of the year on several occasions.

Darnall felt he fulfilled the necessary requirement needed for promotion to full professor. Thus, he submitted his own name for promotion. Whereas ten years before the department chairman submitted Darnall's name for promotion, this time he initiated it himself. To this day, he is not sure whether he had the support of the new department chair as he previously did from Dr. West. He never talked to the chairman regarding this issue. "I have no idea if he/she was asked for a recommendation or not," Dave said. "It was never mentioned to me."

The meeting with the dean took place in Darnall's office at the Fieldhouse. The dean informed him that his promotion was denied. Even though Dave was very successful in the coaching area, it was questioned whether coaching was "teaching." Therefore, academically, it would not be appropriate.

Darnall was furious inside. He did not explode like he thought he would. However, he did let the dean know his dissatisfaction with the committee's decision. He felt that the dean also believed that coaching was not "teaching."

"I disagree with that," Dave argued. "Coaching is like teaching our gifted students. It is no different than an English professor teaching an honor's class in English. Besides, my coaching responsibilities are only one-third of my teaching load. Two-thirds of my teaching load is for teaching in the classroom and other educational responsibilities."

After a few more minutes of discussing the issue, Darnall stated, "I don't know what else I could do to achieve the promotion that does mean a lot to me."

As the dean left the coach's office, he wished Dave good luck in the National Tournament.

"Boy, this is a hell of a note," Dave said to himself as he was headed toward practice. I've got to get my team ready to play in a national tournament just after being turned down for something that I worked hard for, proved I deserved, and wanted."

The dean did tell Dave just prior to leaving that the decision didn't mean that he couldn't be considered later on.

For Darnall, the whole incident became a motivational tool. Not that he really needed one. Going for the National title, a dream come true, was enough, especially since this was his last year of coaching. He knew there would be no more chances. He wanted to prove the committee wrong. He wanted to show them they "screwed up." What a better way than to win the championship he thought.

It was soon after he returned to campus with the National title that Dave had to take care of some business in the dean's office. The dean appeared and anxiously congratulated him on the national championship and being named NAIA II National Coach of the Year.

"You know, Dean, you motivated me when you told me I was denied my promotion. I wanted to prove the Committee wrong. Now maybe this championship and my selection as NAIA National Coach of the Year will prove I am a good teacher," Dave said.

Not much more was said, but Dave felt he did get some satisfaction out of the disappointing decision.

A year later, Dave again applied for full professorship. This time he enclosed a statement from a physical education methods textbook stating that "coaching was teaching." He also enclosed an article from *The Pantagraph* regarding Illinois Wesleyan's Head Basketball Coach, Dennis Bridges, being promoted to full professor at the university for his success and service to the school. The committee had also taken on a new perspective. Coach Sweitzer still remained as the chairperson of the Faculty Status and Development Committee and was a believer in coaching as teaching. A new member was Dr. Loren Logsdon. He was a stout basketball fan and had actually made the trip to Idaho to watch his beloved Red Devils. A side attraction was that his son and daughter and their families lived in Boise! Dr. Logsdon had advised Dave previously that he thought coaching was teaching.

The promotion was granted, and Dave became Professor Dave Darnall. Even though he had received several prestigious coaching awards, this promotion meant as much to Darnall as any of the others.

"I now feel my professional status is complete. Who could ask for more—National Coach of the Year and full professorship," said Dave. "I think my dad would be proud of me. He would never believe this." Perhaps that was also a driving force behind Dave.

As much as Darnall disliked change, a few more were in store. This time he was in control. In 1994, Coach Darnall announced his retirement from basketball effective at the end of the 1994 season.

The president recognized a need to recruit female athletes and suggested that Dave become an athletic counselor. His responsibilities were to recruit lady volleyball, basketball and softball student-athletes. He would also continue to recruit men's basketball players, teach some classes and supervise student teachers. Darnall liked this new position. For the final years of Darnall's employment at Eureka College, he enjoyed "peace of mind."

A second change came as a result of the first. His office was moved from the first in a row of six to the last at the back door. He would now share a small office with several others. Coach Dighton moved from the back to the front after replacing his former "boss." Dave often kidded, "I moved from the front to the back of the bus. How soon do they forget!"

Darnall actually understood the switching of offices. In fact once he was out of coaching, he liked the back. He could then just step outside the multi-purpose office and slide out the back door of Reagan. The worst part of the switch was moving the room full of pictures and clippings collected over twenty years and the gigantic bulletin boards containing newspaper clipping which hung outside the office.

"It was a little hard to be told to move out of your office after twenty years," Darnall said, "but I understood. It was just the swiftness that disturbed me a little especially after just winning the National Championship and being named NAIA II National Coach of the Year. It's like giving up your home and identity. Maybe that's what the Native American's felt."

Chapter 14

Rebuilding to Respectability

T HE DISASTROUS SEASON LEFT COACH DARNALL WONDERING. Could the team bounce back? Which players would have to improve? Which freshmen would be able to contribute early? Could the team stay away from injuries? What kind of recruiting year would he have? Lastly, how much longer could he last? The four consecutive wins at the end of the season gave him some hope.

"I can't stand to have a season like last year," Darnall told his assistants Dighton, Cox, and Knoerle before the opening of practice. "We got to have better luck and do some things differently. Some players really have to come through for us."

One move Darnall did make to "spruce up" the program was to use ball boys. Bradley University had ball boys, and Dave thought they added a little class to the program. In fact, Bradley's Head Coach Jim Les was once a ball boy for Bradley. Darnall's first ball boy was Nate Wertz, "Scout" Wertz's nephew.

Dave's children had brought some happiness and proud moments to the misery of the past season. He only wished he could have watched them perform more. Derek had a great junior year in three sports—football, basketball, and track. However, it was in basketball that Derek made his father proudest.

Derek had been named First Team All Conference in the Blackhawk Conference. The five-foot-nine guard was selected Honorable Mention All-

State by the Illinois Basketball Coaches' Association. He was also named to the All-Tourney Team at the Hawk Holiday Classic at Prairie Central High School.

"I'm really sorry I wasn't able to watch Derek more in his athletic activities. With my extremely busy schedule, I was only able to see him play basketball about six times. I truly regret that. It bothers me to think I had time to watch other fathers' sons play, but not my own. That's why a season like last year makes me wonder if it was all worth it," Dave explained.

Tiera equally made her parents proud. The ISU cheerleader was selected Second Runner-up in the Miss Illinois State University pageant. That was the second pageant award within a year. Earlier, she had been named Miss Woodford County.

Following the disastrous basketball season, Dave had been able to watch Derek participate in track. One of Dave's greatest thrills was watching his son qualify for the State meet in four events at the District track meet. That was the maximum any athlete could participate in at the State meet held at Eastern Illinois University.

One of the events was the 110-meter high hurdles. That had been Dave's favorite event when he was running track. It was also Tiera's favorite event. A four-time Woodford County champion, she also participated in the State track meet in the hurdles. It was an accomplishment Dave couldn't reach.

"Watching Derek run at the State meet made me awfully proud," Dave said. "Who would have known that it would be the last time I would see him run. He decided not to go out for track his senior year. Four years of football, basketball, and three of track took its toll. I think he just got tired."

Fortunately, Coach Darnall was able to watch his son quarterback his last year of interscholastic football before his Red Devil playing season started. Derek teamed up with Wes Sears to make one of the best combinations in small high school football in Central Illinois. The team finished the season with a 6 to 3 record. The Hornet quarterback was selected to the Blackhawk All-Conference Team.

1988–1989

IT WAS NOW TIME TO FACE A NEW YEAR and basketball season, and there were twelve new faces greeting the coaching staff when the 1988-1989 official basketball season began. Two more players rejoined the team after being red-shirted the previous year. Darnall ended up with another good recruiting class.

The coaches were relying on Dooley, Bickett, and Wooters for leadership. The three veteran starters were "class kids" and could lead the Red Devils back to respectability. They were members of the 1987 National Tournament team and wanted to return to the "Big House."

Disaster struck the Red Devils early. Team leader and top player, Tom Dooley, was out for the season. For the second consecutive year, Dooley was struck with a major injury. He broke his foot in practice a couple weeks before the Red Devils were scheduled to open their season in the Wheaton Invitational Tournament. Dooley had to red-shirt the season.

An article written by Dave Reynolds of the Peoria *Journal Star* entitled "Eureka still in rebuilding mode" best summed up the fifteenth year coach's season outlook. The article read in part:

> When your house burns down, it takes a while to get back to the point where you were before the fire.
>
> It's been two years now since Eureka College coach Dave Darnall's team was living life to the hilt in the high-rent district, posting a 26 - 3 record, winning the District 20 tournament and advancing to the NAIA national tournament for the first time in school history.
>
> Now after plummeting to 10 - 16 last season, he's still surveying the wreckage.
>
> "This year, if we have a .500 season, it would be an outstanding season for us," Darnall said. "We had a championship team, but because of that, we didn't have outstanding recruiting years when those kids were there. Who wants to sit for three or four years?"
>
> The only link to that 1986-87 team is senior forward Tom Dooley, a starter then and the Red Devil's leading scorer last year at 14 points per game after he returned from breaking his hand. But Dooley, one of only two seniors on this season's club, may not play at all. He broke his foot in preseason practice, is expected out until at least Christmas and would like to Red-shirt and return to a stronger team next year.
>
> In the meantime, Darnall may have to endure a lot of growing pains . . .
>
> "We have to look at it as a complete rebuilding year. The best thing we have on our team is our attitude. We've established our 'Together We Win' philosophy. Last year we didn't have that. "That's been the real key to our program the last 13 years and it's back this year."
>
> Whether a good attitude can translate into a competitive club is something the Red Devils are going to find out in a hurry . . .

Eureka's first game of the Wheaton Tournament was against St. Xavier, a consistent NAIA playoff team. The EC starters were Mark Blunt at center, DeLeon Lavender and Jeff Wooters at forwards, and Mike Coffman and Kevin Root at guards. Brad Bickett was the "John Havlicek" (sixth man) of the team. Speaking about Bickett, Darnall said, "Bickett is definitely good enough to start. In fact, he is probably the best player on the team since Dooley has been shelved for the season. But, we need him to come off the bench and give the team the lift it needs in order to win. He'll end up being the best 'Havlicek' I've ever had at Eureka."

St. Xavier was as good as publicized. Despite a twenty-four-point performance from Brad "Havlicek" Bickett, the Cougars defeated the Red Devils, 77 to 67. The loss proved to be only the first bad news of the tournament. The Red Devils lost the third place game to host Wheaton College, 78 to 75, despite Mark Blunt's thirty-two points and eleven rebounds.

Eureka returned to action at Concordia College in River Forest. Coach Darnall was hoping his team could gain their first victory of the season before having to play the bigger school, Northeast Missouri State. He got his wish. Junior Mike Coffman led his team to their first win, pumping in twenty-four points.

However, the winning way did not last long. Eureka lost to the NCAA II institution, never really able to make a serious run after trailing 40 to 33 at halftime. The final score was 84 to 63 in favor of the home team.

Coach was asked about his team's 1 to 3 record. "We are definitely going in the wrong direction," Dave said. "I sure as hell hope we don't have another season like last year. A good performance at the Judson Tournament is extremely important. We can't afford to lose two there."

In the meantime, the Darnall household was having success on another end. Tiera was now cheering for the men's basketball team at ISU. She had been a mascot for many of her dad's teams as a little girl, and her goal was to cheer at a large university. The first game of the year was a road trip for ISU to Indiana. Tiera was able to witness Bobby Knight and his team in action. Her dream had been fulfilled.

The Red Devils' first opponent in the Judson Invitational Tournament was one of the best teams in the state. Rosary College had a 7 to 0 record and was rated second in the state in NAIA. They were also able to claim a victory over McKendree College in the past 1988 NAIA District 20 State Championship.

Coach Darnall had one of his "patented" pre-game talks. He challenged his team to prove they were better than what their record showed. "I don't give a damn who we have played," Darnall shouted to his players. "The bottom line is we're 1 to 3. We are going to have another season like last year if we don't get our asses out there and play some ball. If you think you're good, prove it."

The team took the floor. "Dighton, I hate talking to them like that," Dave said to his assistant as the coaches remained in the locker room. He headed to the "john" for about the fifth time and continued, "It seems that is the only way I really get them to play. It's like now they want to prove something to me."

"I know," Dighton replied. "If that's what it takes to win, let it be."

Dighton left the locker room to observe the team in warm-up. Dave finally left the bathroom and joined his team on the floor. "What do you think, Dennis?" Dave asked his assistant.

"Coach, they seemed pumped up. I think maybe they're ready," Dighton replied.

"I sure as hell hope so," said Darnall.

The team matched Coach's challenge. The Red Devils jumped out to a 39 to 24 lead at intermission. Balanced scoring and an effective 1-2-2 adjustable zone defense provided Eureka with the fifteen-point lead at halftime. The Red Devils maintained their intensity for a great win.

"We really needed that," Darnall said after the game. "We couldn't afford another loss this early in the season if we had any hope for post-season play. This will really help our Dunkel rating."

Eureka had four players score in double figures. Mark Blunt's twenty-two points led the way. The Red Devils won the rebounding battle, 35 to 26, led by Bickett's ten rebounds. Root had eleven assists for the winners.

The team was staying at the Elgin Holiday Inn. The motel had an excellent indoor recreational center including a large pool, shuffle board, putting green, and game room. The players enjoyed an evening of recreation with their fans after their impressive win.

Several of the families of the players including the Bicketts, Wooters, Roots, Blunts, Browns, Schafers, Crafts, Coffmans, and Van Weeldens accompanied their sons on the trip. The Wertzes, Murisons, Dan Harrod, Kroehnke, and Bonnie were among the fans that joined the players' parents for a post-game social at the motel. It was finally like "old times"— "Together We Win."

Eureka played the host school for the championship. Darnall, again, challenged his team in his pre-game talk, but not to the degree as the night before. Maybe he should have. The Red Devils trailed at the intermission, 38 to 31.

"Here we go," Darnall yelled at his players at halftime. "I let you have a little fun after the big win, and look where we are now. Do I have to

390

give you an ass chewing before every game in order to get you guys to play the way you're capable, okay? I'm tired of this crap. I shouldn't have to raise hell with you in order for you to play at your potential. We won't change anything. Just start executing and busting your butt. You don't want to be standing there when they cut down the nets and get the first place trophy. It will be a long ride home. This game is worth two. You're either 2 to 4 or 3 to 3. Now get the hell out there and show me you want the championship," finished Darnall.

The Red Devils answered the call. Eureka fought back from the seven-point half-time deficit to down Judson, 69 to 66. Sophomore Mark Blunt led the way with twenty points for EC to escort the championship trophy home.

The feeling of victory was short lived; the Red Devils lost a heartbreaker at Clarke College. Darnall felt the officiating was so bad that, for the first of only two times in his college coaching career, he followed the officials off the floor to their locker room to give them a piece of his mind.

"It's too damn bad that you guys have to take a game away from the kids," Dave yelled.

"Get the hell out of here!" one replied.

"That's the worst call I have seen in fifteen years of coaching. That's terrible," Dave shouted. "What a bunch of shit!"

SLAM! The door shut in the angry coach's face.

"You'll never officiate one of our games again," Darnall yelled through the closed door.

Keith Sander hit an eighteen-foot shot at the buzzer to give the hosts a victory over the Red Devils. Eureka had taken an 83 to 82 lead with thirty seconds left as Scott Schafer scored from inside the lane. Clarke then came down and missed a shot. A Red Devil grabbed the rebound but was called for traveling. That is what had set off the coach's fuse.

Darnall's explanation was, "What actually took place was when my player clutched the long rebound on the baseline, he was literally shoved out of bounds. It should have been a foul. It sure as hell wasn't traveling."

Clarke got the ball under the Red Devil basket with just seconds left for Sander's dramatic shot. The loss dropped Eureka under the .500 mark.

Coach Darnall and the Eureka team were anxiously awaiting their home opener. However, this would have to wait until after they competed in the Aurora Tournament. Eureka, playing in its third season tournament, was matched against the much larger Roosevelt University. Dave did not know how his Red Devils would respond after the disheartening loss to Clarke. He soon found out. They raced to a 12 to 2 lead and were never in trouble. Behind Brad Bickett's twenty-one points, EC claimed a 79 to 68 victory.

Both head coaches were interviewed following the game. "They played a 1-2-2 zone as well as you can play it," said Laker coach Carl Dasko. "We didn't have the intensity; they got the rebounds, came down and stuck it in our craw."

Coach Darnall called Eureka's win, "Our second best game. Our best was in the Judson Tournament when we beat Rosary when they were 7 to 0. Our kids really played well. We just came off a heartbreaker the other night; a one-point loss on a last second throw up. It's a long way from Eureka to Dubuque, and I just didn't know if our kids would respond."

"We played a really good zone defense tonight, and I think we frustrated them a little early, going inside against their players," he continued. "Once we got the lead and by playing good defense, it built our confidence."

Aurora College slipped past Spring Arbor, 76 to 70, setting up a showdown between the Spartans and Red Devils for the championship. An article by Dan Murr, Sports Editor for *The Pantagraph* entitled "Eureka leaves AU in shambles" best described the action in the title game. Portions of the article read:

> In the case of multiple choice, pick nightmarish, embarrassed, humiliated. There you have it - Aurora University's basketball team this morning.
> Coach Don Holler and his Spartans (3-4) could only watch as Eureka College, led by Most Valuable Player Brad Bickett, took turns cutting down AU's nets in AU's Thornton Gymnasium after the Red Devils won AU's Spartan Classic Saturday afternoon.
> The Red Devils didn't just win it. No prisoners ruled in this 91 - 65 bashing that left the Spartans in a shambles in their own place of business.
> And Coach Dave Darnall's 15th Eureka team, not having the luxury of a home court advantage nine games into the season, won its second straight tournament, this one in a breeze.
> Eureka put on a shooting clinic, hitting 39 of 58 shots for a blistering 64 percent mark, including 5 for 8 (62.5 percent) from the three-point range.
> They also displayed what a team can do when it's together.
> "We're not very big, we're not very physical and we're not the type of team that scares anybody—that's for sure," said Darnall. "But the kids execute the offense very well and they do play very good as a team."

"Our kids are very close and we have a slogan, 'Together We Win,' and that's on and off the floor," he said. "We're coming off the worst season we've ever had. Last year we were 10 - 16, so some of these kids went through a miserable year after winning the state NAIA title two years ago."

Mike Coffman, who shot brilliantly in the championship game, making 12 of 15 field goal attempts, led the Red Devils with 24 points while 6-1 sophomore point guard Kevin Root and the 6-2 Bickett, who was 4 for 5 from three-point range, each scored 21. Mark Blunt, 6-6 sophomore, had 13 points . . .

"It was an avalanche you just couldn't stop," Holler said. "They're a very good basketball team; they have very good players. That was an absolutely unbelievable team."

Welcome Home! Eureka College fans were anxiously waiting to greet their tournament champions. The opponent was the old menace, Iowa Wesleyan.

The Red Devils held a one-point margin lead at the intermission, 39 to 38. Coach Darnall instructed his team to switch from the 1-2-2 zone to a man-to-man defense starting the second half. It worked. The defensive move helped Eureka beat the visitors, 92 to 62. DeLeon Lavender, the six-foot-four forward, led his team in scoring with twenty-four points and fifteen rebounds. Bickett had twenty-two points, and Kevin Root contributed to the winning effort with five steals and five assists.

Christmas break came and went. The Red Devils headed to St. Louis for a two-game, three-day trip. There they split. A lopsided win over Sanford-Brown preceded a pretty good "spanking" by NCAA II University of Missouri-St. Louis, 96 to 70.

The remainder of the season consisted mostly of Conference games except for four. The Red Devils opened their Conference play with a win over Greenville before losing a heartbreak non-conference game against highly respected McKendree College.

Six seconds were left in the game with Eureka up 81 to 79. McKendree called for a timeout. The lead had changed hands frequently throughout the game. Two well-matched teams were battling.

The hometown crowd was cheering wildly, believing the Red Devils had this one. The Bearcats threw the ball into play from the centerline. McKendree's Kevin Schwartz received the ball and let one go from outside the three-point line at the buzzer. It left the Reagan gym fans in stunned silence. The ball had hit nothing but net. Coach Darnall was in total shock. McKendree won, 82 to 81.

Darnall turned to Dighton, "I guess they owed us that one. They missed the shot two years ago that would have truly killed us."

Despite the nightmare, there was a good turnout at the post-game gathering at the Darnalls' home. The mood was somber. In fact, most of the evening's conversation was about the two tournament championships and what were the chances for a Conference title. Very little discussion included the heartbreak loss or the Dunkel ratings. Dave, however, thought the loss would not affect the Dunkel points since McKendree had a high Dunkel rating. In fact, McKendree had been favored to win. Even so, it was a devastating defeat for the Eureka coaching staff.

The Red Devils bounced back with a good home win over Conference foe MacMurray College. The hometown fans again showed up to support the team. It was the boost the players needed.

The thrill of the MacMurray win was short. The Red Devils traveled to Blackburn College to take on the tough Beavers. They were too much.

Following the disappointing loss to Blackburn, Eureka went on a short three-game winning streak. Two wins were over Conference opponents, Principia College and Greenville College. A victory over Rockford College was sandwiched between the two league wins.

EC lost a close road rematch game at MacMurray College, 69 to 64, despite a twenty-two-point performance by then starter Brad Bickett. Bickett was forced into the starting lineup due the to ineligibility of a starter. No more "John Havlicek." That was Eureka College's last regular season loss. They finished their season with six consecutive victories.

The biggest Conference win came against Blackburn College at home. Only six players played in the game, but all scored in double figures as the Red Devils beat the Beavers, 72 to 60. The two institutions shared the Prairie College Conference title with 8 to 2 records. That marked the third time in four years Eureka had captured or shared the Conference championship.

In an interview with *The Pantagraph*'s Sports Editor Bryan Bloodworth prior to the last regular season game against the prestigious Westminster College, Darnall commented on his team's season.

"I'm really proud of what this team has accomplished," said Darnall. "We figured this to be a rebuilding year because we were coming off a 10 to 16 record last year with only two seniors on the team. Then we lost one of our seniors, (All-Conference guard) Tom Dooley, to an injury before the season started and DeLeon Lavender went ineligible the second semester."

"It would have been easy to quit because those two were our leading scorers and rebounders. But, the players never did, and I've been very pleased with their performances," concluded Darnall.

Mike Coffman "tickled the twine" for twenty-seven points as the Red Devils delighted their home-court crowd with a 79 to 60 victory over Westminster. The final regular-season post-game party at the Darnalls' was highly attended. Toasts were made for not only the Conference championship, but also for the team's overall 18 to 8 record. Much of the evening's discussion was regarding the up-coming NAIA District 20 Playoff, something the fans missed out on the previous year.

The pairings were to be determined at the District's spring meeting the following day. Coaches Darnall and Dighton were there to hear the "good news." Eureka College captured the No. 4 seed and would host a first-round game against Northeastern Illinois.

The Eureka coach was asked by a *The Pantagraph* staff member about his team's selection. "We're the only school of the eight that doesn't give athletic scholarships, and all of Northeastern's players are getting full-rides because they're moving to NCAA Division I next year," pointed out Darnall.

"We know it will be tough, but we're hoping to get a home game. First because we've seen in the past that it's tough to win on the road in the playoffs, and then it has been a big goal of ours to get a home game."

An article entitled "Red Devils rebuilding ahead of schedule" that appeared in the Peoria *Journal Star* best summarized the playoff picture and Darnall's Red Devils. The unknown writer stated in part:

> Eureka College coach Dave Darnall thought this was going to be a rebuilding year for his basketball team. And that was before returning starter Tom Dooley was lost for the year with a preseason injury.
>
> But the Red Devils finished the regular season with an 18 - 8 record that earned them a spot in the National Association of Intercollegiate Athletics District 20 Playoffs that begin Tuesday. Eureka, seeded fourth in the eight-team tournament, plays host to No. 5 Northeastern Illinois in a 7:30 P.M. quarterfinal-round game at Reagan Center . . .
>
> "It was truly a rebuilding year, even with Dooley here," Darnall said of the only remaining starter from the 26 - 3 national tournament team. "I really thought (Dooley's injury) took any chances away from us of making the playoffs . . .
>
> "These kids have really come a long ways," said Darnall, whose team was 10 - 16 last season. "With only one senior, these kids have accomplished a lot." . . .

Northeastern Illinois, a school of 10,000 in Chicago, is in its final year as a NAIA basketball school. The Golden Eagles will be a NCAA Division I school next season.

The hometown fans were ready for the playoff contest against the Chicago school. However, it was evident that the Golden Eagles were not ready for either the Red Devils or the standing-room-only crowd. Eureka jumped out to an eleven-point half-time lead and cruised to an 83 to 54 victory over the much larger school. Coach Johnson and his team were stunned.

An article by Joe Bates for the Peoria *Journal Star* entitled "Unsure Eureka proves itself; gains semifinal" best described the game. It read in part:

> Dave Darnall wasn't sure if his Eureka College basketball team was going to be able to compete Tuesday with visiting Northeastern Illinois University of Chicago. But after the first nine minutes, Coach Darnall had a pretty good idea.
>
> The Red Devils had a 16-point lead less than eight minutes into the game on the way to an 83 - 54 victory in the quarterfinal round of the National Association of Intercollegiate Athletics District 20 playoff game at Reagan Center.
>
> "To be quite honest, the whole game was a surprise to me," Darnall said. "I think the start of the game really set the tempo. After the kids knew they could play with them, they gained confidence.
>
> Eureka, fourth-seeded in the eight-team tourney, meets No. 1 seed Olivet Nazarene in the semifinals Saturday at Kankakee.
>
> The Red Devils (19 - 8) placed all five starters in double figures, led by 19-point scorer Kevin Root.
>
> "That's the way this team plays," Darnall said of the balanced scoring. "Sometimes when it comes to talent, we might be limited, but as far as playing together as a team . . .
>
> "I think the kids played beyond themselves the first few minutes just because of the surroundings," Darnall said, referring to the play-off atmosphere in Reagan Center that included a boisterous crowd.
>
> "This was a big step in getting our program back on top," Darnall said.

Eureka College next had to play Olivet Nazarene on the road. The Red Devils had only won one NAIA Playoff game away from home: the 1987 championship game against McKendree. Darnall knew Olivet would be a true challenge for his young club. The team left the day before the game so as to practice on the game floor. It gave no advantage. Eureka lost to the No. 1 seed team.

Joe Bates' article "Eureka falls short in NAIA semifinal game" for the *Journal Star* again gave game insight. Portions read:

> Time and again the Olivet Nazarene University basketball Team had Eureka College on the ropes in Saturday's NAIA District 20 semifinal playoff game at Birchard Gym.
>
> And although the Tigers could never deliver the knockout punch, they did hold on for a 70 - 59 decision to advance to Wednesday's championship game . . .
>
> "There were times they could've put us away but our kids kept coming back and that's the kind of kids we've got," Eureka coach Dave Darnall said. 'I think that's a tribute to the way our kids work hard and never quit." . . .
>
> "I thought Eureka did a nice job because there would have been a bunch of other teams that would've cracked with the pressure of being down so many times," Olivet coach Ralph Hodge said. "Eureka's got solid people that play the game very hard and they showed that."

The season was no sooner over than the press was asking Coach Darnall about his recruiting prospects and his outlook for next year. A portion of an article by Ray Driskell for the *Woodford County Journal* entitled "Eureka College concludes surprising season" reported on this.

> Darnall is now recruiting for next year's team, and said he has talked to at least eight high school players so far.
>
> "I don't think that if you are going to be competitive that you can sit back," he said. "I try to be very aggressive."
>
> That aggressive recruiting commitment has meant many miles of travel for Darnall. His car is only three years old but already has 97,000 miles on it, and he expects to travel another 25,000 miles this year on recruiting trips.
>
> He also has somewhat of a disadvantage against other colleges because Eureka does not offer athletic scholarships.
>
> But when Darnall recruits, he said he stresses some of the benefits of attending Eureka, such as smaller classes and closer contact between faculty and students. He also points out that Eureka is the only school in Illinois that competes in both NCAA Division III and the NAIA. By playing in the NAIA, he added, Eureka is playing the second highest level of the college basketball in the nation.
>
> Looking to next year, Darnall said the Red Devils can expect another year of "rebuilding."
>
> "This year we started out with two seniors and ended with only one, so when you do that you are rebuilding," he said. "We still have some young players, so this year was also considered a rebuilding year."

At the same time that the 1988-1989 Eureka basketball team was treating its coach to some satisfaction and relief over the previous year, Derek was also treating his father to a rewarding basketball season. It was Derek's senior year, and his dad made a point to see as many games as possible—actually quite a few. The younger Darnall was named a unanimous pick to the Blackhawk Conference All-Star team for the second straight year. He also had a great Regional tournament even though the Eureka Hornets lost the championship game to Central Catholic of Bloomington.

In the first game of the tournament Darnall was more than instrumental in the win over Roanoke-Benson. The Rocket coach pinpointed in a *Journal Star* article, "Eureka holds off Rockets," what his Roanoke-Benson boys' basketball team was missing Tuesday in a 60 to 58 loss to Eureka. Wiseman watched Eureka point guard Derek Darnall control the game. The senior, who made eight of thirteen shots from the field and five of six free throws, finished with twenty-one points and five assists. The article quoted Roger Wiseman. "He's the key to their team, even when he doesn't score," Wiseman said. "That's the kind of thing we're missing."

Two nights later, Derek followed with another outstanding performance against El Paso in the second round of the tournament. A headline in the Bloomington's *The Pantagraph* read "Darnall helps left Eureka." Part of the article read:

> Just when it looked like a twist of fate was going to relegate him to the role of extra, Derek Darnall stole the show last night in the semifinals of the Roanoke-Benson Class A basketball Regional.
>
> Darnall, a regular starter who was forced to the sidelines when he twisted an ankle during physical education class yesterday, came off the bench to star in Eureka's 64 - 52 triumph over El Paso. Eureka, 21 - 5, now moves into tonight's 7:30 title game against Central Catholic.
>
> "Without a doubt Derek was our spark," said Eureka coach Tim Meiss, whose team had claimed a 74 - 70 win at El Paso earlier this season. "He really gave us a lift—he made things happen."
>
> Darnall a 5-foot-9 senior, sat out a first quarter which saw Eureka fall behind, 15 - 10. The Comets upped the margin to 21 - 10 with 5:22 left in the first half before he came off the bench to assume his normal point guard position.
>
> Darnall's leadership seemed to ignite the Hornets, who scored the next 10 points before El Paso regained its composure and held on for a 25 -23 half-time lead.
>
> Darnall opened the second half by knifing through the lane for a lay-in. On El Paso's next possession, he made a fine defensive play to tip the

ball to teammate Bob Gold, whose lay-up gave Eureka a lead it would never relinquish.

"Darnall changed the ballgame," said El Paso coach Dave Orr, whose team bowed out at 18 - 7. "He came in and penetrated and took us out of our defense."

Darnall finished with just six points, but had eight assists and three steals.

Coach Darnall had recognized his son's floor savvy and ability to make things happen on the basketball floor. And, as a father-coach, he had always hoped he would eventually be able to coach his son. It was not to be. Derek did not want to go to college in Eureka. He was anxious to be "his own person." He had been contacted by several small colleges, but was determined that if he wasn't going to play for his dad, he wasn't going to play against him. He chose to further his education at Illinois State University, his parents' alma mater and where his sister was a senior. Dave was disappointed but respected his son's decision.

1989–1990

THE 1989-1990 BASKETBALL SEASON continued the rebuilding process. Coach Darnall's recruiting efforts had paid good dividends. Twelve of the twenty varsity candidates that greeted the sixteen-year coach when official practice opened were freshmen. Leading the list of newcomers was First Team All-Stater Jon Guderjan. Jon's sharp shooting would make an immediate contribution to his new team.

Darnall had several returning players, but it was Tom Dooley that Coach was most anxious to see. The future EC Athletic Hall of Fame member was a starter on the 1987 District champion team but had suffered sidelining injuries the past two seasons.

Paul King's article for the Peoria *Journal Star*, "Eureka's Magnificent Seven—Unique scenario gives team seven starting players," described Darnall's unique situation and the players contributing to it. It read:

> Can the Magnificent Seven propel Eureka College to its fourth Prairie Conference championship in the last five seasons? Coach Dave Darnall would not be totally surprised.
>
> All Darnall has back is five of his top six scorers from a 19 - 9 season and a first-place conference tie last year, plus, talented senior guard

Tom Dooley, who missed last season with a broken foot, plus, 6-foot-4 forward DeLeon Lavender, a two-year starter who fell victim to a classroom problem the second semester.

"I've got seven starters and it's going to be a tossup each game which five are going to start," says Darnall. "I haven't got a first five, but a first seven. I've never had a group like this before."

The other five are senior guards Mike Coffman and Brad Bickett, junior guard Kevin Root and two 6-6 front-liners, junior center Mark Blunt and sophomore forward Scott Schafer . . .

Darnall cannot just say enough good things about his seven. "Dooley is just a great competitor who jumps and shoots well. Bickett was a first team-state NAIA player, a hustler, a good shooter. He's wherever the ball is.

"Coffman is an extremely good shooter, our best from out. Root is a super passer, the best we've ever had here.

"Lavender is the best jumper on the team. He can slam it and he's got good inside moves. Blunt boards fairly well and shoots well for a big man.

"Schafer is a lot stronger this year. He was basically a scorer when he came out of high school, but he's really improved his rebounding.

"They play together as a team, they complement each other, they look for each other and they get along extremely well. They're close both on and off the court."

Eureka College opened its season with two non-conference home victories over Concordia College and Barat College. Barat College was in its first year of the college basketball competition, and the final score of 149 to 37 attested to it. The Red Devils established school records for most points scored in a single contest and margin of victory in the win. Uncharacteristically, Darnall played seventeen players with nine scoring in double figures. DeLeon Lavender paved the way with nineteen points while freshman Jon Guderjan contributed eighteen.

The next two contests' results were not so pleasant. Eureka College lost both games at the Judson Invitational Tournament, losing to the hosts in the third-place game after dropping to St. Xavier in the opening round.

EC bounced back after their poor tournament performance by winning two out of the next three games. The Red Devils started with a nine-point half-time deficit against Clarke College. Finally, the Red Devils came to life after a half-time ceremony that honored Coach Darnall. Eureka College President George Hearne announced at intermission that Darnall had been chosen for induction into the Illinois Basketball Coaches' Association

Kevin Root goes up for a shot while teammates Brad Bickett (24) and DeLeon Lavander position for the rebound as Mark Blunt (50) trails the play.

Hall of Fame. Dave's team went on to outscore Clarke, 48 to 33, in the second half to earn the victory, 85 to 79. It was a sweet revenge after the previous year's one-point devastating loss in Dubuque

"I was really honored by the award at half time, but if it wasn't for the victory, it wouldn't have meant anything," Darnall said immediately after the game. "The game was more important than the award." Does that sound like a typical coach?

Asked later about the comment, Darnall explained, "It is a great honor. Something that I only dreamed of. You know coaches in the heat of battle; they'll say almost anything."

Coach Darnall celebrated both the victory and his future induction into the IBCA Hall of Fame with parents, friends, and fans of the Red Devils back at his home.

Eureka was next on the road to the Rose-Hulman Tournament. Eureka lost to the host school, 64 to 55, in the championship game despite a twenty-five-point performance by Brad Bickett. The Red Devils qualified for the title game by defeating an old foe, Aurora College.

Eureka concluded its pre-Christmas schedule with three non-conference wins. It would be a month before the team would return to action.

Coach Darnall and Coach Dighton spent the majority of that time recruiting. The Eureka College coaches made appearances at the traditional basketball classics. Nine players on the EC squad being either juniors or seniors necessitated a big recruiting push. That meant both quality and quantity.

The Red Devils opened their second half of the season with a two-game, four-day trip to the St. Louis area. The first opponent was NCAA II Southern Illinois-Edwardsville. SIU-E gave Eureka College a financial guarantee to help offset their expenses. However, they would not make a return trip to Eureka.

The team traveled to St. Louis the day before the game in order to have a practice on the game floor. By the time the team returned to the Marriott in downtown St. Louis after a practice at Edwardsville, some of the parents, fans, and Bonnie had arrived at the hotel. Dave had graciously been given the Cunningham Room. What an environment to host a social gathering! The Marriott had generously provided the Eureka Coach with a special room for quite a few years.

The team executed Darnall's game plan to perfection the first half. Trailing only 22 to 21 at intermission, the team played excellent 1-2-2 adjustable zone defense and ball control offense. The Red Devils waited until fifteen seconds were left on the shot clock before they started to look for a good shot. The plan duplicated the 1987 championship McKendree game.

"The second half made me sick," Coach Darnall said after the game. Every time we got right there, the officials made a foul call. That's part of the damn home court advantage. It's why they won't play at Eureka," a frustrated Darnall commented.

What Darnall was complaining about was that SIU-Edwardsville shot thirteen free throws including two technical foul shots in the second half. Those were on Darnall who had the audacity to question some of the officials' calls even though the "home" coach had questioned the officials numerous times throughout the game. For a game total, the host school had shot seventeen free throws compared to only five for Eureka College. The Red Devils dropped the first game of the second half of the season, 63 to 48. They would have to bounce back in two nights.

It was on this trip that the Eureka College men and women players and coaches, along with a few friends, experienced a once in a lifetime occasion when several St. Louis alumni hosted a dinner for them at the prestigious Missouri Athletic Club in downtown St. Louis.

It was a very impressive evening at the exclusive club whose membership has included many St. Louis professional sports personalities such as Stan Musial and Jack Buck. Reverend Raymond McCallister and a few Eureka College Board of Trustees secured the facility and acted as the hosts to the teams. The head coaches of their respective teams, Coach Darnall and Coach LaCursia, spoke to the group about their seasons and introduced each member of their teams.

Eureka College knocked off Concordia-St. Louis to return home from the trip 1 and 1. The team was scheduled to open its Conference play against Maryville College. However, the St. Louis area institution refused to compete against Eureka. A news release headline in a local paper stated: "Maryville College drops out of the Prairie College Conference." It stated, "Eureka College Athletic Director Warner McCollum announced that Maryville College has notified him that they have dropped out of the Prairie College Conference and will not honor their commitment to play at Eureka on February 8. Based on their decision, Eureka has cancelled their January 20 trip to Maryville."

"You might hear otherwise," Darnall said when asked about the withdrawal, "but the bottom line is they didn't want to get their butt beat." It's too bad that two NCAA III institutions couldn't play.

"Even though we participate in the NAIA post-season play if selected, we still go by the NCAA III rules. They don't believe that. It's too bad they can't understand that hard work can produce the kind of teams we have without athletic scholarships. Besides, I don't think they understand why we have to play the Dunkel. You have to try to get home-court advantage in the playoff.

The next week proved difficult for the Red Devils. They lost two of the next three games. The losses came on the road to the always tough McKendree Bearcats by three and to MacMurray College by only two.

403

Eureka College's record was then nine wins and six losses. Would their losses be fatal to the Red Devils' quest to make the NAIA Playoffs? Darnall knew that a couple more losses would definitely eliminate his squad from any post-season play.

The coach challenged his players in the locker room after the MacMurray defeat. Sparing no words, Darnall expressed his disappointment in the direction the team was headed. They were 0 to 1 in Conference play. It was a long ride home for both the coaches and players following the MacMurray game. Wasn't this to be a rebuilding year? They needed to build!

The team took a day off before a hard practice prior to the first game of nine remaining on the regular schedule. The players responded to their coach's plea. The Red Devils reeled off nine consecutive victories.

A non-conference win, three Conference wins, and another non-conference win, 75 to 63, over Rockford College gave Eureka an overall record of 14 to 6 to that point. Darnall felt his Red Devils would still have to win at least three of the next four games in order to gain a berth in the NAIA post-season field.

Eureka College had three consecutive league games before finishing their season with a contest against the distinguished Westminster College. The Red Devils revenged their only Conference loss by defeating MacMurray, 72 to 62, in front of a spirited home crowd. As he had done most of the season, senior Brad Bickett led his team in scoring with twenty-seven points. Mark Blunt had chipped in with twenty. Bickett has also "tickled the twine" with seven treys.

"I think if we win two out of the last three games, we'll sneak in," Darnall told his visitors after the game at his home. "If we win all three, we'll make it," he assured the eager Red Devil fans. He, however, warned his listeners that winning two out of the three remaining games would not be an easy task. "Playing Blackburn College for the Conference title on the road and finishing the season at Fulton, Missouri, will be difficult," he cautioned.

He went on to say that fan support would be extremely important. The Red Devil loyal followers responded to his urging, and the players didn't disappoint them. EC won a barnburner, beating Blackburn, 79 to 78, in overtime. It damn near killed the highly emotional Eureka coach.

EC trailed, 36 to 32, at the intermission despite eight treys. Bickett had netted four of them, while Dooley had accounted for three. The Red Devils came from behind to knot the score at 69 all at the end of regulation time. It was freshman Jon Guderjan who engineered the second-half comeback. Guderjan came off the bench to lead Eureka's second-half scoring attack with ten points. Guderjan was called into play when Brad Bickett, who had already scored seventeen, was injured early in the second half. The injury was a serious blow to Eureka's ultimate goal, a NAIA District 20 Championship and a return trip to Kansas City. Bickett's career came to an abrupt halt.

Guderjan did not let his injured teammate or the rest of the squad down. His three-point field goal with three seconds left in regulation had been what put the game into overtime. In the extra period, senior Mike Coffman hit two free throws with nine seconds remaining to give Eureka a 79 to 76 lead. The home team scored an uncontested last second basket to account for the final score. The win clinched the Prairie College Conference Championship.

Coach Darnall was mentally and physically drained but still enjoyed the ride home. There was nothing worse than a long, cold trip home after a loss. Second-guessing would be ongoing along with a sleepless night. Most of the time, even close wins like this one produced a restless night.

Eureka College returned home for a lopsided victory over Conference foe Principia College before traveling to Westminster for the regular season finale. The team was able to travel by charter bus because of the six-hour drive, importance of the game, and the Lady Red Devils were also playing in Fulton. That was a blessing for two reasons. First, the coaches didn't have the pressure of driving the vans. Second, the NAIA District meeting was to convene the following day. The charter would allow Darnall to get some rest before the team was expected back on campus around 4:00 A.M. and he had to deal with the District selections.

Whether it was the long trip, the loss of the team's top scorer, or the Westminster crowd, but the Red Devils came out flat. Eureka trailed at intermission, 38 to 30. Darnall was extremely dissatisfied with his team's first-half performance.

The Red Devil coach raised hell during his half-time lecture and warned his players a loss would most likely result in their failure to obtain a playoff berth. The season would be a failure. He stressed better defense, shot selection, and execution of the offense. He once again challenged his team to prove they were champions, and again they responded with a valiant effort. Scott Schafer's two free throws with twelve seconds left put the Red Devils ahead 75 to 71. Westminster's Kevin Schroeder came down and made a three-pointer, but Eureka College held the ball until the clock ran out for the gratifying 75 to 74 victory.

It was a great trip home for the coaches and the victorious players. Dave recalled his lecture to his team after the MacMurray loss. He challenged his team to turn the season around. They accepted their coach's challenge and finished the season with nine consecutive wins and the Conference championship. The Red Devils guaranteed themselves a playoff bid. Where would they be seeded?

The No. 5-seeded Eureka College basketball team, minus All-State guard Brad Bickett, opened the NAIA District 20 Playoff at fourth-seeded Rosary College.

"We've flip-flopped between fourth and fifth with them a few times this year," Darnall told an unidentified *The Pantagraph* reporter. "They returned all of their players from the team we played last year. They're going to be tough on their home floor. It's really difficult to beat teams that give athletic scholarships, especially on the road."

The team left for the game site, as usual, a day before the contest. Darnall, again, wanted a practice on the game floor before tournament play. The trip also provided an opportunity for the coach to reunite with several of his former players. The team stopped in Joliet to pick up EC Hall of Fame member Mike Sain who made the overnight trip with the Red Devils. He, Rob Kroehnke, Jeff Cassidy, and Keith Kovanda were able to visit with the coaching staff at the motel after the players took curfew. It is the relationship with all his former players that Darnall has truly cherished.

The Red Devils came out ready to play. They held a slim 35 to 34 lead at intermission. The second half, however, was a different story. Darnall was fit to be tied not only at his team's eleven turnovers, but also at the officiating. Both officials were from the Chicago area. He felt at least one should have been from Central Illinois. Two Eureka starters fouled out while two others had four fouls each. Rosary made twenty-one out of twenty-eight free throws, whereas, Eureka made nine out of thirteen. The Red Devils actually outscored their opponent from the field by two goals. EC dropped the tournament game 92 to 75.

Coach Darnall, overall, felt his team had a successful season. They were working their way back to becoming one of the best small college basketball programs in the state. They ended with an 18 to 7 record, were Conference champions and undefeated at home. They led the NAIA District 20 in defense, field goal percentage, and rebounding percentage. Eureka also was ranked in the Nation both NAIA and NCAA III in seven categories. Brad Bickett was named to the NAIA All-District 20 Team for the second consecutive year.

Darnall and Dighton spent many hours on the road throughout the season and during the spring. Their recruiting efforts again produced a great bunch of players. "Perhaps this is my best recruiting class," Darnall ventured when asked about his recruiting. "Time will tell." The rest would be history!

The long, emotional season along with the hours spent recruiting, scouting opponents, teaching classes, preparing and directing three camps, and the turmoil concerning his teaching schedule left the coach exhausted. Dave was looking forward to some rest and fun with his family at their condo in Fairfield Bay, Arkansas, starting in July. It did not happen! Instead he found himself recuperating from a heart attack. The stress finally took its toll.

1990–1991

COACH DARNALL DIDN'T REALIZE HE would be leaving the game he loved the same year this outstanding freshman class would graduate. The most celebrated of the young stars in the new recruited crop were Chris Eaton, Dennis Huttenlocher, Chris Peterson, Duane Schmedeke, and Troy Tyler. Peterson, Schmedeke, and Tyler were ex-campers from Darnall's summer camps.

The frail and slow-moving coach greeted twenty-four players as official practice began. Out of character, the normally enthusiastic, energetic coach found himself quite passive. Dave designated more responsibility to his loyal assistant coach, Dennis Dighton. Darnall and Dighton handled the varsity team while student assistant Mike Heavilin was solely responsible for the junior varsity squad. Dave made personnel decisions, offense and defense selections, and prepared the practice schedules. Coach Dighton directed the floor practices.

Seniors Kevin Root, DeLeon Lavender, Mark Blunt, and Todd Ritsema attempted to lead the team back to the NAIA Playoffs. The coaching staff expected the six-foot-four center Lavender and six-foot-six power-forward Blunt to provide most of the inside scoring. Root, one of the best passers in small college basketball, was expected to "thread the needle" with his sharp passes to the veteran front-liners. Darnall thought his sophomores, Jon Guderjan and Steve Weemer could provide some "fire power" in the offense.

The Red Devils opened the 1990-1991 campaign at home against NAIA opponent Trinity Christian. The two promising sophomores did not let their coach down. They led the club's scoring attack with Guderjan pumping in nineteen points and Weemer contributing fourteen.

Eureka traveled to Concordia College-River Forest for its second contest of the year. Freshman forward Troy Tyler came off the bench to score twenty points, leading the Red Devils to a lopsided 64 to 36 victory. That was just the beginning of a fabulous career for the Washington, Illinois, native.

Two twenty-point-plus victories over Barat College and Westminster College occurred before Eureka participated in the Judson Invitational Tournament. EC drew the host school in the first round.

The Red Devils were outscored by six points in the final twenty minutes to drop a nail biter in spite of taking a 31 to 27 lead at half time. They lost their first game of the season by a narrow 72 to 70 margin. Darnall's club bounced back in the third-place game to gain a thirty-eight-point victory over Pillsbury College.

Two more victories were acquired before Christmas break. They were both against Iowa institutions. Sharpshooter Jon Guderjan pumped in twenty-one points as Eureka beat the always tough Iowa Wesleyan Tigers before a near capacity crowd at Reagan Fieldhouse. The Red Devils went on to finish their first half of the season with a thirty-seven-point victory over Mt. St. Clare. Guderjan, along with senior DeLeon Lavender, led EC in scoring with nineteen points each.

Sporting a 7 to 1 record concluding the first half of the season made the recuperating coach extremely happy.

Coach Dighton did most of the recruiting at the usual holiday tournaments during the three-week lay-off. Dave and his family spent some time together at their condo in Arkansas. He was nearly back to his normal weight after regaining the thirty pounds he had lost following his heart attack in July.

Eureka had two tough road trips to open the second half of the season.

The Red Devils battled back from an early deficit to post a hard-fought, 66 to 64, victory over NAIA affiliated Marion (Wisconsin). Eureka fell behind by as much as nine points in the first half before pulling to within five, 37 to 32, at intermission. A 10 to 0 run with ten minutes left in the contest gave EC a 48 to 47 lead. The game see-sawed back and forth until two free throws by Steve Weemer sewed up the win. It was a great six-hour trip home for the victors.

The next game was against Southern Illinois-Edwardsville. The game the previous year had been unpleasant and upsetting to Darnall. Again,

EC lost the game but under different circumstances. The bigger, more talented NCAA II team convincingly took the 75 to 64 victory. The Red Devils completed the road trip with a win over St. Louis Concordia before returning to Eureka.

Then on the road again. Next was Chicago-area Lake Forest. The game was almost postponed due to the United States' attack in the Persian Gulf. Lake Forest administrators spoke with both coaches about postponing the game that was scheduled to begin shortly. It was decided to delay the game until after President Bush's address to the nation was broadcast to all in attendance. The tip-off occurred about an hour later than the regularly scheduled time. Jon Guderjan pumped in twenty-three points to lead his team to a fifteen-point victory over Lake Forest.

It was time for the Red Devils to take on the NAIA District 20 top-rated team, McKendree College. Darnall's team was in the running for a playoff berth, and he knew the game meant a lot in the Dunkel ratings. His team had not beaten the annual powerhouse since the 1987 District championship game.

Jon Guderjan led the team to an unbelievable win in front of the hometown fans. The sophomore guard scored a career-high twenty-six points, including six three-pointers, to lead the Red Devils past the Bearcats, 75 to 69. The win boosted Eureka's record to 12 to 2 for the season.

A sportswriter for *The Pantagraph* asked Coach Darnall to comment on the victory. "It was a great win for us tonight, probably in the top five of my career here," replied Darnall. "They are a quicker, more physical team than we are, but our defense really did an outstanding job."

The Red Devils had held McKendree scoreless in the first six minutes of the game en route to a 34 to 30 half-time lead and never trailed again.

The post-game party at the Darnalls' home seemed like old times. A great win over an excellent team, a house full of Red Devil fans, and with Darnall physically nearly back to normal, the champagne flowed. The conversation overheard among the joyous fans included the night's win, Conference championship, and NAIA Playoffs. Were they back? Time would tell.

The next game started league play. It was the final year of the Prairie College Conference since a couple more Conference schools refused to play Eureka after the current season. Maryville had dropped out the year before.

As jubilant as the Red Devils and their fans were after the McKendree game, the team and their supporters were unbelievably shocked and disillusioned after their first Conference game. Eureka College experienced one of the most devastating losses in Darnall's tenure as head coach. It lost to the then consistent cellar-dweller Principia College on the road. Eureka's twenty-nine percent first-half shooting dug a nine-point half-time hole. Darnall went berserk in his half-time talk. Over extending himself, the coach criticized his team for its over-confident attitude.

"See what I told you," Darnall yelled. "Beating McKendree doesn't mean a damn thing if you lose tonight. The Dunkel points will kill you. Anybody can beat you. You got to be ready for every game. If you don't get your asses in gear, the Conference championship will go down the damn drain. Get the hell out there and play some damn ball. Show them you are one of the best teams in the State."

The lecture was to no avail. The Red Devils rallied to tie at 60 but couldn't overtake the home team. EC dropped a 75 to 67 decision to the host school. The Red Devil locker room was one of anger and disbelief. Darnall was stunned and sick to his stomach.

"You'll never understand the magnitude of this loss," the coach quietly told his players. "Someday you'll understand what I mean when I tell you that you have to be ready for every game regardless who we are playing. Get your showers and let's get the hell out of here."

It was a long, quiet trip home. Darnall was noticeably upset and stressed. The only good thing about the trip was that the team had traveled by charter bus as the Lady Red Devils had also played Principia. The coaching staff, at least, didn't have to drive the vans. That was something Darnall probably couldn't have done.

Coach conducted two hard days of practice before the Blackburn game in which both teams were "co-favorites." The practices weren't to punish his players, but to let them know that only hard work would pay dividends. His team had the difficult task of beating Blackburn on the road. A second loss would probably cost them the Conference championship.

As forecasted, the game was a battle. Despite thirteen points each by Lavender and Guderjan, the Red Devils could do no better than go into the intermission with a 38 to 38 tie. Darnall again reminded his team of the importance of the game. In an emotional speech, coach pleaded for his players to "give their all."

The team responded. Behind Guderjan's career-high twenty-nine points, the Red Devils outscored their opponents by ten in the second half for a final score of Eureka, 80 and Blackburn, 70.

Not only had Darnall's players responded to his half-time plea to play hard and give it their all for the rest of that game, but they also adopted that philosophy for the remainder of the season. Darnall's team conquered eleven consecutive opponents, including the Blackburn game. They went undefeated the remainder of the regular season schedule. That meant going 6 to 0 in Conference play, including a 121 to 53 shellacking of Principia College to revenge their only Conference loss. It also gave Darnall and his team their third consecutive Conference championship. It was their last as the Conference was disbanding only to reform with nearly all the same members excluding Eureka.

The winning streak included one very special game. It took place on February 7th. Coach Darnall's Red Devils gave their coach his 300th college career win by defeating Conference foe Greenville College, 88 to 66. Immediately following the contest, President George Hearne presented his coach with a plaque recognizing his coaching accomplishment. A real feel of the evening and of Darnall's seventeen-year career at Eureka College was expressed in two separate newspaper articles.

Jim Benson for *The Pantagraph* wrote one article entitled "Win No. 300 brings out 'Old' Darnall." It read:

President Hearne presents Coach Darnall with 300th Career Win Plaque.

When it was over and victory No. 300 was in hand, Dave Darnall almost apologized last night.

The Eureka Coach was back to his bubbly old self on the sidelines as the Red Devils beat Greenville, 88-66, at the Reagan Physical Education Center.

He was working the officials. He was screaming at his players.

"I shouldn't get like that," he said afterwards.

Coach Dave Darnall (above) making a point with his players during the game that gave him his 300th career victory. A perfect illustration of a foot-stomping, gesturing, whirl of frowns, yelling Coach Darnall. (Photo by Steve Smedley of *The Pantagraph*)

Darnall has tried to calm down since suffering a "mild" heart attack last summer. Mike Ditka may have been able to do it, but for this occasion Darnall just couldn't.

No one really expected him to anyway.

The victory gave Darnall, in his 17th season with Eureka College, a 300 - 137 mark at the school. At the end, he was teary eyed when Eureka College president George Hearne presented him with a plaque as the crowd came to its feet.

"Coach has been a little on edge the last few days," said senior guard Kevin Root. "We knew it (No. 300) was important to him. We wanted to give it to him as soon as we could."

Jon Guderjan, who put on a show with eight 3-pointers, led Eureka College with 26 points.

The 49-year old Darnall had plenty of time to reflect on his life last June when he spent a week in the cardiac unit at St. Francis Medical Center in Peoria. Darnall suffered the heart attack while speaking at his basketball camp.

412

"As I lay there, I thought how much I've sacrificed my family for this job," he said. "I'm gone almost every night of the week. But if you want to win, that's what you have to do."

Darnall's stay at Eureka College has lasted a little longer than he originally thought upon arriving in 1974.

"When I started my basketball career, my philosophy was to go somewhere, try to build the program and leave when I was on top," he said.

So, starting in 1965, that's what he basically did at Stanford, Gridley, Roseville, and Momence High Schools.

But Eureka College and the community grew on the Darnall family, which includes wife Bonnie, daughter Tiera, and son Derek.

It was small, with a current enrollment of 450 students, and it offered the type of 'togetherness' Darnall found at his high school stops.

The Darnall house is the official spot to gather after Eureka College home games. Players, parents, faculty, students and community members all come and mingle.

"It's something I did when I started at the small schools because in a small community, the No. 1 social activity is the athletic program," said Darnall, who has lost 35 pounds.

"When I go out recruiting, I talk to parents about this. I mention to them that you've watched your son play for four years, and now that he's going to the college, you won't feel part of the program anymore, but at Eureka, you will."

Darnall, an associate professor in the physical education department, plans to coach three more years before retiring.

"I think 20 (years) has a nice ring to it," he said.

The other article, written by Scott Heiberger of the *Journal Star*, was entitled "Darnall gets milestone memory—twenty-five years of success adds up to 300 wins for Eureka coach." It read in part:

The traditional courtside image of Eureka College Basketball coach Dave Darnall is a fiery one: A foot-stomping, gesturing, whirl of frowns, yells and tension.

This is a guy who's had ulcers since he was 25 years old. He blacked out after leaping for joy at the end of his greatest victory in 1987—then quickly revived and conducted interviews.

But a heart attack last summer quieted the 48-year-old Darnall more effectively than any referee could have. Although it was a relatively mild attack, it made him think about his lifestyle.

He lost 35 pounds, began walking regularly and changed his diet. That was the easy part. The toughest change has been to lower his intensity level to a notch below blast furnace.

"It's hard to change your personality after 25 years of coaching," Darnall said. "But now when I feel a little tightness building, I know I've had enough and have to back off."

The attack might have tempered Darnall's drive, but it hasn't changed the direction of it. He's still racking up the wins.

Darnall got his 300th Eureka win Thursday with an 88 - 66 decision over Greenville at the Reagan Physical Education Center.

Some coaches might downplay such a milestone, but not Darnall. He's excited. Victories are payback for his dedication.

Mementos of his 17 years at Eureka - and nine years at the high school level - fill a room in his ranch-style home, located five blocks from the gym.

"Two framed telegrams from Eureka's most famous alum, President Ronald Reagan, congratulate Darnall on Eureka's 1987 state title win at McKendree (the blackout game) and his 200th win during the 1985-86 season.

Action photos of former Eureka players seem to jump off the walls . . .

"He's an excellent recruiter," said six-year assistant coach Dennis Dighton. "He works very hard. He sells his program, sells his college and sells the atmosphere."

Darnall attracts players not normally associated with a school of 500 students. Five former Red Devils went on to play professionally in Europe.

Darnall scouts every opponent personally, even if it is a 10-hour round trip on a school night. Friend Chuck Wertz often drives.

"We do those kinds of things to win basketball games, and some of the other coaches at our level don't do that," Darnall said. "They think

414

we're giving aid, but we don't give a dime. I think we just outwork them."

Dighton shares more of the workload this season. The heart attack made Darnall willing.

"I don't call him my assistant coach. I call him my associate coach," Darnall said. "For the first time, I'm probably using him the way I should . . ."

Darnall, who came up with the motto, "Together We Win," likes to share the excitement. That's why he and Bonnie open their house after all home games to players, their families and other friends.

Players come back to visit years after they've graduated. So do some of their folks.

"When I see all those people come back it shows that once you know Dave, you can't forget him," Wertz said.

And you can't forget his record, either.

Numerous Red Devil supporters gathered for the celebration party at the coach's house following the 300th win. Following Darnall's 200th win, it became a ritual to pull a number off Bill Eaton's "Countdown to 300" wooden flip chart after each victory. It reached 300 on that memorable Thursday evening. Five days later, Darnall received a special letter. It was from former President Ronald Reagan. It read:

February 11, 1991

Dear Coach Darnall:

I was delighted to learn of your recent accomplishment on February 7, 1991. To set a record for coaching Eureka's 300th win in basketball is something to be quite proud of! You may take this accomplishment with pride. Because of your hard work and dedication this record has been set.

As coach, to our young people, you have been another parent and a close friend, the person who makes difficult tasks seem easy. You have taught them to work as a team and to work well together. I applaud your achievements and wish you many more years of happiness and success.

Nancy joins me in sending our best wishes.

Sincerely,
Ronald Reagan

The Eureka College men and women's basketball teams both received bids to the NAIA District 20 State Playoff Tournament. The men were seeded third and faced sixth-seeded Rosary College. The Red Devils had a chance to avenge last year's first-round tournament loss.

Eureka had never lost a playoff game at home. A standing-room-only crowd greeted the Red Devils as they took the floor twenty minutes prior to tip-off. Darnall felt his team was ready, especially after the last play-off loss to Rosary.

Jon Guderjan shot the lights out of the gym for a Eureka College advancement. "Eureka advances in NAIA playoffs" by Joe Johnson for the *Journal Star* emphasized Guderjan's spectacular performance.

Sophomore star Jon Guderjan in action. (Eureka College file photo)

Rosary College knew what Jon Guderjan could do prior to Wednesday night's NAIA District 20 basketball tournament game.

"Our game plan was to stop Guderjan," Rosary coach Bill Brucks said. "He had hit 91 of 191 from three-point range."

You can make that 101 of 205 for Guderjan this season.

The Eureka College sophomore bettered his own school record with 10 three-points and finished with 36 points as the Red Devils rolled to an 89 - 70 victory Wednesday night.

The Red Devils also avenged a 92 - 75 playoff loss to the Rebels last season.

Eureka, 24 - 3, continues its post-season work on Saturday at Olivet Nazarene, an 88 - 51 victor Wednesday over Judson.

Dick Lien, the sportswriter from the Peoria *Journal Star*, who traveled with the 1987 team to the National Tournament in Kansas City, witnessed Eureka's win over Rosary. He also attended the Red Devil's first practice following the victory. Intrigued by this year's team and the memory of the 1987 team, he wrote about both teams in "Eureka hangs an old banner, and it's like '87 again." Portions of the article read:

Even the maroon and gold banner on the north wall of the Reagan Center is the same. Welcome N.A.I.A. State Play-Offs. The Eureka College basketball team has been this way before.

"He thought the sign was lost," Bonnie Darnall said as workmen hung the banner this week while her husband ran the Red Devils through an afternoon practice, "but I put it away."

The road back to Kansas City and the 32-team NAIA National tournament began Wednesday night for Eureka with an 89 - 70 victory over Rosary College of River Forest.

"I want 40 minutes of bust-a-basketball," Coach Darnall had told the players before practice Monday. "That's how those guys five years ago got there . . . Bust-a-basketball."

Carried by guards Greg Nunn and Rick Taylor—"Sugar" and "Ice," everyone called them—the '86-87 Red Devils won three playoff games to make the school's sole appearance in the NAIA.

"Ice and Sugar would lead and we all followed," said point guard Kevin Root, a fifth-year player from Hoopeston who was a reserve on the '86-87 team.

". . . I learned a lot from those guys. I came here thinking I was a scorer, but Greg Nunn made me see I was a role player."

Now Root leads. But even as a starter who holds every Eureka assist record, he remains the ultimate role player.

"I'm comfortable with that," he said. "Now, I just get upset when someone cuts in the lane, I hit him (with the pass) and he misses the lay-up."

417

Root would like to see more of KC, where he was a short-timer in '87—leaving town the morning after the Red Devils lost their opener to Auburn-Montgomery.

"These guys ask about going there . . . I remember playing in Kemper Arena the same year the (NCAA) Final Four was there, watching teams kill other teams and thinking what unbelievable talent there was," he said.

So with one playoff game down: Is this Eureka team as good as that one? "I don't know," Root said. "Sugar and Ice were great players—and they got there."

But that team won only two more games than the Red Devils of '90-91. "We've got a chance," Root said. "We're a team that plays pretty well together."

Which, of course, is largely his fault.

The team left the day before the game so as to practice on the game floor, a tradition Dave started in the middle seventies.

Darnall knew his team was in for a battle. Olivet was looking to win a third straight NAIA District 20 championship. The scholarship institution was almost impossible to beat at home.

Olivet came out of the locker room smoking. Shooting well from the field and playing excellent man-to-man defense, the Tigers took a 37 to 28 half-time lead. The Red Devils, who trailed by as many as seventeen points, roared back to within three after a steal by Troy Tyler and a bucket by Lavender with thirty-five seconds left to play. That was in spite of what Darnall felt was some bad calls by the officials, including a technical foul on one of his players. Olivet advanced in the playoffs with an 87 to 83 victory.

The Eureka locker room was subdued; not many dry eyes. The team finished the season with an outstanding 24 to 4 record but felt they could have gone further. Coach Darnall painfully reminded his ailing team of the Principia loss. He felt that loss cost his team the second seed. The night's game could have been played at Eureka. That was especially true since they had beaten No. 1 seed McKendree College. The Red Devils were undefeated at home. As much as the reminder hurt, Coach wanted his players to remember the importance of every game regardless the opponent. Even though his team would lose several outstanding players, Darnall felt he would field an excellent team the following year. Hopefully, this empty feeling they were experiencing in the losing locker room would make an impact on their attitude and performance the next year.

The 1990-1991 team was ranked nationally in several categories at the end of the year. In NAIA National statistics, they were second in Team Rebounding Percentage, third in Team Field Goal Percentage, fourth in Team Scoring Margin, and fifth in Team Scoring Defense. In NCAA III National statistics, the Red Devils were fifth in Team Scoring Margin and fifth in Scoring Defense. Overall, not bad for an institution that did not give athletic scholarships.

Several members of the team received NAIA honors including Coach Darnall. DeLeon Lavender was named on the NAIA District 20 All-District Team. Kevin Root and Jon Guderjan were named Honorable Mention All-District. Coach Darnall was named NAIA District 20 Co-Coach of the Year along with Harry Statham of McKendree College. The Illinois Basketball Coaches' Association also named Darnall Coach of the Year.

Chapter 15

The Red Devils Are Back

THE NEXT TWO YEARS OF EUREKA COLLEGE basketball were so exciting that an entire book could be written on just them. The title could someday be "On the Brink of Greatness." The combined record for the 1991-1992 and the 1992-1993 seasons were forty-nine wins and nine losses. That included an astonishing 26 to 1 home record. The loss came in the 1991-1992 season opener against Goshen College. That meant Eureka had twenty-five consecutive at-home wins over those two years.

There was question whether Dave Darnall was capable of mentoring the Eureka College basketball program to the level it had reached during the 1986-1987 season. The disastrous 1987-1988 season only reinforced the doubters. However, the two years covered in this chapter detail the Red Devils' return to the "promised land."

The NAIA's decision to move to two divisions was not only logical, but also the right thing to do in Darnall's mind. In most cases, the larger NAIA schools that gave "full" athletic aid with an emphasis on basketball remained in NAIA Division I. Whereas, the smaller schools that could give full, partial, or even no financial aid, like Eureka, declared NAIA Division II. Coach Darnall felt a NAIA II national appearance was a realistic goal for his Red Devils.

Prior to the 1991-1992 school year, the Darnalls spent a few weeks in Fairfield Bay. While there, Dave learned of a special honor he was about to receive. Not in his wildest imagination, had he thought of this.

420

The phone rang at the Darnalls' condo in Arkansas. Dave answered the phone. "Hello, Tiera, how are you doing?" Dave asked his daughter on the other end.

"Fine, Dad," Tiera answered. "An official looking envelope from Illinois State University came in the mail today. What do you want me to do with it?"

Tiera normally gathered her parents' mail and sent it to Fairfield Bay while they were there for the summer.

"Open it and see what it is," Dave instructed. A few minutes passed.

"Dad! You aren't going to believe this. You've been selected by the ISU Athletic Hall of Fame Committee to be inducted into the Hall of Fame on Saturday, September 21st," Tiera enthusiastically told her father.

Stunned, Dave let a few minutes pass. "You've got to be kidding me," Dave answered.

"No, Dad. The letter is from Ron Wellman, Athletic Director. There are some forms you need to fill out and send back," Tiera replied.

"Bonnie," Dave shouted to his wife who was watching the evening news on TV. "Guess what? Here, talk to Tiera; she said I was selected to ISU's Hall of Fame."

It was not unusual for Tiera to call her parents. She and her mother talked at least every other day. Bonnie instructed her daughter to send the letter down with the other mail as they finished their conversation and hung up.

"This is damn hard to believe," Dave told his wife. "For a person who never participated in college sports, it's unbelievable, especially when it took me five years and four summers to graduate. My dad would never believe this," Dave continued in amazement. "I need a beer," he told Bonnie as they continued to discuss the development.

Dave then decided he needed to call his good friend Don Raycraft to tell him what had just occurred. Dave remembered "Ray," who had received his advance degrees from ISU, had mentioned something about writing a letter to the athletic office submitting his name. However, because of his ISU background, Darnall had not given it any more thought.

As the time neared for the actual honor to be bestowed, Dave asked many of his friends from his past to share his experience. He felt it was one of the most special honors a sports enthusiast could receive, being inducted into his/her alma mater's Athletic Hall of Fame. Old friends from Argenta, Normal, Momence, Gridley, and Eureka joined all of Dave's family and friend, Hoyt Crawford who had traveled from Fairfield Bay, to witness his induction. The distinguished ceremony took place at Redbird Arena. It was a place David had never had the opportunity to play or coach in.

Darnall's friend Gene Jontry, a former ISU basketball player and noted area school administrator was one of the five inductees. Mike Pryor, then in his seventh season in the NFL; Roger Weller, former ISU Head Track and Cross Country Coach; and, Ray Morelli, a former ISNU football great, were the other three honorees. Jo Workman received the "Stretch Miller Award" for her long dedication and service to the ISU women's athletic program. Each honoree was asked to select a presenter for their individual award. How fitting it was that Darnall asked one of his childhood idols, Duffy Bass, to be his. The successful ISU baseball coach and teacher had crossed paths with Dave numerous times during Darnall's coaching career.

ISU Athletic Director Ron Wellman and presenter Duffy Bass congratulating Coach Darnall.

Following the impressive ceremony, the Darnalls hosted a reception at the Normal Holiday Inn for their guests. The Holiday Inn also acts as the home for the Illinois Basketball Coaches Association Hall of Fame. Dave had previously been inducted into this Hall of Fame. The IBCA's was the first of five Halls of Fame of which Coach Darnall would become a distinguished member. Bonnie, Tiera, and Derek presented Dave with a very special gift to commemorate the ISU honor—an ISU Hall of Fame ring, which is depicted on the title page of this book.

1991–1992

IN THE 1991-1992 NAIA MEN'S Basketball Division II Pre-season Poll, Eureka College was ranked eighth in the nation. A ranking in the top ten was something for which Darnall had striven since his Red Devils' participation in the 1987 NAIA National Tournament in Kansas City. The first- ever Division II basketball championship tournament was going to be held at Tarleton State University in Stephensville, Texas, that season.

Junior Jon Guderjan and sophomore Troy Tyler led the eight returning lettermen on the nationally ranked team. Chris Hopwood headed a promising freshman class. Six-foot-eight Scott Schwab, the son of Rick Schwab—the college's former leading scorer—had transferred from Northeast Missouri State. The Red Devils did lose an important player when junior to be Steve Weemer transferred to Eastern Illinois University.

Eureka opened its season at home against Goshen College, Indiana. The Maple Leaves had been scouted (remember Scout Wertz' story), but it was to no avail. The bigger and stronger Indiana team left the Red Devils with their heads hanging, 97 to 85.

The game seemed like a road game to the Eureka players. There were very few EC supporters in attendance, but the gym was filled with Goshen fans. The Maple Leaf coach had graduated from nearby Olympia High School, a consolidated school district located just outside of Stanford. The disbanded Stanford High School had been Dave's first basketball coaching position. Also, Goshen affiliated with the Mennonite church, had several of its players from the Central Illinois area and drew loyal supporters from their church communities. Most of the Eureka fans were in Ohio to support the record-setting, undefeated Red Devil football team that was participating in the NAIA post-season playoff.

Coach Darnall was not happy with the performance of his team, fans or no fans. He felt his team played "half-assed" and without emotion for a nationally ranked team.

"Tonight we played like a bunch of damn individuals, everyone for themselves. There was no team effort. I don't give a damn how many fans

423

we had," Darnall shouted to his team in the locker room following the game. "We better in hell get back to the 'Together We Win" philosophy.'"

Normally, Dave said very little to his team following a defeat. He usually waited until the next day's practice. However with a second game coming within twenty-four hours, he knew he had better get their attention before the season went "right down the damn drain." Back-to-back home losses would be a nightmare—a possible "suicide"—instant retirement for the coach.

The next night's home game was again sparsely attended. The football team had lost earlier in the day, but many Red Devil fans still had not returned to campus. Not only was it unusual to have two consecutive home games, but it was unheard of having four of the first five in Reagan Fieldhouse. The early home schedule wasn't the only unique thing that happened during that year. The 1991-1992 season became a year of "firsts."

The Red Devils not only came roaring back against Concordia and beat the visitors, 82 to 54, but also went on to win sixteen straight contests. That period ran from November 23rd to February 1st. Guess Darnall's post-game locker room lecture made an impact. On the other hand, perhaps the Concordia win was the result of the Coach's pre-game talk. Most likely, it was a combination of both!

"If you guys lose this damn game," Darnall warned his team before they took the floor against Concordia, "we'll have a practice after the game. We'll be here 'til midnight if we have to, but we're going to get this turned around."

It appeared the boys didn't like that idea as they jumped out to an eighteen-point lead by intermission, 35 to 17.

Both of the post-game parties at the Darnalls' were scantly attended, but don't feel bad for the Darnalls. That would soon drastically change.

The third game's starters against Trinity Christian were Scott Schwab at center, six-foot-seven Dave VanWeelden, and six-foot-four Troy Tyler at the forward positions, and a pair of six-foot-two guards, Jon Guderjan and Lance Craft. Sophomore six-foot-seven Chris Eaton was usually the first man off the bench. Kevin Brown, a six-foot-two senior, gave relief at the guard position.

The Red Devils started the road game off slowly, trailing by one at intermission. With Chris Eaton starting the second half and Dave VanWeelden playing the best game of his career, EC came back to gain a 79 to 62 victory. Jon Guderjan made twelve for twelve from the charity line in the second half on the way to game-high twenty-two points. Troy Tyler chipped in with twenty-one, while VanWeelden netted seventeen.

Eureka returned home to take on two prestigious NCAA III institutions in Lake Forest and St. Norbert. Chris Eaton got his first start of his career against Lake Forest. He had an excellent attitude and was having some great practices.

Coach Darnall was able to give thirteen Red Devil players some action in the lopsided, 101 to 50, victory over Lake Forest. Often criticized by both opponent and Eureka fans, including parents of some of the players that were not receiving a lot of court time, Darnall was delighted that ten different players contributed in the scoring attack. Guderjan led the way with nineteen, while Eaton and VanWeelden scored seventeen and sixteen points respectively.

Darnall constantly reminded his critics that post-season play was based on the Dunkel Rating System. The previous year's loss against Principia was an example. A win would have possibly meant a second round NAIA tournament game played in Eureka instead of at Olivet Nazarene. It was usually tenths of points that separated the eight seeded teams. Eureka College, remember, had never lost a home playoff game and only had won one on an opponent's floor.

Claiming a 62 to 59 home victory over St. Norbert, Wisconsin, the Red Devils returned to the road for two difficult match-ups. Lance Craft and Troy Tyler, each, pumped in twenty-two points to lead their team to a 68 to 62 win over Blackburn before claiming an 82 to 72 victory over Clarke College, Iowa. Junior guard Jon Guderjan sank seven of eleven shots from the three-point range, scoring a total of thirty-one points. Newly starting, Chris Eaton contributed eighteen points, while grabbing the same number of rebounds.

"It was an excellent win for us," Dave said after the game. "Any time you beat Clarke at their place, you've done a good night's work. It makes the long trip home a little easier."

Even after the five-hour ride home from Iowa and the excellent victory, the Red Devil mentor couldn't sleep. Even winning was causing stress. He woke Bonnie to tell her of his concern.

"You know, I get ill before every game. I get sick to my stomach," Dave stated. "I get the dry heaves. I'm on the toilet five or six times before the game. I am extremely tired before the game. On the road, I have to lie down. Like tonight, as soon as I got into the locker room before the game, I had to lie down on the trunks. I tried to help lay out the uniforms, but had to lie down," Dave continued.

"Even after we won tonight, I couldn't enjoy it. All the way home I worried about the game against Olivet at the Judson Tournament. I'm all broke out. The damn rash is killing me. I'd give anything to get rid of it. I don't know how much longer I can take this," he worried.

Bonnie knew the torment Dave was going through, but she also knew much was self-generated. "You have got to try to not let it get to you so much," she encouraged.

"You know, when we play here, I can't get out of bed until about six. I just feel depressed and tired. I don't know what I am going to do. I don't know how much longer I can stand this," the exhausted coach concluded.

"You've got to get yourself under control. This is not good for you or us. Try to get some sleep now, and then we will talk about it some more tomorrow," she replied. There was little else she could say to him. Dave eventually drifted off.

Darnall knew he had an outstanding sophomore class and wanted to see them through. He had promised the fellows upon their recruitment that he would remain through until they graduated. That meant two more years. Could he make it? Time would tell.

Some coaches under the stress of the profession could "pull back" a little, but not Dave. It was "full blast"—all out—100%, or not at all. He also worried that another heart attack could be fatal, just like his father's second. It has been said the winning causes just a much stress and anxiety as losing. Darnall agreed. There was no real pressure from the administration or community to win; it came from within. Dave hated to lose, and he wanted one more trip back to the nationals.

Even with a 6 to 1 record, Darnall's team had dropped from eighth in the NAIA II polls to fifteenth. That was with Olivet Nazarene, a top NAIA I team in the country over the past three years, coming up next. It didn't look very promising to retain even that ranking.

The team left campus around noon for the three-hour trip to Judson College. Many Red Devil fans and parents made the trip to support the boys and made a point to stay at the same Holiday Inn as the team. They knew that the first game of the tournament against Olivet was big for the Red Devils.

As Darnall stated, "This game can make us or break us in the Dunkel. A win against Olivet and later against McKendree on the road would be huge in the national rating system. What would be the odds of that?"

426

Coach had finished his short but stern pre-game talk when Jon Guderjan asked if he could have a couple minutes with the team. Guderjan was only a junior, but he had become the leader of the team. He pulled out several sheets of paper from his duffel bag. He passed them out to his team-mates and coaches telling his team it was time to pay back Olivet for the losses over the last several years. Jon asked those around him to read the following note before sitting down. The players said nothing as they were concentrating on the papers before them. The locker room was absolutely silent.

Remember 86 - 83 Olivet
Remember 86 - 83 Olivet
Remember 86 - 83 Olivet
Remember 86 - 83 Olivet
Olivet beats Eureka 2 out of the last 4 years in the NAIA State
Playoffs

On Friday morning think about what Olivet has taken away
from you three seniors -
2 opportunities to go to the National Tournament.
Olivet has dominated Eureka Basketball for the 4 years - DOMINATE!
IT IS TIME FOR A CHANGE!!!

D efense
O ffensive execution
M an to man pressure
I n their face every time they pick up the ball
N ever say die attitude
A nother one bites the dust - this is the song
     Olivet played after they beat us last year
T WW
E C BASKETBALL

We have paid the price for the last 4 years and now it's pay back
time—
LETS MAKE OLIVET PAY THE PRICE!
This is something we have waited for a long time and we finally got
the chance. Think about all those long hours in the gym since
August—this is what it's all about—the hard work, the sacrifice, and
the dedication.
40 minutes on Friday afternoon isn't a long time,
and the minutes will be temporary—
BUT THE MEMORIES COULD LAST FOREVER!!
Let's make them good ones.

It seemed that all heads raised at once. Twenty-one pairs of eyes glaring in the still dressing room. The coach asked for his ten seconds of silence and the heads again turned downward. Seconds later, Darnall shouted, "Let's kick some ass. We owe them!"

That's what the EC players wanted to hear. The silence erupted into a roar of "EC - EC - EC" as the spirited Red Devils rushed to the doorway that led to the hall and out into the gym. They were ready.

"Oh, I wish this was over," Darnall thought as he followed the footsteps of his team.

Coach Darnall made a line-up change because of Olivet's quickness and sticky defense. He inserted his "John Havlicek," six-foot-two senior Kevin Brown, for six-foot-seven Dave VanWeelden at one forward position. Brown, an excellent defensive player as well as a potential scorer, was assigned to stop the Tigers' top scorer.

As publicized, the first half proved to be a nail-biter. Two of the state's top small college basketball teams were at battle. One institution gave full ride athletic scholarships and the other none. With Craft and Tyler leading the way, Eureka held a slim two-point lead at the intermission.

Whereas Darnall had been pretty low-key in his pre-game talk, he was extremely vocal in his half-time speech. Uncustomary for Coach, he cheered and challenged his players to play well and win what would be one of the biggest games in the college's history. Much of the time, he was "chewing ass" and raising hell with them. Tonight, there was 100 percent effort by all players, both on the floor and on the bench. There was no need to get after them. Could it have been Guderjan's note to the team?

The Red Devils, again, came out of the locker room fired up. They jumped out to a six-point lead in the first few minutes of the second half. Lance Craft was having a career night. He went on to pump in twenty-three points to lead his team to a spectacular, 67 to 53, victory. The locker room was in pandemonium.

"If there was an example of the 'Together We Win' philosophy, it was tonight," Coach Darnall excitedly told the press following the game. Guderjan sacrificed his scoring for the benefit of the team. Olivet thought if they could stop him, we would crumble. We proved we're a complete team."

Guderjan had only one basket and a total of three points.

The following day one unidentified newspaper headline stated, "Eureka avenges Olivet in tourney." Portions of the article read,

Elgin - The Olivet Nazarene University men's basketball team was haunted by past successes Friday. . . . The Tigers, winners of three straight NAIA District 20 titles, were tamed by Eureka, 67 - 53, in the first round of the Judson College Tournament.

The Peoria *Journal Star* headline stated, "Red Devils finally beat Tigers, 67 to 53." The first sentence of the article read, "Eureka ended its years of frustration against Olivet Nazarene on Friday."

The rumor was that Nazarene's coach was so frustrated that he held a practice late that night after the team arrived back on Olivet's campus, some seventy miles away. Darnall often threatened to do the same, but never did.

What a celebration party the loyal fans enjoyed at the Holiday Inn. Coach Darnall warned his team that the night's victory would be meaningless if they got beat in the championship game. The players understood. After visiting with their fans and families for a short period of time, they headed to bed for the next night's challenge.

Eureka College would compete against Judson for the title of the tournament. Judson had beaten the Red Devils by two in the first round of the Classic the previous year. Could Coach Darnall, again, use the revenge factor in his pre-game motivational talk?

The Red Devils started where they left off the night before. Chris Eaton paved the way with fifteen first-half points, and Eureka jumped out to a 37 to 21 lead at intermission. Not only was Eaton unstoppable in the middle, but EC played excellent man-to-man defense. Eureka continued its onslaught on the hosts the second half to claim a 75 to 53 victory for the championship. The win gave Darnall's team an overall 8 to 1 record going into the Christmas break. The only loss being the first game of the season.

It would be four weeks before the Red Devils played their next game. Dave was worn out. He spent the week prior to Christmas recruiting. Then, the Darnall family headed to their condo in Arkansas.

The team had good reason for wanting to resume play. They were on an eight-game winning streak. With two excellent road victories against Brescia College, Kentucky, and Westminster College, Missouri, the Red Devils returned for a quick home game against Aurora University before hitting the road for two more.

The Eureka College men and women's teams traveled together by charter bus for the four-day Kentucky-Missouri trip. They stayed in one of the most popular hotels in Kentucky, the Rivermont Executive Inn. Some of the nation's top country-western performers highlighted the hotel's entertainment roster.

Prior to leaving for the two-game trip, Coach Darnall was asked by Peoria *Journal Star* sportswriter Scott Heiberger about his thoughts for the season to-date and what the next few games would be like. Portions of the article "Break for Red Devils came at a bad time" gave both Darnall and Heiberger's thoughts.

"I am very surprised at the success of our team so far," said Darnall, whose team averages 78 points per game and yields 63.

"We were pre-season rated eighth in NAIA Division II, but that was based mostly on the success of last year's program and the program we've had in the past. I didn't think we were in the top 25."

The Red Devils wish they could have kept playing while the streak was hot. "As my assistant Coach Dennis Dighton said, 'It's too bad we didn't have just a couple days off,'" said the 18-year coach Darnall.

"The biggest surprise is Chris Eaton," Darnall said. "He has been the turning point. You see him in practice doing things, then you see him at the game, and it's like, 'Gosh, is this the same kid?'"

"He's been playing a ton right now," Tyler said. "He's owning the lane."

The Red Devil coach thinks the next few games will be critical to his squad's development and national ranking. Six of the next nine games are on the road.

"If we can keep our heads above water the next three weeks, then I think we can have another pretty good year," Darnall concluded.

The Lady Red Devils played their game prior to the men's contest. The men's team supported the women's team and vise-versus. Coach Schuster's team was trailing by some ten points with a couple minutes remaining in the contest. The head coach decided to substitute with young players to provided experience, but Bescia's coach stayed with the starters, completely out-matching the young Lady Red Devils. The home team won by over twenty points.

Both Eureka College basketball teams shared the same small locker room. The two head coaches crossed paths.

"What the hell was going on?" Coach Schuster asked the veteran men's coach. "He didn't substitute! He ran up the score!"

"Welcome to the Dunkel Rating System," Coach Darnall explained to the dejected coach. "They're a very good team, and he was playing the point spread. You know Dunkel points are, basically, based on winning and losing and the point spread?" Coach Darnall asked the puzzled Lady's coach.

"I don't understand," Coach Schuster told Dave.

"After we feed the kids tonight, let's get both coaching staffs together, and I'll explain," replied Darnall. "We'll meet in the lounge."

The Dunkel was complicated, but Darnall felt he somewhat knew what was expected. In fact, ever since the system was implemented to determine the playoff field, Dave had studied it. That's why he knew the Olivet game and the up-coming game against McKendree were huge in the Dunkel system.

On the way to Westminster College, the EC team made a layover in St. Louis. The college students enthusiastically welcomed the day of relaxation at the St. Louis Downtown Marriott. They enjoyed the motel's indoor pool and found the visit to the "Arch" fascinating. The night was topped off with a walk to the "Spaghetti Factory" located in the Landing on the Mississippi River for dinner. The old surroundings were intriguing to the travelers. It was the first time that most of the young adults had visited the historical section of St. Louis.

When the Red Devils returned home to play Aurora, the team did not disappoint its fans. Three players scored in double figures as Eureka trounced the Spartans, 91 to 49. Guderjan led the attack with twenty-one points, while Eaton and Tyler made twenty and eighteen respectively.

"After six road games, it was nice to play in front of the hometown crowd," Darnall said after the game. "It's been a while since we have had a post-game party at our house. We were able to share the wins at the Judson Tournament and those on the Kentucky-Missouri trip with our fans that were able to make the trips, but it's nothing like after home games in Eureka."

Eureka College jumped four places to No. 11 in the NAIA Division II poll. The stress and worrying about keeping the team winning and living up to its national ranking kept Darnall physically and mentally drained.

"For those who think there is no pressure on a coach when his team in winning, they have never been a winning coach," Darnall said. "Once you have your team on the top, you want to keep it there, especially, if your team is ranked. I fear losing."

Two changes took place on the Red Devil roster just prior to the Aurora game. Gerald Monroe, a six-foot-five forward, rejoined his teammates after participating in the basketball program his first two years at Eureka College.

Second, Chris Peterson, the highly recruited guard from Brimfield who had not returned to Eureka the beginning of his sophomore year for personal reasons, transferred back to EC. When Chris failed to come back, the coaching staff had not been overly concerned. Boy, would he prove to them that they should have been.

Even though "Pete" had a lot of talent, his attitude had been questionable. The coaches felt he was not very coachable, not a Eureka College-type player—"Together We Win."

Chris missed his former teammates, campus life, and now the disciplined Red Devil program. The coaching staff agreed to allow Peterson to return to the team at the beginning of the college's second semester. Chris left a junior college after completing a semester of academic work, but had not participated on its basketball team during that time. Chris' "homecoming" was a blessing.

It was then back on the road for two, including an enormous game with the nationally renowned McKendree Bearcats.

In the first of the two, Dave VanWeelden and Troy Tyler, each, pumped in twenty points as EC "spanked" Harris-Stowe University in St. Louis, 87 to 58. It was then time for the Red Devils' second showdown with a top NAIA Division I team in the nation—Harry Statham's McKendree Bearcats. Only once in two decades had Eureka College beaten McKendree on its home floor. The 1987 win was unbelievable!

Two of the top NAIA teams in the nation were about to tangle. One, a NAIA I team that gave athletic scholarships, and the other a NAIA II institution that gave no athletic aid. McKendree, with a 20 to 1 record and ranked No. 5 in the latest Division I poll was going against Eureka College, with a 12 to 1 record and recently moved to No. 8 in the most current NAIA Division II poll. EC had won twelve consecutive games after losing its season opener. McKendree was a scoring machine as usual, ranked No. 12 in Division I by averaging 97.9 points per game. Eureka relied heavily on its defense and was ranked No. 4 in Division II, yielding just 63.1 points per game.

The team left campus around 2:00 P.M. for the four-hour drive to Lebanon, including a stopover at the Springfield Bonanza for a pre-game meal. The Red Devils were hoping for a duplication of their performance against Olivet Nazarene. They arrived at the college close to 6:00 P.M. While the coaching staff laid out the uniforms, the players strolled around the gym. Some removed their shoes and shot around, while others just lay back in the bleachers.

Coach Darnall helped his staff for a few minutes and then lay down on the traveling trunks for his now usual pre-game nap. Pre-game syndrome had set in. Perhaps tonight, it was even worse. What an important game!

After receiving a low-key pre-game talk from their coach, the players took the floor for their biggest game of the year. Darnall, basically, told his guys to play hard, smart, execute the game plan, and not to lose their heads regardless of the score. He then requested the traditional ten seconds, "Let's take our ten seconds. Each one is an individual. Think what you want to think, or you don't need to think at all, as long as we are quiet, and we do it together—TWW."

What a first twenty minutes of play! The home team held a slim, 39 to 37, lead at the intermission. Darnall reminded his players to do the same things they had been doing the first half. They were executing the game plan to a "T." He added, "Don't quit, and be patient. You don't know what might happen if you win this game. This might be the biggest game of your career." As the players sprinted to the locker room door, Coach shouted, "Let's go do it!"

The Red Devils posted a tremendous upset. Jon Guderjan nailed a three-pointer with two minutes left to put his team ahead to stay. Kevin Brown sank five free throws down the stretch to help seal the victory.

Dave talked to the press immediately following the game. "This has to be right up there in the top three of biggest wins in my 18-years of coaching," said the Red Devil coach. "They are a run-and-gun type of team, and I told my kids if we could hold them to under 70 points, we would win. We really played very good defense."

The bench players and EC fans swarmed their heroes on the floor—a repeat of five years earlier. It just didn't last as long.

In the locker room, Coach Darnall enthusiastically congratulated his team on their accomplishment, telling them how proud he was of them. The coach told his jubilant winners that the "sky was now the limit."

"You can go as far as you want. Play hard and keep the "Together We Win" attitude, and we can go the Nationals," Darnall assured his boys.

The trip home was one even Dave could find somewhat relaxing and enjoyable. The players were given the now post-game meal of two ham sandwiches, a bag of chips, a couple cookies, and a can of soda that had been prepared by the college's food service. The Red Devils were going home as real "winners."

Coach Darnall drove the lead van, while Coach Dighton rode "shotgun" working on the game stats. Coach Blunt drove the second van with administrative assistant Steve Bosch sitting alongside. The trainer and upper-classmen rode in Blunt's van. Darnall and Dighton escorted the young players. They had the privilege of listening to the "Oldies but Goodies." They could not wait until they "graduated" to the other van.

The trip back to Eureka went quickly. The fairly new expressway between Lincoln and Morton made the trip a little shorter. The two-vehicle caravan merged onto Interstate 74. Ten miles later, they spotted the exit sign for Goodfield and another that read "Eureka College Home of President Ronald Reagan." It was about 1:30 A.M. and only seven more miles to Eureka. However, as the vans approached the Goodfield four-way stop intersection, Coach Dighton noticed a couple county sheriff squad cars located in a parking lot at the intersection.

"They must be looking for someone," Coach Darnall told Dighton. "I hope nothing has happened in Eureka."

"Maybe they're getting ready for a drug bust," one of the players offered.

"I don't know," Dave replied, "but something is going on."

Making sure he stopped at the stop sign for several seconds, Darnall drove on through. The second van repeated the same procedure, but as the vans gained speed, the patrol cars sped toward them with their sirens on and lights flashing.

"I hope to hell they don't think we have drugs in here," Darnall said of the unmarked van he was driving. About that time, one patrol passed the vans and slowed down. The others fell in behind the second van.

"Hell, I think we are being escorted to Eureka," the surprised head coach shouted. "I don't believe this. This has never happened to me before," Darnall commented.

Those sleeping players abruptly woke up. Dave turned the interior lights on. The now alert players were giving high-fives. Darnall was wondering what was happening in the following van. He thought all of this had to impress the upperclassmen.

Upon reaching town, Dave was wondering what the people in bed must have been thinking by all the commotion. The escorted vans turned off Route 17 onto Reagan Drive for the four-block drive to the Reagan Field-house. As the small caravan passed the TKE House just before turning into the parking lot, the victorious Red Devils saw several of their frat brothers outside cheering. Pulling in front of the fieldhouse, the passengers saw a small crowd of cheering fans. In the center of the group was President

George Hearne. The smiling, but surprised, EC team departed the vans to greet their fans and the president. Congratulations were exchanged, and then the students left for their resident halls. It was past 2:00 A.M.

Coach Darnall conversed with the president, describing the game and expressing his surprise at the escort from Goodfield. Dave thanked Hearne for organizing and participating in the "welcome home" gesture. It was the first time in Darnall's tenure that had happened.

Four days later, the Red Devils played Clarke College, the first of three home games before returning to the road. Darnall had his boys ready to play in front of their anxious home fans. Tyler and Eaton scored twenty-five and twenty-three points respectively, but it was six-foot-seven Dave Van Weelden that Darnall felt was the key player in the Red Devils, 85 to 52, victory over Clarke.

"VanWeelden played the most complete game in his career," Darnall said. "If we're going to go anywhere, we need him to play well because he gives us two big boys. When both he and Eaton play together, it really helps us."

VanWeelden banged home sixteen points and grabbed seventeen rebounds in helping his team gain its fourteenth consecutive win.

An overflow crowd showed up at the Darnall home after the Clarke game. People wanted to hear all the details of the exciting McKendree win as well as celebrate the night's victory over Clarke. Before the night was over, the conversation turned to the topics of national ranking and Dunkel points. Unfortunately, Coach Darnall was only able to make a guess. *The Pantagraph*'s article that appeared three days later would help answer the question Darnall could not at the after-game party.

"Eureka College No. 3" was the headline in the January 28, 1992, edition. Portions read:

One win did quite a bit for the Eureka College men's basketball team. The Red Devils, 14 - 1 overall, rose from No. 8 to No. 3 in the NAIA Division II poll released yesterday. The Red Devils, who also gained a first-place vote, are 22 points behind No. 2 St. Joseph's of Maine and 69 points behind leader King College of Tennessee.

The main thrust behind the jump was a 77 - 70 win at McKendree College last week. McKendree was ranked fifth in the Division I poll.

"The win over McKendree was one of the biggest wins in my career," Eureka College coach Dave Darnall said. "That had to be a factor when people saw us take a team which averaged 98 points a game and hold them almost 30 under their average and beat them at their place."

Eureka College, which had never been ranked before this season, has its coach as the most surprised of all.

"More people were sold on my team than I was," he said. "This is surprising since we lost four starters from last year.

"The bottom line is that the kids have the right chemistry. Maybe they don't have the overall talent we've had in the past, but the togetherness is there."

The high ranking also gives the Red Devils a safety zone when the playoffs begin at the end of February. The Red Devils have a Dunkel ranking of 45.5, which is nearly 20 points higher than Trinity Christian, the state's next highest Division II school.

"That's the highest Dunkel (which ranks schools based on strength of schedule, won-loss record and point margin) ever," Darnall said. "Unless we have a total collapse, we should be able to host both rounds in the state playoffs if we continue to win."

Not only did the article summarize the NAIA II National ranking, but it also summarized the Dunkel ratings that determine the District Playoff field. For several years, Darnall had "played" the Dunkel Rating System to many people's displeasure.

"It is the only way to make it back to the national tournament," Dave would tell his critics.

With two more wins "under their belt," the Red Devils took their annual trip to Edwardsville to complete against NCAA Division II, full scholarship Southern Illinois-Edwardsville. SIU-E would not travel to Eureka for a game but did give the much smaller school a financial guarantee to play on their campus.

The team and some of their fans left Eureka around noon the day before the game. Dave wanted his players to get a "feel" of the large arena before Saturday's afternoon game. Following an hour or so practice concentrating on the game plan and shooting, the Red Devil team returned to their motel to visit with their families, friends, and fans.

Later with the players in bed, the coaching staff joined player fathers John Tyler, Larry Guderjan, Ron Craft, Jon Hopwood, Nyle Schmedeke, Bob Brown, and super supporters Chuck Wertz and Dan Harrod in the motel's lounge to discuss the team's new national ranking and the following day's game. Former player DeLeon Lavender, who lived nearby, joined the group for the evening. There were some agreements and some disagreements, but it was the young female bartender that drew the fellows' attention. Approximately an hour later, the female members of the entourage joined the men in the lounge. Unenthusiastically, the "big boys" left the bar and joined the women at a large table in the middle of the room, but a good time was had by all until heading off to bed themselves.

The players knew the game plan. It definitely was not what some of the players, their parents, and other fans liked or wanted to see, but it was what Coach Darnall thought needed to be done to have a chance to win against a team of SIU-E's stature on the road. The fastest way for a player to see "pine time" in the day's game would be not to follow the coach's game plan.

In his pre-game talk, Dave was pretty calm. He reminded his team to stay with the plan, the importance of the game regarding Dunkel points, and the national ranking. The team took their ten seconds of silence.

"Keep you heads. Play hard. Do what you're told," Darnall instructed his players as they began to leave the locker room for the long trip down the hall, down the stairs, and through the lower hall to the gym. Coach remained behind for a final bathroom visit.

Darnall was not happy with the score at intermission, but he was satisfied with the way the team was playing. Even though they missed a couple of easy shots that had to be made if EC was going to beat a quality NCAA II team, the players stayed with the game plan. The fans, both Cougar and Red Devils, didn't like the style of play that Darnall was employing. Eureka was controlling the tempo of the game. It was slow and deliberate, just what spectators hated to watch.

Trailing 25 to 19 at the break, Coach Darnall told his team not to change a thing, just play a little better defense and make a couple more of their open shots. Again, the Eureka Coach informed his players, "Be patient, work hard, and don't let the fans or officiating effect your play," as they started for the locker room door.

The players did as instructed. The game was close the entire second half, but the Red Devils trailed by eight points with 2:30 left when Jon Guderjan hit two consecutive three-pointers.

Kevin Caldwell had a chance to ice the game for SIU-E, but he missed a bonus opportunity leaving the "door open" for a possible Eureka shot. The Red Devils rebounded the missed free throw and with only seconds left got the ball into the hands of Troy Tyler who was standing directly in front of the EC bench. Tyler received the pass and turned and shot. He was hit by a Cougar defender, but no call was made. Darnall went crazy. Jumping off the bench, he shouted at the officials to call the foul. Meanwhile, Tyler's game winning three-pointer hit nothing but net. However, the shot at the buzzer was ruled to have come too late as NCAA Division II Southern Illinois University-Edwardsville was given the 48 to 46 victory.

Darnall went berserk. Not only was his player definitely fouled as the potential winning basket was scored, but now there was the question of the made shot. The three officials dashed off the floor. Darnall, for the second time in his career, sprinted after them. Remember the Clarke, Iowa, game? The EC players were dismayed. Startled at the two spontaneous home court calls, they were in instant shock. They, also, starting yelling at the streaking officials.

The officials were faster than the angry coach. Dave could not catch them, but that didn't stop him from screaming. "He was fouled, he was fouled, call the damn foul. You took that game away from my kids," the raving coach yelled as he pursued the "deaf ear" officials. Running off the floor while chasing the game officials, Darnall did not return. His players shortly followed after him. There was no shaking the opponents' hands.

Reaching the locker room, the steaming coach slammed the entrance door behind him to wait for his heroic team.

"We got _ _ _ _ _ _ screwed," he shouted as his dejected players sat on the locker room benches with their bowed heads in their hands. "We'll never come back here," Dave yelled. "It's too damn bad that a school like SIU has to beat a tiny school like us on that kind of call. I'm proud as hell of you. You proved to me you're for real."

Darnall walked around, patting the players on their backs as they sat on the benches, and individually reinforcing his pleasure with their efforts. Meanwhile, the assistant coaches were beginning to pack the team's warm-ups.

"You guys had this one taken away from you, but Dunkel point wise, you were a big winner. Remember, Southern averaged 90 points a game. You held them to 48. Only one other team held them under 50 points and that was Division I South Carolina at home," praised the coach. "This was a great effort. Let's get your showers and get the hell out of here. We'll stop in Litchfield for supper," Darnall concluded.

"I don't know about the shot. I didn't see it. I was yelling at the officials. I damn well know that Troy was fouled. It was directly in front of me. I could have reached out and touched them," the still irate coach told the press later. "Troy should have had three free throws at least. No wonder they don't want to play us at Eureka."

"I could hear some of the bench players saying the basket was good. So were our fans yelling behind our bench, but I don't honestly know," Darnall said in concluding his interview with the press.

Coach Darnall tried to keep up beat. He didn't want his players to be "down." However, he felt that they had deserved the win. The forty-five minute drive to the Maverick Steak House seemed like hours. Darnall was internally dejected. In fact, Coach Dighton was doing the driving.

"Coach, I don't know how much longer I can take this crap," Dave told his assistant. "Damn officiating is driving me out of coaching. It's hard enough to lose, but like this? I can't stand it."

Coach Dighton just kept driving, not really responding because missed calls also upset him a great deal. The rest of the van was quiet. The young players still seemed to be in shock.

Upon arriving back at Eureka College campus, Coach Darnall again told the players how pleased he was with their performance. He told them regardless what anyone says, they played the game the proper way. The game plan had worked.

"Enjoy the day off tomorrow," Dave told his departing players. "Forget about basketball. We're okay."

Even though Dave told his players to forget about the happening, he couldn't. He was still angry. It would be a sleepless night.

"Thank God, tomorrow is Sunday," Dave told Bonnie. "I don't think I could make it to school."

He was right. Feeling extremely tired and depressed, the coach spent the entire day in bed.

Forty-eight hours after the disheartening loss, the players reported to practice. Athletes seem to bounce back after tough losses better than coaches. Even though Coach Darnall was still troubled over the disappointing loss, the players seemed to be in a pretty good mood. Darnall appreciated that.

"Fellows, we've got to forget about Saturday's game," Coach Darnall told his players in his pre-practice talk. "What would be a real tragedy would be to play a game like that and then come home and lose to Hannibal-LaGrange. Your effort against SIU-E will go right down the drain if we lose tomorrow night. Let's have a good practice and kick the hell out of LaGrange."

Normally after a practice, Coach Darnall traveled to a college game to scout with Wertz or to a high school game with an administrative assistant to recruit. However, this particular night was exceptional. After a good practice, the coach was able to stay home. Still beat after Saturday's tough loss, he was happy he did not have to go on the road. All future opponents had either already been scouted or weren't scheduled to play. High school games are played on Tuesdays, Fridays, and Saturdays.

"It was meant to be" that Coach Darnall was home on that Monday, February 3rd, chilly evening. With Dave lying in bed watching TV, the phone rang. As usual, Bonnie answered it.

"It's for you," Bonnie shouted to the bedroom for Dave.

"Congratulations!" the caller said. "You guys are rated No. 1."

Dave, nearly falling out of the bed, responded. His comments to an unidentified *The Pantagraph* sportswriter appeared in an article entitled "Eureka College No. 1" in the Tuesday morning issue of the paper. It best explained Darnall's impression of the shocking news and how the rating came about.

> Dave Darnall has been climbing a mountain during his 18-year tenure as Eureka College's basketball coach.
>
> Yesterday, he got to the top and liked the view.
>
> The Red Devils were ranked No. 1 in the NAIA Division II poll. Eureka College and King College of Tennessee each received five first-place votes, but the Red Devils totaled 373 poll points to King's 367. Both teams have 16 - 2 records.
>
> "I am absolutely in shock," said Darnall last night. "I didn't think in my wildest dreams that I would ever be coaching the No. 1 team in the country. It doesn't matter what level.
>
> "This is so great for the team and Eureka College."
>
> The Red Devils moved up from No. 3 despite a 48 - 46 loss at Division II Southern Illinois-Edwardsville Saturday . . .
>
> Obviously, voters in the poll knew the challenge Eureka College faced and weren't swayed by the loss . . .
>
> This is the first year for an NAIA Division II poll and national tournament, which will be March 12 through March 17 at Stephensville, Texas.
>
> Eureka College has a comfortable lead in the Dunkel ratings, which determine home teams for the state playoffs . . .
>
> There are 16 Division II districts in the country. Those champions advance to the national tourney, as well as eight at-large teams.
>
> "If we stay in the top eight and should we get upset (in the playoffs), we could still make it. That's also why this is important," said Darnall.
>
> Because Eureka College also is an NCAA Division III member, it cannot give scholarships.
>
> "If you look at the top 25 teams, there's probably not five like us," said Darnall. "The other 20 give aid. That makes it even better."

A couple hours later the Darnalls heard the startling news on a local television sports newscast. They weren't the only ones watching. Within seconds of the TV announcement, the Darnalls' phone started to ring. It seemed like continuous calls came in—from the Red Devil players, their parents, local fans, and Eureka College personnel—over the next two hours or so.

A dream had come true. Darnall's understanding and "playing" the Dunkel Rating System had finally paid dividends. He was definitely a happy man. He could finally get past the Southern Illinois-E loss. Eureka had also climbed to the top of the entire NAIA District 20 basketball hill with the best Dunkel rating among all of the NAIA I and NAIA II schools. The Red Devils jumped from 42.4 to 45.1, passing up McKendree in the overall ratings. McKendree remained the top ranked team in Division I with 39.2. Oh, by the way, notice the day of the month that Darnall's team reached the top of the pedestal in both the state and national ranking—February *third*!

The ranking inspired the players. Many of them had gotten up early in the morning and went to IGA or Hucks for a newspaper. They were ready to play that night. Their coach did not have to say a word. The team just wanted their ten seconds of silence, and then he turned them loose.

A huge crowd welcomed the No. 1 NAIA II team in the nation as their heroes took the floor for warm-up. There was more press attending the game than Reagan Fieldhouse had ever seen.

Coach Darnall's Red Devils did not disappoint their cheering fans or the press. An article in the Peoria *Journal Star* written by Mike Murphy who had witnessed the game was entitled "Eureka proves the polls right." Portions read:

> On Monday, NAIA pollsters voted Eureka College as the top Division II men's basketball team for the first time in school history.
>
> On Tuesday, the Red Devils got their first chance to defend the ranking and were successful in a 73 - 45 victory over Hannibal-LaGrange, MO.
>
> Led by Washington graduate Troy Tyler's 20 points and Mid-County alum Jon Guderjan's 19, the Red Devils improved to 17 -2 at Reagan Center.
>
> "I was probably more nervous than the players," Eureka coach Dave Darnall said. "I've had an upset stomach ever since I heard we were No. 1.
>
> "I've been here 18 years and we're finally on the top, but we also know that the first time we lose we'll topple . . . so there's more pressure now . . ."
>
> "It'll be nice to have a day off Wednesday to enjoy what we've accomplished," Darnall said. "This is a dream come true, because the kids can say at one time they made it to the top.
>
> "We know the only way you can go is down, but we made it to No. 1 and no one can take that away."

In the six-game winning streak under way, Coach Darnall felt the Iowa Wesleyan game at Mt. Pleasant was the most difficult. Beating a well-coached Greenville team on the road and knocking off Cornell College, Iowa at home was not an easy task. However, conquering Iowa Wesleyan on their undersized floor in their tiny packed gym by the score of 89 to 62 was a magnificent win for the No. 1 team in the nation.

Darnall worried so much about the game that he asked Dean of Students Dale Martin to support a student fan bus for the game. The coach felt it was the most critical game on the remaining season schedule in regards to the state and national playoff seeding. The Red Devil fans, students and adults alike, responded to the call. The charter bus was completely full. Supporting a fan bus to an away game was a rarity for the college.

Dave had reason to worry about the game. There was not a seat available in the five-row bleacher gym. The balcony encircling the playing floor also contained five rows of bleachers. It, too, was crammed with standing-room-only spaces filled.

The Tiger fans, aware of their opponents' national ranking, were all over the Red Devil players from the moment they took the floor until they were on the bus to head home. The game was extremely rough with the Iowa players inspired by their rowdy fans. Players were "jawing."

To get an idea of how rough the game was there were fifty-three free throw attempts total with Eureka shooting thirty-two. The atmosphere of the contest carried over to after the game, mostly by the Tiger football players.

"While my players were going off the floor, they were standing at the gym doorway and on the stairway that led to the locker room, taunting my players. They wanted a fight," said Darnall. "Some of the players' fathers —Tyler, Guderjan, Brown, VanWeelden, and Craft—all fairly "big boys" themselves, and other supporters guarded my players as they tried to get down to the locker room," an angry Darnall related.

But it wasn't over yet. As the players were leaving the locker room twenty or so minutes later, they could see both their fathers and the Iowa Wesleyan football players at the top of the stairs. Reaching the building's main doorway, halfway between, the players could see more Iowa Wesleyan students outside on the sidewalk leading to the waiting bus. With Coach Darnall leading the way, the Red Devils left the gym with the escort of the fathers and other EC fans. The yelling students still wanted "action" with the Eureka players.

Coach Darnall was just glad to get the hell out of there. "I won't be back," he told the escorting crew as he followed the team up the steps of the bus. It was his last trip to Mount Pleasant.

Eureka College split the last two games of the season. They dropped an 80 to 68 decision at NCAA Division II Quincy College before securing an 82 to 49 home victory over Greenville College.

Coach Darnall was asked about the scheduling of two NCAA II full-ride scholarship schools.

"I really didn't want to schedule Quincy," Coach said. "Their guarantee wasn't as good as SIU-E's, but I couldn't find anyone else to play. Many schools our size won't schedule us. I wanted a full schedule."

Eureka ran into the same difficulty at Quincy as it had at SIU-E. Darnall made the mistake of sticking up for one of his players and was assessed a technical foul.

"I can't believe it," Darnall said after the game when asked about the technical. "Every time we got close, a call was made that hurt us. Eaton got three quick fouls called on him. Yet, every time he got the ball in the middle, he got hammered, but no foul was called. Damn officials are killing me. My big boy doesn't get to play—theirs does," he lamented shaking his head.

The season finale with Greenville left the Red Devils with a 23 to 3 record and still in No. 1 position, but Dave knew that would change within the next couple of days. Yes, it did!

A *Pantagraph* article headline read "Eureka College drops to fourth in NAIA Division II poll." Portions of the article stated:

> The Eureka College men's basketball team moved up to No. 1 in the NAIA Division II poll several weeks ago largely because of a 48 - 46 loss at NCAA Division II Southern Illinois-Edwardsville.
> Ironically, losing on the road to another NCAA II school, Quincy College, has knocked the Red Devils out of the No. 1 spot.

In the meantime, the excited Red Devil fans passed bottles of champagne at the last post-game party to celebrate the great season and in anticipation of the No. 1 seed for the District 20 playoff, meaning home court play. The announcement came the next day. Eureka would host fourth-seed Judson College that they had already defeated, 75 to 55, earlier in the season. The No. 1-seeded team was now guaranteed home-court advantage throughout the playoffs. The other two qualifying teams were Trinity College and Trinity Christian College.

Coach Darnall was a little worried about his team. He thought they seemed a little tired both mentally and physically. Chris Eaton was his biggest concern.

Dave told the press, "The big redhead seemed to labor the second half of the Greenville game. His timing was off. He wasn't getting up and down the floor in his normal manner. Perhaps a couple of day's rest would help."

Coach Darnall gave his team two complete days off with a third day for shooting only. That allowed for two hard days of practice followed by a light one before the first round Saturday game.

An article entitled "EC men gear up for state playoffs" by Alan McNeil gave some before game thoughts. It read in part:

> Crowds at Reagan Physical Education Center are routinely sell-outs, standing room only.
>
> Any of the teams playing Eureka will have to enter one of the loudest arenas in the area, a building where Eureka almost never loses, a building where the college fraternities try to outdo each other with their outlandish schemes to destabilize the opposing teams, a building where a single mistake by an opposing player can, and does, lead to a never-ending barrage of catcalls from the stands (which are only 2½ feet away from the court, allowing for maximum volume) . . .
>
> Many of the students at Eureka are making plans to follow the team to Texas. The school-sponsored spring break trip has a detour to Texas planned, and some of the athletic boosters are also sponsoring a Texas-bound trip.
>
> Red Devil fever is extremely contagious, and the entire campus has got it, as the multitude of posters, banners, and signs across campus attest.
>
> There is only one group of people on campus who aren't looking ahead to the national finals—the team itself. The men are focusing on one game at a time, not looking past Judson to the state finals, nor looking past that to the national title game. This team is focused on one goal, winning on Feb. 29.

A boisterous, standing-room-only crowd greeted the Red Devils as they took the floor for what the fans hoped was not the last time. It was a good thing!

The following morning's *The Pantagraph* article "Eureka College avoids upset bid" described the previous evening's game. Portions read:

Eureka College is one victory away from the NAIA Division II National Basketball Tournament.

And the Red Devils might be just hanging on.

Judson almost derailed fourth-ranked Eureka College in the first round of the NAIA District 20 playoffs last night at Reagan Center. But the Red Devils used a 22 - 1 advantage at the free throw line to register a 62 - 59 victory . . .

"We're not playing well. We might have peaked, and I hate to say that," said Eureka College coach Dave Darnall, whose team beat Judson by 22 points in December. "We're not executing offensively nearly as well as we were . . ."

Coach Darnall was happy as hell that his team had the home court advantage and stated, "I don't feel guilty about any home-court advantage. Not when I play at Southern Illinois-Edwardsville, Quincy, or Olivet Nazarene. That's not counting all those other years we played playoff games on the road. In all the years we have played in the NAIA playoffs, we have only won once on the road. That's why we "play" the Dunkel Rating System all year—to get the home-court advantage in post-season play," Darnall concluded.

Trinity Christian, playing at home, beat Trinity College to become Eureka's next foe. The winner would head for Texas. Jim Benson of *The Pantagraph* staff reported on the game. "Eureka College on its way to nationals" read in part:

The celebration was in full force. Nothing was going to spoil the fun. Parents, students, and fans were mobbing the Eureka College's basket-ball team after its resounding, 93 - 41, victory over Trinity Christian last night . . .

Then came the dreaded announcement.

"Remember, we have finals tomorrow," boomed a voice over the public address system.

There was a slight groan from the giddy student body. Then it was time to cut down the nets.

"We came out like a team on a mission," said sophomore forward Troy Tyler of Washington, who paced Eureka College with 30 points. "A lot of times we have a slow first half, but not tonight."

It was close for awhile—like five minutes . . .

The Red Devils took a 41 - 20 halftime lead. They outscored Trinity Christian 16 -2 to start the second half and began thoughts of the trip to Texas . . .

"I would say this is our best game in the last 10," said Guderjan. "Ever since we were ranked No. 1, we were playing not to lose instead of to win. Coach said to go out hard for 40 minutes and have fun."

As soon as Darnall finished with the press, he hurried home to the already on-going party. As usual, the Eureka College basketball team supporters didn't hold off partying until the coaches arrived. This was their first real NAIA District 20 state championship party. The fans had celebrated following the 1987 win, but nothing like this night.

Since Dave would never pre-plan a trip to a national tournament before actually qualifying, there were many arrangements that needed to be attended to. The first question to answer was: How would the team get to Tarleton State at Stephensville, Texas? Tarleton was hosting the first twenty-team NAIA Division II National Tournament.

Coach Darnall hated to fly and remembered how nice it was to have had a charter at their disposal in Kansas City in 1987. However, many players had never flown and thought the fastest way to Texas was the only way to go. Coach informed them that the last fifty miles would require vans.

Dave needed a scheme. How could he convince his team that the slow, long way was best? He remembered that an old acquaintance, Ken Trickey, was Head Basketball Coach and Athletic Director at Oral Roberts University. Wouldn't it be nice to be able to leave a couple days early, take time to sightsee a little, and stay over in Tulsa for a practice at Oral Roberts? Maybe that would work.

Darnall contacted his former clinic speaker. The hospitable Trickey said, "Bring the boys down. We'll take care of them."

Dave now had some "fire power." The team would practice at Oral Roberts and stay in the Grandview Hotel, considered one of the town's finest. After some tough persuasion, the players agreed to join their coach on the red-and-white Peoria charter.

A small crowd of well-wishers gathered in the lobby of Reagan Fieldhouse for the Red Devil send-off. Most were college personnel since the student body was on break. Some had already left for Texas on a school-sponsored trip. Pat Bayles and Lynn Woolen from the Business Office presented each traveling member a silk yellow rose for "good luck." Dan Harrod provided the players with a tape of "The Yellow Rose of Texas." Dan had also supplied the Red Devils with tapes of "Lean on Me" and "Kansas City" for the 1987 trip.

Arriving in Tulsa around 6:00 P.M., the team checked into its motel and then proceeded on to Oral Roberts for the scheduled practice. Coach was pleased with his team's effort but was extremely concerned about his big

446

center's health. Chris Eaton was ill and did not participate in the practice. Uncharacteristically, the six-foot-seven sophomore was unable to eat during the day and looked pale to the coaches.

The team returned to the motel after a late dinner at Shoney's. The final leg of the trip to Texas would start early the next morning.

Since the team traveled by bus instead of plane, they were one of the first teams to arrive at the tournament site. What a difference in the weather! The guys left Eureka in jackets and arrived in Stephensville in shorts. Their home away from home was a Holiday Inn. The players were ready to head for its outdoor pool or just to lie around for a while.

That evening, the Red Devils held a practice at Tarleton State University. Eaton accompanied his teammates but did not participate. Junior Scott Schwab was replacing the stricken Red Devil.

He was not getting better. The coaches ran back and forth between their coaches' meeting that night and Eaton's room. It was a long night for both Darnall and Dighton. They alternately worried between who their opponent would be—thirteenth-seed George Fox, Oregon, or fourteenth-seed Missouri Valley, Missouri—and whether their six-foot-seven starting center would be able to play. There was still two days before tip-off.

The coaches and trainer Tim Murphy went to Chris's room around 10:00 the next morning. Eaton was awake but looked terrible. He hadn't eaten for a couple days, was pale, weak, had a sore throat, was stiff all over, and extremely tired. The symptoms were not good.

Coach Darnall suggested they call their assigned sponsor—Harris Methodist Erath County to make arrangements for Chris to see a doctor. They were told to bring Chris immediately to their facility. It was definitely the right place to go—a hospital. Chris was diagnosed with mononucleosis. What a devastating blow!

The team, again, practiced at Tarleton that afternoon. That night was the Tournament Tip-Off Banquet. It was a very special event where all the twenty competing teams were honored. The banquet was a very impressive affair. The teams' sponsors purchased the banquet tickets and treated their teams to the night's dinner.

Coach Darnall held an hour-long practice Thursday morning, the first day of the tournament. After practice the team returned to the motel for lunch, and a few then went to the hospital to visit their fallen comrade.

In mid-afternoon, the second Peoria charter arrived. Among the loyal Red Devil fans, parents, and students were Bonnie, Dan Harrod, Rich

Beer, and the Wertz family. Senior citizen supporters, the Bob Paxsons and eighty-year-old Russell Roseman, also braved the long trip. Dave's home-game announcer, Jim Finch, along with Chad Ruback from the Alumni Office, and John Roberts, sports announcer for Eureka's WCRI radio station also were on the bus. Several parents had elected to drive themselves.

One surprise passenger was Mrs. Eaton. The single mother had originally not been able to make the trip. However, with Chris so ill, it was arranged for her to receive time off from her work and join the others on the chartered bus. Everyone was pleased that it had been arranged for her to get to Texas.

Darnall's children, Tiera and Derek, flew in on game day. Also flying in on the same day to Dallas and then driving on to Stephensville was Peoria *Journal Star* sportswriter, Scott Heiberger. Scott wanted to do an interest piece on the ill Red Devil.

"All isn't well for Eureka," appeared shortly after in the *Journal Star*. It read in part:

> With an intravenous needle stuck in his left arm and a tissue in his right hand, Eureka College center Chris Eaton still couldn't believe the bad timing of it all.
>
> "It's crazy," said the 6-foot-7 Eaton, his feet dangling over the end of the hospital bed. "You work so hard to get down here, and then you can't enjoy it."
>
> Eaton was diagnosed with mononucleosis Wednesday afternoon and admitted to Harris Methodist Hospital on the eve of the NAIA Division II basketball tournament . . .
>
> "I hoped I'd be able to play at least one game," he said.
>
> Eureka coach Dave Darnall said Eaton's loss will be tough for his 25 - 3 team to overcome.
>
> "If I can't make it out there for the game, I can at least say I saw the gym," Eaton said. "I guess this just gives me that much more incentive for next year."

The opening ceremony was one of the highlights of the National Tournament. All competing teams lined up in single file and marched out onto the main arena floor when their school's name was announced. The top twenty teams in the nation formed a giant "NAIA" on the playing court. Three teams had already been eliminated earlier in the day but still participated in the "Parade of Champions." Coach Darnall was glad his team had not yet played.

"It would be miserable to be in the 'Parade of Champions' if you had already lost," Dave said. "It would be very anticlimactic."

The final game of the evening was significant to Eureka College. The winner of the George Fox-Missouri Valley game would provide their competition the following evening. The players sat in the bleachers observing the contest. Coach Dighton charted one team while faithful scout, Chuck Wertz, scouted the other. The starting five sat next to Darnall so that he could make comments to them regarding both teams. Other members of the team surrounded them and their coaches.

Mid-way through the second half, Coach Darnall was satisfied that their opponent would be George Fox and suggested that the team leave for a late dinner. There was no hesitation from the players. By the time they had finished pizza at Muzzio's and returned to the motel, it was close to midnight. Coach instructed his players to go directly to bed. Tomorrow would be a busy day.

Their game was scheduled for 9:45 P.M. Coach knew his players would get plenty of rest, but with Eaton out, they would have to "step it up a notch" and go full blast for forty minutes.

Prior to leaving for their first tournament action, the team attended a reception in the motel's Poco Bueno Room sponsored by the college's Alumni Office. Besides the alumni that had come from Eureka, several others lived in the Dallas area. Plus, Scott Runyen, Dave's nephew and also an alum, drove from New Mexico to attend.

The team boarded the charter around 7:30 P.M. for their long-awaited participation in the national tournament. Coach wanted his players to see possible future opponents, Tarleton State and Northwestern, Iowa. The team had a surprise passenger. Chris Eaton had been released from the hospital earlier in the day and would join his teammates on the bench.

By the time the Red Devils took to the floor in the final game of the second day of the tournament, only nine teams remained in contention for the national championship. When asked about this, Coach Darnall said, "I guess you could say we're in the top nine in the country. However, that doesn't mean a damn thing if we don't win tonight. I am glad, though, we got a bye in the first round. Our game tonight will be really tough for us. Their seven-footer is extremely good. Without Eaton, we could be in trouble. Their guards are at least two inches taller than ours are. Their overall size will cause us problems."

The Eureka College fans were boisterous and supportive, especially the younger group. However, it was to no avail. Even though the Red Devils gave gallant effort, as predicted, the Bruins' overall size and depth were too much for EC.

Heiberger's article "Red Devils ousted from NAIA—George Fox gains victory in second round of tournament, 85 - 77" in the *Journal Star* explained the night's action. Portions of the article read:

> The Eureka College Red Devils used 3-point shots and hustle to stay within striking range of George Fox (Ore.) College on Friday night, but it wasn't enough.
> George Fox eliminated Eureka from the NAIA Division II National Championship Tournament with an 85 - 77 second-round decision at Wisdom Gymnasium.
> Eureka trailed at halftime and by 14 with 9:39 left in the game. The Red Devils whittled the deficit to 81 - 77 when Kevin Brown made two of three free throws, but George Fox stayed ahead with its own free throws . . .
> George Fox's full-court pressure gave Eureka trouble throughout the first half, and helped the Bruins extend their lead.
> Brown sparked Eureka's outside shooting with two treys early in the second half and Jon Guderjan buried his first basket of the game to cut the deficit 49 - 44 with 14:19 left in the game . . .
> But George Fox stabilized with a flurry of lay-ups to take a 65 - 51 lead with 9:39 left.
> Eureka unleashed more treys, including three more by Brown, to stay close.
> Brown finished his last game as a Red Devil with 24 points before fouling out with 24 seconds left.
> Eureka sorely missed 6-foot-7 center Chris Eaton.

The post-game locker room scene was one of extreme disappointment and dejection. There were very few dry eyes. As usual after tough losses, Coach Darnall was in an extremely bad mood. He hated to lose. He felt bad for his players, the college, and his coaching staff. The team had worked so hard for such negative results.

In Darnall's depressed mood, he noticed one player that he thought the loss didn't seem to bother. While the others were sitting on the locker room benches with their heads in their hands, Chris Peterson had dressed and was headed for the door.

"Where in the hell are you going?" Darnall asked his player.

"I'm going to see my cousin," Peterson replied.

"Not yet," Darnall yelled. "You'll wait 'til we all leave. We're all together."

"Not me," Chris answered.

"The hell you're not," Coach shouted.

Coach Dighton and a couple players, seeing the confrontation between the headman and their teammate, stepped in to cool them both down. Minutes later the players left the locker room to meet their waiting fans. Darnall and Dighton remained in the room.

"That kid is done. He doesn't give a damn about the team. He only worries about how much playing time he gets," Coach Darnall screamed at his assistant. "I thought his attitude would change when he came back here, but it didn't. He won't be playing for me next year."

"Just because he didn't play tonight doesn't mean he shouldn't care that we lost. I could tell he was upset when he was sitting on the bench during the later part of the game, but I sure and hell didn't think this would happen," the frustrated coach continued. In reality, Darnall used only seven players in his team's eight-point loss.

The coaches finally left the locker room to join the team and their faithful fans. Darnall had promised that the team would join the fans for a late snack at a local pizza parlor. He instructed the bus driver to take the team there, while the fan bus followed and the parents fell in behind. It looked like a small caravan from "Hoosiers."

The coaching staff made a decision to stay in Stephensville until around 5:00 P.M. the next day. Coach Darnall felt the players deserved a little fun around the pool during the day. The driver could sleep during the day and drive throughout the night. The fan bus made the same plans. It seemed to be a very good decision. Everyone enjoyed the day. Even Darnall was at ease, and Eaton was finally beginning to move around. Perhaps it would be an enjoyable ride home even if it was a bit long. That could be blamed on Darnall.

The Eureka College caravan left as planned around 5:00 P.M. Coach Darnall had made reservations for a private room at a supper club about an hour away for dinner and a team celebration party to celebrate a dream season.

It was a season of honors for the team, individual players, and Coach Darnall. The team finished with a 25 to 4 record, ending the season rated No. 4 in the country NAIA Division II and the NAIA District 20 state champions. They finished high in several national statistical categories in both NAIA and NCAA III.

Jon Guderjan, Chris Eaton, and Troy Tyler were selected NAIA Division II All District 20 players. Coach Darnall was selected NAIA

Division II District 20 Coach of the Year and named NAIA Coach of the Year by the Illinois Basketball Coaches Association.

1992–1993

THE DARNALL FAMILY HAD A BUSY SUMMER before Dave's nineteenth year as Eureka College Head Basketball Coach began. There was the three weeks of the Dave Darnall's Eureka College Basketball Camps, a couple of weeks of relaxation at their condo in Arkansas, and the wedding of their daughter. Tiera and her long-time boyfriend, Brett Charlton, were married August 1st.

Coach Darnall ended up having a good recruiting year even though he got way behind because of his team's participation in the NAIA National Tournament. Seven freshmen and two successful junior college players comprised the new crop of Red Devils. Randy Begole left the playing ranks to become the head junior varsity coach. Scott Raycraft, the youngest son of Dave's good friend Dr. "Ray," became an administrative assistant.

The extremely successful 1991-1992 basketball team would be hard to follow. Craft, VanWeelden, and Brown would be hard to replace, and their loss would be felt. The coaching staff had to depend on the previous year's starters Guderjan, Tyler, and Eaton for both leadership and productivity. Juniors Dennis Huttenlocher, Duane Schmedeke, and sophomore Chris Hopwood had to "step up to the plate." Freshmen Adam Ferguson and Greg Clore and the return of Chris Peterson gave Darnall some good candidates to choose from for the two remaining positions.

Yes, Chris Peterson, the guy that Coach Darnall said would never play for him again or any Red Devil team. However, Peterson impressed both Darnall and Dighton. From the day the 1991-1992 team arrived back on campus from Stephensville, Chris was in the gym every weekday sometime between 3:00 and 8:00 P.M. for at least an hour. While most of the other players were not in the gym (or if they were, they were engaged in a full-court scrimmage), Peterson was working on his basic fundamentals. Not doing the fun things, the six-foot-two junior was working on dribbling drills, ball handling drills, shooting drills, and defensive footwork drills. The coaches definitely noticed but did not say anything. They were still unsure of "Pete's" attitude. Boy, were they wrong! Chris's attitude and contribution to the team in the future would be invaluable. Dave and Chris Peterson became very good friends. The same held true for Coach Dighton.

Prior to the start of the season, the 1993 NCAA Record Book was released. Coach Darnall was listed among the national leaders for NCAA Division III coaches. Darnall's .707 win percentage ranked him fourteenth in the nation while his eighteen-year record of 332 to 142 at Eureka ranked the coach twenty-fifth nationally among his peers for total victories.

Official practice started with a "Midnight Madness" scrimmage at 12:01 A.M. on Saturday, November 1. The NCAA pushed back the starting date of practice from October 15 to November 1. Coach Darnall felt he needed every practice he could get in before the season opener on November 21. A good crowd attended the benefit game. Spectators were asked to bring a food donation for the Eureka Food Pantry.

An article written by Peoria *Journal Star* sportswriter David Vecsey entitled "A return ticket—successful Eureka team wants another shot at national tourney" described the Red Devils' season outlook. Portions read:

> You ain't never seen a group of the college guys so anxious to go to Idaho for spring break as these Eureka Red Devils.
>
> Their hunger is not so much for potatoes as for a return trip to the NAIA Division II National Tournament, hosted by Northwest Nazarene College in Nampa, Idaho. The Red Devils still haven't shed frustrations of the first-round loss in last year's first Division II tournament in Stephensville, Texas.
>
> "I'll do anything legal it takes to get back," said center Chris Eaton, whose sudden case of mononucleosis forced him to miss the loss to George Fox University.
>
> "To work your butt off all year long and end up in the hospital . . . I can't even put into words what that was like. I'm not going to be satisfied with nothing else if we don't get back."
>
> So don't anyone tell Eaton and Co. that Coach Darnall is calling this a rebuilding year. Though returning three starters and 48.6 points per game, Eureka is a new team with a pack of eight competing for the final two starting spots.
>
> "I'm not even going to worry about the national tournament right now," Darnall said.
>
> "People see that we have three kids who were all-state last year. I don't think they realize that you don't win with three people. You win with seven or eight . . .
>
> "With all the new kids playing, it's hard to tell whether our strength will be on defense or offense," Darnall said. "I want a winning season—and that's as far as I'll go right now."
>
> His team has higher visions.

They tasted a national tournament last year, but left with a sour taste in their mouths when a 7-footer abused them in the absence of their big man Eaton.

"We want to prove to the NAIA that that wasn't the real Eureka team last year," said Guderjan.

With the season opener just a few days away, Darnall had yet to determine his starting line-up or who would be the team's "John Havlicek." Coach looked upon that role as the most important aspect of personnel selection.

Dave was looking at Dennis Huttenlocher as a potential replacement for VanWeelden at the power forward position. The six-foot-four junior reminded Darnall of a shorter "Kronk" off the 1987 team. Both players had great attitudes and understood what a "role" player was supposed to do.

Then tragedy nearly took place. While driving to the bucket in a practice, Huttenlocher went up for a lay-up. Somehow an opposing teammate got under the upward moving Huttenlocher. As Huttenlocher came down, he landed on the defensive player's back and then tumbled hard to the floor landing on his head. His body started to convulse. Then the injured player "went out." A frightened Darnall yelled for trainer Murphy as Dennis' teammates gathered around. Murphy dashed to the side of the fallen Red Devil. Shortly after, he was transported to Eureka Hospital. Even though practice resumed, it was not the same. The coaches and players were worried about Huttenlocher. Coach Darnall finally decided to call off practice.

The accident determined the fifth spot in the starting line-up. Peterson, Guderjan, Tyler, and Eaton were certains. By "default," freshman Adam Ferguson got the starting nod.

Coach Darnall and "super scout" Chuck Wertz had gone to River Forest just prior to their opener against Concordia College to watch their upcoming opponent participate in a scrimmage game against a local junior college. The scrimmage took place in the evening and was attended by some students and a few other observers. Darnall had watched Concordia's preseason scrimmages with junior colleges for several years. He had no reason to hide or to believe it would be a problem. He was wrong.

Near the conclusion of the scrimmage and just as the two scouts were walking down the bleachers, the Concordia coach sprinted toward them, raising hell about "them being there." Uncomplimentary words were exchanged. Darnall now knew that the season opener at Concordia in a few days would not be good.

The Eureka College basketball team was ranked fourteenth in the pre-season NAIA II poll. They were ranked eighth the previous year and ended the season ranked fourth.

The Alumni Office planned a "post-game" "Slam-Dunk Celebration" at Doc Ryan's in Forest Park after the Concordia game for all the alumni in the Chicago area and the fans that would travel to the game. Coach disliked this type of function because if the team happened to lose, it was like he and the team had let the alumni down. Being the competitor he was, Darnall took defeats extremely hard and was not really in any mood to visit following a loss. Some may say he was a poor loser. However, he knew this was good for the college, and it did give recognition to the basketball program. Therefore, he supported the effort by the Alumni Office.

The only good thing about the season opener, in Darnall's mind, was the team traveled by charter bus instead of those "damn vans." Freshman Adam Ferguson made his first career start. Huttenlocher, who had suffered a mild concussion on his high-flying fall, played the "John Havlicek" role, but saw only limited action.

Coach Darnall was fit to be tied following his team's 77 to 64 loss.

"Nobody better ever complain about officiating at Eureka," the angry coach said. He was referring to Concordia shooting thirty-two free throws to his team's thirteen.

"Hell, even the real John Havlicek would've been able to help us tonight. He would have fouled out too. Tonight, it was terrible," Darnall told the press.

Darnall was extremely unhappy after the game. "He got me," Darnall said referring to Concordia's fairly new coach. "I can see why he won't come back down to Eureka next year."

The two teams were not scheduled to play during the 1993-1994 season for the first time in numerous years. However, at the printing of this book, both institutions are members of the Northern Illinois-Iowa Conference.

The Red Devils went to Doc Ryan's for the alumni gathering, but the only celebration that night was the post-game jubilation by the Concordia players and fans on their court. They had just knocked off the fourteenth ranked team in the nation. What had happened was just what Coach Darnall had feared. All of the pre-season press, rankings, and hopes for a great year had "gone right down the drain." Coach Darnall and his team would now have to step back and reload.

Behind the thirty-point performance of Troy Tyler, the Red Devils bounced back with a three-point margin win over Rockford College on the road.

It was time for a quick home game before heading to Judson College. Tyler, again, led his team in scoring as Eureka pleased the Reagan Fieldhouse crowd with a convincing 94 to 66 victory over Clarke College. Even though Troy was the leading scorer, it was the performance of Dennis Huttenlocher that impressed the coach most. Starting his second game, the six-foot-four junior showed no evidence of his earlier head injury. Hopefully, the chemistry would begin. The starting line-up was now set, and Ferguson had become the "Havlicek spark plug."

The first post-game party at the coaches' home was highly attended. The conversation varied between the night's win and the opening season loss at Concordia. The effect the first three games would have on Eureka's Dunkel was also a hot topic of discussion. That would be the first of many discussions on the Dunkel throughout the year.

With wins over the next two opponents, Judson College and Blackburn College, Eureka prepared for their one and only invitational tournament appearance. The tournament was at Franklin College, Indiana. The Red Devils' first opponent was highly regarded Defiance College, Ohio. Eureka College started the game with a 16 to 2 run, but led only be one at the intermission.

The second half was a seesaw battle with the Red Devils drawing within one point on a three-point basket by Chris Peterson with just seconds left. After a Eureka foul on the in-bound play, Defiance missed the free throw but was able to pull down the missed carom to "ice" the game. The final score was 69 to 68.

It was an extremely disheartening defeat for Coach Darnall and his players. To have such an early lead and let it get away was hard to swallow. The Red Devils fell 4 to 2 overall. That was not the start Darnall expected, especially for a top-ranked team in the country. Things were going to have to change in a hurry if EC expected to return to the national tournament.

In the locker room following the game, Darnall had a little discussion with his team. He talked about "killer instinct" and playing with some emotion. The team had to realize they were "marked" and, thus, had to play hard for forty minutes. The basketball court was their "workshop."

Finishing his talk, Dave instructed his players to get showered and dressed so they could get back to the motel for pizza. Former Eureka College Assistant Basketball Coach Paul Brown and his family, who lived in Columbus, Indiana, were going to treat the team to pizza. That was going to be a nice change for the players.

Even though he was depressed about losing the game, Dave knew he should visit with the Red Devil fans that had made the trip to Indiana to support the team. He was able to relax in the motel's lounge for a while with some of the men—Paul Brown, Larry Guderjan, John Tyler, Chuck Wertz, Dale Coleson, Dan Harrod, John Hopwood, and Ron Craft and son, former player Lance. What a bunch! It was hard to break away, but Darnall knew the next day would be difficult. His team would have to bounce back against old foe Greenville College.

Dave said very little to his players in his pre-game talk against Greenville. His message was that the early afternoon game was probably the most important game of the year. If they had any pride and wanted any post-season action, they had better play their butts off.

The team did! Playing great man-to-man half-court pressure defense, the Red Devils held the Panthers to only sixteen first-half points, while scoring forty-six. A thirty-point lead at intermission pleased their coach. However, the third-place trophy did not. He had wanted the championship hardware.

With victories over two St. Louis area schools—Sanford-Brown and Harris-Stowe State University—Eureka College took an overall record of 7 to 2 into Christmas break. The Red Devils had a three-week lay-off before their next competition.

Coach Darnall was ready for the break. He felt drained and stressed. The pressure of living up to the pre-season expectation and his own personal desire to return to the national tournament had put a tremendous amount of pressure on him. In fact, Coach Darnall did not make the trip to St. Louis to direct his team's seventh win of the season. Coach Dighton guided the Red Devils to a 106 to 71 victory over Harris-Stowe, while Darnall was being released from the local hospital. Dighton had made his boss proud. That was the coach's only absence from any of his teams' games in his twenty-seven years of coaching, including when his father past away during Dave's first year of coaching in 1966 at Stanford High School.

Dave had felt a disturbing pain in his chest along with lightheadedness and dizziness while attending a Christmas party at the home of Rich and

457

Lynn Beer. He had arrived at the party around 10:00 P.M. following a recruiting trip to the Peoria area. He had only been at the social less than thirty minutes when he began to feel ill. Grabbing his chest, he sat down on the nearest kitchen chair. Dr. Mike Toliver, Professor of Biology came to his colleague's aid as well as Bonnie who was in another room. Dave was ashen and starting to sweat. The two quickly escorted Dave to the car for the short ride to Eureka Hospital. Dave was scared and did not say much to them on the way. Doesn't everyone who has had one heart attack worry about having another?

The emergency room doctor and nurses began administering to him immediately upon arrival. He was given oxygen and tests were started. Fortunately, the tests showed no evidence that Dave had suffered another heart attack, but the doctor wanted him admitted for observation. They continued the oxygen and connected him to a monitoring machine for the night. President Hearne and his wife, who had come to the hospital, along with Bonnie reassured Dave that everything could proceed without him just fine the next day—that Coach Dighton and his boys could handle the situation. Dave was dismissed from the hospital the following day around noon, just an hour before his team was to depart for St. Louis. The coach wisely took his doctor's advice and stayed home.

Dave did not want to die on the "floor." He knew he had told the now juniors that he'd stay until they graduated. Darnall planned to fulfill that promise. Besides, the ring of saying, "I was Head Basketball Coach at Eureka College for twenty years" sounded good. Somehow, he was going to make it. It meant a great deal to him.

The Darnalls were able to spend several much-needed days in Arkansas before the players reported back to campus for two-a-day practices. The relaxation was good for Coach.

An article appeared in *The Pantagraph* the day Eureka resumed play written by Randy Scharer entitled "Darnall at the heart of Eureka College basketball program" described the intensity of the Red Devil coach and the demands he made of his players and himself. Portions of the article read:

> Dave Darnall pours his heart into Eureka College and that, according to his doctor, isn't such a good thing.
> Darnall, in his 19th season as Red Devil basketball coach, recently had a flare-up of the heart problems which began 2½ years ago with a heart attack.

That recent setback came after watching various prospects play 16 games in 13 days. It caused him to miss a Eureka College game Dec. 19, his first absence in 28 years as a head coach.

"It was a depressing day," said the man who had once coached a game the night of his father's funeral.

Darnall knows he should ease up on trying to keep his winning percentage at Eureka College at .698 (337 - 146).

"I can't change," confessed Darnall, who admits his medical history is scary. His heart attack came at the same age as his father's first attack. His father died six years later.

The 51-year-old Darnall claims to be feeling better . . .

Coaching a team, for Darnall, means driving many miles to see prospects and to scout opponents.

"Every night of the season, if we're not playing, if there is a high school game, I'm there or if there's a game to scout, I'm there," said Darnall, who credits associate coach Dennis Dighton for being a major part of the program's success. "I think we outwork any other school.

"It has taken its wear and tear. I think it will probably cause me to get out of the game earlier than what I would normally do."

Guard Jon Guderjan, the Red Devils' lone senior, remembers Darnall attending 24 of his 26 games as a Mid-County High School senior. 'If I had to do it over again, I'd be here again. He's a great coach and also a great friend."

Guderjan said Darnall is demanding. His 2½ hour practices aren't for the lazy. "He expects a lot out of us. I'd say he's a perfectionist."

Center Chris Eaton, a 6-7, 210-pound junior averaging 17.4 points, said picking Eureka College was the best decision of his life.

"He got started (recruiting me) early in the season my senior year," Eaton said. "He hounded me night and day. I wouldn't want to be anywhere else."

The Red Devils returned to action following term break with four consecutive victories. Two came at home at the expense of the prestigious institutions Wabash College and McKendree.

The Red Devils trailed 36 to 31 at the intermission, but bounced back the second half against Wabash to claim an 82 to 71 victory. All five starters scored in double figures with Guderjan's nineteen paving the way.

It was then showdown time between two of the top NAIA teams in the state—the scholarship NAIA Division I McKendree Bearcats with a 13 to 3 record against the non-scholarship NAIA Division II Eureka College Red Devils with a 10 to 2 record. Everyone knew McKendree's reputation.

"Eureka knocks off old rival McKendree—Red Devil center scores 27 points, grabs 10 rebounds in victory" was the headline in the Peoria

Journal Star the following morning. The article by Duane Brienen described the battle the night before between the two teams. Portions read:

> The host Red Devils took their NAIA Division II national ranking against the big boys Tuesday night.
> So 11th-ranked Eureka turned to its biggest boy in defeating Division I McKendree 67 - 60 in a non-conference men's game.
> The Red Devils' Chris Eaton had 27 points and 10 rebounds.
> "We knew this was the biggest game so far this year," Eaton said. "They were scoring almost every time down (in the first half), so I knew I couldn't miss much."
> During one stretch, the 6-foot-7 Eaton made 11 straight from the field before finishing 12 of 14.
> But Eaton wasn't the only Red Devil big man to come up big. Dennis Huttenlocher had 12 points and 11 boards and Troy Tyler added 17 points, as Eureka's starting frontline outscored the Bearcats frontline 56 - 30.
> "Dennis kept us in the game in the first half," Eureka coach Dave Darnall said of Huttenlocher who had 10 points and 11 rebounds in the first half.

The post-game party at the Darnalls' home was the most enthusiastic gathering of the year. The night's win gave the Eureka fans the confidence that their team could make a return trip to the national tournament. Many of the full-house supporters stayed until the wee hours of the morning. In fact, Coach Darnall who had been instructed by his physician to walk a mile a day convince John Tyler, Troy's father, that he should stay and take a walk with him. It was close to 3:00 A.M. when the two strollers started their journey.

The Red Devils played three games before they traveled back to Southern Illinois University-Edwardsville for a contest with the NCAA Division II institution. That's right, SIU-E, the team Coach Darnall vowed he would never play again. However, still unable to fill his schedule since so many colleges Eureka's size refused to play them, Dave decided to take his team back. Besides, SIU-E again gave a good guarantee. The Red Devil fans also enjoyed the atmosphere of playing the larger school.

Eureka College's menace Greenville College sent the Red Devils back to reality. Coach Darnall had warned his players about being over confidant after the great McKendree win. The Panthers knocked off their guests, 80 to 65. It was now time for a little "soul searching."

EC bounced back with two wins and then headed to Southern Illinois -Edwardsville. The game strategy was the same as in the past—ball control, slow the pace down, shoot the ball only with fifteen seconds or less on the shot clock, and play great defense.

The Red Devils executed their game plan flawlessly the first twenty minutes of the game and held a surprising, 23 to 22, lead at the intermission. However Ty Margenthaler, the coach's son, hit two three-pointers near the end of the seesaw second half to give the home team the 56 to 46 victory. Perhaps this time, the best team won.

Darnall knew that losing two of the last four games was going to hurt their Dunkel points. The year before they lost by two to SIU-E and gained points, but the ten-point loss would definitely hurt. Not only did Eureka, with a 13 to 4 overall record, drop in the Dunkel, but it also dropped to sixteenth in the NAIA Division II national poll. Northern State from South Dakota received 395 points to claim the No. 1 spot. Remember the name Northern State.

With eight regular-season scheduled games left, Coach Darnall knew his team had to win at least six or possibly seven to remain on the top of the NAIA Division II playoff poll according to the Dunkel system. That, of course, was extremely important in order to achieve a home-court advantage in the post-season tournament. Eureka College had never lost a home game in the NAIA state playoffs.

The team pleased its coach. It won all eight remaining games.

The Red Devils made a two-game, four-day trip to Wisconsin. The first game was a Sunday afternoon contest against Northwestern College in Watertown. They were not a particularly good team that year, but Darnall will never forget the game because of their unbelievable student fans. In fact, when the game was over, the Red Devil players went to the home team's student section and gave them "high-fives" and visited with them. The students, all dressed in different outfits, stood the entire game to cheer on their overmatched Trojans. Their enthusiasm really impressed the EC players.

The Red Devils had a few loyal supporters themselves, including Dave's brother Bruce and his family who lived only fifteen minutes away. In fact, Dave gave his brother some credit for the win as Bruce had scouted the opponent for him.

Following the game, the team had their traditional McDonald's meal before heading to Green Bay. While at the restaurant, the conscientious Chris Eaton, in front of the entire team, asked his coach about his possible up-coming 350th career win. Dave had not talked about the personal milestone to his team, but Eaton had figured it out and knew his coach was getting very close. The Northwestern win had been 348.

With the 349th "under his belt" as the result of the Red Devils' impressive, 66 to 44, win over St. Norbert, Dave was looking for 350 against Iowa Wesleyan when the team returned home.

NEITHER THE RED DEVILS NOR their supporters had forgotten the problem the previous year in Iowa. Eureka College was anxious to meet on its floor. The contest would fulfill the contract and end the heated rivalry between the two institutions.

An article in *The Pantagraph* entitled "Eureka College rolls; Darnall gets 350th win" commented on the milestone and the game. It also described a "patent" Darnall timeout—the kind he had once been chastised for by a former college president. It read in part:

> Longtime Eureka College basketball coach Dave Darnall doesn't have a certain number of victories he hopes to reach before retiring, but each milestone he reaches is sweet, nonetheless.
>
> Darnall's Red Devils rolled to a 104 - 62 victory over Iowa Wesleyan last night at Reagan Center, giving the coach his 350th win at the school.
>
> "The 300th win was a big deal, but to be able to last long enough to get No. 350 is definitely a nice honor," said Darnall, whose team improved its record to 18 - 4.
>
> "I don't have any goals for a number of wins. I've been here 19 years and I'll be here next year, so we'll just go from there."
>
> Iowa Wesleyan (10 - 12) owned a two-point lead six minutes into the game, prompting Darnall to call timeout. The Red Devils responded by scoring the next 20 points.
>
> Chris Eaton poured in 30 points and grabbed 15 rebounds to pace the Red Devils. Troy Tyler added 20 points and Jon Guderjan and Chris Peterson chipped in 15 apiece.

The twenty-two-point revenge victory was especially sweet for Coach Darnall and his players. The happy Red Devil fans toasted the victory at the Darnalls' following the game. Those who had traveled to Iowa the previous year were especially gratified.

Eureka College finished its season with home wins over Mount St. Claire, Judson, and Greenville.

The win over Judson meant EC would possibly have to beat Judson for the third time in order to qualify for the plane ride to Idaho. Most coaches will tell you that beating any team three times in a season is hard to do.

The team ended its regular season schedule with a 21 to 4 record. It moved up three spots to No. 13 in the NAIA II National poll. Oh, those numbers three and thirteen! Coach Schuster's Lady Red Devils joined Darnall's team in the NAIA II post-season play.

The Eureka College men's basketball team was seeded No. 1 in the National Association of Intercollegiate Athletics Division II District 20 Tournament. That was what Coach Darnall had been working for all year.

"You have to 'play' the Dunkel," Dave said of his team's ranking.

The Red Devils were scheduled to play No. 4-seed Trinity Christian. The Trolls had one game left on their schedule, so Dave decided to take his top eight players, Wertz, and Dighton to the game. The van full of Red Devils arrived just before tip-off.

"Coach was hoping our crew wouldn't be spotted, but we were," said senior leader Jon Guderjan. "He told us not to wear our Eureka College jackets, but they knew we were there."

However, the Red Devils were more concerned about the knowledge they could gain by scouting.

"I think it helped everyone to see who they'd be matching up with and what they like to do," Chris Eaton told a *Journal Star* sportswriter. "Coach does a lot of scouting, and he can tell you things, but it's not the same as seeing it for yourself," said the redhead, dubbed "Rooster" by his teammates.

The trip north was not in vain. Troy Tyler and Dennis Huttenlocher combined for thirty-five points to lead the Red Devils to a 73 to 48 victory over the Chicago school in front of a capacity crowd at Reagan Center.

It was now show time with Judson College, as predicted, for the playoff championship. The Eagles qualified by knocking off Greenville College. Could the third encounter with Judson (Dave's number three) be lucky for Darnall once more? The NAIA Division II championship game took place on Wednesday, the third day of the month in the third month of the year against a team his Red Devils would play for the third time. The superstitious Coach sure hoped so.

Scott Heiberger's article for the *Journal Star* set the stage for the important showdown. It was entitled "Red Devils 'Jungle' scary for visitors —Eureka puts 25-game home winning streak on line for trip to nationals." Portions read:

> The song "Welcome to the Jungle" cuts through the public address system whenever the Eureka College men's basketball team trots onto the court at Reagan Center.

The Eureka College "Jungle"—home to many Red Devil victories aided by raucus fan support.

The hard-edged Guns n' Roses rock tune usually foreshadows pain and misery for opponents. Eureka is 46 - 1 at home during the past four seasons and has won 25 consecutive times on its floor . . .

The gym holds about 2,000 fans and is expected to be packed as the Red Devils try to clinch their second consecutive trip to the NAIA Division II national tournament. This season's national site is Nampa, Idaho, March 11 - 16.

"You can really feel it when the place gets loud," Eureka forward Troy Tyler said. "You can tell the other team is in trouble when the crowd gets into it and they have to call a timeout."

The victory over Judson was exciting and relief for Coach Darnall and his players. They had worked so hard all season to reach that plateau and make the next step to the national tournament.

"Guderjan's shot saves victory for Eureka College" was the headline in *The Pantagraph* the day after the game. Bob Warth gave the account of the game. It read in part:

There was a sign on the wall at Eureka College's Reagan Center thanking senior guard Jon Guderjan for four years of memories.

Last night, in his final home game, the NAIA District 20 championship game against Judson College, Guderjan provided the home folks with one last memory.

With his team clutching to a one-point lead with 3:43 left in the game after leading 17 points, Guderjan drilled a 3-pointer that built the Red Devils' lead to four . . .

Peterson missed a shot with 13.4 seconds left and Russell was fouled driving to the basket with 2.1 seconds remaining.

Darnall called a timeout to ice Russell, which proved successful when Russell missed his first attempt.

"I usually don't call timeouts to ice players," said Darnall. "This time it worked, even though I didn't think it would. Guderjan's 3-pointer and that timeout were the keys."

Huttenlocher added a free throw with 0.3 seconds left for the final score.

The bench players and "die hard" Red Devil fans dashed to the floor swarming their exhausted teammates and excited head coach. Eureka College was heading back to the NAIA II National Tournament for the third time.

"Where's Nampa?" someone asked at the wall-to-wall people celebration at the Darnalls' home.

"I don't know. I hear it's close to Boise," Dave replied. "Hell, I don't even know for sure where Boise is. I'll look it up tomorrow. I was too damn superstitious to check it out before we earned it," he concluded.

It was then time to pass the champagne bottles among the scores of fans. "Together We Win" was the saying of the evening. When asked about how the team would get to Idaho, the smiling coach said, "I do know the players will fly. It's a hell of a long way out there. I am not sure what I'll do."

The coach paused. "Maybe I'll leave a couple days earlier and have someone drive me. I hate to fly," Darnall somewhat kiddingly said.

It was decided the traveling EC party would consist of twenty members. Darnall unenthusiastically agreed to accompany his team on the cross-country flight. Any parent or Red Devil fan who wanted to join the official group was welcome. Several did, including Bonnie. Tiera, the Guderjans and their friends, the Colesons, would join the EC group by flying out the following day. The trip would be the first time any Eureka College team had traveled to a game site by plane.

Coach Darnall had a good "down to earth" talk with his players at the team meeting just before the last practice prior to leaving for the tournament.

"We worked all year for this plane trip. We prayed for a return to the nationals. Now that we got it, let's do something about it. I am not planning on going out there for a vacation—not one game and come home," Darnall emphasized to his team. "Our opponents will be Tarleton State University, Texas. They are the largest school in the tournament—over 6,000 students, full scholarships, very athletic," Coach said.

"I have got a scouting report from one of the teams they played this year. I'll give you starters your assignments later in practice. We must control the tempo of the game, have good shot selection, and get back on defense. Their center averages several dunks a game. He can sky," Darnall informed his players.

Before Coach Darnall dismissed his team for practice, he reached into his practice folder and pulled out a letter. It was from the college's most distinguished alumnus, President Ronald Reagan. The coach proudly read the letter to his players. He felt it would serve as a motivation for his team throughout the tournament.

The Eureka entourage left in the dark by Peoria charter for the short journey to the Greater Peoria Airport. The "John Madden" of basketball was hesitant, but with Bonnie at his side and his faithful friend Air National Guard pilot Dan Harrod nearby, the coach boarded. The plane left Peoria and made a quick stop at Moline before proceeding on to Denver. Dave hated the "ups and downs" of the ride. Even though it was still morning, the coach ordered a cold beer. He thought he needed it. Maybe he could now relax.

A coaches' meeting for all tournament participating head coaches was scheduled for 4:00 P.M. that day at Northwest Nazarene College. Coach Darnall did not want to miss the assembly. However, he damn near did.

Arriving at Denver International Airport, the team's plane could not land due to a backlog of flights and had to circle Denver for over forty-five minutes before landing. Once the passengers entered the terminal, they learned that their connecting flight to Boise had just left the runway. Dave was upset. It was just like he had lost a game. He had no idea of what to do next. But it was pretty clear to him that he would probably miss the coaches' meeting. That really "T'd" him off.

Thank God for Larry Clore, father of promising freshman Greg Clore, and Dan Harrod—both experienced flyers who were able to take charge. The group was first offered a deal where six to eight passengers could leave immediately on another flight with the remainder of the team and fans leaving later. Coach Darnall rejected the plan.

"The team will stay together," Dave told the two negotiators. "We'll wait until we can go together, even if I have to miss the meeting."

Coach Darnall felt responsible for the entire team and did not want to break them up. A proof of his "Together We Win" philosophy.

An hour of wheeling and dealing by Clore and Harrod finally paid off. The entire Eureka College entourage had tickets. Two were for first class with the remaining in coach. How had Harrod pulled that? He talked Coach into sitting with him in first class. Both decided they needed another beer.

The team finally arrived at Boise Air Terminal. Their tournament sponsors, Frank Mattern and John Danielson, representing Albertson Foods greeted them. The two honorary coaches hustled Coach Darnall and Dighton to Nampa to attend the coaches' meeting. The Red Devil coaches were late but were still able to obtain significant information needed for their team's participation in the NAIA Division II National Tournament.

Student coach Randy Begole and trainer Tim Murphy drove the players to their motel in the two complimentary vans provided by the tournament committee. The team stayed at a Shilo Inn-Boise Riverside. The fans spent their time at the Super 8 motel in Nampa, some eight miles away. The team and their supporters did not see each other until the "Tip-off Banquet" the following night.

The "Tip-off Banquet" was held at the Nampa Civic Center. The capacity crowd of over a thousand people paid fifteen dollars each to witness the evening's program. Their sponsors assumed the teams' expenses. Albertson's representatives Mattern and Danielson joined the Red Devils at their assigned table. The special guest speaker was Governor Cecil Andrus, who welcomed the twenty teams and other guests to the State of Idaho. There were dignitaries from the NAIA, local government, and the host school Northwest Nazarene College that took their turn at the podium.

With the banquet completed, the honorary coaches suggested that the Eureka College coaches and any interested adult supporters join them for a cocktail at a nearby lounge. They wanted to meet some of the Red Devil fans and visit with the coaching staff.

Coach Darnall, knowing that his team did not play for two days, thought it was a great idea. He needed a little relaxation. There would be sleepless nights to come. He also wanted a chance to talk with Frank and John. They seemed to be great guys. It would also be the last chance to visit with any of the fans for a while. The student assistants Begole and Bosch were also able to join the group. Fathers Tyler, Guderjan, Hopwood, Clore, Schmedeke, and supporters Coleson and Harrod were more than willing to accompany. It was the "duty" of trainer Murphy and student administrative assistant Scott Raycraft to chaperone the players at the motel. Losing their first game of the tournament the year before, Darnall felt he did not have to worry about the behavior of his players. They were on a mission. They would get their rest and be ready to play the bigger, stronger Texans of Tarleton State on Friday.

Thursday was a busy day for the Eureka College basketball team. The players were able to sleep in before they had brunch and then traveled to a local high school for a 12:30 P.M. practice. Then came a quick trip back to the Boise Riverside Inn to prepare for an early dinner at Albertsons' Home Office in Boise. The Eureka College team was a guest of John and Frank for a sit-down affair. The meal had to be the best of the entire trip to Idaho. The hosts gave the EC student-athletes a tour of the office building. That was an experience the players still talk about.

It was next a jaunt to Montgomery Physical Education Building on the campus of Northwest Nazarene College for the tournament's opening night ceremony. All twenty teams marched onto the floor to form a huge "NAIA" as their respective institution's name was called. As the year before, three teams had already been eliminated from the tournament field by the time the marching ceremony took place.

Darnall had wanted his team to watch the first game of the evening session. The host school, Northwest Nazarene, was paired against St. Joseph's Maine. The winner of the game could possibly become a third-round opponent of the winner between Eureka and Tarleton State. Members of the starting five surrounded Coach Darnall and listened to his comments concerning both teams. Student coaches Begole and Bosch charted Nazarene while Coach Dighton scouted St. Joseph.

At the conclusion of the opening ceremony, the Eureka College basketball team and their fans went to Denny's Restaurant for a late-night meal. Denny's was located directly across the street from the fans' Super 8 motel. For Coach Darnall, it seemed like that was all the players did—eat! In reality, the team had only eaten three meals that day. It was the times of the meals that were unusual. The first meal was around 11:00 A.M.—brunch. The second occurred around 4:00 P.M.—dinner. And then the third meal taking place late in the evening.

The first couple of nights at Boise were not too stressful for Darnall. However, that night was difficult. It was the normal night-before-the-game syndrome.

"Was it all worth it?" he asked himself as he lay in bed wide awake, tossing and turning, following the coaches' meeting in his room earlier. He finally drifted off an hour or so before dawn.

The mood around the community of Eureka and the college campus was upbeat. Many college students, personnel, and area fans were anxiously waiting for the radio broadcast of that was to be that night's game. The supporters back home had sent faxes to the team wishing them well. That meant a great deal to the coach and his players. Darnall used the messages as motivational tools, reading them to the players during the team meeting. Some of the faxes could have been stimulated by an article entitled "National Tourney clippings bound for Darnall's office" by Randy Sharer for *The Pantagraph*. Parts read:

> Just where Dave Darnall's way of life ends and where Eureka College basketball begins is hard to determine.
> But it's safe to say that whatever documentation exists of Darnall's 19 years with Red Devil roundball—be it a photo or newspaper clipping—it has been affixed to the walls of his office in Reagan Center.
> "He keeps track of past and present players. He lets everybody know what's going on with his program. I think he's really proud of it. It's kind of like a mess, but it'sorganized in his way. It's nice to see your face up there," said junior Chris Eaton.
> The next clippings bound for Darnall's walls will relate to the National Association of Intercollegiate Athletics Division II national tournament at Nampa, Idaho, on the campus of Northwest Nazarene.
> The key to victory may be the 6-foot-7, 230-pound Eaton, whose 17.3 scoring average is second on the team to the 20.7 mark of Washington native Troy Tyler.
> "Eaton has to play," Darnall said. "In the couple of games we've lost, he been in foul trouble."
> Eaton, who is averaging a team-high 9.1 rebounds, is a key because Tarleton State is the tallest foe the Red Devils will have to face.

The team arrived at the tournament site two hours before tip-off. The players had to be ready to shoot around at the half of the preceding game. Shortly, it would be the showdown between the larger scholarship seventh-seeded Tarlton State and the small non-scholarship tenth-seeded Eureka College. Coach Darnall was his normal self before a game—very tired, sick to his stomach, and on the toilet.

"It's a good thing our players aren't like me before a game," Darnall told his assistant Dighton. "Hell, we'd never win a game."

Dave and his staff felt they had their team ready for the uphill battle against the very talented Texans. They just hoped the players would execute their offense and defense—be very patient on offense and "pack down" the defense inside.

"If you're going to get beat, get beat by 20," Coach told his anxious Red Devils. "Now, let's take our ten seconds. Each one is an individual.

Think what you want to think, or you don't need to think at all, as long as we are quiet, and we do it together."

The Red Devils, led by the smallest player on the team, Chris Hopwood, took the floor in front of their small but vocal following. Eureka was ready to go.

In the huddle, just prior to tip-off and after the starting line-up was announced, Coach Darnall warned his players not to let their big man, six-foot-seven Sean Walker, dominate the game. He was known for his slam-dunks. It was said that he had an ungodly number during the season, fifty or so.

Hell, Eureka probably did not have a team total of ten. Coach Darnall was not a dunk enthusiast. In fact, if a player missed a dunk, he got benched. The way Darnall substituted, once a player got benched, he might not get back into the game. No wonder they had less than ten dunks all season.

Walker got the tip over Eaton. Could this be a battle of big men?

It took only ten seconds for Eureka to fall behind. Walker received a pass about ten feet from the left side of the basket and took it to the hole. The "jumping jack" skied right over the shocked redhead from Eureka for a slam-dunk. Exactly what Darnall said he did not want to happen.

The Red Devils struggled to stay close. The athletic ability of the talented Texans showed. Eureka trailed 33 to 26 at the intermission.

Darnall was "fit to be tied." He felt his team was giving a half-ass performance.

"There's no damn reason why you guys can't play with them," Dave shouted. "Last year we had an excuse. This year we don't. You're just getting your ass kicked. They're out working you. You've got to start playing some damn defense."

"Put pressure on their shooter," (Chris Givens) Darnall screamed. "Start rebounding. Don't let the big boy hurt you on the boards. Block him out."

"Get you ass out there and play some ball. A lot of people paid a lot of money to come out here and watch you play. Don't let them down," he instructed.

Wow! What a difference! The Red Devils came out to play. Coach Darnall's ass chewing must have done some good. His team made a complete turn-around. Eureka College claimed a great, 63 to 54, victory over the largest institution in the tournament. The Red Devils had made the "Elite 8."

The Pantagraph gave an excellent review of the game and some of the thoughts of the players for the fans back home in Illinois. Portions of "Red Devils rally to beat Tarleton State" read:

The Eureka College men's basketball team used a 15 - 0 run midway through the second half to post a come-from-behind, 63 - 54, victory over Tarleton State yesterday in the second round of the National Association of Intercollegiate Athletics Division II national tournament . . .

Junior center Chris Eaton, who didn't play in the national tournament last season because he had mononucleosis, led the way with 22 points and a game high 13 rebounds. Troy Tyler and Jon Guderjan added 14 points each for Eureka College . . .

"We fell behind but the kids did a gut check and came out in the second half and played great defense. And our shot selection was as good as it's been all season.

"When you're playing a team that is this good, you need to have one of your best efforts of the year. And we got that in the second half," said Coach Dave Darnall.

"I have to give them a lot of credit," said Tarleton State coach Lonn Reismann. 'They came back in the second half and shut us down offensively. They put great defensive pressure on us.

"If they play like they did in the second half, there's no reason they can't win this whole tournament."

There was a scene of total emotion as the clock ran out. Coach Darnall ran to the floor to congratulate his ecstatic players. Bench players were hugging anyone they could find. High-fives and pats on the back were taking place everywhere. Honorary coaches Frank and John were just as jubilant. The Red Devil cheerleaders and fans finally made their way to the floor to celebrate with their heroes.

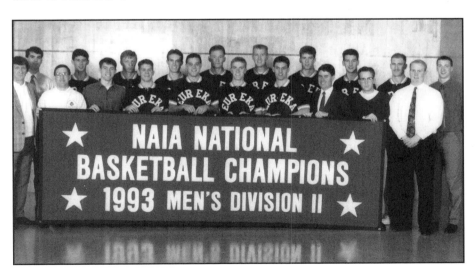

For the first time in the school's history, a Eureka College team won a NAIA National Tournament game. It took three tries—there's that number three again. The win was a "monkey off Darnall's back." Coach called Denny's to reserve a room for the Red Devils and their supporters to eat a late dinner around 9:30 P.M., but first there was work to do. The host school was still to play against the No. 2 seed Grace College, Indiana. The game had to be scouted.

With ten minutes or so left in that contest, the Eureka College entourage left for dinner. Even though Grace had been seeded higher in the tournament, Dave felt it would be more difficult to beat Northwest Nazarene on their own court. As the group was leaving the gymnasium, several fathers questioned Dave about their sons' next opponent.

"It's very difficult to defeat anyone on their own floor. That's why I feel a neutral site would be better," Dave said. "It may be worse here. They've got those thousand screaming fans. Some seem pretty zealous. I don't know if anyone can beat Nazarene."

Joining the Red Devils at dinner were the Red Devil cheerleaders. Dean Dale Martin had driven the cheerleaders some 2,000 miles in his own van so that they could support the team.

"That's great dedication, don't you think?" Dave asked. "They really helped us tonight."

The coaching staff met in Darnall's room after returning from Denny's to discuss a game plan.

"I worry about the team, but the home crowd and the officiating really concern me," Dave said. "There are really good officials here, but remember the SIU-E game last year."

The team had its pre-game meal around 2:00 P.M. That was four hours before tip-off. The Red Devil played the opening game of the evening session. Actually, by the time Eureka College played their game, there were only six teams remaining in contention for the championship.

As Darnall kiddingly said before the game, "I guess you can say we're now in the top six in the country. If we can win, we'll be in the "Final Four."

Following the traditional pre-game talk and the ten seconds of silence, the Red Devils took the floor to the cheers of the sparse Eureka fans. Moments later, the Crusaders jogged out of their locker room to the astounding roar of a capacity crowd of 4,000.

"Damn, Dighton, they're loud. I don't think our players will be able to hear us on the floor. We could be in trouble," Coach said. "Some how we have got to get the crowd out of the game. Maybe a quick lead would do it," Darnall concluded.

There was no big lead. The team struggled. A seesaw battle took place for the first half with Eureka trailing, 31 to 29, at the intermission. Coach Darnall did not chew out his players as he often did during his half-time talks when his team was not performing to its capability. Instead, he just used words of encouragement.

"Stay in there. Keep working. We're okay. We've just got to start executing our offense better the second half," Dave told his team. "The game could be close at the end. Don't let the crowd rattle you. Don't make any stupid fouls and make those damn free throws."

Coach Darnall did not keep his team in the locker room very long. He wanted his top six players to return to the floor to take some shots. Shooting poorly the first half, they needed the extra time to get warmed up.

The second half was a carbon copy of the first—a seesaw battle. No team was really controlling the game. With seven minutes left, Coach Darnall felt his team might pull the upset of the year—beating Nazarene on its own floor.

Eureka took a 54 to 51 lead with 6:36 remaining on a lay-up by Eaton, but the Crusaders regained the lead for good at 55 to 54 on a rebound shot by Eric Spencer. Eaton drew his fourth foul on the play. Darnall was beside himself. He could not believe the call. Coach Dighton had to restrain the main man from getting a technical. That definitely would have taken the Red Devils out of the game.

The "bomb dropped" a few seconds later. After EC missed a shot, Nazarene got the defensive rebound and pushed it down the floor. It was then that the "curtain fell." Eaton picked up his fifth foul trying to block a Brian Locke shot. To Darnall, it was a stupid foul, but he also felt it was the result of frustration by Eaton for the call a few seconds earlier. This was a fatal blow.

The Red Devils did not give up; it just wasn't to be. The players were now out-matched. They missed several open shots and missed some crucial free throws before Troy Tyler fouled out late in the game. Eureka College dropped the 69 to 60 decision to the host school. It was a gallant try, but this was not the year.

Coach Darnall felt bad for his only senior Jon Guderjan. Dave said of his standout leader after the game, "He'll be leaving the program a little short. If everything goes right for us, we could be back next year with more experience under our belt. I would give anything to have him with us. We'll really miss him."

The team and its fans returned to Denny's for another late dinner following the game. Coach Darnall had made reservations for the private dining room the night before. John and Frank, their sponsors who had become friends with the coaching staff and fans, were able to join them. They were proud to have had their team go that far.

As the previous year in Stephensville, the post-game meal started off as a sad affair. The players knew they hadn't reached their goal—a national championship. They had felt that they were capable of achieving that objective, and it was defeating to have failed.

With the meal over, the fathers and other adult male fans slipped off to the adjacent lounge. A short period of time had passed when the fellows wanted to have a toast with their sons and the coaching staff for a great year. Eventually, everyone joined together to celebrate an overall successful season.

Bad weather throughout the country caused a nationwide chaos in flights. That evening, while the players were eating, Coach Darnall, Dale Martin, and Larry Clore were communicating with their travel agent regarding the Eureka College's entourage returning home. The travel agent returned a call to Denny's to inform them that he was able to obtain a few tickets for a flight out of Boise early the next morning. It was decided that the adults that needed to get back for work would go first. The team wanted to stay together.

"When one goes, we all go. If we can't all go at once, we'll just stay here," an upperclassman stated. "Remember, 'Together We Win.'"

"Great attitude," Darnall thought. "This group is really learning the meaning."

One very special and outstanding honor was announced that day. Troy Tyler was notified that he was named as the winner of the National Association of Intercollegiate Athletics Frank Hesselroth Leadership Award. Tyler was the sole recipient of the award, selected from NAIA Division I and II nominees from across the nation. The award took into consideration athletic ability, academic achievement, and community service. Tyler, who carried a 3.78 grade point average and majored in the science and math areas, was to receive a personal award at the NAIA Division I Men's Basketball Tournament Tip-off Banquet on March 15 in Kansas City, Missouri. Eureka College would receive $1,000 to be applied to the general scholarship fund.

With both him and his father in Idaho, Troy asked Athletic Director Warner McCollum to accept the national award on his behalf.

The team left Boise early Tuesday morning after spending a full week in Idaho. Switching planes in Chicago to a small commuter plane for the final leg into Peoria scared the hell out of Darnall.

"Boy, I am glad to be back here," Dave said upon his arrival at the college's campus. "I don't know if I'll ever fly again."

Would he have to?

Later that afternoon a victory rally for all of Eureka College's successful programs was held. The men's basketball team, the lady's basketball team, the swim team's national qualifiers, and the college Academic Bowl team were honored.

There were many honors bestowed upon members of the Red Devil basketball team. Troy Tyler was selected the Most Valuable Player in District 20. Joining him on the All-District team were Jon Guderjan and Chris Eaton. Tyler was also selected Second Team All-American while Eaton was named Third Team All-American.

Chris was also selected on the National Tournament All-Tourney Team. He was Eureka College's first player to be named to the team. Troy was named an Academic All-American.

Eaton, Guderjan, Tyler, and Chris Peterson would all become future members of the Eureka College Athletic Hall of Fame.

Coach Darnall was named both the NAIA Division II District 20 Coach of the Year and the Illinois Basketball Coaches Association NAIA Coach of the Year. That was the third consecutive year Darnall had received the IBCA award.

Darnall's team had won twenty-six consecutive home games and was 47 to 1 at home over the past four years. He boasted an overall college record of 356 to 147 in his nineteen-year tenure at Eureka.

Dave still had one point of business he needed to attend to. He organized and scheduled the world famous "Platters" for a concert eleven days after returning from Boise. The "Platters" were Darnall's favorite singing group while growing up. He met the group at an engagement in Fairfield Bay and became acquainted with the drummer of the group.

Being an antique car buff, Dave also wanted to have an antique car show and cruise coincide with the concert. He turned to his local car club, the Rusty Rockers, for assistance. After ten years, Darnall was able to drive his '55 Chevy for the first time in the forty-plus vehicle cruise.

The "Platter" concert proved to be an extremely successful event with near capacity crowd of approximately 1,000 spectators clapping and swaying to the music. Following the concert, all of the members of the "Platters" except one, including the band members went to the Darnalls' for a post-concert party. Over two hundred people gathered in the house, garage, and deck to welcome their guests. It was a long, fun night.

Coming to Eureka College
The Fabulous Buck Ram "Platters"
March 27, 1993

Chapter 16

The Final Season

EUREKA COLLEGE WAS FRANTICALLY SEARCHING for conference affiliation before the season actually began. The NAIA no longer was composed of districts. The National field would come from Conference champions and Regional tournament champions. The NAIA Division II National Tournament was increased by four teams to twenty-four. There would be eighteen automatic conference bids to the tournament. The other six spots would be filled by regional tournament champions and the tournament host school.

Eureka College was scrambling for a place to "belong." They had been independent the past couple of years. Besides, the conference they had been affiliated with was composed of mostly NCAA Division III institutions. EC had to join a conference of NAIA schools or participate in a regional tournament. Coach Darnall did not want the latter option. Finally after a month of maneuvering, preparing, and late-night rescheduling by Athletic Director Warner McCollum and Darnall, Eureka joined five other schools—Barat, Indiana Tech, Judson, Trinity Christian, and Robert Morris—in the Chicagoland Conference. The Conference would have one of the eighteen automatic bids to the National Tournament.

It had been agreed that the Conference would hold a post-season tournament with the winner advancing to the Nationals in Nampa, Idaho. All teams did not play each other during the regular season due to the late for-

477

mation of the Conference. That made a post-season tournament necessary. The tournament would be seeded according to the Dunkel Rating System. Coach Darnall would be forced to "play" the Dunkel again even though parents, fans, and opponents despised it.

Eureka College earned the No. 8 National ranking in the NAIA II pre-season basketball poll. Dave was asked by a *The Pantagraph* sportswriter his reaction to his team's ranking.

"I kind of thought we would be anywhere between No. 5 and No. 8," said Coach Darnall. "We made it to the Elite Eight last year and that impressed a lot of people, especially when they saw we started four juniors," Darnall continued. "You know me; I'm very cautious. It does not make a difference to me if we're rated or not, but it's good for the college and our players. But, it does put a lot of pressure on us."

Northern State of South Dakota took the No. 1 spot with the help of ten first-place votes. Defending champion Willamette (Oregon) was second. Tarleton State University, the team Eureka beat in the National Tournament the previous year, was ranked fifth.

Coach Darnall had recruited nine new prospects for what would become his last basketball team. Heading the list of new recruits were six-foot guard Stote Reeder, six-foot-six center Doug Hattermann, six-foot-five forward Chris Carter, and six-foot-four forward Mike Norris.

Jon Guderjan was the only player lost from the previous year's outstanding team, and what a loss that was! The coaching staff and Red Devil fans were extremely optimistic about the coming season. They had high hopes.

An outlook of the new season appeared in an article by David Vecsey for the Peoria *Journal Star* entitled "Finding a wheel—Eureka has four starters back; replacing the fifth might be key."

Most people would look at the Eureka College men's basketball team and see four starters returning from a 24 - 5 season in which the Red Devils made the quarter-finals of the NAIA Division II National Tournament.

Dave Darnall, an automobile buff, sees a pretty nice car returning from the auto show with a wheel missing.

"Anytime you take even one player away, it can mess up the chemistry," the coach said.

"We're a veteran ballclub, so everybody might think we can just pick up where we left off. That's not always the case."

Eureka's missing wheel is Jon Guderjan, the school's fifth all-time leading scorer who helped lead the Red Devils national-tournament appearances the last two seasons.

478

He was the only senior on last year's club and the only starter not returning this year, which the Red Devils begin as No. 8 in NAIA Division II.

So while the Red Devils seek a new chemistry, they take heart in the fact that they do return some heavy firepower.

Senior Troy Tyler (1,506) is third on the all-time scoring list and just 162 points away from the record of Mike Sain (1979-83). Tyler is coming off surgery on his left knee, but expects to start the season.

Also returning is 6-foot-8, 215-pound center Chris Eaton, whose 275 rebounds last year was a school record.

Filling Guderjan's spot will likely be 6-3 sophomore Adam Ferguson, who shined late last season. His jumping ability will put him down low and Tyler will move out to the perimeter.

"When I talked with Coach (as a high school senior), one of the things I looked at was how things were set up in terms of openings," Ferguson said. "He never made any promises, which I respect him for.

"But, one of the things I noticed was that there would be an opening my sophomore year."

Starting the season, *The Official 1994 NCAA Basketball Record Book* listed Eureka College's Head Men's Basketball Coach Dave Darnall among the nation's leaders for NCAA Division III coaches. Darnall held a .709 win percentage which ranked him fourteenth nationwide in the "Winningest Active 1993-94 Division III Men's Coaches by Victories" category. He had a 356 to 147 record in nineteen years at Eureka. His victories ranked him twenty-fourth in the nation for the "Winningest Active 1993-94 Division III Men's Coach by Victories" category.

The Red Devils would open the 1993-1994 campaign at Columbus, Ohio, participating in the Capital Classic on the campus of Capital University. The team left early Thursday morning, stopping at Earlham College, Indiana, for a short practice before proceeding on to Columbus for the Classic banquet that night.

Eureka College's first-round opponent was the host school. The starters for the first game of the year were seniors Eaton, Tyler, Peterson, Huttenlocher, and sophomore Adam Ferguson.

Despite a fifteen-point first-half performance by six-foot-seven Chris Easton, the "good guys" were down by six at the intermission. The much larger institution went on to beat its guest, 89 to 74, in a high scoring affair.

For the third consecutive year, the Red Devils lost their season opener. The two previous years, they still made the National Tournament field. It made for an up-hill battle, but maybe it was an omen of things to come.

"Since the number three is one of my favorite numbers, maybe something special will happen toward the end of the season. I'll take a loss the first game of the season any day if I can win the last game of the year," Darnall said after the game. "So far, we haven't won the last game of the season, but maybe the third year will be a charm."

Eureka College played Tusclum College from Greenville, Tennessee, for third place. EC's top players Tyler, Eaton, and Peterson scored over twenty points each as the Red Devils bounced back from their opening night loss. It was only the beginning that the trio would be heard from.

The Red Devils' twenty-eight-point margin victory was to the satisfaction of their coach. "Maybe since we beat them by such a large margin, we won't lose too many Dunkel points going home with a one-and-one record," Darnall said after the game. "I hope people get use to this Dunkel crap because we're going to play it all year. If we plan to make it back to Idaho, we're going to have to have the highest Dunkel points in the Conference."

The Eureka College home crowd got a chance to see their favorite team for the first time that season in the game against Rockford College.

Chris Peterson and Chris Eaton propelled their team to a lopsided 117 to 77 win by pouring in twenty-one and nineteen points respectively. Uncharacteristically, fourteen players saw some action in the contest. That was unusual since Darnall was found to limit his substitutions because of having to play the Dunkel.

The Red Devils claimed a road victory over Clarke College and was then ready for a revenge meeting with Concordia-River Forest. Last year's season opening loss at the hands of the Cougars haunted the players for a year. Coach Darnall said very little in his pre-game talk to motivate his team. The players remembered Concordia shot thirty-two free throws the previous year at their place while EC had only shot thirteen. Besides, Darnall let his team know the Concordia coach became very upset when "Scout" Wertz and he scouted their opening scrimmage with a junior college team. The EC players were ready to "kick butt."

Coach Darnall and the hometown Red Devil fans got their wish. The team came out of the locker room "smoke'n." Chris Peterson made seven three-point shots to lead his team to a 41 to 25 half-time advantage. Chris Eaton had a game-high twenty-nine points with twenty-one coming in the second half to pace Eureka to a 105 to 64 clobbering of their opponent. Senior guard Duane Schmedeke came off the bench to score fourteen second-half points, including four three-point shots. The Red Devils made a total of fourteen three-point baskets. For the second consecutive game, Darnall was able to substitute freely. A total of fifteen players saw action with eleven aiding the final score of 105.

Following the game, Jeffrey Shelman of the Peoria *Journal Star* asked Coach Darnall and Chris Peterson about the game.

"We played good ball the first three minutes, but we let them back in the game," Coach Darnall said. "Peterson really made two or three big baskets. We weren't executing our offense. Peterson has been playing outstanding basketball for us. He has been the most consistent player we have."

"I was just getting open shots," Peterson said. "I didn't shoot in the second half and that's fine with me. If they concentrate on me, we have Tyler and Eaton."

This was the same guy, or is it, that two years prior Coach Darnall said would never play again at Eureka College because of his attitude. Now he is the team leader and example of Coach Darnall's slogan "Together We Win."

"In the second half, we had a lot more balanced scoring and we began to play like we are capable," said Coach Darnall. "All the kids seem to think, 'I have to do it.' When this happens, we don't play very well."

"If we can get Troy and Chris Eaton to play 40 minutes, we'll have a pretty nice team," Darnall said.

The next two games were very important for the Red Devils. They were Conference games. The post-season Conference tournament would determine who qualified for the National Tournament. However, beating Conference teams during the regularly scheduled season influenced the Dunkel Rating System. That is what would be used to determine the seeding of each team. Eureka was going for No. 1.

The Red Devils traveled to Judson College for a rematch of the previous year's District 20 championship game. Coach Darnall knew it was going to be a "different game." In his pre-game talk, he reminded his players that they were going to have to play hard and stay out of foul trouble.

"Don't make any damn stupid fouls," Darnall instructed his players. "You're going to have to play forty minutes of basketball. Don't let the crowd get into the game. You know how important this game is. Play like it."

"Let's take our ten seconds. Each one is an individual. Think what you want to think or you don't need to think at all as long as we are quiet, and we do it together." Silence filled the locker room. "Now go out there and kick ass," Darnall emphasized.

The team dashed out of the locker room, down the hall, and through the doors leading to the gym floor.

"I hope like hell they're ready," Dave remarked to Assistant Dighton as he headed to the "john" for the last time.

"Me too, we'll see," Dighton responded as he left the locker room leaving Coach alone.

Troy Tyler pumped in thirteen first-half points as Eureka College took a slim one-point lead into intermission. Darnall, again, stressed the same points at half time as he did in his pre-game talk. He did, however, instruct his players to apply more pressure and play better defense. "We might not always be able to shoot good," Dave told the team, "but we can always hustle, bust our butts, and play good defense."

The players responded to the coach's "words of wisdom." They held the home team to only twenty-five second-half points while scoring thirty-nine themselves to claim a 71 to 58 victory over Judson. It was a great win and made for a good three-hour ride home for Darnall and his team.

The Red Devils returned home to take on their second Conference foe, Trinity Christian. It was another rematch. Eureka has played Trinity in the first round of the 1992-1993 District 20 Playoffs. Tyler shelled out thirty points while Peterson "tickled the twine" for twenty-seven as the Red Devils out-manned the Trolls, 102 to 58.

Coach Darnall was asked to comment about the future Eureka College Athletic Hall of Fame member's performance. "Troy looked a lot smoother tonight," he said. "He seemed more fluid. He injured his knee while working a summer basketball camp, and it required surgery in early October. He's just now beginning to play at full strength."

Eureka College participated in only one invitational tournament that season. It was the prestigious Pete Thorn Invitational Tournament held at Wabash College (Indiana). Their first opponent was Purdue Calumet. Purdue Calumet was a member of the Chicagoland Collegiate Athletic Conference the same as Eureka. However, there was a difference. Purdue Calumet offered athletic scholarships and was NAIA Division I. Eureka, on the other hand, offered no athletic scholarships and was NAIA Division II. The other Division II schools in the Conference also offered some type of athletic aid. The Red Devils had to be the underdog.

Coach Darnall decided to make a change in his lineup for this game by inserting Duane Schmedeke in the spot of sophomore Adam Ferguson. "I'm making this change for several reasons," Coach Darnall explained when asked about the move. "First of all, I need a third potential scorer from outside. Duane gives us that. Teams will soon start over-playing Tyler and Peterson because we don't have the third outside scorer. With Schmedeke starting the game, teams will have to play us straight up. He can light it up."

Darnall continued, "We are going to lose some quickness, overall size, and rebounding, but it's Huttenlocher's job to rebound and play defense. He'll just have to get a couple more rebounds a game. Also, this means Tyler moves from the guard position to a forward. Troy is a good jumper. He'll be able to pick up a couple more rebounds a game from his new position. Beside, I think Ferguson makes for a better 'John Havlicek.' He's a great leaper and a more exciting player. He'll add 'fire' to the team when he comes in."

The game was billed to be a close affair. The billing was correct. The Red Devils broke a 34 to 34 half-time tie by scoring the first five points of the second half. Chris Eaton scored sixteen points of his game-high twenty-one points in the final twenty minutes as Eureka downed the much larger Purdue Calumet, 72 to 65.

Four of the five starters scored in double figures. That is what Coach Darnall was hoping for. Huttenlocher and Schmedeke were going to have to contribute to the scoring attack when the opponents concentrated on one or two of their teammates. Tyler got only eight points, but Huttenlocher and Schmedeke scored fourteen and ten points respectively. The whole effort re-enforced Coach Darnall's slogan, "Together We Win."

The team watched the Wabash vs. Ohio Dominican game following their sweet win. Coach Dighton scouted Wabash while Coach Wertz scouted Ohio Dominican. Yes, "Coach" Wertz! Wertz normally only scouted for Coach Darnall but acted as an assistant coach that weekend due to the absence of Coach Begole.

Chuck was well qualified to serve as an assistant coach. He knew the Red Devil players, knew Darnall's system, and had scouted Purdue Calumet with Darnall just a week prior.

Wabash was a NCAA Division III school while Ohio Dominican was a NAIA II school. Wabash was led by the previous year's tournament MVP six-foot-four forward David Wallace. The Little Giants also had three solid seniors that Coach Mac Petty could depend on. Wabash had won the last two tournament championships.

Ohio Dominican had plenty of height with forwards at six-foot-five and six-foot-six and two centers at six-foot-eight and six-foot-nine. The Panthers' best player, however, was NAIA II All-American candidate Jerry Lanier. The six-foot-one, super-quick guard was a scoring machine. Lanier could not only drill the three-point shot, but he could also take the ball to the bucket for a slam-dunk.

When asked which team he would prefer to play for the championship, Coach Darnall said, "Even though it's harder than hell to beat a team at home, I don't think we have anyone who can stop Lanier. Both teams are well coached. Wabash is more disciplined and has more of a balanced scoring attack. Ohio Dominican has a great player, is more athletic, and quicker. I don't know. They'll both be tough as hell. We'll have to play our best game of the year in order to win. Whoever we play, if we can win it, it will really help our Dunkel rating."

As it turned out, Eureka would play Wabash for the championship. Could they prevent Wabash from winning their third consecutive championship?

Coach Darnall's team had a 7 to 1 record, but the pressure to continue winning and trying to get back to the Nationals were taking their toll on the Red Devil coach. Darnall was getting very little sleep, felt extremely tired, depressed, and stressed. When his team played on consecutive nights, he got no rest. The coaches met in Darnall's motel room after the second game to prepare a game plan for Wabash. He began to feel ill. The other coaches returned to their rooms. Dave was up most of the night sick to his stomach, breaking out with a rash, and being extremely nervous. It was the night that he decided this could be his final year at the helm of the Eureka College Basketball Program.

The championship game proved to give no relief. It was an extremely important game for the Dunkel rating points, and Darnall knew it. During his pre-game talk, Coach Darnall preached on the importance of playing hard for forty minutes and executing the offense. "Playing on the road will be no excuse for a poor performance," Darnall told his team. "You guys keep telling me you want to go back to Idaho. If that is the case, then get your asses out there and prove you can beat good teams like Wabash. Now, let's take our ten seconds."

It was a great contest for the spectators and the kind that drives some coaches from the game. There was a championship atmosphere. The gym was over half full with the noise level extremely high. The spirited Wabash male students sat directly behind the Red Devil bench. They let the Eureka College coach know he was on the road.

Shortly after tip-off, several of the Red Devils' fathers left their seats and intermingled with the Little Giant fans behind the Red Devil bench. A few of them were pretty "big boys" themselves and actually intimidated the college fellows. The ribbing of the Eureka College players and coaches ceased. It was then just good old-fashioned cheering by both the Wabash College students and the Red Devil fathers.

The first twenty minutes was a seesaw affair with neither team really taking charge of the game. Eureka College did hold a slim four-point, 39 to 35, half-time lead. Darnall, however, was not totally happy with his players' first-half performance. The more he spoke during his half-time talk, the more upset he became.

Coach Darnall found himself excited and emotional. To this day, he is not sure if it was a spontaneous or a planned performance that got out of control. In either case, Coach Wertz was totally amazed at Darnall's half-time antics. The players were leaving the locker room and heading to the gym floor while Darnall headed to the toilet again. From there, Darnall could hear Wertz ask Assistant Dighton, "Is he always like that at half time? I can't believe what I just saw and heard. I don't know how in the hell he does it."

"I've seen him do and say a lot of different things, but nothing like that," Dighton said. "But he wants the kids to play hard all the time. We hate to lose."

The team was warming up as several of the players' fathers walked to the end of the bench to ask the "weekend" coach how the halftime went. "Are the players ready to play?" one dad asked.

"I don't know, but they better," Wertz replied. "You won't believe what I just saw and heard. Darnall went nuts."

This is "Coach" Wertz's description of that memorable locker room display.

I had heard that Coach Darnall often got very vocal during the half-time recess. Sure, I thought, all coaches do. I did a few times while coaching Biddy Basketball and freshman ball. I would soon find out that college ball was different and that Coach was more descriptive and more dramatic than one could imagine.

EC had played absolutely terrible in the first half. The defense was horrendous and the game was extremely close at halftime. The players entered the locker room first, then assistant Dighton, and I followed.

The players were talking among themselves when Coach burst into the room. He slammed the door without looking behind him, and it closed hard right in the face of the trainer, Tim. Tim decided quickly that this was not the time to enter, so he waited outside.

Coach began telling the team how terrible they had played, the mistakes they had made, and the longer he talked, the louder he became. Everything was wrong. Not one player played up to his capability. The box in which towels were carried was sitting on the floor next to Coach. He must have kicked this box in disgust three or four times. Each time, it skidded across the floor towards Dighton. Almost unbelievably, each time, Dennis would push the box back to Coach. I tried not to laugh and thought that Dennis would eventually put the box somewhere else where Coach couldn't get to it. But after the fourth kick, Dighton pushed it back again. Coach Darnall was saying, "No one is taking charge out there. Everyone is pointing his finger at someone else and not taking responsibility for his own sloppy play."

At this juncture in the tirade, Coach, without actually thinking, decided to emphasize his point. He said, "You have to step up, take a look at yourself in the damn mirror, and say, 'It's me, damn it, it's me!'"

As he mentions the mirror, he picks up the box and instead of holding it out in front of him as a mirror, he *sticks* his head in it. Not just partway, but his head disappeared inside the box. The whole time, of course, he's ranting, cussing, and screaming out instructions. Dave removed the box and flung it across the room. Again, it lands right next to Dighton. This time though, he elects to push it behind him, out of Coach's reach.

Everyone, myself included, was almost in tears. Without laughing out loud, the players looked at me, biting their tongues. On the way out of the locker room for the start of the second half, Peterson and Eaton walked past me. They both were still trying hard not to laugh.

"So now you know," said Pete.

"One of the best half-time displays I've ever seen," commented Eaton.

You know, I don't remember if we won or lost that game, but I'll always remember the half-time show during my college-coaching debut.

The players made their coach a happy man. Troy Tyler banged home a three-pointer with fifty seconds remaining to break a 79-all tie and lift the Red Devils past Wabash, 90 to 81, in the Pete Thorn Invitational Tournament. Eureka converted on several free throws down the stretch to produce the final margin. All starting five of the Red Devil players scored in double figures. Darnall was looking for a balanced scoring attack. That's why he inserted Duane Schmedeke into the starting line-up at the beginning of the tournament. The strategy worked!

Tyler, who poured in twenty-nine points, became Eureka College's all-time leading scorer with 1,683. Mike Sain, who played for Coach Darnall from 1979 to 1983, had held the previous record.

"This is my twentieth season at EC, and this has to rate as one of the best invitational tournament championships we have won," said Coach Darnall when speaking to the media at the post-game news conference. "There were some good teams here. This is a very pleasant surprise. The kids worked hard for the championship."

Chris Peterson averaged 18.5 points for the two games and was named the tournaments Most Valuable Player. Tyler was named to the All-Tournament Team. However, the players weren't the only ones who worked hard for the victory. So did Coach Darnall. If there is any question about that, just ask Chuck Wertz.

Later, several EC fans asked Coach about the half-time incident. "I believe I am feeling the pressure. It's my own pressure. I really want one more try at the Championship. I know the players do. This is the third year for the NAIA Division III National Championship. With three being my lucky number, maybe this will be our year," Coach said.

Eureka College had one game remaining on its schedule before Christmas break. The team traveled to Deerfield, Illinois, for what the coaches knew would be an extremely difficult battle against a quality Trinity College team. University of Illinois transfer six-foot-six forward Marc Davidson led Trinity. Davidson had played two years for U of I. The high school All-stater was one of the top NAIA II players in the country. He and his teammates made Trinity College a top NAIA II team in the Midwest.

Trinity provided an opportunity for the Red Devils to gain precious Dunkel points. That type of game was especially stressful for Darnall. He felt extremely tired and sick to his stomach. The numerous trips to the toilet before the game became very monotonous. He agonized over the pre-game syndrome. He finally took his pre-game nap on the traveling trunks.

The pressure to win and keep Eureka College basketball as one of the top small college programs in the country was getting to him. Winning wasn't worth the fear of losing. Darnall had not lost many games over the past five years, but when his club did, it almost killed him. Some symptoms of depression were creeping in. Difficulty getting out of bed in the morning, always tired, and not eating properly were a few. "The thrill of victory wasn't worth the agony of defeat"

Darnall woke up in time to speak to his players. In a rather low-key speech, the coach reminded his team of the importance of the game. Coach Dighton gave a few defensive pointers as the players prepared to leave the locker room. "It was showtime!"

A few seconds after the start of the game, Coach Darnall's good friend and former Chicago Bull center, Dave Corzine, and his friend, Elise, entered the gym to witness the intense battle between two top NAIA II teams in the country. Corzine and the other Red Devil fans were not cheated. They definitely got their money's worth.

The crowed actually got to see a game and a fourth. Eureka College finally won in a double overtime. The game, however, was the "straw that broke the camel's back." Darnall made his decision to retire!

The key to the game was Dennis Huttenlocher, an often forgotten player to some, but not to the coaching staff. The outcome of the game was determined by how well he performed his specialties—rebounding and defense, this time on Davidson. Thank God! For the sake of his teammates, the coaches, and the Red Devil fans, Dennis performed spectacularly. He held the All-American to only four baskets.

Trinity jumped out to an early lead with Davidson hitting a coupe three-pointers. Coach Darnall jumped off the bench and called a quick time-out. It was the Darnall of old! Snorting at his players, he met them midway out on the court. There was no sitting down for the participating players. They knew their asses were in trouble. It was his "patented" timeout when he was pissed! Coach was animated. It was a good thing that the substitute players were surrounding the five starters with Darnall in the middle. He was tired no longer. This game was too important for him to hold back. Coach gave them hell for their lack of hustle, aggressiveness, and non-execution of their offense. Darnall also reminded Huttenlocher why he was playing.

Dennis got the message. Eureka went into the half-time break trailing 41 to 35, but the All-American forward only made one more basket the first half after Darnall's timeout.

Coach was still full of vigor at the intermission. His voice wasn't quite as loud as it was during the timeout, but his message was the same. He got his players attention!

The second half was a defensive gem on the part of both teams. Eureka was able to tie the score early in the second period of the seesaw battle. Trinity scored only twenty-two points in the second half while Eureka scored twenty-eight. In reality, the two teams played evenly for the first forty-five minutes. In the second OT, Duane Schmedeke took over, hitting a three-pointer with 1:26 left to give Eureka a 74 to 70 lead. Schmedeke then hit another basket with fifty-three seconds to play giving the Red Devils a 76 to 70 lead which Trinity could not overcome. The final score was 79 to 73.

It was a joyous assembly of Red Devils on the host's floor. Everyone congratulated each other on a job well done. Coach Darnall met his players on the court with congratulating hugs and handshakes. Then came a sigh of relief. The emotionally charged game was finally over. It was a huge win!

Darnall commented to a *The Pantagraph* reporter after the game, "This is a real big victory for us going into the Christmas break. Hopefully, this will give us a lift for the rest of the season."

Bonnie had made the three-hour trip to Deerfield with the Wertzes. The plan was if the team won, Dave would join them and Corzine after the game. If they lost, he would go back with the team. The Darnalls, Wertzes, Corzine, and his friend were able to spend time together at a little sports bar in nearby Lake Forest. It was a well-known establishment often frequented by members of the Chicago Bears when practicing in Lake Forest. The win had given everyone a nice evening and a great beginning to the holidays.

The Darnalls spent a few days at Fairfield Bay with some of their friends from Eureka. It gave Dave a chance to play a little golf and think. While there, he informed Bonnie that he had made one of the biggest decisions of his life. He was going to step down as Head Basketball Coach at Eureka College at the end of the current season. He was retiring from coaching. He loved coaching basketball and loved Eureka College, but the stress of maintaining Eureka as one of the top small college basketball programs had taken its toll. Darnall felt his health was slipping and wanted to spend more time with Bonnie and his children.

Not all small college coaches put as much time into their profession as Darnall. He was obsessed with personally seeing (scouting) all future opponents. Thank God, he had a good friend in Chuck Wertz to help him. When Chuck was not available, he either went by himself or with a student administrative assistant. At times he would persuade Bonnie to go with him. Coach Dighton conducted practice. Dave wanted to match his players with the future opponent players. He could also begin the game plan process. He had to see the actual game. Viewing a game tape was not sufficient. Dave was convinced that this was the only way his team would win; they had to be prepared.

"If I can't do what it takes to keep the program where it is, then I am cheating the college, the players, and myself. I keep telling my players to work hard and give it all you have or don't expect to play. I feel the same way about my coaching. If I can't work hard and give it my all, then it's time to get out." Dave told Bonnie. "When we get back I'll call the President's Office and set up an appointment with George. I want to continue teaching, directing my camps, and would like to still recruit. Hopefully, everything will work out. Don't tell anybody about this."

The players reported back to campus on January 2nd for five days of double practices before leaving on the seventh for Owensboro, Kentucky. The Red Devils were scheduled to open the second half of their season against Brescia College on the eighth.

It was over those five days that Coach Darnall informed Assistant Coach Dennis Dighton that he had definitely decided to step down at the conclusion of the season. Coach had broached this with his assistant on several occasions before. Darnall wanted to know if he would be interested in the position. He felt Dighton had an excellent basketball mind and after nine years as an assistant coach, he deserved the job. It would provide for an easy transition for the underclassmen and stability in the successful program.

Coach Darnall phoned the President's Office to arrange a meeting with President Hearne. George was the last person still connected with the college that had anything to do with his hiring. The up-coming meeting kept him tense for the next twenty-four hours. Dave was unsure what his future would be with the college. He did not want to leave. He felt that President Hearne knew his dedication and loyalty to the school and would be supportive.

The meeting took place the following day. Darnall informed the president of his decision. Mr. Hearne was surprised but supported his retirement submission. Dave thanked the president for his support over the years and expressed his appreciation for understanding why he was stepping down. Darnall also expressed his interest in helping recruit student-athletes as well as maintaining his teaching responsibilities and directorship of the basketball camps. President Hearne suggested that Dave replace his coaching duties by serving as an "Athletic Counselor." His major responsibility would be to help in the recruitment of women student-athletes. Coach Darnall would also continue to recruit men's basketball players for the new coach. Darnall was hoping that would be Coach Dighton.

The president suggested they keep Dave's decision quiet until the first of February. He had to be out of town for a couple weeks and wanted to be on campus when the official announcement was made. Dave left the office somewhat relieved. It was a weight off his shoulders. He could not concentrate on his main concern, his basketball team.

Coach Darnall had told the president, "I can leave this game and not feel cheated. I have been fortunate enough to win three District titles and participate in three NAIA National Tournaments. Very few coaches win a National Championship. It is something I never considered necessary in order to feel I have had a successful career. My biggest concern the last couple years was to be able to say I coached at Eureka College for twenty years —more than any other coach."

In Coach Darnall's mind, there were two Eureka College coaching legends that he hoped to someday be compared with. Ralph McKenzie coached basketball from 1921 to 1937 with a 121 to 131 won-loss record. Leo Traister, whom Darnall replaced in 1974, coached basketball from 1957 to 1974 with a 168 to 193 won-loss record. Traister served as basketball coach for seventeen years while McKenzie coached sixteen years.

The day before the team was to leave for Brescia College, Coach Darnall received a surprising letter. It was from Dr. B. Michael Higgins, president of the Greater Peoria Sports Hall of Fame. Dave was informed the Board of Directors of the Hall of Fame had selected him as the Tri-County Male Coach of the Year for 1993. This was the result of his last year's team's success. Coach Darnall was to be honored at the Greater Peoria Sports Hall of Fame's annual banquet held on February 20, 1994, at the Peoria Civic Center. It would be the day following the conclusion of the Red Devil's regular season schedule.

The team left for Owensboro, Kentucky, on an early Friday morning for a Saturday afternoon game to start the second half of the season. They checked into the Rivermont Executive Inn and then proceeded on to Brescia for a short practice. The main emphasis was to work on how to stop Brescia's sharp-shooting guard Scott Schoen. Darnall thought he might possibly be the best pure shooter they would face all year. He had a quick release and great range. He could be a one-man scoring machine.

The Red Devils came out of the locker room ready to play. Schoen pumped in twenty first-half points, but Eureka still held a 44 to 31 lead at intermission. Chris Peterson countered with fifteen first-period points by hitting on five three-point shots. Coach switched defensive assignments for guarding Schoen throughout the first twenty minutes between Peterson and Schmedeke, but it was to no avail. The sharpshooter still got his twenty.

The second half was a nightmare for the EC coaching staff. In the greatest single performance by any opposing player in Dave's tenure, the

Brescia guard single-handedly beat the nationally ranked Red Devils. Darnall assigned different players the entire second half to the unconscious shooter, even inserting sophomore Greg Crider, to try to slow down the scoring machine. However, no one could stop him. Schoen scored fifty-four points, including the winning basket with fifteen seconds remaining on the clock to give Brescia an 89 to 88 victory. Eureka had possession of the ball following Schoen's shot only to have it knocked out of bounds with four seconds remaining. EC called timeout to set up a special play. It didn't work; they could not get a shot off before time ran out. Chris Peterson led Eureka with thirty points.

Coach Darnall was pissed in the locker room following the game. Very seldom did he say anything to his players after a loss. Today it was different. It was a humiliating defeat for Coach Darnall and his team. The winners had only a 5 to 10 record. Basically, one player had beaten the entire Red Devil team. The home team had wanted the victory more! The loss haunted Darnall the remainder of the season. How would it affect the Dunkel? Needless to say, it was a long five-hour ride home.

Next would come the only two consecutive home games that EC would have that year. They could not have come at a better time. The one-point loss to Brescia was devastating. Could the hometown fans rally their beloved team?

Thank goodness the Red Devils rebounded and beat a mediocre Harris-Stowe University team by a lopsided score of 126 to 52. The following day, the NAIA II poll was released. How much would the Brescia loss hurt? To Coach Darnall surprise, his team climbed from eighth to fifth in the national rating.

Dave was asked about his team's new ranking by the local press. "I don't know if we've played as well as we are capable," he said. "Tomorrow we play Aurora, which has beaten both Millikin and Illinois Wesleyan Universities. That is going to be a big game for us. If we win, we'll be able to hold on to our new ranking. If not, we'll probably fall."

A milestone in Eureka basketball had been reached. Prior to the tip-off of the Aurora game, Troy Tyler was honored in front of a near-capacity crowd for surpassing Mike Sain as the college's All-time Leading Scorer. Coach Darnall presented a game ball with Troy's accomplishments printed on it to Mike Sain, who in turn, presented it to Troy. It was good to see the two great scorers on the floor together. Darnall hoped the ceremony would motivate his team to play one of its best games of the year.

Troy Tyler honored for surpassing Mike Sain as Eureka College's All-Time Leading Scorer with 2,119 points.

Could Eureka College beat one of the top small college teams in the state? The following article by Scott Heiberger from *The Pantagraph* "Eureka shoots down Aurora" gave the answer. It read in part:

When Aurora University came out in a 1-3-1 zone defense, Eureka shooters got into a zone of their own.

"I can't see too many teams coming in here and beating us playing zone," said Eureka forward Troy Tyler. "We just have too many good shooters."

The Red Devils never trailed in beating highly-regarded Aurora 111 - 60, Wednesday night in a non-conference game at Reagan Center.

"They were hitting them five feet beyond the line," said Aurora coach Don Holler, who coached at Flanagan High School in the 1960s. "It didn't matter if we were playing zone or man."

Tyler . . . led the Red Devils with 29 points and added seven rebounds . . . Peterson scored 25 and Chris Eaton added 22 points and a game-high 13 rebounds.

Eureka coach Dave Darnall said it was the best his team has played this season . . . "We needed this," Darnall said.

The outstanding victory brought out the largest attended celebration party at Coach's house of the year. The win over the Spartans was as sweet as the loss to Brescia was bitter. The Red Devil fans were ready to toast the near perfect performance of their ranked team. Perhaps the post-game lecture at Brescia had paid off! Coach Darnall had been so agonized by the heartbreak loss in Kentucky that he briefly wished he had retired at the end of the first semester. Tonight's win over Aurora University had made Darnall glad he had not.

The NAIA II National fifth ranking troubled Coach Darnall. He was afraid it would "add fuel" to the Lindenwood coach's pre-game motivational talk. A win over Eureka College would make Lindenwood College's season. He also worried that his team might be overlooking the St. Charles, Missouri, school in favor of the highly regarded McKendree Bearcats.

His fears were realized. The Lindenwood game was played in an extremely small gym with a very sparse crowd. In fact, Eureka was probably represented more than the home team. When Darnall saw Lindenwood dressed only eight players, he knew his team would think they were weak. They also had no height.

Lindenwood had no surprises for the Eureka coach. He had scouted them and knew they were very quick with a couple outstanding players, especially a guy named Braswell. Coach resoundingly warned his players in his pre-game talk not to take their opponent lightly. He stressed Lindenwood would be extremely patient on offense and probably would spread Eureka out. They were quick on defense and would put a lot of pressure on his shooters, especially Peterson and Tyler.

"If you guys don't go out there and play some ball, you'll get your asses beat," Coach Darnall shouted. "Everything you did will go right down the damn drain. Remember the feeling after the Brescia game. You sure as hell don't want that again. Now, let's take own ten seconds . . ."

The Red Devils just weren't ready to play. Lindenwood was! It was one of those games that caused Coach Darnall's early retirement. The headman called two quick timeouts to try to get his team going, but it was no use. Eureka trailed at the intermission, 37 to 31. Coach Darnall continued his outrage at halftime. Finally, totally lost for words and exhausted, he turned the team over to Coach Dighton. Dighton continued where Darnall left off. Now it was up to the players.

Perhaps the most significant happening of the contest was when EC Assistant Coach Dighton was assessed a technical foul. With less than seven minutes remaining, Dighton was whistled for a technical foul for protesting from the bench area several missed calls he could no longer tolerate. The Red Devil coaches didn't know which were worse, their players or the officials. Probably a combination.

The technical sparked what had been a sluggish Red Devil effort. The result was a rally from a ten-point deficit that culminated in a Chris Peterson twelve-foot baseline jumper with five seconds remaining to lift Eureka College over Lindenwood.

The locker room scene was subdued. The coaches were tired. The players were just glad to have the damn game over. There was no celebration. Everyone wanted to forget the game and just get home. The cold-cut sandwiches and chips didn't even sound appetizing. It was a long ride back to Eureka.

Three days later was the "big game" with NAIA I McKendree College. Prior to the game, Eureka College moved two spots to No. 3 in the NAIA II poll. The Red Devils, 12 to 2, received 438 points. Willamette, Oregon, the defending National Champion, remained in first with Bethel, Indiana, moving into second. Darnall, again, worried the announcement could make the players overconfident. The coaching staff hoped the players would redeem themselves for their poor showing at Lindenwood by knocking off the 1993 NAIA I District Champion.

The Red Devils came out of the locker room "smokin'." Everything that went up, went down. That lasted, however, for only the first twelve minutes of the game. Eureka held a nine-point lead when the momentum swung to the home team. Darnall called timeout to regroup his troops, but McKendree's comeback did not stop. EC trailed at halftime by five, 25 to 20.

It was McKendree's strategy to shut down Eureka's outside game. The Red Devils were one of the top teams in the Nation both NAIA II and NCAA III in the three-point shot. Eureka had only one such basket in the first twenty minutes. In fact, the majority of the scoring came from the center position. Eaton had seventeen points.

The Red Devils managed to tie the score at 66 with 4:08 remaining. McKendree's Brian O'Neil provided the decisive blow when his three-point shot ended the scoring at the two-minute mark. The visitors' last shot was a missed three-pointer by Troy Tyler with thirty-seven seconds left in the game. Despite Chris Eaton's career-high forty-three points and thirteen rebounds, Eureka College fell to an excellent McKendree team, 73 to 72.

Coach Darnall said very little to his players in the locker room following the defeat. His players were feeling the pain, and so was he. They gave it their "all." It's harder than hell to win on the road. The loss was the second in the last five games and another game that the Red Devils could have lost. Things had to change for a return trip to the National Tournament. They did!

The Red Devils came alive with six consecutive victories. Three were over Conference teams and three were non-conference. Two wins over Barat and one over Judson had kept the Red Devils perfect in league play. A great road rematch victory over Wabash was followed by a win over Greenville and then a shellacking of Moody Bible, 100 to 25.

It's hard enough to beat a good team once on the road, let alone twice. That was, however, the challenge Eureka had to face at Wabash. As expected, the first half was a seesaw affair as both teams played well. Chris Eaton pumped in twelve points in the first twenty, but EC still trailed at intermission by three. Darnall was fairly calm during the half-time talk. It wasn't like at Lindenwood where the team was just going through the motions and failing to execute their offense. This time, they were playing a quality team that knew how to play them. Coach emphasized the importance of the game regarding the Dunkel rating points. He reminded his players how nice it was the previous year at the National Tournament in Idaho. Darnall challenged his players in their desire to become National Champions. He also adjusted the offense in order to get more shots from the perimeter players, Tyler, Peterson, and Schmedeke. It worked!

The team came to life the second half. "Changes in the offense, defense and desire were changes for the better," said Darnall. Eureka College was able to withstand thirteen three-point bombs by the Little Giants to gain a rewarding 88 to 79 victory. Chris Peterson had led the way with thirty points while Chris Eaton and Troy Tyler chipped in nineteen and seventeen respectively. The nine-point win proved that the Pete Thorn Tournament Championship was no fluke.

Eureka College fell one spot to No. 4 in the NAIA II poll. The Red Devils, who were 14 to 3, had received 403 points. Willamette remained No. 1 and Bethel No. 2. Sioux Falls, South Dakota, moved up to the No. 3 spot.

"I am really somewhat surprised we didn't fall further than one spot," said Darnall. "With the loss to McKendree and near loss to Lindenwood, a mediocre team, and our struggle against Wabash, we are lucky we didn't."

After a lopsided 100 to 25 win over Moody Bible, the Red Devils traveled to Greenville to play the always-troublesome Panthers. Eureka got off to a very unusual good start and held a 39 to 33 lead at halftime. They went on the gain a 79 to 43 victory.

February 1st was now almost there and Darnall's pending retirement announcement. The Director of College Relations, Lynn Beer, arranged a press conference at the college's Melick Library. News personnel from the Bloomington-Normal, Peoria, and Eureka areas attended. With Bonnie, Tiera, Dave's players, and many other interested spectators, President Hearne stepped to the podium to speak to those gathered.

Randy Kindred of *The Pantagraph* reported the event in "Reluctantly, Darnall to step down." It read:

> To anyone who had met Dave Darnall, the image is as clear as a slam-dunk, as sharp as a backdoor cut.
>
> It is a man head over heels in love with his job, a man whose drive and dedication are matched only by the endless energy used to set them in motion.
>
> It is a image Darnall has spent 20 years carving out . . . year by year, mile by mile, victory by victory. He cant't stand the thought of it being altered, or perhaps destroyed.
>
> With that in mind, an emotional Darnall announced yesterday he will retire as Eureka College men's basketball coach at the end of the season.
>
> The 52-year-old Darnall cited stress and its related health problems as major factors in his decision to end the longest and most successful tenure in school history.
>
> He will remain at Eureka College as an associate professor of physical education and in the newly created position of College Athletic Counselor, in which he will counsel and recruit prospective student-athletes in men's and women's basketball, women's softball and women's volleyball.
>
> "I don't feel I can still do the things it takes to maintain Eureka as one of the top basketball programs in the nation," said Darnall, whose 20th Red Devil squad has a 16 - 3 record and is ranked fourth nationally in NAIA Division II.
>
> "I want to go out on top and be remembered as a hard worker, not someone who kind of slides out and is not able to maintain the program Coach Dighton (assistant coach Dennis Dighton) and I have developed."
>
> The Red Devils have a 372 - 150 record under Darnall, a .713 winning percentage, and have won five conference championships and three NAIA District 20 (state) titles. Eureka College has reached the NAIA playoffs 13 times since 1974, the year Darnall succeeded Leo Traister . . .

Coach Darnall officially announcing his retirement as Head Basketball Coach effective at the end of the season.

Eureka College President George Hearne had this to say, "There is no adequate way to describe the impact Dave Darnall has had on Eureka College's athletic program and recognition.

"I understand and accept his decision to step down," Hearne added. 'But I cannot do so without expressing my personal regret, and that of the entire Eureka College family, that he will not be on the floor next year, leading us to another great season . . ."

It was an emotional time for Coach Darnall and his family. This was something they knew would happen someday but were not looking forward to. Basketball was so much a part of their lives—the games, post-game parties, and the life-long friends they had made with both players and parents. It definitely would seem quieter around the Darnall house now. "If only walls could talk," said Darnall. "There was enough conversation, gossip, and celebration here over the past twenty years to write a very interesting book."

Randy Kindred of *The Pantagraph* reflected in "Along for the ride on Darnall's date with destiny." Randy had been assigned to cover the 1987

McKendree vs. Eureka game at Lebanon. In the article he remembered his assignment:

> It promised to be a long drive and a longer game, but the assignment sheet on the bulletin board read: "Eureka College at McKendree—Kindred."
>
> Clearly, almost painfully, duty called. An throughout the 2½-hour trip to Lebanon, visions of a blowout grew sharper with each mile marker.
>
> But what I did not know—what no one knew—was that Dave Darnall had a far different vision, one that a few hours later would seem eerily predestined . . .

The rest of that game was history. Kindred's article continued with the retiring Darnall.

> That is how it is with Dave Darnall: full speed ahead, 100 percent, all or nothing.
>
> If you're going to play a game, go all out to win it. If you're going to have a party, make it an all nighter, and if you're going to coach, do whatever it takes to build and maintain a winning program.
>
> That's the one that troubled the 52-year-old Darnall this season, even haunted him. With a heart that already has sustained one attack, and a skin condition brought on by the self-inflicted pressure to win, he felt his health slipping and feared his coaching would do the same.
>
> "I know I could not have gone another year this way," said Darnall, who has fretted away 15 pounds since Christmas. "I could tell it. It's the right decision."
>
> Applaud him for making it. It could not have been easy, particularly at a time when his team is 16 - 3 and ranked fourth nationally in NAIA Division II, but it is even more difficult to think of the Red Devils without Darnall.
>
> He has not simply coached Eureka College basketball. He has lived it, breathed it, become it . . .

There were only six games remaining on the regular season schedule. One game was also guaranteed in the post-season Conference tournament. Coach Darnall was looking at the possibility of roaming in front of the Eureka College basketball bench on only seven more occasions.

Judson was the first contest for Eureka College following Darnall's retirement announcement. Both his players and the Red Devil fans were fired up for the game. Eureka jumped out to a 25 to 3 lead before Judson scored it first field basket at the midway point of the first half. The Red Devils went on for an easy 79 to 45 win with senior forward Troy Tyler leading the way with twenty-three points.

Kevin Bergquist of the Peoria *Journal Star* asked the coach to comment on his team's first game since he announced he was stepping down at the conclusion of the season. "Anytime you hold a team the first ten minutes without a basket, you have to be satisfied," Darnall said. "We came out and played good defense, but we weren't real happy with our offense. As the game continued, our offense began to perk up."

The Darnall house was full of Red Devil fans after the game, but the tone was just a little different. All knew it was coming to an end. Two more home scheduled games and at least one post-season game would provide the short time for parents, former players, college personnel, town people, camp coaches, and friends of Eureka College basketball to gather together. Such a cross section of people would no longer meet. No more "Together We Win."

Eureka College stood at 17 to 3 after the Judson win and dropped to fifth in the NAIA II National poll. Bethel, Indiana, took over the No. 1 position with Willamette dropping to second. Taylor, Indiana, moved to third and Northwestern Iowa was fourth.

Coach Darnall insisted annually that he would never schedule Southern Illinois University-Edwardsville again. Every year, he did. The reason was his inability to fill his schedule with colleges similar to Eureka. In addition, the financial guarantee that the state NCAA II institution offered permitted Eureka to take an overnight trip to the St. Louis area staying in a nice motel. It was good for recruiting purposes. Besides, many EC players had not been to St. Louis and seen the "Arch." The SIU-E trip was the last overnight scheduled trip for the Red Devils. A large entourage of EC basketball fans made the journey to Edwardsville.

Coach Darnall had scheduled a short practice the day the team arrived in the St. Louis area. The loyal fans were at the motel to greet the team upon return from practice. This was the last time the players and their supporters were to be on the road together this season. Or would it be? The players and fans enjoyed the evening together in a small private room. Much of the talk was about the season and what the possibilities were for post-season play.

The team arrived at the SIU-E fieldhouse about an hour before tip-off. Coach didn't have to say much in his pre-game talk. The players knew the magnitude of the game. Darnall reviewed the scouting report Wertz and he accumulated. Now it was time to execute the game plans from the report.

It was a little different than in previous years. Instead of waiting until fifteen seconds left on the shot clock before taking a shot, the players were able to shoot whenever they were open. However, it must be a good shot. Darnall always emphasized good shot selection.

The first half was a "dandy." Both teams played very well. Coach Darnall was happy with the execution of both his team's offense and defense. The halftime score verified the first half seesaw battle. It was tied at 36. Chris Peterson led the Red Devil assault with thirteen points. Darnall was very positive during his half-time speech. He, basically, emphasized to keep up the intensity, work hard, keep executing the offense and defense, and not let the officials affect their play. He told them to prepare for a close game at the end.

Darnall was right. Southern Illinois-Edwardsville rallied in the final minutes to claim a 74 to 70 victory. The Cougars trailed 70 to 69 with 1:30 left when Eureka center Chris Eaton missed the front end of a one-and-one free throw situation. Coach Darnall's heart nearly fell out. SIU-E rebounded the miss, and Matt Fridley drilled his fifth 3-pointer of the game with 1:10 remaining to give his team a 72 to 70 lead. Eureka brought the ball down the floor and patiently worked a good shot. A shot was taken. It hit the rim and fell off. The hosts got the defensive rebound, and Anthony Smith's basket with twenty seconds left sealed the win for SIU-E.

Following the game, the disheartened Coach told his players how proud he was of their performances, how hard they worked, and they deserved a better outcome. He did, however, warn them that it's the little things that make the difference. If they planned to be a champion, they had to make pressure free throws, hit the big baskets, and grab the key rebounds. That's what it takes to be a National Champion.

Darnall also reminded his team that the biggest game of the year was going to be the next day. It was the make-up contest against the highly respected Westminster College. "Even though you lost today, you didn't lose any Dunkel points," Coach Darnall told his players. "But your effort today won't mean a damn thing if you get beat tomorrow. We got to go out and kick some butt early. Let's get dressed now and head to Litchfield for supper."

Coach Darnall held another brief team meeting outside the field-house when arriving back on campus. "Fellows, we got to bounce back tomorrow. We can't lose any Dunkel points. Indiana Tech is really good and they are right there with us. We don't want to have to go over there to play. If we do, it could be like it was today. Go back to your dorms and get your rest. We got to be ready tomorrow."

Darnall's boys were ready to go. So was the near capacity Sunday afternoon crowd. The fans cheered loudly the moment the Red Devils took the floor until the sound of the horn indicated the end of the game. They let the team know that the SIU-E loss hadn't hampered their enthusiasm and optimism of going back to Idaho.

Chris Peterson hit five three-point baskets plus a two-pointer for a combined seventeen points in the first twenty minutes of play to give Eureka a huge, 48 to 16, half-time lead over the out-manned Westminster team. The Red Devils went on to double the score on their opponent and claimed a 100 to 50 victory for their nineteenth win of the season.

Regardless of it being a Sunday afternoon, the Red Devil fans still gathered at the Darnall home for the traditional post-game party. Much of the conversation had to do with what effects the two weekend games would have on the Dunkel points. Everyone knew that the points separating Eureka and Indiana Tech were slim. The team with the highest point rating would be guaranteed the host court advantage throughout the post-season Conference Tournament. That was a must for any team having aspirations of going to the NAIA II National Tournament. Darnall had "played" the Dunkel game for years. He knew the top seed position would be close. Both institutions had a good record, good personnel, and were ranked high in several national statistical categories.

Coach gave his players the following day off. That gave them a little rest and a day to prepare for Mount St. Claire in Clinton, Iowa. His concern was not necessarily Mount St. Claire's personnel, but where the game was being played.

Darnall was proven wrong. He should have been concerned about Mount St. Claire's players and his own team's motivation, or maybe lack of motivation. Trailing 42 to 41 at halftime, Coach Darnall had an absolute fit. Snatching a piece of chalk, he threw it at the blackboard. He blasted his team's work ethic, especially on defense.

"I told you guys we had better be ready to play tonight. They got nothing to lose and everything to gain. Beating you will make their season. This team can't hold a candle to those in Idaho. So, you think you can win a national championship. Like hell you can," Darnall shouted.

He was going berserk. The whole damn season was going down the drain. His career was coming to an end. *Now*, he thought, *Indiana Tech will be seeded No. 1.*

With blood vessels popping in his neck, Darnall continued the onslaught. He had to challenge his players. He had to make them prove him wrong. They just couldn't have to play Indiana Tech on their home court. "You guys don't deserve to be ranked fifth in the Nation. There's no way you're better than Indiana Tech. They'd kick your butt. If you think you're half as good as you think you are, then prove it," Darnall bellowed.

"Dighton, you talk to 'em. I'm tired of it. Hell, they don't care," Darnall shouted.

Coach walked away, still worried, but he knew he had gotten their attention. He felt he'd done his job. If he were a betting man, he'd bet the fans would see a different Red Devil team on the floor the second half. He then let Assistant Dighton talk to the team about defensive adjustments and a slight change in the offense. Coach Darnall continued the "silent treatment act," avoiding the players and not saying anything else as they prepared to return to the floor. *Let them think a little; can't make up yet,* he thought.

Coach Darnall's only words to his players as they gathered in front of the bench to begin the second half were, "Prove me wrong. Show me you want to go to Idaho."

They did. Trailing at the intermission, the Red Devils came out and played a determined twenty-minute second half. They outscored the home team, 51 to 26. Hard work on defense, balanced scoring, hustling all over the court, and an attitude adjustment made the difference. Four players scored in double figures. Eaton had twenty-nine points, Tyler had twenty-five, Schmedeke had eighteen, and Peterson had fourteen.

Darnall was exhausted following the game. He praised his players for their comeback play and headed to the toilet. Not only did he spend time in the "john" before the game, but now he was also there after the game. It was time to get out!

The ride home was quiet. It seemed extremely long. The players and coaches were mentally and physically drained. Dave knew it was a "big win." It was the team's twentieth victory. With only a home game left of the regular schedule, they should finish the year with twenty-one wins. Hopefully, a 21 to 4 season would give them the No. 1 seed in the post-season Conference Tournament. The winner goes to the National Tournament.Dave knew the Saturday afternoon game against arch rival Greenville would be an emotional affair. There would be a "packed house" at Reagan Center. The afternoon would also include "Senior Day," Dave's last regular season game, and a "Blast from the Past" game. A game among

Darnall's former players from his nineteen previous teams was played just prior to the regular game. It was a great affair. Players ranging from Coach Darnall's first recruit, Tim McGuire, to the previous year's only senior, Jon Guderjan, participated in the game. Forty-six former players and student administrative assistants returned to the Eureka College campus. That was the first ever alumni game of Coach Darnall's former players. Some were back on campus for the first time since graduating. The names of these players who made that trip back to Eureka to honor their former coach are listed in Appendix E.

There was excitement in the air that Saturday afternoon. It was a true "Together We Win" atmosphere. An article by Kevin Bergquist for *The Pantagraph* entitled "Taking the floor one more time—Darnall to coach last regular-season game at Eureka today" read in part:

> Looking at a game program Friday titled "Together We Win: 1974 - 1994" made Eureka College men's basketball Coach Dave Darnall realized the end is near.
> Darnall, coach of the nations No. 6 rated NAIA II team, is retiring at the end of the season after 20 years at Eureka . . . "It will be different for me," Darnall, who is two wins shy of his 500th career coaching victory, said. "Seeing all of the former players will be very emotional, but once the game gets going, we will be all right . . ."
> "The players really want to go back to the national tournament, and they are trying to keep all of the emotion toward going to Idaho," Darnall said.
> A win today would also give Darnall the chance to get his 500th career coaching victory at home next Saturday.
> "It would be great, but I don't like to think about it," Darnall said. "If something happens and I go out at 499 wins, I don't want to take away from anything we have accomplished here."

Prior to the game, perhaps the best assembled group of seniors during Darnall's tenure and their parents were introduced to the capacity crowd. They were Chris Eaton, Dennis Huttenlocher, Ryan Markley, Chris Peterson, Duane Schmedeke, and Troy Tyler. Two-year student assistant Randy Begole was also graduating. Coach Darnall and his entire family were introduced as well.

Greenville played a good first half in front of a full house of Red Devil fans but still trailed at intermission, 35 to 27. Eureka gradually increased that lead during the second half finishing with an 87 to 67 victory. Three Red Devils scored twenty points or more. Peterson pumped in twenty-five while Tyler and Schmedeke each tallied twenty. It was a great way to end the regular season. Now it was the "waiting game." Who would be seeded No. 1 in the post-season Conference Tournament?

A tradition was changed that night. The post-game party was moved from the Darnall home to a private room at The Outpost. There were too many people for the Darnall home. There were the forty-six former players and their families; the current players and families; the Darnall family including Dave's mother, sisters, and brother; the loyal Red Devil fans; family friends from Momence including the Clarks and Monks; and Dave's childhood friends—the Raycrafts, Drapers, Phillips, and LeRoy Moyer. So many stories and reminiscing. It was a night Dave and his family will not forget, definitely a night of "Together We Win."

Eureka College was notified the following day that they were seeded No. 1 in its Chicagoland Conference Playoff Tournament. That was the news Darnall wanted to hear. Playing the Dunkel point system the whole season had paid dividends for Darnall and his players. The coach was often criticized for his non-substituting practices and running up the score on opponents. Darnall defended by saying, "As a coach, I had to do what it took to get this No. 1 rating."

The coach and several of his players were also informed of Chicagoland Conference honors. Dave was named Conference Coach of the Year, Chris Eaton was selected Conference Player of the Year, and Chris Peterson and Troy Tyler were named First Team All-Conference.

It was now time to prepare the way Dave always did for his opponents—scout! The coaches concluded practice on a Thursday at 5:00 P.M. and hustled to Elgin for the 7:30 P.M. first-round game of the tournament. Dighton scouted Judson while Darnall watched Barat. Judson won the contest and, thus, became Eureka's first Conference Tournament foe. If Eureka beat Judson, Dave anticipated his team would play Indiana Tech for the championship. Darnall and "Super Scout" Wertz had seen the Indiana school in early December. Coach, however, felt they need to be scouted again. He had sent Wertz and Coach Begole to Fort Wayne in early February to observe them the second time. The effort eventually paid off.

A pre-game article appeared in the *Journal Star* by Scott Heiberger entitled "Red Devils prepare for playoff pressure—Eureka counting on experience to keep the season going."Portions of it read:

The upcoming retirement of Coach Dave Darnall and impending graduation of a senior-dominated lineup meant the end of an era for Eureka College men's basketball. But the Red Devils hope the era lasts another few weeks.

"Our experience should help," senior Chris Eaton said. "At the same time the pressure is on because the expectations are just that much higher . . ."

The Red Devils have advanced to nationals two seasons in a row, reaching the quarterfinals last year.

"The seniors feel pressure," Eaton said. "But I think everyone is trying to stay relaxed and let coach do the worrying."

The ability to worry is one reason why Darnall, who announced he'll retire after this 20th season, has a record of 377 - 151 at Eureka.

"It's tough to beat any team three times," Darnall said of Saturday's matchup.

It's tough to beat Eureka, especially at home. The Red Devils are ranked No. 6 in NAIA II and have not lost at Reagan Center since the first game of the 1991-92 season - a string of 36 regular-season and playoff games . . .

The game was played on a Saturday evening in front of a near-capacity, vocal crowd. The Red Devil fans anticipated a return trip to Idaho. Coach Darnall had a sleepless night and a very agonizing day. He did not want to end his lifetime career until he guided his team one more time to the National Tournament.

Coach was surprisingly calm in his pre-game talk. There was no ranting, raving, or worrying about the Dunkel. In fact, he only told his players to not embarrass themselves and reminded them that there would be no "tomorrow" if they lost.

"A lot of people out there have confidence you'll win the Conference Championship. Don't let them down. What's more important, don't let yourselves down. You'll never forget it," Darnall said.

Don Baker summarized the game in an article for the Peoria *Journal Star*. "Eureka, Darnall end up winners—coach gets 500th career victory as Red Devils jump all over Judson, 75 - 54" read in part:

> It was not a good day for Eureka College men's basketball coach Dave Darnall, but it was a great night. Darnall worried about all that was on the line in this game.
>
> With Eureka College's 75 - 54 victory Saturday over Judson College in the Chicagoland Conference Tournament semifinal, his team advanced to the title game. It also gave Darnall his 500th victory in high school and college coaching.

Eureka (22 - 4) hosts Tuesday's title game at 7:30 P.M. Against Indiana Tech (20 - 7), a 109 - 93 winner over Trinity Christian. The two teams have not met this season.

Troy Tyler led the Red Devils with 29 points. Chris Peterson added 21 and Chris Eaton 14.

"Tyler played his best game of the year," Darnall said. "And I told him that three or four times during the game and afterwards. He really came down like a thoroughbred tonight and not just because he scored. He did everything we needed done—his diving on the floor, his rebounding, his assists . . ."

Eaton set a school record for career rebounds with 866. His first rebound broke the old record held by Craig Gerdes (1967-71). This is also the third consecutive year Eaton has taken the single-season rebounding honors. He holds the top three spots for single-season totals . . .

Can you guess what the topic of conversation was at the Darnall home after the game? Of course the night's win was celebrated, but it was the up-coming title game that kept the packed house buzzing. How good was Indiana Institute of Technology? Did the No. 1 NAIA II offensive team in the country beat Trinity Christian? Curiosity was killing the coach and house full of fans. Darnall called the Bloomington's *The Pantagraph* Sports Department for the score. IIT had won!

The Red Devil team had only two practices to prepare for the highly potent offensive Fort Wayne team. Darnall also had another problem. Star point guard Chris Peterson had sprung his ankle in Eureka's win over Judson. Would he be ready to go? In Sunday's practice, Chris Hopwood and Adam Ferguson had to fill in for the injured Peterson. Darnall saw the season coming to an end with the single-season scoring leader on the bench.

"Eureka one step from nationals—Red Devils must defeat top scoring team in nation for third consecutive trip to NAIA tourney" headed an article by Scott Heiberger for the *Journal Star* on Tuesday, March 1, 1994. It gave an excellent preview of the evening's game. It read in part:

The NAIA Division II men's basketball tournament is nine days away, but Eureka College coach Dave Darnall predicts tonight's game against Indiana Tech will generate national tournament atmosphere.

"I look at this game as the first round of the national tournament," said Darnall, whose team plays host to Indiana Tech at 7:30 P.M. in the championship game of the Chicagoland Collegiate Conference Tournament.

"I think whoever wins this game will make it to the Elite Eight at nationals," Darnall said.

The winner gets a automatic berth in the 24-team national tournament, March 10 - 15, in Nampa, Idaho.

Eureka (22 - 4), ranked No. 6 nationally, seeks it third trip in a row to nationals.

Indiana Tech (20 - 7), ranked No. 25, is a pressing, running team that leads the nation in scoring at 109.3 points per game . . .

Point guard Chris Peterson will figure greatly in Eureka's ability to break the press and hit open shots.

The senior from Brimfield averages 20.4 points per game, just ahead of returning all-Americans Troy Tyler (20.0 ppg) and Chris Eaton (19.4 ppg) . . .

Indiana Tech is led by 6-6 forward Rick "Sugar" Foster (24 ppg, 5.5 rpg). He's followed by Dwayne Tubbs (21.9 ppg, 4.2 rpg, 5.6 assists, 4.8 steals) and Dale Blassingame (19 ppg, 8.5 rpg).

Darnall had an extremely stressful day. It also followed a sleepless night. All he could think about was how he might be coaching his last basketball game. Twenty-nine years of coaching and living in the fast lane might come to an end. No more walking the sidelines in front of his players and fans, no more people over after the home games, and no national championship.

Bonnie drove her husband to Reagan Fieldhouse as she normally did on home game nights at 6:00 P.M. Coach Dighton had already prepared the game equipment by the time the head coach arrived. Darnall went directly to his office where he remained until his pre-game talk in the upper-floor classroom at 6:40. This was his team's pre-game meeting room for twenty years. He made several trips to the faculty restroom before his final forty-foot walk to the classroom. The agonizing journey seemed like miles.

He addressed his solemn team. The coach was more subdued than his normal fussy mood. He felt this probably was his last team meeting with any team. His players would have to play "the game of their careers" to beat the highly athletic Tech team. He knew they could, but there weren't many "takers." In the past, Darnall realized that each season would end in a loss unless his team didn't qualify for the playoffs, but there was always next year. Now, there was no "tomorrow."

"This year's past season play was like being on death row. You know the end is coming, but you just don't know when," Darnall said. "Maybe that's why I'm against capital punishment. It's hell waiting and not knowing when it will be over. I guess that's why I treasured the wins so much."

Dave asked his players to play hard, execute their offense, not let the officials affect their play, and play the best game of their lives. "This game is the first round of the National Tournament," Coach informed his players. "Whoever wins tonight can definitely get into the Elite Eight. You can't win a national championship without winning tonight. No Eureka team has ever lost a NAIA post-season game here at home. Why should you? That standing-room-only crowd is for you. Don't let them down."

Coach Darnall paused to do something very unusual. He read a letter from a former player. Jon Guderjan, the previous year's only senior and one of the most respected players to ever wear the maroon and gold, had written a letter to his former teammates. It was a message from his heart to his buddies. Two years prior, as a member of the team, Guderjan had written another note "Remember 86 to 83 Olivet" to his teammates. Coach had read the letter prior to playing Olivet Nazarene in the Judson Tournament. The Red Devils had gone on to defeat Olivet for the first time in Darnall's tenure at Eureka College, 67 to 53. Jon challenged his former teammates as Darnall had numerous times. "Next year when most of you get out of school and in the years to come for the rest of you guys, you will realize how athletics, your coaches, and your parents have played a major role in making you the person that you are. They pushed you to the limit for a reason, and now it is time to push yourselves to the limit. Don't take any one play for granted because it could be the last game you play for the season; for some of you— the last game of your career. Like Coach Darnall always says, you should be able to look in the mirror after the game and be able to say to yourself that you gave absolutely everything you had for 40 minutes."

"Now let's take our ten seconds. Each one is an individual. Think what you want to think or you don't need to think at all as long as we are quiet, and we do it together."

A few moments of silence passed. "I'm proud of what you guys did this year. I hope we'll get to take another ten seconds again. Now, let's go kick some ass. 'Together We Win,'" were Darnall's departing words.

The players left the room. Dave remained upstairs while the players walked down the hall, down the stairs, and then dashed through the gymnasium's double doors to a tremendous ovation from the standing-room-only crowd. Hearing this from the upper hall, Darnall walked around the corner, as he did numerous times, to the faculty men's bathroom for the final time. It was here, sitting on the "john" all alone in this small exclusive hideaway that Dave truly realized the end was here. No more games. No more times in there.

Following a few moments of isolation, Coach duplicated the path his players had taken just a few moments before. This time, however, there was no applause. Darnall walked past the players' empty chairs to his customary third chair from the scoring table. Recall, three was his lucky number.

Three outstanding players, five-foot-ten junior guard Dwayne Tubbs, six-foot-three forward Dale Blassingame, and six-foot-six senior forward Rick Foster led the Warriors. Michael Terry, a five-foot-ten guard, and six-foot-five center Ramon Batts rounded out the starting five.

Indiana Institute of Technology was very athletic. They could run, jump, and shoot. Their No. 1 national ranking in offensive output was proof of their worth. The super quick team depended a great deal on the fast break for scoring. Their quickness supported a full-court man-to-man defense throughout the game.

In contrast, Eureka College was basically a half-court team. They were very patient on offense, only employing the fast break on sure opportunities, and played half-court defense. This being Darnall's 1-2-2 adjustable zone or pressure man-to-man. No pressing. The game was a clash of strategy and philosophy. Indiana Tech's fast pace and shoot-when-open philosophy versus Eureka's patient offense and pressure half-court defense. In Dave's mind it was a replay of the 1987 NAIA District 20 Championship game against high scoring McKendree College. The only difference in tonight's game was that it was being played at home, not on the road. Thanks to Darnall's "playing" of the Dunkel system.

The buzzer sounded. The teams went to their respective benches for last-second instructions from their coaches. Mary Finch sang the National Anthem. Jim Finch, public address announcer, began to introduce the starting line-ups to the standing, cheering crowd.

Eureka College's starters were the same five outstanding seniors, Eaton, Peterson, Tyler, Schmedeke, and Huttenlocher that had started most of the season. Then there was the tip-off!

The first half was as predicted—a seesaw battle between two of the better NAIA II teams in the country. Eureka College held a one-point lead with just seconds left in the first half when Troy Tyler hit a three-point shot. This gave the Red Devils a 40 to 36 lead at the intermission. Tyler paved the way for the home team with seventeen first-half points.

Darnall knew the score would be close throughout the entire game. That's what happens when two good teams are matched. He was satisfied with his team's first-half play. He was also extremely calm at halftime for such an important game. He, basically, just encouraged his team to continue their good play. He ended his last half-time talk by reminding his players the rewards of a victory and the severe agony of watching Tech cut down the nets after receiving the championship trophy. They sure as hell didn't want to witness that.

In spite of the noisy crowd cheering its team, the Red Devils fell nine points behind the mighty Warriors with approximately eight and one-half minutes remaining on the clock. Darnall looked over to his assistant. "Dennis, I think it's over. We're not going to come back. I can't believe it."

Dighton didn't respond. He just kept yelling at their players to apply more pressure on defense. Darnall stood and started to pace the floor.

The final minutes of this game is best described by Robert Warth, sportswriter for *The Pantagraph* in "Eureka College digs deep, rallies for emotional win." It read in part:

> During a timeout Tuesday night at Reagan Center, the starting five for Eureka College's basketball team, which had played all 31 minutes and 45 seconds of the game, started thinking about the possibility of defeat.
>
> The Red Devils trailed by nine points against an explosive Indiana Tech team that appeared on the verge of breaking the championship game of the Chicagoland Conference Playoffs wide open.
>
> Yet the five seniors amazingly found the courage to pull together and shut out the highest scoring team in NAIA Division II for the final 8:15 of the game, pulling out a 75 - 69 triumph and sending the Red Devils to the NAIA National Tournament for the third straight year.
>
> Leading 69 - 60, Indiana Tech proceeded to miss its final nine shots and commit one turnover as Eureka College slowly climbed back.
>
> "We knew we'd better dig down deep and play defense like we'd never played before," said senior guard Chris Peterson, whose 17-foot jumper tied the game 69-all with 4:30 remaining.
>
> "We played good defense and made sure they got only one shot," said senior guard Duane Schmedeke, who grabbed five rebounds during the stretch.
>
> "We did not want to lose our last game on this floor," said senior center Chris Eaton, whose lay-up off an assist from Troy Tyler with 1:25 left gave the Red Devils a 71 - 69 lead.
>
> "Half-court defense and rebounding were 'the whole key.'" said Eaton. "Getting second the third shots gave them the lead. Holding them to one shot was what won the game for us."
>
> "When we were down nine, the character of the kids came out," said an emotional Eureka College coach Dave Darnall, who wept for several moments on his wife Bonnie's shoulder after the game. "When we won (the district) in 1987, I fainted, and tonight, I cried."
>
> Eaton finished with 21 points and 17 rebounds, Schmedeke had 17 points and nine rebounds and Peterson tallied 16 points . . . Tyler scored all 17 of his points in the first half.

Coaches Begole and Dighton and player Ryan Markley look on as Coach Darnall shows concern with his team's deficit.

The fieldhouse scene was one of hysteria following the buzzer. It was undoubtedly the greatest game ever played in the fieldhouse and the best home victory in Darnall's career. "Welcome to the House that Darnall Built" were words printed on a huge banner hung high on the north wall of the gym. Tonight's win—it was meant to be!

The bench players dashed to the center of the court to congratulate the players that would take them back to Idaho. Darnall was stunned. It was an extremely emotional time for the coach. His last game at home, a win, another trip to Idaho, and another game to coach.

Regaining his composure, Darnall also sprinted to the floor to hug his fabulous five. By the time he reached them, the court was full of yelling, screaming Red Devil fans. Dave found it difficult to reach his players. They were surrounded by family, friends, and fans.

The Indiana Tech Warriors were in a state of shock. How did they let this one get away? What happened? Coach Darnall did feel for Coach Dan Kline. Kline was a good guy, a class act. Dave knew how he would feel after such a devastating loss. Thank God, he didn't have to.

A twenty-minute celebration by the players and their fans occurred on court after the presentation of the Conference Championship plaque. There was still one more tradition to take place. That was to cut down the winning nets. Substitute players hoisted the seniors individually in the air to snip the souvenirs. To finish the removing of the nets, the seniors lifted their coach for the final cut.

The players finally headed to the locker room to hear from their coach. It was the first time Coach Darnall had his team alone since the conclusion of the game. He knew they were anxious to get out of the locker room and celebrate with their fellow classmates. Coach thanked his players for their efforts and congratulated them again for their outstanding performances. He reminded them that finals were coming up the next day or so. However, at that time, that was probably the last thing on their minds.

A dedicated, loyal Red Devil fan, Professor Loren Logsdon later commented on the memorable game calling it a "miracle." In watching the pre-game warm-up, he had thought that Tech was the most talented opponent to play at Eureka since 1991. "Even on the best of days, I tend to be a guarded pessimist, and that night I thought that Eureka would have to play extra hard to beat this team."

"I don't know what Coach Darnall told the players in the time out. Whatever it was, it must have been inspirational and effective. The players came out fired up and determined. Suddenly our defense was there; we were all over the Tech players, causing them to hurry their shots and even getting a charging call on their guard," he continued.

"The last nine minutes of that game had to be the most amazing team play I have ever witnessed in any athletic contest. When the game ended, and we had won 75 to 69, I could not believe what our team had done. We had not only overcome a nine-point deficit, but we had held a highly talented team without a score. I remember clearly the two thoughts I had when the final buzzer went off: Dave is a genius, or someone in this crowd is proficient in the use of the hex. That victory was so miraculous."

The coaches had left for Darnall's house to join the party already in progress. There were so many in attendance that some fans had to stand outside on the deck. It was only fitting, after twenty years, that the last postgame party was held here. The place had seen so many!

Champagne was flowing generously. Many toasts were being made. It was a cold beer, however, that Coach Darnall really wanted. The party lasted well into the night; some might say the wee-hours of the morning. No one wanted the night or the season to end. It very well could be the last win for Darnall and his troops; the last time the team and their fans would feel the "thrill of victory."

The conversations were varied but several kept rising. How did the team keep the Warriors from scoring the last eight minutes of the game? Who would be the team's next opponent? Where would they be seeded? When would the team be leaving for Idaho? Where would they be staying? Most of those questions could not be answered. Time would tell.

Coach Darnall served as one of twenty-two national NAIA II basketball raters throughout the season. "Coach" Wertz and he ranked the teams and faxed their rankings to the National office each Sunday. Wertz reflected on the procedure.

"Since I had always watched the scores of opponents in the paper on a daily basis, I was Coach's natural assistant for this job. Ranking the teams involved gathering as many game scores as possible at the end of the week and comparing teams across the country. We then had to decide the ranking of each team, #1 through #25. The NAIA office supplied forms weekly. I would watch the paper daily and write down all the pertinent scores in both NAIA and NCAA in my little blue diary. On Sunday mornings, with our wives and two newspapers, we would meet at Kim's restaurant to do the rankings. Not only would we do the rankings, but we would re-analyze EC's last game, as well as plan our scouting schedule for the following week. You know, I don't miss tracking all the scores, but I do miss those Sunday morning breakfasts at Kim's."

Coach Darnall had to call the NAIA National office that night to inform them of their Conference Tournament Championship result. He then received a fax with the names of the twenty-four institutions that had qualified for the National Tournament. The excited Red Devil fans were now informed of whom had made the tournament field.

Darnall and Wertz then had to rank those twenty-four qualifying schools in order to obtain a seeding order for the National Tournament. The tournament pairing would be released the following day. Wertz, John Tyler, Dan Harrod, and Coach finally shut down the Darnall house at "who knows when" that morning.

Coach Darnall had mixed feelings about the seeding results and pairings. Eureka College could possibly face defending champion Willamette University and host school Northwest Nazarene College. Both would be difficult tasks. The top eight teams as seeded for the NAIA II National Tournament were Taylor, Indiana; Northwestern, Iowa; Willamette, Oregon; Northern State, South Dakota; Bethel, Indiana; Eureka, Illinois; Alice Lloyd, Kentucky; and Lewis & Clark, Oregon.

Coach Darnall gave the players two well-deserved days off. The team resumed practice on the Friday following the completion of final exams.

A meeting was held between the coaches and the college administration to finalize all travel arrangements. It was, basically, a duplicate of the previous year.

The Eureka College basketball team and the fans accompanying them left by Peoria Charter from Reagan Fieldhouse at 11:30 A.M., Tuesday, March 8, for Nampa. The bus ride was to Chicago O'Hare with a flight on to San Francisco and then to Boise, Idaho.

Prior to leaving campus, an informal send-off was held in the gym and lobby area of the fieldhouse. The college was on term break so most of the well-wishers were college personnel, including President Hearne and his wife, parents, and fans from the community. Several newspaper sportswriters, TV sports personnel, and the local radio station's sports director were also on-hand. An article by Randy Sharer summarized Darnall's and his players' attitudes. It was entitled "Darnall hits road for last time—Eureka College ready for Coach's final tournament" and appeared in the next morning's issue of *The Pantagraph*. It read in part:

Claustrophobic Dave Darnall has a fear of heights.

That explains why it was a mixed blessing for his Eureka College basketball team to qualify for the NAIA Division II National tournament at Nampa, Idaho.

The No. 6 nationally ranked Rd Devils (23 - 4) play at 1:30 P.M. (CST) Friday against the winner of Thursday's 1:00 P.M. game between No. 13 Westbrook, Maine (30 - 4) and No. 14 Ohio Dominican (23 - 9).

Being in an airplane thousands of feet above terra firma en route to a tournament is just one of many difficulties Darnall has aced while building a 379 - 151 record in 20 years at Eureka College.

But this will be Darnall's last trip as head coach as he will step down after this season. He will remain at the school as an associate professor of physical education and as College Athletic Counselor.

Even if the Red Devils don't win a game at the National Tournament, Darnall is viewing the chance to play in it as a storybook ending to his career.

"To say we did it my last year, is very rewarding," Darnall said. "We beat one of the better teams in the nation (Indiana Tech, 75 - 69) in order to make it."

Should Eureka College win the national crown, it would be a fairy-tale ending even Darnall would find too good to be true.

That possibility is not so far fetched because this year's team, like many other Darnall squads, has bought into the slogan he invented while coaching at Momence High School: Together We Win (TWW) . . .

Red Devil senior guard Chris Peterson said the motto is especially applicable to this year's team, which has six seniors, five of who start.

"We've been together for four years and we've developed close friendships," Peterson said. "We're always together."

The fact this is Darnall's last season is being used as a motivational factor by the players.

"We would love more than anything to give him a national championship," Peterson said. "Think that would pretty much cap off his career."

Senior guard Troy Tyler, a Washington native, said TWW is "reflected in the way we play so unselfishly." . . .

. . . "This may be the best team I've seen here," said President Hearne. "They are so unselfish and well balanced."

Chapter 17

A National Championship

T HE TEAM ARRIVED AT MONTGOMERY Physical Education Building on the campus of Northwest Nazarene College a few minutes before 11:00 A.M. Friday, March 11, 1994. Eureka's first game of the tournament was set for 12:30. That was the Red Devil's second consecutive appearance in the NAIA Division II National Tournament in Nampa and its third in the three years of the Division II's tournament's existence. Coach Darnall was hoping that his favorite "3" would be significant, and they would be able to capture the main prize on their third try.

The team parked their two courtesy vans behind the fieldhouse and entered the gym's back door. They strolled down the long hallway, around the corner, through the main lobby, and into their dressing room. It was located under the east stands below the scorer's table.

The St. Ambrose vs. Northern State 10:45 A.M. game was in progress. With only ten minutes between games, the next game's opponents were allowed to shoot around at halftime of the on-going game. Dave wanted his players shooting during that time.

Coach Darnall felt his players were in the proper frame of mind. They realized each game would be a challenge. They had to play a "career" game each time as they proceeded through the tournament.

Scott Heiberger, sportswriter for the Peoria *Journal Star* made the trip to Nampa with the team. He attended a team practice, and while there

517

interviewed the starting five seniors. Their comments appeared in an article entitled "Eureka's country boys can survive—Small-town Red Devils have big dreams at national tournament." It read in part:

They came from places where people waive to one another in their cars and the name of the town is painted on the water tower.

The starting five for the eureka College men's basketball team have more in common than Red Devil uniforms. They share a small-town background and big-time dreams.

Four of the starters are from towns with populations listed at less than 2,000.

"I think it pulls us closer together," said Eureka forward Dennis Huttenlocher, who grew up in Stockton, located in the northwest corner of Illinois.

"We do everything together," Huttenlocher said. "We've all been to each other's homes, and we've all seen each other's old high school basketball teams play."

Now they're here at the NAIA Division II tournament, trying to parlay their bond into a national championship . . .

The Eureka starters, all seniors, are playing in their third consecutive national tournament. They made the quarterfinals here last year before losing to host Northwest Nazarene.

"The thing that's different about this tournament is that it's the last chance for us," said swingman Troy Tyler, a resident of Washington. Washington, with a population of more that 10,000, is a metropolis when compared to the hometowns of other Red Devil starters.

"Troy is from a bigger town, but he's still a good ol' country boy at heart," said guard Chris Peterson from Brimfield. "He's the one I go hunting and fishing with."

The recruiting class of 1990—starters Huttenlocher, Tyler, Peterson, center Chris Eaton of Wyoming, and guard Duane Schmedeke of Morrisonville—have helped Eureka post a 96 - 17 record since they came on board.

"I focused on the best players who I thought we had a shot at," said Eureka coach Dave Darnall, who is retiring after this season. "And most of them were Class A (small schools) players. Needless to say, that was a really good recruiting year."

"I think that was a big reason why all of us came to Eureka," Schmedeke said. "There was a feeling of togetherness."

Schmedeke grew up on a farm outside Morrisonville, 25 miles southeast of Springfield. He honed his 3-point skills by firing at a basket his father erected in a machinery shed.

"I put tape down on the cement to make a 3-point arc. When chores are done there's not much to do in the country, so I shot baskets," Schmedeke said.

The starters not only come from similar backgrounds, but four of them—all but Tyler—belong to the Tau Kappa Epsilon fraternity.

"I think you can tell when we're playing that we're close friends off the court," Peterson said.

Said Eaton, "You always know there's someone to back you up out there on the floor. Just like being in a small town or belonging to the same fraternity, you know someone is always there to look out for you."

Darnall's feeling about his team's readiness was reinforced by the comment his player made in the article. He felt perhaps they were on a mission.

The Red Devil team gained additional supporters when a charter bus carrying Dean of Students Dale Martin, cheerleaders, and faithful fans such as Dave's nephew, Travis, arrived just in time for the opening game. Otis Meadows who had driven many of the Red Devil charters over the years had driven the bus. He had been requested by the travelers to drive them on the two-day journey to Idaho.

"Otis traveled a lot of miles with the boys. We were glad they assigned him to come out here," Darnall said when Scott Heiberger told him that Otis and his passengers had arrived.

Coach Darnall had his typical pre-game syndrome, feeling tired and sick at his stomach. He was extremely nervous as he began his pre-game talk. Darnall began by reminding his players of the offense and defense they were to use as well as reviewed each of the Panther's players' personal characteristics. He felt his players were capable of winning, but he did not want them to get complacent. They had seen Ohio Dominican play a good game in the opening round of the tournament, but also witnessed a not so good performance at the Wabash Tournament.

Twice during his pre-game speech, Darnall got an upset stomach and had to stop talking and dash to the bathroom. He, however, did not stop talking. From the toilet stall he continued making comments to his players as Coach Dighton was speaking. To this day, those incidents are the players' most favorite memories of their coach.

Some fans and players wanted to tape what might become Darnall's final locker room talk. Darnall felt restricted in what he could say if taped. He was also superstitious as hell and did not like to change things. Since he had never had a locker room speech taped, he felt it could bring bad luck.

Dave "caved in" to the constant pressure. He allowed an administrative assistant to video some of the pre-game locker room scene and portions of his pre-game talk. However, the half-time lecture was a taboo. That became a wise decision as the game progressed. Coach was in no mood for any "nonsense." This was serious shit!

The traditional ten seconds of silence was taken. The team and coaching staff took the floor. Darnall returned to the toilet one last time. Sitting in tranquility, the coach's mind raced a mile a minute. Twenty years of college coaching flashed through in seconds. Would this be the last time he walked out of a locker room to the noise of a crowd, seeing black-and-white-striped shirts, and greeting a handful of anxious fellows in shorts and jerseys? Was this the last game he would coach, stomp his foot, or leap for joy after another Red Devil victory? He finished and walked slowly through the locker room.

"Please, one more," he prayed as the door flung open leading to the hallway that would take him to his "workshop" for twenty-eight years. Dave was nervous!

The Red Devils were supported by some fifty fans that made the trip from Eureka. They also gained a few extra supporters as Professor Logsdon's daughter and son and their families lived in the Boise area. Additional fans came aboard in the form of Northern State University supporters. The parents and other fans from both institutions were staying at the same Super 8 in Nampa and had become friends. They crossed paths at both the motel and at the Denny's Restaurant located directly across the street from the Super 8. The cheerleaders, fans, and players of the two schools cheered for each other's team. Then, of course, there were the team sponsors, Frank and John, and their families.

The Ohio Dominican Panthers started two forwards and three guards against the sharp-shooting Red Devils. They were led by NAIA II All-American Jerry Lanier. The six-foot-four junior guard averaged twenty points a game. Coach Darnall countered with his normal five senior starters, Eaton, Huttenlocher, Tyler, Schmedeke, and Peterson. Sophomore Adam Ferguson and junior Chris Hopwood were the first two players off the bench. The Panthers relied on their athleticism and quickness while the Red Devils depended on their defense, patient offense, and three-point shots. Senior Ryan Markley became ill, requiring medical attention and, unfortunately, saw limited action throughout the tournament.

The scene had a championship tournament atmosphere—the crowd; the red championship banner with white lettering bordered in blue suspended at the north end of the gym; the huge official tournament bracket board hanging on the same wall; various NAIA pennants and signs dangling throughout the gym; and the official NAIA score table.

The Red Devils were ready for tip-off. They had worked all season for that moment. The nervousness ceased as soon as the ball left the official's hand. There was work to do. Eureka opened in a half-court, man-to-man pressure defense while Dominican employed a full-court press. Darnall knew his team had to overplay and contain Lanier and six-foot-three guard Mike Bell if they had any chance to win. Both teams used a form of the "motion" offense when in possession of the ball.

The first ten minutes of the game saw both teams trading baskets. Midway through the first half, Eureka pulled away with back-to-back steals and a three-pointer by Troy Tyler. That sparked a scoring drive that pushed the Red Devils to a 29 to 19 lead.

That lead, however, was short-lived. With a little less than a minute remaining in the half, the Panthers closed the gap to two points. One last surge by the Red Devils gave them a 43 to 38 lead at intermission.

In the locker room, Darnall was extremely vocal to his players. He didn't like the fact of having a ten-point lead and letting it slip away. That was especially true when he questioned the shot selection of a couple shots taken in the last five minutes of the half. Coach prided himself on the disciple his players normally had in choosing what shots to "let fly" and which one to pass up.

"You guys now know you can play with these guys," Coach Darnall yelled. "You've got to do better on the press offense. Don't dribble so damn much. Pass the hell out of the ball, we can get some fast-break baskets from it. Reverse the ball a little more on offense. I think we can get some good open three-point shots backside. Peterson, Schmedeke, if you've got the open three, nail it."

"You guys have got to put more pressure on the ball on defense. Don't give 'em the open shot. Also, get your asses back on defense. No more fast-break baskets," Darnall continued. He then stopped to catch his breath and stepped closer to the starters sitting on the locker room benches. "We don't want to go back to Eureka tomorrow. You guys said you want 'the ring.' Well, prove it! Get the hell out there and play some damn ball," shouted Darnall as the players dashed from the locker room.

The Red Devil players were ready to play. Within the first six minutes of the second half, Eureka surged ahead, 54 to 42. From then on, their lead only increased.

The press offense was working successfully. The "good guys" were getting some easy fast-break baskets. The Red Devils were controlling the boards, allowing the Panthers only one shot while getting several second shots themselves.

Darnall's team, playing inspired basketball, went on to an impressive 92 to 71 victory. The Red Devils, showing a balanced scoring attack, had four players scoring over nineteen points a piece. Eaton and Tyler led the way with twenty-four each. Even though Dennis Huttenlocher had only four points, he fulfilled his role exceptionally well; that was to rebound, play defense, and set picks for Eaton.

Eureka College had duplicated the previous year's accomplishment. They reached the quarterfinals. Only eight teams remained in contention for the National Championship. They were the Elite 8!

An article written by Scott Heiberger describing the great Red Devil win appeared in the Peoria *Journal Star*. "Next step huge for Eureka—Red Devils defeat Ohio Dominican to return to NAIA Division II quarterfinals," read in part:

> Ohio Dominican guard, Jerry Lanier doesn't want to be like Mike. He wants to be like Eureka College.
> "Hopefully we can eventually be like Eureka, consistently making it to nationals and not just making it on a fluke," Lanier said.
> Tradition-rich Eureka beat upstart Ohio Dominican 92 - 71 Friday to advance to the quarterfinals of the NAIA Division II tournament in front of 2,100 at Montgomery Fieldhouse.
> The Red Devils opened their third consecutive trip to the tournament with a team effort, shooting 64 percent from the field nd limiting the Panthers to their fourth-lowest scoring output of the season.
> Eureka, seeded sixth, will face defending champion Willamette (Ore.) at 4 p.m. today. Willamette, seeded third, advanced by beating Tabor (Kan.), 92 - 61.
> Eureka was glad to get the first game out of the way.
> "We're really confident, but not over-confident," Peterson said.
> "I have to believe they've come here to be a true challenger," Darnall said of his team. "I think they'd be really disappointed not to get to the Final Four."

The bench players and coaches met the active players on the floor just after the final buzzer to congratulate them on a job well done. No big court celebration. The job was not completed. The players did not have much time to savor their victory. Their next opponent was about to play. They had about ten minutes to shower and join their coaches in the stands to observe the Willamette-Tabor game.

Coach Dighton scouted one team, and Chuck Wertz charted the other. Darnall sat between the scouts surrounded by the players. The starting five sat next to their coach so he could make comments to them concerning both teams. It was obvious late in the game that defending National Champion Willamette University would win. Since it was dinnertime and the players were extremely hungry, Dave thought he would treat them to a smorgasbord. The players liked the idea and were ready to leave the building.

The team returned to the Nampa Suites Hotel following dinner instead of reappearing at Montgomery Fieldhouse to watch more tournament play. Coach felt his players needed some free time to relax. Waiting for them were many congratulatory faxes and well-wishes for the up-coming game from people back home. Coach distributed several of them that evening but kept others to read at the team meeting in the morning. He wanted to maximize the words of inspiration.

When the team was on the road, curfew was 11:00 P.M. the night before a game. That night was no different regardless of the great win. The mission was not completed.

The coaching staff went next door to O'Callahan's to relax and prepare the next day's game plan for the contest with Willamette. Not only was this done, but the day's schedule was also drawn up. The Eureka-Willamette tip-off was scheduled for 3:00 P.M., meaning a busy day for the Red Devils.

Darnall slept very little that night. The adrenaline was still flowing. He lay awake in bed, continuing to review the scouting report on Willamette with the noise of the TV in the background. The win, playing the reigning National Champion the next day, and one more victory to get into the Final Four. Who would believe?

Coach knew the game would be like looking into a mirror. The Red Devils and Bearcats were very similar teams. The team from Salem, Oregon, overall, was a little taller. They played straight man-to-man defense, normally picking up their man crossing the centerline. They normally played straight up; no switching. They pressed very seldom, and if they did, it usually was a man-to-man full-court press. The Bearcats liked to fast break, but it was a controlled break. On offense, they ran a flex type offense which Darnall referred to as a "Continuity." Coach Darnall often ran a similar offense called the "Wheel."

Willamette's front line was big and strong, averaging close to six-foot-six. The big boys set hard picks, and all five players made good cuts. The starters were six-foot-five Gavan Scanlan and six-foot-six Jason Thompson as forwards; six-foot-three Steve Raze and six-foot-one Dave Snyder at guards, and six-foot-six Scott Baker at the pivot. Willamette's sixth man was six-foot-three R.J. Adelman, son of Portland Trail Blazer Head Coach Rick Adelman.

Coach Darnall would counter with his regular five seniors. The game plan was to start in a half court man-to-man defense; run the four-man motion with Eaton inside. If that didn't work, switch to the "Wheel offense." Use the control fast break if opportunities arise. Play hard and hit the boards.

"Doesn't that sound a lot like Willamette?" Coach Darnall asked. "Both teams are similar in all aspects of the game. The winner will be the team that executes the similar style of play the best." That was what kept Dave up most of the night. Could his team execute its offense and defense the best? If he had known the answer, he might have gotten a good night's sleep.

The players woke up late, had breakfast and returned to the hotel for their team meeting. Darnall started the meeting by telling the players how happy he was for them to be back in the Elite 8. However, history could be made that afternoon by being the first Eureka College team to make the Final Four. Darnall then went over the individual assignments, matching his starting five with Willamette's. He discussed the individual characteristics of each Bearcat player and then turned the meeting over to Coach Dighton.

The assistant explained the offenses and defenses they would employ. Darnall and he both diagrammed Willamette's offensive alignment on the board and drew the various options the players should look for. Dave finished the meeting by reading several of the faxes he had received from the fans back home. The fans had listened to the first game on radio station WIVR Eureka. Some, further from Eureka, were unable to gain reception in their homes but could do so from their car radios. The Student Center on campus provided a place where the college community gathered to listen to the game together. There they cheered their heroes to victory. Numerous faxes originated from that gathering.

The coaching staff had been notified earlier of the results of the other games that had taken place the previous evening and during the day. No. 11 and host Northwest Nazarene, Idaho, upset No. 7 Alice Lloyd, Kentucky, in the 8:00 P.M. game. That was no surprise to Darnall. Other winner to comprise the Elite 8 were No. 1—Taylor, Indiana; No. 8—Lewis & Clark,

Oregon; No.16—Huron, South Dakota; No. 4—Northern State, South Dakota; No. 3—Willamette, Oregon; No. 6—Eureka, Illinois; No.11—Northwest Nazarene, Idaho; and No. 2—Northwestern, Iowa.

Eureka's game was the second game of the afternoon session. The Red Devils arrived at Montgomery Fieldhouse a little less than an hour before warm-up. Since there was only four games that day, the normal twenty-five-minute warm-up was being allowed. Putting their gear into a locker room beneath the west stands, the players then left for a quick peek at the ongoing game. The Red Devil fans were already in the stands cheering on Northern State. State defeated Huron, 102 to 96; thus, would take on Lewis & Clark who upset No. 1 seed Taylor in the quarterfinals. Darnall remained in the locker room experiencing his customary pre-game syndrome.

A short period of time passed, and the players returned to the dressing room to prepare for battle. Dave was more serene than prior to the Ohio Dominican game. Coach reminded his players of the offense and defense they were going to use. He told them to work hard, not to let themselves, their fans, or the college down, that many people had faith in them, that they had to believe in themselves and just go out and do it.

"Fellows, work hard, get back on defense, be patient on offense, take only good shots, bust your butts on defense, and hit those damn boards," Darnall instructed.

"Now let's take our ten seconds. Each one is an individual. Think what you want to think, or you don't need to think at all as long as we are quiet, and we do it together," requested Coach Darnall.

Following the few moments of silence, Darnall stated, "TWW, now go out and kick some ass." Those few words must have stimulated the boys. Their orneriness came out. They were ready to go.

The Red Devils played a flawless first twenty minutes. The man-to-man pressure defense was perfect. They allowed only twenty-six first-half points from the defending champions while scoring thirty-three. Eaton led the first half assault with fifteen. When the Bearcats applied pressure on the good shooting Eureka College perimeter players, Peterson, Schmedeke, and Tyler provided Eaton the opportunity to roam in the lane where he either had a good close shot or got fouled. Chris made seven of eight free throws during the first half of play.

Darnall seemed more like a cheerleader than a coach in his half-time talk. His team was enjoying a seven-point, 32 to 26, lead over Willamette. He praised his players for the defensive effort and their execution of the motion offense. Their team play was outstanding, and their patience on offense was precisely what Coach was wanting all year. Darnall instructed his players to continue exactly what they had done the first half.

"Don't change a thing," Coach emphasized. "Only twenty more minutes and you'll make history. The best team in Eureka's history. Now get your butts out there and do it." Those were the only harsh words Darnall said during the entire halftime. That was unusual. However, if the team had played like that all year, there wouldn't have been any reason to.

As time would tell, maybe he should have been a little more aggressive. During the first six minutes of the second half, the Red Devils were not the same team they had been earlier. Perhaps the talented Bearcats were going to prove why they were the National Champions.

Willamette caught the Red Devils flat-footed and roared back to tie the game several times throughout the first nine minutes of the second period. A patent Darnall timeout was called. Coach met his players on the court. This timeout talk was dramatically different from his one at halftime. Darnall shouted at his players like a coach would when his team blew a seven-point lead. Challenging their effort, Darnall also switched the motion offense to the "Wheel." Hopefully, changing the offensive outlook might confuse the opponent a bit.

The Red Devils immediately became a different team for the last ten minutes of play. They began to play like they had the first half. Tied at 41 all, Troy Tyler nailed a three-pointer, and Duane Schmedeke followed with a short jumper, sparking a 19 to 9 run. The timeout had worked!

Eureka College went on to a 71 to 63 thrilling victory. As the final buzzer sounded, the bench players and coaching staff dashed onto the floor bear hugging and giving high-fives to their five heroes. Some of the exuberant Red Devil fans followed along as well as sponsors Frank and John. Whereas there had been little emotion displayed following the Ohio Dominican game on the floor, this afternoon there was a celebration taking place on Northwest Nazarene's gym floor.

Why not? It was historic and an exhilarating victory for Eureka College. It had gained a berth in the NAIA Division II Final Four by defeating the reigning National Champions—that's right the National Champions! Who would believe? Several minutes of shouting congratulations, shaking hands, and hugging occurred before the Red Devils headed toward their dressing room with the applause of their faithful fans ringing in their ears. The over two thousand-mile trip to Nampa, Idaho, was now truly worth it for all.

To get a better account of the impressive Eureka College win, a review of an article entitled "Eureka eliminates defending champs—Devils down Willamette in quarterfinals" by Rob Lundgren that appeared in the Idaho *Press-Tribune* is included in part.

Will the third game be the charm? Eureka College, the team with a mission, certainly hopes so.

The Red Devils took a giant step in the right direction Saturday afternoon when they shocked defending NAIA Division II Champ Willamette 71 - 63 in the quarterfinals.

Eureka (25 - 4) now plays host Northwest Nazarene (26 - 7) in Monday night's second semifinal at 8:30.

"Our goal was to get in the Final Four," said Eureka coach Dave Darnall, whose team lost in the first round two years ago and in the second round last year.

"This year we also kept more focused," he explained. "There's a burning desire in these kids. They're paying $15,000 because we have no athletic scholarships. What a tribute to these kids!"

Saturday's victory was especially satisfying to Peterson, who tossed in 20 points, dished out five assists, hit five key free throws and played all 40 minutes along with Eaton who finished with a game-high 24 points and 11 rebounds.

"Last year was all new to us; we never realized what was going on," Peterson recalled. "This year we knew what we had to do. We weren't overwhelmed by the crowd. We were pumped. We wanted to make the Final Four."

Schmedeke and Tyler also finished in double figures for the winners with 12 and 10 points respectively.

Dave congratulated each member of his team in the locker room before they showered and prepared to go to dinner. It was a joyous mood in the winner's locker room. When the team left the locker room and exited the back door of the gymnasium, they were greeted by cheering loyal fans and cheerleaders.

The team returned to the smorgasbord for dinner, as it was the best place for the players to get all they wanted at a reasonable cost. They had not eaten since the pre-game meal at 11:00 A.M.

The team then headed back to the Nampa Suites to freshen up before returning to Montgomery Fieldhouse. Coach wanted his players to observe the 8:00 P.M. game between Northwest Nazarene and second-seed Northwestern Iowa. He knew it would be a hell of a game with the winner becoming their opponent on Monday.

The manager and desk clerk both shouted congratulations to the Red Devil team as they came through the lobby door. They told Coach numerous faxes had again been received from the fans back home. The college community had again listened to the game in the Student Center.

The team arrived at Orrin E. Hills Center Court in time to see the second half of the 6:00 P.M. contest between No. 1 Taylor and Lewis & Clark. The winner could be a future opponent. The main attraction for EC was the Northwestern Iowa and Northwest Nazarene game. Northwestern was a legitimate contender for the National Championship. Northwest Nazarene had to be reckoned with for several reasons. Mainly they had the great advantage of playing on their own floor. Eureka College's home record of 50 to 1 over the past four years was proof of that. The Crusaders were also an excellent team playing in front of a standing-room-only crowd that supported them.

Coach Darnall, thinking the host team had such a homecourt advantage as knowing the floor, the home crowd, the officiating, and players able to sleep in their own beds, stated, "I'd love to host the National Championship Tournament. Since we have never lost a home NAIA playoff game, I think we would be a legitimate contender each year."

Dave had nothing but praise for the organization, operation, and promotion of the NAIA II National Tournament by the Northwest Nazarene personnel and NAIA National office. He just felt the tournament should be held on a neutral floor like the NAIA I tournament. "I think Northwest Nazarene ran an outstanding tournament. The Boise-Nampa area really supported it," Darnall concluded.

The gym was crammed full. The Eureka College entourage, including the team, had to sit high in the southeast corner of the balcony. The crowd noise was unmerciful—loud, vocal, and biased.

"I would much rather play the No. 2 seed Northwestern Red Raiders than Northwest Nazarene. Their fans are brutal. The crowd noise is so damn loud my players won't be able to hear me on the court," Dave said. "Believe me, I know. We had to go through it last year."

As usual, the starting five sat around Coach Darnall as Coach Dighton and Chuck Wertz charted the two participating teams. Dighton took Nazarene while Wertz scouted Northwestern. Dave did not get his wish. Not unexpected, the host team beat the No. 2 seeded club, 85 to 75.

The Red Devils and their fans left the final game of the evening with five minutes remaining in the contest. Coach had seen all he wanted to see.

It was enough for him to start to torment about the Monday night game forty-eight hours away.

"Thank God we are off tomorrow," Dave told Dighton as the team left the gym. "I don't think our players or I would be ready to go tomorrow. We need to stop and catch our breath." He was exhausted and knew his players also had to be mentally and physically drained. He decided there would be no Sunday practice. In fact, there wasn't even going to be a "skull session." Hopefully, the fellows would get a lot of rest and put their tired legs in the whirlpool.

The team headed for the Denny's Restaurant located across the street from the Super 8 Motel where the Red Devil supporters were lodged. The fans and cheerleaders frequented it often. Now it was the players' turn. They enjoyed their meals while being surrounded by family, friends, and fans. Darnall had reserved a private room for Monday and Tuesday nights, regardless of the outcomes of their games, but tonight they had to settle for sitting in proximity of each other in the main dining room.

The team returned to the Nampa Suites with about a half-hour left before lights out. Curfew had been moved to midnight since tomorrow was a day off. The players were tired and anxious to go to their rooms to relax. The "tube" was the extent of the rest of the night's entertainment. They had guaranteed their Idaho stay for at least three more days with that day's victory.

With the players in bed, the coaches enjoyed a few cool drinks at O'Callahan's. Darnall and Begole had cold beers and Dighton screwdrivers. The coaches were plotting Sunday's daily schedule along with celebrating the great win over Nazarene. There was no game or practice the following day, but a full day of activity was still scheduled. The all-important Final Four Banquet and a trip to John Danielson's home were to be the highlights. Danielson, one of the team's sponsors, lived about two miles north of Boise in the foothills and had invited the team and the players' parents to his home for dinner and a celebration cake. For three years, the dream of the seniors was to make the Final Four and enjoy the prestigious banquet that went with it. The players were looking forward to both.

The players had an excellent breakfast buffet at O'Callahan's and returned to the Suites to prepare for their 12:30 twenty-mile trip to Boise. They were looking good—slacks, sport coats, sweaters, and ties. The Final Four Banquet was scheduled for 1:00 P.M. at the Red Lion Riverside Motor Inn in Boise. A capacity crowd gathered in a large banquet room in the classy inn. Each in attendance paid $20.00 with the individual team's sponsor picking up the tab for their team. The banquet room was decorated to reflect the full flavor of the tournament. Four huge eight-foot wooden pennants with the final four respective institutions being honored hung on the wall behind the head table. Dignitaries from the NAIA, host school, and the four remaining coaches in the tournament sat at the raised-platform table.

After dinner, Master of Ceremony, channel KTVB Sports Director Larry Maneely, introduced each coach, who gave a fifteen-minute presentation on his respective institution. The four head coaches were Ed Weidenbach of Northwest Nazarene College with an enrollment of 1,218; Bob Olson, Northern State University with an enrollment of 3,000; Bob Gaillard, Lewis & Clark College with an enrollment of 1,650; and Dave Darnall, Eureka College with an enrollment of 450.

Coach Darnall stressed several issues in his presentation. The first being that the seniors had great grades with three starters on the Dean's List; that nine of his players had a 3.0 grade point average or better. Then he talked about the college being a member of both NAIA and NCAA. Therefore, it was governed by the strictest rules of each. That was quite unique. Very few colleges in America were dual members. The bottom line of dual membership meant no athletic aid was given to the student-athlete.

Dave gave a little history of Eureka College including its religious affiliation, where it was located, and the school's most famous alumnus, President Ronald Reagan. The Coach then turned to basketball, talking about his great five starting seniors and his talented sixth senior, Ryan Markley—their closeness, academic inclinations, attitude, work ethic, and basketball accomplishments.

Coach then explained the team's slogan, "Together We Win." Darnall finished his phase of the program by thanking Albertson's for sponsoring them and in particular John Danielson and Frank Mattern for their support and friendship.

Dr. Eric Forseth, Athletic Director at the host school and the NAIA Tournament Director made a few special acknowledgements. Dave had nothing but high praise for Forseth. Dr. Gay Frederick, NAIA Vice President of Champions, concluded the ceremonial dinner with some closing remarks. A press conference for sportswriters, radio and TV personalities followed.

Several outstanding articles regarding the up-coming contest with Northwest Nazarene was the result of the press conference. One was entitled "Eureka steps up to the buffet—after snacking on NAIA field, Final Four meal is on the table," written by *Journal Star* sportswriter, Scott Heiberger. It read in part:

> It is possible to measure progress in the NAIA Division II National tournament in terms of banquets. Eureka College and 23 other men's basketball teams were feted Wednesday on the eve of competition in a massive, welcome-wagon type affair.
>
> But just four teams sat down to lunch Sunday at Red Lion Hotel in nearby Boise. The exclusiveness of the company began to hit Eureka guard Troy Tyler before salads arrived.
>
> "I think it's just starting to sink in right now," Troy said, looking around at the few remaining players.
>
> The sixth-seeded Red Devils (25 - 4), first-time visitors to the Final Four, will face 11th seeded host school Northwest Nazarene (26 - 7) at 9:30 tonight at Montgomery Fieldhouse.
>
> "We're too close to winning a national championship to be complacent," guard Chris Peterson said.
>
> Eureka was eliminated in the quarterfinals last season by Northwest Nazarene, 69 - 60, aided by a sellout hometown crowd of more than 3,500. Another sellout is expected.
>
> "I don't think their team bothers me as much as the location of the game and the crowd," Eureka coach Dave Darnall said. "Every team is evenly matched at this stage."

A second excellent article about the match-up appeared in the *Idaho Statesman* written by Stephen Dodge. It was entitled, "NW Nazarene hopes to continue shooting streak against Eureka" and read in part:

> It was a day of rest—and the atmosphere showed it.
>
> The intensity of the first three rounds of the NAIA Division II national basketball tournament was replaced by smiles, jokes, and a steak dinner.
>
> It was the NAIA Final Four Luncheon at the Red Lion Riverside. Not a bad way to spend a sunny Sunday afternoon . . .
>
> Today, of course, are the semifinals. In the early game, Lewis & Clark of Portland will meet Northern State of Aberdeen, S.D . . .
>
> The feature attraction will be the host Crusaders battling sixth-seeded Eureka (Ill.) at 8:30. If you plan on attending, get there early—last spring's national semifinals, also held at Montgomery Fieldhouse, left people standing three deep in the doorways.
>
> After playing a trio of run-and-gun teams in the early rounds, Northwest Nazarene will see a different approach from Eureka. The Red Devils are a Boise State clone, patiently working the ball for a good shot and focusing on defense.
>
> "We're going to be tested," NNC coach Ed Weidenbach said. "They're our toughest opponent by far. They are so disciplined that we're going to have to do just an excellent job defensively."

"I don't know that much about them except that they are really patient and just will not take a stupid shot," NNC Todd Schumacher said. "That will make it all the tougher for us."

But don't pity Northwest Nazarene just yet. The Crusaders have been playing their best basketball of the season lately, averaging more than 100 points for the tournament and shooting 45 percent from 3-point range.

Portions of a third article that appeared in the *Idaho Press-Tribune* entitled "Four remain with dream of NAIA crown" by Barry Miller had some good quotes by both head coaches. Portions of the article read:

The dream of a national title is still alive for four teams . . .

"I think any one of the four could win it," NNC coach Ed Weidenbach said. "I know Eureka is better than last year and we've been playing great basketball, especially last month. Monday is going to be a great evening of basketball."

"I anticipate the same type game we had last year," said 20th-year Eureka head coach Dave Darnall, who will retire at the end of the season. "I expect it to hopefully be a close game. Just being in the Final Four is the important thing for us and I don't want a loss to spoil the most successful team in Eureka College history."

The Devils led the nation in three statistical categories—3-point field goal percent (48.0), scoring margin (24.2) and rebounding (a 15.5 margin)—and continues to excel in those areas at the national tournament. Eureka has made 16 of 33 treys and is outrebounding its two tourney foes by an 11.5 average.

"We're both pretty similar to last year, but they haven't played as deep," said Weidenbach referring to Eureka using only six players and four seeing almost full-time action. "We need to make sure we really use our depth by playing aggressive defense and hopefully we can somehow wear them down.

"I'm really impressed with their discipline on offense, they execute well and are physical," he added. "They really work for open shots inside with (Chris) Eaton, their guards set a lot of back picks and they run a lot of motion."

"It's going to take a lot of luck and us playing well to beat them," Darnall said. "They are quick, get the ball up and down the floor, are aggressive and big inside. They are just a complete ballclub."

The eight-foot wooden pennant was removed from the wall after the banquet. The underclassmen placed the huge board on top of their heads in the van for the trip back to the hotel. Thank heaven they had a spectator bus for the trip back to Eureka. It eventually arrived on campus and was displayed on the north wall of Reagan Fieldhouse.

The team and some fans next moved on to the Danielsons' home tucked in the foothills of Boise. The gathering gave the players a chance to get to know their sponsors 'as well as the opportunity to visit with their parents. The players, so far, had spent very little time with them. They were just too busy with "work."

The group spent several hours conversing, eating, playing on the computer, and *even* shooting hoops on the outdoor court. The highlight of the afternoon was when a large "victory cake" was served. The multi-colored cake had a large Red Devil and basketball on it. It read "Red Devils—Go Coach Dave—Final Four—NAIA." It was a memorable evening and appre-

Red Devil team with congratulatory Final Four cake and well-wishers for next game.

ciated by all. It left a lasting impression of how gracious both John and Frank and their families were.

Returning to the motel, the players spent the rest of evening relaxing until curfew at 11:00 P.M. Many enjoyed the pool and whirlpool. Others stayed in their rooms, playing cards and watching TV.

The coaching staff again converged at O'Callahan's to prepare the game plan against the host school. O'Callahan's had become "tournament central" for Darnall and his assistants. The coach knew the up-coming game against Nazarene could be more difficult than the championship game. The crowd and the familiarity of the floor presented a great advantage for the Crusaders. The Red Devils remembered what it was like the previous year against them.

Northwest Nazarene planned to start five-foot-ten Todd Schumacher and five-foot-ten Rolando Garcia at guards. The super quick Garcia was considered an All-American candidate. Six-foot-four Sheldon McLain and six-foot-five Emiko Etete were the forwards. Etete, a great leaper who could score, was also considered an All-American candidate. The center was six-foot-ten senior Eric Spencer.

Offensively, the Crusaders like to fast break. They really tried to push the ball up the floor every chance they had. If they didn't get a quick basket, they'd run a motion offense from various alignments. The Crusaders cut and screened extremely hard. They liked to double screen and reverse the ball for their outside shooters. Their running game was in great contrast to what EC did.

Defensively, Northwest usually employed a tough, aggressive man-to-man defense. At times, they may switch out front. The Crusaders occasionally showed a 1-2-2 zone.

Coach Darnall would counter with his reliable five seniors. The Red Devils would start in their half court man-to-man pressure defense. If needed, they could switch to their 1-2-2 adjustable zone.

Offensively, EC planned to open with their four-man motion offense. That kept the big redhead, Eaton, close to the basket, and gave Huttenlocher the responsibility to set a lot of picks for his fraternity brother. It should be repeated that four of the five starters were members of the Tau Kappa Epsilon fraternity—Reagan's fraternity. Only Tyler was not.

If the motion offense was ineffective, the "Wheel" offense would be employed. If opportunities became available, the Red Devils would fast break. However, it would be controlled. No helter-skelter break.

The coaches' meeting concluded, and Dave instructed Coach Begole to order and pick-up a late-night snack for the players. Each received two cheeseburgers, fries, and a large Coke from McDonald's. The players would love the treat. "Anything to keep the boys happy for the next couple days," Darnall thought.

Darnall thought once his team qualified for the Final Four, he would be able to stop worrying long enough to get some sleep. Who was he fooling? He was, as usual, up most of the night fretting over the up-coming game. Sometime in the early hours of the morning, the sleeping pill finally took effect and he drifted off.

The players slept until around 10:00 A.M. Breakfast was again at O'Callahan's at 10:30. Following breakfast, Coach Dighton and Coach Begole took the players to Montgomery Fieldhouse for an hour of shooting around. Coach Darnall felt it would be good to get the players out of the hotel and get some shooting in since they had not been on the court since Saturday afternoon's game.

Dave met his team in the Nampa Suite's conference room upon its return for a "skull session." He had had his typical game-day syndrome besides being extremely tired from the night before so had skipped breakfast and the shoot around. Darnall and Dighton covered the game plan. Dave also gave a little motivational speech and read some of the faxes that the team had received on Sunday.

At 4:15 P.M. the team walked next door for the pre-game meal. Dave was still extremely tired, nervous and sick to his stomach. He knew that the night might very well be his last game as a coach, the last time ever, after twenty-nine years of coaching, that he would walk the side-line. That saddened him.

Coach was a little hungry since he had not eaten for almost twenty-four hours. He felt at the time, however, that eating was not the answer. He could wait for dinner. Perhaps he would feel like eating then. Dighton and Begole took the players for their pre-game meal while Darnall remained at the hotel. Coach Dighton did bring back a piece of coconut pie, Darnall's favorite, and a glass of milk.

The team left the hotel at 5:15 P.M. for Orrin E. Hills arena. As bad as Coach Darnall hated to, he felt the team needed to watch the Northern State-Lewis & Clark game, just in case. Dave did not mind his players watching a potential opponent; he just didn't like to do it immediately before one of their games. He felt both the players and he needed to concentrate on their game, not someone they may play. Following one of their games is fine to scout a perspective opponent.

The team arrived at the tournament site right at 5:30. They entered the back-pass door and walked a few feet to the same locker room they had been assigned when playing Willamette. The players put their gear into lockers and went directly to the stands to watch the game in progress. Chuck Wertz took Lewis & Clark and Coach Dighton scouted Northern State. Darnall, again, sat among his starters.

At halftime, the players, Trainer Brown, Begole, and Darnall went to the dressing room. Brown was busy taping ankles, and the players were dressing while Darnall laid down on a locker room bench to get a little rest before the emotional game. Dighton and Wertz remained in the stands, scouting.

The Red Devil locker room was quiet. There was very little talk among the guys. It was all business. That's how Darnall was, and that attitude carried over to most of his players. They were there to win!

Coach was pretty low-key in his pre-game talk. He was so nervous and exhausted that his energy level was low. However, once on the floor and the game got underway, the adrenaline would flow again. Dave would become his normal emotional self, yelling instructions to his players or at the officials for unpopular calls as he kneeled in front of his chair. When Darnall really got upset, he'd stomp his right foot and stroll the sideline. He would be back at it.

Coach reviewed the offense and defense he wanted his players to utilize. He then turned his attention to what he said later was the key to the game, the crowd and officials. The five seniors knew the type of game Northwest Nazarene played. They knew their personnel. All the Red Devil players had to do was execute. However, they couldn't control the crowd or officials. That's what bothered Darnall.

"Don't worry about the damn officiating. Just play the game. Don't let the crowd take you out of your game. Get out there and get a lead. Don't let them run the court or get early baskets. That will help take the crowd out of the game," Darnall sternly said.

"We owe then one. Remember last year? Let's play one more game. Only two teams in the United States can do that, Northern State and the winner of our game. Let's make that us! Now let's take our ten seconds."

The team dashed out of their safe haven to the roar of the standing-room-only home crowd as the Crusaders were also running onto the floor. Darnall turned and headed for the toilet, his last moment of peace before the battle. He again wondered if this would be his last time. He walked back through the silent locker room to the dressing room door. Opening the door, he proceeded to possibly to his last night of work still worrying about the crowd and officiating.

An article that appeared that day in the Peoria *Journal Star* by Scott Heiberger entitled "Hostile home crowd awaits," explained Darnall's concern. It read in part:

The Eureka College Red Devils remember the roar.

Eureka will face Northwest Nazarene and a capacity crowd of more than 3,500 hostile Crusader fans at 9:30 tonight in the semifinals of the NAIA Division II national tournament.

"It would be nice to send thousands of people home disappointed," Eureka guard Duane Schmedeke said . . .

"It was something I've never played in front of before," Eureka forward Dennis Huttenlocher said of the throng. "At first, I think it took us out of our game, but as things went along, I think it helped fire us up."

Verbal communication can be a problem in a loud gym, but Eureka's all-senior lineup thinks it can communicate fine without words.

"A lot of times we just have to look at each other," Huttenlocher said. "Like Troy (Tyler), for instance. He'll make a fake one way, we'll make eye contact and then he'll go back door."

Dr. Loren Logsdon, who had traveled to Idaho to support the Red Devils, also had his concern about the crowd and the home court advantage. He expressed it this way,

Lou Holz feared Navy, and I feared Northwest Nazarene. I was so nervous about the game that my wife refused to sit with me. I was so nervous that I was afraid to speak to Bonnie Darnall before the game for fear of jinxing the team. I was so nervous that I wasn't watching the seating arrangements and ended up sitting with my son and son-in-law in the midst of a group of outspoken fans from NNC. The NNC fans were cocky and loud. I heard them making snide remarks about the fact that we had beaten Moody Bible Institute, 125 - 25. The NNC fans were suggesting that we played an easy schedule. Finally, I had had enough. I turned around and said, "Listen, I saw that game against Moody, and it was the most awesome defensive performance I have ever witnessed. Eureka was so tough that Moody couldn't even get the ball across the time stripe much of the night. They were a good team, but our defense just killed them." I know that it is wrong to tell a lie, but I just couldn't sit quietly and let those loud fans deprecate our team. I concluded by saying to the NNC fans, "You just watch; you haven't played against a defense like ours."

The strongest memory that I have about the NNC game is that I had never before felt the power of the home crowd as strongly as I did here. Frankly, it was a bit scary and intimidating.

Coach Darnall sat down in his chair gazing at the enormous crowd. He realized that this is what is was all about. This was his dream, making the final four in the country and playing in front of a sellout crowd, just like the "big boys." It was something he truly didn't ever think would happen. Very few small college coaches ever do.

The public-address announcer called the teams to their respective benches. The National Anthem was sung. The announcer introduced the teams. The crowd was on its feet, four thousand for Northwest Nazarene—a hundred for Eureka.

In the jump circle was six-foot-five Etete and six-foot-eight Eaton. Both teams' bench players were standing and clapping. Darnall was sitting. The ball went up. The game was finally underway. The winner plays for the National Championship!

NNC got the tip and rushed the ball toward the north basket where Garcia took a shot that missed. Eureka grabbed the rebound and brought the ball down slow, setting up in their half-court four-man motion offense. The complete house was still standing, no one settling in just yet.

Eaton received the ball with his back facing the south-end basket and took his patent "baby hook" from the right side of the bucket for the first two points of the game.

The Crusaders hurriedly pushed the ball to their end of the court where Eric Spencer missed a turn-around twelve-footer. The Red Devil's Huttenlocher snatched the carom, and Eureka headed toward its end of the floor. Running the four-man motion, Schmedeke came off a screen and got open for a three-pointer. That gave the Red Devils a 5 to 0 lead.

The Crusaders, running their man-to-man offense got an open baseline fifteen-footer from Spencer, but it hit the iron and Eaton grabbed the rebound. Eureka returned the ball to its forecourt where Tyler got a backdoor pass. However, on a great defensive move, his shot was blocked, setting up a Nazarene fast break. Emiko Etete went for a lay-up, getting fouled by Eureka's Huttenlocher. Etete made the second free throw to break the ice for the home team and put them on the scoreboard.

Overall, the first half seemed like a shooting contest. Eureka College made seven three-point shots. Northwest Nazarene countered by making seven of eleven from three-point range. The game was close throughout the first twenty minutes, but the Crusaders went into the intermission with a four-point lead, 41 to 37.

Despite the roar from the gigantic Nazarene crowd, the Red Devil players proved to their crowd that they could play with the home team. The inspired Darnall was enthusiastically yelling praise and encouragement to his gamers in their locker room at halftime.

Eueka's center, Cris Easton (53) battles NNC's Eric Spencer (54) for the ball while Peterson (30) looks on. (Photo by Chris Butler of the *Idaho Statesman*)

"We need twenty more minutes of bust your butt. We're only four down. Keep patient. Take good shots. Nail 'em. Don't make stupid fouls. Keep your head. Forget the crowd. Just play hard. You guys can do it. Let's play one more game. Let's go! Get out there and get some shots in. We can do it!" Darnall shouted with enthusiasm.

539

The players left the locker room. "Dighton, keep me in this game. You go on out," Darnall instructed his assistant as he headed for the bathroom.

The second half was absolutely phenomenal. It was the game of all games for Coach Darnall—the significance of the game, the crowd, the emotion, and the result. To get a true account of the happening, the articles by three sports writers who witnessed the game are reviewed.

Barry Miller of the *Idaho Press-Tribune* described what he saw in "Red Devils defy Crusaders for spot in finals—Eureka hits record sixteen three-pointers to overcome crowd, NNC, 83 to 67." It read in part:

> Character and a hot hand from 3-point land. Those were the two key ingredients that helped Eureka College overcome tremendous odds to knock off host Northwest Nazarene College, 83 - 67, Monday night in the semifinals of the NAIA Division II Men's Basketball Championship.
>
> The Red Devils from Eureka, Ill., hit an unbelievable 16-of-21 shots from behind the 3-point arc and didn't fold when the Crusaders made their final run to advance to tonight's title game against last year's runner-up, Northern State (S.D.).
>
> Eureka coach Dave Darnall said, "This win showed the character of our team because we were up 13 and twice we throw it away so they can cut it to four. With 4,000 people rooting for them, we could have very easily choked."
>
> But they didn't thanks to back-to-back treys from Chris Peterson and Duane Schmedeke that ended NNC's short-lived rally and increased Eureka's lead to 67 - 57 with 5:39 remaining. The Crusaders never got closer than eight points the rest of the way, and when Peterson nailed his tournament record tying ninth trey (in 11 attempts) with 1:42 left for a 78 - 64 lead, it was all over.
>
> NNC head coach Ed Weidenbach, whose team had similar shooting nights in its first two tournament wins, was a bit shell-shocked after the game when he looked over the final statistics.
>
> "They just played lights out and when you shoot 76 percent on your threes, you're going to win some games," he said.

Stephen Hauge wrote an article for the same paper entitled "Eureka gives NNC taste of own medicine." He stated:

> The festivities continue one more night, but the show is over. The host hit the wall. The rim shrunk. And the NAIA championship game tonight has lost its ring for most of the fans jammed into Montgomery Fieldhouse on Monday night.
>
> Eureka College yanked the wheels off the Northwest Nazarene Crusader fun bus to the NAIA title game, parking it 83 - 67 in the semifinal contest.

"Actually I was thinking, 'Boy, I now know what it felt like to be playing us,'" said Todd Schumacher.

He wasn't kidding, either. Bill it as a role-reversal.

The Crusaders shot 37 treys in their first three games. And though they had nine more Monday night, it all paled in light of Eureka's Chris Peterson.

He sizzled.

The senior sent nine of his 10 attempts from the 3-point line through the net. For the game, Eureka hit 16 of 21 in front of a hostile 4,000 fans.

The bell began to toll for the Crusaders when the second half began. Ahead by four points at 41 - 37, the Crusaders went into a deep freeze, shooting 29 percent from the field for the second half.

But behind by 13 points, the Crusaders made one more valiant run, and the crowd made one more valiant call. Sparked by senior Rolando Garcia, NNC closed the gap to four points at 61 - 57 with 6:50 to go in the game.

And the decibel rating went through the roof.

Said Garcia, "We sensed the crowd getting loud and we got intense . . . but Eureka answered every time."

"I couldn't hear, my ears were ringing," said Peterson.

But it didn't seem to phase him. Two quick Peterson treys and "we just couldn't fight back," said Schumacher.

Scott Heiberger, the sportswriter for Eureka's team in the Peoria *Journal Star* gave his account of the game in "Eureka on brink of NAIA title." It read in part:

When the Eureka College Red Devils walked into jam-packed Montgomery Fieldhouse on Monday night to face hometown Northwest Nazarene in the NAIA Division II semifinals, they already had laid claim to the title of most successful team in school history.

But the Red Devils aren't through making history yet. Tonight they play for the national championship.

Chris Peterson scored 31 points, including a 9-for-10 effort on 3-point goals; Chris Eaton scored 20 and Duane Schmedeke tallied 17 as Eureka defeated Northwest Nazarene, 83 - 67, and sent an overflow crowd home unhappy from the 3,500-seat arena.

Eureka outshot Northwest Nazarene 57 percent to 40 percent. The Red Devils, who led the nation in regular-season 3-point shooting, converted an astonishing 16 of 21 (76 percent) 3-point shots.

"They played lights out," shaken Northwest Nazarene coach Ed Weidenbach said. "And every time we made a run, they responded. That's the mark of a good team."

As the final buzzer sounded, pandemonium broke out in the small but boisterous Red Devil cheering section. The remaining standing-room-only crowd was silent and shocked. For the first time all evening, the small but mighty Eureka crowd could be heard.

The Red Devil players on the floor were exhausted and stunned. Darnall was in a brief state of shock, sitting in his chair with quiet tears in his eyes. An emotional Peterson, also with tears in his eyes, headed directly toward his coach and sat down.

The bench players were on the floor giving high fives, bear hugs, and shaking hands. However, the starting seniors were just too tired to celebrate. They just wanted to sit down and reflect. It was a load off their minds. It was a dream come true. But at the same time, they couldn't believe what they had just accomplished—a very small college located among the corn-fields of Central Illinois that offered no athletic aid would be playing for the NAIA Division II National Championship. It would also be their coach's last game of his career.

Several minutes of shock, calmness, and catching their breaths passed before the "fabulous five" and Darnall joined in the celebration of

Coach Darnall and players recoverd to celebrate their win over Northwest Nazarene.

bench players and Red Devil fans. Twenty minutes later, the Eureka team finally made its way to the locker room. While in a team huddle Coach, still somewhat dazed, congratulated his players on their achievement expressing how proud he was of their performance. He then suggested that they shower quickly so they all could head to Denny's for a well-deserved dinner.

The players left by the back fieldhouse door to be greeted by clapping and cheering Red Devil supporters. Again, there were hugs, hand shaking, and well wishing. The team then boarded their vans for the short ride to dinner.

Professor Logsdon was also absolutely delighted with what the Red Devils had just pulled off. He exuberantly stated, "Early in the second half, Troy Tyler stole the ball and drove the length of the court to score a dunk lay-up. I have never been fond of that shot, agreeing with Coach Ralph Miller when he called the slam-dunk 'The Idiot's Delight.' I have always felt that basketball was not originally intended to be played that way, that the slam-dunk reduced the game to an absurd level. However, when Troy slam-dunked that lay-up, I began to appreciate the value of the shot. The NNC crowd was completely silenced for the first time in the evening. Later, when Troy stole the ball again and drove for a lay-up, I heard an NNC fan behind me say, 'Here it comes again.' The effect on the crowd was palpable, almost as if they were witnessing a burial. After those two slam-dunks, I now appreciate the strategic value of that shot, and I loved it when Troy did it the second time to NNC.

"The second half of the NNC game was a masterpiece as far as Eureka was concerned. Our defense really was outstanding in holding NNC to only twenty-six points. Our offense was almost as perfect. At the end of the game, I actually believed that we had won the tournament because in defeating NNC we had climbed a mountain that I did not believe we could climb. I know that Northern State is a good team; they have three outstanding players. However, I have no fears about them the way I did before the Indiana Tech and the NNC games. Bring on Northern State! We will defeat them and then go home as the champs," concluded the loyal Logsdon.

A round of applause went up for the team as it entered Denny's. It came from their boosters as well as the Northern State fans that had supported Eureka in the night's second game. Eureka College fans had attended the first game of the evening and had cheered for Northern State. The two groups had developed a mutual admiration and respect over the time they had spent at the same motel and eating at Denny's. In fact, they had even partied together in the motel's "party room"—the laundry room. What a coincidence they would now be playing each other for the "ultimate"—the National Championship! A short comment in the Peoria *Journal Star* emphasized the unique relationship. It read, "Fans of Eureka College and Northern State University joined forces at the Nampa Denny's Restaurant cocktail lounge the night before their teams met for the championship and belted out karaoke versions of songs like Garth Brooks' 'I've Got Friends in Low Places.'"

Northern State normally started three guards and two inside players. The three perimeter players were the six-foot-one Kline, six-foot-two Lance Luitjens, and six-foot-one Scott Boekelheide. Scott's twin brother, Chad, was the first guard off the bench. The two inside players were the six-foot-seven Burckhard and six-foot-seven Paul Sather.

The Wolves were a very aggressive fast break team. They worked hard at both ends of the floor. Burckhard, Sather, and Kline were aggressive on the boards. Northern State played a lot of straight up man-to-man defense with very little switching. They also employed a match-up zone when needed. On offense, the Wolves ran a motion offense from a 1-4 stack, a 1-2-2, or 2-3 alignment. All players played all offensive positions except for Sather who stayed inside. Once in a while, the continuity may be used, usually starting from a 2-3 alignment.

Eureka would counter with its then well recognized "fabulous five." Darnall planned to open with their pressure man-to-man defense, picking up the opponent at the three-point line. If needed, their 1-2-2 adjustable zone defense could always be used. The Red Devils planned to open up in their four-man motion offense, looking for back screens. Six-foot-eight center Chris Eaton would remain inside. Huttenlocher's main responsibility, again, would be to pick for the All-American while Peterson, Schmedeke, and Tyler would cut and set screens for each other. If that failed, EC would switch to their "Wheel" offense. As with all games, the Red Devils were ready to set up their press offense if needed.

Coach Darnall's assistant left his room around 2:00 A.M. Darnall had hoped to get some well-needed sleep, but it was futile. He was up the remainder of the night. The thought that his team was actually playing for the National Championship, realizing it would be his last game as a coach, worrying about the Northern State game, and reliving the night's unbelievable victory over the host school Northwest Nazarene kept his mind in an extreme turmoil with no shutoff button to be found. The hours passed slowly. Lying all-alone in his darkened hotel room, reality and sentimentality took over the coach's wandering mind. The career he loved would be over. Would the game he knew be forgotten? Would the players with whom he treasured being associated be lost? The college that meant so much and he would someday part. In addition, his family's sacrifices, the many things he missed out on as his children grew up because of his basketball obligations, and his health were also thoughts that flashed through the retiring coach's head. Finally, Dave switched on the nightstand's light and reached for the scratch pad and pen that lay by the phone. He had to write down his final thoughts. Perhaps that would relieve the turmoil in his head. Maybe peace would finally come. Darnall jotted down his own "game plan."

Daybreak came as Dave had undoubtedly dozed off. He could now hear people in the halls. The sun was peeking through the drawn drapes. The Eureka College Head Basketball Coach had surely found a short period of peace, but for how long? Not long!

The half-dressed coach went to the hotel's lobby to fetch an *Idaho Press-Tribune* and an *Idaho Statesman* newspaper. Dave needed to make sure everything that had happened the night before was true and not just a dream. There it was. The headlines from the newspapers gave the verification he was looking for.

With newspapers in hand, Darnall was headed to the elevator when he was summoned to the front desk for more faxes that had just been received that morning. Again, they were from Central Illinois.

Dave returned to his room and stretched out on the bed. All of the other Red Devil rooms were still quiet. With the curtains still shut, coach reached for the nightstand light. He noticed the poem he had written only a short time earlier. It seemed so foggy to him. He read it but would share it with no one. There would be a time. When would that be? Now was not the proper time; there was still work to be done. The appropriate time would emerge. It was meant to be!

Championship game day had arrived. It would be almost a duplicate of the previous day. The players had wake-up at 10:00 A.M. They gathered in the hotel's lobby for the short walk to O'Callahan's for breakfast. Then there was the hour's shoot around at Orrin E. Hills Center Court. Meanwhile, Dave remained in seclusion.

The team returned to the Nampa Suites around 1:00 P.M. It was time for the daily "skull session" held in the hotel's conference room. Coach

Darnall and Coach Dighton presented the all-important game plan. Dave thanked his players for the great year and for allowing him to coach this final game in his last year of coaching. He then read some of the faxes from back home.

Darnall finished the meeting with a small motivational speech. He told his players, "A win tonight will give you something no other basketball team from Eureka College will probably ever do—win a National Championship. You'll go down in history as the best team ever at Eureka. You will become a Hall of Fame team in several Halls of Fame. A victory tonight will bring some of you unbelievable honors. It will mean that the big red, white, and blue championship banner will hang high from the rafters of Reagan Fieldhouse forever. Finally, it will give you the prize all college and professional athletes covet—the championship trophy and those championship rings!

The team meeting was over. The players left for their rooms. A few headed for the pool and whirlpool to comfort their aching and tired legs. Darnall and Dighton were the only two remaining. Dave turned to his faithful companion of nine years, "Dennis, do you believe this? We are playing for the National Championship. Keep me in the game. We've worked too hard to let this get away. I want you to take over for me next year."

"I will Coach," Dighton replied as they left the room.

Coaches Dighton and Begole went to the room they shared to lay out the players' uniforms and warm-ups. Dave returned to his room and went to bed. As usual, game day syndrome was taking hold. As he lay in bed, his mind again raced with a million thoughts.

At 4:00 P.M. the team, minus Darnall, walked next door to O'Callahan's for the pre-game meal. By then, the employees had begun to know some of the players and seemed to be pulling for them.

The players had until 6:30 to rest and get ready to leave for Montgomery Physical Education Building. The team left the Nampa Suites Hotel on their final trip of the season precisely on time. For the six seniors and Darnall, it was their final trip ever to the college hardwood. A sad thought!

Arriving at the arena, the Red Devils entered the back-pass door and again walked to the same locker room. It now seemed like "home." It was the third consecutive game they would take their "ten seconds of silence" in that room. Oh, that number three again!

It was 7:00 P.M. on March 15, 1994; only one hour before the biggest game a Eureka College basketball team would ever play and the game that would bring to a close Darnall's career. The end of the road for the coach would come just three days short of when it began fifty-two years earlier. Why does that number (3) always connect to significant happenings? Was it meant to be?

The game was being billed as "offense against defense." Northern State's potent offense was averaging over 103 points a game in tournament play, versus Eureka College's stingy defense allowing opponents only sixty-seven points. It was large school against small school. State's enrollment of over 3,000 students compared to Eureka's fewer than 500. A school located in Aberdeen, South Dakota, with a population of 25,000 overshadowed Eureka, Illinois, at 4,500. A school that had a fieldhouse with a capacity seating of 8,000 to a fieldhouse that held 2,200. Northern State offered athletic scholarships while Eureka couldn't. State had a basketball program with a nice-sized budget; Eureka's was limited.

Coach Darnall was informed that Northern State's Head Coach Bob Olson and he were to report to the court for a taped interview by telecasters Ross Cook and Mike Boyle to be shown at halftime. Darnall was interviewed by Boyle. He asked Coach Darnall his thoughts about his last game as a coach and about his senior players.

"We climbed the mountain. All we have to do now is go over the top. Hopefully, we'll be able to do that," Darnall said. "We have a slogan, 'Together We Win' and that's the way they believe. Very unselfish people. They play hard. They play their hearts out. It's a great feeling to be associated with a class group of guys. They're a class act. They are just great kids!"

It was then back to the business at-hand—the determination of the NAIA II National Champion. As with the previous night, the Red Devil locker room was quiet. Very little talking was going on by the players as they were dressing. Coach Darnall was sitting on a corner table while Coach Dighton moseyed around the locker room. The atmosphere was like going into a battle where there were possibilities of casualties. There was no more tomorrows. This was it. The game of twenty years!

Coach Darnall actually appeared quite calm as he prepared to address his players with his last-ever pre-game talk. However, he was extremely nervous, not just about the game result, but also would he say the right things in this final speech?

"Fellows, there are only two teams in the entire United States, NAIA Division II, that has not completed their seasons—you and Northern State. Only one team will end its year with a win. I think that will be us," Darnall said. "Prove me right!"

"Ever since your sophomore year, you seniors have been waiting for this moment. Don't screw it up. You have been trained and conditioned to play the whole game. Show 'em what you are made off."

"Don't worry about the damn officiating. In fact, it's been pretty good. You won't have the crowd to worry about like you did last night. No reason to be nervous; we're here. Just play!"

"The only thing you have to do is play hard and execute. Take good shots, rebound, don't make stupid fouls, and make your free throws," Darnall instructed.

You've got all Central Illinois pulling for you. Can you imagine what it would be like to win the National Championship? It would be a dream. You'll never experience anything like it again. Let's go do it!"

"Now, let's take our ten seconds," Darnall said. "Each one is an individual. Think what you want to think or you don't need to think at all, as long as we are quiet, and we do it together."

"TWW, let's do it!" Darnall shouted as his team exited the locker room. Coach Dighton followed the players. Darnall headed to the "john" for the final time before a game! It was his last time to have his private thoughts before the game. How could this really be happening? Could he accomplish something only a handful of coaches ever had—win a National Championship after announcing retirement? Legendary coaches John Wooden, Al McGuire, and Larry Brown were among them. Could Dave Darnall join the group?

It seemed like hours, but actually it was only minutes before Dave joined his team on the court. As he left the locker room and entered Hills Arena, there was a feeling of emptiness—not in the crowd sitting in the bleachers, but the feeling one gets when something is over, but was not completed. That scared him as he strolled to his customary third seat in line.

The NAIA Division II National Championship game was being televised by TCI Sports nation wide. Telecaster Mike Boyle described both coaches as being extremely nervous and anxious to get the game started when they were interviewed prior to the game. When asked about his pre-game disposition, Darnall agreed with the telecaster. "The wait is worse than the game," he had said. That's partially the reason Dave had such a tough time on game day—nervousness, upset stomach, tiredness, itching, depression.

A near-capacity crowd witnessed the third NAIA Division II National Championship game. It wasn't the same standing-room-only crowd that watched the Red Devils defeat the home team, but it was an outstanding turnout considering Nazarene was not playing. The people in the Nampa-Boise area should be given credit. Eureka College had its loyal seventy-five fans, six cheerleaders, and the Red Devil mascot. But, they were without the other Super 8 supporters from the previous night. Those fans were now cheering for their own team, the Northern State University Wolves.

The wish of all the people staying at the Super 8 was that their two institutions would play for the championship. They got their wish—no animosity—just great competition. Both teams were already winners. Even though the players from the two teams never actually met and talked with each other, there was the feeling that they knew each other because of the relationship of their fans. The mutual admiration and respect had been passed to the teams.

The starters for both teams were as predicted. EC played a flawless first half. In Coach Darnall's words, "That was the best twenty minutes of play from any team I have ever coached at Eureka College. It was damn near perfect!"

The Wolves six-foot-seven center Paul Sather jumped against the six-foot-eight Red Devil center. Eaton tipped the ball back to his star point guard, Chris Peterson. The game was underway. Eureka had the opportunity to break out on top. Peterson dribbled the ball up court. He got open for a two-pointer. The shot was missed, but Pete was fouled. Calmly, he stepped up to the free throw line and swished two. Eureka took a 2 to 0 lead.

The Wolves brought the ball back to the end of the floor. Before they could get their first shot off, EC's Schmedeke made a clean steal to reclaim the ball, but it was wasted. Huttenlocher shot an air ball in the lane, and Northern State had its second chance to score.

It didn't happen. Kevin Burckhard missed a turn-around, and Tyler grabbed the rebound. Troy, dribbling the ball down the court, found himself open. He nailed the three-pointer.

The Wolves looked to their All-American guard Eric Kline for their first basket of the game, but he missed. Eaton snatched the rebound, and Eureka set up its four-man motion offense. Schmedeke, coming off a great screen, got open for a three-point shot. It hit nothing but net. The Red Devils had jumped out to an unbelievable, shocking eight-point lead. Coach Darnall and the Eureka bench were going crazy. They were going nuts.

"I don't believe this," Darnall told Dighton. "I hope to hell this isn't an illusion."

With Peterson kicking the ball out of bounds, Northern State got the ball under its own basket. Kline got open in the right corner for a jumper to score the Wolves' first two points of the game.

The Red Devils came right back. From a sharp pass from Peterson, Eaton got open in the lane for a lay-up and was fouled. Eaton missed the charity toss, and Northern State got the carom. Kline missed a baseline shot, and Eaton rebounded.

Executing the motion offense, Duane Schmedeke got open again from the right side of the circle and "tickled the twine" for another three-pointer. Northern State called a timeout with seventeen minutes left in the first half, trailing 11 to 2. The Red Devils were playing good defense and making their shots on offense.

Following the timeout, the Wolves set up their box inbound play under their basket. Burckhard missed a fifteen-footer, and Peterson got the rebound.

As the telecaster reported, "Eureka is playing textbook basketball—allowing only one shot on defense."

An EC turnover gave the ball back to Northern State with Luitjens driving the lane and drawing a foul from Schmedeke. The six-foot-two guard made both charity shots. Eureka returned the ball to its end of the floor where Eaton finished off with a rebound lay-up after a missed jumper by Peterson. That made the score 18 to 4. An unbelievable fourteen-point Eureka College lead with a little over fifteen minutes left in the first half.

The Red Devils went on to maintain a fourteen-point margin throughout the first half and led at the intermission, 50 to 36. Troy Tyler, playing an outstanding first half, led Eureka in scoring with eighteen points. Eaton contributed to the scoring cause with twelve.

The game wasn't over yet. Whereas, the first twenty minutes of the contest belonged to Eureka College, the second twenty was reversed. It, basically, was owned by State.

In Coach Darnall's final half-time talk to any team, his demeanor was calm. Extremely excited about his team's first half play, the coach did not have to rant and rave as he often did.

"Fellows, don't let up. You're doing a great job. Just twenty more minutes." Dave told his players. "You've got to keep working hard. Don't let 'em back in the game. Stay on those damn boards. They get only one shot. Keep your heads. If the game gets close, the team that keeps its head in the game will win. Make your damn free throws. The team that makes its free throws in crunch time will come out on top. Don't make any damn fouls. Make them beat you from outside."

He stopped. He looked at Dighton. Dighton looked back. "Okay, fellows, let's do it! Let's take it back to Eureka. Let's get that banner. We want those rings," Darnall shouted to get the adrenaline flowing again.

"TWW—now go out there and get some shots in," Darnall instructed his players. Dighton and Begole followed the team out. Darnall headed for the "john." It was a habit he would not miss.

By the time Coach got to the Red Devil bench, the buzzer had sounded for the players to meet with their respective coaches. Dighton had the Red Devils gathered around. Darnall said a few departing words as it was back to "battle."

Eureka started the second half with the ball and promptly scored the first two points of the second half when Tyler flashed the lane for a layup.

Luitjens missed an easy close-in shot, and Tyler grabbed the rebound. Eureka, running its motion offense, got a good three-point shot from Peterson, but it drew only iron. The Wolves got the rebound, and Sather nailed a two-pointer in the lane. That was the beginning of Northern State's comeback.

Throughout the next fourteen minutes, the Wolves steadily narrowed the Red Devils' once sixteen-point second half lead. With fifteen seconds remaining in the game, Northern State had finally tied the score. The tide had turned.

Eureka had been missing field shots and free throws as well as not getting offensive rebounds. Whereas, the Wolves had been making the majority of their shots, and when they did miss, they were getting offensive rebounds and second shots. In the first ten minutes of the second period, the Red Devils had eleven misses while the Wolves had only four. That hurt! Northern State had also increased the tempo of the game. They were shooting on the first open opportunity and were nailing most of them. Turnovers had also taken a toll on the Red Devils. Its intense pressure defense was slacking. In addition, Dennis Huttenlocher had picked up his fourth personal foul with twelve minutes to play and had to be replaced by sophomore Adam Ferguson. Was Eureka folding? Was the pressure finally getting to the players? Were they tired?

The final five minutes of the championship game was not for anyone who had a weak heart, including the Devils' head coach. The momentum had definitely swung in Northern State's direction. After All-American guard Eric Kline and Chris Peterson, who should have been, traded three-point baskets, EC held a slim two-point lead, 69 to 67, with 5:10 showing on the score clock.

On an inbound play under their own basket, Red Devil center Chris Eaton got a sharp inland pass from Huttenlocher, who was then back in the game, for a quick "two." That gave the Red Devils a four-point lead, but the Wolves countered with a lay-up from Scott Boekelheide to draw Northern back within two.

On the next possession, Troy Tyler was fouled in the lane while shooting a fourteen-footer. He stepped to the line to make a pair. With 3:43 remaining, the Red Devils held a 73 to 69 lead as a TV timeout was called.

The Wolves immediately brought the ball down the floor and drew a foul from Huttenlocher. The six-foot-four senior fouled out. Adam Ferguson again replaced him.

Northern State took the ball out under their basket and got a quick three-point score from Kline. That brought them to within one. Following that basket, Northern threw up a full court man-to-man press. Fortunately, the Red Devils had no trouble breaking it.

Darnall wanted his team to look for a good shot. No bad shots now. With less than five seconds left on the shot clock, Schmedeke got open on the top of the key and nailed a three-pointer. The patience of the Red Devils to look for a wide-open shot had the TV telecasters calling Eureka a "precise basketball team."

On their next possession, the Wolves had the ball stolen by Peterson. The six-foot guard made two free throws to give his team a 78 to 72 lead with 2:30 left. Kline next missed a shot, and Peterson grabbed the rebound. Eureka, again working the shot clock, got an open shot from Schmedeke who proceeded to shoot an "air ball." As the ball was going out-of-bounds, Adam Ferguson leaped high in the air and tossed the ball back into play as he fell off court. "What a great play!" Darnall said to Dighton.

The ball landed in the hands of Eaton who promptly passed to Peterson who immediately nailed a trey. Ferguson's outstanding effort proved to be one of the "plays of the game." He was an "unsung hero." The total play had the telecasters remarking, "That had National Champion written all over it." Darnall sure hoped so!

With 1:42 left in the contest, Eureka held a nine-point lead. As Northern State got the ball in its forecourt, Tyler made a steal and drove the length of the floor for a lay-up. Troy missed the "bunny" but was fouled and received two free throws. Known as a good free throw shooting team, that pleased the screaming Red Devil fans. There was 1:37 left. Tyler stepped to the free throw line following a timeout. He missed both! Oh, shit!

The Wolves, rebounding the ball, quickly advanced the ball to their end of the floor where Scott Boekelheide nailed a three-pointer with 1:15 left in the action.

On the inbound pass, Peterson threw the ball away. Northern State's Scott Boekelheide recovered the ball and immediately took a wide-open three-pointer. The ball drew iron, and Eaton rebounded. He was fouled by All-American Kevin Boekelheide. It was his fifth. Boekelheide fouled out with sixteen rebounds and twenty-two points. Eaton was awarded two free throws. The six-foot-eight senior center missed both! That was four missed free throws in the last thirty seconds. Darnall had a headache!

The Wolves got the rebound and pushed the ball down the floor for a quick three-pointer by Lance Luitjens. He hit nothing but net. It was a three-point game with fifty-five seconds remaining in the contest.

On the inbound pass, Peterson was fouled immediately. He calmly stepped to the line and swished two. Northern State, again, advanced the ball quickly to their forecourt where Luitjens took another three-point shot from the top of the circle. Even though he missed the shot, he was fouled by Peterson and was awarded three charity tosses. Coach Darnall about died on the bench. The one thing he did not want with a five-point lead was the clock stopped by a foul.

Luitjens stepped to the line and made all three. That cut the lead to only two with forty-six seconds left. What a "big play" that had been.

On the inbound pass, Peterson was again fouled. He duplicated what he had done just seconds before. He sank both tosses. Coach Darnall wanted the ball in his superstar guard's hands. What a clutch player!

Northern State came right back down, and Luitjens hit another three-pointer. The six-foot-two guard from Custer, South Dakota, was taking over. Eureka held only a one-point lead with thirty-seven seconds remaining in the game. Breaking the full court man-to-man press, EC ran their spread offense. Coach wanted the ball in the hands of Peterson. He was fouled again—this time with twenty-seven seconds left. The man with "ice in his veins" stepped to the line following Northern's timeout. Chris had two charity tosses. He made both, giving Eureka a three-point lead. However, the Wolves were not dead yet. They immediately pushed the ball up the court looking for a three-pointer. Who would take it—Boekelheide, Luitjens, or Kline?

It was their All-American. With fifteen seconds left, Kline got the ball on the right side of the circle and went up for his famous jumper. It hit nothing but net. The game was tied, 87 to 87.

Eureka inbounded the ball, and Peterson brought the ball down the right side of the court. Timeout was called to set up a last second shot. Tyler threw the inland pass. Eureka was running what Coach Darnall called his "Roseville sideline out-of-bounds play." The ball went to Schmedeke. He drove the circle for a fourteen-foot jumper, trying to draw a foul. The ball hit the rim and bounced about twelve feet out where Eaton grabbed it and put it back up at the buzzer. The ball fell off the right side of the rim. The game was going into overtime!

Coach Darnall was stunned. His team let the championship get away. He was hoping Peterson would get the last shot. The Red Devils had had two open shots, but they just wouldn't fall. Maybe Eureka just wasn't meant to beat the larger school. A few seconds passed, and Darnall gathered his thoughts. Coach Dighton and he had to plot what they wanted to do for the next five minutes. There was no change. It was going to be man-to-man defense and motion offense. Darnall pleaded with his players not to give up and to continue to work hard. He told his team to remain patient on offense and to step up to the line and make those damn free throws.

Sather jumped against Eaton. The six-foot-eight senior redhead tipped the ball back to Peterson. Eureka College had the first opportunity to score. Running the four-man motion offense, Troy Tyler drove the lane for a close-in shot but was fouled. Lance Luitjens had just picked up his fifth personal foul!

Tyler swished the first throw but missed the second. Northern State got the rebound and hurriedly advanced the ball to their end of the court. Kline got open on the left baseline for a three-point shot. He nailed it. The Wolves took the lead for the first time in the game. How could this happen? Could the Red Devils come back after trailing?

Eureka brought the ball to its end of the floor. They were in their four-man motion offense. Schmedeke got an open three on the left side of the circle but missed. Tyler snatched the rebound, but Chad Boekelheide stole the ball and raced down the floor passing to an open Kline. Kline missed a "three!" Northern's Chad Boekelheide grabbed another offensive rebound and threw the ball to Chad McGough who drove the right baseline. He was fouled by Adam Ferguson. McGough calmly made two free throws to give Northern State a 92 to 88 lead with 3:38 remaining in the game.

Eureka's Troy Tyler took a three-point shot but missed. Ferguson grabbed the offensive rebound and dished it back to Tyler who had followed his shot and was breaking to the basket. Tyler missed a lay-up but was fouled. The senior forward stepped to the line again. He missed the first one but came back to sink the second.

The missed free throw made Coach Darnall walk the sideline. Normally, Coach was a "squater," not a walker. Squating in front of his chair helped hide the emotional coach from the fans behind him.

Northern State set up their motion offense and patiently looked for a good shot. Kline spotted Sather under the basket and hit him with a brisk pass for a lay-up. With 2:55 left, the Wolves had a five-point lead. Were the Red Devils dead? Did they have the heart to fight back?

Darnall seeing what had just transpired, looked over to his assistant and said, "Dighton, we've just _ _ _ _ _ up the National Championship!" Coach Dighton made no reply.

Coach put his head in his hands. "The dream won't come true. How did I let this get away? To be so close to the ultimate—a national championship and not get it," thought Darnall.

The shot clock was running down with the Red Devil offense "out of sink." All of a sudden, Schmedeke noticed Peterson in the *deep* left corner. How did he spot Pete in all the court turmoil? With only two seconds left on the shot clock and Scott Boekelheide in his face, Peterson let one fly. It hit nothing but net. Eureka was still in the game! Coach Darnall called Peterson's shot the most incredible he had seen in his coaching career. Pete had been deep in the corner behind the rim, a defensive player in his face, and falling out of bounds as he made the shot. He had brought his team back within two with 2:20 left in the contest.

With just over two minutes left, Schmedeke fouled Kline who was attempting a three-point shot. That brought Darnall off the bench. For the second time in the game, one of his players had fouled an opponent who was in the process of a three-point shot. That had never happened before in the coach's tenure. However, the official ruled that Kline had been fouled after the shot. What a break for the Red Devils! Dave quickly "forgave" any bad calls he thought may have been made against his team earlier and retracted any negative remarks he may have made about the officials. Kline made the first free throw but missed the second. The missed free throw became a loose ball. A jump ball was called. It was Northern State's ball.

The Wolves threw the ball in from underneath their own basket. Moving the ball around out front for several seconds, Scott Boekelheide broke away for a lay-up. It rolled off the rim, but he retrieved his own rebound. The Wolves had another chance at it with the clock running down and holding a three-point lead, 95 to 92. With 1:30 remaining, Kline shot a three-pointer, but it rebounded long. Red Devil Adam Ferguson went high in the air for the long rebound and was fouled by Scott Boekelheide.

The sophomore forward stepped to the free throw line for two shots. He converted both to Darnall's great relief. It was now a one-point game with 1:20 remaining to play.

The Wolves slowly brought the ball to their forecourt, looking for a good percentage shot. Scott Boekelheide, handling the ball, picked up his dribble on the top of the circle. Schmedeke and Peterson went for the steal. Schmedeke knocked the ball away. While going after the loose ball, Peterson was fouled by Boekelheide. Another break for the Red Devils!

Calmly, the player of the tournament in Darnall's mind swished two. For the first time since the beginning of the overtime, Eureka had taken the lead, 96 to 95. The Red Devils had not quit. They didn't point fingers at teammates when they missed shots, missed free throws, or made turnovers. TWW—they climbed back on top with a little over a minute to play in the most crucial basketball game in Eureka College's history.

Northern State brought the ball up-court and set up their motion offense. As the shot clock was running down to just a few seconds, Chad McGough attempted a three-pointer. It drew iron. The Red Devils' Troy Tyler leaped high in the air to snatch the missed shot. Eureka regained the ball with thirty-five seconds left and a one-point lead.

Coolly, Chris Peterson brought the ball up the court. Coach Darnall had the man handling the ball that he wanted. With nineteen seconds left in the contest, All-American Eric Kline fouled his counterpart. Peterson would prove why he should have been selected an All-American. Northern State called a timeout. Pete went to the charity line. For the eleventh and twelfth consecutive time, he swished them. Only a three-pointer would be able to tie the game.

Darnall called a timeout following Peterson's free throws. He wanted to set up the defense. The Wolves brought the ball down the floor looking for the trey. Eureka was willing to give up the two-pointer, but not the three.

With six seconds left, Scott Boekelheide was open briefly in the lane, but the Eureka defense recovered to knock the ball out of bounds.

Northern State threw the ball in from under their basket. It came into Chad Boekelheide along the left side baseline. He let a three-pointer fly. The ball hit the rim, and Schmedeke went high in the air to grab the missed shot. Eureka College was the 1994 NAIA National Champions. They had won, 98 to 95, in overtime.

Pandemonium broke out. The players on the court were jumping with raised arms. The bench players leaped high from their chairs and dashed to the floor to grab their heroes. Bear hugs and high fives could be seen all over the court.

Tiera leading Red Devil fans in cheering for their heroes' victory.

Coach Darnall turned and saluted the Red Devil fans sitting directly behind the Eureka bench. They were shouting, "We're No. 1! We're No. 1!" Bonnie was looking for Dave. Tiera and Derek were following their mother.

Emotions were expressed in so many ways. The most obvious were Bonnie and Dave embracing and finishing with a kiss; Chris Peterson was hugging his step-father, Chuck Schaffer in relief; the cheerleaders were swarming the players; and, of course, the players were pointing their finger to the rafters and chanting, "We're No. 1! We're No. 1!"

While the Red Devils were hooting and hollering on the court, the Northern State University players and coaches were sitting solemnly on their bench, stunned, and pondering the fact that for the second consecutive year, they had come in second. This time it was to a small, non-scholarship school from Central Illinois. Several players could be seen with their heads buried in their hands. Others were staring into space or just watching what was taking place on the floor. What did they have to do to celebrate a championship? When would it be their turn?

After several minutes of celebration, order was finally restored. Second place individual plaques and the second place National Tournament trophy were presented to the Northern State University players and coaches.

In front of the huge red, white, and blue National Champion pennant, the Red Devils were presented the National Championship trophy. Each member of the team was presented an individual championship plaque and a NAIA championship hat.

As the Eureka College basketball team stood behind the NAIA championship pennant, facing their fans and official scoring table, honors were bestowed upon several members of the Red Devil team.

Well-deserving superstar Chris Peterson was selected the tournament's Most Valuable Player. Chris Eaton was named on the All-Tournament team. Coach Darnall was named NAIA Division II National Coach of the Year. He was honored when Dan Klein, Head Coach of Indiana Institute of Technology and member of the NAIA National Tournament Committee presented him with his plaque. Darnall had a great deal of respect for Coach Klein. Chris Eaton was also named First Team All-American. Troy Tyler was named Second Team All-American. Where was Peterson? That's what Coach Darnall wanted to know.

Chris Eaton reached the ultimate for any college player. He was selected the NAIA Division II National Player of the Year.

Northern State's Eric Kline and Kevin Burckhard were selected to the All-Tournament team as well as being named First Team All-Americans.

The Red Devil team members went to the goals to cut down the nets. The last time this traditional ceremony occurred was when Eureka beat Indiana Tech to advance to the National Tournament. Who ever thought while those Reagan Fieldhouse goal nets were being cut that the Red Devils would actually repeat it one more time?

Players hoisted players for the cutting of the nets, while the Eureka fans mingled joyfully on the court with their heroes. Pictures and interviews were taking place all over the floor.

John Roberts of radio station WCRI, Eureka, interviewed Coach Darnall and his seniors from the Center's balcony. The numerous listeners in Central Illinois wanted to hear from the victorious coach and his amazing senior players. Coach thanked all the people back in Central Illinois for their support and faxes. He explained that, when he had read their messages to the players, the players were anxious to bring the NAIA Division II National Championship trophy and pennant back to the Eureka College campus.

Becky Duffield, Athletic Department Secretary, recalled listening to the championship game and interviews. "I was listening to John Roberts broadcast the game live on the local radio station. I received a telephone call near the end of the game, and it was several members of the Eureka College men's baseball team. The team was on their spring trip to Florida, and they were calling me from their hotel room to find out if I knew the score of the game in Idaho. I turned the volume up and held the telephone to the radio. The team in Florida was able to hear when Chris Peterson shot the three-pointer and the last few minutes of the game. I can still hear them yelling excitedly over the phone," said Duffield.

Thirty minutes of celebrating on Orrin E. Hills Center Court went by quickly. The Eureka College basketball team headed to their dressing room under the west stands. It was there that sophomore Greg Crider led his team-mates in a celebration conga-line dance. As the players circled the lockers, they chanted, "Uh, huh; uh huh," while raising their index finger signifying No. 1.

Coach Darnall did something special at the conclusion of the single-line dance around the jubilant locker room. He said, "Pete, would you lead us in a 'thank you' prayer for the guidance, watching over us, and helping us achieve the ultimate goal—the National Championship?" It was the first time that this had taken place after a game. Chris Peterson gave a grateful and moving prayer. It was the last time the Red Devils were "quiet and did it together." Together We Won!

Several journalists who witnessed the thrilling championship reported on the game and comments made by the Red Devil players. "Eureka! Devils win NAIA title in OT—Northern St. settles for second again after 98 - 95 thriller" by Barry Miller appeared in the *Idaho Press-Tribune*. It read in part:

> It was a storybook ending for Eureka College basketball coach Dave Darnall and his senior ironmen Tuesday night in the title game of the NAIA Division II National Men's Championships.

But the destiny of the Red Devils was almost dashed by a gutsy comeback from a Northern State squad that was trying to avoid being runner-up for the second consecutive year.

Eureka which had three players averaging more than 40 minutes per game for the tournament, avoided a hellish ending after losing all of an 18-point lead by scoring nine of the final 10 points of overtime for a thrilling 98 - 95 victory over the Wolves in Montgomery Fieldhouse.

"Coach had a great season and this is the pinnacle of his career," said Eureka senior guard and tournament MVP Chris Peterson about Darnall coaching his final game after 20 years in the business. "We had 99 wins in our career here and we knew this would be the 100th. What a way to hit 100!"

Peterson, who almost single-handedly led the Devils past host Northwest Nazarene College in the semifinals Monday by hitting 9 of 10 shots from 3-point range, came alive in the second half and overtime to help Eureka (26 - 4) overcome an amazing comeback by the Wolves (24 - 9).

He hit six straight free throws after four consecutive losses by his teammates in the final 53 seconds of regulation and nailed four more in the extra period after his trey and a pair of shots from the line by reserve Adam Ferguson knotted the game at 94.

"I just told myself it's just like shooting them in practice and tried to forget it was the championship game of the national tournament," Peterson said. "When we were struggling and missing those free throws, I was really worried because they were hitting some amazing shots. We got lucky that a couple shots fell and got a couple of turnovers. It's too bad someone had to lose this game." Peterson was 14-of-14 from the stripe and finished with a game-high 36 points after scoring 31 on Monday against NNC. He got plenty of help from Tyler, who scored 29, and All-American center Chris Eaton, who netted 17.

"I don't know how I could go out any better; this is a wish come true," Darnall said as he carted the first-place trophy and one of the nets off the court. "We had an uphill battle the whole way, but we did prove ourselves by beating the defending national champions (Willamette 71 - 63 on Saturday), the host school and the No. 2 team last year within three days."

"Eureka College wins crown—Darnall goes out as national champion" was the headline of an article by D.M. Bomar, a correspondent for the Bloomington, Illinois, *The Pantagraph*. It read in part:

Dave Darnall didn't just leave college basketball coaching a winner Tuesday night, he left a national champion.

In Darnall's final game as Eureka College coach, the Red Devils claimed the NAIA Division II national championship with a 98 - 95 overtime victory over Northern State (SD) before a crowd of 3,500.

"It's a storybook ending. I may even write a movie on it," said Darnall, who had announced his retirement from coaching effective at the end of the season.

"We had to beat the defending national champions, Willamette, the tournament host, Northwest Nazarene, and last year's runner-up, Northern State, to get here. I guess we did prove we're the best team in the nation."

Darnall was selected NAIA Division Coach of the Year.

"He had a great career," Peterson said of his coach. "He goes out of the way for us all the time. This is the only way for him to go out."

A second article that appeared in the *Idaho Press-Tribune* by Rob Lundgren gave insight to the Red Devil seniors and their coach. The human-interest story, "Seniors send coach out with a bang," read in part:

They came from Brimfield, Lakota, Wyoming—the town not the state—and Northville.

These towns and others such as Washington, Custer, and Aberdeen are the places where Tuesday night's champions, Eureka College of Illinois, and runners-up Northern State University from Aberdeen, S.D., come from. Just a microcosm of small-town America.

But these were definitely not small-time players.

Led by NAIA tournament MVP Chris Peterson and his teammate Troy Tyler, the Red Devils outlasted the Wolves in overtime, treating basketball fans to an excellent championship game.

Afterwards, while the Eureka starting five gathered around the radio microphone to talk to the folks back home in Illinois, several reflected on their winning the championship, despite entering the tourney as the sixth seed.

"I think they were on a mission," noted head coach Dave Darnall, who will enjoy retirement all the more with a championship trophy. "They didn't quit; I think we as coaches almost did, but they showed they did have the character."

Peterson, who finished up with 67 points and a perfect 18-for-18 in the free throw department in his final two games, admitted he was a little worried when the Wolves came back.

"I was getting worried," he said, "because they were hitting some amazing shots."

Teammate Chris Eaton, who made the NAIA All-American team first team, said coming to Eureka from a small high school actually helped.

"We've got five guys playing together and nothing can overcome that," he said. "We're always picking each other up. It helped coming from a small school because you learned to play together."

Eaton's Wyoming High had only 150 students, while Peterson's was around the 200 mark. By contrast, senior Troy Tyler's high school in

Washington, Ill., just 12 miles distant from the Eureka campus is quite
cosmopolitan with a student body of 1,200 . . .

Small-town basketball? Hardly.

The players showered and finally began to filter out of the locker
room to the gymnasium. Numerous Red Devil fans were still wandering
around. The players gathered the two large tournament bracket boards that
were hanging on the fieldhouse walls. The also received the two small score
board name panels. The bracket boards and the large wood final four pennant
were sent back to Eureka on the Peoria Charter fan bus.

Dave Darnall was the last to leave the Eureka College locker room.
While all the other members of the team had left, Dave stayed behind to
reflect. He knew that once he walked through the locker room door his career
was over. It was hard for him to comprehend they had just climbed to the top
of the basketball world. His career ended in a "blaze of glory" as telecaster
Ross Cook said, "It's a Cinderella Story. Hollywood, it don't get any better
than this," referring to the National Championship game and the way it concluded. "There is a precise basketball team," said Cook.

Coach Darnall had flashbacks of his coaching tenure at Eureka College. The great wins like the 1987 playoff championship game against
McKendree, the previous night's win against Northwest Nazarene, and of
course, the biggest victory of all—that night's. He also thought of the disheartening losses, the long recruiting and scouting trips, and the hours away
from home.

There had been ups and downs over the past twenty years. Thank
God, there had been a great deal more ups than downs. There were numerous team awards, many individual awards earned by his players, and those
bestowed upon Darnall. He realized that he had just joined a select few
coaches that had announced their retirement before the conclusion of the season and went on to win a major national championship.

The night was "frosting on the cake." There would be no more National
Championships or National Coach of the Year awards—just great memories of
a gratifying career. As Darnall exited the locker room, his thought was not
"Together We Win" but "Together We Won!" It was all over. He shut the locker room lights off. It was now dark. A final thought rushed through his mind, "I
wonder what my dad is saying now. I know he had to see it."

Dave switched his mood so he could enjoy the "fruit of his labor"
and the evening's unbelievable ending as he joined his assistant and players

on the gym floor. Finally, they exited the back fieldhouse door to a group of cheering Red Devil fans. Darnall was grasping the National Championship trophy and game ball as if a burglar was going to steal them. They boarded the team vans that led the caravan to Denny's for a late dinner followed by a well-deserved celebration party.

The private dining room at Denny's was waiting. Darnall had made reservations for dinner regardless the game's outcome. There was going to be a celebration of the absolutely unbelievable and phenomenal season one way or the other. The Eureka College group was going to be together, win or lose. The NAIA II National Championship title made it GREAT!

Chapter 18

It Was Meant to Be

I T HAD BEEN SEVEN HOURS SINCE the players had eaten their pre-game meal. For Darnall, who knew how long it had been? Food sure would taste good. Isn't it funny how much better food tastes after wins? In Darnall's case, it sure did! Dave actually hadn't eaten much since the previous night. Coach Dighton did bring his boss a piece of pie and a glass of milk following the team's pre-game meal, but that was all. The coach was now ready for his last post-game meal ever.

However hungry Darnall was, he was actually thirstier. All of the hollering, screaming, and sweating had made him dry. Besides, John, Frank, the players' fathers, and most of the male adult fans were also thirsty. They wanted the coach and his staff to join them in the lounge for a quick cold beer before the late, late dinner. The jubilant coach obliged.

The team and its fans were enjoying an outstanding meal, while discussing the evening's happenings when Scott Heiberger, Peoria *Journal Star* sportswriter dropped by Denny's Restaurant to observe the celebration. He wanted to visit with Coach Darnall and his champion players. His reaction to what he saw and heard was related in an article entitled "Eureka title: Meant to be—To win it all, Red Devils had to beat them all—and they did."

Heiberger learned in his conversation with Darnall that Coach felt "it was meant to be" regarding the final chapter of his career and the conclusion of the fabulous season for his seniors. Dave could not explain why it happened or why he believed that someone above wanted it to happen. The article read in part:

> Less than two hours after he walked off the court for the last time as Eureka College head coach, Dave Darnall sat amongst dozens of players, friends and family at the Denny's Restaurant here.
>
> Darnall had an easier time grasping his fork than gripping what had happened earlier Tuesday evening.
>
> Twenty years after Darnall took over at Eureka, he posted his 383rd and most memorable victory, a 98 - 95 overtime decision against Northern State of Aberdeen, S.D., to capture the NAIA Division II national basketball championship.
>
> "We beat the defending national champion, then we beat the host school, and then we beat the defending runner-up," Darnall said, recounting the Red Devil's path to the top. "My God, how can you imagine that?"
>
> The Red Devils seeded sixth with an all-senior starting line-up, opened by beating Ohio Dominican 92 - 71. They followed with a victory over defending champion Willamette (Ore.) and an 83 - 67 semifinal victory against host Northwest Nazarene in front of almost 4,000 hostile fans.
>
> Then Eureka, a private school that does not offer athletic scholarships, faced defending runner-up Northern State, a public school that awards athletic aid. The Wolves were ranked No. 1 at the start of the season.
>
> "Don't ask me how or why, but I believe some things are just meant to be," Darnall said . . .
>
> The senior starters—best friends—Peterson, Eaton, Tyler, Huttenlocher, and guard Duane Schmedeke—played virtually every minute of the tournament, catching their breath during free throws and while walking the ball upcourt.
>
> They helped Eureka to a 100 - 17 record and three national tournament appearances during their careers. Victory No. 100 capped an era and earned a championship banner that will hang in Reagan Center, where the journey began.
>
> "Nobody could've written a better ending," Huttenlocher said. "It's like the movie *Hoosiers*. We started with small high school backgrounds and coach pulled us all together."

Perhaps the National Championship was the result of Darnall's slogan, "Together We Win." Dave thinks so. Could some special "Being" want mankind to know that the TWW belief would result in good things? It was now, "Together We Won."

Congratulations and praise were generously spread throughout the lounge and private dining room. Laughter and cheering drifted out into the regular dining room. Poses were taken and cameras were flashing.

Tiera celebrating the evening with her father.

After spending an hour in the reserved room, the adult male fans began drifting back into the lounge area adjacent to their dining room. The coaches and other fans soon followed. It wasn't long before the players and cheerleaders also joined the jovial group. Only a few people remained in the banquet room where they could see and hear the festivities close by.

Even though there were several other patrons in the lounge, the Eureka College entourage was predominant. Toasts were given, champagne was flowing, and sons were having beers with their fathers. It was students with adults, players with coaches, and officials with players. Yes, the officials who had worked the night's final game were also there. They had a few cold ones with the Red Devil group. The officials were very complimentary to the players for both their play on the court and the way they conducted themselves on the floor.

566

Father and son—Dave and Derek enjoying a cold one together.

Soon karaoke began. The three songs the team and their fans wanted to sing were "We Are the Champions," "Put Me in, Coach," and "American Pie." Before the night was over, there were several good trios and quartets, but no good solos! Concluding the evening of singing, the whole team stepped forward and sang, "We Are the Champions." The entire bar joined in with the jubilant winners.

"The camaraderie of my players and their fans in this setting is something no one in attendance will ever experience again," Darnall said, as he was about to depart. The evening went extremely fast, and no one wanted it to end. It was around 2:00 A.M. when the management informed the partygoers that they would have to leave. It was closing time.

Still in the mood to celebrate, the fans staying across the street in the Super 8 suggested the party continue in its "party room"—the laundry room. John and Frank, having to work in the morning, bid their winning team farewell until the next day and left for home. The others walked across the street to continue the celebration.

Red Devil players dumping the traditional "ice bucket" on their winning coach.

The tiny room was "bulging at the seams." A few partygoers were forced to stand in the hallway. Joining the team and fans were none other than the game officials. Not ready to quit yet, plus enjoying the company, the officials had accepted the invitation to join the Eureka College group at the Super 8. Wonder if that invitation would have been offered if the result of the game was different? Probably—the Red Devil fans had class. Approximately 4:00 A.M., Coach Darnall decided that he should get the team back to the Nampa Suites Hotel located two miles away. A couple busy days would be coming.

Wednesday was a full day for the Eureka College Red Devils. Before the players were up, student assistant Coach Randy Begole and Trainer Shane Brown traveled throughout Nampa gathering four-by-three-foot red, white, and blue NAIA Championship paper pennants posted at various businesses. They gave one to the coaches and one each to the six seniors. One was kept for display at Reagan Fieldhouse.

The players woke around 10:00 A.M. and began to pack. They were to meet the coaches in the hotel lobby at 10:30 to walk next door to O'Callahan's for the final time. The team enjoyed a delicious buffet brunch. Upon returning to the Shilo Inn-Nampa Suites, the team said farewell to their hosts for the week and checked out.

The fans that were accompanying the team back to Eureka were already waiting in their vans in the Nampa parking lot. The two team vans led the small caravan to the Boise air terminal. The Peoria Charter bus carrying the student fans, the basketball boards, and large wooden Final Four pennant had left earlier in the morning. It would be several days before they would reach Eureka. Frank and John, Albertson sponsors greeted the team and their traveling fans at the airport. Several minutes of departing words were taken before the Eureka College entourage boarded the United Airlines for the flight to Chicago. Their journey would soon be over—just the road to Eureka would remain.

The team left Boise mid-afternoon, scheduled to arrive in the "Windy City" between 6:30 and 7:00 P.M. It was Darnall's last flight as a college coach or as a private citizen. The non-flyer made it through the flight with Bonnie and good friend, Dan Harrod, nearby. He held onto the Championship trophy throughout the trip, but everything seemed like a dream.

The plane arrived at Chicago O'Hare Airport shortly after 7:00 P.M. The first person to greet the Champions was Coach Dave Gilliland. Gilliland lived in nearby St. Charles. He was a good friend of both the Darnalls and the EC players, the high school coach of Adam Ferguson and student assistant Randy Begole, an EC basketball camp coach, and a staunch Red Devil fan. Students who lived in the Chicago area also welcomed their heroes back. A big red-and-white decorated Peoria Charter bus awaited the National Champions for the last leg home.

The Eureka College basketball team looked classy in their traveling suits and NAIA Championship caps. They hurriedly grabbed their luggage from the baggage area and headed to the awaiting charter. They were ready to get home.

The bus had signs taped to the windows facing outward as well as some facing the inside for the passengers. Shellie Schwanke, from the Office of College Relations, had directed the Chicago Charter pick-up and "Welcome Home Celebration" set to take place at Reagan Fieldhouse later that night. She had talked to Dave by phone several times over the past few days. Once the team made the Final Four, Shellie had started the planning for the team's return to the Eureka College campus.

When the coaches and players saw the decorated bus, they had a sense of pride and accomplishment. The signs had various slogans printed on them. Among those were: "Thanks for the 'Thrills' all year long," "We'll Polish the Gold and Wave the Maroon," "The Championship Trophy Will Be in Eureka Soon," "Good Job, EC Red Devils," "The Victory Lane Runs from Idaho to Illinois," "EC No. 1," "EC Basketball, the TEAM with Class," "40 Minutes of Hard Work = a Lifetime of Memories," "40 Hearts Greater than 4,000 Mouths," "Eureka College Red Devils NAIA Division II National Champs," and "UR The Champs." The signs meant a lot to the EC team.

Everyone had boarded when Coach Darnall approached the front seat by the door and instructed the driver, Charles Lyons, "to head south to Eureka." The "dressed-up" charter added a spark to its tired passengers. Coach Darnall had Coach Dighton insert a tape of the Championship game into the video. John had given it to him at the airport. A friend of John's had taped the game the night before from his TV. The entire busload anxiously awaited the two-hour tape to begin.

It took an hour and a half drive on Interstate 55 for the charter to reach Route 24 at Chenoa. The bus exited and approached the Route 24 stop sign. Coach Darnall and driver Lyons noticed a car parked along the side of the road with two men holding a large sign. As the charter got closer, Dave recognized the two gentlemen. The charter stopped. Ed Thomas, Head Football Coach at Chenoa High School and Ray Hoselton, owner of Union Roofing, walked toward the bus with the large sign. Their wives, Bobbie and Sharon, joined them. The Thomases and Hoseltons were friends of the Darnalls from their high school coaching days. The large sign read: "NAIA Champs—Congrats! Coach Darnall & Eureka College Red Devils—From Hoseltons' & Thomas' Families"

Dave, Bonnie, and Tiera stepped from the charter to greet their friends with hugs and handshakes. After visiting briefly, Dave asked the four if they would drive the thirty miles to Eureka for a celebration at the Darnalls' home. They were more than willing to oblige.

The bus passed through El Paso. It was now only fifteen miles from Eureka. As it left the city limits, a Woodford County Sheriff's car was spotted parked along the side of the highway. As soon as the team bus passed, the officer turned on the red light and siren to pull the bus over. What was happening?

The sheriff's car caught the charter quickly. It passed the bus and led it on to Eureka. The team was literally being escorted to the college campus. It brought excitement among the travelers.

Coach Darnall knew there was going to be a "Welcome Home" of some type, but he did not know to what extent until he saw the waiting escorts. As the bus reached the outskirts of Eureka, a fire truck and rescue squad vehicles pulled in front of the charter. It was now a six-vehicle caravan. As the vehicles approached the one and only stoplight in the center of Eureka, people were standing on sidewalks and at the Shell gas station. It was a scene of jubilation on the charter. The players and fans were laughing, crying, clapping, and waving. Those on the streets were waving and shouting. The bus driver honked his horn as passing cars blared theirs. The bus reached Reagan Drive and turned left for the short final leg to the Fieldhouse. It was the last five blocks for Dave Darnall as Head Basketball Coach. As the charter got within two blocks of its destination, the passengers could see cars lining the roadway and some students standing in front of the TKE House cheering and waving. The bus made its final turn into the Fieldhouse parking lot and pulled in front of Reagan. It was close to 10:00 P.M., thirty minutes later than expected. Two hundred people had waited to greet the National Champions. Most in attendance were community fans since the college was still on term break, and the students were gone. An all-campus celebration was scheduled after their return.

Bright floodlights lit up the area as if it were a movie set. Shellie Schwanke stepped onto the bus to congratulate Dave and the team. She also asked Dave to follow an exiting order that she had planned. Dave's family would depart first, followed by the fans that had accompanied the team to Idaho. The coaches and players would exit last. Many had "goose bumps" as they exited the bus to blaring sounds of Queen's "We Are the Champions" and cheering fans. Coach's mother, Ola, and nephew, Lance greeted him as he stepped off the bus carrying the National Trophy. Lance had driven his grandmother ten hours from Arkansas after they were notified of the reception that morning. Ola wanted to be with her son and his family upon their return to Eureka. Dave gave his mother a big hug and kiss.

The players followed their coach from the charter. Don Baker of the Peoria *Journal Star* best described their departure. "Then the video cameras started and the flash cameras illuminated the sky as the smiling National Champions disembarked slowly and proudly."

Jim Michels, a Physical Plant employee and the "disk jockey" for EC home basketball games, was acting as Master of Ceremony. He was able to shout congratulatory remarks over the public address system.

Even before Coach Darnall had a chance to greet the noisy crowd, he was whisked away to an outdoor site a few feet away from the motor

571

Coach Darnall got a "Welcome Home" kiss from his mother, Ola. Jeff Tyler followed. (Photo by David Proeber of *The Pantagraph*)

coach for a live sport newscast on Channel 19. Sports Director, Jim Mattson, had followed the Red Devils' basketball faithfully for the past five years.

Channel 19 was not the only television station that covered the homecoming. Channels 31 and 25, both of Peoria, also had representatives on hand. Newspaper personnel from the Peoria *Journal Star*, *The Pantagraph* of Bloomington, and the local *Woodford County Journal* were present and talking to the team members. Local radio station WCRI had not only broadcast the games from Idaho, but was also giving live coverage of the homecoming.

The guys looked so good standing in their black traveling suits and Championship caps in front of the decorated Fieldhouse as a background. Duplicates of the signs in the charter bus were displayed on the building. One sign stretching completely across the Fieldhouse front read, "NAIA Div. II Nat. Champions."

Coach Darnall worked his way through the joyous crowd to the public address system following his interviews. Michels was then able to officially congratulate Darnall and his players on a job well done. Before Michels introduced the coaches and team, he turned the microphone over to Dave's nephew to speak. Unknowing to Coach, Lance represented the Darnall family in thanking the players for winning the National Championship and helping Dave earn the National Coach of the Year award in his twentieth and last year of coaching.

Coach Darnall took over the microphone and relived moments of tension and those of joy. He distributed several bags of tournament souvenirs such as "Final Four" caps and tournament t-shirts. He also thanked the fans for their support and faxes. He then turned the microphone over to the six seniors and junior Chris Hopwood. Peterson addressed the crowd first. The rest followed. The six seniors thanked their fans for all the support over the entire season and told them that they were inspired by all the faxes they had received while in Idaho. Chris Hopwood spoke on behalf of the underclassmen. He thanked the seniors for their accomplishment and stated that he hoped the returning players could fill their shoes.

In concluding the planned portion of the celebration, Michels announced that a formal reception would be held at 8:00 P.M. on Monday in Reagan Center. The student body would be back on campus, the fans on the bus from Idaho would be back, and President Hearne would have returned from a fund-raising tour.

A request came from the crowd that the team "huddle up" one last time. The players formed a circle and raised one arm in the air with hands touching to give their traditional chant before taking the floor for tip-off. They shouted, "Hustle - Hustle - Defense!" What a fitting way to finish the team's official involvement! That is what brought Eureka College its first NAIA National Championship in any sport.

Informal conversation and congratulations continued as the team members, coaches, and Red Devil fans mingled for another half-hour. The press corp continued to talk to the team members.

Don Baker of the Peoria *Journal Star* asked Coach Darnall his thoughts about the evening. "Seeing the crowd waiting for us was really the first time we realized what this is about," Darnall said. "We were shell-shocked. We didn't expect to see that large of a crowd waiting for us."

A firsthand account of the welcome home celebration was described in an article by Randy Gleason of the Bloomington's *The Pantagraph*. "Red Devils cheered on return" was accompanied by a picture of Coach Darnall stepping off the bus and receiving a hug and kiss from his mother, Ola, and a cartoon of cheering fans. The article read in part:

Amid cheers and screams of support, the Eureka College basketball team Wednesday night made a triumphant return to campus after capturing the NAIA Division II national championship.

Most of the college's 500 students were out of town because of spring break, but about 200 faculty, administrators, college staffs and town residents showed up at Reagan Center on campus to praise the Red Devils, who beat Northern State (S.D.) 98 - 95 Tuesday night.

Coach Dave Darnall, who announced in January that he would retire at the end of the season, thanked everyone for their support and enthusiasm.

"What this team has achieved is something we don't recognize ourselves yet," said Darnall, who was selected NAIA Division II Coach of the Year.

Team member Chris Peterson, the tourney MVP, thanked the more than 200 supporters and said, "If it wasn't for you fans, none of this would have been possible." The Red Devils finished with a 27 - 5 record.

The celebration continued at the Darnall home. Dave was extremely tired after a strenuous week, but the adrenaline was flowing. It resembled a victorious game night. The evening's festivities had him already missing coaching. Joining several of the fans that had made the trip to Idaho with the team were other fans from the community that had attended the homecoming. Darnall's friends from Chenoa and lifelong friends from Normal, Don and Carol Raycraft and Bill Draper, also stopped by. Believe it or not, it was Draper and the Raycrafts who were the last to leave the Darnalls' sometime after 5:00 A.M.

Several bottles of champagne from fans who were unable to attend the tournament but listened to the games on the radio were passed around for all to have a swig. Everyone wanted to see the tape of the game. It was another long night of celebrating. The previous night, it was in the Super 8's laundry room in Idaho and twenty-four later, it was at the home of the Darnalls' in Eureka some 2,000 miles apart. The marvel of air travel!

The next several days brought rest and recuperation for the coaches and players since school was still not in session. Dave received numerous congratulatory phone calls, letters, and cards. Several establishments in Eureka, such as at Yoder Oil Company, Hardees, and Wuethrich-Sanckin Auto Repair, posted signs that demonstrated the town's appreciation of the Red Devils' accomplishment.

Monday evening was a very special night in the history of Eureka College. Approximately 700 well-wishers showed up to honor the NAIA Division II National Champions and witness the hoisting of the huge red, white, and blue National Championship banner to its permanent home high in the rafters of Reagan gymnasium. Lynn Beer and Shellie Schwanke organized an evening to remember.

The gym walls were lined with congratulatory signs. The pep band from Eureka High School was playing "Welcome to the Jungle" as Darnall and the team lined up in the outer hallway. The gym had been nicknamed the "Jungle" and the song had been played by Michels at home games for several years. As the team was announced and entered the darkened gym, the members were followed by two huge spotlights. Coach Darnall led his team into his workplace for the last time to a rampageous, cheering crowd.

The team sat in on their padded white game chairs placed at center court facing the full west side of the stands. Portable bleachers were arranged at the south end of the facility for special guests. Among them were Dave's family, friends, dignitaries, and special friends of Eureka College.

The ceremony began with Mary Finch singing the National Anthem as she had done for Dave and the college before every home game for several years. Master of Ceremony, Athletic Director Warner McCollum introduced the Mayor of Eureka, Joe Serangeli. A week earlier, Mayor Serangeli had proclaimed the month of March 1994 as "March Madness Month" in the city of Eureka in honor of the unprecedented success of its basketball teams —the Eureka College Men's and Woman's teams, the Eureka High School Boys' and Girls' teams, and the Eureka Middle School Boys' team.

The Lady Red Devils, under the leadership of Coach Sandy Schuster and Assistant Coach Karen Sweitzer had the best record in the history of women's basketball at Eureka College. They finished with a 22 to 5 record. Head Basketball Coach Tim Meiss had led his boys' team to a second place finish in the Class A State Tournament. Head Girls' Coach Ron Eeten led the lady Hornets to a Sectional Title and an overall record of 24 to 3. Craig Gerdes, Head Middle School Coach, had concluded his season with another outstanding record.

A representative from the Bloomington's *The Pantagraph* presented Coach Darnall with the printing plates from the article proclaiming Eureka College the NAIA Division II National Champions. He also gave each member of the team an issue of the paper that had a special section dedicated to Eureka College Men's Basketball.

McCollum then introduced President George Hearne. The president officially saluted the players and Coach Darnall for their outstanding achievement on behave of the Trustees, faculty, student body, and friends of the college. He apologized for not being able to attend the tournament because of his previous college commitments in Arizona.

Turning the microphone back to McCollum, the Master of Ceremony just simply said, "The Man." Coach Darnall approached the podium. His first official function was to present President Hearne and Eureka College with the National Championship trophy. He then talked about mixed emotions—the emotion of leaving the game he loved by retiring as Head Basketball Coach at Eureka College, how immensely he was going to miss the players and Eureka College. On the other hand, he felt he had made the right decision. Then came the emotion of winning the National Championship.

Darnall then requested President Hearne and Mayor Serangeli to come forward. "On behalf of the basketball team and coaches, I would like to present you these 'Final Four' caps. Since there were only 20 National Championship caps, you'll just have to be happy with these," said Coach Darnall.

The team and individual awards were going to be placed on a cloth-covered table in front of the podium so that the spectators could view them

Coach Darnall presenting President Hearne the NAIA II National Championship trphy to be placed in a special display case in the lobby of Reagan Fieldhouse.

after the ceremony. Coach Darnall asked the tournament's Most Valuable Player, Chris Peterson, to come forward and bring his MVP trophy. He then presented Chris with a game ball for becoming the college's all-time single season scoring leader with 653 points. He also read an official letter just received that day from the NCAA inviting Chris to participate in a three-point shooting contest against a player from the NCAA I and NCAA II. Chris would represent the NCAA III. The three players would shoot at halftime of the NCAA Division I All-star game at Charlotte, North Carolina, during the Final Four weekend. Needless to say, at that time no one knew who the winner would be, but Chris went on to win the contest by making sixteen of twenty three-point shots to proclaim him the top three-point shooter in the country.

Next, Chris Eaton was asked to come forward. The six-foot-eight redhead sauntered to the podium as Coach announced his honors. The First Team All-American was also named the NAIA II National Player of the Year. What an honor! He was also the first player ever from Eureka College to be selected as a First Team All-American. In addition, Eaton was named to the All-tournament Team for the second consecutive year.

Troy Tyler followed Eaton to the podium. The Second Team All-American and First Team Academic All-American, both for the second consecutive year, brought with him the individual championship plague each member of the team had received.

577

Coach Darnall thanked the fans that had accompanied the team to Idaho and expressed gratitude for the financial burden they incurred in order to make the trip. He also thanked Dean Dale Martin, the cheerleaders, and other students who made the long trip by charter bus.

Dean Martin stepped to the microphone next. He thanked Coach Darnall and the team for their effort and for winning the 1994 NAIA II National Championship. Martin told the crowd of the exciting games and the positive image the team portrayed in Idaho. He summarized the win over the host school, Northwest Nazarene, in front of 4,000 screaming hometown fans, and the come-from-behind win over the larger, scholarship school, Northern State for the championship. Martin then turned his attention to the retiring head basketball mentor. "Dave, as your last season as head coach of the Red Devils—what a way to go out—on top—a national champion! You were a Eureka legend before this tournament, and you definitely have added to that legend now. To share with this crowd what was announced at the National Tournament, it is my privilege to introduce President George Hearne to bestow upon you a very special award."

President Hearne stepped to the podium. He had Dave join him at the center of attention. President Hearne displayed the NAIA Division II Coach of the Year Plaque that Dave had received at the championship game's post-game ceremony. Receiving the plaque, Coach Darnall placed it upon the table with the other National Tournament awards.

Dean Martin acknowledged another person who had worked hard during the tournament making signs, megaphones, and making arrangements. He called her Dave's greatest supporter. He asked Bonnie to come forward to accept a gift from college—a bouquet of roses. Martin called Bonnie a "silent warrior" as Dave presented her the roses and gave a small kiss.

The pep band played as the cheerleaders and crowd stood and clapped.

The microphone went back to the Master of Ceremony. McCollum then introduced Coach Darnall for some farewell remarks and a summation of the tournament. Darnall started off by thanking his family for all the years of understanding and support in order to make this evening possible. He then thanked Coach Dighton, Coach Begole, Coach Prosser, the trainers, and of course, the players for putting up with him and for all the hard work and dedication that brought the championship.

"I don't think any of us really realized what the impact of our slogan 'Together We Win' had, but this team is a real example of what togetherness is. Whether you're black or white, rich or poor, five-five or six-five, handsome or average looking, Protestant or Catholic, none of this makes a difference. The only thing that makes the difference is that you care about each other on and off the floor. It doesn't mean you have to be buddies, but it does mean you must care about each other," said Darnall.

"I think our players do, I think our administration does, I think our coaches do, and I hope our general student body does, because that's what makes Eureka great and that's what made this team great. If you think of what they did," Darnall said. "They had the great come-from-behind win over Indiana Tech here, the victories over Ohio Dominican, Willamette, who was the defending champion, Northwest Nazarene with its overwhelming fan support, and the overtime championship game against Northern State. Pete's amazing shot from deep in the corner behind the rim with the team trailing by five and only two and a half minutes left in the game was remarkable. It is the one shot of my entire career that I will always remember."

Coach Darnall went on the explain the Final Four banquet's large wooden pennant and the red, white, and blue paper banners that Coach Begole and Trainer Brown had gathered from Nampa area businesses along with the tournament bracket board that were all now hanging on the north end wall of Reagan Fieldhouse.

Dave also mentioned that the only free time that the players had with their fans and families was during the four hours on Sunday afternoon spent at John Danielson's home. He emphasized how lucky and thankful they were to have Frank and John from Albertson's as their sponsors for the second year. Other than those four hours, the players and coaches were practicing, playing, conducting skull sessions, scouting, eating, or resting. The team was focused and dedicated to win and was on a mission. The final result brought about the honor of being able to hoist the National Championship banner in our own gym.

As Coach Darnall continued, he talked about the image that the Eureka College players and team left in Nampa, Idaho. "I would like to say that these are a great group of kids. Every year we got better and better until we won the championship. I think people will remember two things about Eureka College. One was our conduct on the floor. People were amazed at the way we handled ourselves. They were amazed at our defense because a lot of the teams were quicker and jumped higher, but we had great defense. When we got down, we never quit. Second, our composure and self-confidence were at the highest level. I think that was one thing that all the newspaper sportswriters and TV people talked to me about and what impressed them about Eureka College basketball."

"These guys have taken Eureka College basketball to a height that none of us in our lifetime ever thought would happen. I never really thought it could be possible because you have to have so many breaks and be so lucky. But let me say, when I made my retirement announcement the last of January, that was the hardest thing for me to do. There was no way I thought we would be National Champions. I knew these guys could get to Idaho and possibly get to the Final Four, but there is no doubt in my mind that this was meant to be. It was meant to be for Eureka College, it was meant to be for President Hearne, it was meant to be for the players, and it was meant to be for me at the end of my career. I think the most amazing thing about this is, honest to God, I believe it was meant to be. It was fate that brought this Eureka College team the NAIA II National Championship," Coach Darnall concluded.

Darnall turned the microphone over to his six seniors and Chris Hopwood for their remarks. They in turn thanked their faithful supporters and commented about the "togetherness" of the team. Hopwood, who again spoke on behalf of the underclassmen, thanked the seniors and pledged to do their best to maintain the basketball program at its current level.

At that point, the National Champion red banner with white letters and blue border was hoisted to the rafters high above the scorer's table for its permanent home as the crowd sang the Eureka College Alma Mater.

President Hearne returned to the podium. He talked about Coach Darnall's exciting and successful coaching career and his love for Eureka College. "His heart has been with Eureka College and for that we will ever be grateful. We have had twenty marvelous years. We celebrate tonight the final one of those years with a present, and it was a wonderful present, with a National Championship. But for those of us who can reach back two years, four years, eight years, or the full twenty years, we have so many memories that we thank you for and that have become a part of the tradition at this college forever. So we thank you for the present; we thank you for the past; and, we thank you for building a tradition, for building pride, and building a program that's going to take us into the future and carry on that tradition. Coach Darnall, all of us thank you and wish you well as you retire from coaching but continue to be so much a part of us," said President Hearne.

The lights dimmed, "We Are the Champions" began playing, and a video presentation was made to the tremendous approval of the audience. It contained clips of the flight to Idaho, after game celebrations, eating at Denny's, the Red Devils' locker room conga-line dance, in the charter bus, the homecoming reception, and of course, the team standing behind the championship banner minutes after the conclusion of the championship presentations.

The final announcement of the evening came from President Hearne. He announced that Dennis Dighton would be taking over as the new Head Basketball Coach at Eureka College. Dave was happy for his assistant of nine years and 1975 Eureka College alum. The appointment was what Darnall had wanted. He felt it was best for the college, the team, and of course, for Coach Dighton. The returning players also had expressed their desire to have Dennis as their new head coach.

All facets of the media covered the event—radio, TV, and newspapers. In talking to Scott Heiberger, Darnall said, "It's been an eventful two months since I announced my retirement. The National Championship, I believe, was meant to be."

An article entitled "Eureka College's champions saluted," written by Randy Gleason, in *The Pantagraph* reported on the evening. It read in part:

> It was official a week ago when the buzzer sounded in Nampa, Idaho. But the Eureka College basketball team and its fans learned what it meant Monday night, during the unveiling of the trophy and the raising of the banner that proclaimed the team NAIA Division II national champions. Dale Martin, dean of students, told the capacity crowd at the college's Reagan Center that the Eureka College players and coaches proved they were better than everyone else.
>
> Eureka College President George Hearne had appointments in Arizona and couldn't make the tournament. But he managed to listen to the championship game by calling home and having someone put the phone receiver next to the radio speaker.
>
> He is going to have a major phone bill, but "It was worth it," he said.

The Eureka College basketball fans had one final opportunity to go to a post-event party at the "Coach's" house. That time the players were also invited. They finally got to see what they had been missing the past four years. With a house full of guests, it was a grand night of congratulatory remarks, reminiscing the season, especially the trip to Idaho, wishing each other well in the future, and saying good-bye. Many toasts were given. For

Dave and Bonnie, it was sad. It was the last basketball party after twenty-eight years of Eureka College post-game gatherings.

A short article appeared in *The Pantagraph*'s Editorial section that summarized the happening in Eureka. A cartoon that Coach Darnall thoroughly enjoyed accompanied the piece. "Eureka! They found gold!" had just a little different twist. It opened with and read in part:

> When the gold miners of old found the mother lode, they shouted, "Eureka!" An aptly named Central Illinois community has struck gold of another sort.
> Eureka College brought home the NAIA Division II national championship less than a week after Eureka High School captured the second place trophy in the Illinois Class A boys' basketball championship . . .
> Congratulations to all involved.
> By the way, with the good fortune smiling on Eureka lately, how many Illinois State Lottery retailers does the community have? The odds seem to be with Eureka.

There were numerous team, individual, and coaching honors that followed the season. The Red Devils were ranked high nationally in many

Dave found humor in his reference to Michael Jordan.

statistical categories. They were first in the NAIA II Team Rebounding Percentage and Scoring Margin; second in three-point Field Goal Percentage; and third in Team Scoring Defense. In NCAA III statistics, Eureka College was first in three-point Field Goal Percentage; second in Scoring Margin; and fifth in three-point Field Goals Made Per Game. They were also ranked nationally in both NAIA II and NCAA III other categories.

Coach Darnall was named "College Sport" magazine's NAIA Men's Coach of the Year. Darnall was especially honored by this selection as it included both NAIA Divisions. He was selected Chicagoland Collegiate Athletic Conference Coach of the Year as well as being named the Illinois Basketball Coaches Association's State of Illinois NAIA Coach of the Year. This was the fourth consecutive year Darnall had received that award.

The NAIA Digest section of the *College Sports* magazine featured an article by Brendan Healey entitled "Men's Coach of the Year" detailing Darnall's honor.

Dave received another personal compliment in the fall when Indiana Tech's Head Coach Dan Klein asked him to be a guest speaker at the Kesslers and Nike First Annual Basketball Clinic. Another guest speaker was Purdue University's well-known coach, Gene Keady. Coach Gilliland, Kevin Root, and Bonnie accompanied Dave to the Indiana clinic.

Coach also had many other speaking engagements, but his "Road to Destiny" would end with a "Dave Darnall Roast." This special event was directed by Lynn Beer from college Relations Office with the support of the administration. It was the first major event to be held at the recently build Cerf Center. The new building contained the student union, bookstore, post office, secretarial services, student development office, chaplain's office, banquet and meeting rooms, the president's private conference room, auditorium, and housed the Ronald Reagan Museum.

It was a very special April evening for the Darnall family. A near capacity crowd attended. The Roast drew a conglomerate of people, family, parents of players from both Dave's high school and college career, childhood friends, former college players, camp coaches, personal friends, college personnel, and Red Devil basketball fans.

The NAIA II National Championship banner had been lowered and served as a background to the elegant white cloth covered head table. Fantastic drawings by artist Kelly Brasel, a former Eureka College student, of Coach Darnall and his team flanked the red, white, and blue banner.

Paul Brown, Dave's former assistant and family friend, served as Master of Ceremony. Roasters were Tim McGuire, Jeff "Little Butch" Cassidy, Mike Sain, Rob Kroehnke, and Leo "Doc" Traister. The roasters had a great time "nailing" the former coach. However, it was "Little Butch" who stole the show. As an assistant and traveling companion for two years, he knew Darnall well. Cassidy stated:

> Without a doubt Dave's organizational skills and work ethic made him a very good practice coach. Coach was always double checking and analyzing his preparations in the car, in the bar, at the office, at the supper table, everywhere. By the time it came to putting it to the test at practice, he had his plans fine tuned and was confident of each and every breakdown and drill he was going to use. Dave loved practices because he had control and always knew what was coming next and for how long it was going to take place.
>
> On the other hand, he hated the nervousness of games at which he had limited control. Seriously, Dave told me more than once how upsetting games were for him. He felt that he was vulnerable at games because he was on display and there wasn't much he could do if the players did not perform.
>
> Coach always used note cards to organize everything, and I mean everything. Every practice would be on note cards with the time span of

drills, the drills, offenses, defenses, and also little side notes about specific players of ours or our opponents. At times you could even find notes about personal things, i.e. Bonnie's B-day, Derek's game, etc. . . . Dave was not very confident in his memory so he would constantly drive himself crazy by either going over these note cards or adding to them. Think about it; it you constantly were double checking yourself, you'd have about 3 or 4 heart attacks a year.

Tom Cassidy, known as "Big Butch," made sure his parents were able to attend the special occasion for Coach Darnall. His parents were especially fond of Coach Darnall who had coached both Tom and his baby brother, Jeff.

Chris Peterson made a special salute to his coach on behalf of the 1994 National Champions. Pete thanked Dave for guiding them to the championship. He talked about the closeness of the players and stressed how meaningful Coach's motto "Together We Win" was. He stated that even though the players did not agree with every move Darnall made, they realized he out-worked all other small college coaches. He always had them prepared to play the next opponent.

Coach Dennis Dighton spoke on his nine years as Dave's assistant. He also thanked those responsible for his being named Darnall's successor.

President George Hearne took the podium to talk of Dave's career at Eureka College. He spoke of Dave's love, commitment, and service to the college. He also commented on his successful basketball program before turning his remarks to the National Championship Team. He praised the Red Devil players and coaches for their dedication and hard work in order to bring the 1994 NAIA II National Championship to Eureka College.

Rob Nicks, a former football player at the college, made a special presentation from the Eureka College Alumni Association. He gave Dave the several wonderful drawn and framed pictures by Brazel that were on display at the Roast. The pictures are very special to the Darnalls and are scattered throughout their new home in Fairfield Bay, Arkansas.

The college gave the retiring coach a huge glassed collage of memorabilia, including a jersey with the No. 20 for his twenty years at the college. It was proudly hung over the fireplace in the downstairs family room at "the Bay."

Last, Paul Brown presented Darnall a white basketball with a full length drawing of him wearing his familiar gray-blue plaid sport jacket. Some of Dave's career accomplishments at Eureka College were printed on the ball also.

Coach Darnall thanked all those who were responsible for making the evening so meaningful for him. He acknowledged all those in attendance for sharing the very special occasion with him and his family. Dave also thanked President Hearne for his support and friendship over the past twen-

Coach Darnall addressing the audience with Bonnie sitting to the right. President Hearne and Mr. and Mrs. Paul Brown are seated on the left. Former Coach Leo Traister and wife, Betty, are sitting in front.

ty years. He especially thanked the president and all of the friends of college who purchased the National Championship rings for all members of the Red Devil team. The rings were magnificent—a dream come true.

A maroon stone with NAIA inlaid in gold in the center served as the face. The bezel surrounding it read "1994 National Champions" in gold letters on a black background. The player's name, a gold basketball player figure, and the player's jersey number was placed on the left shank. On the right shank was placed "Eureka Basketball," with a gold basketball hoop beneath. The most important symbol of the championship was placed below—"TWW" in gold letters. When asked what they would like to have on their rings, their first request was to have TWW displayed as a symbol of their togetherness.

Coach became sentimental. He knew it was getting late and the end was near. The last time he would officially be called "COACH" was here. He once again thanked all the members of his family for their understanding, sacrifices, and support during his coaching career. He then turned his attention to his players.

All members of the 1994 NAIA II National Championship team were sitting at a table to the speaker's right. Coach Darnall turned to face his team. He thanked them for their effort, hard work, and for fulfilling a dream that he never thought possible or that would ever happen—A National Championship. The "Road to Destiny" had been completed. Dave expressed that he was going to miss coaching, especially at Eureka College. He felt it was only fitting that he go out with this incredible group of seniors.

In closing, Coach Darnall told the audience of the poem he had written in the wee morning hours before the championship game in the solitude of his motel room. It had given him some comfort that night to jot down his thoughts but did not know when he would share it. This night seemed very appropriate. "It summarizes my feelings," Coach Darnall said. "This is dedicated to my family, friends and former players." As he began to read, a tear could be seen in the eye of the man who had just completed the "whole journey."

THE RETIRING COACH
Why do we wait for the end to come near
Before we can care for those so dear?
As we go through our career,
Sometimes we forget the ones so near.
Time flies by oh so fast
Before we realize the fun of the past.
We never think of the lives we touch
Because we worry about winning so much.
We even often forget the real bunch.
But now that the end is here
May we be thankful for each year.
And we now will spend our time
With those oh so dear.

Wouldn't Dave's father be proud of him now? The room turned dim. The lights were turned off. "Together We Won"

Eureka College's national champions

Dave Darnall

Darnall concludes his final season of coaching as the NAIA Division II National Coach of the Year. In his 20-year reign as head coach, the Red Devils posted a 383-151 record for a .717 winning percentage.

Dennis Dighton

Dighton is in his ninth season as assistant coach at the varsity level. Dighton, a native of Springfield, is a 1975 graduate of Eureka College. He also serves as the school's assistant baseball and volleyball coach.

Randy Begole

Begole is the head junior varsity basketball coach and assistant varsity coach. Now in his second season with the Red Devils, Begole played for two years in the Eureka College program.

Chris Eaton

The 6-7 senior forward from Wyoming made the national all-tournament team by averaging 21.2 points and 10.2 rebounds in four games. Led Eureka College in rebounding (11.6) and was third in scoring (19.6). He ends his career as the school's all-time leading rebounder with 942.

Chris Peterson

He was the most valuable player of the national tournament by averaging 26.7 points. He made 22 of 32 shots (68.7 percent) from 3-point range and 29 of 30 free throws. The 6-0 senior guard from Brimfield led Eureka College with a 21.0 scoring average.

Troy Tyler

A 6-4 senior forward from Washington, who was second on the team in scoring (19.7) and rebounding (6.9). He ends his career as the school's all-time scoring leader with 2,119 points.

Dennis Huttenlocher

A 6-4 senior center who averaged 5.7 points and 5.5 rebounds. The Stockton native was the team's best defensive player last year.

Duane Schmedke

The 6-2 senior guard from Morrisonville averaged 11.8 points and 4.3 rebounds. He had 102 assists this year. He led the team in assists last season.

Ryan Markley

The 6-3 guard from Watseka played two years for the Red Devils after transferring from Kankakee Community College. Last year he was selected as the Tri-Best team player.

Adam Ferguson

Ferguson appeared in all but one game this season and averaged 4.2 points and 2.7 rebounds. The 6-3 sophomore was the team's most valuable substitute last year.

Mike Norris

The 6-3 freshman forward from Niantic-Harristown averaged 24 points and 9 rebounds his senior year of high school. He played in 9 games this season at Eureka College with the varsity.

Greg Crider

A 6-0 sophomore guard from Dunlap who saw action in 13 games. He is Dunlap's all-time assists leader.

Pete Vaughn

The 6-6 sophomore forward, a graduate of University High School in Normal, saw action in 24 games this year. He averaged 1.2 points and 1.3 rebounds.

Chris Hopwood

The 5-11 junior point guard from Shabbona appeared in 26 games. He also was selected as a Tri-Best team player last season.

Jeff Tyler

The 6-3 sophomore forward from Washington is the younger brother of Troy Tyler. Jeff played in 11 games this season.

The road to the championship

L Capital, 74-89
W Tusculum, 93-65
W Rockford, 117-77
W Clarke, 70-43
W Concordia, 105-64
W Judson, 71-58
W Trinity Christian, 102-58
W Purdue-Calumet, 72-65
W Wabash, 90-81
W Trinity Christian, 79-73 (2 OT)
L Brescia College, 88-89
W Harris-Stowe, 126-52
W Aurora, 111-60
W Lindenwood, 67-65
L McKendree, 70-73
W Barat, 88-57
W Wabash, 88-76
W Moody, 100-25
W Greenville, 79-43
W Judson, 79-45
W Barat, 94-56
L SIU-Edwardsville, 70-74
W Westminster, 110-50
W Mount St. Claire, 92-68
W Greenville, 87-67
W Judson, 75-54
W Indiana Tech, 75-69
W Ohio Dominican 92-71
W Willamette (Ohio) 71-63
W NW Nazarene (Idaho) 83-67
W North. State (S.D.) 98-95 (OT)

Final record: Won 27, Lost 4

The Pantagraph photo.

Epilogue

DAVE AND BONNIE HAVE BOTH RETIRED from the education profession. They spend most of their time in their new home at beautiful Fairfield Bay, Arkansas. However, they still maintain a small home in Eureka, Illinois, to serve as a home base while visiting their children and grandchildren.

Tiera is a Human Resource Specialist with State Farm Insurance Company. Her husband, Brett, is a teacher and Head Cross Country and Track Coach at Eureka High School. He has won five Class A State Cross-Country titles. That is a state record for Class A. They have three children, Brett, seven; Carraghan, four; and Alexis, one year old at the time of this writing.

Derek is a member of the Illinois Bar and has served nearly four years as a police officer with the City of Seattle. He will be leaving Seattle to become a Chicago policeman.

The 1994 NAIA Division II National Championship team will celebrate its tenth anniversary by being honored by the host school, College of the Ozarks, at the NAIA Division II National Tournament held in Branson, Missouri in March 2004.

The 1987 team, which was the first Eureka College team to ever qualify for a National Tournament will be recognized for its participation in the NAIA National Tournament in Kansas City.

Both the 1994 and 1987 teams will be joined by other members of Darnall's squads over his twenty years of coaching at Eureka College in a celebration at both Fairfield Bay and Branson.

Dave's brother, Bruce, now retired, maintains a home in Lake Mills, Wisconsin, as well as having a vacation condo in Fairfield Bay. His sister Lucia and husband, Russ, also have a home in Fairfield Bay. Judy and her husband, Chuck, still reside in the Argenta-Oreana area. Dave's mother, Ola, resides in her own home in Oreana. Dave's father and Bonnie's parents are deceased.

Dave has been inducted into three more Halls of Fame since retirement—the Greater Peoria Sports Hall of Fame, the Eureka College Athletic Hall of Fame, and the Bloomington-Normal Officials' Association's Hall of Fame. Dave was also honored as the recipient of the Illinois State University's 1996 Alumni Achievement Award.

Dennis Dighton followed Darnall as Head Basketball Coach at Eureka College for five years and is currently teaching and coaching at Eureka High School.

Dave Corzine retired from the NBA after thirteen seasons, ending his career with the Chicago Bulls. He is currently owner of two appliance outlets located in the western suburbs of Chicago.

President George Hearne retired from college in 2003, ending a career that spanned forty-three years.

Dr. Don Raycraft and his wife, Carol, continue to reside in Normal besides owning a beautiful condo in Florida. Don and Carol own and operate the "Third Sunday Market," recognized nationally by antique dealers and collectors.

Chuck and Jane Wertz still live in Eureka and are now huge Peoria Rivermen hockey fans.

Dan Harrod continues to practice law in Eureka and remains a big Red Devil fan.

Coach Dave Darnall's Won-Lost Record

High School Record

YEAR	SCHOOL	WON	LOST
1965-66	Stanford	5	18
1966-67	Stanford	11	13
1967-68	Gridley	13	10
1968-69	Gridley	17	7
1969-70	Roseville	25	4
1971-72	Momence	14	12
1972-73	Momence	14	11
1973-74	Momence	22	5
	Overall Record	121	80

Eureka College Record

YEAR	WON	LOST
1974-75	9	16
1975-76	19	6
1976-77	20	7
1977-78	15	10
1978-79	20	4
1979-80	21	5
1980-81	17	9
1981-82	19	6
1982-83	16	11
1983-84	16	10
1984-85	17	10
1985-86	21	5
1986-87	26	3
1987-88	10	16
1988-89	19	9
1989-90	18	7
1990-91	24	4
1991-92	25	4
1992-93	24	5
1993-94	27	4
Over All Record	383	151

NAIA Men's Basketball National Championship Results

YEAR	CHAMPION	SCORE	RUNNER-UP
1937	Central Missouri	35-24	Morningside, IA
1938	Central Missouri	45-30	Roanoke, VA
1939	Southwestern, KS	32-31	San Diego State, CA
1940	Tarkio, MO	52-31	San Diego State, CA
1941	San Diego State, CA	36-32	Murray State, KY
1942	Hamline, MN	33-31	Southeastern Oklahoma
1943	Southeast MO State	34-32	Northwest Missouri State
1944	NO TOURNAMENT HELD		
1945	Loyola, LA	49-36	Pepperdine, CA
1946	Southern Illinois	49-40	Indiana State
1947	Marshall, WV	73-59	Mankato State, MN
1948	Louisville, KY	82-70	Indiana State
1949	Hamline, MN	57-46	Regis, CO
1950	Indiana State	61-47	East Central, OK
1951	Hamline, MN	69-61	Millikin, IL
1952	Southwest MO State	73-64	Murray State, KY
1953	Southwest MO State	79-71	Hamline, MN
1954	St. Benedict's, KS	62-56	Western Illinois
1955	East Texas State	71-54	Southeastern Oklahoma

1956	McNeese State, LA	60-55	Texas Southern
1957	Tennessee State	92-73	Southeastern Oklahoma
1958	Tennessee State	85-73	Western Illinois
1959	Tennessee State	97-87	Pacific Lutheran, WA
1960	Southwest TX State	66-44	Westminster, PA
1961	Grambling, LA	95-75	Georgetown, KY
1962	Prairie View A&M, TX	62-53	Westminster, PA
1963	Pan American, TX	73-62	Western Carolina, NC
1964	Rockhurst, MO	66-56	Pan American, TX
1965	Central State, OH	85-51	Oklahoma Baptist
1966	Oklahoma Baptist	88-59	Georgia Southern
1967	St. Benedict's, KS	71-65	Oklahoma Baptist
1968	Central State, OH	51-48	Fairmont State, WV
1969	Eastern New Mexico	99-76	Maryland-Eastern Shore
1970	Kentucky State	79-71	Central Washington
1971	Kentucky State	102-82	Eastern Michigan
1972	Kentucky State	71-62	Wisconsin-Eau Claire
1973	Guilford, NC	99-96	Maryland-Eastern Shore
1974	West Georgia	97-79	Alcorn State, MS
1975	Grand Canyon, AZ	65-54	Midwestern State, TX
1976	Coppin State, MD	96-91	Henderson State, AR
1977	Texas Southern	71-44	Campbell, NC
1978	Grand Canyon, AZ	79-75	Kearney State, NE
1979	Drury, MO	60-54	Henderson State, AR
1980	Cameron, OK	84-77	Alabama State
1981	Bethany Nazarene, OK	86-85ot	Alabama-Huntsville
1982	SC-Spartanburg	51-38	Biola, CA
1983	Charleston, SC	57-53	West Virginia Wesleyan
1984	Fort Hays State, KS	48-46ot	Wisconsin-Stevens Point
1965	Fort Hays State, KS	82-80ot	Wayland Baptist, TX
1986	David Lipscomb, TN	67-54	Arkansas-Monticello
1987	Washburn, KS	79-77	West Virginia State
1988	Grand Canyon, AZ	88-86ot	Auburn-Montgomery, AL
1989	St. Mary's, TX	61-58	East Central, OK
1990	Birmingham-Southern, AL	88-80	Wisconsin-Eau Claire
1991	Oklahoma City	77-74	Central Arkansas
1992	Oklahoma City - Div I	82-73ot	Central Arkansas
	Grace, IN - Div II	85-79ot	Northwestern, IA

1993	Hawaii Pacific - Div I	88-83	Oklahoma Baptist
	Willamette, OR - Div II	63-56	Northern State, SD
1994	Oklahoma City - Div I	99-81	Life, GA
	Eureka, IL - Div II	98-95ot	Northern State, SD
1995	Birmingham-Southern, AL		
	- Div I	92-76	Pfeiffer, NC
	Bethel, IN - Div II,	103-95	Northwest Nazarene, ID
1996	Oklahoma City - Div I	86-80	Georgetown, KY
	Albertson, ID - Div II	81-72ot	Whitworth, WA
1997	Life, GA - Div I	73-64	Oklahoma Baptist
	Bethel, IN - Div II	95-94	Siena Heights, MI
1998	Georgetown, KY - Div I	83-69	Southern Nazarene, OK
	Bethel, IN - Div II	89-87	Oregon Tech
1999	Life, GA - Div I	63-60	Mobile, AL
	Cornerstone, MI - Div II	113-109ot	Bethel, IN
2000	Life, GA - Div I	61-59	Georgetown, KY
	Embry-Riddle, FL - Div II	75-63	Ozarks, MO
2001	Faulkner, AL - Div I	63-59	Science & Arts, OK
	Northwestern, IA - Div II	82-78	MidAmerica Nazarene, KS
2002	Science & Arts, OK - Div I	96-79	Oklahoma Baptist
	Evangel, MO - Div II	84-61	Robert Morris, IL
2003	Concordia, CA - Div I	88-84ot	Mountain State, WV
	Northwestern, IA - Div II	77-57	Bethany, KS

Appendix C

NAIA National Coach of the Year

1954	Sam Hindsman	Arkansas Tech
1955	Leroy Morley	Western Illinois
1956	John Lance	Pittsburg State, KS
1957	Bloomer Sullivan	Southeastern Oklahoma
1958	John McLendon	Tennessee State
1959	Bob Davis	Georgetown, KY
1960	Milt Jowers	Southwest, Texas, State
1961	Rex Pyles	Alderson - Broaddus, WV
1962	Charles "Buzz" Ridl	Westminster, PA
1963	Fred Hobdy	Grambling, LA
1964	Sam Williams	Pan American, TX
1965	Dick Campbell	Carson-Newman, TN
1966	Ted Kjolhede	Central Michigan
1967	Bob Bass	Oklahoma Baptist
1968	Jack Dobbins	Northeastern State, OK
1969	Joe Retton	Fairmont State, WV
1970	Dean Nicholson	Central Washington
1971	Lucias Mitchell	Kentucky State
1972	Ken Anderson	Wisconsin-Eau Claire
1973	Archie Porter	Sam Houston State, TX
1974	John Collier	Hanover, IN

1975	Ed Messbarger	St. Mary's, TX
1976	Joe Retton	Fairmont State, WV
1977	Nield Gordon	Newberry, SC
1978	Edsel Matthews	Drury, MO
1979	Lonnie Nichols	Cameron, OK
1980	Ken Anderson	Wisconsin-Eau Claire
1981	Ken Anderson	Wisconsin-Eau Claire
1982	Howard Lyon/	
	Dave Holmquist	Biola, CA
1983	Merv Lopes	Chaminade, HI
1984	Dick Bennett	Wisconsin-Stevens Point
1985	Bill Morse	Fort Hays State, KS
1986	Ron Slaymaker	Emporia State, KS
1987	Bob Chipman	Washburn, KS
1988	Larry Chapman	Auburn-Montgomery, AL
1989	Buddy Meyer	St. Mary's, TX
1990	Don Meyer	David Lipscomb, TN
1991	Paul Patterson	Taylor, IN
1992	Darrell Johnson	Oklahoma City - Division I
	Jim Kessler	Grace, IN - Divison II
1993	Gerald Stockton	Midwestern State, TX - Division I
	Gordie James	Willamette, OR - Division II
1994	Jim Reid	Georgetown, KY - Division I
	Dave Darnall	Eureka, IL - Division II
1995	Rick Byrd	Belmont, TN - Division I
	Mike Lightfoot	Bethel, IN - Division II
1996	Jim Reid	Georgetown, KY - Division I
	Warren Friedrichs	Whitworth, WA - Division II
1997	Roger Kaiser	Life, GA - Division I
	Mike Lightfoot	Bethel, IN - Division II
1998	Happy Osborne	Georgetown, KY - Division I
	Scott Fleming	Mount Vernon Nazarene, OH - Division II
1999	Scott Sanderson	Mobile, AL - Division I
	Kim Elders	Cornerstone, MI - Division II
2000	Roger Kaiser	Life, GA - Division I
	Steve Ridder	Embry-Riddle, FL - Division II

2001	Jim Sanderson	Faulkner, AL - Division I
	Kris Korver	Northwestern, IA - Division II
2002	Harry Statham	McKendree, IL - Division I
	Steve Jenkins	Evangel, MO - Division II
2003	Ken Ammann	Concordia, CA - Division I
	R. Clair Oleen	Bethany, KS - Division II

Basketball Players and Administrative Assistants in the Program a Minimum of Two Years

Allen	Mike	Paxton
Bange	Greg	Homer
Bangert	Bruce	Quincy
Begole	Randy	St. Charles
Bell	Flamond	Chicago Heights
Bickett	Brad	Ohio
Blair	Michael	Lanark
Blakeley	Benjamin	Chicago
Blakesley	Kip	East Peoria
Blanton	Reginald (Hughley)	Momence
Blunt	Mark	Mascoutah
Bosch	Steve	Brimfield
Brady	Ed	Grayslake
Brandau	Jim	Ohio
Brown	Doug	Mazon
Brown	Kevin	Lexington
Brown	Paul	Brooklyn, NY
Brown	Shane	Effingham
Bryson	Elton	Peoria

Buchhaas	Jeff	Tinley Park
Buerkett	Eric	Hillsboro
Burgess	Scott	Girard
Butler	John	Mundelein
Butler	Mike	Peoria
Callaway	Keith	Paris
Carlson	Carl	Winnebago
Carson	Jay	Markham
Carter	Chris	Bloomington
Carter	Jeff	Chicago
Cassidy	Jeff	Mendota
Cassidy	Tom	Mendota
Chandler	Dave	Chrisman
Coffman	Mike	Decatur
Cowan	Joe	Wellington
Cowan	Joel	Marengo
Cox	Chris	Sesser
Craft	Lance	Oakland
Crider	Gregory	Dunlap
Deitz	David	Chicago
Dighton	Dennis	Monticello
Doehring	Cary	Vandalia
Doehring	Kirk	Vandalia
Dooley	Tom	Vandalia
Eaton	Chris	Wyoming
Echols	Alonzo	Chicago
Ferguson	Adam	St. Charles
Fernandez	Mark	Collinsville
Ferrell	Jerome	Chicago
Ferrenburg	Dave	Danvers
Fisher	Tom	Decatur
Fuchs	Pat	Girard
Gerling	Randy	Germantown
Gibson	Dave	Wellington
Gonzalez	Dave	Chicago
Goodman	Curtis	Chicago
Gorham	Jason	Belvidere
Gorman	Steve	Bradford

Greene	Jason	El Paso
Gray	Jeff	Granite City
Griffin	Tyronne	Danville
Griffith	Robert	Kilbourne
Guderjan	Jon	Varna
Haile	Robert	Chicago
Hall	Jon	Dwight
Harper	Ernie	Chicago
Harris	Michael	Chicago
Hattermann	Doug	Bartonville
Hayes	Pat	Gridley
Heavilin	Mike	Gibson City
Holmes	Reginald	Chicago
Holmes	Troy	Pekin
Hopwood	Chris	Lee
Hunsinger	Henry	Round Lake
Hunt	Greg	Decatur
Huttenlocher	Dennis	Stockton
Johnson	Dennis (J.J.)	New York, NY
Johnson	Gregg	Abingdon
Jones	Doug	Aledo
Jones	John	Hazel Crest
Jones	Larry	Union City, TN
Kerestes	Mike	Streator
Knoerle	Mike	Toluca
Kovanda	Keith	Arlington Heights
Krieger	Matt	Ottawa
Kroehnke	Rob	Wheaton
Kuzel	Gerard	Chicago
Larson	Ben	Toulon
Lavender	DeLeon	Alton
Layendecker	Bob	Springfield
LeMoine	Rich	Normal
Markley	Ryan	Watseka
Martin	Derrick	Chicago
McClain	Maurice	Centralia
McGuire	Tim	Forrest
Meyer	Wayne	Watseka

Micetich	Joel	Coal City
Missavage	Paul	Kirkwood
Monroe	Gerald	White Hall
Moore	Tony ("T")	Chicago
Mueller	Steve	Sibley
Myers	Mike	Streator
Nafziger	Dan	Mackinaw
Nimrick	J.D.	Georgetown
Norris	Mike	Harristown
Nunn	Gregory (Sugar)	Markham
Ogryzek	Larry	Fox Lake
Oliver	Aaron	O'Fallon
Opiela	Larry	Hometown
Payne	Paul	Indianapolis, IN
Paynic	Brian	Wood River
Peterson	Chris	Brimfield
Pillow	Dave	Lyle
Potter	Chris	Princeton
Prosser	Stan	Villa Grove
Quigley	John	Glen Ellyn
Rabelhofer	Mike	Spring Grove
Raney	Mike	Farmer City
Raycraft	Scott	Normal
Redman	Steve	Chrisman
Reed, Jr.	Sam	Chicago Heights
Reeder	Stote	Sullivan
Ricketts	Tim	Cullom
Rinker	Dave	Toluca
Rinker	John	Toluca
Ritsema	Todd	Lansing
Robertson	Marc	Hamilton
Rohl	Van	Monticello
Root	Kevin	Hoopeston
Roschnofsky	Randy	Millstadt
Royse	Mike	Galesburg
Runyen	Scott	Oreana
Sain	Mike	Decatur
Sallee	Marty	Decatur

Samo	Curt	Malta
Sanders	Steve	Momence
Schacht	Jeff	Galesburg
Schafer	Scott	Sandwich
Schelling	Jeff	Leaf River
Schmedeke	Duane	Morrisonville
Schulte	Clarence	Highland
Schultz	Dave	Normal
Schultz	Bill	Oak Lawn
Schumacher	Glen	Herrin
Scotti	Brian	Pekin
Shelly	Tony	Chicago
Slimack	Joe	Belleville
Smith	Damon	Brookport
Smith	Jeff	Easton
Sroka	Dave	Cary
Stafford	Darrell	Eureka
Steffens	Gordon	Saunemin
Stephens	Jeff	Bethalto
Stephens	Jeff	Mendon
Stone	Ian	Downs
Taylor	Rick	Alton
Taynor	Leroy	Bethalto
Teegarden	Terry	East Peoria
Tepen	Dave	Meppen
Thomason	Larry	Bartonville
Topp	Chuck	Rockford
Trimpe	Tracey	Havana
Tuttle	Tony	Greenview
Tyler	Jeff	Washington
Tyler	Troy	Washington
VanWeelden	Dave	Flanagan
VanWinkle	George	Heyworth
Vaughn	Peter	Normal
Vigna	Dean	Gardner
Vogel	Bill	Streator
Vowels	Jim	Joliet
Wadsworth	Larry	El Paso

Walker	Darryl	Momence
Washington	Calvin	Maywood
Weemer	Steve	Tuscola
Westbrooks	Jerome	Momence
Whaley	Jeff	Broadview
White	Jerome	Momence
Wilmington	Mark	Plainfield
Witherspoon	Bill	Danville
Wooters	Jeff	Shelbyville
Wright	Alan	East St. Louis
Zimmerman	Shaun	Bellflower

The author sincerely apologizes if anyone was inadvertently left from the list.

Appendix E

Former Red Devil Basketball Participants, 1974 to 1994, Who Attended Alumni Game—"Blast from the Past"—February 19, 1994

Dan Nafziger	(74-75)
Kip Blakesley	(74-75)(77-79)
Dennis Dighton	(74-77)(85-94)
Gregg Johnson	(74-77)
Jeff Smith	(74-77)
Tim McGuire	(74-78)
Jerome "Spanky" White	(74-78)
Stan Prosser	(75-79)(91-94)
Mike Butler	(76-78)
Jeff Stephens	(76-78)
Joe Slimack	(76-79)
Paul Missavage	(76-79)
Reginald "Hughley" Blanton	(76-80)
Tony "T" Moore	(76-80)
Henry "Hank" Husinger	(76-80)
Dave Chandler	(77-79)
Joel Micetich	(77-80)
Bruce "Preacher" Bangert	(77-81)
George VanWinkle	(78-80)

Tom Fisher	(78-80)
Mike Sain	(79-83)
Mark Scherer	(80-83)
Greg Bange	(80-84)
Scott Burgess	(81-83)(83-85)
Rodney Todd	(82-85)
Michael Harris	(83-86)
Robert Haile	(83-86)
Calvin Washington	(83-86)
Jeff "Shakey" Whaley	(83-86)
Curtis Goodman	(83-86)
Greg Nunn	(83-87)
John Jones	(84-86)
Tim Ricketts	(85-87)
Bob Kroehnke	(85-87)(87-88)
Eric Buerkett	(85-86)(86-87)
Jeff Wooters	(85-89)
Tom Dooley	(85-90)
Donald "Jay" Carson	(86-88)
Brad Bickett	(86-90)
Kevin Root	(86-91)
Todd Ritsema	(86-91)
Chris Cox	(87-88)(88-89)
DeLeon Lavender	(87-91)
Mike Heavilin	(87-91)
Mark Blunt	(87-91)(91-92)
Mike Allen	(88-92)
Kevin Brown	(88-92)
Dave Vanweelden	(88-92)
Jon Guderjan	(89-93)

Professional Coaches Who Have Worked a Dave Darnall Eureka College Basketball Camp

Bruce Abbott
Marty Abbot
Ryan Ackerman
Mike Adams
Scott Adreon
Mike Allen
Mark Artcher
Lori Ash
Mark Astle
Robbie Axsom
Steve Baker
Gary Barlow
Gary Bartell
Don Becker
Randy Begole
Rob Behrens
Kurk Bell
Roger Bell
Tod Berger
Mark Berry
Jane Bertolino

Brad Bickett
Amy Birch
Erik Black
Kip Blakesley
Reginald "Hughley" Blanton
Brian Bloomhurst
Doug Bloyd
Jason Bohm
Mike Boles
Steve Bosch
Rod Bourne
Deb Braatz (Martin)
Kirk Brandenburg
Mark Branscum
Dave Brown
Doug Brown
Kevin Brown
Eric Buerkett
Scott Burgess
Randall Bushue
Cathy Camargo

Antoinette Campbell
Claxton Cantrell
Dan Carie
Don Carlson
Gary Carlton
Paul Carlton
Chris Carter
Dave Chandler
Mike Chandler
Brett Charlton
Kevin Chase
Carol Chasteen
Tom Cirks
Jim Cleven
Brian Cluskey
Chad Cluver
Cathy Compton
Lisa Connell (Toole)
Anita Conrad
John Coon
Amy Copple (Heller)
Glenn Corbly
Joe Cowan
Chris Cox
Ken Cox
Jim Cozzolino
Doug Craig
Greg Crider
Dan Cronin
Tod Crose
Lynn Cross
Dennis Crouse
John Cullick
Dave Culvey
Jeff Curley
Dana Dale
Bill Danner
Bruce Darnall

George David
Julie Davis
Steven Delicath
John DeMay
Larry Denzel
Dean Derango
Dennis Devino
Rachelle DeWerff
Huck Dewitt
Doug Diemer
Dennis Dighton
John Dodd
Angela Dorks
Rebecca Duncan
Pat Durley
Chris Eaton
Derek Eaton
Kevin Edens
Mitch Edlund
Jane Eeten (Brooks)
Ron Eeten
Mike Eigenbrod
Larry Engle
Margaret Erskine
Roger Essmann
Zack Ettelbrick
Kyle Evans
Tim Fairchild
Harold Fay
Chad Fazel
Brandon Fenton
Dave Ferrenburg
Terry Ferris
Tony Finan
Fred Fox
David Franke
Jon Fromi
Betty Gardner

Russ Garey
Greg Geick
Craig Gerdes
Kurt Gibson
Dave Gilliland
Mike Gittleson
Jack Gleich
Bob Gold
Dave Gonzales
Steve Gould
Doug Graven
Jason Greene
Jack Gronholz
Max Gross
Roger Gualandi
Jon Guderjan
Mark Haberkorn
Kris Hagberg (Kruse)
Doug Hageman
Jeff Hamer
Delores Hanner
Michelle Hanson (Latsch)
Kirk Haring
Clay Haurberg
Ernie Harper
Bill Harrison
Rod Hart
Pat Hartzler
Pat Hauser
Brenda Hayes
Pat Hayes
Harrison Hearne
Mike Heavilin
Paul Heidenrich
Gary Heider
Brett Helm
Phil Hilti
Pat Hise

Linda Hocker
Brian Hodge
Reginald Holmes
Roger Horton
Maury Hough
Jeff Houston
Bonita Howard
Laura Howell (Darnall)
Anna Hoyt
Velma Hubbs (Wilson)
Lance Huber
Jan Hughes
Henry Hunsinger
Dennis Huttenlocher
Jonathon Immel
Ken Ingold
Dave Jacobs
Lyndon Jason
Todd Jefferson
Bob Jiles
Britta Johnson
Carol Johnson
Chad Johnson
Craig Johnson
Dennis Johnson
Gregg Johnson
Norm Johnson
Valerie Johnson
Wendy Johnson
Jeannie Jones
R. C. Jones
Diane Kane
Bill Kauth
Steve Kelly
Terry Kelly
Dave Kilbelkis
Tony King
Steve Kirby

Mike Kirkham
Chris Kleine
Al Klunick
Sandy Knack
Herb Knoblauch
Rich Knowles
Ryon Kramer
Scott Krause
George Kridner
Rob Kroehnke
John Krone
Harry Kunsch
Aaron Kunz
Chris Kurtenbach
Sandy Kuzniewski (Socha)
Nancy LaCursia
Shelly Lange
Linda Langston (Kahle)
Kathy Larson (Pratt)
Mary Lauwerens
DeLeon Lavender
Tim Lee
Ray Leng
Rich Lessen
Bob Liggett
Eugene Link
John Link
Jim Lisk
Steve Litteral
Pete Logan
Kevin Long
Terry Lootens
Darren Loschen
Albert Lowe
Bonita Lytel
Tom Magan
Paul Manahan
Steve Marshall

Deb Martin
Greg Martin
Ron Martin
Jim Matta
Charles McBurney
Dick McCammack
Tony McCoy
Carla McDonald
Dave McFadden
Tim McGuire
Scott McMullen
Pete Meiss
Tim Meiss
Zach Meiss
Jim Melton
Shelly Merritt (Coats)
Stan Messmore
Joel Micetich
Ken Miller
Ken W. Miller
Terry Milt
Paul Missavage
Dennis Moehring
Bob Montgomery
Tony Moore
Dave Moors
Phil Morrison
Randy Moss
Mike Mueller
Matt Mulholland
Bill Mulvaney
Steve Mundle
Tim Murphy
Dan Neuberger
Phil Nevels
Jennifer Nigg
Dana Noble
Coy Nunn

Dave Oleson
Ron Oloffson
Mark O'Neill
J. D. Orwig
Shelley Osborne
Tim Paddock
Harry Park
Barb Parker
John Patty
Tim Pearison
Marj Pertzborn (Slotten)
Ross Pesch
Chris Peterson
Greg Peterson
Ray Phillis
Allen Pickering
Bruck Placek
Richard Powell
Stan Prosser
Mike Pryor
Chris Puckett
Lee Purchatzke
John Quigley
Kris Quinlan
Karen Randall
Mike Raney
Greg Rasmuson
Alex Razzo
Dave Rebmann
Liz Rebmann
Bill Reed
Stote Reeder
Josh Rich
Jim Riley
Narcissa Roberts
Don Robinson
Dwayne Roe
Jim Roesch

Jim Rolando
Kevin Root
Larry Rosenthal
Dale Ross
Pat Ruff
Scott Runyen
Foz Ryan
Tim Sanders
Steve Sash
Diane Savage (Vandemore)
Jeff Schacht
Mark Scherer
Rick Schertz
Duane Schmedeke
Sherry Schmidgall (Bryan)
Mike Schmidt
Troy Schmidt
Jerry Schmitt
Todd Schneider
Luke Schroeder
A. J. Schroff
Sandy Schuster
Tom Scott
Eric Seifert
Rich Shadburne
Ron Shank
Chris Sharkey
Don Shields
Clayk Shoufler
Dale Skelton
Marge Slotten
Mike Smargiassi
Tom Smargiassi
Jeff Smith
Roger Smith
Tim Smith
Betsy Specketer
Rich Spenn

Gordan Steffens
Robert Steiger
Jeff Stephens
Brad Stewart
Russ Stewart
Lyle Stine
Mike Stoecklin
Dick Stoltz
Eric Stone
Dan Sullivan
Davy Summers
LuAnn Swanberg
Vince Swanson
Harry Sward
Karen Sweitzer
Vince Swynson
Carla Taylor (Bayles)
Bob Thomas
Kevin Thomas
Rocky Thomas
Shelli Thomas
Rich Thompson
Mike Thornton
Don Thorton
Rodney Todd
Ray Toland
Ryan Tompkins
Mike Trame
Shari Traughber
John Tully
Andy Turner
Ted Turner
Joe Turngren
Tony Tuttle
Andy Underwood
Jim Valla
Rich Vana
Karen Vandemore

Linda VanDerLeest
George VanWinkle
Mark VanWinkle
Dan Vaughn
Dan Veach
Marsha Vitiello (St. Peter)
Stan Voudrie
Lori Voyles
Don Wallace
Joel Wallace
Neil Wallner
Glenda Warmbir
Roy Webb
Rodney Wecker
Bruce Weldy
Joe Wenskus
Ken Wenzel
Chuck Wertz
Chuck West
Jerome Westbrooks
Norm Westerdahl
Doug Whiskers
Tom Whitaker
Dustin White
Jim White
Kevin White
Dave Whiteman
Dave Wiley
Dan Williams
Amy Wilson
Jerry Wilson
Van Wilson
Roger Wiseman
Don Wohlers
Brian Wojtysiak
Larry Woods
Gene Wyatt
Susan Wynn

Bonnie Yocum
George Young
Doug Zimmer

The author sincerely apologizes if anyone was inadvertently left from the list.